STATE	REGISTRATION DEADLINE BEFORE ELECTION	EARLY VOTING PERMITTED?	IDENTIFICATION REQUIRED TO VOTE?*	MORE INFORMATION
Nevada	Fourth Tuesday prior to election in person or by mail; Thursday before early voting begins online; Election-Day registration permitted	Yes (all voting by mail)	No	nvsos.gov
New Hampshire	6–13 days (varies by county); Election-Day registration permitted	No	ID requested; photo not required	sos.nh.gov
New Jersey	21 days	Yes	No	njelections.org
New Mexico	28 days by mail or online; in-person Election-Day registration permitted	Yes	No	sos.state.nm.us
New York	25 days	Yes	No	elections.ny.gov
North Carolina	25 days	Yes	No	ncsbe.gov
North Dakota	No voter registration required	Yes	ID required; photo not required	vote.nd.gov
Ohio	30 days	Yes	ID required; photo not required	sos.state.oh.us
Oklahoma	25 days	Yes	ID requested; photo not required	ok.gov/elections
Oregon	21 days	Yes (all voting by mail)	No	sos.oregon.gov
Pennsylvania	15 days	Yes	Only for first-time PA voters	votespa.com
Rhode Island	30 days; Election-Day registration permitted for presidential races only	Yes	Photo ID requested	elections.ri.gov
South Carolina	30 days	No	ID requested; photo not required	scvotes.org
South Dakota	15 days	Yes	Photo ID requested	sdsos.gov
Tennessee	30 days	Yes	Photo ID required	tn.gov/sos/election
Texas	30 days	Yes	Photo ID requested	votetexas.gov
Utah	11 days by mail or online; no in-person deadline	Yes (all voting by mail)	ID requested; photo not required	elections.utah.gov
Vermont	No registration deadline; Election-Day registration permitted	Yes (all voting by mail)	No	sos.vermont.gov /elections/voters/
Virginia	22 days by mail or online; in-person Election-Day registration permitted	Yes	ID requested; photo not required	elections.virginia.gov
Washington	8 days by mail or online; Election-Day registration permitted	Yes (all voting by mail)	ID requested; photo not required	sos.wa.gov/elections/
West Virginia	21 days	Yes	ID requested; photo not required	sos.wv.gov
Wisconsin	20 days by mail or online; Election-Day registration permitted	Yes	Photo ID required	myvote.wi.gov
Wyoming	14 days; Election-Day registration permitted	Yes	ID required; photo not required	sos.wyo.gov

SOURCES: Project Vote Smart, www.votesmart.org/elections/voter-registration (accessed 10/5/22); National Conference of State Legislatures, www.ncsl.org (accessed 10/5/22).

*In states where an ID is "requested," voters who do not bring ID to the polls may be required to sign an affidavit of identity, vote on a provisional ballot, have a poll worker vouch for their identity, or take additional steps after Election Day to make sure their vote is counted.

NOTE: Voter registration requirements and deadlines may be altered at any time in accordance with changes in state law. Please go to vote.org or your secretary of state's website to learn more about how to vote in your state.

Essentials
EDITION

14

We the People

An Introduction to American Politics

Essentials
EDITION

14

We the People

An Introduction to American Politics

BENJAMIN GINSBERG
THE JOHNS HOPKINS UNIVERSITY

THEODORE J. LOWI
LATE OF CORNELL UNIVERSITY

MARGARET WEIR
BROWN UNIVERSITY

CAROLINE J. TOLBERT
UNIVERSITY OF IOWA

ANDREA L. CAMPBELL
MASSACHUSETTS INSTITUTE OF TECHNOLOGY

MEGAN MING FRANCIS
UNIVERSITY OF WASHINGTON

ROBERT J. SPITZER
SUNY CORTLAND

W. W. NORTON & COMPANY
Celebrating a Century of Independent Publishing

W. W. Norton & Company has been independent since its founding in 1923, when William Warder Norton and Mary D. Herter Norton first published lectures delivered at the People's Institute, the adult education division of New York City's Cooper Union. The firm soon expanded its program beyond the Institute, publishing books by celebrated academics from America and abroad. By midcentury, the two major pillars of Norton's publishing program — trade books and college texts — were firmly established. In the 1950s, the Norton family transferred control of the company to its employees, and today — with a staff of five hundred and hundreds of trade, college, and professional titles published each year — W. W. Norton & Company stands as the largest and oldest publishing house owned wholly by its employees.

Editor: Peter Lesser
Project Editor: Laura Dragonette
Editorial Assistant: Tichina Sewell-Richards
Managing Editor, College: Marian Johnson
Senior Production Manager: Stephen Sajdak
Media Editor: Spencer Richardson-Jones
Associate Media Editor: Lexi Malakoff
Media Project Editor: Marcus Van Harpen
Media Editorial Assistant: Quinn Campbell
Managing Editor, College Digital Media: Kim Yi

Ebook Producer: Kate Barnes
Marketing Manager: Ashley Sherwood
Design Director: Debra Morton-Hoyt
Senior Designer, College: Marisa Nakasone
Director of College Permissions: Megan Schindel
Permissions Consultant: Elizabeth Trammell
Photo Editor: Thomas Persano
Composition: Graphic World, Inc.
Illustrations: Kiss Me I'm Polish
Manufacturing: Transcontinental

Permission to use copyrighted material is included in the credits section of this book.

ISBN 978-0-393-88784-6

W. W. Norton & Company, Inc., 500 Fifth Avenue, New York, N.Y. 10110
www.wwnorton.com

W. W. Norton & Company Ltd., 15 Carlisle Street, London W1D 3BS

1 2 3 4 5 6 7 8 9 0

To:

Sandy, Cindy, and Alex Ginsberg
David, Jackie, Eveline, and Ed Dowling
Dave, Marcella, Logan, and Kennah Campbell
Horace, Annette, and Peter Francis

Brief Contents

Contents

PART II
POLITICS

PART III

INSTITUTIONS

Appendix

Preface

When we wrote the First Edition of this book, our concern was to explain to students why they should be interested in government and politics. But today our pedagogical priorities are different. After two years in which our nation has been confronted with a terrible pandemic, severe racial strife, an attack on the Capitol, allegations of stolen elections, and nuclear threats from Russia's leader, many, if not most, students know that politics can have a direct impact upon their lives. Indeed, they see every day that politics can be a matter of life and death, and that democracy itself may be in peril. Today's students are eager to learn what they need to know about politics and how they can affect the political world. In this book we endeavor to provide students with a core of political knowledge and to show them how they can apply that knowledge as participants in the political process.

As events from the past several years have reminded us, "what government does" inevitably raises questions about political participation and political equality. The size and composition of the electorate, for example, affect who is elected to public office and what policy directions the government will pursue. Challenges to election administration, from the reliability of voting machines to the ability of local officials to handle the many complications of running a voting operation during a global pandemic, became important in the 2020 election. Many questions arose about the integrity of the voting process, from fears of foreign attacks to concerns that there was not enough mail-in voting—or too much. Fierce debates about the policies of the Trump and Biden administrations have heightened students' interest in politics. Other recent events have underscored how Americans from different backgrounds experience politics. Arguments about immigration became contentious as the nation once again debated the question of who is an American and who should have a voice in determining what the government does. Debates about who benefited from pandemic relief legislation—and who slipped through the cracks—raised questions about which interests have effective voices in government policy. And concerns that the police sometimes use excessive force against members of minority groups have raised questions about whether the government treats all Americans fairly. Reflecting all of these trends, this new Fourteenth Edition shows more than any other book on the market (1) how students are connected to government, (2) why students should think critically about government and politics, and (3) how Americans from different backgrounds experience and shape politics.

What's New in the Fourteenth Edition

To help us explore these themes, Professor Megan Ming Francis has joined us as the most recent in a group of distinguished coauthors. Professor Francis's scholarly work focuses on the way all Americans, but especially communities of color, have mobilized to foment change in the American political system. In teaching the introduction to American politics course at the University of Washington, Professor Francis is committed to cultivating a learning environment where students of all backgrounds and political persuasions see themselves in the course content and feel empowered to speak and learn together. Among her many contributions to the Fourteenth Edition are a broadened perspective on American political values to include justice—as expressed in the Constitution and recent mass movements (Chapter 1); an expanded examination of how Native land dispossession and slavery underpinned the development of the Constitution (Chapter 2); a heavily revised and modernized chapter on civil rights that focuses on the strategies of social movements and includes a longer and more expansive civil rights timeline (Chapter 5); and a thoroughly updated chapter on the federal courts, with greater emphasis on the importance of circuit courts and new coverage of partisanship and the Supreme Court today (Chapter 13).

In order to highlight the book's emphasis on the citizen's role in government and politics, Professor Andrea Campbell continues to write and revise engaging chapter introductions that focus on stories of individuals and how government has affected them. Many Americans, particularly the young, have difficulty understanding the role of government in their everyday lives. The Fourteenth Edition features 13 new chapter openers that profile various individuals and illustrate their interactions with government, from a high school student taking what she saw as a violation of her right to free speech all the way to the Supreme Court (Chapter 4), to college Democrats and Republicans working to overcome internal disagreements to support presidential candidates (Chapter 8), to a whistleblower calling out Facebook for what she saw as harmful algorithms and business practices (Chapter 10), to people fighting groundwater contamination from "forever chemicals" around local military bases (Chapter 12).

Several other elements of the book also help show students why politics and government should matter to them. These include:

- **Who Are Americans? infographics**—many new and updated for the Fourteenth Edition—ask students to think critically about how Americans from different backgrounds experience politics. These sections use bold, engaging graphics to present a statistical snapshot of the nation related to each chapter's topic. Critical-thinking questions are included in each infographic.

- **How To guides** feature interviews with political experts to provide students with concrete advice about how to participate in politics. These guides offer easy-to-follow instructions about getting involved in politics in effective ways.

- **America Side by Side boxes** in every chapter use data figures and tables to provide a comparative perspective. By comparing political institutions and behavior across countries, students gain a better understanding of how specific features of the American system shape politics.

- **Up-to-date coverage** features more than 20 pages and numerous graphics on the 2022 elections, including a 12-page section devoted to analysis of these momentous elections in Chapter 9, as well as updated data, examples, and other information throughout the book. Revised by Caroline Tolbert, a retitled and thoroughly updated chapter, The Media and Political Information (Chapter 7), presents students with a contemporary view of who makes the news, how it is delivered, and how the interplay between content and platform affects partisanship and political knowledge. Professor Tolbert also provides updated coverage of political parties (Chapter 8), focusing on parties as factions and growing political polarization in the United States. Voting access has become a key issue since the 2020 election. Chapter 9 provides up-to-date information on state election laws directly affecting the ability of Americans to vote, such as mail voting, in-person early voting, automatic voter registration, voter identification laws, and more. A new discussion highlights the importance of election administration—wait times, availability of polling places, polling place staff, invalidated votes, and more.

- **For Critical Analysis questions** are incorporated throughout the text. These questions in the margins of every chapter prompt students' own critical thinking about the material in the chapter, encouraging them to engage with the topic.

- **What Do You Think? chapter conclusions** ask students to relate the chapter content and the personal profiles that begin each chapter to fundamental questions about the American political system and to reflect on the significance of government to the lives of individuals.

- **This Fourteenth Edition is accompanied by a Norton Illumine Ebook** that encourages students to check their understanding of each section and provides a richer, more immersive reading and learning experience through embedded animated infographics and interactive data exercises.

- **InQuizitive**, Norton's award-winning formative, adaptive online quizzing program, accompanies this Fourteenth Edition. The InQuizitive course for *We the People* guides students through questions organized around the text's chapter learning objectives to ensure mastery of the core information and to help with assessment. Additional information and a demonstration are available at digital.wwnorton.com/wethepeople14ess.

We miss working with past contributors Theodore Lowi, Margaret Weir, and Robert Spitzer but continue to hear their voices and to benefit from their wisdom in the pages of our book. We also continue to hope that our book will itself be accepted as a form of enlightened political action. This Fourteenth Edition is another chance. It is an advancement toward our goal. We promise to keep trying.

Benjamin Ginsberg
Caroline J. Tolbert
Andrea L. Campbell
Megan Ming Francis

October 2022

A Note from New Author Megan Ming Francis

To my colleagues:

When the Norton editorial team approached me to become a coauthor of *We the People*, I was hesitant at first. I hadn't found the perfect textbook for my intro American government course. In fact, I was unsure whether a textbook could capture the richness and diversity in American political life that I wanted to emphasize in my teaching. Ultimately, I realized that if I wanted a better textbook experience for my students, and for students across the country, I should do something about it. And working on *We the People* has been a wonderful journey.

Credit: Jonathan Pilkington.

The changes I focused on spring from my research and my teaching at Pepperdine University and the University of Washington. In my own course, students from various racial and ethnic backgrounds often come to my office hours and ask why they could only see themselves reflected in the chapter on civil rights. And my research in American politics has taught me that race has played a central role in the development of this nation—from the Founding to the present. A major goal of this edition was to integrate scholarship from the subfield of race, ethnicity, and politics into the textbook in a more consistent way. While you will see substantial changes in the chapters I took the lead on—1: Americans and Their Political Values; 2: The Founding and the Constitution; 5: Civil Rights; and 13: The Federal Courts—there is more on race throughout the book, at key moments.

In addition, my revisions focused on amplifying *We the People*'s hallmark themes: that the citizen's role is central to American democracy and that participation matters. No longer is history a disembodied march of court cases and institutional action. I have focused on highlighting the people and social movements that made their voices heard and pushed political elites to support and make change. I hope that through these examples and stories, students from all backgrounds and political persuasions will see that their participation is critical to supporting the issues they believe in, and to sustaining democracy itself.

One of the keys to the success of *We the People* has been the sustained interaction and feedback between instructors, authors, publishers, and students. I hope that when you see the Fourteenth Edition, you share your thoughts and experiences with me. A great textbook, like American democracy, is always unfinished, always in the process of being perfected.

Thank you for your help and support,

Megan

Megan Ming Francis
G. Alan and Barbara Delsman Associate Professor
of Political Science
University of Washington
meganmf@uw.edu

Acknowledgments

We are pleased to acknowledge the many colleagues who had an active role in criticism and preparation of the manuscript. Our thanks go to:

* Fourteenth Edition reviewer

Marisa Abrajano, The University of California, San Diego*
Amy Acord, Lone Star College–CyFair
Janet Adamski, University of Mary Hardin-Baylor
Craig Albert, Augusta University
Maria J. Albo, University of North Georgia
Andrea Aleman, University of Texas at San Antonio
Stephen P. Amberg, University of Texas at San Antonio
Molly Andolina, DePaul University
Lydia Andrade, University of the Incarnate Word
Milan Andrejevich, Ivy Tech Community College
Greg Andrews, St. Petersburg College
Steve Anthony, Georgia State University
Brian Arbour, John Jay College, CUNY
Phillip Ardoin, Appalachian State University
Gregory Arey, Cape Fear Community College
Juan F. Arzola, College of the Sequoias
Julia Azari, Marquette University*
Joan Babcock, Northwest Vista College
Ellen Baik, University of Texas–Pan American
Ross K. Baker, Rutgers University
Thomas J. Baldino, Wilkes University
Evelyn Ballard, Houston Community College
Robert Ballinger, South Texas College
Alexa Bankert, University of Georgia
Antoine Banks, University of Maryland, College Park*
M. E. Banks, Virginia Commonwealth University
Mary Barnes-Tilley, Blinn College
Nathan Barrick, University of South Florida
Robert Bartels, Evangel University

Nancy Bednar, Antelope Valley College
Christina Bejarano, University of Kansas
Paul T. Bellinger, Jr., Stephen F. Austin State University
Annie Benifield, Lone Star College–Tomball
Donna Bennett, Trinity Valley Community College
Andrea Benjamin, University of Missouri–Columbia
Sarah Binder, Brookings Institution
David Birch, Lone Star College–Tomball
Daniel Birdsong, University of Dayton
Jeff Birdsong, Northeastern Oklahoma A&M College
Paul Blakelock, Lone Star College–Kingwood
Rachel Blum, University of Oklahoma*
Melanie J. Blumberg, California University of Pennsylvania
Louis Bolce, Baruch College
Chris Bonneau, University of Pittsburgh*
Jeremy Bowling, University of Nevada, Las Vegas
Matthew T. Bradley, Indiana University–Kokomo
Amy Brandon, El Paso Community College
Phil Branyon, University of North Georgia
Tyler Alexander Branz, Valencia College West Campus*
Mark Brewer, University of Maine
Lynn Brink, Dallas College–North Lake
Gary Brown, Lone Star College–Montgomery
Melissa Buehler, Miami Dade College
Sara Butler, College of the Desert
Joe Campbell, Johnson County Community College
Bill Carroll, Sam Houston State University

xxix

Niambi Carter, Howard University*
Jim Cauthen, John Jay College, CUNY
Jason Casellas, University of Houston*
Dina Castillo, San Jacinto College Central
    Campus*
Neilan Chaturvedi, Cal Poly Pomona*
Ed Chervenak, University of New Orleans
Jeffrey W. Christiansen, Seminole State College
Gary Church, Dallas College–Mountain View
Mark Cichock, University of Texas at Arlington
Adrian Stefan Clark, Del Mar College
Jennifer Clark, University of Houston
Andrew Clayton, McLennan Community College
Dewey Clayton, University of Louisville
Jeff Colbert, Elon University
Cory Colby, Lone Star College–Tomball
Annie Cole, Los Angeles City College
John Coleman, University of Wisconsin–Madison
Darin Combs, Tulsa Community College
Greg Combs, University of Texas at Dallas
Sean Conroy, University of New Orleans
Amanda Cook Fesperman, Illinois Valley
    Community College
Paul Cooke, Lone Star College–CyFair
Tracy Cook, Central Texas College*
Cassandra Cookson, Lee College
Kevin Corder, Western Michigan University
McKinzie Craig, Marietta College
Brian Cravens, Blinn College
Christopher Cronin, Methodist University
John Crosby, California State University–Chico
Jesse Crosson, Trinity University*
Justin Crowe, Williams College*
James Curry, University of Utah*
Todd Curry, University of Texas at El Paso*
Anthony Daniels, University of Toledo
Courtenay Daum, Colorado State University
Kevin Davis, North Central Texas College
Paul Davis, Truckee Meadows Community College
Terri Davis, Lamar University
Vida Davoudi, Lone Star College–Kingwood
Jennifer DeMaio, California State University–
    Northridge
Lena Denman, Blinn College*
Louis DeSipio, University of California–Irvine
Darin DeWitt, California State University–Long
    Beach
Robert DiClerico, West Virginia University
Corey Ditslear, University of North Texas
Peter Doas, University of Texas–Pan American
Leanne Doherty, Simmons University*
Kathy Dolan, University of Wisconsin–Milwaukee
John Domino, Sam Houston State University
Doug Dow, University of Texas at Dallas
Jeremy Duff, Midwestern State University
Jenna Duke, Lehigh Carbon Community College
Francisco Durand, University of Texas at San
    Antonio
Christopher D'Urso, Valencia College
Bruce R. Drury, Lamar University

Bryan M. Dubin, Oakland Community College*
Denise Dutton, University of Tulsa
Daphne Eastman, Odessa College
Carrie Eaves, Elon University
Sheryl Edwards, University of Michigan–Dearborn
Lauren Elliott-Dorans, Ohio University
Ryan Emenaker, College of the Redwoods
Emily Erdmann, Blinn College*
Heather Evans, Sam Houston State University
Andrew I. E. Ewoh, Texas Southern University
Hyacinth Ezeamii, Albany State University
Dennis Falcon, Cerritos College
William Feagin, Jr., Wharton County Junior
    College
Otto Feinstein, Wayne State University
Leslie Feldman, Hofstra University
Kathleen Ferraiolo, James Madison University
Del Fields, St. Petersburg College
Glen Findley, Odessa College
Bob Fitrakis, Columbus State Community College
Brian Fletcher, Truckee Meadows Community
    College
Paul M. Flor, El Camino College Compton Center
Elizabeth Flores, Del Mar College
Paul Foote, Eastern Kentucky University
Peter Francia, Eastern Carolina University
Brandon Franke, Blinn College
Heather Frederick, Slippery Rock University
Adam Fuller, Youngstown State University
Maria Gabryszewska, Lone Star College–CyFair*
Frank Garrahan, Austin Community College
Steve Garrison, Midwestern State University
Michael Gattis, Gulf Coast State College
Jason Ghibesi, Ocean County College
Patrick Gilbert, Lone Star College–Tomball
Kathleen Gille, Office of Representative David
    Bonior
James Gimpel, University of Maryland at
    College Park
Jill Glaathar, Southwest Missouri State
    University
Randy Glean, Midwestern State University
Jimmy Gleason, Purdue University
Donna Godwin, Trinity Valley Community
    College
Jessica Gracey, Northwest Missouri State
    University*
Christi Gramling, Charleston Southern University
Matthew Green, Catholic University of America
Naima Green-Riley, Harvard University*
Steven Greene, North Carolina State University
Jeannie Grussendorf, Georgia State University
Matt Guardino, Providence College
Zoltan Hanjal, The University of California,
    San Diego*
Precious Hall, Truckee Meadows Community
    College
Sally Hansen, Daytona State College
Tiffany Harper, Collin College
Allison P. Harris, Yale University*

Todd Hartman, Appalachian State University

Mary Jane Hatton, Hawaii Pacific University

M. Ahad Hayaud-Din, Brookhaven College

Virginia Haysley, Lone Star College–Tomball*

David Head, John Tyler Community College

Barbara Headrick, Minnesota State University, Moorhead

Julia Hellwege, University of South Dakota*

David Helpap, University of Wisconsin–Green Bay

Frederick Michael Hemker IV, Antelope Valley College*

Rick Henderson, Texas State University–San Marcos

Shaun Herness, George Washington University

Rodney Hero, University of California–Berkeley

Richard Herrera, Arizona State University

Thaddaus Hill, Blinn College

Alexander Hogan, Lone Star College–CyFair

Justin Hoggard, Three Rivers Community College

Gary Hollibaugh, University of Pittsburgh*

Steven Holmes, Bakersfield College

Kevin Holton, South Texas College

Steven Horn, Everett Community College

Joseph Howard, University of Central Arkansas

Glen Hunt, Austin Community College

Teresa L. Hutchins, Georgia Highlands College

John Patrick Ifedi, Howard University

Anika Jackson, Los Angeles City College

Cryshanna A. Jackson Leftwich, Youngstown State University

Robin Jacobson, University of Puget Sound

Amy Jasperson, Rhodes College

Mark Jendrysik, University of North Dakota

Krista Jenkins, Fairleigh Dickinson University

Catherine L. Johnson, Weatherford College*

Loch Johnson, University of Georgia

Annie Johnson-Benifield, Lone Star College–Tomball*

Anthony Jordan, Central Texas College

Joseph Jozwiak, Texas A&M University–Corpus Christi

Carlos Juárez, Hawaii Pacific University

Mark Kann, University of Southern California

Demetra Kasimis, California State University–Long Beach

Eric T. Kasper, University of Wisconsin–Eau Claire

Robert Katzmann, Brookings Institution

Nathan Kelly, University of Tennessee*

Nancy Kinney, Washtenaw Community College

William Klein, St. Petersburg College

Casey Klofstad, University of Miami

Aaron Knight, Houston Community College

Kathleen Knight, University of Houston

Robin Kolodny, Temple University

Melinda Kovacs, Missouri Western State University

Nancy Kral, Lone Star College–Tomball

Douglas Kriner, Boston University

Thom Kuehls, Weber State University

Ashlyn Kuersten, Western Michigan University

Milosz Kucharski, Lone Star College–CyFair

Rick Kurtz, Central Michigan University

Paul Labedz, Valencia College

Christina Ladam, University of Nevada*

Chryl Laird, Bowdoin College*

Elise Langan, John Jay College of Criminal Justice

Boyd Lanier, Lamar University

Jennifer L. Lawless, American University

Jeff Lazarus, Georgia State University

Jeffrey Lee, Blinn College

Alan Lehmann, Blinn College

Julie Lester, Middle Georgia State University

LaDella Levy, College of Southern Nevada

Steven Lichtman, Shippensburg University

Robert C. Lieberman, Columbia University

Timothy Lim, California State University–Los Angeles

Kara Lindaman, Winona State University

Mary Linder, Grayson College

Samuel Lingrosso, Los Angeles Valley College

Kelley Littlepage, University of Houston*

Mark Logas, Valencia Community College

Fred Lokken, Truckee Meadows Community College

Timothy Lynch, University of Wisconsin–Milwaukee

William Lyons, University of Tennessee at Knoxville

Scott MacDougall, Diablo Valley College

Shari MacLachlan, Palm Beach State College

David Mann, College of Charleston

Prakash K. Mansinghani, Laredo College

Katie Marchetti, Dickinson College

David A. Marcum, Laramie County Community College

Christopher Marshall, South Texas College

Guy Martin, Winston-Salem State University

Laura R. Winsky Mattei, State University of New York at Buffalo

Mandy May, College of Southern Maryland

Phil McCall, Portland State University

Michael McConachie, Collin College–Wylie Campus*

Kelly McDaniel, Three Rivers Community College

Larry McElvain, South Texas College

Seth McKee, Oklahoma State University*

Corinna R. McKoy, Ventura College

Elizabeth McLane, Wharton County Junior College

Eddie L. Meaders, University of North Texas

Rob Mellen, Mississippi State University

Marilyn S. Mertens, Midwestern State University

Suzanne Mettler, Cornell University

Eric Miller, Blinn College

Lisa L. Miller, Rutgers University*

Michael Miller, Barnard College
Michael Minta, University of Minnesota*
Don D. Mirjanian, College of Southern Nevada*
R. Shea Mize, Georgia Highlands College
Justin Moeller, West Texas A&M University
Fred Monardi, College of Southern Nevada
Dana Morales, Montgomery College
Nicholas Morgan, Collin College
Vincent Moscardelli, University of Connecticut
Matthew Murray, Dutchess Community College
Paul Musgrave, University of Massachusetts Amherst*
Christopher Muste, University of Montana
Jason Mycoff, University of Delaware
Carolyn Myers, Southwestern Illinois College–Belleville*
Sugumaran Narayanan, Midwestern State University
Jalal Nejad, Northwest Vista College
Adam Newmark, Appalachian State University
Stephen Nicholson, University of California–Merced
Joseph Njoroge, Abraham Baldwin Agricultural College
Larry Norris, South Plains College
Anthony Nownes, University of Tennessee at Knoxville
Julie Novkov, University at Albany*
Patrick Novotny, Georgia Southern University
Elizabeth Oldmixon, University of North Texas
Anthony O'Regan, Los Angeles Valley College*
Harold "Trey" Orndorff III, Daytona State College
John Osterman, San Jacinto College–Central
Cissie Owen, Lamar University
Richard Pacelle, University of Tennessee at Knoxville
Randall Parish, University of North Georgia
Christopher Parker, University of Washington*
Michelle Pautz, University of Dayton
Mark Peplowski, College of Southern Nevada
Maria Victoria Perez-Rios, John Jay College, CUNY
Robert L. Perry, University of Texas of the Permian Basin
Gerhard Peters, Citrus College
Michael Petri, Santa Ana College
Michael Pickering, Tulane University
Eric Plutzer, Pennsylvania State University
Sarah Poggione, Florida International University
Andrew Polsky, Hunter College, CUNY
Christopher Poulios, Nassau Community College
Michael A. Powell, Frederick Community College
Suzanne Preston, St. Petersburg College
Wayne Pryor, Brazosport College
David Putz, Lone Star College–Kingwood
Donald Ranish, Antelope Valley College
David Rankin, State University of New York at Fredonia
Grant Reeher, Syracuse University

Molly Reynolds, Brookings*
Elizabeth A. Rexford, Wharton County Junior College
Richard Rich, Virginia Polytechnic
Glenn W. Richardson, Jr., Kutztown University of Pennsylvania*
Sara Rinfret, University of Wisconsin–Green Bay
Andre Robinson, Pulaski Technical College
Jason Robles, Colorado State University
Rene Rocha, University of Iowa*
Paul Roesler, St. Charles Community College
J. Philip Rogers, San Antonio College
Susan Roomberg, University of Texas at San Antonio
Stella Rouse, University of Maryland*
Auksuole Rubavichute, Dallas College–Mountain View
Andrew Rudalevige, Bowdoin College
Ionas Aurelian Rus, University of Cincinnati–Blue Ash
Ryan Rynbrandt, Collin College
Robert Sahr, Oregon State University
Mario Salas, Northwest Vista College
Michael Sanchez, San Antonio College
Amanda Sanford, Louisiana Tech University
Elizabeth Saunders, Georgetown University
Mary Schander, Pasadena City College
Thomas Schmeling, Rhode Island College
Laura Schneider, Grand Valley State University
Ronnee Schreiber, San Diego State University
Ronald Schurin, University of Connecticut
Kathleen Searles, Louisiana State University*
Jason Seitz, Georgia Perimeter College
Jennifer Seitz, Georgia Perimeter College
Jennifer Selin, University of Missouri
Allen K. Settle, California Polytechnic State University
Subash Shah, Winston-Salem State University
Greg Shaw, Illinois Wesleyan University
Kelly B. Shaw, Iowa State University
Mark Shomaker, Blinn College
John Sides, Vanderbilt University
Andrea Simpson, University of Richmond
Shannon Sinegal, University of New Orleans
Tracy Skopek, Stephen F. Austin State University
Roy Slater, St. Petersburg College
Captain Michael Slattery, Campbell University
Brian Smentkowski, Southeast Missouri State University
Daniel Smith, Northwest Missouri State University
Don Smith, University of North Texas
Michael Smith, Sam Houston State University
Matthew Snyder, Delgado Community College
Chris Soper, Pepperdine University
Thomas Sowers, Lamar University
Bartholomew Sparrow, University of Texas at Austin

Scott Spitzer, California State University–
Fullerton
Laurie Sprankle, Community College of
Allegheny County
Jim Startin, University of Texas at San Antonio
Robert Sterken, University of Texas at Tyler
Maryam T. Stevenson, University of
Indianapolis
Debra St. John, Collin College
Dara Strolovitch, University of Minnesota
Barbara Suhay, Henry Ford Community College
Bobby Summers, Harper College
Steven Sylvester, Utah Valley University
Kirstine Taylor, Ohio University*
Ryan Lee Teten, University of Louisiana at
Lafayette
John Theis, Lone Star College–Kingwood
Herschel Thomas, University of Texas at
Arlington
John Todd, University of North Texas
Dennis Toombs, San Jacinto College–North
Delaina Toothman, University of Maine
Austin Trantham, Jacksonville University
Linda Trautman, Ohio University–Lancaster
Elizabeth Trentanelli, Gulf Coast State College
Jessica Trounstine, The University of California,
Merced*
David Trussell, Cisco College
Stacy Ulbig, Southwest Missouri State
University
Rosalinda Valenzuela, Collin College*
Ronald W. Vardy, University of Houston
Justin Vaughn, Boise State University
Linda Veazey, Midwestern State University
John Vento, Antelope Valley College*
Kevin Wagner, Florida Atlantic University
Sophia Jordán Wallace, University of
Washington*

Jeremy Walling, Southeast Missouri State
University*
Rachel Walker, Collin College*
Timothy Weaver, State University of New York
at Albany
Aaron Weinschenk, University of Wisconsin–
Green Bay
Matthew Weiss, College of Southern
Nevada*
Eric Whitaker, Western Washington University
Corena White, Tarrant County College–
Trinity River
Clay Wiegand, Cisco College
Nelson Wikstrom, Virginia Commonwealth
University
Clif Wilkinson, Georgia College
Donald Williams, Western New England
University
Lucas Williams, Texas Southern University*
Walter Wilson, University of Texas at
San Antonio
Christopher Witko, Penn State University*
Christina Wolbrecht, University of
Notre Dame
Carolyn Wong, Stanford University
John Wood, Rose State College
Laura Wood, Tarrant County College
Robert Wood, University of North Dakota
Terri Wright, California State University–
Fullerton
Peter Yacobucci, Buffalo State College
Alixandra B. Yanus, High Point University*
Kevan Yenerall, Clarion University
Michael Young, Trinity Valley Community
College
Tyler Young, Collin College
Rogerio Zapata, South Texas College
Julian Zelizer, Princeton University

We are also grateful to Daniel Fuerstman of State College of Florida Manatee-Sarasota, who contributed to the America Side by Side boxes.

Perhaps above all, we thank those at W. W. Norton. Editor Steve Dunn helped us shape the book's first five editions in countless ways. Ann Shin carried on the Norton tradition of splendid editorial work on the Sixth through Ninth Editions and on the Eleventh Edition. Lisa McKay contributed smart ideas and a keen editorial eye to the Tenth Edition. Peter Lesser brought intelligence, dedication, and keen insight to the development of the Twelfth, Thirteenth, and Fourteenth Editions. For our InQuizitive course, digital resources for learning management systems, and other instructor support, Spencer Richardson-Jones has been an energetic and visionary editor. Stephen Sajdak, Alexandra Malakhoff, Quinn Campbell, and Tichina Sewell-Richards also kept the production of the Fourteenth Edition and its accompanying resources coherent and in focus. Nancy Green copyedited the manuscript, and our superb project editor Laura Dragonette and media project editor Marcus Van Harpen devoted countless hours to keeping on top of myriad details.

We thank Lynn Gadson for finding new photos and our photo editor Thomas Persano for managing the image program. We thank Marisa Nakasone for the stunning new interior and cover design. And we thank Ashley Sherwood for her dogged and creative marketing work. Finally, we thank Roby Harrington and Michael Wright, the former and current heads of Norton's college department, who provided guidance and support through many editions.

—*B.G., C.J.T., A.L.C., M.M.F.*

About the Authors

Benjamin Ginsberg is the David Bernstein Professor of Political Science and Chair of the Center for Advanced Governmental Studies at Johns Hopkins University. He is the author, coauthor, or editor of more than 30 books, including *The Fall of the Faculty*; *Presidential Government*; *Downsizing Democracy*; *The Captive Public*; *Politics by Other Means*; *The Value of Violence*; *How the Jews Defeated Hitler*; *America's State Governments: A Critical Look at Disconnected Democracies*; *What Washington Gets Wrong*; *The Imperial Presidency and American Politics: Governance by Edicts and Coups*; *Speaking Truth to Power: Expertise, Politics and Governance*; and *Warping Time: How Political Forces Manipulate the Past, Present, and Future*. Ginsberg received his PhD from the University of Chicago in 1973 and was Professor of Government at Cornell until 1992, when he joined the faculty at Johns Hopkins.

Caroline J. Tolbert is Distinguished University Professor of Political Science at the University of Iowa, where she regularly teaches American government and social media and politics. She was named a 2021 Andrew Carnegie Fellow for her research on voting and elections. She is coauthor of *Accessible Elections: How State Governments Can Help Americans Vote* (2020) and *Choosing the Future: Technology and Opportunity in Communities* (2021), both with Oxford University Press. *Accessible Elections* examines absentee/mail voting, early voting, and same-day registration. Tolbert is coauthor of three other books on technology and politics: *Digital Cities, Digital Citizenship*, and *Virtual Inequality: Beyond the Digital Divide*. *Digital Citizenship* was ranked one of 20 best-selling titles in the social sciences by the American Library Association. Her research has been funded by the National Science Foundation and other nonprofit and technology partners. She has served on the Council for the American Political Science Association. Her work is driven by an interest in strengthening American democracy and inclusive participation in politics, the economy, and society.

Andrea L. Campbell is the Arthur and Ruth Sloan Professor of Political Science at Massachusetts Institute of Technology. Professor Campbell's interests include American politics, political behavior, public opinion, and political inequality, particularly their intersection with social welfare policy, health policy, and tax policy. She is the author of *Trapped in America's Safety Net: One Family's Struggle* and *How Policies Make Citizens: Senior Citizen Activism and the American Welfare State* and is coauthor of *The Delegated Welfare State: Medicare, Markets, and the Governance of Social Provision* and *Policy Feedback: How Policies Shape Politics*. She holds an AB degree from Harvard and a PhD from the University of California, Berkeley. Her research has been funded by the National Science Foundation, Robert Wood Johnson Foundation, and Russell Sage Foundation. She is an elected member of the American Academy of Arts and Sciences and the National Academy of Social Insurance and served on the National Academy of Sciences Commission on the Fiscal Future of the United States.

Megan Ming Francis is the G. Alan and Barbara Delsman Associate Professor of Political Science and Associate Professor of Law, Societies, and Justice at the University of Washington. She is also a Senior Democracy Fellow at the Ash Center for Democratic Governance at the Harvard Kennedy School. Francis specializes in the study of American politics, with broad interests in criminal punishment, Black political activism, philanthropy, and the post–Civil War South. She is the author of the award-winning book *Civil Rights and the Making of the Modern American State*. Francis serves as the editor for the Race, Ethnicity, and Politics Elements series at Cambridge University Press. Her research and commentary have been featured on ABC and NPR, in the *New York Times, LA Times*, and the *Washington Post*, and she has conducted a TED talk with over 2 million views. Francis is a proud alumnus of Seattle Public Schools, Rice University, and Princeton University, where she received her MA and PhD in Politics.

Theodore J. Lowi was John L. Senior Professor of American Institutions at Cornell University. He was elected President of the American Political Science Association in 1990 and was cited as the political scientist who made the most significant contribution to the field during the decade of the 1970s. Among his numerous books are *The End of Liberalism* and *The Pursuit of Justice*, on which he collaborated with Robert F. Kennedy.

Margaret Weir is Professor of Sociology and Political Science at the University of California, Berkeley. She has written widely on social policy in Europe and the United States. She is the author of *Politics and Jobs: The Boundaries of Employment Policy in the United States* and coauthor (with Ira Katznelson) of *Schooling for All: Class, Race, and the Decline of the Democratic Ideal*. Weir has also edited (with Ann Shola Orloff and Theda Skocpol) *The Politics of Social Policy in the United States*.

Robert J. Spitzer is Distinguished Service Professor of Political Science at the State University of New York College at Cortland. He is the author of 15 books, focusing in particular on the presidency, gun policy, and the Constitution. Spitzer's books include *The Presidential Veto; President and Congress; The Presidency and the Constitution* (with Michael Genovese); *The Politics of Gun Control; The Right to Bear Arms*; and *Saving the Constitution from Lawyers*. His most recent book is *Guns across America*. He is also a regular contributor to the Huffington Post and many newspapers.

We the People

An Introduction to American Politics

1

WHAT GOVERNMENT DOES & WHY IT MATTERS

High school student Hayat Muse worked 15 to 20 hours per week at a coffee shop near her home in Minnesota to help her mother with the bills for their family of nine children plus a grandmother. When the Covid-19 pandemic hit, it shut down both her high school and her job. Expenses were up at home—with Hayat and her siblings attending school remotely, the grocery bill rose, as did internet usage—and Hayat followed the path of millions of American adults during the pandemic: she filed for unemployment benefits. At first she received aid, both from the state of Minnesota and from the federal government. But the state soon informed her that it had made a mistake: under a 1939 law, Hayat was not eligible for unemployment benefits. Minnesota was one of a few states that bars high school students from receiving benefits. The state wanted its money back. And because the state had applied the same rule to the federal pandemic unemployment aid, it wanted Hayat to repay that as well.

Hayat felt the law was unfair but repaid the state money. When it came time to repay the federal funds,

Americans & Their Political Values

she appealed and got the repayment waived. But she also worked with a local nonprofit, Youthprise, which spent a year organizing on social media, linking students with others in the same predicament and partnering with other organizations to overturn the law. Perhaps Minnesota's law made sense back when high school workers were earning pocket money, the students argued. But with many young people now working to supplement their families' incomes, the law was outdated. When efforts to pass a new bill stalled, Youthprise and the students sued the Minnesota Department of Employment and Economic Development for prohibiting the federal aid to high school students. In December 2020, they won. The state had to pay them the federal unemployment benefits. Cole Stevens, who had spent months making phone calls and organizing with other high school students, was shocked by the decision: "I think the number one thing I learned is that it's possible for someone like myself, 18 years old, no assets, family has no assets. No social capital, nothing at all. When I went into this, I was literally just a kid who was broke, lost his job and didn't like what the government did to me."[1]

Every day, government affects our lives. Sometimes that is welcome, as when the federal government disbursed federal aid to states to help with their pandemic responses. Sometimes people disagree with government activity, like the high school students who felt they should receive unemployment insurance just like other laid-off workers—and the

▲ The work of Hayat Muse and other students to change a Minnesota law around pandemic relief payments highlights the importance of the citizen's role in American democracy.

people who feel that the government should not spend as much money on unemployment benefits or pandemic relief in the first place.

Because the United States is a democracy, ordinary people play a significant role in government and politics. Individuals can act alone through voting, writing letters to elected officials, participating at local community meetings, and signing petitions. But often, participation is more effective when people work together.

Thus, government affects us all in ways big and small. The purpose of this book is to show what government does, how, and why—and what you can do about it.

CHAPTER GOALS

Differentiate among forms of government (pp. 5–10)

Describe the rights and responsibilities that citizens have in a democracy (pp. 11–12)

Describe the social composition of the American population and how it has changed over time (pp. 13–20)

Describe how foundational values of liberty, equality, and justice influence the U.S. system of government (pp. 20–26)

Summarize Americans' attitudes toward government (pp. 27–28)

Government

Government is the term generally used to describe the formal institutions through which a territory and its people are ruled. A government may be as simple as a town meeting in which community members make policy or as complex as the vast establishments found in many large countries today, with extensive procedures, laws, and bureaucracies. In the history of civilization, thousands of governments have been established. The hard part is establishing one that lasts.

government institutions and procedures through which a territory and its people are ruled

politics conflict over the leadership, structure, and policies of governments

Even more difficult is developing a stable government that is true to the core American political values of liberty, equality, and justice. Though in principle these three values are endorsed by most Americans, in practice each of them means different things to different people, and they often seem to conflict with one another. This is where politics comes in. **Politics** refers to conflicts and struggles over the leadership, structure, and policies of governments.

Is Government Needed?

Government is needed to provide services, sometimes called "public goods," that citizens all need but probably cannot provide adequately for themselves—such as defense against foreign aggression, maintenance of public order, a stable currency, enforcement of contractual obligations and property rights, and some measure of economic security. Government, with its powers to tax and regulate, is viewed as the best way to provide public goods. However, there is often disagreement about which public goods are essential and how they should be provided.

Much of what citizens take for granted every day is in fact affected by government. Throughout the day, for example, a typical college student relies on a host of services and activities organized by national, state, and local government agencies (see Table 1.1).

Different Forms of Government

Two questions are of special importance in determining how governments differ: Who governs? And how much government control is permitted?

Some nations are governed by a single individual—a king or dictator, for example. This system is called **autocracy**. Where a small group—perhaps landowners, military officers, or the wealthy—controls most of the governing decisions, that government is an **oligarchy**. If citizens

autocracy a form of government in which a single individual — a king, queen, or dictator — rules

oligarchy a form of government in which a small group — landowners, military officers, or wealthy merchants — controls most of the governing decisions

TABLE 1.1	The Presence of Government in the Daily Life of a Student at "State University"

TIME	SCHEDULE
7:00 A.M.	Wake up. Standard time set by the national government.
7:10 A.M.	Shower. Water courtesy of local government, and supplied by either a public entity or a regulated private company.
7:30 A.M.	Have a bowl of cereal with milk for breakfast. "Nutrition Facts" on food labels are a federal requirement.
8:30 A.M.	Drive or take public transportation to campus. Airbags and seat belts required by federal and state laws. Roads and bridges paid for by state and local governments.
8:45 A.M.	Arrive on campus of large public university. Buildings are 70 percent financed by state taxpayers.
9:00 A.M.	First class: Chemistry 101. Tuition partially paid by a federal loan (more than half the cost of university instruction is paid for by taxpayers), chemistry lab paid for with grants from the National Science Foundation (a federal agency) and smaller grants from business corporations made possible by federal income tax deductions for charitable contributions.
Noon	Eat lunch. College cafeteria financed by state dormitory authority on land grant from federal Department of Agriculture.
2:00 P.M.	Second class: American Government 101 (your favorite class!). You may be taking this class because it is required by the state legislature or because it fulfills a university requirement.
4:00 P.M.	Third class: Computer Science 101. Free computers, software, and internet access courtesy of state subsidies plus grants and discounts from Apple and Microsoft, the costs of which are deducted from their corporate income taxes; internet built in part by federal government. Duplication of software prohibited by federal copyright laws.
6:00 P.M.	Eat dinner: hamburger and french fries. Meat inspected for bacteria by federal agencies.
7:00 P.M.	Work at part-time job at the campus library. Minimum wage set by federal, state, or local government.
8:15 P.M.	Go online to check the status of your application for a federal student loan (FAFSA) on the Department of Education's website at studentaid.gov.
10:15 P.M.	Watch TV. Networks regulated by federal government, cable public-access channels required by city law. Weather forecast provided to broadcasters by a federal agency.
Midnight	Put out the trash before going to bed. Trash collected by city sanitation department, financed by user charges.

or the general adult population have **popular sovereignty**—the power to rule themselves—that government is a **democracy**.

Governments also vary considerably in terms of how they govern. In the United States and some other nations, such as the United Kingdom and France, constitutions and other laws limit what governments can do and how they go about it. Governments limited in this way are called liberal or **constitutional governments**.

In other nations, including some in Latin America, Asia, Eastern Europe, and Africa, the law imposes few real limits. Government is nevertheless kept in check by other political and social institutions that it cannot control—such as self-governing territories, organized religions, business organizations, or labor unions. Such governments are generally called **authoritarian**.

In a third group of nations, including the Soviet Union under Joseph Stalin, Nazi Germany, and North Korea today, governments not only lack legal limits but also try to eliminate institutions that might challenge their authority. Because these governments typically attempt to control all of a nation's political, economic, and social life, they are called **totalitarian**.

popular sovereignty a principle of democracy in which political authority rests ultimately in the hands of the people

democracy a system of rule that permits citizens to play a significant part in the governmental process, usually through the election of key public officials

constitutional government a system of rule in which formal and effective limits are placed on the powers of the government

authoritarian government a system of rule in which the government recognizes no formal limits but may nevertheless be restrained by the power of other social institutions

totalitarian government a system of rule in which the government recognizes no formal limits on its power and seeks to absorb or eliminate other social institutions that might challenge it

Today, by one measure, 68 percent of the global population lives in electoral and closed autocracies, and only 14 percent enjoy true liberal democracy with free and fair elections, the rule of law, and constraints on the executive (president or prime minister); 19 percent live in more limited democracies.[2]

Limiting Government

The founding generation of the young United States established many of the principles that would come to define individual liberty for all citizens—freedom of speech, of assembly, and of conscience, as well as freedom from arbitrary search and seizure. Notably, the Founders generally did not favor democracy as we know it today. Despite calls for liberty and freedom, many of the delegates to the Constitutional Convention owned enslaved Black people and sought to protect the brutal system of slavery.[3] In addition, they supported property requirements and other restrictions for voting and for holding office so as to limit political participation to the White male middle and upper classes. Once these institutions and the right to engage in politics were established, however, it was difficult to limit them to the economic elite. Through mass movements that also found political allies in Congress and the courts, voting rights have significantly expanded since the Founding era (see Chapters 2, 3, and 5).

America's Founders were influenced by the English thinker John Locke (1632–1704). Locke argued that governments need the consent of the people.

Democracy in the United States

What type of government exists in the United States? Most people respond with one word: democracy. Yet this is not the complete answer.

A system that permits citizens to vote directly on laws and policies is a **direct democracy**. However, Founders like James Madison were concerned that in a direct democracy, the majority could trample over the rights of the minority. So the Founders focused on creating a democracy based on the principle of **majority rule** with **minority rights**.

Majority rule means that the wishes of the majority determine what government does. The House of Representatives—a large body elected directly by the people—was designed to ensure majority rule. But the Founders feared that popular majorities might turn government into a "tyranny of the majority"; thus, concern for individual rights and liberties has been a part of American democracy from the beginning.

Today, the U.S. government is a **representative democracy**, or a **republic**, in which citizens have the opportunity to elect top officials. At the national level, citizens select government officials but do not vote directly on legislation. Some states and cities, however, do provide for direct legislation through initiatives and referenda. These procedures allow citizens to collect petitions, or legislators to pass bills, requiring a direct popular vote on an issue. In 2021 more than 2 million Californians signed a petition in an effort to recall the governor, Gavin Newsom. Many Californians were unhappy with his leadership, especially his handling of the coronavirus pandemic. In 2022, 137 statewide ballot measures were certified for the ballot, many addressing hot-button issues such as the legalization of medical or recreational marijuana, taxes, abortion access and funding, election policies such as redistricting, voting requirements, and criminal trials.[4]

direct democracy a system of rule that permits citizens to vote directly on laws and policies

majority rule, minority rights the democratic principle that a government follows the preferences of the majority of voters but protects the interests of the minority

representative democracy (republic) a system of government in which the populace selects representatives, who play a significant role in governmental decision-making

political power influence over a government's leadership, organization, or policies

Participation in Government Is How People Have a Say in What Happens

As Harold Lasswell, a famous political scientist, once put it, politics is the struggle over "who gets what, when, how."[5] In this book *politics* will refer to conflicts over who the government's leadership is, how the government is organized, or what its policies are. Having a say in these issues is called having **political power** or influence.

AMERICA | SIDE BY SIDE

Forms of Government

The question of whether a country is democratic or authoritarian is complex. Every year, countries are rated on a scale from "Full Democracies" to "Authoritarian" systems based on expert evaluations of five factors: electoral processes, political culture, respect for civil liberties, political participation, and functioning of government. In 2016, for the first time, the United States was classified as a "Flawed Democracy" in response to declines in public confidence in governance and a rise in polarization.

1. Is there a geographic pattern between the countries labeled "Full" or "Flawed" democracies and those that are labeled "Hybrid" or "Authoritarian" systems? What factors, historical, economic, geographic, or otherwise, might help explain this pattern?
2. What do you think separates a "Full Democracy" from a "Flawed Democracy"? The United States' categorization as a "Flawed Democracy" happened during the Obama administration and persisted during the Trump and Biden administrations. What changes have you seen in the past few years that might explain this shift? How concerned should Americans be by this categorization?

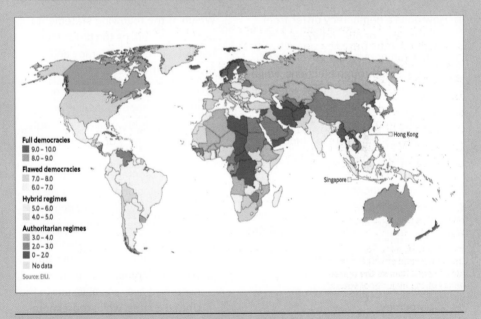

SOURCE: "Democracy Index 2021," The Economist Intelligence Unit.

pluralism the theory that all interests are and should be free to compete for influence in the government; the outcome of this competition is compromise and moderation

An individual's participation in politics can take many forms, including voting, donating money, signing petitions, attending political meetings, tweeting and commenting online, sending emails to officials, lobbying legislators, working on a campaign, and participating in protest marches and even violent demonstrations.

Groups and organized interests also participate in politics. Their political activities include providing funds for candidates, lobbying, and trying to influence public opinion. The pattern of struggles among interests is called group politics, or **pluralism**. Americans have always had mixed feelings about pluralist politics. On the one hand, the right of groups to support their views and compete for influence in government is the essence of liberty. On the other hand, groups may sometimes exert too much influence, advancing their own interests at the expense of larger public interests (see Chapter 9).

Check your understanding

1. How does a democracy differ from an autocracy or oligarchy?

   a) In a democracy, the government is chosen through elections, while the government is never selected through elections in an autocracy or oligarchy.

   b) Few legal limits are in place to limit government in a democracy, while constitutions place limits on government in an autocracy or oligarchy.

   c) In a democracy, citizens rule themselves, while a single individual or small group controls most governing decisions in an oligarchy or autocracy.

   d) In a democracy, citizens always vote directly on policies, while in an autocracy or oligarchy, citizens indirectly affect policies through their elected officials.

2. Which of the following statements best characterizes the difference between direct democracy and representative democracy?

   a) According to James Madison, direct democracy always protects minority rights, while representative democracy does not protect minority rights.

   b) In a representative democracy, voters select individuals to act on their behalf, while direct democracy involves citizens voting directly on legislation, such as through initiatives and referenda in some states.

   c) Direct democracy tends to be exercised over social issues in the United States, while representative democracy is used for fiscal or monetary policies.

   d) Direct democracy always results in policies that reflect what the public wants, while representative democracy always results in what special interests want.

Citizenship Is Based on Participation, Knowledge, and Efficacy

Describe the rights and responsibilities that citizens have in a democracy

In a democracy, **citizenship** can be defined as membership in a political community that provides legal rights and carries participation responsibilities.[6] Civil liberties and rights such as freedom of speech, freedom of worship, and trial by jury are identified in the Constitution—particularly in the Bill of Rights (see Chapters 2 and 4). Citizens also have responsibilities, such as upholding the Constitution; obeying federal, state, and local laws; paying taxes; serving on juries when called; and being informed about issues.[7]

> **citizenship** membership in a political community that confers legal rights and carries participation responsibilities
>
> **political knowledge** information about the formal institutions of government, political actors, and political issues

One key ingredient for political participation is **political knowledge**. Democracy functions best when citizens have the knowledge needed to engage in political debate. It is also important to know the rules and processes that govern political institutions and the principles they rest on, *and* to know them in ways that relate to your own interests.

Without political knowledge, citizens cannot be aware of their stakes in political disputes. For example, during the 2017 debate about whether to repeal the health care reform enacted in 2010, one-third of Americans did not know that "Obamacare" and the "Affordable Care Act" (ACA) are the same thing.[8] Therefore, some people who had enrolled in "Obamacare" didn't realize their access to health insurance would be affected if the ACA were repealed.

Surveys show that large majorities of Americans get political information online, although inequalities in internet access by income, education, geographic region, race, and age remain. Despite the internet making it easier than ever to learn about politics, actual political knowledge in the United States remains spotty. Even with greater access to information, most Americans know little about current issues or debates, or even the basics of how government works. For example, in 2021 only 56 percent of those surveyed could identify all three

Politics sometimes involves rallies or protests to draw attention to issues like immigration, seen here.

disinformation false information that is shared intentionally to reach a political goal

political efficacy the belief that one can influence government and politics

branches of the federal government, and only 35 percent knew the term of office for a senator is six years.[9] In addition, **disinformation**— false information shared intentionally to reach a political goal—complicates the process of acquiring valid political information (see also Chapter 7).[10]

Another ingredient in participation is **political efficacy**, the belief that ordinary citizens can affect what government does. The feeling that you *can't* affect government decisions can lead to apathy, declining political participation, and withdrawal from political life. Americans' sense of political efficacy has declined over time. In 1960 only 25 percent felt shut out of government. In 2019, 71 percent of survey respondents said that elected officials don't care what ordinary people think.[11] Moreover, 52 percent disagreed with the idea that the "government is really run for the benefit of all the people."[12] Research shows that efficacy and participation are related: a feeling that one can make a difference leads to participation, and joining in can increase one's efficacy.[13]

Check your understanding

3. Why are political knowledge and political efficacy important ingredients for a democracy?

   a) An informed and engaged public that participates and serves as a check on government is vital for ensuring that government is responsive to the public.

   b) Extensive knowledge is required since citizens must vote directly on policies before they are enacted.

   c) Elected officials generally only engage citizens with high levels of knowledge and efficacy since they usually have resources.

   d) Most Americans have extensive knowledge about politics and have a high level of political efficacy, and this means they almost always participate in elections.

4. Which of the following statements about Americans' knowledge and involvement in politics and government is true?

   a) Americans are generally highly knowledgeable about politics and the workings of government given the wide accessibility of information.

   b) Most Americans feel that government cares what they think and works for the public good.

   c) Americans' level of efficacy has steadily increased over time, leading to significant increases in voter turnout among the public.

   d) Americans' level of efficacy has declined over time, and political involvement and knowledge is generally low among the public.

Who Are Americans?

Describe the social composition of the American population and how it has changed over time

While American democracy aims to give the people a voice in government, the meaning of "we the people" has changed over time. Who are Americans? Throughout the nation's history, citizens have puzzled and fought over the answer to this fundamental question.

Immigration Has Changed American Identity

The U.S. population has grown from 3.9 million in 1790, the year of the first official census, to 333 million in 2022.[14] At the same time, it has become more diverse on nearly every dimension imaginable.[15]

In 1790, when the nation consisted of 13 states along the Eastern Seaboard, 81 percent of Americans traced their roots to Europe, mostly Britain and elsewhere in northern Europe, and nearly 20 percent, the vast majority of whom were enslaved, were of African origin.[16] Only 1.5 percent of the Black population were free. There were also an unknown number of Native peoples, the original inhabitants of the land, not counted by the census because the government didn't consider them Americans. The first estimates of Native Americans and Latinos in the mid-1800s showed that each group made up less than 1 percent of the total population.[17]

Fast-forward to 1900. The country stretched across the continent, and waves of immigrants, mainly from Europe, had boosted the population to 76 million. It still predominantly comprised people of European ancestry, but it now included many from southern and eastern as well as northwestern Europe; the Black population stood at 12 percent. Residents who traced their origin to Latin America or Asia each accounted for less than 1 percent of the population.[18] The large number of new immigrants was reflected in the high proportion of foreign-born people in the population, which peaked at 14.7 percent in 1910.[19] As immigrants from southern and eastern Europe crowded into the nation's cities, anxiety mounted among those of British and other northwestern European ancestry, who feared losing their long-dominant position in American society and politics.

After World War I, Congress responded to nativist fears about immigration with new laws that sharply limited how many people could enter the country each year. It also passed the Immigration Act of 1924, which used a national origins quota system, based on the nation's population in 1890, before the wave of eastern and southern European immigrants arrived.[20] Supporters of these measures hoped to restore an earlier America in which northern and western Europeans dominated. The new system set up a hierarchy of admissions: northern and western European countries received generous quotas for new immigrants, whereas eastern and southern European countries were granted very small quotas. And almost all immigrants from Asian and African countries were banned.[21] By 1970 these guidelines had reduced the foreign-born population in the United States to an all-time low of 5 percent.

The use of ethnic and racial criteria to restrict the country's population and to draw boundaries around "American" identity began long before the national origins quota system, however. Most people of African descent were not deemed citizens until 1868, when the Fourteenth Amendment to the Constitution granted citizenship to formerly enslaved people (see Chapter 2). Native Americans weren't officially recognized as citizens until the Indian Citizenship Act of 1924, but this did not include suffrage. Efforts to limit nonwhite immigration and citizenship dated back to the Naturalization Act of 1790—a law stating that only free White people could become naturalized citizens, a ban not lifted until 1870. Even then, different restrictions applied to Asians: the Chinese Exclusion Act of 1882 outlawed the entry of Chinese laborers to the United States, a limit lifted only in 1943, when China became America's ally during World War II. And after the Japanese attack on Pearl Harbor in 1941, virtually all Japanese Americans were denied their basic rights of citizenship and were incarcerated for the duration of the war.

With laws about citizenship linked to "Whiteness," questions arose about how to classify people of Latino origin. In 1930, for example, the census counted people of Mexican origin as nonwhite, but a decade later it reversed this decision after protests by those affected and by the Mexican government. Then, in 1960, the census classified immigrants from Latin America as White. Only after a lengthy campaign by Latino activists and business leaders did the census adopt a "Hispanic" classification category in 1970, noting also that people identifying as Hispanic could be of any race.[22] (The census uses the term *Hispanic*, but we will generally use the term *Latino* to refer to people of Spanish or Latin American descent.)

Who Are Americans in the Twenty-First Century?

Race and Ethnicity Recent immigration patterns have profoundly shaped the nation's current racial and ethnic profile. The primary cause was Congress's decision in 1965 to lift the tight restrictions of the 1920s, allowing expanded immigration from Asia and Latin America (see Figure 1.1). Census figures for 2020 show that Latinos (who can be of any race) constitute 18.7 percent of the total population, and Asians make up 6 percent. The Black, or African American, population is 12.4 percent of the total, while the non-Hispanic White population accounts for 61.6 percent. More than 33 million Americans, about 1 in 10, now identify

WHO ARE AMERICANS?

An Increasingly Diverse Nation

Since the Founding, the U.S. population has grown rapidly and people living in the United States have become increasingly diverse. Dramatic changes in population, demographics, and geography often drive changes in American government and politics.

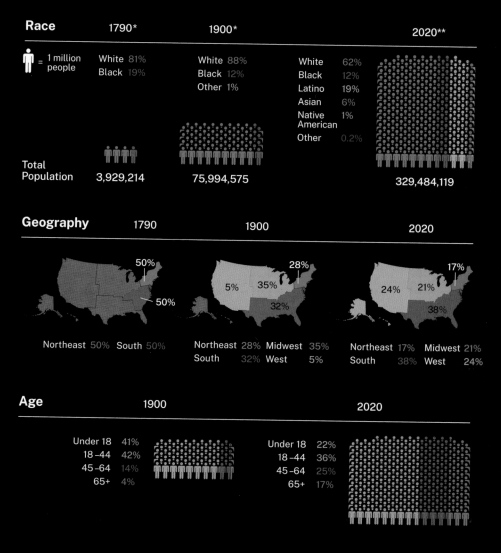

Race

	1790*	1900*	2020**
= 1 million people	White 81%	White 88%	White 62%
	Black 19%	Black 12%	Black 12%
		Other 1%	Latino 19%
			Asian 6%
			Native American 1%
			Other 0.2%
Total Population	3,929,214	75,994,575	329,484,119

Geography

1790

50%

50%

Northeast 50% South 50%

1900

28%

5% 35%

32%

Northeast 28% Midwest 35%
South 32% West 5%

2020

17%

24% 21%

38%

Northeast 17% Midwest 21%
South 38% West 24%

Age

	1900		2020
Under 18	41%	Under 18	22%
18–44	42%	18–44	36%
45–64	14%	45–64	25%
65+	4%	65+	17%

* The 1790 census does not accurately reflect the population because it only counted Black people and White people. It did not include Native Americans or other groups. The 1900 census did not count Latino Americans.

** Numbers may not add up to 100 percent due to rounding.

SOURCE: U.S. Census Bureau, American Community surveys, data.census.gov (accessed 12/6/21).

FIGURE 1.1 | Immigration by Continent of Origin

Where did most immigrants come from at the start of the twentieth century? How does that compare with immigration in the twenty-first century?

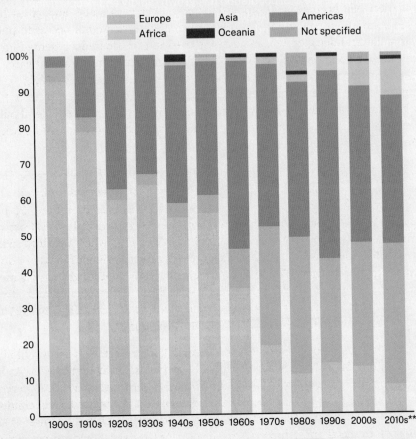

PERCENTAGE OF IMMIGRANTS*

Legend: Europe, Asia, Americas, Africa, Oceania, Not specified

*Less than 1 percent not shown.

**Through 2018.

NOTE: Figure shows those who have obtained "lawful permanent resident status" by continent of origin.

SOURCE: Department of Homeland Security, www.dhs.gov (accessed 1/19/20).

as being of "two or more races," a category that was added in 2000.[23] Notably, in 2019, for the first time, more than half of Americans under age 16 identified as a member of a racial or ethnic minority group. The United States is continuing to diversify and is projected to become a majority-minority country by 2050.

Large-scale immigration means that many more residents now are foreign-born. In 2020, 13.2 percent of the population were born outside the United States, a figure comparable to that in 1900.[24] About half came from Latin America and the Caribbean—almost 1 in 10 from the Caribbean, just over one-third from Central America (including Mexico), and 1 in 15 from South America.[25] Those born in Asia made up 31.3 percent of foreign-born residents.[26] In sharp contrast to the immigration patterns of a century earlier, just 10.9 percent came from Europe.[27]

Estimates are that 12 million immigrants live in the country without legal authorization—the majority from Mexico and Central America.[28] This unauthorized population has become a flashpoint for controversy as states and cities have passed a variety of conflicting laws regarding these immigrants' access to public services. Several decades ago, some states tried to exclude undocumented immigrants from public services such as education and emergency medical care, but in 1982 the Supreme Court ensured access to K–12 education in its *Plyler v. Doe* ruling, and Congress guaranteed access to emergency medical care in a 1986 law.[29] Today, undocumented immigrants remain ineligible for most federal public benefits, but some states allow them to obtain driver's licenses or in-state tuition at public colleges and universities.[30]

Religion New patterns of immigration have combined with differences in birth rates and other social changes to alter the balance of Americans' religious affiliations. By 2021, only 35 percent of Americans identified as Protestant, 22 percent as Catholic, 10 percent as Christian (nonspecific), 2 percent Jewish, 1 percent Mormon, and 6 percent "Other" (this includes Muslims, who constitute nearly 1 percent of the population). Moreover, a growing number identify with no organized religion: 21 percent of the population in 2021.[31] Although many Americans think of the United States as a "Judeo-Christian" nation—and indeed it was 95 percent Protestant, Catholic, or Jewish as recently as 50 years ago—by 2021 this number had fallen to 69 percent of the adult population.[32]

Age As the population has grown and diversified, the country's age profile has shifted with it. In 1900 only 4 percent of the population was over age 65. As life expectancy increased, so did the number of older Americans: by 2020, 16 percent of the population was over 65. During the same period, the percentage of children under age 18 fell, from 44 percent in 1900 to 22.4 percent in 2020.[33] However, the population of racial and ethnic groups is younger than the American population overall: 32 percent of the Latino population and 26 percent of the Black population are under 18, compared to 19 percent of the White population. As a group, Americans are still younger than the populations of many other industrialized countries. The share of the population age 65 and over is 21 percent in the European Union and 28 percent in Japan.[34] But an aging population poses challenges. As the elderly population in the United States grows relative to those of working age, the funding of "safety-net" programs such as Social Security becomes more difficult.

Geography Over the nation's history, Americans have mostly moved from rural areas and small towns to large cities and suburbs. Before 1920 less than half the population lived in urban areas; today over 80 percent does.[35] As a result, the national political system created when the population was still largely rural underrepresents urban Americans. Providing each state with two senators, for example, overrepresents sparsely populated rural states and underrepresents those with large urban populations (see Chapter 2).

The population has also shifted regionally. During the past 50 years especially, many Americans have left the Northeast and Midwest and moved to the South and Southwest, with congressional seats being reapportioned to reflect the population shift.

Socioeconomic Status For much of U.S. history, most Americans were relatively poor working people, many of them farmers. A new, extremely wealthy elite emerged in the late 1800s, a period called "the Gilded Age." By 1928 nearly one-quarter of total annual national income went to the top 1 percent of earners; the top 10 percent took home 46 percent of the total. In the mid-twentieth century, the distribution of income and wealth shifted away from the top. A large, predominantly White middle class grew after New Deal programs helped counteract the Great Depression of the 1930s, and it grew further with the postwar economic boom of the 1950s and '60s.

In the 1960s, the enactment of civil rights legislation and new social programs helped shrink the income disparity between those at the bottom and those at the top. Since then, however, economic inequality has again widened in what some call a "new Gilded Age."[36] Factors like deindustrialization, globalization, slow growth in wages, technological change, and the Great Recession of 2007–09 have accelerated this trend.[37] After a period of recovery, the Covid-19 pandemic contributed to a widening of long-standing economic divides. By 2021 the top 1 percent earned 27 percent of total household wealth. During that same time, the middle 60 percent of households saw their wealth drop to 26.6 percent—the lowest in three decades. In other words, the top 1 percent hold more wealth than America's middle class.[38] At the same time, there has been an increase of people who live below the poverty line, to 11.4 percent of the population (see Figure 1.2).[39]

But there are significant racial differences among levels of income and wealth. Wealth is defined as the difference between a household's assets (what you own that contains economic value, like houses and stock) and debt. The term "racial wealth gap" refers to the disparity in assets of typical American households across racial and ethnic groups. According to recent data, the median White household had $188,200 in wealth, compared to just $36,100 for the median Latino household and $24,100 for the median Black household.[40]

Population and Politics Population growth and shifts have spurred politically charged debates about how to apportion the population among congressional districts and how to draw those districts. These conflicts have significant implications for the balance of representation among different regions of the country and between urban and rural areas. Representation of other demographic and political groups may also be affected, as evidence shows that Americans are increasingly divided from one another geographically according to education, income, marriage rates, and party voting.[41] In addition, immigration and the resulting cultural and religious changes spark passionate debate today, just as they did 100 years ago. (You can read about valuable debate tips in the How To feature on pp. 24–25.)

FIGURE 1.2 | Wealth in the United States

While the wealth of most Americans has risen only slightly since 1989, the wealth of the richest Americans (the top 10 percent) has increased dramatically. In 2022, the top 10 percent of Americans had more than double the total amount of combined wealth held by the middle 40 percent and bottom 50 percent of Americans. Does the growing economic gap between the richest groups and most other Americans conflict with the political value of equality?

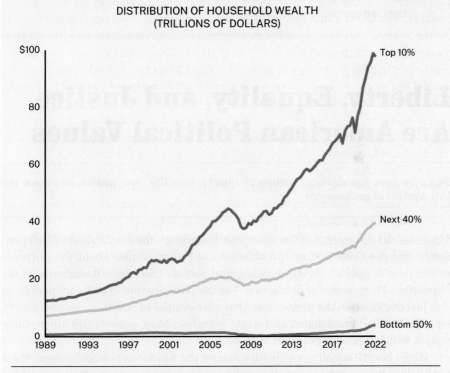

DISTRIBUTION OF HOUSEHOLD WEALTH
(TRILLIONS OF DOLLARS)

SOURCE: Federal Reserve, "Distribution of Household Wealth in the U.S. since 1989," www.federalreserve.gov/releases/z1/dataviz/dfa/distribute/chart/ (accessed 9/22/22).

Check your understanding

5. Which of the following statements best characterizes population changes in the United States over time?

a) Americans have moved from large cities and the suburbs to small rural towns.

b) The American population has become more racially and ethnically diverse.

c) There has been a steep decline in the foreign-born population.

d) Non-Hispanic White Americans have become a minority of the population.

6. What effect has the changing composition of the American population had on politics and government?

   a) It has ensured widespread political participation among different groups.

   b) It has made governing easier and ensured that all groups in American society are represented equally.

   c) It has produced more agreement and consensus in American politics.

   d) It raises contentious debates about balance of representation among different regions of the country and between urban and rural areas.

Liberty, Equality, and Justice Are American Political Values

Describe how foundational values of liberty, equality, and justice influence the U.S. system of government

The essential documents of the American Founding—the Declaration of Independence and the Constitution—proclaimed a set of principles about the purposes of the new Republic: liberty, equality, and justice. (See these documents in the appendix.) The practice of democracy—or the participation of ordinary people, as was just discussed in the previous section—is essential to how these values (liberty, equality, justice) are debated and made manifest. Most citizens still affirm these values, which form our **political culture**.

While liberty, equality, and justice anchor the American political system, these core values have not been equally applied over time. Despite the influence of the Founding principles on the practice of government, certain undemocratic traditions—nativism, racism, and sexism—have also been influential. Examining the impact of these traditions on American political culture allows a deeper understanding of how far this nation has come and the challenges that still lie ahead.

political culture broadly shared values, beliefs, and attitudes about how the government should function; American political culture emphasizes the values of liberty, equality, and justice

liberty freedom from governmental control

Liberty Means Freedom

Liberty is one of America's central political values. The Declaration of Independence identified three "unalienable" rights: "Life, Liberty and the pursuit of Happiness." The Constitution likewise identified the need "to secure the Blessings of Liberty." For Americans, **liberty** means both personal freedom and economic freedom.

Both are closely linked to the idea of **limited government**.

The Constitution's first 10 amendments, known collectively as the Bill of Rights, delineate individual personal liberties and rights. In fact, the word *liberty* has come to mean many of the freedoms guaranteed in the Bill of Rights: freedom of speech and the press, the right to assemble freely, and the right to practice religious beliefs without interference from the government.

> **limited government** a principle of constitutional government; a government whose powers are defined and limited by a constitution
>
> **laissez-faire capitalism** an economic system in which the means of production and distribution are privately owned and operated for profit with minimal or no government interference

Throughout American history, the scope of personal liberties has expanded as laws have become more tolerant and individuals have successfully used the courts to challenge restrictions on their personal freedoms. Far fewer restrictions exist today on the press, political speech, and individual behavior than in the nation's early years. Even so, conflicts emerge when personal liberties violate a community's accepted standards of behavior. For example, a number of cities have passed "sit-lie" ordinances, which limit the freedom of individuals to sit or lie down on sidewalks. Designed to limit the presence of people who are homeless and to make city streets more attractive to pedestrians, the ordinances have also been denounced as restrictions on individual liberties.

Liberty also extends into the realm of economics. The American concept of economic freedom supports capitalism, free markets (including open competition and unrestricted movement of goods), and the protection of private property.[42] During the nation's first century, support for capitalism often meant support for the principle of *laissez-faire* (French for "allow to do"). **Laissez-faire capitalism** allowed the national government very little power to regulate commerce or restrict the use of private property. Today, however, federal and state governments impose many regulations to protect the public in such areas as health and safety, the environment, and the workplace.

Equality Means Treating People Fairly

The Declaration of Independence declares as its first "self-evident" truth that "all men are created equal." However, equality has been an even less well-defined ideal than liberty, because people interpret it in such different ways. Few Americans have wholeheartedly embraced the ideal of full equality of results (that everyone deserves equal wealth and power), but most share the ideal of **equality of opportunity** (that all people deserve a fair chance to go as far as their talents will allow). Yet it's hard to agree on what constitutes equality of opportunity. Furthermore, in contrast to liberty, which requires limits on the role of government, equality implies an *obligation* of the government to the people.[43] But how far does this obligation extend? Must a group's past inequalities be redressed to ensure equal opportunity in the present? Should legal,

> **equality of opportunity** a widely shared American ideal that all people should have the freedom to use whatever talents and wealth they have to reach their fullest potential

political, and economic inequalities all be given the same weight?

Americans do make clear distinctions between social or economic equality and **political equality**, the right of a community's members to participate in politics on equal terms. Though America started with a very restricted definition of political community, which included only White men who owned a certain amount of property, the nation has moved much closer to an ideal of political equality that can be summed up as "one person, one vote." Most Americans agree that all citizens should have an equal right to participate and that government should enforce that right.

Many Americans see economic inequality as largely the result of individual choices, so they tend to be more skeptical of government action to reduce it (compared to government action to reduce political inequality). Income inequality rose on the political agenda during the coronavirus pandemic. The economic slowdown most affected lower-income workers without employee benefits, including those in the restaurant, retail, and gig economy sectors. As Congress deliberated economic stimulus measures and policy changes during the Covid-19 pandemic, debates about the role of government reemerged. Should greater resources be directed at helping workers or employers? Would increased unemployment benefits lead to better jobs for workers or disincentivize returning to work? Such debates appear even under the toughest economic circumstances.[44]

The Fight for $15 — a nationwide effort to increase the minimum wage to $15 an hour — first gained traction in 2013, increasing public awareness of income inequality in the United States. By 2022 many states had increased their minimum wage above the federal minimum wage, but few had reached the $15 threshold that workers had protested for.

Justice Is an Unfinished Project

Justice is the first of five political objectives high-lighted in the Constitution: "We the People of the United States, in Order to form a more perfect Union, establish Justice, insure domestic Tranquility, pro-vide for the common defense, promote the general Welfare, and secure the Blessings of Liberty." How-ever, as with liberty and equality, what constitutes justice is contested and has been debated over time.

While the Founders valued the *concept* of jus-tice, the *practice* of justice was more complicated. Numerous aspects of the Founding period were unjust, such as the taking of land from Native nations, the enslavement of Black people, and the absence of voting rights for women and other groups.

Some of the most intense battles over the meaning of justice have occurred through the judicial branch. In the Founders' view, the judicial branch would have the responsibility of ensuring that justice is carried out. Justice was, and is, closely linked to the principle of **fairness**.[45] Ensuring a fair process is key to how we get to a just outcome. In order for the judicial branch to do its job, courts must apply the law fairly. Today, many disputes over the meaning of justice are decided in the Supreme Court. For example, in the landmark case *Obergefell v. Hodges* (2015), the Court ruled that banning same-sex marriage represented a grave injustice and that fairness required its legalization.[46]

But justice is not exclusively determined by judges, nor does it always necessitate a change in laws. Conceptions of justice arise from the people, and efforts to realize those visions can take many different forms. Over time, organized groups of Ameri-cans have used the language of justice—especially **social justice**—to advocate for change.[47] Examples include the disability justice, environmental justice, and crim-inal justice reform movements. Some-times the change being sought is about present challenges, and other times it is focused on redressing past wrongs. The movement for racial justice inspired over 20 million people to take to the streets during spring 2020 to draw attention to persistent racism directed at Black peo-ple.[48] Protesters sought the transformation of policing, housing, and the economic system. In response, in many cases police reforms were instituted, cities provided help to families that needed housing, and corporations pledged resources to help improve race relations.[49] And as with other

justice the fairness of how rewards and punishments are delivered, especially by gov-ernments and courts, but also in society

fairness impartial decision-making; the quality of treating people equally, free from discrimination

social justice the just alloca-tion of wealth, opportunities, and privileges within a society

Justice is one of America's most important political values. In fact, justice is so central to the mission of the Supreme Court of the United States that engraved in marble on its building is the famous phrase "Equal Justice Under Law."

HOW TO

Debate Respectfully

APRIL LAWSON, THE DIRECTOR OF DEBATES FOR BETTER ANGELS

Government by the people functions best when individuals discuss ideas, share their preferences, and talk about what government is doing. But political discussion and debate can be uncomfortable, particularly among people who disagree or when politics is polarized, as it is in the current era. In order to have a productive discussion, it is important that people are respectful of others from different backgrounds, who might hold different political views.

To learn how to engage others and to debate respectfully, we spoke with April Lawson, the director of debates for Better Angels, a national organization that works with individuals from across the political spectrum to "combat polarization and restore civil dialogue across America." She offers these tips for successful and civil political conversations:

1 **The most important thing is the presumption of good faith.** If someone says something you can't stand, know that the other person is trying, just like you are, to address hard questions. Assume that the other person is smart and that they are moral.

2 **Say what you actually believe.** Genuineness and sincerity are crucial. You could debate either by making a case no one could disagree with or by sharing what you really feel about the issue. The latter will make for a more productive exchange of ideas.

3 **How can you launch such a conversation and set the tone?** A good technique is to start with a question of genuine curiosity for the other person, which reassures them that you want to know what they believe. Another tip is to paraphrase what they have said before you respond, to make sure the other person feels heard.

4 When you respond, it helps if you express some doubt or nuance in your own argument, or mention that you agree with some aspect of the other person's position. You do not need to agree with everything they have said, but you can pick something reasonable the other person said and affirm, "You said X, which makes sense because of Y."

5 Know that you may need to be the bigger person in the conversation. In order to be an ambassador of civility, you may need the patience to ask several genuine questions of curiosity before the other person believes that you are actually interested in what they have to say. And you need to control your own emotions and triggers, to manage your activation, because you know these rules for civil engagement, and they may not.

6 Finally, realize that you have agency. Prepare yourself for these tough conversations by telling yourself, "I will probably have feelings about this. But I can be patient and manage them." Remember, you're not trapped. You can take a break. You can change topics. Or you may want to have a conversational exit in mind. If it's Thanksgiving and you're speaking with your combative uncle, you might pivot to the football game.

Debating respectfully requires coming to the table with a posture of openness and helping the other person feel heard. In America, at the talking-point level, which is a surface level, we don't agree at all. But if you can go down even one level to political values, or even one more level to moral values, then there's a lot of common ground. With these conversations, we're not trying to change how you see the issue; we're trying to change how you see the other person.

protests advocating for change, those who disagreed with the calls for racial justice held counterdemonstrations.

Another recent example of a social justice movement is the landback movement led by Native nations.[50] Landback leaders point to centuries of land dispossession by the U.S. government and assert that justice will be achieved when government and private land are returned to the stewardship of Native Americans. However, because some of the land is now privately owned or part of national parks, detractors argue that the movement's goal is unfair to current landowners and to the public.

These examples show that despite Americans' reverence for justice, its meaning and practice are often deeply contested.[51] Some people understand it as closely related to liberty and requiring limitations from government intrusion. For others, it overlaps more closely with equality and requires government to intercede on behalf of citizens to address deep-seated inequalities. Just as we can say that the concept of justice is not static, we can consider all of American politics to be an unfinished project: the Founders established lofty guiding principles such as liberty, equality, and justice, but it has been the responsibility of successive generations of Americans to realize these ideals more fully.

Check your understanding

7. Which of the following statements regarding the values of liberty, equality, and justice is true?

   a) While Americans are deeply committed to equality, Americans have shown less commitment to the values of liberty and justice.

   b) Liberty, equality, and justice are contested values and their meaning has changed over time.

   c) Most Americans support the idea of equality of results because it is necessary for both liberty and justice.

   d) While liberty was a value explicitly mentioned by the Founders, justice and equality as political values were not introduced until after the Civil War.

8. How have the values of liberty, equality, and justice shaped the U.S. political system?

   a) In the United States, the equality of results has significantly stronger support than equality of opportunity, and support for liberty and justice has declined over time.

   b) Justice has been addressed exclusively through the judicial system and has remained a static concept over time, while liberty and equality primarily have been defined by the legislative branch and remain fairly static concepts.

   c) Liberty, equality, and justice are core values that have not been equally applied over time, yet continue to inform debates around important issues like press freedom, income inequality, and criminal justice reform.

   d) The values of liberty, equality, and justice have had an influential role in government passing policies that have eliminated economic inequality.

What Americans Think about Government

Summarize Americans' attitudes toward government

Since the United States was established as a nation, Americans have been reluctant to grant government too much power, and they have often been suspicious of politicians. But they have also turned to government for assistance in times of need and have strongly supported it in periods of war. In 1933 the government's power began to expand to meet the crises created by the stock market crash of 1929, the massive business failures and unemployment of the Great Depression, and the threatened failure of the banking system. Congress passed legislation that brought government into the businesses of home mortgages, farm mortgages, credit, and relief of personal financial distress. More recently, when the economy suffered a deep recession in 2008 and 2009, the federal government took action to stabilize the financial system, oversee the restructuring of failing auto manufacturers, and provide hundreds of billions of dollars in economic stimulus.

Trust in Government Has Declined

A key characteristic of contemporary political culture is low *trust* in government. In the early 1960s three-quarters of Americans said they trusted government "most of the time or always." By 2021 only 24 percent said they did.[52] Importantly, trust in government has been found to increase among members of the party that controls the presidency. For example, Republicans exhibited higher levels of trust when Trump was president (36 percent), while Democrats' trust fell (12 percent). In contrast, Democrats' trust in government increased to 36 percent during the Biden administration while Republicans' plummeted to 9 percent.[53]

While Americans' trust in the federal government has fallen over recent decades, trust in local and state governments has stayed relatively high. Even during the pandemic, with people objecting to policies from their state and local governments, confidence continued to be higher than in the federal government. The differing levels in trust are likely related to the fact that citizens can exert greater influence on local and state politics.

Level of trust also differs across groups: Black people and Latinos express more confidence in the federal government than do White people. And there is a generational difference in levels of trust: Baby Boomers (those born between 1946 and 1964) express greater confidence in the federal government than those from Generation Z (born after 1996).[54]

Does it matter if Americans trust their government? Yes. As we've seen, most Americans rely on government—federal, state, and local—for a wide range of services and protections. Long-term distrust in government can result in opposition to the taxes necessary to support such programs and can also make it difficult to attract talented workers to public service.[55] Likewise, a weakened government can do little to help citizens weather periods of tumultuous economic or technological change. Public confidence in government is vital for the health of a democracy.

Check your understanding

9. Overall, which statement best describes Americans' views about government?

   a) Republicans generally support a larger role for the federal government, while Democrats support a limited role of government.

   b) Nearly every American supports a larger role for government, while also being skeptical of government.

   c) The power and size of government has decreased over time as an overwhelming majority of Americans support a smaller role for government.

   d) Americans are deeply divided over the scope of government with Democrats supporting an enlarged role and Republicans preferring limited government.

10. Which statement best characterizes Americans' trust in government?

   a) Americans' trust in the federal government has been declining, though their trust in state government has remained relatively consistent.

   b) Americans have much more trust in the federal government than state or local government.

   c) Democrats always overwhelmingly trust government, while Republicans generally have low levels of trust in government.

   d) White Americans have higher levels of trust in the federal government compared to Latinos and Black Americans.

WHAT DO YOU THINK?

AMERICANS AND THEIR POLITICAL VALUES

This chapter has examined various components of American ideals, traditions, and values. Many Americans support the political values of liberty, equality, and justice, but how we put them into practice sparks many of the debates that shape American political life. In addition, the makeup of the population deeply influences the nation's politics. Race, gender, and class divisions foster disagreement and debate and, as we will see throughout this book, influence how government and politics function.

At the start of this chapter, we introduced Hayat Muse and Cole Stevens, workers who supported their families but who were denied unemployment benefits when they were laid off during the coronavirus pandemic because they were high school students. Given what you learned in this chapter about Americans and their political values, take a closer look at the account of the students' activism on pp. 2–4 and consider the following questions:

- Given your political values—your beliefs about liberty, equality, and justice— what do you think of the unemployment benefit case? If you were to contact an elected official about this issue, which American values would you emphasize? What values do you think Hayat and Cole underlined?

- In what ways does the diversity of the American people represent a strength for American democracy? In what ways is it a challenge?

- How important do you think participation, knowledge, and efficacy are for the functioning of American democracy? What would make you more engaged in government? How do you imagine Hayat and Cole would answer these questions? Are your friends, family, or fellow students engaged in politics? Why, or why not?

Use 🐇 INQUIZITIVE to help you study and master this material.

2

WHAT GOVERNMENT DOES & WHY IT MATTERS

For nearly 200 years—since 1834—a statue of Thomas Jefferson has stood in New York City Hall, residing in the city's Council Chambers since 1915. A debate has been simmering for two decades about removing the statue. Many of the Founders, including Jefferson, owned enslaved people even as they were formulating the nation's founding documents such as the Declaration of Independence and the U.S. Constitution, which uphold the ideas of liberty, justice, equality, and the pursuit of happiness. On one side of the debate are members of the city council's Black, Latino, and Asian caucus, who described the statue as "oppressive" and "racist," and who, in a letter to the mayor, argued that it serves as "a constant reminder of the injustices that have plagued communities of color since the inception of our country."[1] Council member Inez Barron said that Jefferson "felt that Blacks were inferior to Whites— in his own words," and that he had removed Native peoples from their ancestral lands.[2] Those urging that the statue remain in City Hall had a different view. In a

The Founding & the Constitution

letter to the city's Public Design Commission, Princeton historian Sean Wilentz argued that "the statue honors Jefferson for his greatest contribution to America, indeed, to humankind: the basic idea, radical then, radical now, that all men are created equal."[3] Raymond Lavertue, a historian from the University of Oxford, testified that "removal is a very simple solution that will erase the debate" and that although Jefferson was "massively flawed," his ideas on equality should "be grappled with daily."[4]

In October 2021, the city's Public Design Commission decided to remove the statue. It will be moved to the New-York Historical Society, whose president and chief executive, Louise Mirrer, planned to create an exhibition examining "the relationship between the founding ideals of freedom and equality set down by Jefferson and their lived experience, which included supporting slavery and owning enslaved people."[5]

The Declaration of Independence explained the American colonists' right to revolt against England. Abraham Lincoln called it a "rebuke . . . to tyranny and oppression." The U.S. Constitution lays out the purposes of government: to promote justice, to maintain peace at home, to defend the nation from foreign foes, to provide for the "general welfare" of Americans, and, above all, to secure the "blessings of liberty" for them. It also spells out a plan for achieving these objectives, including institutions to exercise legislative, executive, and judicial powers and a division of

▲ A statue of Thomas Jefferson as it stood in the city council chambers in New York's City Hall.

powers among the federal government's branches and between the national and state governments.

The debate over removing statues and monuments to Founders also reminds us that these documents were written by men whose legacy is complex. The Constitution was the product of conflict and intense bargaining among competing interests. The values of liberty, equality, and justice encapsulated in it and in the Declaration were contested then, and they are contested now.

Although many Americans believe strongly in the values of liberty, equality, and justice, the ways those values are defined and implemented by the institutions that the Constitution created have generated much controversy. As this chapter will show, the Constitution reflects high principles as well as political self-interest. How those principles have been realized over time— and which groups have benefited and which groups have suffered—is an enduring theme of American governance.

CHAPTER GOALS

Explain the conflicts and coalitions that led to the Declaration of Independence and the Articles of Confederation (pp. 33–39)

Describe the political context of the Constitutional Convention and the compromises achieved there (pp. 39–46)

Describe the principles of governance and the powers of the national government defined by the Constitution (pp. 47–58)

Differentiate between the Federalists' and Antifederalists' stances on the ratification of the Constitution (pp. 59–62)

The First Founding: Interests and Conflicts

Explain the conflicts and coalitions that led to the Declaration of Independence and the Articles of Confederation

To understand dynamic historical eras such as the Founding of the United States, it is helpful to focus on the different perspectives of the people that were present. In American politics, the Founders—people like James Madison, Thomas Jefferson, and Alexander Hamilton—usually take center stage and are revered for articulating American values and ideals such as individual liberty, equality, justice, and the pursuit of happiness.

However, recent scholarship has highlighted the importance of incorporating two additional processes in our understanding of the Founding: land removal from Native nations and enslavement of Africans.[6] In fact, both practices are directly connected to some of the crucial conflicts that led the 13 colonies to declare independence. While it may be difficult to reconcile the lofty ideals of the Founders with the unfair and inhumane treatment of two groups of people, it is necessary to acknowledge the complexity of the Founding period.

Native Nations and Colonial Life

Before the first colonists arrived, the land that would come to be known as the United States was not empty.[7] Hundreds of independent Native nations and millions of Native peoples were already there. Colonists from England set up the first successful colony in America in 1607 in Jamestown, Virginia. In 1620 the second colony was established in Plymouth, Massachusetts. In both places, the colonists settled on land that was occupied at the time by powerful Native nations (among them the Pequot, Narragansett, and Algonquin), who were already practicing a form of democratic self-governance. In fact, there were 60,000 Native Americans living in what would later become the New England colonies. The colonists brought desirable new goods to trade with the Native nations, but they also brought foreign diseases such as smallpox, to which the Native population had no immunity. As a result, their numbers were quickly decimated. For example, of an estimated 12,000 Native Americans when Jamestown was settled in 1607, only 1,000 were left by 1700.[8] For this reason and others, the initially cordial relations between colonists and Native peoples worsened steadily.

Subsequent waves of English settlers rejected Native land ownership and forcibly confiscated land for themselves, displacing Native nations.[9] This unauthorized taking of land, a process known as **settler colonialism**,[10] made possible the growth of the colonies. After all, land was the most valuable commodity in early America. The

> **settler colonialism** a form of colonialism that seeks to remove Native peoples from land and replace them with a new settler population

vast amount of land on the North American continent enticed Europeans to establish and expand colonies. Though Native peoples initially welcomed European newcomers with trade and diplomacy, as the settler populations swiftly grew, especially in the English colonies, land dispossession increased. Soon, lands once controlled by Native nations became bustling colonial merchant areas in the northeast and lucrative agricultural plantations in the southeast.

British Taxes and Colonial Interests

During the first half of the eighteenth century, Britain ruled its American colonies with a light hand. British rule was hardly evident outside the largest towns, and colonists avoided most taxes levied in London. Beginning in the 1760s, however, debts and other financial problems forced the British government to search for new revenue sources. This search quickly led to the North American colonies. Here the colonists were divided into two groups: the radicals (small farmers, shopkeepers, and artisans) and the colonial elite (merchants, planters, royalists). The radicals tended to have fewer economic resources and were distrustful of the British. In contrast, many elites benefited from British rule and supported the Crown. However, its aggressive new tax and trade policies split the elites, enhancing the radicals' political influence and setting off a chain of events that culminated in the American Revolution.[11]

At that time, governments relied mainly on tariffs, duties, and other taxes on commerce to raise revenue. In particular, the Stamp Act of 1765 imposed taxes on many printed items in the colonies, and the Sugar Act of 1764 taxed sugar, molasses, and other commodities. Many colonists saw these moves as detrimental to their livelihoods and a challenge to the colonies' autonomy. United under the slogan "No taxation without representation," they organized demonstrations and a boycott of British goods that ultimately forced the Crown to rescind most of its hated new taxes.

Political Strife Radicalized the Colonists

Ongoing colonial strife was the background for the events of 1773–74. With the Tea Act of 1773, the British government granted the politically powerful East India Company a monopoly on the export of tea from Britain, eliminating a lucrative trade for colonial business interests. Worse, the company planned to sell the tea directly in the colonies instead of working through the colonial merchants. Because tea was an extremely important commodity during the 1770s, these British actions posed a serious threat to New England business interests.

In response, the radicals joined the elites to protest the Tea Act. In three colonies, antitax Americans blocked the unloading of taxed tea, resulting in its return to Britain. However, the most dramatic response was a protest that came to be known as the Boston Tea Party. When the royal governor of Massachusetts refused to allow three shiploads of unsold tea to leave Boston Harbor, the colonists seized this opportunity: on the night of December 16, 1773, fifty of them, some "disguised" as Native Americans, boarded the vessels and threw all 342 chests of tea into the harbor. In response, Parliament closed the port of Boston to

The British helped radicalize colonists through bad policy decisions in the years before the Revolution. For example, Britain gave the ailing East India Company a monopoly on the tea trade in the American colonies. Colonists feared that the monopoly would hurt colonial merchants' business and protested by throwing East India Company tea into Boston Harbor in 1773.

commerce, changed the colonial government of Massachusetts, and removed accused persons to Britain for trial. Most important, Parliament restricted colonists' movement to the west.

These acts of repression further radicalized the new Americans and set in motion a cycle of provocation and retaliation that in 1774 resulted in the convening of the First Continental Congress. An assembly of delegates from 12 colonies, the group called for a total boycott of British goods and, under the radicals' prodding, began considering the possibility of ending British rule. As relations with Britain further deteriorated, there was mounting public pressure from the colonies to declare independence.

Enslaved Africans and the Colonial Economy

While the calls to end British rule were spurred by crushing taxes, repressive measures, and representational concerns, economic forces within the colonies were also at play. Key among these were issues related to **enslavement**—the system of holding people for the purpose of forced labor so that slaveowners could extract profit. In fact, profits gained through slavery were critical to the early development of the colonial economy and made it possible to imagine a future without the British. In

> **enslavement** a system of slavery in which individuals are held as property for the purpose of forced labor so that profit can be extracted

1619 a small group of 20 to 30 enslaved Africans was delivered to Jamestown, Virginia. Their arrival marked the beginning of the transatlantic slave trade in the new colony. Though, at the time, slavery was much more significant in the West Indies, over time the system would grow throughout North America.[12]

Under this dehumanizing system, enslaved African men, women, and children had no legal rights. They were considered "property" with a monetary value and could be insured, bought, and sold.[13] Ultimately, enslaved labor was responsible for the major agricultural and mineral exports of the colonial period, including tobacco, rice, sugar, coffee, silver, and gold. Slavery was vital to manufacturers in places like New York, the largest slave-owning colony in the north. And enslaved labor was essential for the building of sprawling southern plantations, some of which were home to colonial leaders such as George Washington and James Madison.[14] Although some people argued that slavery was inhumane and should be restricted or abolished, it was widely accepted because enslaved people were essential to sustaining the colonial economy.

The Declaration of Independence Explained Why the Colonists Wanted to Break with Great Britain

As the slave trade took hold, mounting tensions led to violent skirmishes between British soldiers and American militia at Lexington and Concord that ultimately erupted into the Revolutionary War. In 1776, more than a year after the war commenced, the Second Continental Congress appointed a committee to draft a statement of American independence from British rule. Thomas Jefferson of Virginia, who drafted the majority of the document, had the daunting task of legitimizing separation from Britain and announcing the creation of a new nation to the rest of the world. After revisions by other delegates, on July 4, 1776, the Second Continental Congress voted to officially accept the document and declare independence. (The Declaration is reprinted in the appendix, pp. A1–A4.) Politically, the Declaration was remarkable because despite the colonists' differences along regional, economic, and philosophical lines, it focused on principles, goals, and grievances that might unify the various groups.

The first section begins with a sweeping statement of human rights: "We hold these truths to be self-evident, that all men are created equal, that they are endowed by their Creator with certain unalienable Rights, that among these are Life, Liberty and the pursuit of Happiness." In the world of 1776, in which some kings still claimed a God-given right to rule, this was a dramatic statement. The Declaration then states that the purpose of governments is to secure the aforementioned rights and that governments derive "their just powers from the consent of the governed." Therefore, when governments violate these rights—when governments no longer have the support of the people—the people have a duty to overthrow them.

The second part of the Declaration lists 27 grievances against King George III. The long list of grievances made clear to the global community that the colonists could not reconcile with Britain.

Yet, even while the Founders were issuing this document that extolled the importance of freedom and self-government, the burgeoning self-sovereign nation was at the same time limiting sovereignty for Native nations. Of particular concern to the colonists was Native resistance to white settlers advancing on the frontier. They were especially worried those Native nations would form an alliance with the British against the colonies. In fact, the last grievance cited in the Declaration accuses the king of colluding with Native peoples. Black people were also excluded from the Founders' belief that all men were created equal. At the time of the signing of the Declaration, slavery was legal in all 13 colonies, and most of the signatories, including Thomas Jefferson, enslaved Black people.[15]

The final paragraph of the Declaration is an assertation of independence. Overall, the document both reviewed a history and identified a set of principles that, together, would forge a new national identity.[16] Today, the Declaration is recognized as a key document from the Founding period, marking the transition from a group of colonies into an independent nation.

The European Enlightenment Influenced the Founders

In describing the expectations of good government in the Declaration, Jefferson drew heavily from philosophers associated with the European Enlightenment. Indeed, while America's leaders were first and foremost practical politicians, they also read political philosophy and were influenced by the important thinkers of their day, including Hobbes, Locke, and Montesquieu. In comparison to what the Americans experienced under British rule, the Enlightenment writings concerning the relationship between organized government and the people presented an exciting alternate future.

The seventeenth-century British philosopher John Locke (1632–1704) advanced the principles of republican government by arguing not only that monarchical power was not absolute but that such power was dangerous and should therefore be limited. Locke held that the people retain rights despite the social contract they make with the monarch. Preserving safety in society is not enough; people's lives, liberty, and property also require protection. Further, Locke wrote in his *Second Treatise of Civil Government* that the people of a country have a right to overthrow a government they believe to be unjust or tyrannical. This key idea shaped the thinking of the Founders, including Jefferson, who said that the Declaration of Independence was "pure Locke." Locke advanced the important ideas of limited government and consent of the governed.

Another British political thinker, Thomas Hobbes (1588–1679), was no advocate of democratic government, but he wrote persuasively in *Leviathan* about the necessity of a government authority as an antidote to human existence in a government-less state of nature, where life was "solitary, poor, nasty, brutish, and short." He also believed that governments should have limits on the powers they exercised and that political systems are based on the idea of "contract theory"—that the people of a country voluntarily give up some freedom in exchange for an ordered society. The monarchs who rule that society derive their legitimacy from this contract, Hobbes argued, not from a God-given right to rule.

Baron de la Brède et de Montesquieu (1689–1755) was a French philosopher who advocated the idea that power needed to be balanced by power as a bulwark against tyranny. This could be achieved through the separation of governing powers. This idea was already in practice in Britain, where legislative and executive powers were divided between Parliament and the monarch. In *The Spirit of the Laws*, Montesquieu argued for the separation and elevation of judicial power, which in Britain was still held by the monarch. Montesquieu did not argue for a pure separation of powers; rather, basic functions would be separated, but there would also be some overlap of functions. These ideas were central in shaping the three-branch system of government that America's Founders would later outline in the Constitution of 1787.

The Articles of Confederation Created America's First National Government

Articles of Confederation
America's first written constitution; served as the basis for America's national government until 1789

confederation a system of government in which states retain sovereign authority except for the powers expressly delegated to the national government

Having declared independence, the colonies needed to establish a government. In November 1777 the Continental Congress adopted the **Articles of Confederation**—the United States' first written constitution. Eventually ratified by all the states in 1781, it functioned as the country's constitution until the final months of 1788.

The colonists' experience with the powerful British government made them fearful of establishing a powerful central government of their own. Thus, the first goal of the Articles was to limit the powers of the central government; as provided under Article II, "each state retains its sovereignty, freedom, and independence." (These attributes define a **confederation**.) Given that there was no president or other presiding officer, the entire national government consisted of a Congress with very little power. Its members were little more than messengers from the state legislatures: their salaries were paid out of the state treasuries; they were subject to immediate recall by state authorities; and each state, regardless of its population, had only one vote. All 13 states had to agree to any amendments to the Articles of Confederation after it was ratified.

Congress was given the power to declare war and make peace, to negotiate treaties and alliances, to issue currency, to borrow money, and to regulate trade with the Native nations. Any laws it passed, however, could be carried out only by state governments. Congress could also appoint the senior officers of the U.S. Army—but there was no such army, because the nation's armed forces consisted only of the state militias. Finally, Congress had no power to collect taxes. These extreme limits on the national government made the Articles of Confederation hopelessly impractical.[17]

Check your understanding

1. Which of the following motivated the colonists' desire for a stronger central government leading to the Declaration of Independence?

   a) the desire of the colonists to establish a national religion
   b) disagreements with King George III over England's support of slavery
   c) the desire of the colonists to pursue westward expansion against the wishes of King George III and Native peoples
   d) disagreements with King George III over England's poor treatment of Native nations

2. Which of the following descriptions of the Articles of Confederation is accurate?

   a) The Articles of Confederation established a president but no Congress due to the Founders' fear of a strong legislative branch.
   b) The Articles of Confederation granted virtually no power to the states.
   c) The colonists established a strong national government in the Articles of Confederation that would enable taxation to pay off war debt.
   d) The colonists established a weak central government in the Articles of Confederation, reflecting their fear that a strong government would infringe upon individual liberty.

The Failure of the Articles of Confederation Made the "Second Founding" Necessary

Describe the political context of the Constitutional Convention and the compromises achieved there

As we have seen, the Americans prevailed and won the Revolutionary War, thereby securing their independence. However, a series of developments following the armistice in the 1780s highlighted the shortcomings of the Articles of Confederation in holding the former colonies together as an independent and effective nation-state. These shortcomings led to what was essentially a second founding.

First, the United States had great difficulty conducting its foreign affairs successfully, as there was no national military and competition among the states for foreign commerce allowed the European powers to play them off against one another. At one point, John Adams, who had become a leader in the independence struggle, was sent to negotiate a new treaty with Britain, one that would cover disputes left over from the war. The British Parliament responded that since the United States under the Articles was unable to enforce existing treaties, it would negotiate with each of the 13 states separately.

Second, the power that states retained under the Articles of Confederation began to alarm well-to-do Americans—in particular, New England merchants and southern planters—when radical forces gained power in a number of state governments. As a result of the Revolution, one key segment of the colonial elite—the royal land, office, and patent holders—was stripped of its economic and political privileges. While the elites were weakened, the radicals had gained strength and now controlled key states, including Pennsylvania and Rhode Island, where they pursued policies that struck terror in the hearts of business and property owners throughout the country. The central government under the Articles was powerless to intervene.

Continuing international weakness and domestic economic turmoil led many Americans to consider revising their newly adopted form of government. In the fall of 1786, the Virginia legislature invited representatives of all the states to a convention in Annapolis, Maryland. It was established at the Annapolis Convention that a future constitutional convention would need to address how to create a stronger central government.

Shays' Rebellion

It's quite possible that the Constitutional Convention of 1787 in Philadelphia would never have taken place except for Shays' Rebellion. In the winter following the Annapolis Convention, Daniel Shays, a former army captain, led a mob of debt-ridden farmers in an effort to prevent foreclosures on their land. A militia organized by the state governor and funded by a group of prominent merchants dispersed the mob, but Shays and his followers then attempted to capture the federal arsenal at Springfield. Within a few days, the state government regained control and captured 14 of the rebels. But later that year, a newly elected Massachusetts legislature granted some of the farmers' demands.

Daniel Shays' rebellion proved the Articles of Confederation were too weak to protect the fledgling nation.

George Washington summed up the effects of the incident on the new nation's leaders: "I am mortified beyond expression that in the moment of our acknowledged independence we should by our conduct verify the predictions of our transatlantic foe, and render ourselves ridiculous and contemptible in the eyes of all Europe."[18] The Congress under the Confederation had shown itself unable to act decisively in a time of crisis. In response to the escalating crisis surrounding the Articles, the states were asked to send representatives to Philadelphia to discuss constitutional revision. Delegates were eventually sent by every state except Rhode Island.

The Constitutional Convention and the Great Compromise

The delegates who convened in Philadelphia in May 1787 had political strife, international embarrassment, national weakness, and local rebellion on their minds. Recognizing that these issues were symptoms of fundamental flaws in the Articles of Confederation, the delegates soon abandoned the plan to revise the Articles and committed themselves to a new founding—a transformed, and ultimately successful, attempt to create a legitimate and effective national system of government. This effort would occupy the convention for the next five months.

The Great Compromise Supporters of a new government fired their opening shot on May 29, 1787, when Edmund Randolph of Virginia offered a resolution proposing sweeping corrections and additions to the Articles of Confederation. Randolph represented the Virginia delegation, which also included James Madison and George Washington. The proposal, drafted by the Virginia delegation, provided for virtually every aspect of a new government.

The most controversial portion of Randolph's motion was called the **Virginia Plan**. It provided for representation in the national legislature to be based on the population of each state or the proportion of each state's revenue contribution to the national government, or both. Randolph also proposed a second chamber of the legislature, to be elected by the members of the first chamber. Therefore, Congress would have two chambers and take the form of a **bicameral legislature**. Since the states varied enormously in population and wealth, the Virginia Plan was heavily biased in favor of the large states.

While the convention was debating the Virginia Plan, opposition to it began to mount as more delegates arrived in Philadelphia. William Paterson of New Jersey introduced a competing resolution, the **New Jersey Plan**. Its main proponents were delegates from the less populous states, including Delaware, New Jersey, Connecticut, and New York, who asserted that the more populous states—Virginia, Pennsylvania, North Carolina, Massachusetts, and Georgia—would dominate the new government if representation were determined by population. The smaller states argued that each state should be equally represented regardless of its population. Under the New Jersey Plan, there would be one chamber, a system known as a **unicameral legislature**.

The issue of representation threatened to wreck the entire constitutional enterprise. As factions maneuvered and tempers flared, the Union was on the verge of falling apart. Finally, the debate

Virginia Plan a framework for the Constitution that called for representation in the national legislature based on the population of each state

bicameral legislature a legislative assembly composed of two chambers or houses

New Jersey Plan a framework for the Constitution that called for equal state representation in the national legislature regardless of population

unicameral legislature a legislative assembly having only one chamber or house

Great Compromise the agreement reached at the Constitutional Convention of 1787 that gave each state an equal number of senators regardless of its population but linked representation in the House of Representatives to population

was settled by the Connecticut Compromise, also known as the **Great Compromise**. Under its terms, there would be a bicameral legislature. Yet in one chamber of Congress—the House of Representatives—seats would be apportioned according to population, as delegates from the large states had wished. But in a second chamber—the Senate—each state would have equal representation, as the small states preferred.

The Constitution and Slavery

The institution of slavery was crucial to the colonial economy. However, by the late eighteenth century, attitudes toward the acceptability of slavery, especially in northern cities, was shifting. And calls to end the transatlantic slave trade and slavery in

Crispus Attucks, a man of Native and African descent, is considered to be the first person killed by British forces in the American Revolution.

America became louder after the Declaration of Independence declared that "all men are created equal." But it's important to recognize that pressure also came from enslaved people themselves.

Enslaved Black people strategically resisted their treatment through both obvious and subtle ways. The more explicit forms of resistance included running away and armed mass uprisings. Other discreet acts of rebellion included secretly learning how to read, destroying tools, and slowing down work pace.[19] Together, these forms of resistance were instrumental in pointing out the brutality of the institution of slavery and how it ran counter to the professed democratic ideals of the young country.

The discomfort around slavery became more pronounced with the onset of the Revolutionary War. After the British encouraged enslaved Black people

FOR CRITICAL ANALYSIS

1. Compare the demographic data of the framers of the Constitution with the overall population data from the time. Do these data confirm or contradict what you know about the framers? Use the data to explain your answer.

2. Do you think the Constitution would be different if the framers were more representative of the population? How so? How well did the framers of the Constitution represent the people?

WHO ARE AMERICANS?

Who Were the Framers of the Constitution?

During the drafting and ratification of the Constitution, the demographics of the framers were quite different in comparison to the overall population of the United States. The 55 delegates to the 1787 Constitutional Convention were all White and male, whereas the American people were more diverse. The contrast between who was writing and designing the Constitution (a document that emphasized freedom, equality, and justice) and the composition of the U.S. population overall illustrates the contradictions in American political life and provides the foundation for conflicts and debates we have seen throughout American history.

The Delegates to the Constitutional Convention (1787) and the U.S. Population (1790)

Race*

- Free White people
- All other free persons**
- Enslaved people

80% 100% 2% 18%
United States   Delegates

Slaveowners†

- Slaveowners
- Non-slaveowners

17% 36% 64% 83%
United States families   Delegates

Gender††

- Women
- Men

49% 100% 51%
United States   Delegates

Occupation

- Farming
- Non-farming

74% 26% 75% 26%
United States   Delegates

* The 1790 census had no category to count Native peoples living in the general population, even though an estimated 600,000 Native peoples lived in the United States.

** The 1790 census defined "all other free persons" as free Black people, people of mixed race, and a small number of Native peoples who lived among White people.

† For this graphic, slaveowning delegates are delegates who owned slaves at the time of the 1787 Constitutional Convention.

†† The 1790 census only recorded gender data for the White population.

NOTE: Numbers may not add up to 100 percent due to rounding.

SOURCES: 1790 census, full data tables, p. 4: www.census.gov/library/publications/1793/dec/number-of-persons.html; Russell Thornton, *American Indian Holocaust and Survival: A Population History Since 1492* (University of Oklahoma Press, 1990); Dorothy S. Brady, ed., "Output, Employment, and Productivity in the United States after 1800," NBER, 1966.

to fight on the British side in exchange for their freedom, many of the 13 colonies countered that enslaved people who served in the Continental Army could have their freedom. In fact, Crispus Attucks, a man of African and Native background who had escaped from slavery, was the first person killed in the American Revolution. The active involvement of thousands of Black soldiers, fighting alongside the colonists, weakened support for slavery.[20] Indeed, northern colonies such as Vermont, Rhode Island, Massachusetts, and Pennsylvania outlawed slavery after the War.

As the process of drafting a new constitution began, the Founders faced a nation divided over slavery.[21] Many of the conflicts that emerged during the Constitutional Convention reflected fundamental differences between southern and northern states related to slavery. From an economic perspective, southerners wanted to protect slavery, and while it made northerners uneasy, many of them benefited from investments in the institution. From a moral perspective, the issue was more complicated. There was widespread acknowledgment that slavery was incompatible with democratic principles and should not be legitimized in the Constitution. Embarrassment about protecting the institution of slavery led to the omission of the words "slavery" and "slave" from the document. Despite this, constitutional experts have drawn attention to two important provisions related to slavery: the Three-Fifths Compromise and the extension of the slave trade.

Three-Fifths Compromise Slavery was at the center of the debate about representation in the House of Representatives. More than 90 percent of the country's enslaved people lived in five states (Georgia, Maryland, North Carolina, South Carolina, and Virginia), where they accounted for 30 percent of the total population. Delegates from these states wanted enslaved people to be counted as free persons for the purposes of determining representation in the House of Representatives. Were they to be counted as part of a state's population even though they weren't citizens, thereby giving southern states increased representation in the House?

While delegates from the northern states held a range of opinions about the morality of slavery, most opposed counting the population of enslaved people in the apportionment of congressional seats, although this did not necessarily mean they opposed slavery itself. James Wilson of Pennsylvania, for example, argued that if enslaved people were counted for this purpose, other forms of property should be as well. But southern delegates insisted they would never agree to the new government if the northerners refused to give in. Northerners and southerners eventually reached agreement through the **Three-Fifths Compromise**: seats in the House of Representatives would be apportioned according to a "population" in which "three-fifths" of enslaved people would be counted (Article 1, Section 2). As a result, the southern states gained added influence in the House of Representatives, but not as much as they wanted and not as much as the northern states feared. The Three-Fifths Compromise would remain in effect until the Fourteenth Amendment repealed it in 1868.

Three-Fifths Compromise
the agreement reached at the Constitutional Convention of 1787 that stipulated that for purposes of apportioning congressional seats only three-fifths of enslaved people would be counted

Despite the Founders' emphasis on liberty, the new Constitution allowed slavery, counting three-fifths of all enslaved people in apportioning seats in the House of Representatives. In this 1792 painting, *Liberty Displaying the Arts and Sciences*, the books, instruments, and classical columns at the left contrast with the kneeling enslaved people at the right — illustrating the divide between America's rhetoric of liberty and equality and the reality of slavery.

Extension of the Slave Trade After the issue of representation was resolved, the question arose of how long the trade of enslaved Africans would continue. The slave trade was violent. It involved forcibly removing people from their African homelands (often tearing them from their families), transporting them across the Atlantic Ocean in brutal, inhumane conditions, selling those who survived in slave auctions, and threatening them with violence and death if they attempted to escape. Many delegates were appalled at the idea of accommodating an extension of the slave trade in the new Constitution; others considered it key to their future economic livelihood. In hopes of protecting their economic interests, the South Carolina delegates proposed to ban the federal government from regulating the importation of enslaved Africans.

At the time of the Convention, 10 states had already outlawed the importation of African captives. Delegates from these states objected to the South Carolina proposal. But in the end, protecting the slave trade proved pivotal to keeping the union intact. Delegates from the three states where it was legal—Georgia, North Carolina, and South Carolina—threatened to walk out of the Convention if the Constitution banned it. To keep these states in the union, a deal was struck whereby the trade or "importation" of enslaved Black people was allowed to continue uninterrupted for another 20 years (Article 1, Section 9, Clause 1). As part of this compromise, the federal government was granted increased authority to tax the imports of enslaved Africans.

The compromises the Founders made at the Constitutional Convention around slavery have had lasting consequences. First, by allowing the slave trade to continue, the Constitution entrenched and protected a dehumanizing institution that violated the liberties of Black people. According to a new study, more than 1,700 men who served in the U.S. Congress in the eighteenth and nineteenth centuries owned enslaved Black people.[22] Second, it wove white supremacy into the fabric of the new nation, solidifying a system of racial hierarchy that is still in the process of being unraveled (this will be discussed more in Chapter 5). Even Madison acknowledged: "The institution of slavery and its consequences form the line of discrimination."[23]

Check your understanding

3. During the Constitutional Convention, the delegates disagreed over how representation should be determined, resulting in

   a) a bicameral legislature in which one chamber would be apportioned based on state population and in the other states would receive equal representation.

   b) a unicameral legislature with state representation based on population.

   c) a unicameral legislature with equal representation for each state.

   d) a bicameral legislature in which one chamber's representation is based on the state's gross revenue and the other contributions to the federal government.

4. How was the debate surrounding the counting of enslaved Black people for purposes of representation in the House of Representatives resolved?

   a) An agreement was reached through the Virginia Plan, which created a bicameral legislature.

   b) Southerners agreed that enslaved Black people would not count for purposes of representation in the House of Representatives.

   c) Northerners and southerners eventually agreed only three-fifths of enslaved people would be counted.

   d) Northerners agreed to allow enslaved Black people to count fully for purposes of representation in the House of Representatives.

The Constitution Created Both Bold Powers and Sharp Limits on Power

Describe the principles of governance and the powers of the national government defined by the Constitution

Together, the Great Compromise and the Three-Fifths Compromise showcase the difficulty in uniting a geographically diverse group of people and creating a national government that is representative of all. But with these important principles in place, delegates at the Convention moved to fashion a constitution consistent with their economic and political interests.

In particular, the framers wanted a new government that, first, would be strong enough to promote commerce and protect property from radical state legislatures. This goal led to the constitutional provisions for national control over commerce and finance, for national judicial supremacy over state courts, and for a strong presidency. (See Table 2.1 for a comparison of the Articles of Confederation with the Constitution.)

Second, the framers wanted to prevent what they saw as the threat posed by the "excessive democracy" of both state and national governments under the Articles of Confederation. This desire led to such constitutional principles as

TABLE 2.1	Comparing the Articles of Confederation and the Constitution	
MAJOR PROVISIONS	**ARTICLES OF CONFEDERATION**	**CONSTITUTION**
Executive branch	None	President of the United States
Judiciary	No federal court system. Judiciary exists only at state level.	Supreme Court
Legislature	Unicameral legislature with equal representation for each state. Delegates to the Congress of the Confederation were appointed by the states.	Bicameral legislature consisting of Senate and House of Representatives. Each state is represented by two senators, while apportionment in the House is based on each state's population. Senators are chosen by the state legislatures (changed to direct popular election in 1913) for six-year terms and members of the House by popular election for two-year terms.

Continued

TABLE 2.1 | Comparing the Articles of Confederation and the Constitution—cont'd

MAJOR PROVISIONS	ARTICLES OF CONFEDERATION	CONSTITUTION
Fiscal and economic powers	The national government is dependent upon the states to collect taxes. The states are free to coin their own money and print paper money. The states are free to sign commercial treaties with foreign governments.	Congress is given the power to levy taxes, coin money, and regulate international and interstate commerce. States are prohibited from coining money or entering into treaties with other nations.
Military	The national government is dependent upon state militias and cannot form an army during peacetime.	The national government is authorized to maintain an army and a navy.
Legal supremacy	State constitutions and state law are supreme.	National Constitution and national law are supreme.
Constitutional amendment	Must be agreed upon by all states	Must be agreed upon by three-fourths of the states
Slavery	No mention	Enslaved people count as 3/5 of a state's total enslaved population, and trade of enslaved people is allowed for 20 years.

checks and balances mechanisms through which each branch of government is able to participate in and influence the activities of the other branches; examples include the presidential veto power over congressional legislation, the Senate's power to approve presidential appointments, and the Supreme Court's power of judicial review of congressional enactments

Bill of Rights the first 10 amendments to the U.S. Constitution, ratified in 1791; they ensure certain rights and liberties to the people

a bicameral (or two-chambered) legislature; **checks and balances** among the three branches of government; staggered terms in office; and indirect election (selection of the president by an electoral college and of senators by state legislatures, rather than directly by voters).

Third, lacking the power to force the states or the public to accept the new form of government, the framers wanted to identify principles that would help gain support for it. This goal became the basis of the constitutional provision for direct popular election of representatives and, later, of the addition of the **Bill of Rights** to the Constitution.

Finally, the framers wanted to ensure that the government they created did not pose an even greater threat to its citizens' liberties and property rights than did the radical state legislatures they despised. To prevent abuses of power, they incorporated principles such as the **separation of powers** and **federalism** into the Constitution.

The Legislative Branch Was Designed to Be the Most Powerful

In Article I, Sections 1–7, the Constitution provides for a Congress consisting of two chambers: a House of Representatives and a Senate. Members of the House of Representatives were given two-year terms in office and were to be elected directly by the people. Members of the Senate were to be appointed by the state legislatures (a provision changed in 1913 by the Seventeenth Amendment, which instituted direct election of senators) for six-year terms. These terms were staggered so that the terms of one-third of the senators would expire every two years.

The Constitution assigned somewhat different tasks to the House and Senate. Though the enactment of a law requires the approval of both, the Senate alone is given the power to ratify treaties and approve presidential appointments. The House, on the other hand, is given the sole power to originate revenue bills.

The character of the legislative branch was related to the framers' major goals. The House was designed to be directly responsible to the people, with all members serving two-year terms, to encourage popular support for the new Constitution and thus enhance the power of the new government. At the same time, to guard against "excessive democracy," the power of the House was checked by that of the Senate, whose members were to be appointed by the states for long terms rather than elected directly by the people for short ones. The purpose of this provision, according to Alexander Hamilton, was to avoid "an unqualified complaisance to every sudden breeze of passion, or to every transient impulse which the people may receive."[24] Staggered terms in the Senate were intended to make that body even more resistant to popular pressure. Since only one-third of the senators would be selected every two years, it was thought that the institution would be protected from changes in public opinion transmitted by the state legislatures.

The issues of governmental power and popular consent are important throughout the Constitution. Section 8 of Article I specifically lists the powers of Congress, which include the authority to collect taxes, borrow money, regulate commerce, declare war, and maintain an army and navy. By granting Congress these powers, the framers indicated clearly that they intended the new government to be far more powerful than its predecessor under the Articles of Confederation. At the same time, by assigning its most important powers to Congress, they promoted popular acceptance of this critical change by reassuring citizens that their views would be fully represented whenever these powers were used.

As a further safeguard that the new government would pose no threat to the people, the Constitution implies that any powers not listed were not granted at all. This is what Chief Justice of the Supreme Court John Marshall named the

expressed powers specific powers granted by the Constitution to Congress (Article I, Section 8) and to the president (Article II)

elastic clause the concluding paragraph of Article I, Section 8, of the Constitution (also known as the "necessary and proper clause"), which provides Congress with the authority to make all laws "necessary and proper" to carry out its enumerated powers

doctrine of **expressed powers**: the Constitution grants only those powers specifically expressed in its text. But the framers intended to create an active and powerful government, so they also included the necessary and proper clause, also called the **elastic clause**, which declares that Congress can write laws needed to carry out its expressed powers. This clause indicates that expressed powers could be broadly interpreted and were meant to be a source of strength to the national government, not a limitation on it. In response to the charge that they intended to give it too much power, the framers included language in the Tenth Amendment stipulating that powers not specifically granted by the Constitution to the federal government were reserved to the states or to the people. As we'll see in Chapter 3, the resulting tension between the elastic clause and the Tenth Amendment has been at the heart of constitutional struggles between federal and state powers.

The Executive Branch Created a Brand-New Office

The Articles of Confederation had not provided for an executive branch. The president under the Articles was the official chosen by the Congress to preside over its sessions, not the chief executive of the national government. The framers viewed the absence of an executive as a source of weakness. Accordingly, the Constitution provides for the presidency in Article II. As Hamilton commented, the article aims toward "energy in the Executive."[25] It does so in an effort to overcome the natural tendency toward stalemate that was built into the separation of the legislature into two chambers and of governmental powers among the three branches. The Constitution affords the president a measure of independence from both the people and the other branches of government—particularly the Congress. However, unlike the legislative branch, for which the Constitution enumerates explicit powers, executive branch powers are often implied. Throughout the nation's history, presidents have interpreted executive power in many different ways, as we'll see in Chapter 13.

In line with the framers' goal of increased power for the national government, the president is granted the power to accept ambassadors from other countries— to "recognize" other governments—as well as the power to negotiate treaties, although their acceptance requires approval of the Senate by a two-thirds vote. The president also has the power to grant reprieves and pardons except in cases of impeachment, appoint major departmental heads (e.g., Agriculture, Defense, Energy, Justice), convene Congress in a special session, and veto bills it passes. The veto power is not absolute, since Congress can override it by a two-thirds vote, reflecting the framers' concern with checks and balances.

The framers hoped to create a presidency that would make the federal government rather than the states the agency capable of timely and decisive action to deal with national issues and problems. At the same time, however, they tried to

AMERICA | SIDE BY SIDE

Democratic Systems

Executive authority is vested in different positions in different countries. In parliamentary systems the prime minister is both the chief executive and the head of the legislature. In presidential systems, such as in the United States, the executive and legislative branches are separate. Some countries use a semi-presidential system in which there is a president who heads the executive branch and has limited authority, and a prime minister who heads the legislative branch. Parliamentary systems can be more efficient, as the prime minister can wield a lot of authority, but only if their party has a sizable and stable majority in Parliament. Presidential and semi-presidential systems can lead to more gridlock, as there are multiple seats of power.

1. Does one system seem to be more common than another? Why might one country have a parliamentary system while its neighbor has a presidential system?
2. What do you think would be the advantages to having executive and legislative authority vested in the same individual? What are the advantages to a system such as that of the United States, where powers are separated in independent branches? Do you think the advantages of one system over another are different today than they were 250 years ago at the Founding of the United States?

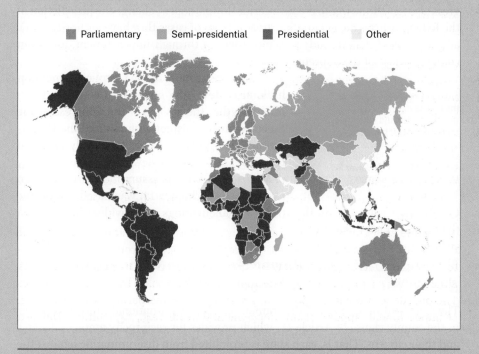

SOURCE: CIA World Factbook, "Government Type," www.cia.gov/the-world-factbook/field/government-type (accessed 10/17/21).

help the presidency withstand excessively democratic pressures by establishing an electoral college through which to elect the president.

The Judicial Branch Was a Check on Too Much Democracy

In establishing, in Article III, that "the judicial Power of the United States" resides in the Supreme Court, the Constitution reflects the framers' preoccupations with nationalizing governmental power and checking radical democratic impulses while preventing the national government itself from interfering with liberty and property ownership. The most important expression of this intention is granting the Supreme Court the power to resolve any conflicts between federal and state laws. In particular, it can determine whether a power is exclusive to the national government, exclusive to the states, or shared between the two.

In addition, the Supreme Court is assigned jurisdiction over controversies between citizens of different states. As the country developed a national economy, it came to rely increasingly on the federal judiciary, rather than state courts, to resolve disputes.

Federal judges are given lifetime appointments to protect them from political or public pressure and from interference by the other branches. The judiciary isn't totally free of political considerations of the other branches, however, for the president appoints the judges and the Senate must approve the appointments. Congress also has the power to create inferior (lower) courts, change the jurisdiction of the federal courts (the geographic area or types of cases they have authority over), add or subtract federal judges, remove judges through impeachment, and even change the size of the Supreme Court.

judicial review the power of the courts to review actions of the legislative and executive branches and, if necessary, declare them invalid or unconstitutional; the Supreme Court asserted this power in *Marbury v. Madison* (1803)

The Constitution doesn't explicitly mention **judicial review**—the power of a court to determine whether the actions of the Congress or the executive are consistent with law and the Constitution. The Supreme Court eventually assumed the power of judicial review in the case *Marbury v. Madison* (1803). Its assumption of this power, as we'll see in Chapter 13, was based not on the Constitution itself but on the strategic maneuverings of individual justices and the politics of later decades.

National Unity and Power Set the New Constitution Apart from the Old Articles

The Constitution addressed the framers' concern with national unity and power in the comity clause of Article IV, which provides for reciprocity among all states and their citizens. That is, each state is prohibited from discriminating against the citizens of or goods from other states in favor of its own citizens or goods, with the Supreme Court being charged with deciding cases where such discrimination is alleged. The Constitution thus restricts the power of the states so as to give the national government enough power to ensure a free-flowing national economy.

The framers' concern with national supremacy was also expressed in Article VI, whose **supremacy clause** provides that national laws and treaties "shall be the supreme Law of the Land." This means that laws made under the "Authority of the United States" are superior to those adopted by any state or other subdivision and that the states must respect all treaties made under that authority. The supremacy clause also binds all state and local as well as federal officials to take an oath to support the national Constitution. Therefore, they must enforce national law over state law if the two conflict.

> **supremacy clause** Article VI of the Constitution, which states that laws passed by the national government and all treaties are the supreme law of the land and superior to all laws adopted by any state or any subdivision
>
> **amendment** a change added to a bill, law, or constitution; the process of making such change through constitutional procedure

The Constitution Establishes the Process for Amendment and Ratification

The Constitution establishes procedures for its own **amendment** in Article V. The requirements are so difficult that, as we'll see below, the amending process has succeeded only 17 times since 1791, when the first 10 amendments were adopted. The rules for ratification, or adoption, of the Constitution are set forth in Article VII. Of the 13 states, 9 would have to ratify it in order for it to go into effect.

Figure 2.1 outlines the ways in which the Constitution can be amended. Since 1789, more than 11,000 amendments have been formally introduced in Congress. Of these, Congress officially proposed only 29, and 27 were eventually ratified by the states. Historically, most amendment efforts have failed because they attempted to use the constitutional amendment process, instead of legislation, to address a specific public problem. The successful amendments, on the other hand, are concerned with the broader structure or composition of government—not with specific policies (see Table 2.2). This pattern is consistent with the dictionary definition of *constitution* as the makeup or composition of something. And it's consistent with the concept of a constitution as "higher law," whose purpose is to establish a framework within which the processes of governing and making ordinary law can take place.

There is great wisdom in this concept. A constitution ought to make laws and policies possible, but not determine what they ought to be. For example, property ownership is one of the most fundamental and well-established rights in the United States—not because it is recognized as such in the Constitution, but because legislatures and courts, working within an agreed-upon constitutional framework, have made it a crime for anyone, including the government, to trespass on or take away property without compensation. A constitution is good if it leads to just legislation, courts that protect citizens' liberties and rights, and appropriate behavior of public officials. Its principles can be a citizen's dependable defense against the abuse of power. Since the Founding, debates have raged as to whether the United States Constitution achieves these goals for all Americans.

FIGURE 2.1 | Four Ways the Constitution Can Be Amended

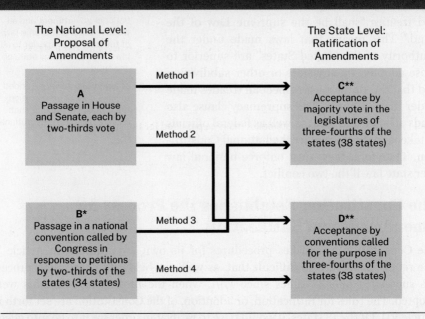

The National Level:
Proposal of
Amendments

The State Level:
Ratification of
Amendments

A
Passage in House
and Senate, each by
two-thirds vote

Method 1

Method 2

B*
Passage in a national
convention called by
Congress in
response to petitions
by two-thirds of the
states (34 states)

Method 3

Method 4

C**
Acceptance by
majority vote in the
legislatures of
three-fourths of the
states (38 states)

D**
Acceptance by
conventions called
for the purpose in
three-fourths of the
states (38 states)

*This method of proposal has never been employed. Thus, amendment methods 3 and 4 have never been attempted.

**For each amendment proposal, Congress has the power to choose the method of ratification, the time limit for consideration by the states, and other conditions of ratification. The movement to repeal Prohibition in the Twenty-First Amendment was the only occasion in which method 2 was used successfully.

TABLE 2.2 | Amendments to the Constitution

AMENDMENT	PURPOSE
I	Congress is not to make any law establishing a religion or abridging free exercise of religion, speech, press, assembly, or petitioning the government for redress of grievances.
II, III, IV	No branch of government may infringe on the right of people to keep arms (II), arbitrarily occupy homes for a militia (III), or engage in the search or seizure of evidence without a court warrant swearing to belief in the probable existence of a crime (IV).
V, VI, VII, VIII	The courts' are not to hold trials for serious offenses without provision for a grand jury (V), a petit (trial) jury (VII), a speedy trial (VI), presentation of charges (VI), confrontation of hostile witnesses (VI), immunity from testimony against oneself (V), and immunity from more than one trial for the same offense (V). Neither bail nor punishment can be excessive (VIII), and no property can be taken without just compensation (V).

TABLE 2.2 | Amendments to the Constitution—cont'd

AMENDMENT	PURPOSE
IX, X	All rights and powers not enumerated are reserved to the states or the people.
XI	Federal courts have limited jurisdiction over suits involving the states.
XII	A separate ballot must be provided for the vice president in the electoral college.
XIII	Slavery and the right of states to treat persons as property are eliminated.
XIV	The principle of national citizenship is asserted and the states are prohibited from infringing upon the rights of citizens of the nation, no matter that they happen to live in that state. States are prohibited from denying voting rights to male citizens over the age of 21.**
XV	Voting rights are extended to all races.
XVI	National power to tax incomes is established.
XVII	Provision for direct election of senators.
XVIII	The manufacture, sale, transportation, or export of alcohol is prohibited.
XIX	Voting rights are extended to women.
XX	"Lame-duck" session of Congress is eliminated.
XXI	The Eighteenth Amendment is repealed.
XXII	Presidential term is limited.
XXIII	Voting rights are extended to residents of the District of Columbia.
XXIV	Voting rights are extended to all classes by abolition of poll taxes.
XXV	Presidential succession is provided in case of disability.
XXVI	Voting rights are extended to citizens age 18 and over.
XXVII	Congress's power to raise its own salary is limited.

*These amendments also impose limits on the law-enforcement powers of federal and (especially) state and local executive branches.

**In defining *citizenship*, the Fourteenth Amendment actually provided the constitutional basis for expanding the electorate to include all races, women, and residents of the District of Columbia. Only the "18-year-olds' amendment" should have been necessary, since it changed the definition of citizenship. The fact that additional amendments were required following the Fourteenth suggests that voting is not considered an inherent right of U.S. citizenship. Instead, it is viewed as a privilege.

Constitutional Limits on the National Government's Power

Although the framers wanted a powerful national government, they also wanted to guard against possible misuse of that power. Thus they incorporated two key principles into the Constitution—federalism and the separation of powers. A third set of limitations, the Bill of Rights, was added in the form of 10 amendments proposed by the first Congress and ratified by the states. Most of the framers had thought a Bill of Rights unnecessary but accepted the idea during the ratification debates after the new Constitution was submitted to the states for approval.

The Separation of Powers No principle of politics was more widely shared at the time of the 1787 Founding than that power must be used to balance power. Although the separation of powers is not explicitly stated in the Constitution, the entire structure of the national government was built precisely on Article I, the legislature; Article II, the executive; and Article III, the judiciary (see Figure 2.2).

The method adopted to maintain that separation became known as "checks and balances" (see Figure 2.3). Each branch is given not only its own powers but also some power over the other two branches. Among the most familiar checks and balances are the president's veto power over Congress and Congress's power over the president through its control of appointments to high executive posts and to the judiciary. Congress also has power over the president with its control of

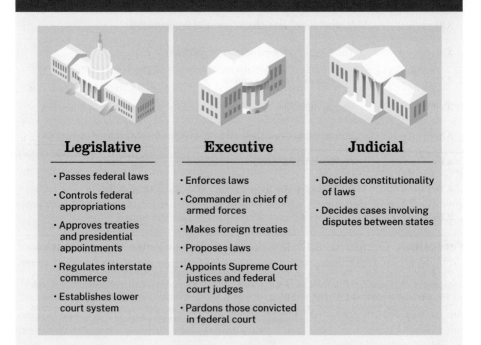

FIGURE 2.2 | The Separation of Powers

Legislative

- Passes federal laws
- Controls federal appropriations
- Approves treaties and presidential appointments
- Regulates interstate commerce
- Establishes lower court system

Executive

- Enforces laws
- Commander in chief of armed forces
- Makes foreign treaties
- Proposes laws
- Appoints Supreme Court justices and federal court judges
- Pardons those convicted in federal court

Judicial

- Decides constitutionality of laws
- Decides cases involving disputes between states

FIGURE 2.3 | Checks and Balances

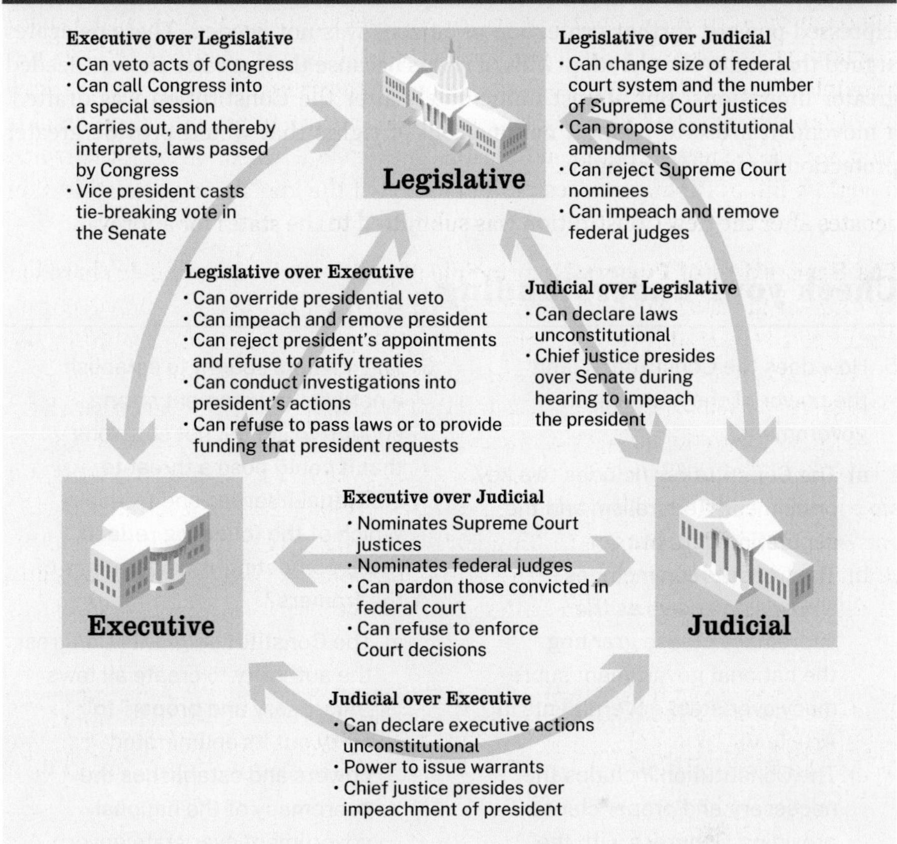

Executive over Legislative
- Can veto acts of Congress
- Can call Congress into a special session
- Carries out, and thereby interprets, laws passed by Congress
- Vice president casts tie-breaking vote in the Senate

Legislative

Legislative over Judicial
- Can change size of federal court system and the number of Supreme Court justices
- Can propose constitutional amendments
- Can reject Supreme Court nominees
- Can impeach and remove federal judges

Legislative over Executive
- Can override presidential veto
- Can impeach and remove president
- Can reject president's appointments and refuse to ratify treaties
- Can conduct investigations into president's actions
- Can refuse to pass laws or to provide funding that president requests

Judicial over Legislative
- Can declare laws unconstitutional
- Chief justice presides over Senate during hearing to impeach the president

Executive over Judicial
- Nominates Supreme Court justices
- Nominates federal judges
- Can pardon those convicted in federal court
- Can refuse to enforce Court decisions

Executive

Judicial

Judicial over Executive
- Can declare executive actions unconstitutional
- Power to issue warrants
- Chief justice presides over impeachment of president

appropriations (the spending of government money) and the requirement that the Senate ratify treaties. The judiciary has the power to declare actions of the other two branches as unconstitutional.

An important aspect of the separation of powers is that each branch is given a distinctly different constituency—with the president being chosen, indirectly, by electors; the House, by popular vote; the Senate (originally), by state legislatures; and the judiciary, by presidential appointment. Through these means, the occupants of each branch would develop very different outlooks on how to govern, different definitions of the public interest, and different alliances with private interests.

Federalism Compared with the decentralizing principle of the Articles of Confederation, federalism was a step toward greater concentration of power. The delegates to the Constitutional Convention agreed that they needed to place more power at the national level without completely undermining the power of the state governments. Thus, they devised a system of two sovereigns, or supreme powers—the states and the nation—with the hope that competition between them would effectively limit the power of each.

The Bill of Rights Late in the Convention, a motion to include a list of citizens' rights in the Constitution was almost unanimously turned down. Most delegates sincerely believed that since the federal government was already limited to its expressed powers, further protection of citizens was not needed. These delegates argued that states should adopt bills of rights because their greater powers needed greater limitations. But almost immediately after the Constitution was drafted, a movement arose to adopt a national bill of rights that would provide greater protection for individual rights.

Check your understanding

5. How does the Constitution limit the power of the national government?

   a) The Constitution includes two key principles — federalism and the separation of powers.

   b) The Constitution includes a provision known as the supremacy clause granting the national government supremacy over state governments in Article VI.

   c) The Constitution includes the necessary and proper clause providing Congress with the authority to make all laws "necessary and proper" to carry out its enumerated powers.

   d) The Constitution established a judicial branch with the authority of judicial review.

6. The framers sought to establish a national government strong enough to act yet not so strong that it could pose a threat to individual liberties and freedom. Which of the following reflects these competing considerations of the framers?

   a) The Constitution grants Congress the authority to create all laws "necessary and proper" to carry out its enumerated powers and establishes the supremacy of the national government over state governments in Article VI.

   b) The Constitution creates a president with the authority to negotiate treaties and grant pardons who shares powers with the legislative and judicial branches and is chosen through indirect election.

   c) The Constitution establishes a judicial branch with the authority of judicial review.

   d) The Constitution establishes a process of amendment in Article V that makes it very challenging to succeed, only doing so 17 times.

Ratification of the Constitution Was Difficult

Differentiate between the Federalists' and Antifederalists' stances on the ratification of the Constitution

The first hurdle faced by the proposed Constitution was ratification by state conventions of delegates elected by voters. This struggle for ratification included 13 separate state campaigns, each influenced by local as well as national considerations.

Two sides faced off in all the states, calling themselves **Federalists** and **Antifederalists** (see Table 2.3). The Federalists (who more accurately could have called themselves "Nationalists") supported the Constitution and preferred a strong national government. The Antifederalists opposed the Constitution and preferred a more decentralized federal system. The Federalists were united in their support of the Constitution, whereas the Antifederalists were divided over possible alternatives.

Federalists those who favored a strong national government and supported the Constitution proposed at the American Constitutional Convention of 1787

Antifederalists those who favored strong state governments and a weak national government and who were opponents of the Constitution proposed at the American Constitutional Convention of 1787

Federalist Papers a series of essays written by Alexander Hamilton, James Madison, and John Jay supporting ratification of the Constitution

Federalists and Antifederalists Fought Bitterly over the Wisdom of the New Constitution

Thousands of essays, speeches, pamphlets, and letters were presented for and against ratification of the proposed Constitution. The best-known pieces in support were the 85 articles published in New York City newspapers by Alexander Hamilton, James Madison, and John Jay. These *Federalist Papers*, as they are known today, defended the principles of the Constitution and sought to dispel fears of a strong national government. Meanwhile, the Antifederalists, including Patrick Henry and Richard Henry Lee, argued in their speeches and writings that the new Constitution betrayed the Revolution and was a step toward monarchy.

Representation One major area of contention between the two sides was the nature of political representation. The Antifederalists asserted that representatives must be "a true picture of the people . . . [possessing] the knowledge of their circumstances and their wants."[26] This could be achieved, they argued, only in small republics such as each of the existing states, whose people were relatively similar to one another. In their view, the size and diverse population of the entire nation made a truly representative form of government impossible.

Federalists saw no reason that representatives should be exactly like those they represented. In their view, one of the great advantages of representative government over direct democracy was precisely the possibility that the people would

TABLE 2.3	Federalists versus Antifederalists	
	FEDERALISTS	**ANTIFEDERALISTS**
Who were they?	Property owners, creditors, merchants	Small farmers, frontiersmen, debtors, shopkeepers, some state government officials
What did they believe?	Believed that elites were most fit to govern; feared "excessive democracy"	Believed that government should be closer to the people; feared concentration of power in hands of the elites
What system of government did they favor?	Favored strong national government; believed in "filtration" so that only elites would obtain governmental power	Favored retention of power by state governments and protection of individual rights
Who were their leaders?	Alexander Hamilton, James Madison, George Washington	Patrick Henry, George Mason, Elbridge Gerry, George Clinton

choose individuals with experience and talent greater than their own to represent them. In Madison's words, rather than mirroring society, representatives must be "[those] who possess [the] most wisdom to discern, and [the] most virtue to pursue, the common good of the society."[27]

tyranny oppressive government that employs cruel and unjust use of power and authority

Tyranny A second issue dividing Federalists and Antifederalists was the threat of **tyranny**—unjust rule by the group in power. The two sides, however, had different views of the most likely source of tyranny, and thus different ideas about how to keep it from emerging.

For the Antifederalists, the great danger was the tendency of republican governments to become gradually more "aristocratic," with members of the small group in authority using their positions to gain more and more power over other citizens. In essence, Antifederalists feared the few would tyrannize the many. For this reason, they sharply criticized those features of the Constitution that created governmental institutions without direct responsibility to the people—such as the Senate, the presidency, and particularly the federal judiciary, with its lifetime appointments.

The Federalists, in contrast, viewed the danger particularly associated with republican governments not as aristocracy but as tyranny over the few by the many. They feared that a popular majority, "united and actuated by some common impulse of passion, or of interest, adverse to the rights of other citizens," would "trample on the rules of justice."[28] From their perspective, those features of the Constitution that the Antifederalists attacked as potential sources of tyranny actually offered the best hope of preventing it. They saw the nation's size and diversity as further protection because these characteristics would make it harder to unite a tyrannical majority.

Governmental Power A third divisive issue concerned how to place limits on governmental action. Antifederalists favored **limited government** and proposed limiting and spelling out the powers granted to the national government in relation both to the states and to the people at large. To them, its powers ought to be "confined to certain defined national objects"[29] so that it did not "swallow up all the power of the state governments."[30] Antifederalists bitterly attacked the supremacy and elastic clauses of the Constitution as dangerous surrenders of power to the national government.[31] They also demanded that a bill of rights be added to the Constitution to limit the government's power over the people.

In reply, Federalists such as Hamilton acknowledged the possibility that every power could be abused, but argued that the risk was worth taking in order to give the government the powers needed to achieve essential national goals. In addition, the various checks and controls on power incorporated into the Constitution would minimize the risks of abuse. As Madison put it, "the power surrendered by the people is first divided between two distinct governments (state and national), and then the portion allotted to each subdivided among distinct and separate departments. Hence, a double security arises to the rights of the people. The different governments will control each other, at the same time that each will be controlled by itself."[32] The Federalists' concern with avoiding unwarranted limits on governmental power led them to oppose a bill of rights as unnecessary.

Debates over the meaning of the Constitution continue to this day. Some critics of mask mandates instituted during the coronavirus pandemic pointed to the Constitution's protections of individual liberty as reason to protest the mandates.

Compromise Contributed to the Success of the New System

While the Federalists ultimately prevailed, the Antifederalists did have a lasting impact on the Constitution by making a persuasive case for the inclusion of a bill of rights. During the first Congress, in June 1789, Madison introduced a proposed bill of rights. Three months later, Congress sent a final list of amendments to the states, and in December 1791 the states ratified the Bill of Rights—the first 10 amendments to the Constitution. Intended to protect individual rights and liberties from government overreach, these include the freedom of speech, the right to bear arms, protection from unreasonable searches, and the right to a fair trial. Initially, the amendments applied only to the federal government; not until passage of the Fourteenth Amendment in 1868 were many of the protections extended to states. At the end of the ratification

limited government a principle of constitutional government; a government whose powers are defined and limited by a constitution

fight, the Federalists did secure passage of the Constitution, and the compromise around a bill of rights made for a stronger governing document—one that has endured to the present. (We'll say more about the Bill of Rights in Chapter 4.)

Check your understanding

7. How did the perspective of the Federalists differ from that of the Antifederalists?

   a) The Federalists feared a government that could become too aristocratic where a few would tyrannize the many, while the Antifederalists feared tyranny over the few by the many.

   b) The Federalists asserted that representatives must be a true picture of the people, while the Antifederalists believed that government did not necessarily need to reflect the people.

   c) The Federalists supported granting the state governments an absolute veto right over all legislation, while the Antifederalists were opposed to an absolute veto right being granted to the state governments.

   d) While the Federalists supported a stronger national government, the Antifederalists favored limited government.

8. While the Federalists ultimately prevailed, the Antifederalists had a lasting impact on the Constitution by making a persuasive case for the inclusion of

   a) the supremacy clause.

   b) the necessary and proper clause.

   c) the right to privacy.

   d) the Bill of Rights.

WHAT DO YOU THINK?

THE CONSTITUTION

Many Americans cherish the nation's founding documents as symbols of the great American "experiment for promoting human happiness,"[33] as George Washington termed it. But the system of government that emerged was the subject of intense debate and of compromise between competing factions with differing interests along regional, economic, and philosophical lines. The meaning of the values encapsulated in the institutions of American government as set out in the Constitution were the subject of debate as well — and continue to be contested to this day.

The Founders placed individual liberty ahead of all other political values. They feared that too much democracy could degenerate into tyranny of the majority. They feared that economic or social equality would inspire the have-nots to interfere with the liberty of the haves. As a result, they designed many of the Constitution's key provisions, such as separated powers, internal checks and balances, and federalism, to safeguard liberty, and they designed others, such as indirect election of senators and the president and the appointment of judges for life, to limit democracy and the threat of majority tyranny. These features continue to influence the nature of representation in the United States.

By championing liberty, however, the framers virtually guaranteed that the fight for justice and equality would mark the history of the United States. The degree to which different groups of Americans have enjoyed liberty, equality, and justice has varied across time and place. But because liberty promotes political activity and participation, it encourages people and groups to fight for their rights and interests and for justice. In so doing, they may achieve greater equality.

- What do you think about the values of liberty, equality, and justice? Which is most important to you? Which do you think is most important to New York City council member Inez Barron, or Professor Sean Wilentz? How might your life be different if you lived in a country with different commitments to these values?

- Advocates arguing for a particular policy position often invoke cherished values such as liberty, equality, and justice to support their positions. What kinds of arguments could both supporters and opponents of removing statues of the nation's Founders make using these three values?

- Are there policy areas where you are frustrated by the slow policy-making process created by the separation of powers and the system of checks and balances? Or policy areas where you are relieved that changes that you opposed were slowed or halted? What are your views on the pros and cons of the nation's constitutional structure?

Use 🐰 **INQUIZITIVE** *to help you study and master this material.*

Mail Ballot
Hand Delivery

ENTER HERE

3

WHAT GOVERNMENT DOES & WHY IT MATTERS

Brittany Hyman of Harris County, Texas, wondered how she could vote safely in the November 2020 election. Her schedule was hectic—she had just accepted a new job as executive director of marketing and communications, and the coronavirus pandemic had shut down her toddler's school, forcing her to homeschool. More importantly, she wanted to avoid crowds to protect her family from the virus; Brittany was pregnant, and the entire family had been quarantining carefully to protect the new baby. Fortunately, her county had recently created drive-through voting, by which voters remain in their cars, show a photo ID and verify their voter registration, and cast their ballots on portable voting machines. The closest location was just minutes away. "What was really great was that I was able to tie the experience to my daughter's homeschooling," Brittany said. "I am by no means a teacher, but I was able to work in a lesson about voting—what voting is and why it's important. She was able to ride with me and see me vote and then they gave her a sticker."[1] Despite the pandemic, Texas experienced one of its highest voter turnouts in recent history, especially among Black and Latino voters.

Federalism

Less than a year after the 2020 election, however, the Texas legislature passed a law to ban drive-through voting. Signed by Republican governor Greg Abbott, this law contains a variety of restrictions on how and where citizens can vote. Voting advocates say that the changes will disproportionately affect the ability of Black, Latino, disabled, and older voters to cast their ballots. Texas was able to make these changes because in 2013 the Supreme Court struck down a provision of the Voting Rights Act of 1965 that required localities and states with a history of voter discrimination (like Texas and others) to get federal approval for any proposed changes affecting voting.

The new Texas law set up a profound fight over federalism, the allocation of responsibilities across the nation's different levels of government. On one side were state lawmakers, often Republicans, who championed the ability of states to set their own voting rules. On the other side were voter advocates who urged national legislation that would protect ballot access, including the John Lewis Voting Rights Advancement Act, named after the civil rights activist and long-time U.S. representative who died in 2020. The act would restore preclearance and prevent laws with a disproportionate impact on racial, ethnic, or language minority groups.

These struggles over voting standards engage some of the oldest questions in American government: What is the responsibility of the

▲ Because of federalism, voting rules and procedures vary by state. In 2020 many states, like Texas, made voting easier, and many people, like Brittany Hyman, took advantage. After the 2020 elections, however, some states made moves to tighten voting rules.

federal government, and what is the responsibility of the states? Some responsibilities, such as international relations, clearly lie with the federal government. Others, such as divorce laws, are controlled by state governments. In fact, most of the rules and regulations that Americans face in their daily lives are set by state and local governments. But subnational control raises another question of federalism: When should there be uniformity across the states, and when is it better to let states and localities adopt their own policies based on the needs and desires of their own population?

Given overlapping responsibilities and policy variation across subnational units like cities and states, the American form of federalism inevitably brings conflict. At its heart, federalism is about power. And the debate about "who should do what" remains one of the most important discussions in American politics.

CHAPTER GOALS

Describe how the Constitution structures the relationships among the national, state, and local governments (pp. 67–76)

Explain how the relationship between the federal and state governments has evolved over time (pp. 76–82)

Analyze what difference federalism makes for politics and government (pp. 83–90)

Federalism Is Established by the Constitution

Describe how the Constitution structures the relationships among the national, state, and local governments

Federalism is a system of government in which power is divided between a central government and regional governments. Federalism contrasts with a **unitary system**, in which lower levels of government have little independent power and primarily just implement decisions made by the central government. As we saw in Chapter 2, federalism was a central element of America's Constitution of 1787, which assigned specific powers to the national government and left others to the states.

federalism a system of government in which power is divided, by a constitution, between a central government and regional governments

unitary system a centralized government system in which lower levels of government have little power independent of the national government

The United States was the first nation to adopt federalism as its governing framework. By granting "expressed powers" to the national government and reserving the rest to the states, the original Constitution recognized two authorities: state governments and the federal government.

The nations most likely to have federalism are those with diverse ethnic, language, or regional groupings, such as Switzerland and Canada and certainly the United States. At the time of America's Founding, the new nation consisted of diverse economic and political interests. Federalism was a way of assuring these interests, particularly southern plantation owners, most if not all of whom owned enslaved Black people, that their views would not be submerged in the new nation. The multiple governments at the national, state, and local levels present many opportunities for citizens to express their preferences, promising to maximize democratic participation. Because states and even localities have their own taxing, spending, and policy-making powers (especially in the United States), policy experimentation and innovation is another feature, as is the tailoring of policy to local preferences. And competition among states and localities to attract individuals and businesses promises to maximize the efficiency of government services.[2] But federalism can produce problems as well. Slavery and segregation hid behind the banner of federalism, and, today, opponents of measures that might mitigate the Covid-19 pandemic have seized upon the rhetoric of local control and states' rights.

In the American version of federalism, state and local governments have even more policy-making responsibilities than in most federal systems. The result is wide variation in policies and a centuries-long tug-of-war between the national and state governments, and between state and local governments. The federal structure's division of labor across the levels of government makes **intergovernmental relations**—the processes by which those levels of government negotiate and compromise over policy responsibility—one of the most characteristic aspects of American government.

Political Ramifications of Federalism

American federalism not only affects political power; it has significant implications for policy outcomes as well. Because of the policy variation made possible by the sovereignty of state and local governments, where you live determines the age at which you can get a license to drive or get married, the amount you pay for public college tuition, the licensing requirements to work as a barber or accountant or athletic trainer, and, if you were out of work, whether you would get unemployment benefits and how much. But federalism has important effects on American politics as well.

Political preferences arising from federalism are not set in stone. Although conservatives typically support a smaller federal government or a return of power to the states, once in power they find at times that federal power can be used to advance conservative policy goals. For President George W. Bush, for example, the importance of a strong federal government became apparent after the terrorist attacks in 2001. Aware that the American public was looking to Washington for protection, Bush worked with Congress to pass the USA PATRIOT Act, which greatly increased the surveillance powers of the federal government. A year later he created the enormous new federal Department of Homeland Security. Bush also increased federal control and spending in policy areas far removed from security. The 2001 No Child Left Behind Act (NCLB) introduced unprecedented federal intervention in public education, traditionally a state and local responsibility, through detailed new requirements for states' testing of students and treatment of failing schools.

Democratic presidents, too, have sometimes made decisions about national–state responsibilities that defy the usual ideological expectations. As president, Obama released the states from the federal NCLB mandates, and in 2015 he sponsored a new law called Every Student Succeeds that returned power to the states to evaluate schools—a move that might have been expected more from a conservative president. A second important political implication of federalism concerns individuals' democratic participation and the accountability of government to the people. The multiple layers of government provide many opportunities for ordinary citizens to vote, contact elected officials, and engage in "venue shopping"—seeking policy change at a different level of government if stymied at first. But federalism can also demobilize individuals. The overlapping policy responsibilities facilitated by federalism make it difficult for individuals to figure out which government is responsible for the problem that concerns them, and they may give up; it is difficult for individuals to demand answers from government if they can't determine which government is in charge.[3]

The Powers of the National Government

As we saw in Chapter 2, the **expressed powers** granted to the national government are found in Article I, Section 8, of the Constitution. These 17 powers include the power to collect taxes, coin money, declare war, and regulate commerce. Article I, Section 8, also contains another important source of power for the national government: the **implied powers** that enable Congress "to make all Laws which shall be necessary and proper for carrying into Execution the foregoing Powers." Not until several decades after the Founding did the Supreme Court allow Congress to exercise the power implied in this **necessary and proper clause**. But as we shall see later in this chapter, this power allowed the national government to expand considerably—if slowly—the scope of its authority. In addition to these expressed and implied powers, the Constitution affirmed the power of the national government in the supremacy clause (Article VI), which made all national laws and treaties "the supreme Law of the Land."

expressed powers specific powers granted by the Constitution to Congress (Article I, Section 8) and to the president (Article II)

implied powers powers derived from the necessary and proper clause of Article I, Section 8, of the Constitution; such powers are not specifically expressed but are implied through the expansive interpretation of delegated powers

necessary and proper clause Article I, Section 8, of the Constitution, which provides Congress with the authority to make all laws "necessary and proper" to carry out its expressed powers

reserved powers powers, derived from the Tenth Amendment to the Constitution, that are not specifically delegated to the national government or denied to the states

concurrent powers authority possessed by *both* state and national governments, such as the power to levy taxes

The Powers of State Government

One way in which the framers preserved a strong role for the states in the federal system was through the Tenth Amendment to the Constitution, which says that the powers the Constitution does not delegate to the national government or prohibit to the states are "reserved to the States respectively, or to the people." The Antifederalists, who feared that a strong central government would encroach on individual liberty, repeatedly pressed for such a "**reserved powers** amendment."

States also share with the national government **concurrent powers** to regulate commerce and the economy—for example, they can charter banks, grant or deny charters for corporations, grant or deny licenses to engage in a business or practice a trade, regulate the quality of products or the conditions of labor, and levy taxes. Wherever there is a direct conflict of laws between the federal and state levels, the issue will most likely be resolved in favor of national supremacy.

A very important power of the states is control of voting rights and the process of elections. States, for example, draw congressional district boundaries, establish voter registration requirements, decide whether absentee voting is allowed, and organize the casting and counting of ballots. The struggle over voting rights, to be discussed in Chapter 5, has been an effort to loosen restrictive state requirements

AMERICA | SIDE BY SIDE

Federal and Unitary Countries

Worldwide, unitary systems of government are much more common than federal systems. Geographically they may appear to be roughly even on this map, but that is because larger countries such as the United States and Russia often use federal systems. In fact, fewer than 15 percent of the world's countries use federal systems. Each type of system brings its own strengths and drawbacks: unitary systems can be more efficient, but federal systems can allow for more regional autonomy and policy innovation.

1. What explains why a country might use a federal or a unitary system? Why would a country with a large amount of territory to govern, such as Canada or Brazil, prefer a federal arrangement? Are there any geographic or regional patterns that you see? What might lead to countries on a continent being more likely to have similar government arrangements?
2. What are some of the other advantages to having a unitary system? In what ways might a federal system be more responsive? If you were designing your own country, which would you prefer and why?

that tend to reduce participation on the part of poor people and people from racial and ethnic minority groups. Today, Republicans control a majority of state governments. Accordingly, congressional Democrats support legislation that would reduce the states' power over voting rules while congressional Republicans support the status quo.

The Police Power America's federal system leaves a great deal of power in the hands of the individual states. The most fundamental power that the states retain is that of coercion—the power to develop and enforce criminal codes, administer health and safety rules, and regulate the family through marriage and divorce laws. States also have the power to regulate individuals' livelihoods; physicians, attorneys, plumb-

As businesses like this bakery in Arizona pushed the limits of stay-at-home orders during the coronavirus pandemic, police officers stepped in to enforce the state's authority to regulate the public health and safety of citizens.

ers, hairdressers, and those wishing to practice a host of other occupations must obtain licenses from their state. Even more fundamental, the states have the power to define private property. Private property exists because state laws against trespass and theft define who is and who is not entitled to use a piece of property. Ownership of a house or piece of land, for example, means that the state will enforce the owner's possession by prohibiting others from occupying the property without the consent of its owner. At the same time, under its power of eminent domain (see Chapter 4), the state may seize private property for anything it deems to be a public purpose. If the state, however, does seize such property, it is required by its own constitution and the federal constitution to compensate the owners for their loss. The decision to take the property, though, is well within the states' recognized powers.

A state's authority to regulate these fundamental matters, commonly referred to as the **police power**, encompasses its power to regulate the health, safety, welfare, and morals of its citizens. Policing is what states do: they coerce individuals in the name of the community in order to maintain public order. When an individual is issued a traffic ticket, or taken into custody for most other crimes, the state is exercising its police power, often through the agency of a county or city police officer. (Counties and cities are effectively agencies of their states.)

Though Americans tend to look to the federal government for help in times of crisis, the states, and especially their governors and executive departments, are the actual primary responders when Americans are threatened by natural or human-made disasters. Every year, the states deal with floods, hurricanes, fires, shootings, and public-health problems.

> **police power** power reserved to the state government to regulate the health, safety, and morals of its citizens

States' Obligations to One Another

The Constitution also creates obligations among the states, spelled out in Article IV. By requiring the states to recognize or uphold governmental actions and decisions in other states, the framers aimed to make the states less like independent countries and more like components of a unified nation. Article IV, Section 1, calls for "Full Faith and Credit" among states, meaning that each state is normally expected to honor the "Public Acts, Records, and Judicial Proceedings" of the other states. So, for example, if a restraining order is placed on a stalker in one state, other states are required to enforce that order as if they had issued it.

full faith and credit clause provision from Article IV, Section 1, of the Constitution requiring that the states normally honor the public acts and judicial decisions that take place in another state

privileges and immunities clause provision, from Article IV, Section 2, of the Constitution, that a state cannot discriminate against someone from another state or give its own residents special privileges

Nevertheless, some courts have found exceptions to the **full faith and credit clause**: if one state's law is against the "strong public policy" of another state, that state may not be obligated to recognize it.[4] The history of interracial marriage policy shows how much leeway states once had about recognizing marriages performed in other states. In 1952, 30 states prohibited interracial marriage, and many of these also refused to recognize such marriages performed in other states.[5] For example, in the 1967 Supreme Court case of *Loving v. Virginia*, which successfully challenged state bans on interracial marriage, Mildred and Richard Loving, a Black woman and a White man, were married in the District of Columbia. However, when they returned to their home state of Virginia, it refused to recognize them as a married couple.[6]

Until recently, same-sex marriage was in a similar position to interracial marriage. Thirty-five states had passed "Defense of Marriage" acts, defining marriage as a union between one man and one woman, or had adopted constitutional amendments to this effect. In 1996, Congress passed a federal Defense of Marriage Act, which declared that states were not required to recognize a same-sex marriage from another state and that the federal government did not recognize same-sex marriage even if it was legal under state law.

In 2015, however, the Supreme Court ruled that the Fourteenth Amendment guaranteed a fundamental right to same-sex marriage. The case, *Obergefell v. Hodges*, challenged four home states' refusals to grant same-sex marriage licenses or recognize same-sex marriages performed out of state.[7] The Court's decision meant that all states must now offer marriage licenses to two people of the same sex and recognize same-sex marriages licensed by other states. In one stroke, same-sex marriage turned from a state-level policy choice to a nationally recognized right.

Article IV, Section 2, known as the "comity clause," also seeks to promote national unity, by providing that citizens enjoying the "**privileges and immunities**" of one state should be entitled to similar treatment in other states. This has come to mean that a state cannot discriminate against someone from another state or give special privileges to its own residents. For example, in the 1970s the Supreme Court struck down as unconstitutional an Alaska law that gave Alaska residents preference over nonresidents for jobs on the state's oil and gas pipelines.[8] The comity clause also regulates criminal justice among the states by requiring states to return fugitives to the states from which they have fled.

Local Government and the Constitution

Local government occupies a peculiar but very important place in the American system. It has no status in the U.S. Constitution. Instead, state constitutions define local government structures and responsibilities. Thus, local governments are subject to ultimate control by the states.

This imbalance of power means that state governments could legally dissolve local governments or force multiple local governments to consolidate into one. Most states have amended their constitutions to give their larger cities **home rule**—a guarantee of noninterference in various areas of local affairs.[9] In recent years, however, as discussed later in the chapter, some local governments have passed laws making policy on matters from minimum wage to public broadband, only to have state legislatures preempt, or remove, that authority.

home rule power delegated by the state to a local unit of government to manage its own affairs

Check your understanding

1. How does the distribution of national and state power in a unitary system compare to that of a federal system of government?

   a) In a unitary system, state governments establish most policies, and the national government lacks the authority to tax, while in a federal system, the national government can determine most policies.

   b) In a unitary system, the national government holds most policy-making authority, and in a federal system, policy-making authority is shared among the national government and regional or state governments.

   c) In a unitary system, foreign policy is determined by the national government and states determine domestic policy, while in a federal system, the national government is responsible for domestic policy and the state governments determine foreign policy.

   d) In a unitary government, state governments retain all policy-making authority, while in a federal system, the national government holds all policy-making authority.

HOW TO

Make Your Voice Heard at a Local Meeting

DOMINGO MOREL, COFOUNDER OF THE RHODE ISLAND LATINO POLICY INSTITUTE AND ASSISTANT PROFESSOR AT RUTGERS UNIVERSITY–NEWARK

How can you change policy in your community? There are over 90,000 local governments in the United States, including school boards, city councils, county boards, and special districts for public transportation, utilities, libraries, parks, police, fire, water, and more. Domingo shared his advice for making your voice heard in local government:

1 **Figure out which governmental entity has jurisdiction over your issue and get on its agenda.** Most school boards, city councils, and other local government entities have an online sign-up to speak at their meetings.

2 **Do research on your issue.** Local governments often do not have staffs to do research. Many local officeholders have day jobs. You can be an effective advocate and partner by supplying the research they can't do. Young people would be surprised to learn how far that can get them.

3 **Prepare your statement.** Your time will be limited, so lay out your issue concern and suggested solution succinctly. The most effective statements don't just articulate an argument but also attach a personal narrative about why this issue is important and convey that to the people who are in power.

4 **Follow up.** Email the members of the board or council. Broadcast your issue concern and proposals on social media. Monitor the agenda and attend subsequent meetings. Build relationships with local officials.

5 Consider that collective action may be even more powerful. I recall a mother who attended Newark school board meetings for four months, urging, without success, that Muslim holidays be added to the school calendar. In the fifth month she said, "Today I brought my community. Can all of the Muslims in attendance please stand up?" Seeing an auditorium full, the school board changed the policy. I advise bringing friends, finding out what groups may already work on your concerns, or creating your own group if needed (see How to Start an Advocacy Group on p. 250).

6 Work across the generations. Seek the advice of elders and community leaders who worked on such issues in the past. In turn, recruit younger people to keep the effort going, giving them information so they don't have to start over. It's not easy getting engaged, it's not easy to go out there and be an activist on the individual or collective level, but once you get to that place, it's important to ensure you're recruiting others.

7 Work the federal system. Many issues are addressed at multiple levels of government. Strategize about the best level for addressing your particular concern. And if you make no headway at one level, target another. Federalism brings its challenges but also has its advantages.

2. How does the U.S. Constitution establish the authority of the national government and state governments?

a) The U.S. Constitution sets out expressed powers for the national government and state governments to avoid confusion over who has jurisdiction over particular issues.

b) The U.S. Constitution establishes the powers of the state governments and reserves all other powers for the national government.

c) The U.S. Constitution establishes expressed powers for the national government in Article 1, Section 8, and it establishes reserved powers to the states in the Tenth Amendment.

d) The U.S. Constitution only establishes the powers of the national government and avoids mentioning state and local governments.

National and State Powers Have Shifted over Time

Explain how the relationship between the federal and state governments has evolved over time

The federal framework is not static; it changes over time as competing forces seek to make use of different levels of government to pursue their interests. Yet the federal framework does create both restraints and opportunities for political action and helps to determine how the country evolves. At the time of the Founding, the states far surpassed the federal government in their power to influence the lives of ordinary Americans. In the system of shared powers, they played a much more active role in economic and social regulation than the federal government, which tended toward a hands-off approach. Although Supreme Court decisions gradually expanded its authority in this area, not until the New Deal of the 1930s did the national government gain vast new powers. Since then, the states have asserted themselves at certain times and in certain policy areas, sometimes aided by the courts. But at other moments a crisis shifts power toward the national government again, as during the September 11, 2001, terror attacks, the fiscal crisis that began in 2008, and the coronavirus-induced economic crisis in 2020.

Restraining National Power with Dual Federalism

dual federalism the system of government that prevailed in the United States from 1789 to 1937 in which most fundamental governmental powers were shared between the federal and state governments

Historically, **dual federalism** has meant that states have done most of the fundamental governing. We call this state-centered federalism the "traditional system" because it prevailed for much

TABLE 3.1 | Governmental Functions in the Traditional Federal System, 1789–1937

NATIONAL GOVERNMENT POLICIES (DOMESTIC)	STATE GOVERNMENT POLICIES	LOCAL GOVERNMENT POLICIES
Internal improvements Subsidies Tariffs Public land disposal Patents Currency	Property, estate, and inheritance laws Commerce and banking laws Corporate, occupations and professions, and insurance laws Family, morality, public health, and education laws Penal and criminal laws Eminent domain, construction, land use, water, and mineral laws Local government, election, and civil service laws	Adaptation of state laws to local conditions Public works Contracts for public works Licensing of public accommodation Zoning and other land-use regulation Basic public services

of American history. Under this system, the national government was quite small and very narrowly specialized in the functions it performed (see Table 3.1).

What do the functions of the national government reveal? First, virtually all of them were aimed at assisting commerce, such as building roads or protecting domestic industries with tariffs on imported goods. Second, virtually none of them directly coerced citizens. The emphasis was on promotion and encouragement—providing land or capital needed for economic development.

State legislatures were also actively involved in economic regulation during the nineteenth century. American capitalism took its form from state property and trespass laws and from state laws and court decisions regarding contracts, markets, credit, banking, incorporation, and insurance. Until the Thirteenth Amendment abolished slavery, property law extended to slavery, with the fugitive slave clause of the Constitution (Article IV, Section 2) requiring even "free states" without slavery to return freedom-seeking enslaved people to the states from which they had escaped.

How the Supreme Court Responded to Demands for a Larger Federal Role

In the first several decades after the Founding, the Supreme Court decided several critical cases that expanded federal powers when there was a conflict between the states and the federal government, removed interstate barriers to trade, and laid the groundwork for a national economy. These early decisions to expand federal power rested on a pro-national interpretation of Article I, Section 8, of the Constitution. That article enumerates the powers of Congress, including the power to tax, raise an army, declare war, establish post offices, and "regulate commerce with foreign nations, and among the several States and with the Indian tribes." Though its scope initially was unclear, this **commerce clause** would later form the basis for expanding federal government control over the economy.

The first and most important such case was *McCulloch v. Maryland* (1819), which involved the question of whether Congress could charter a national bank—an explicit grant of power nowhere to be found in Article I, Section 8.[10] Chief Justice John Marshall answered that this power could be "implied" from other powers expressly delegated to Congress, such as the power to regulate commerce. His decision rested on the necessary and proper clause of Article I, Section 8, which gave Congress the power to enact laws "necessary and proper" for carrying out its delegated powers. Marshall also concluded in *McCulloch* that any state law conflicting with a federal law is invalid because the Constitution states that "the Laws of the United States . . . shall be the supreme Law of the Land."

Another major case, *Gibbons v. Ogden* (1824), reinforced this nationalistic interpretation of the Constitution. The issue was whether New York State could grant a monopoly to Robert Fulton's steamboat company to operate an exclusive service between New York and New Jersey. In arguing that the state lacked the power to do so, Chief Justice Marshall had to define what Article I, Section 8 meant by "commerce among the several states." He insisted that the definition was "comprehensive," extending to "every species of commercial intercourse." However, this comprehensiveness was limited "to that commerce which concerns more states than one." *Gibbons* is important because it established the supremacy of the national government in all matters affecting what later came to be called "interstate commerce."[11]

Later in the nineteenth century, though, any effort of the national government to *regulate* commerce in such areas as fraud, product quality, child labor, or working conditions or hours was declared unconstitutional by the Supreme Court. The Court said that with such legislation the federal government was entering workplaces—local areas—and attempting to regulate goods that had not yet passed into interstate commerce. To enter local workplaces was to exercise police power—a power reserved to the states.

No one questioned the power of the national government to regulate businesses that by their nature crossed state lines, such as railroads, gas pipelines, and waterway transportation. But well into the twentieth century the Supreme Court used the concept of interstate commerce as a barrier against most efforts by Congress to regulate local conditions. Thus, federalism, as interpreted by the Supreme Court for 70 years after the Civil War, enabled business to enjoy the benefits of national policies promoting commerce while being shielded by the courts from policies regulating commerce by protecting consumers and workers.[12]

This barrier fell after 1937, however, when the Supreme Court issued a series of decisions that laid the groundwork for a much stronger federal government. Most significant was the Court's dramatic expansion of the commerce clause. By throwing out the old distinction between interstate and intrastate commerce, the Court converted the clause from a source of limitations to a source of power for the national government. The Court upheld acts of Congress that protected the rights of employees to organize and engage in collective bargaining, regulated the amount of farmland in cultivation, extended low-interest credit to small businesses and farmers, and restricted the activities of corporations dealing in the stock market.[13]

The Court also upheld many other laws that contributed to the construction of the modern safety net of social programs created in response to the Great Depression. With these rulings, the Court decisively signaled that the era of dual federalism was over. In the future, Congress would have very broad powers to regulate activity in the states.

The New Deal: New Roles for Government

The economic crisis of the Great Depression and the nature of the government response signaled a new era of federalism in the United States. Before this national economic catastrophe, states and localities took responsibility for assisting people in poverty, usually channeling aid through private charity. But the extent of the depression quickly exhausted their capacities. By 1932, 25 percent of the workforce was unemployed, and many people had lost their homes. Elected in 1928, the year before the depression hit, President Herbert Hoover steadfastly maintained that the federal government could do little to alleviate the misery caused by the depression. It was a matter for state and local governments, he said.

When Franklin Delano Roosevelt took office in 1933, he energetically threw the federal government into the fight against the depression through a number of proposals known collectively as the New Deal. He proposed a variety of temporary relief and work programs, most of them to be financed by the federal government but administered by the states. In addition, Roosevelt presided over the creation of several important federal programs designed to provide future economic security for Americans. The New Deal signaled the rise of a more active national government.

Cooperative Federalism and the Use of Categorical Grants

The Roosevelt administration programs typically offered states **grants-in-aid**, money provided on the condition that it be spent for a particular purpose defined by Congress, such as financial assistance to poor children. Congress added more grant programs after World War II to help states fund activities such as providing school lunches and building highways. Sometimes state or local governments were required to match the national contribution dollar for dollar, but in programs such as the development of the interstate highway system, the congressional grants provided 90 percent of the cost.

These types of federal grants-in-aid are called **categorical grants**, because the national government determines the purposes, or categories, for which the money can be used. One of the most important—and expensive—was the federal Medicaid program, which provides grants to pay for

grants-in-aid programs through which Congress provides money to state and local governments on the condition that the funds be employed for purposes defined by the federal government

categorical grants congressional grants given to states and localities on the condition that expenditures be limited to a problem or group specified by law

medical care for people in poverty, disabled people, and many nursing home residents. Over time the value of categorical grants has risen dramatically, increasing from $54.8 billion in 1960 to an estimated $1,111 billion in 2022 (see Figure 3.1).

The growth of categorical grants created a new kind of federalism. If the traditional system of two sovereigns—the federal government and the states—performing highly different functions could be called dual federalism, historians of federalism suggest that the system since the New Deal could be called

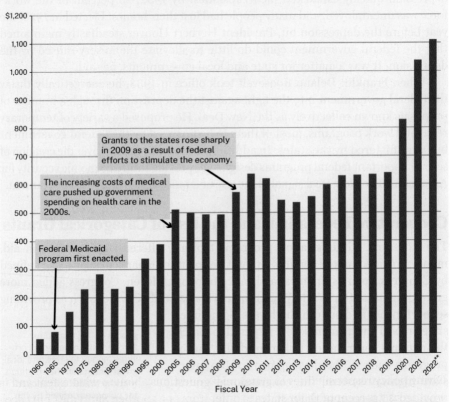

FIGURE 3.1 | Federal Grants-in-Aid,* 1960–2021

Federal spending on grants to state and local governments has grown dramatically since 1980. Today, most state and local governments are heavily dependent upon such grants to implement their policy goals. How might such dependence affect the autonomy of state governments and the character of American federalism?

TOTAL IN BILLIONS OF CONSTANT 2012 DOLLARS

Grants to the states rose sharply in 2009 as a result of federal efforts to stimulate the economy.

The increasing costs of medical care pushed up government spending on health care in the 2000s.

Federal Medicaid program first enacted.

Fiscal Year

*Excludes outlays for national defense, international affairs, and net interest. Data in constant (fiscal year 2012) dollars.

**Estimate.

SOURCE: Office of Management and Budget, U.S. Budget for Fiscal Year 2020, "Historical Tables: Table 12.1," www.whitehouse.gov/omb/historical-tables/ (accessed 1/21/20); White House, "Aid to State and Local Governments," www.whitehouse.gov/wp-content/uploads/2021/05/ap_11_state_and _local_fy22.pdf (accessed 5/10/22).

FIGURE 3.2 | Dual versus Cooperative Federalism

In layer-cake (dual) federalism, the responsibilities of the national government and state governments are clearly separated. In marble-cake (cooperative) federalism, national policies, state policies, and local policies overlap in many areas.

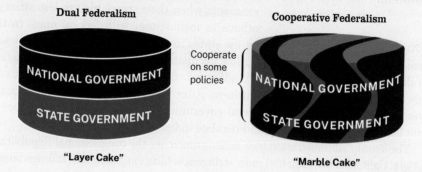

Dual Federalism

Cooperative Federalism

Cooperate on some policies {

NATIONAL GOVERNMENT

STATE GOVERNMENT

"Layer Cake"

NATIONAL GOVERNMENT

STATE GOVERNMENT

"Marble Cake"

cooperative federalism. The political scientist Morton Grodzins characterized this as a move from "layer cake federalism" to "marble cake federalism,"[14] in which intergovernmental cooperation and sharing have blurred a once-clear distinguishing line, making it difficult to say where the national government ends and the state and local governments begin (see Figure 3.2).

As important as the states were in this new system of grants, some new federal grants, particularly during the War on Poverty of the 1960s, bypassed the states and instead sent money directly to local governments and even to local nonprofit organizations. One of the reasons for this shift was discriminatory treatment of African Americans in the South. As the civil rights movement gained momentum, the southern defense of segregation on the grounds of states' rights confirmed the belief in Washington that the states could not be trusted to carry out national purposes.

cooperative federalism a type of federalism existing since the New Deal era in which grants-in-aid have been used strategically to encourage states and localities (without commanding them) to pursue nationally defined goals; also known as *intergovernmental cooperation*

regulated federalism a form of federalism in which Congress imposes legislation on states and localities, requiring them to meet national standards

Regulated Federalism and the Rise of National Standards

Giving policy responsibilities to states raises questions about to what extent and in what areas it is acceptable for states to differ from one another. Supreme Court decisions have provided important answers to many of these questions, typically pushing for greater uniformity across the states. But in other policy areas, the national government has created greater uniformity by offering incentives or imposing rules.

As Congress in the 1970s began to enact legislation in new areas, such as environmental policy, it resorted to another tool: regulations on states and localities, called **regulated federalism,**[15] in which the national government began to set standards

preemption the principle that allows the national government to override state or local actions in certain policy areas; in foreign policy, the willingness to strike first in order to prevent an enemy attack

of conduct for the states. As a result, state and local policies in environmental protection, social services, and education are more uniform from coast to coast than are other nationally funded policies.

Sometimes the federal government takes over areas of regulation from state or local governments when their standards are less strict or otherwise inconsistent with federal ones. In the 1970s, such **preemption** required the states to abide by tougher federal rules in areas including air and water pollution, occupational health and safety, and access for disabled people. The regulated industries often opposed preemptions because they increased the cost of doing business. After 1994, however, when Republicans took control of Congress, the federal government used its preemption power to limit the ability of states to tax and regulate industry.

The Trump administration took actions much like the congressional Republicans of 1994. California has long had more stringent vehicle emissions and mileage targets than the federal government, but the administration moved to prohibit any state from setting standards different from federal ones. In 2019, California and 22 other states sued to keep their ability to set stricter regulations in place.[16] The suit was unsuccessful. In 2022, however, the Biden administration restored the rights of states to set their own emission standards even if these were more strict than federal standards.

Check your understanding

3. Which of the following statements concerning the evolution of the national government's power is true?

   a) In the 1930s, the Court increased the power of the national government through its expansive interpretation of the commerce clause, and the national New Deal policies further expanded the government's scope.

   b) The Court's decisions in *McCulloch v. Maryland* and *Gibbons v. Ogden* limited the power of the national government.

   c) During the New Deal, state power expanded considerably at the expense of the national government's power as states were provided funding with no strings attached.

   d) The U.S. Constitution and the federal framework it creates produce a system in which national power is static and narrowly interpreted by the expressed powers in Article 1, Section 8.

4. One way that the national government has exerted influence over state governments is

   a) through imposing home rule on the states.

   b) defunding state legislatures when they fail to enact policies the national government supports.

   c) by restricting the amount of property taxes states may collect.

   d) by giving money to state and local governments if they agree to spend it for the purposes Congress specifies.

Federalism Today Is as Important as Ever

Analyze what difference federalism makes for politics and government

Debates about the appropriate role for each level of government—national, state, and local—continue. Intergovernmental tensions have shifted and even increased. The significant role for the states in particular raises important questions. Might states be sources of experimentation and innovation, the "laboratories of democracy," as Supreme Court Justice Louis Brandeis suggested?[17] Which responsibilities are states capable of managing and financing? Does interstate competition enhance or impede efficiency? Who prefers national rather than state control? And do multiple levels of government in fact promote citizen engagement?

States' Rights

The Tenth Amendment, which reserves to the states the powers the Constitution does not specifically delegate to the national government, has been used over time to bolster the role of the states in the federal system. For much of the nineteenth century, when federal power remained limited, the Tenth Amendment was used to argue in favor of **states' rights**. The extreme version of this position, known as nullification, claimed that the states did not have to obey federal laws that they believed exceeded the national government's constitutional authority.

> **states' rights** the principle that the states should oppose the increasing authority of the national government; this principle was most popular in the period before the Civil War

Prior to the Civil War, sharp differences between the North and the South over tariffs and slavery gave rise to nullification arguments that were most fully articulated by South Carolina senator John C. Calhoun. (Calhoun was a slaveowner and white supremacist, and his political positions were often informed by his support of the expansion of the institution of slavery.) Such arguments were voiced less often after the Civil War. But the Supreme Court continued to use the Tenth Amendment to strike down laws that it thought exceeded national power, including the Civil Rights Act passed in 1875, which would have eliminated discrimination against African Americans in public accommodations and transportation.

By the late 1930s, the Supreme Court had expanded federal power—so much so that the Tenth Amendment appeared irrelevant. Yet the idea that some powers should be reserved to the states did not go away.

For example, in the 1950s, southern opponents of the civil rights movement revived the idea in order to maintain racial segregation. In 1956, 96 southern members of Congress issued a "Southern manifesto" in which they declared that southern states were not constitutionally bound by Supreme Court decisions outlawing segregation. With the eventual triumph of the civil rights movement, the slogan "states' rights" became tarnished by its association with racial inequality. The 1990s, however, saw a revival of interest in the Tenth Amendment and important Supreme Court decisions limiting federal power. Much of the interest stemmed from conservatives who believed that a strong federal government encroached on individual liberties. They favored returning more power to the states through the process of devolution, as we'll see later.[18]

For example, in *United States v. Lopez* (1995),[19] the Court, stating that Congress had exceeded its authority under the commerce clause, struck down a federal law that barred handguns near schools. This was the first time since the New Deal that the Court had limited congressional powers in this way.

State Control over National Policies

devolution a policy to remove a program from one level of government by delegating it or passing it down to a lower level of government, such as from the national government to the state and local governments

block grants federal grants-in-aid that allow states considerable discretion in how the funds are spent

New Federalism attempts by Presidents Nixon and Reagan to return power to the states through block grants

general revenue sharing the process by which one unit of government yields a portion of its tax income to another unit of government, according to an established formula; revenue sharing typically involves the national government providing money to state governments

Since the 1970s, the idea of **devolution**—transferring responsibility for policy from the federal government to states and localities—has become popular. Its proponents maintain that states are potential innovators and experimenters, whose good ideas might spread horizontally to other states and even vertically to the federal government. Devolution's supporters also assert that governments closer to the people can better tailor policies to local needs than can the federal government in "far-off" Washington, D.C.

An important tool of devolution is the **block grant**, federal funding that states have considerable leeway in spending. President Nixon led the first push for block grants in the early 1970s as part of his **New Federalism** initiative, when programs in the areas of job training, community development, and social services were consolidated into three large block grants. In addition, Congress provided an important new form of federal assistance to state and local governments, called **general revenue sharing**, which had no strings attached; recipients could spend the money as they wished.

In his version of New Federalism in the 1980s, President Reagan also looked to block grants to reduce the national government's control and return power to the states. But, unlike Nixon, he used them to cut federal spending as well. The 12 new block grants enacted between 1981 and 1990 cut federal spending in those areas by 12 percent.[20] Reagan's view was that states could spend their own funds to make up the difference if they chose to do so.

The Republican Congress elected in 1994 took devolution even further through more block grants and spending cuts in federal programs. Their biggest success was the 1996 welfare reform law, which delegated to states important new responsibilities.

Those who argue for state policy control note that states have often been important sources of policy innovations that have diffused to other states or to the federal government. For example, Minnesota first created charter schools in 1991; now 44 states and the District of Columbia permit them.[21] In 1990, San Luis Obispo, California, became the first city to ban smoking in bars and restaurants. The state of California followed with a statewide ban on smoking in enclosed workplaces in 1995, and the federal government banned smoking on commercial flights in 1998. The Massachusetts health care reform of 2006 became the template for the federal Affordable Care Act of 2010 ("Obamacare").

States often complain about **unfunded mandates**—requirements on states imposed by the national government without accompanying funding. For example, a 1973 federal law prohibiting discrimination against disabled people required state and local governments to make public transit accessible. But the legislation provided no funding for the wheelchair lifts and elevators that would be necessary, leaving states to cover the multibillion-dollar cost.[22]

Additional concerns with state responsibility are variation in policy outcomes and questions of who benefits or suffers from government action or inaction. For example, Congress enacted major welfare reform in 1996 that changed welfare from a combined federal–state program into a block grant, giving the states more responsibility for programs that serve people in poverty. Supporters of the change hoped to reduce welfare spending and argued that states could experiment with many different approaches to find those that best met the needs of their citizens.

Minnesota adopted an incentive-based approach that offers extra assistance to families that take low-wage jobs, while six other states imposed very strict time limits on receiving benefits, allowing welfare recipients less than the five-year lifetime limit in the federal legislation (the lifetime limit is shortest in Arizona: 12 months).[23] As of 2021, cash welfare benefits per month for a family of three were $712 in Rhode Island, $512 in Ohio, $308 in Texas, and

The federal government frequently passes laws that impose mandates on the states, such as the 1990 Americans with Disabilities Act, which protects against discrimination based on disability. States were required to pay for changes to meet federal standards for accessibility in public transportation and public facilities.

unfunded mandate a law or regulation requiring a state or local government to perform certain actions without providing funding for fulfilling the requirement

$260 in Mississippi.[24] After the passage of the 1996 law, welfare rolls declined dramatically—on average, by more than half from their peak in 1994. In 12 states the decline was 70 percent or higher.

Federal–State Tensions in Two Issue Areas

One source of federalism-based controversy concerns whether states and localities have to enforce federal immigration laws. For example, the Secure Communities program, launched in 2008 and expanded under President Obama, required state and local authorities to check the fingerprints of people being booked into jail against a Department of Homeland Security database. The program led to a record number of deportations in 2009 and 2010 and then to several states and localities pulling out of it on the grounds that too many of the undocumented immigrants being detained had not committed a crime. The Obama administration softened its deportation policy in 2011 and ended the Secure Communities program in 2014, replacing it in 2015 with one containing a more limited deportation policy.[25]

Having campaigned on promises for more rigorous immigration enforcement, President Trump signed an executive order days after his inauguration restarting Secure Communities and expanding the types of immigrants considered a priority for deportation, from those convicted of felonies or multiple misdemeanors (as under Obama) to those accused or convicted of minor crimes as well.[26] In response, a growing number of cities, counties, and states declared themselves "sanctuaries" that limit their cooperation with federal enforcement of immigration law. Trump pledged to withhold federal grants from these jurisdictions, but a federal judge's ruling blocked him from doing so.[27] In 2019 a federal appeals court ruled that the Trump administration did have authority to withhold Community Oriented Policing Services (COPS) grants from sanctuary cities.[28] President Biden promised a thorough overhaul of immigration policies and has ended several Trump-era programs.

With regard to marijuana policy, federal authority has also been upheld by the courts. In 2005 the Supreme Court upheld the right of Congress to ban medical marijuana, even though 11 states had legalized its use. The Court found that the commerce clause gave the federal government the power to regulate marijuana use. Nonetheless, by 2022, 37 states and the District of Columbia had

FOR CRITICAL ANALYSIS

1. Which states receive significantly more in federal government expenditures than their citizens pay in federal taxes? Which states pay more federal taxes than they receive in government spending?

2. Fiscal federalism involves the federal government influencing public policy in the states using federal government dollars. What are some explanations for those differences? Why would states pay more in federal taxes than they receive in government spending?

WHO ARE AMERICANS?

Who Benefits from Federal Spending?

Federal Grants to State and Local Governments, 2022 (estimated)

Health
$618 billion

Transportation
$101 billion

Other
$198 billion

Income security
$195 billion

Education
$107 billion

Although Americans often think they pay a lot in federal taxes, they receive much in return in the form of federal money for state and local programs. Federal outlays for grants to state and local governments have grown from $68.2 billion in 1960 to $1.229 trillion in 2022.

Fiscal Transfers between the States and the Federal Government, 2019

Federal spending
per tax dollar

- $2.00+
- $1.51–2.00
- $1.01–1.50
- ———— $1.00
- < $1.00

Every U.S. state contributes to the federal government through the federal taxes paid by the state's citizens, and every state receives money from federal spending. Federal spending is a broad category that includes the grants described above as well as spending on military bases and federal procurement. Not every state receives the same amount from the federal government, however. The map above shows how much federal spending each state received for each dollar paid in federal taxes in 2019.

SOURCES: Office of Management and Budget, Historical Table 12.3, www.whitehouse.gov/omb/budget/historical-tables; Rockefeller Institute of Government, 2021, "Who Gives and Who Gets?," https://rockinst.org/issue-areas/fiscal-analysis/balance-of-payments-portal (accessed 4/18/22).

FIGURE 3.3 | Marijuana Laws across the States

While buying, selling, and possessing marijuana remain federal crimes, states have adopted policies that conflict with federal laws. Should this be allowed?

- ■ Marijuana legalized for recreational and medical use
- ■ Marijuana legalized only for medical use
- ■ No broad laws legalizing marijuana

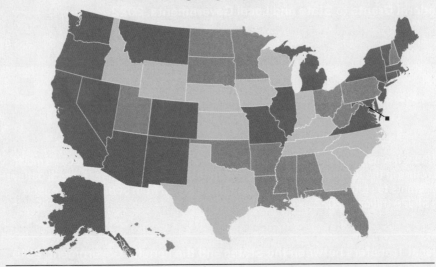

SOURCE: "State Medical Cannabis Laws," National Conference of State Legislatures, www.ncsl.org /research/health/state-medical-marijuana-laws.aspx (accessed 11/9/22).

legalized medical marijuana and several had legalized it for recreational use (see Figure 3.3). Amid this legal confusion, a medical marijuana industry began to flourish, and a number of states went further by legalizing recreational marijuana. The mismatch between federal and state laws has precipitated federal raids on marijuana dispensaries and growers, even if their states have legalized the practice.[29]

A third area in which federal–state tensions and, perhaps, conflicts among the states are likely to arise in the coming years is the matter of abortion. As we discuss in Chapter 4, in the case of *Dobbs v. Jackson* (2022), the U.S. Supreme Court over-turned its own 1973 *Roe v. Wade* decision, which had safeguarded abortion rights for the past half century. The *Dobbs* decision did not outlaw abortion. Rather, it left the individual states free to restrict (or not restrict) abortion as they saw fit.

Soon after the *Dobbs* decision, 13 states enacted nearly total bans on abortion and 5 imposed significant restrictions. Abortion remained fully legal in 12 states and legal but with some limitations in 9 states. In several states, constitutional amendments were proposed either guaranteeing abortion rights or restricting abortions.

This patchwork of state policies may eventually produce conflicts between the federal government and the states. At the federal level, Democrats have pro-posed legislation that would establish a federal guarantee of abortion rights, while

Despite the Charlotte City Council's ordinance prohibiting sex discrimination in public facilities, state preemption allowed for the North Carolina legislature to pass the "Charlotte bathroom bill," which undid the provisions originally set out by the city council.

some Republicans have proposed federal legislation that would severely restrict abortion rights. Either of these federal actions would lead to conflicts between the federal government and the states that chose the opposite path.

Conflicts also may arise between states that permit abortion and those that prohibit it. For example, in Missouri, a state that has outlawed abortion, legislation was introduced that would penalize state residents who traveled outside the state to obtain an abortion. It might seem that such legislation violates the Constitution's full faith and credit clause or the long-established right of Americans to travel from state to state. There are, however, precedents for state power to enforce laws beyond their boundaries (see *Skiriotes v. Florida*, 313 U.S. 69 [1941]). The question of out-of-state abortions could become a major area of conflict in the federal system.

State–Local Tensions

Another notable development in the recent politics of federalism has been the willingness of state governments to preempt local policy. Just as states sometimes seize the policy initiative from the federal government, so too have cities made policy in areas where states have not or where policy preferences in the city differ from those in the state at large. In recent years some cities have set higher minimum wages than are in effect elsewhere in the state, required employers to provide paid sick leave, regulated the "sharing economy" of car- and home-sharing (such as Uber and Airbnb), prohibited gender-based discrimination in public facilities such as bathrooms, and attempted to establish public broadband services.

One of the most contentious areas in the relationship between state and local governments today concerns regulation of firearms. Quite a few states have enacted laws preempting local ordinances restricting the ownership of firearms. However, bowing to local pressure, six states—Colorado, New York, Massachusetts, New Jersey, Connecticut, and Hawaii—have recently repealed their preemption laws, opening the way for strict local gun control ordinances.

In each of these areas, however, some state legislatures have responded with laws preempting (limiting or prohibiting) municipal law or authority. As of 2019, 25 states preempt local minimum-wage ordinances, 23 prohibit local paid-leave ordinances, 44 limit local authority to regulate ride-sharing, and 10 ban local regulation of e-cigarettes. Michigan bans cities from banning plastic bags; Texas bans them from banning fracking. Twenty states prohibit localities from establishing municipal broadband service, and three—most famously North Carolina—preempt local antidiscrimination ordinances.[30]

Check your understanding

5. Which of the following statements regarding states' rights is true?

   a) Devolution resulted in states' policy-making authority being limited and an expansion of the national government's power.

   b) Since the 1970s, states have taken a much more active role in administering large-scale programs with the federal government providing states with block grants that have fewer conditions on how the funds should be spent.

   c) Congress imposed considerable constraints upon state governments through block grants during the New Federalism period.

   d) The states' rights movement during the 1980s impeded policy diffusion and innovation as states were more restricted in policy implementation.

6. Federalism often gives rise to controversies concerning whether the national government or state governments have authority over various issues. When federal–state conflicts have arisen, how have these conflicts been resolved?

   a) The Supreme Court has always ruled in favor of states' rights based on the Tenth Amendment, which establishes the states' reserved powers.

   b) The Supreme Court always rules in favor of the national government based on the supremacy clause, which it believes trumps the Tenth Amendment.

   c) The Supreme Court has generally viewed these controversies as "political questions" and thus has not rendered a ruling.

   d) The Supreme Court has tended to side with the national government, but it can vary depending on the issue.

WHAT DO YOU THINK?

FEDERALISM

As described in the opening of this chapter, conflicts over voting restrictions and rights highlights the tensions inherent in a federal system of government. The United States' history of federalism shows that Americans generally accept the idea that states should have the freedom to enact policies that best serve their residents, within the bounds set by Congress and the courts. But variation across the states may not be desirable in some policy areas. These are perennial questions in American government.

- In what ways is federalism a struggle over power and political ideas?

- Is it fair that a transgender person in California can legally change the sex on their birth certificate, but a transgender person in Tennessee cannot? Is it reasonable that a gun owner can openly carry a handgun in Georgia but not in Florida? Is it fair that voters in some states can use drive-through voting but Brittany Hyman can't in Texas? Why or why not?

- How might your life be different if you lived in a different state? Imagine being a student in a state with very different state-college tuition levels. Or a state with a very different minimum-wage level. For example, in 2022 the minimum wage was $9.20 in Montana and $15.50 in Arizona.[31] Or a state where you can vote early in person or where there is no pre–Election Day in-person voting option.

Use 🐰 *INQUIZITIVE to help you study and master this material.*

4

WHAT GOVERNMENT DOES & WHY IT MATTERS

One of the most important and well-known civil liberties in the United States Constitution is the First Amendment guarantee of "freedom of speech." But what speech is protected? By whom? And in what contexts?

Brandi Levy, a high school student in Pennsylvania, got a firsthand look at the Supreme Court's thinking on free speech. In 2017, when she failed to get promoted to her school's varsity cheerleading squad, she voiced her frustrations on Snapchat. Posting a photograph of herself and a friend making an obscene gesture, she wrote, "F____ school f____ softball f____ cheer f____ everything." The school suspended her from the cheerleading team, but her parents sued, arguing that the punishment of Brandi's speech violated the First Amendment.

It was unclear how the Court might rule. In 1969 the Court had upheld freedom of speech for public school students protesting the Vietnam War, finding that the black armbands they wore to symbolize the protest were not "disruptive" to the educational experience.[1] In subsequent decades, however, the Court had

Civil Liberties

supported limits on student speech. In 2007 it upheld the suspension of a high school student who displayed a pro-drug banner while the Olympic torch rally went through his town.[2] In this and other cases the Court determined that student speech is less protected than adult speech and that public schools can restrict speech that undermines schools' other goals, such as teaching that "the use of vulgar and offensive terms in public discourse"[3] or the use of illegal drugs is undesirable. The Court even said that schools might have an interest in regulating student speech that occurs off campus, if it includes bullying or harassment.

But in a victory for student speech, Brandi Levy won. In 2021 the Court ruled that her Snapchat rant did not meet the Court's "disruptive" standard because Brandi "spoke outside the school on her own time," used her cell phone, and did not target particular members of the school community with abusive language. In the majority opinion, Justice Stephen Breyer wrote that off-campus social media speech differs in three ways: parents, not schools, should regulate off-campus speech; schools cannot and should not regulate students' speech 24/7; and schools should protect even unpopular speech because "America's public schools are the nurseries of democracy."[4]

Free speech, along with the freedoms of assembly, religion, and privacy, is among the civil liberties contained in the Bill of Rights and elsewhere in the Constitution. We often take these liberties for granted.

▲ After a profanity-laced Snapchat post got her suspended from her cheerleading team, Brandi Levy sued and her case ended up in the Supreme Court, where the Court said her post was protected under the First Amendment.

And while swearing about the cheerleading team may seem like a minor controversy, questions about the nature of freedoms in the Constitution raise difficult questions. Under what circumstances can the government restrict Americans' liberties, especially in the realms of speech, assembly, and privacy? Do freedoms for some people, such as free speech, threaten other people? And how should we think about possible trade-offs, as between the free exercise of religion and government restrictions on large gatherings that seek to slow the spread of a contagious disease?

CHAPTER GOALS

Outline the founding debate about civil liberties and explain how civil liberties apply to the federal government and the states (pp. 95–99)

Explain how the Supreme Court has interpreted freedom of religion through the establishment and free exercise clauses (pp. 100–102)

Explain how the Supreme Court has interpreted freedom of speech, assembly, petition, and the press (pp. 103–110)

Explain how the Supreme Court has interpreted the right to bear arms (pp. 110–113)

Explain how the Supreme Court has interpreted the right to due process (pp. 113–118)

Describe how the Supreme Court has identified and interpreted the right to privacy (pp. 119–122)

The Bill of Rights Originated with Opponents of the Constitution

Outline the founding debate about civil liberties and explain how civil liberties apply to the federal government and the states

Civil liberties are related to but different from civil rights, which we will discuss in Chapter 5. **Civil liberties** are *protections from* improper government action. They determine what the government may or may not do to restrict individual freedom. Civil rights are protections of citizen equality *by* the government. The foundations of civil liberties and civil rights are to be found in the state and federal constitutions, which guarantee freedom of speech, freedom of the press, freedom of assembly, and so forth. The Constitution's Bill of Rights includes both liberties and rights.

civil liberties areas of personal freedom constitutionally protected from government interference

habeas corpus a court order that the individual in custody be brought into court and shown the cause for detention; habeas corpus is guaranteed by the Constitution and can be suspended only in cases of rebellion or invasion

When the first Congress under the newly ratified Constitution met in 1789, the most important item of business was the consideration of a proposal to add a bill of rights to the Constitution. Such a proposal had been turned down with little debate in the waning days of the Philadelphia Constitutional Convention in 1787 because, as the Federalists, led by Alexander Hamilton, later argued, it was "not only unnecessary in the proposed Constitution but would even be dangerous."[5]

First, according to Hamilton, a bill of rights would be irrelevant to a national government that was given only delegated powers in the first place. To put restraints on "powers which are not granted" could provide a pretext for governments to claim such powers: "For why declare that things shall not be done which there is no power to do?"[6] Second, to Hamilton and the Federalists the Constitution as originally written amounted to a bill of rights. For example, Article I, Section 9, included the right of **habeas corpus**, which prohibits the government from depriving a person of liberty without an open trial before a judge. Many of the framers, moreover, saw the very structure of the Constitution, including checks and balances, as protective of citizens' liberties.

Antifederalists, most of whom had not been delegates in Philadelphia, argued that the lack of a bill of rights was a major imperfection. They noted that most state constitutions included bills of rights—so why not the federal constitution? The Federalists realized that to gain ratification they would have to add a bill of rights, including a confirmation (in what would become the Tenth Amendment) that all powers not expressly delegated to the national government or explicitly prohibited to the states were reserved to the states.[7]

TABLE 4.1 | The Bill of Rights

Amendment I	Congress cannot make any law establishing a religion or abridging freedoms of religious exercise, speech, the press, assembly, or petition.
Amendments II, III, IV	No branch of government may infringe upon the right of the people to keep arms (II), cannot arbitrarily take houses for militia (III), and cannot search for or seize evidence without a court warrant swearing to the probable existence of a crime (IV).
Amendments V, VI, VII, VIII	The courts cannot hold trials for serious offenses without provision for a grand jury (V), a trial jury (VII), a speedy trial (VI), presentation of charges and confrontation by the accused of hostile witnesses (VI), and immunity from testimony against oneself and immunity from trial more than once for the same offense (V). Furthermore, neither bail nor punishment can be excessive (VIII), and no property can be taken without "just compensation" (V).
Amendments IX, X: Limits on the national government	Any rights not enumerated are reserved to the state or the people (X), and the enumeration of certain rights in the Constitution should not be interpreted to mean that those are the only rights the people have (IX).

Bill of Rights the first 10 amendments to the U.S. Constitution, ratified in 1791; they ensure certain rights and liberties to the people

The House of Representatives approved 17 amendments; of these, the Senate accepted 12. Ten of the amendments were ratified by the necessary three-fourths of the states on December 15, 1791; from the start, these 10 were called the **Bill of Rights** (see Table 4.1).[8]

The Fourteenth Amendment Nationalized the Bill of Rights through Incorporation

The First Amendment provides that "Congress shall make no law. . . ." But this is the only amendment in the Bill of Rights that addresses itself exclusively to the national government. Thus, a fundamental question inevitably arises: Do the provisions of the Bill of Rights other than the First Amendment put limits only on the national government, or do they limit the state governments as well?

The Supreme Court first answered this question in 1833 by ruling that the Bill of Rights limited only the national government.[9] This meant that the actions of state governments were restricted only by their own state constitutions as interpreted by their own courts. But the question arose again in 1868 with the adoption of the Fourteenth Amendment, which reads:

> *No State shall make or enforce any law which shall abridge the privileges or immunities of citizens of the United States; nor shall any State deprive any person of life, liberty, or property, without due*

process of law; nor deny to any person within its jurisdiction the equal protection of the laws.

This language sounds like an effort to extend the entire Bill of Rights to all citizens, in whatever state they might reside.[10] Yet this was not the Supreme Court's interpretation for nearly 100 years. Within 5 years of ratification of the Fourteenth Amendment, the Court was making decisions as though the amendment had never been adopted.[11]

In 1897, the Supreme Court did hold that the amendment's due process clause prohibited states from taking property for a public use without just compensation, a form of deprivation of property that is specifically prohibited in the Fifth Amendment.[12] But even though in both amendments "due process" is required for the taking of life and liberty as well as property, only the provision protecting property was "incorporated" into the Fourteenth Amendment as a limitation on state power.

Civil liberties did not expand through the Fourteenth Amendment again until 1925, when the Supreme Court held that freedom of speech is "among the fundamental personal rights and 'liberties' protected by the due process clause of the Fourteenth Amendment from impairment by the states."[13] In 1931 the Court added freedom of the press to that "fundamental" list; in 1939 it added freedom of assembly.[14] Until the 1960s, that was as far as the Court was willing to go. Indeed, in the 1937 case of *Palko v. Connecticut*, the Court affirmed the states' existing power to determine their own laws on a number of fundamental civil liberties issues. In that case, a Connecticut court had found Frank Palko guilty of second-degree murder and sentenced him to life in prison. Unhappy with the verdict, Connecticut appealed it to the state's highest court, won the appeal, and succeeded in getting Palko convicted of first-degree murder in a new trial. Palko appealed to the Supreme Court on what seemed an open-and-shut case of double jeopardy, which is prohibited by the Fifth Amendment.

The majority of the Court, however, decided that protection against double jeopardy was *not* one of the provisions of the Bill of Rights incorporated into the Fourteenth Amendment as a restriction on the powers of the states. Not until more than 30 years later did the Court reverse this ruling. Palko was eventually executed for the crime. The *Palko* case established the principle of **selective incorporation**, by which each provision of the Bill of Rights was to be considered separately as a possible limit on the states through the Fourteenth Amendment.[15]

Table 4.2 shows the progress of this revolution in the interpretation of the Constitution. Today, only the Third and Seventh amendments remain unincorporated, though it should be noted that almost every state voluntarily complies with the Seventh Amendment's requirement of jury trials.

Though nearly all of the protections from government in the Bill of Rights have been applied to the states, states retain some ability to restrict individual freedoms. For instance, an important civil liberties issue today concerns the power of the government to require citizens to wear masks

selective incorporation the process by which different protections in the Bill of Rights were incorporated into the Fourteenth Amendment, thus guaranteeing citizens protection from state as well as national governments

TABLE 4.2 | Incorporation of the Bill of Rights into the Fourteenth Amendment

SELECTED PROVISIONS AND AMENDMENTS	INCORPORATED	KEY CASES
Eminent domain (V)	1897	Chicago, Burlington and Quincy R.R. v. Chicago
Freedom of speech (I)	1925	Gitlow v. New York
Freedom of press (I)	1931	Near v. Minnesota
Free exercise of religion (I)	1934	Hamilton v. Regents of the University of California
Freedom of assembly (I) and freedom to petition the government for redress of grievances (I)	1937	DeJonge v. Oregon
Free exercise of religion (I)	1940	Cantwell v. Connecticut
Nonestablishment of state religion (I)	1947	Everson v. Board of Education
Freedom from warrantless search and seizure (IV) ("exclusionary rule")	1961	Mapp v. Ohio
Freedom from cruel and unusual punishment (VIII)	1962	Robinson v. California
Right to counsel in any criminal trial (VI)	1963	Powell v. Alabama; Gideon v. Wainwright
Right against self-incrimination and forced confessions (V)	1964	Malloy v. Hogan
Right to counsel (VI)	1964	Escobedo v. Illinois
Right to remain silent (V)	1966	Miranda v. Arizona
Right against double jeopardy (V)	1969	Benton v. Maryland
Right to bear arms (II)	2010	McDonald v. Chicago
Excessive fines prohibited (VIII)	2019	Timbs v. Indiana
Jury trial (VI)	2020	Ramos v. Louisiana

or submit to vaccinations in the face of the deadly Covid-19 pandemic. As we saw in Chapter 3, state governments possess "police powers" and can take emergency actions so long as they are not prohibited by the federal or state constitutions. States almost certainly have the legal power to require Covid-19 vaccinations. The federal government, though, is a government of limited, constitutionally prescribed powers. It can require its employees and contractors to wear masks and accept vaccinations, but it probably cannot issue such requirements for members of the general public.

Check your understanding

1. Which of the following statements best describes the Federalists' and Antifederalists' views on the Bill of Rights?

   a) Neither the Federalists nor the Antifederalists felt the Bill of Rights was necessary since the Constitution placed clear limits on the national government.

   b) While the Federalists felt that a Bill of Rights was unnecessary because there were already restrictions on the national government, the Antifederalists saw its exclusion as a major flaw that needed to be remedied.

   c) Both Federalists and Antifederalists felt that the Bill of Rights was needed, and neither would agree to ratify the Constitution without it.

   d) The Bill of Rights was not discussed during the ratification of the Constitution; rather, it was an issue that was raised after the Civil War.

2. How does the Bill of Rights limit the power of the national government and state governments?

   a) While the Bill of Rights limits the power of the national government, it does not apply to the states, which are subject only to restrictions of their own state constitutions.

   b) The Bill of Rights initially only applied to the national government; however, in the *Palko* case, the Court established selective incorporation with provisions of the Bill of Rights applying to the state governments through the Fourteenth Amendment.

   c) The Court has always taken a very broad interpretation of the Bill of Rights, arguing that it places limits not only on the national government but also on the state governments.

   d) While the national government has always been restricted by the Bill of Rights, the state governments became restricted by the Bill of Rights immediately after the ratification of the Fourteenth Amendment.

The First Amendment Guarantees Freedom of Religion

Explain how the Supreme Court has interpreted freedom of religion through the establishment and free exercise clauses

Congress shall make no law respecting an establishment of religion, or prohibiting the free exercise thereof; or abridging the freedom of speech, or of the press; or the right of the people peaceably to assemble, and to petition the Government for a redress of grievances.

—from the First Amendment

establishment clause the First Amendment clause that says "Congress shall make no law respecting an establishment of religion"; this constitutional provision means that a "wall of separation" exists between church and state

The Bill of Rights begins by guaranteeing freedom of religion, and the First Amendment provides for that freedom in two distinct clauses: "Congress shall make no law [1] respecting an establishment of religion, or [2] prohibiting the free exercise thereof." The first clause is called the "establishment clause," and the second is called the "free exercise clause."

Separation between Church and State

The **establishment clause** and the idea of "no law" regarding the establishment of religion could be interpreted in several ways. One interpretation is simply that the national government is prohibited from establishing an official church. Official "established" churches, such as the Church of England, were common in Europe in the eighteenth century as well as in some of the 13 colonies and were viewed by many Americans as inconsistent with a republican form of government. Indeed, many American colonists had fled Europe to escape persecution for having rejected established churches.

A second possible interpretation is that the government may provide assistance to religious institutions or ideas as long as it does not take sides or show favoritism among them. The United States accommodates religious beliefs in a variety of ways, from the reference to God on currency to the prayer that begins every session of Congress. These forms of religious establishment have always been upheld by the courts.

The third view regarding religious establishment, the most commonly held today, favors a "wall of separation"—Jefferson's formulation—between church and state. For two centuries, Jefferson's words have powerfully influenced Americans' understanding of the proper relationship between government and religion. Despite the seeming absoluteness of the phrase, however, there is ample room to disagree on how high the "wall of separation" should be.

One area of conflict over the appropriate boundary is public education. For example, the Court has consistently struck down such practices in public schools as Bible reading,[16] prayer,[17] a moment of silence for meditation, and pregame public prayer at sporting events.[18] In each of these cases, the Court reasoned that organized religious activities, even when apparently nondenominational, strongly suggest the school is sponsoring them and therefore violate the prohibition against establishment of religion.

In 2022 the Supreme Court heard the case of *Kennedy v. Bremerton*. This case involved a high school football coach in Bremerton, Washington, who made it a practice to pray at the 50-yard line after every game. The school board feared that this practice could be construed as officially sanctioned prayer, ordered the coach to halt the practice, and fired him when he refused. The Supreme Court, however, viewed the case as a matter of free exercise and ruled that the coach had a constitutional right to pray after games.

After the Bremerton, Washington, school board fired high school football coach Joe Kennedy for refusing to stop praying on the field, the coach took his case to the Supreme Court, which ruled in his favor and changed the way the courts would rule on freedom of religion and separation of church and state cases in the future.

The Court used the Kennedy case to abandon the *Lemon* test, which it said had turned the establishment clause into a barrier to the free exercise of religion or free speech, and proposed a new way of assessing establishment cases: "This Court has instructed that the Establishment Clause must be interpreted by 'reference to historical practices and understandings.' . . . 'and faithfully reflec[t] the understanding of the Founding Fathers.'"[19] In other words, the Court said that the decision on whether a practice unlawfully "establishes" religion must take into account the history of that practice and the effect that banning the practice would have on free speech and free exercise rights.

Free Exercise of Religion

The **free exercise clause** protects the right to believe and to practice whatever religion one chooses (and also protects the right to be a nonbeliever). The precedent-setting case involving free exercise is *West Virginia State Board of Education v. Barnette* (1943), which involved the children in a family of Jehovah's Witnesses who refused to salute and pledge allegiance to the American flag in their school on the grounds that their religious faith did not permit it.[20]

More recently, the principle of free exercise has been bolstered by legislation prohibiting religious discrimination by public and private entities in a variety of realms. In *Burwell v. Hobby Lobby Stores*,[21] the owners of a chain of craft stores claimed that a section of the

> **free exercise clause** the First Amendment clause that protects a citizen's right to believe and practice whatever religion they choose

Affordable Care Act (ACA, or "Obamacare") requiring employers to provide their female employees with free contraceptive coverage violated the owners' religious beliefs as protected by the Religious Freedom Restoration Act. This law, enacted in 1993, requires the government to prove a "compelling interest" for requiring individuals to obey a law that violates their religious beliefs. The Supreme Court ruled in favor of Hobby Lobby.

Despite this precedent, free exercise of religion continues to have limits, though those limits are contested. During the Covid-19 pandemic, for example, former New York governor Andrew Cuomo ordered limits on in-person worship services. However, the Supreme Court ruled in a 5–4 decision that the prohibition violated the Constitution's protection of religious liberty.[22]

Check your understanding

3. What is the difference between the establishment clause and the free exercise clause found in the First Amendment of the U.S. Constitution?

   a) The free exercise clause only applies to individuals who practice a religion, while the establishment clause extends protections to nonbelievers.

   b) The establishment clause only pertains to religious institutions, and the free exercise clause pertains to the national government.

   c) The Courts have treated these two clauses as one and the same so there is virtually no distinction.

   d) The free exercise clause safeguards individual religious rights, while the establishment clause restricts government from endorsing a particular religion or giving favor to a certain religion.

4. Which of the following statements regarding Supreme Court rulings on recent religious freedom cases is true?

   a) The Supreme Court has generally held that organized religious activities in public schools, such as moments of silence or public prayer before sporting events, do not violate the establishment clause.

   b) The Supreme Court has consistently ruled that public displays of religious symbols do not violate the establishment clause.

   c) The Supreme Court ruled that the section of the Affordable Care Act mandating employers to provide their female employees with free contraceptive coverage violated the business owners' religious beliefs.

   d) The Supreme Court has consistently ruled that public displays of religious symbols violate the establishment clause.

The First Amendment's Freedom of Speech and of the Press Ensure the Free Exchange of Ideas

Explain how the Supreme Court has interpreted freedom of speech, assembly, petition, and the press

Freedom of speech and freedom of the press have a special place in American political thought. Democracy depends on the ability of individuals to talk to one another and to disseminate information. It is difficult to conceive how democratic politics could function without free and open debate.

Congress shall make no law . . . abridging the freedom of speech, or of the press.

—from the First Amendment

Such debate, moreover, is seen as an essential way to evaluate competing ideas. As Justice Oliver Wendell Holmes said in 1919, "The best test of truth is the power of the thought to get itself accepted in the competition of the market. . . . That at any rate is the theory of our Constitution."[23] What is sometimes called the "marketplace of ideas" receives a good deal of protection from the courts. In 1938 the Supreme Court held that any legislation restricting speech "is to be subjected to a more exacting judicial scrutiny . . . than are most other types of legislation."[24]

This higher standard, which came to be called "strict scrutiny," places a heavy burden of proof on the government if it seeks to restrict speech. Americans are assumed to have the right to voice their ideas publicly unless a compelling reason can be identified to prevent them. But strict scrutiny does not mean that speech can never be regulated. Over the past 200 years, the courts have scrutinized many different forms of speech and constructed different principles and guidelines for each. According to the courts, although virtually all speech is protected by the Constitution, some forms are entitled to a greater degree of protection than others.

Political Speech

Political speech was the form of greatest concern to the framers of the Constitution, even though some found it the most difficult one to tolerate. Within seven years of the ratification of the Bill of Rights in 1791, Congress adopted the infamous Alien and Sedition Acts (long since repealed), which, among other things, made it a crime to say or publish anything that might tend to defame or bring into disrepute the government of the United States.

The first modern free speech case arose immediately after World War I and involved persons convicted under the federal Espionage Act of 1917 for opposing U.S. involvement in the war. The Supreme Court upheld the Espionage Act and refused to protect the speech rights of the defendants on the grounds that their activities—appeals to draftees to resist the draft—constituted a **"clear and present danger"** to national security.[25] This is the first and most famous "test" for when government intervention or censorship can be permitted, though it has since been discarded. Since the 1920s, political speech has been consistently protected by the courts even when judges acknowledged that the speech was "insulting" or "outrageous."

In the important and controversial 2010 case of *Citizens United v. Federal Election Commission*, the Court struck down a ban on corporate funding of political advertisements supporting or opposing particular candidates[26] on the grounds that this spending is political speech that the Constitution prohibits the government from regulating. In 2014 the Court again expanded its protection of campaign expenditures under the First Amendment by overturning limits on the total amount an individual may contribute.[27] As a result of this decision, wealthy donor contributions to presidential candidates skyrocketed in 2016 and 2020.

Fighting Words and Hate Speech

Speech can lose its protected position only when it moves from the symbolic realm to the realm of actual conduct—for example, "expressive speech" that directly incites physical conflict with the use of so-called **fighting words**. In 1942 a man who had called a police officer a "goddamned racketeer" and "a damn Fascist" was arrested and convicted of violating a state law forbidding the use of offensive language in public. The Supreme Court upheld his arrest on the grounds that such words are not protected by the First Amendment because they "are no essential part of any exposition of ideas."[28] This decision was reaffirmed in 1951 in *Dennis v. United States*,[29] when the Court held that there is no substantial public interest in permitting certain kinds of speech, including "fighting words." Since that time, however, the Court has reversed almost every conviction based on arguments that the speaker had used "fighting words."

In recent years, a number of college campuses have confronted the issue of hate speech—forms of expression intended to assert hatred toward one or another group of people, be they African Americans, Jewish or Muslim people, or others. Some students and faculty have demanded that certain public figures (usually conservative and far-right ones) be banned from speaking on the grounds that they promote hatred. There seems little doubt that the Constitution protects the right of individuals to share controversial views. The conflict arises when that right comes up against university policies to emphasize safety—a consideration that not so long ago led to bans on left-wing speakers. Perhaps people of all political persuasions should think about the words of Supreme Court Justice Oliver Wendell Holmes, who said, "If there is any principle of the Constitution that more imperatively calls for attachment than any other, it is the principle of

AMERICA | SIDE BY SIDE

Civil Liberties in Global Perspective

Civil liberties cover a broad swath of rights, from freedom of expression to organizational rights to the functioning of the rule of law. The enshrinement of such protections varies tremendously worldwide, with citizens in some countries enjoying far stronger civil liberties safeguards than others. Freedom House releases an annual report that compiles a scale of civil liberties protections based on scores of 15 subcategories, ranging from freedom from surveillance to due process in civil and criminal matters.

1. Looking at the map, what geographic patterns do you see? Are there some areas that have stronger civil liberties protections than others? Do countries seem to have levels of civil liberties protections similar to those of their neighbors?
2. What factors about a country do you think are likely to correlate with stronger or weaker protections of civil liberties? Why would a country be more or less likely to have protections for freedom of expression and the rule of law? Compare this map with the map in the America Side by Side graphic in Chapter 1. What commonalities and differences do you see?

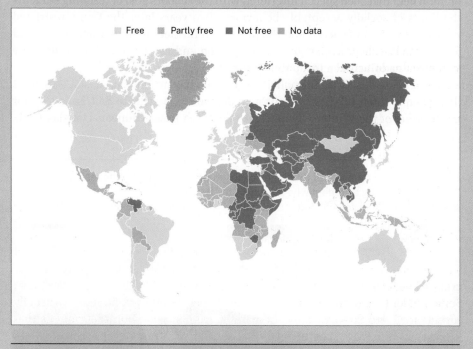

■ Free   ■ Partly free   ■ Not free   ■ No data

SOURCE: Freedom House, *Freedom in the World 2021* Report, Civil Liberties scale, https://freedomhouse.org/countries/freedom-world/scores (accessed 10/22/21).

free thought—not free thought for those who agree with us but freedom for the thought that we hate."[30]

Many of these cases have involved action by the federal or state governments, but what about private action to prohibit various forms of speech? Today, the ability to post messages on social media platforms is critically important to those who want to disseminate their ideas. In 2019, Facebook announced a change in its terms-of-service agreement designed to prevent users from posting hateful commentary and claims. Facebook is a private organization, so the constitutional restrictions on the government's actions may not apply.

Student Speech

As the chapter opener about the cheerleader's Snapchat tirade discussed, one category of speech with only limited protection is that of students in public schools. In the 1969 case of *Tinker v. Des Moines*,[31] the Supreme Court ruled that the First Amendment protected two students who came to school wearing black armbands to protest the Vietnam War. In 1986, however, the Supreme Court backed away from a broad protection of student free speech rights by upholding the punishment of a high school student for making a sexually suggestive speech. The Court opinion held that such speech interfered with the school's goal of teaching students the limits of socially acceptable behavior.[32] Two years later the Court restricted students' freedom of speech and the press even further, defining their speech and journalism in school as part of their education and not protected with the same standard as adult speech in a public forum.[33]

A later case dealt with the policies of a high school in Juneau, Alaska.[34] In 2002 the Olympic torch relay passed through Juneau on its way to Salt Lake City for the opening of the Winter Olympics. As the torch passed Juneau-Douglas High,

---

The Supreme Court has ruled that high school students' speech can be restricted. In a 2007 case involving a student who displayed the banner above, the Court found that the school principal had not violated the student's right to free speech by suspending him.

a student unfurled a banner reading "BONG HITS 4 JESUS." The school's principal promptly suspended the student, who then brought suit for reinstatement, alleging that his free speech rights had been violated. Like most of America's public schools, Juneau-Douglas High prohibits assemblies or expressions on school grounds that advocate illegal drug use. In the Supreme Court's majority decision in 2007, Chief Justice John Roberts said that the First Amendment did not require schools to permit students to advocate illegal drug use.

As we saw in the opener, the Court took a different view of schools' efforts to regulate student speech off campus, ruling in 2021 that Brandi Levy's Pennsylvania school district had violated the First Amendment when it punished her for using vulgar language and gestures in a Snapchat post.

Commercial Speech

Commercial speech, such as newspaper or television advertisements, was initially considered to be entirely outside the protection of the First Amendment and is still subject to limited regulation. For example, the Federal Trade Commission's prohibition of false and misleading advertising is an old and well-established power of the federal government. The Supreme Court has upheld city ordinances prohibiting the posting of all commercial signs on publicly owned property (as long as the ban is total so that there is no hint of selective censorship).[35]

However, commercial speech has become more protected under the First Amendment. For example, in 1975 the Supreme Court struck down a state law making it a misdemeanor to sell or circulate newspapers encouraging abortions; the Court ruled that the statute infringed both on constitutionally protected speech and on readers' right to make informed choices.[36]

Symbolic Speech, Speech Plus, and the Rights of Assembly and Petition

Because the First Amendment treats the freedoms of religion and political speech as equal to those of assembly and petition, the Supreme Court has always largely protected an individual's right to "symbolic speech": peaceful actions designed to send a political message. One example is the burning of the American flag as a protest.

Closer to the original intent of the assembly and petition clause is the category of **"speech plus"**—combining speech with physical activity such as picketing, distributing leaflets, and other forms of peaceful demonstration or assembly. In the 1939 case of *Hague v. Committee for Industrial Organization*, the Supreme Court declared that the government may not prohibit speech-related activities such as demonstrations or leafleting in public areas traditionally used for that purpose, though it may impose rules to protect the public safety at such events so long as they do not discriminate against particular viewpoints.[37] The Court has also ruled

"speech plus" speech accompanied by conduct such as sit-ins, picketing, and demonstrations; protection of this form of speech under the First Amendment is conditional, and restrictions imposed by state or local authorities are acceptable if properly balanced by considerations of public order

that the First Amendment protects freedom of association. In the 1958 case of *NAACP v. Alabama*,[38] the Court blocked the state of Alabama from demanding the NAACP's membership lists for an investigation into the group's activities. Without freedom of association, groups could not organize and advocate for their beliefs. Such "public forum" assemblies have since been consistently protected by courts.

But the same kind of assembly on private property is quite another matter and can in many circumstances be regulated, such as at a shopping center. Even in public areas, assemblies or demonstrations can be restricted under some circumstances, especially when they jeopardize the health, safety, or rights of others.

Freedom of the Press

prior restraint an effort by a governmental agency to block the publication of material it deems libelous or harmful in some other way; censorship; in the United States, the courts forbid prior restraint except under the most extraordinary circumstances

With the exception of the broadcast media, which are subject to federal regulation, the press is protected against **prior restraint**. That is, beginning with the landmark 1931 case of *Near v. Minnesota*, the Supreme Court has held that, except under the most extraordinary circumstances, the First Amendment prohibits government agencies from preventing newspapers or magazines from publishing whatever they wish.[39] Indeed, in the 1971 case *New York Times Co. v. United States* (the so-called Pentagon Papers case), the Supreme Court ruled that the government could not block publication of secret Defense Department documents furnished to the *New York Times* by an opponent of the Vietnam War who had obtained the documents illegally.[40]

Another press freedom issue that the courts have often been asked to decide is whether journalists can be compelled to reveal their sources of information. Journalists assert that if they cannot ensure their sources' confidentiality, the flow of information will be reduced and press freedom effectively curtailed. Government agencies, however, argue that names of news sources may be relevant to criminal or even national security investigations. Nearly 40 states have "shield laws" that protect journalistic sources to varying degrees. There is, however, no federal shield law and no special constitutional protection for journalists.[41]

libel a written statement made in "reckless disregard of the truth" that is considered damaging to a victim because it is "malicious, scandalous, and defamatory"

slander an oral statement made in "reckless disregard of the truth" that is considered damaging to the victim because it is "malicious, scandalous, and defamatory"

Libel and Slander Some speech is not protected at all. If a written statement is made in "reckless disregard of the truth" and is considered damaging to the victim because it is "malicious, scandalous, and defamatory," it can be punished as **libel**. If such a statement is made orally, it can be punished as **slander**.

Most libel suits today involve freedom of the press, but American courts have narrowed the meaning of libel to the point that it is extremely difficult for politicians or other public figures (as opposed to private individuals) to win a libel suit against a newspaper. In the important 1964 case of *New York Times Co. v. Sullivan*, the Supreme Court held that to be found libelous, a story about a public official not only had to be untrue but also had to result from "actual malice" or "reckless disregard" for the truth.[42] In other words, the newspaper had to print false and damaging material deliberately. Because in practice this charge is nearly impossible to prove, essentially the print media have become able to publish anything they want about a public figure.

With the emergence of the internet as a communications medium, the courts have had to decide how traditional libel law applies to online content. In 1995 the New York courts held that an online bulletin board could be held responsible for the libelous content of material posted by a third party. To protect internet service providers, Congress subsequently enacted legislation absolving them of responsibility for third-party posts. The federal courts have generally upheld this law.[43]

Obscenity and Pornography Cases involving pornography and obscenity can be even trickier than those involving libel and slander. Not until 1957 did the Supreme Court try to define obscenity, and its definition may have caused more confusion than it cleared up. The Court's opinion defined obscenity as speech or writing that appeals to the "prurient interest"—that is, whose purpose is to excite lust, as this appears "to the average person, applying contemporary community standards." Even so, the work should be judged obscene only when it is "utterly without redeeming social importance."[44] In 1964, Justice Potter Stewart confessed that, although he found pornography impossible to define, "I know it when I see it."[45] The vague and impractical standards that had been developed meant ultimately that almost nothing could be banned on the grounds that it was pornographic and obscene.

In recent years, the battle against obscene speech has targeted online pornography, whose opponents argue that it should be banned because of the easy access children have to the internet. In 1996, Congress passed the Telecommunications Act. Attached to it was an amendment, called the Communications Decency Act (CDA), designed to regulate the online transmission of obscene material. In the 1997 case of *Reno v. American Civil Liberties Union*, the Supreme Court struck down the CDA, ruling that it suppressed speech that "adults have a constitutional right to receive" and that governments may not limit the adult population to messages fit for children. Supreme Court Justice John Paul Stevens described the internet as the "town crier" of the modern age and said it was entitled to the greatest degree of First Amendment protection possible.[46] In 2008, however, the Court upheld the PROTECT Act, which outlawed efforts to sell child pornography via the internet.[47]

In 2000 the Court extended the highest degree of First Amendment protection to cable (not broadcast) television. In *United States v. Playboy Entertainment Group*,[48] it struck down a portion of the 1996 Telecommunications Act that required cable TV companies to limit the availability of sexually explicit programming to late-night hours.

Closely related to the issue of obscenity is the question of whether governments can prohibit broadcasts or publications considered excessively violent. Here, too, the Court has generally upheld freedom of speech.[49]

Check your understanding

5. Which of the following statements regarding limitations on free speech is true?

a) Political speech has consistently been protected by the courts since the 1920s; however, speech can lose its protected status when it is deemed a "clear and present danger" or incites physical conflict with the use of fighting words.

b) The Court has consistently ruled in a manner that limits the speech of students with the argument that minors do not have the same level of protections as adults.

c) Commercial speech falls outside what is considered protected speech and thus is subject to limitations.

d) Speech plus, including peaceful demonstrations or assembly, has been subject to limitations because the Court viewed these actions as being outside the First Amendment protections.

6. Which of the following statements regarding the freedom of the press is true?

a) The government under no circumstances may restrict what print media publishes.

b) In recent years, the Supreme Court has upheld the government blocking the publication of classified materials in all circumstances with a broadened idea of what constitutes a national security threat.

c) Although many states have shield laws that protect journalistic sources to varying degrees, there is no federal shield law and no special constitutional protections for journalists.

d) Libel and slander are protected forms of speech.

The Second Amendment Protects the Right to Bear Arms

Explain how the Supreme Court has interpreted the right to bear arms

A well regulated Militia, being necessary to the security of a free State, the right of the people to keep and bear Arms, shall not be infringed.

—from the Second Amendment

Some argue that the purpose of the Second Amendment was the maintenance of militias. *Militia* was understood at the time of the Founding to be a military or police resource for state governments to maintain local public order. Others have argued that the Second Amendment also establishes an individual

Mass shootings in the United States, including one at Robb Elementary School in Uvalde, Texas, in which 19 students and 2 teachers were killed, often prompt calls for legislation to limit the availability of guns.

right to bear arms. The judicial record of Second Amendment cases is relatively sparser, and localities across the country have very different gun-ownership standards, the result of a patchwork of state and local laws. For instance, in Wyoming there is no ban on owning any type of gun, no waiting periods to purchase a firearm, and no permits are required. In California, however, there are many more restrictions. Figure 4.1 shows the background check requirements to purchase a firearm across the country.

The Supreme Court's silence on the meaning of the Second Amendment ended in 2008 with the first of two rulings in favor of expansive gun rights. In *District of Columbia v. Heller*, the Court struck down a strict Washington, D.C., law that banned handguns. It ruled 5–4 that the Second Amendment provides a constitutional right to keep a loaded handgun at home for self-defense. In the majority opinion, Justice Antonin Scalia stated that the decision was not intended to cast doubt on all laws limiting firearm possession, such as by felons or people who are mentally ill.[50] In his dissenting opinion, Justice Stevens asserted that the Second Amendment protects the rights of individuals to bear arms only as part of a militia force, not in an individual capacity.

Because the District of Columbia is an entity of the federal government, the Court's ruling did not apply to state firearms laws. However, in the 2010 case of *McDonald v. Chicago*, the Supreme Court applied the Second Amendment to the states, its first new incorporation decision in 40 years. The ruling effectively overturned a Chicago

FIGURE 4.1 | Gun Rights by State

Although state gun laws must conform to the Second Amendment as interpreted by the U.S. Supreme Court, laws concerning gun sales and ownership vary widely from state to state. While federal law requires background checks when purchasing a firearm from a licensed seller, only 21 states require them from unlicensed sellers as well. Should all states require unlicensed firearm sellers to perform background checks? Why or why not?

BACKGROUND CHECKS AT UNLICENSED GUNSELLERS
REQUIRED FOR THE PURCHASE OF . . .

■ All firearms   ■ Only handguns   ■ None

SOURCE: Everytown Research & Policy, "Background Checks on All Gun Sales," https://everytownresearch.org/solution/background-checks/ (accessed 1/24/22).

ordinance that made it extremely difficult to own a gun within city limits. Similarly, in 2022 the Court struck down a New York State statute requiring a person to show a special need for self-protection to receive an unrestricted license to carry a concealed firearm outside the home.[51]

Despite these rulings, the debate over gun control continues to loom large in American politics. The issue of gun laws has been kept firmly on the national agenda by a series of tragic shootings, including the killings of 50 people at a nightclub in Orlando, Florida; 11 worshippers at a synagogue in Pittsburgh, Pennsylvania; and 19 students and 2 teachers at an elementary school in Uvalde, Texas. Proponents of gun control point to these shootings as evidence of the need for stricter gun laws; opponents say they demonstrate that Americans are not safe and should be free to carry arms for self-protection.

Check your understanding

7. What effect did the Supreme Court's ruling in *District of Columbia v. Heller* have on gun ownership rights?

   a) The Court ruled in favor of expansive rights of gun ownership by individuals.

   b) The Court's ruling severely restricted the rights of gun ownership by individuals.

   c) The Court provided a mixed ruling, stating that rifle or shotgun ownership may not be subject to restrictions but handguns could be regulated.

   d) The ruling resulted in a fundamental reinterpretation of the Second Amendment in which protections of individuals' rights to bear arms are allowed only as part of a militia force, not in an individual capacity.

8. What is the significance of the Supreme Court's decision in *McDonald v. Chicago*?

   a) The Supreme Court applied the Second Amendment to the states, a process known as incorporation.

   b) The Supreme Court ruled that the Second Amendment only applied to national government, not state governments.

   c) In this case, the Court established an explicit test for determining when a regulation on handguns constitutes an infringement on Second Amendment rights.

   d) In this case, the Supreme Court offered a strict reading of the Second Amendment in which protections of individuals' rights to bear arms are allowed only as part of a militia force, not in an individual capacity.

Rights of the Criminally Accused Are Based on Due Process of Law

Explain how the Supreme Court has interpreted the right to due process

The Fourth, Fifth, Sixth, and Eighth amendments, pertaining to the rights of the accused, are the essence of the **due process of law**, even though these precise words for this fundamental concept do not appear until the end of the Fifth Amendment.

> **due process of law** the right of every individual against arbitrary action by national or state governments

The Fourth Amendment and Searches and Seizures

The right of the people to be secure in their persons, houses, papers, and effects, against unreasonable searches and seizures, shall not be violated, and no Warrants shall issue, but upon probable cause, supported by Oath or affirmation, and particularly describing the place to be searched, and the persons or things to be seized.

—from the Fourth Amendment

The purpose of the Fourth Amendment is to guarantee the security of citizens against unreasonable (i.e., improper) searches and seizures. In 1990 the Supreme Court summarized its understanding of the Fourth Amendment: "A search compromises the individual interest in privacy; a seizure deprives the individual of dominion over his or her person or property."[52] But how are we to define what is reasonable and what is unreasonable?

The 1961 case of *Mapp v. Ohio* illustrates one of the most important principles to have grown out of the Fourth Amendment—the **exclusionary rule**, which prohibits evidence obtained during an illegal search from being introduced in a trial. Acting on a tip that Dollree Mapp was harboring a suspect in a bombing incident, several police officers forcibly entered Mapp's house, claiming they had a search warrant. They did not find the suspect but, in an old trunk in the basement, did find some materials they declared to be obscene. Although no warrant was ever produced, Mapp was convicted of possessing obscene materials.

The Supreme Court's opinion in the case affirmed the exclusionary rule: under the Fourth Amendment (applied to the states through the Fourteenth Amendment), "all evidence obtained by searches and seizures in violation of the Constitution . . . is inadmissible."[53] This means that even people who are clearly guilty of the crime of which they are accused cannot be convicted if the only evidence for their conviction was obtained illegally.

In recent years, however, the Supreme Court has softened the application of the exclusionary rule, allowing federal courts to use their discretion about it depending on the "nature and quality of the intrusion."[54]

Changes in technology have also had an impact on Fourth Amendment jurisprudence. In the 2012 case of *United States v. Jones*, the Court held that prosecutors violated a defendant's rights when they attached a Global Positioning System (GPS) device to his Jeep and monitored his movements for 28 days.[55] On the other hand, in *Maryland v. King*, the Court upheld DNA testing of arrestees without the need for individualized suspicion.[56] In the 2014 case of *Riley v. California*, the Court held that the police were constitutionally prohibited from seizing a cell phone and searching its digital contents during an arrest.[57]

exclusionary rule the ability of courts to exclude evidence obtained in violation of the Fourth Amendment

grand jury jury that determines whether sufficient evidence is available to justify a trial; grand juries do not rule on the accused's guilt or innocence

The Fifth Amendment

Grand Juries The first clause of the Fifth Amendment, the right to a **grand jury** to determine whether a trial is warranted, is considered "the oldest institution known to the Constitution."[58] A grand jury is a body of citizens that must agree that a prosecutor has sufficient evidence to bring criminal charges against a suspect. Although grand juries do play an important role in federal criminal cases, the provision for them is the one important civil liberties provision of the Bill of Rights that was not incorporated into the Fourteenth Amendment and applied to state criminal prosecutions. Thus, some states operate without grand juries. In such states, the prosecutor simply files a "bill of information" affirming that sufficient evidence is available to justify a trial. For the accused person to be held in custody, the prosecutor must persuade a judge that the evidence shows "probable cause" to justify further action.

Double Jeopardy "Nor shall any person be subject for the same offence to be twice put in jeopardy of life or limb" is the constitutional protection from **double jeopardy**, or being tried more than once for the same crime. The protection from double jeopardy was at the heart of the *Palko* case in 1937, which, as we saw earlier in this chapter, also established the principle of selective incorporation of the Bill of Rights. However, in the 1969 case of *Benton v. Maryland*, the Supreme Court expressly overruled *Palko* and declared that the double jeopardy clause did, in fact, apply to the states.[59]

Self-Incrimination Perhaps the most significant liberty found in the Fifth Amendment is the guarantee that no citizen "shall be compelled in any criminal case to be a witness against himself." The most famous case concerning self-incrimination is one of such importance that Chief Justice Earl Warren assessed its results as going "to the very root of our concepts of American criminal jurisprudence."[60]

In 1963, Ernesto Miranda was convicted and sentenced to between 20 and 30 years in prison for the kidnapping and rape of a woman in Arizona. The woman had identified him in a police lineup, and after two hours of questioning, Miranda confessed and subsequently signed a statement that his confession had been made voluntarily, without threats or promises of immunity. The statement was admitted into evidence and served as the basis for Miranda's conviction.

After his conviction, Miranda argued that his confession had not been truly voluntary and that he had not been informed of his right to remain silent or his right to consult an attorney. In a controversial ruling, the Supreme Court agreed and

No person shall be held to answer for a capital, or otherwise infamous crime, unless on a presentment or indictment of a Grand Jury, except in cases arising in the land or naval forces, or in the Militia, when in actual service in time of War or public danger; nor shall any person be subject for the same offence to be twice put in jeopardy of life or limb; nor shall be compelled in any criminal case to be a witness against himself, nor be deprived of life, liberty, or property, without due process of law; nor shall private property be taken for public use, without just compensation.

—from the Fifth Amendment

double jeopardy the Fifth Amendment right providing that a person cannot be tried twice for the same crime

Miranda rule the requirement, articulated by the Supreme Court in *Miranda v. Arizona*, that persons under arrest must be informed prior to police interrogation of their rights to remain silent and to have the benefit of legal counsel

SPECIFIC WARNING REGARDING INTERROGATIONS

1. YOU HAVE THE RIGHT TO REMAIN SILENT.

2. ANYTHING YOU SAY CAN AND WILL BE USED AGAINST YOU IN A COURT OF LAW.

3. YOU HAVE THE RIGHT TO TALK TO A LAWYER AND HAVE HIM PRESENT WITH YOU WHILE YOU ARE BEING QUESTIONED.

4. IF YOU CANNOT AFFORD TO HIRE A LAWYER ONE WILL BE APPOINTED TO REPRESENT YOU BEFORE ANY QUESTIONING, IF YOU WISH ONE.

| SIGNATURE OF DEFENDANT | DATE |
| WITNESS | TIME |

☐ REFUSED SIGNATURE   SAN FRANCISCO POLICE DEPARTMENT   PR.9.1.4

The case of Ernesto Miranda resulted in the creation of Miranda rights, which must be read to those arrested to make them aware of their constitutional rights.

---

overturned the conviction. *Miranda v. Arizona* (1966) produced the rules the police must follow before questioning an arrested criminal suspect, and the reading of a person's "Miranda rights" became a standard scene in every police station and on virtually every television and film dramatization of police action.

Miranda expanded the Fifth Amendment's protection against coerced confessions and self-incrimination and also confirmed the right to counsel, as discussed below. Although the Supreme Court later considerably loosened the *Miranda* restrictions, the **Miranda rule** still stands as a protection against police abuses.

In all criminal prosecutions, the accused shall enjoy the right to a speedy and public trial, by an impartial jury of the State and district wherein the crime shall have been committed, which district shall have been previously ascertained by law, and to be informed of the nature and cause of the accusation; to be confronted with the witnesses against him; to have compulsory process for obtaining witnesses in his favor, and to have the Assistance of Counsel for his defence.

—from the Sixth Amendment

The Sixth Amendment and the Right to Counsel

Some provisions of the Sixth Amendment, such as the right to a speedy trial and the right to confront witnesses before an impartial jury, are not very controversial. The "right to counsel" provision, however, like the exclusionary rule of the Fourth Amendment and the self-incrimination clause of the Fifth Amendment, is notable for sometimes freeing defendants who seem to be clearly guilty.

Gideon v. Wainwright (1963) involved a disreputable person who had been in and out of jails for most of his 51 years. Clarence Earl Gideon received a five-year sentence for breaking into and entering a poolroom in Panama City, Florida. He was too poor to afford a lawyer, and Florida law provided for court-appointed counsel only for crimes carrying the death penalty. While serving time, however, Gideon made his own appeal on a handwritten petition, and eventually won the landmark ruling on the right to counsel in all felony cases.[61] The right to counsel has been expanded during the past few decades, even as the courts have become more conservative.

The Eighth Amendment and Cruel and Unusual Punishment

Virtually all the debate over Eighth Amendment issues focuses on the last clause of the amendment, because what is considered "cruel and unusual" varies from culture to culture and from generation to generation. In 1972 the Supreme Court overturned several state death penalty laws, not because they were cruel and unusual but because they were being applied unevenly—that is, Black people were much more likely than White people to be sentenced to death, people in poverty more likely than rich people, and men more likely than women.[62] Very soon after that decision, a majority of states revised their capital punishment provisions to meet the Court's standards, and the Court reaffirmed that the death penalty could be used if certain standards were met.[63] Since 1976, the Court has consistently upheld state laws providing for capital punishment, although it also continues to review death penalty appeals each year.

> *Excessive bail shall not be required, nor excessive fines imposed, nor cruel and unusual punishment inflicted.*
>
> —from the Eighth Amendment

Between 1976 and October 2020, states executed 1,524 people. Most of those executions occurred in southern states, with Texas leading the way at 570. As of October 2020, 28 states had statutes providing for capital punishment for specified offenses, a policy supported by a majority of Americans, according to polls.[64] On the other hand, 22 states bar the death penalty, and, since the end of the 1990s, both the number of death sentences and the number of executions have declined annually.[65]

The Supreme Court has long struggled to establish principles to govern executions under the Eighth Amendment. In recent years, the Court has declared that death was too harsh a penalty for the crime of rape of a child,[66] prohibited the execution of a defendant with an IQ under 70 and of a youthful defendant, and invalidated a death sentence for an African American defendant after the prosecutor improperly excluded African Americans from the jury.[67] In 2015, however, the Court upheld lethal injection as a mode of execution despite arguments that this form of execution was likely to cause considerable pain.[68]

The Eighth Amendment also prohibits excessive fines. In the 2019 case *Timbs v. Indiana*,[69] the Supreme Court ruled that this prohibition applied to the states.

In the *Timbs* case, the state confiscated Timbs's car after he was convicted of drug possession. The car was worth much more than the maximum possible fine Timbs could have received. The Indiana Supreme Court agreed that the fine may have been excessive but said this did not matter because the Eighth Amendment had never been applied to the states. The U.S. Supreme Court reversed that decision and added excessive fines to the list of constitutional provisions the states were obligated to recognize.

Check your understanding

9. How has the Supreme Court's interpretation of individuals' Fourth Amendment protections against unreasonable searches and seizures evolved?

   a) The Supreme Court has strengthened the application of the exclusionary rule, further limiting the circumstances in which an intrusion could be justified.

   b) The Supreme Court has maintained that there are no circumstances under which materials obtained without a search warrant would be admissible in court.

   c) The Supreme Court has softened the application of the exclusionary rule, allowing federal courts to use their discretion about it depending on the "nature and quality of the intrusion."

   d) The Supreme Court has changed its position on "anticipatory warrants," now ruling that the police could not conduct searches using them.

10. What is the significance of the Supreme Court's ruling in *Miranda v. Arizona*?

    a) It set criteria of what constitutes "cruel and unusual punishment" and restricted the crimes eligible for the death penalty.

    b) It expanded the Sixth Amendment provision pertaining to the right to counsel to civil cases and a wider variety of criminal cases.

    c) It applied the right to a trial by jury to the states through the Fourteenth Amendment, a process known as incorporation.

    d) It advanced the civil liberties of the accused by expanding the Fifth Amendment's protection against coerced confessions and self-incrimination as well as confirming the right to counsel.

The Right to Privacy Means the Right to Be Left Alone

Describe how the Supreme Court has identified and interpreted the right to privacy

A **right to privacy** was not mentioned in the Bill of Rights. In a 1928 case, however, Supreme Court Justice Louis Brandeis argued in a dissent that the Fourth Amendment's provision for "the right of the people to be secure in their persons, houses, papers, and effects, against unreasonable searches and seizures" should be extended to a more general principle of "privacy in the home."[70]

> **right to privacy** the right to be left alone, which has been interpreted by the Supreme Court to entail individual access to birth control and abortions
>
> **eminent domain** the right of government to take private property for public use

Eminent Domain

One important element of privacy is the possession of private property—property belonging to individuals for their own peaceful enjoyment. The privacy of private property, however, is conditioned by the needs of the public at large. What if the government believes that the construction of a public road or other public project requires that a private home be torn down to make way for the public good? Where does privacy end and the public good begin? The power of any government to take private property for public use is called **eminent domain**.

The Fifth Amendment, through the "takings clause," regulates that power by requiring that the government show a public purpose and provide fair payment for the taking of someone's property. This provision is now observed by all governments within the United States.

Birth Control

The sphere of privacy as a constitutional principle was formally recognized in 1965, when the Court ruled that a Connecticut law forbidding the use of contraceptives (and that forbade information about contraception) by married couples violated the right of marital privacy. The Supreme Court declared the Connecticut law unconstitutional because it violated "a right of privacy older than the Bill of Rights."[71] Justice William O. Douglas, who wrote the majority opinion in the *Griswold v. Connecticut* case, argued that this right of privacy is also grounded in the Constitution because it fits into a "zone of privacy" created by a combination of the Third, Fourth, and Fifth amendments.

Abortion

The right to privacy was confirmed and extended in 1973 in a revolutionary Supreme Court decision: *Roe v. Wade*, which established a woman's right to seek an abortion. The decision prohibited states from making abortion a criminal act prior to the point in pregnancy at which the fetus becomes viable, which in 1973 was the 27th week.[72]

The *Roe* decision touched off a decades-long political battle between pro-choice and anti-abortion rights groups, with Democrats generally declaring their support for abortion rights and Republicans expressing opposition to abortion rights. As Republican appointees became more dominant on the Supreme Court, the legal standard shifted against abortion rights and, in *Dobbs v. Jackson Women's Health Organization* (2022), the Court ruled that the Constitution did not confer the right to an abortion and overturned *Roe v. Wade.* The Court said:

> *Guided by the history and tradition that map the essential components of the Nation's concept of ordered liberty, the Court finds the Fourteenth Amendment clearly does not protect the right to an abortion. Indeed, . . . This consensus endured until the day* Roe *was decided.* Roe *either ignored or misstated this history.*[73]

The *Dobbs* decision did not outlaw abortion. It said, rather, that the states will be free to determine, through legislation, whether and to what extent abortion will be permitted. More conservative states will undoubtedly place severe restrictions on access to abortions, while more liberal states will continue to make abortion services readily available.

Justice Clarence Thomas, in his concurring opinion overturning *Roe v. Wade,* made an observation that prompted concerns about what other rights could be affected: the same rationale that the Supreme Court used to declare there was no right to abortion, he said, could also be used to overturn cases establishing rights to contraception, same-sex consensual relations, and same-sex marriage. However, in the majority opinion written by Justice Samuel A. Alito, the court said that nothing in its decision "should be understood to cast doubt on precedents that do not concern abortion."

Sexual Orientation

In the last three decades, the right to be left alone began to include the privacy rights of people in the LGBTQ community. In the 1986 case of *Bowers v. Hardwick* the Court ruled in favor of a state anti-sodomy law on the grounds that "the federal Constitution confers [no] fundamental right upon homosexuals to engage in sodomy."[74]

FOR CRITICAL ANALYSIS ⟶

1. Should abortion rights vary from state to state? Should individuals from a state that bans abortion be able to secure an abortion in another state?
2. How do you think state laws about abortion rights will change? Which states will impose stricter restrictions? Which states will lessen them?

WHO ARE AMERICANS?

Abortion Rights after *Dobbs*

Access to Abortion, 2022

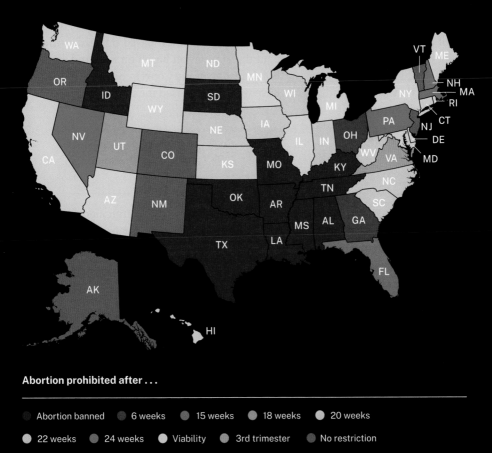

Abortion prohibited after . . .

- Abortion banned
- 6 weeks
- 15 weeks
- 18 weeks
- 20 weeks
- 22 weeks
- 24 weeks
- Viability
- 3rd trimester
- No restriction

In its 2022 decision in *Dobbs v. Jackson Women's Health Organization*, the U.S. Supreme Court overturned *Roe v. Wade*, the 1973 decision that had established a constitutional right to abortion in the United States. The *Dobbs* decision left the states free to enact their own laws on abortion. Several states have banned abortion except where a pregnancy would severely injure or kill the person bearing the child. Several states permit abortion throughout the pregnancy. A number of states do not allow abortions after the fetus is viable or beyond a certain number of weeks of pregnancy.

SOURCE: Data from Guttmacher Institute, www.guttmacher.org (accessed 8/5/22).

Seventeen years later, to almost everyone's surprise, in *Lawrence v. Texas* (2003) the Court overturned *Bowers v. Hardwick* with a dramatic pronouncement that gay people are "entitled to respect for their private lives"[75] as a matter of constitutional due process and that "the State cannot demean their existence or control their destiny by making their private sexual conduct a crime."[76] In 2015 the Court took another important step in the protection of gay rights by declaring that state bans on same-sex marriage were unconstitutional because they violated the Fourteenth Amendment's equal protection and due process clauses.[77] See Chapter 5 for more on same-sex marriage.

In 2020, LGBTQ individuals won a significant victory in the Supreme Court. In a 6–3 decision written by Justice Neil Gorsuch, the Court ruled that the 1964 Civil Rights Act prohibited employment discrimination based on sexual orientation, just as it prohibited employment discrimination based on race and gender.[78] The fact that the decision was authored by one of the Court's conservative justices suggests that LGBTQ individuals have won an increased measure of acceptance in the United States.

Check your understanding

11. How has the government protected the right to privacy?

  a) Although not explicitly mentioned in the Bill of Rights, various Supreme Court cases have recognized the right to privacy through other rights.

  b) The framers explicitly included privacy among the civil liberties listed in the Sixth Amendment of the Constitution.

  c) The federal government has never recognized the right to privacy; states alone have recognized it in a piecemeal fashion.

  d) The right to privacy had extensive protections in the years shortly after the Constitution was adopted, but the Supreme Court has significantly limited the right to privacy since then.

12. Which of these statements regarding a woman's right to seek an abortion is true?

  a) The Supreme Court established the right to an abortion in *Roe v. Wade*, and it has consistently upheld the right to abortion by striking down state-level laws that aim to restrict abortions.

  b) In recent years, the Supreme Court has greatly expanded the right to abortion, arguing that states lack the authority to regulate abortion.

  c) The Supreme Court has ruled that states have the sole authority to regulate abortion.

  d) While the Supreme Court has continued to affirm a woman's right to seek an abortion, it has increasingly limited that right.

WHAT DO YOU THINK?

CIVIL LIBERTIES

The prominent place of civil liberties is one of the hallmarks of American government. The freedoms enshrined in the Constitution and its amendments help define the relationship between government and citizens by limiting what government can do to individuals. But these freedoms also come with trade-offs, as the debate about student speech and public schools' educational interests highlights.

- Have you had experiences where someone else's exercise of freedom interfered with yours? How do you think about the trade-offs between one individual's freedom and the implications for others?

- What do you think about questions concerning the right to bear arms, the use of the death penalty, and religious freedom? What are your rights to act upon your beliefs? What are the rights of people who disagree with you? How do you think Brandi Levy would react to critics of her First Amendment claims?

- How have new technologies affected the government's ability to monitor its citizens? What are your expectations of privacy in your email conversations, your plane tickets, your reading habits?

Use 🐰 **INQUIZITIVE** *to help you study and master this material.*

5

WHAT GOVERNMENT DOES & WHY IT MATTERS

In August 2005, Desmond Meade stood by a railroad track in South Florida, contemplating suicide. Homeless and unemployed, he had difficulty getting a job because of his criminal record, and he could not vote because since 1868 Florida's constitution had banned people who served time from voting. "I didn't see any light at the end of the tunnel. . . . I didn't have any hope or any self-esteem and I was ready to end my life," said Desmond.[1] But no train came that day, and Desmond vowed to change course. He first attended community college and then earned a law degree from Florida International University.

Despite his degrees, his civil rights remained limited. He still couldn't vote, even when his wife was running for the state legislature.[2] Nor could he practice law, because the state's bar association prevented him from sitting for the bar exam. But he put his legal training to use to fight the voting ban. As president of the Florida Rights Restoration Coalition (FRRC), he lobbied policy makers statewide and gathered over 750,000 signatures to place an initiative on the November 2018 ballot to restore voting rights for previously incarcerated people.

Civil Rights

Amendment 4 passed, with over 64 percent of the vote. On January 8, 2019, Desmond walked into the Orange County Supervisor of Elections office to register to vote. "The impact of Amendment 4 will be felt for decades to come," he said.[3] His framed voter registration card hangs in his office above his law degree.

Despite the strong support for Amendment 4, in 2019 Florida enacted a bill undercutting its provisions. The new law requires people with criminal convictions to pay back all their court fees and fines before being eligible to vote, threatening the continued disenfranchisement of hundreds of thousands of people.[4] In response, Desmond's FRRC organization started a fund to help "returning citizens" pay off their financial penalties.

In fall 2021, Desmond's civil rights were restored by a new clemency process the governor established; having paid off his court fees, Desmond was at last cleared to run for office if he chose, serve on a jury, and take the bar exam.[5] He also received a MacArthur "genius" award for his work on ending the disenfranchisement of and discrimination against people with convictions.

But the larger struggle over voting rights continues. In March 2021, the U.S. House passed the For the People Act, which expands voter registration and access and reforms campaign finance, among other provisions. With control of the Senate split evenly between Democrats and Republicans,

▲ In 2018, Amendment 4, a ballot initiative to restore voting rights to people with prior felony convictions, passed in Florida thanks to the efforts of the Florida Rights Restoration Coalition and its executive director, Desmond Meade, pictured here.

however, the bill had no hope of passing, because 60 votes were needed to overcome a Republican filibuster, and Democratic senators Joe Manchin of West Virginia and Kyrsten Sinema of Arizona were firmly opposed to changing the filibuster.

As we saw in Chapter 4, the Bill of Rights speaks of civil liberties as negatives—what government must *not* do. Civil rights, however, involve positives—what government *must* do to guarantee equal citizenship and protect citizens from discrimination. Civil rights regulate *who* can participate in the political process and *how*: for example, who can vote, who can hold office, who can serve on juries, and when and how citizens can petition the government to take action. Civil rights also define how people are treated in employment, education, and other aspects of American society, as this chapter will show.

CHAPTER GOALS

Define civil rights and describe the different strategies that lead to achieving civil rights (pp. 127–31)

Outline the key political and legal developments in the civil rights movement (pp. 131–41)

Explain how different social movements have expanded civil rights (pp. 142–51)

Describe key issues of civil rights that continue to impact American politics (pp. 152–58)

What Are Civil Rights, and How Are They Achieved?

Define civil rights and describe the different strategies that lead to achieving civil rights

Many of the monumental changes to our political system have come about through deeply contested struggles for civil rights. But these rights have not simply been handed down from elected leaders or institutions like the courts. Throughout America's history, organized groups of people have played a key role in improving American democracy.

Defining Civil Rights

Civil rights are guarantees of equal opportunity and protection for all citizens through obligations imposed on government power—what government must do to ensure that citizens are treated equally. The ideals of liberty, equality, and justice embedded in the Declaration of Independence and the Constitution (see Chapter 1) underlie the understanding that government should protect certain rights. Today these include the right to vote, the right to attend desegregated schools, and the right of people with disabilities to be free from discrimination. Civil rights law focuses on granting equal rights of citizenship to members of groups who have historically faced discrimination.

> **civil rights** guarantees of equal opportunity and protection through obligations imposed on government to protect individuals

Two important distinctions between civil liberties (see Chapter 4) and civil rights are (1) the way they were established and (2) the way they are protected. Civil liberties are basic personal freedoms established in the Bill of Rights. In contrast, civil rights have evolved over time as different groups have organized and campaigned for new rights. And although civil liberties are often viewed as *limitations on government action* (conducting unreasonable searches, for example), protecting civil rights often requires an *expansion of government power* to take positive action (as in desegregating public schools).

Americans agree with the basic principle of civil rights but quarrel over their application. Even today the question of what "equal rights" means is hardly settled.

Achieving Civil Rights

Civil rights mainly come about through **social movements**, which are sustained campaigns brought by and on behalf of disadvantaged populations in support of a political goal.[6] Social movements emerge when multiple groups of people and organizations decide to organize around a

> **social movements** sustained campaigns brought by and on behalf of disadvantaged populations in support of a political or social goal

collective action the process of a group of people organizing and acting based on a shared goal

specific injustice. Part of what makes social movements effective in achieving their goals is that they enable individuals to engage with others in **collective action**. It might be difficult for one person to get a new law passed, but thousands of people working together greatly increase the likelihood of it occurring. This is the fundamental understanding of social movements: large, organized groups are stronger than one person in achieving political change.[7] Yet, even when masses of people mobilize, there is no guarantee that a social movement will be successful.

Strategies Used by Social Movements

Social movements focus on establishing a "right" (such as a right to vote) and then fight for government enforcement of that right (such as protection from voter intimidation and violence). In this struggle, groups pursue different tactics depending on the social and political environment. At times, groups follow an "inside strategy" whereby movement leaders work inside the political system to achieve their goal—such as passing legislation, winning a court case, or securing a presidential executive order. However, if there are no opportunities for intervention within the political system, movement leaders pursue an "outside strategy" of organizing in other arenas to transform public opinion—such as peaceful protests and sit-ins. And when the resources are available, social movements pursue both strategies.

Social movements for civil rights pursue strategies that try to build support in public opinion (as in the protests of Native Americans and environmentalists against the Dakota pipeline), with the president (as when Martin Luther King, Jr., Whitney Young, and James Farmer — not pictured — met with President Johnson to discuss African American civil rights), in Congress (as when supporters of the Equal Rights Amendment marched to the Capitol), and in the courts (when James Obergefell and LGBTQ rights organizations pressed their case for marriage equality at the Supreme Court).

Shifting Public Opinion Raising greater awareness about an injustice is often the first step for social movements. While a disadvantaged group may have difficulty gaining access to formal political institutions, low barriers to entry in the public opinion arena make it easier to spread information.

Shifting public opinion is instrumental in convincing political institutions to take action, and the most successful social movements are those that have garnered widespread public support. In fact, studies of protest activity in the 1960s found that voters were directly influenced by protests and activism.[8] But success in shifting public opinion is not the same as actually accomplishing the passage of a new civil rights law. Over time, as movements gain public support, they continue their outside strategies while also expanding their focus to build pressure inside formal political institutions, like Congress, the courts, and the executive branch.

Influencing the President Throughout history, presidents rarely have met with members of a social movement or used their power to implement executive policies on behalf of a movement. However, protest activity and informational campaigns aimed directly at the president can be useful in creating a more receptive political environment.[9] For example, as movements pushed for increased voting rights, in 1965 President Lyndon B. Johnson gave a speech to Congress in support of voting rights legislation while using "We shall overcome," a well-known slogan from the civil rights movement. Johnson also worked behind the scenes to pressure members of Congress to support the legislation. A few months later, Congress passed the Voting Rights Act—landmark legislation that protected voting rights.

Congressional Legislation Social movements have also pressed for civil rights in Congress. But because congressional decision-making involves 435 congressional representatives and 100 senators, it can be frustratingly slow to build a majority in support of civil rights legislation. Social movements that have succeeded in Congress have engaged in activities such as drafting legislation and lobbying legislators to support their goals.[10]

equal protection clause provision of the Fourteenth Amendment guaranteeing citizens "the equal protection of the laws." This clause has been the basis for the civil rights of African Americans, women, and other groups

burden of proof the responsibility of an individual, organization, or government to provide sufficient evidence in support of a claim in court

Supreme Court Decisions With the adoption of the Fourteenth Amendment in 1868, civil rights became part of the Constitution, guaranteed to each citizen through the **equal protection clause**. Yet, while this clause guarantees citizens "the equal protection of the laws," for a considerable portion of American history (and even today), many groups have faced unequal laws and conditions. In fact, what "equal protection" means and which groups should be protected has evolved over time. As a result, groups filing lawsuits and the Supreme Court deciding cases have played important roles in interpreting the constitutional principles set out in the Fourteenth Amendment. In using the equal protection clause to limit discrimination, part of the judicial decision-making process is to determine on whom the **burden of proof** should be placed: the person or organization seeking to show that discrimination has not occurred, or the individual or organization attempting to show that discrimination has occurred.

At times, the Court has appeared more welcoming than the other branches of government to social movements focused on civil rights. For example, in *Brown v. Board of Education* (1954), the Court declared racial segregation in education a violation of the Constitution—ten years before Congress declared legal discrimination unconstitutional.[11]

Yet there are limitations to a court-centered strategy for social movements. Court decisions are not self-enforcing, and there has been considerable opposition and backlash to controversial civil rights cases. The Supreme Court is most effective as a vehicle for social change when public opinion has already shifted.[12]

Check your understanding

1. How do civil rights differ from civil liberties?

   a) While civil rights involve limitations on government, civil liberties are positive actions that government must take to ensure equality.

   b) Civil liberties are found in the Bill of Rights of the Constitution, and civil rights are only found in statutes passed by Congress.

   c) Civil rights are guarantees of equal protection and opportunity for all; civil liberties are restrictions or limitations on what government can do.

   d) Civil liberties only apply to the national government, whereas civil rights apply to the national and state governments.

2. Which of the following statements about the evolution of civil rights in the United States is correct?

a) The ratification of the Fourteenth Amendment immediately established equality for all groups.

b) Court decisions have been more influential in advancing civil rights than legislation passed by Congress since the Court's decisions are self-enforcing.

c) Congress has always taken the lead on civil rights by passing legislation like the Civil Rights Act of 1964.

d) What equal protection means and to whom equal protection applies has evolved over time and still remains a highly contested question.

The Civil Rights Movement, 1600s–1960s

Outline the key political and legal developments in the civil rights movement

In the United States, a strong tradition of individual liberty coexists uneasily with the history of slavery and legalized racial **discrimination** against Black people.

> **discrimination** the use of any unreasonable and unjust criterion of exclusion

By accepting the institution of slavery, the Founders embraced a system fundamentally at odds with the "Blessings of Liberty" promised in the Constitution (see Chapter 2). Their decision set the stage for centuries of struggles to achieve the full rights of citizenship. Black people's journey from being forcibly transported to America as enslaved people to achieving political and legal equality during the twentieth century is our nation's central civil rights story. This struggle is sometimes called "the long civil rights movement."[13]

Slavery and the Abolitionist Movement

The subjugation of Africans kidnapped from their native lands was a practice virtually as old as European colonial settlement: the first enslaved people arrived in Jamestown, Virginia, in 1619, a year before the Plymouth colony was established in Massachusetts. Over time, due to the importance of slavery to the colonial economy in the North and the South, the violent transatlantic and domestic trade of enslaved Africans quickly expanded.

Despite the growth of slavery in the colonies, enslaved people resisted their inhumane treatment in a multitude of ways. Resistance efforts, especially revolts,

Slavery tore the nation apart and ultimately led to the Civil War. The abolition movement organized in the North and pushed to end slavery. Harriet Tubman (far left in photograph) was an abolitionist and formerly enslaved person who helped many people escape bondage through a network of safe houses called the Underground Railroad.

were brutally suppressed by slaveowners and local law enforcement. Enslaved people who pursued the dangerous step of escaping were often aided by the Underground Railroad, a network of individuals (both Black and White) and secret houses that sheltered people as they made their way to free states. Many members of this network were abolitionists—they viewed slavery as an abomination and were committed to ending it. The abolitionist movement grew among White northerners in the 1830s, and its strategies centered on swaying public opinion through speeches and the distribution of antislavery literature. Numerous Black people, including the great abolitionist leader Frederick Douglass, himself a former enslaved person, spoke out against slavery.

While the movement made considerable progress toward civil rights, it suffered a disappointing setback in 1857 with the Supreme Court's infamous decision in *Dred Scott v. Sandford*. Dred Scott was an enslaved person who sued for his freedom because his owner had taken him to Illinois and the territory of Wisconsin, both of which prohibited slavery. The Court, however, ruled that enslaved people—indeed, all Black people—were not citizens of the United States and that Scott was his owner's permanent property, regardless of his having been taken to a free state or territory.[14] This ruling inflamed the tense debate over the future of slavery, splitting the country deeply and helping to precipitate civil war.

The Civil War Amendments and Their Aftermath

Tensions over slavery boiled over into the American Civil War (1861–65). On one side was the United States of America and on the other was the Confederate States of America, a group of 11 southern states that seceded from the United States and supported the institution of slavery. On January 1, 1863, President Abraham Lincoln emphasized the nation's desire to end slavery by issuing the Emancipation Proclamation, which declared that all enslaved people in Confederate states "shall be then, thenceforward, and forever free." However, the Confederate states refused to comply. It took the eventual surrender of the Confederate army and subsequent passage of the **Thirteenth Amendment** (1865) for legal slavery to be abolished. The end of the war led to two additional constitutional amendments meant to protect the rights of the formerly enslaved: the **Fourteenth Amendment** (1868) guaranteed equal protection and due process under the law, and the **Fifteenth Amendment** (1870) guaranteed voting rights for Black men. These three amendments are called the Reconstruction amendments.

Thirteenth Amendment one of three Civil War amendments; it abolished slavery

Fourteenth Amendment one of three Civil War amendments; it guaranteed equal protection and due process

Fifteenth Amendment one of three Civil War amendments; it guaranteed voting rights for African American men

During the period of Reconstruction (1865–77) after the war, Black Americans organized for greater social, economic, and political freedoms. Their quest for a more equitable society was significantly aided by the national government, which sent federal troops to the former Confederate states to enforce their reintegration into the Union and to ensure that they adhered to the promises of the Reconstruction amendments. Especially important was the Civil Rights Act of 1866, which defined as citizens all persons, regardless of race, born in the United States. This was the nation's first federal law affirming that all citizens were equally protected by the law and that no state could pass new laws discriminating between White and Black people. The Civil Rights Act and the Reconstruction amendments provided necessary protections for Black people as they navigated the meaning of freedom and equality within states where they were formerly enslaved.[15]

Black men began exercising their right to vote and gained political power in the South. During Reconstruction, 16 Black men were elected to the U.S. Congress and approximately 2,000 held public office in the region.[16] As voters and public officials, Black Americans found a home in the Republican Party, the party of President Lincoln, which had sponsored the Reconstruction amendments.[17]

The newfound political equality during Reconstruction was short-lived, however. During this period of expanding civil rights for Black people, deep opposition remained. Southern leaders, especially plantation owners and Democratic politicians, worked to undermine the promises of equal protection and bring Reconstruction to an end. They succeeded in 1877 when the national government withdrew its troops from the South and turned its back on Black Americans. After that, southern states erected a "Jim Crow" system of social, political, and economic inequality that made a mockery of the Constitution's promises. The first **Jim Crow laws** were adopted by the southern states beginning in the 1870s, criminalizing racial intermarriage and segregating railroad travel, all public accommodations, and public schools.

Jim Crow laws laws enacted by southern states following Reconstruction that discriminated against African Americans

Jim Crow laws were approved by the Supreme Court as well. In the infamous *Plessy v. Ferguson* (1896)[18] case, the Court upheld a Louisiana law that *required* segregation of the races on trolleys and other public transit (and, by implication, in all public facilities, including schools). Homer Plessy, a man defined as "one-eighth Black," had sat in a trolley car reserved for White people and was found guilty of violating a law providing for "equal but separate accommodations" on trains. In its ruling, the Court held that the racial restrictions did not violate the Fourteenth Amendment's equal protection clause as long as the facilities were equal.

Plessy v. Ferguson legally authorized White people's use of race to exclude nonwhite people and established the **"separate but equal" rule** that prevailed through the mid-twentieth century. Judges in this period generally accepted the false pretense that accommodations for Black people (no matter what the actual quality) were equal to those for White people.

Organizing against Racial Violence

Given Jim Crow laws mandating racial segregation and the lack of a legal basis for "equal protection of the laws," Black people soon faced a long period of racial terrorism. In particular, in an effort to reestablish White political power and Black subordination, lynchings and mob violence directed at Black people increased. The period 1877–1950 saw over 4,000 Black lynching victims.[19] Fewer than 1 percent of White people involved in lynchings were ever convicted of a criminal offense.

In response, Black people formed organizations and devised outside and inside strategies to battle the escalating racial violence. Of particular importance is the National Association for the Advancement of Colored People (NAACP), established in 1909. Initially, NAACP founding member and director of publicity W. E. B. Du Bois was insistent on the power of the press to sway public opinion. In addition to writing news stories, the association supported collective action efforts in the form of mass demonstrations. During subsequent phases of the anti-violence struggle, the NAACP lobbied Congress to pass a federal anti-lynching bill, petitioned three presidents to denounce racialized violence, and won a landmark case about mob violence in the Supreme Court. Safety—the protection from violence—was considered a precursor to all the other important battles the NAACP would eventually wage.[20]

By the mid-1920s, lynchings started to decline nationwide as a result of the mass organizing. In the following decades, the NAACP turned its attention to other areas of civil rights—most notably, education.

The Fight for Education Equality and the Weakening of Jim Crow

Across the South there were separate schools for Black and White students, and this racial segregation was legally enforced under *Plessy*'s "separate but equal" doctrine. But the schools were never equal; Black schools were poorly funded, lacked adequate resources, and did not properly compensate Black teachers. Given these conditions, beginning in the 1930s the NAACP executed a three-pronged plan, focused on the courts, to transform public school education in the South for Black students. Initially, the organization did not directly challenge segregated schools; instead, it demonstrated that existing Black schools were unequal. In doing so, the NAACP opened the door for the idea that separate schools could never be equal.

After success in most of these suits, NAACP lawyers decided the time was ripe to confront the "separate but equal" rule head-on. Key in this phase were the Black parents and students who participated as plaintiffs in the lawsuits. One parent, Oliver Brown, the father of three girls, lived in a racially mixed neighborhood of Topeka, Kansas. Every school day, his daughter Linda took the school bus to Monroe Elementary School, a school for Black children, about a mile away. In September 1950, Linda's father took her to the all-White Sumner School, closer to their home, and tried to enroll her in the third grade, in defiance of state law and local segregation rules. When they were refused, Brown went to the NAACP. Soon thereafter, the case **Brown v. Board of Education** was born.

Brown v. Board of Education the 1954 Supreme Court decision that struck down the "separate but equal" doctrine as fundamentally unequal; this case eliminated state power to use race as a criterion of discrimination in law and provided the national government with the power to intervene by exercising strict regulatory policies against discriminatory actions

In 1954 the Supreme Court ruled unanimously in one of the most important decisions in its history:

> *Does segregation of children in public schools solely on the basis of race, even though the physical facilities and other "tangible" factors may be equal, deprive the children of the minority group of equal educational opportunities? We believe that it does. . . . We conclude that in the field of public education the doctrine of "separate but equal" has no place. Separate educational facilities are inherently unequal.*[21]

The *Brown* decision not only altered the constitutional framework by striking down "separate but equal" as unconstitutional; it also signaled the Court's determination to use the **strict scrutiny** test in cases related to discrimination. That is, the burden of proof would fall on the government to show that the law in question *was* constitutional—not on the challengers to show the law's *un*constitutionality.[22]

strict scrutiny a test used by the Supreme Court in racial discrimination cases and other cases involving civil liberties and civil rights that places the burden of proof on the government rather than on the challengers to show that the law in question is constitutional

Resistance to *Brown* Despite the significance of *Brown*, the decision proved more symbolic than substantive—at least early on. Most states refused to obey the decision until they were sued. In addition, even as southern school boards began to eliminate their legally enforced (**de jure**) school segregation, extensive actual

de jure literally, "by law"; refers to legally enforced practices, such as school segregation in the South before the 1960s

(**de facto**) school segregation remained—in the North and the South—as a consequence of racially segregated housing. Also, discrimination in employment, public accommodations, juries, voting, and other areas of political, social, and economic activity was not directly affected by *Brown*, which focused exclusively on public education.

The Civil Rights Movement after *Brown*

Ten years after *Brown*, fewer than 1 percent of Black children in the Deep South were attending schools with White children,[23] making it clear that the goal of "equal protection" required not just court decisions but also positive—or affirmative—action by Congress and government agencies. Given massive southern resistance and only lukewarm northern support for racial integration, progress also required strategies of intense, well-organized support.

Organized demonstrations began to increase slowly but surely. By the 1960s, a number of Black-led civil rights organizations—notably the Southern Christian Leadership Conference (SCLC), the Student Nonviolent Coordinating Committee (SNCC), and the Congress of Racial Equality (CORE)—had built networks capable of launching large-scale nonviolent direct-action campaigns against southern segregationists. The movement used the media to attract nationwide attention and support: images of protesters being beaten, attacked by police dogs, and set upon with fire hoses won broad sympathy for the cause of Black civil rights and discredited governments in the South. The civil rights movement then used the shifting of public opinion to make broader claims about how the federal government needed to intercede to protect Black people's civil rights.

Montgomery Bus Boycott (1955–56) Due to segregation under Jim Crow, Black people had to sit in different sections on public transportation: the front section of buses was reserved for White passengers and the back for Black passengers. On December 1, 1955, Rosa Parks, a Black woman who was active in the NAACP, boarded a bus and sat down in the first row of the Black section. However, when the bus filled up with passengers, the driver demanded she give up her seat to a White man. Parks refused. As a result, she was arrested. Her act of defiance set the spark for the Montgomery bus boycott, during which 40,000 Black bus riders came together—the majority of the city's bus riders—and boycotted the buses. This protest campaign lasted until March 30, 1956, when the Supreme Court declared that Montgomery's segregated buses were unconstitutional.

Student Sit-Ins (1960–61) The sit-in movement began when four Black college students asked to be served at a "Whites only" lunch counter in a Woolworth's department store in Greensboro, North Carolina, on February 1, 1960. The sit-ins quickly spread to include over 70,000 participants and became one of the most effective examples of collective action. College students, both Black and White, would walk into a segregated establishment, ask to be served, and refuse to leave when denied service. Such coordinated resistance resulted in the integration of many establishments across the South.

March on Washington for Jobs and Freedom (1963) In the March on Washington of August 28, 1963, over 200,000 demonstrators and many civil rights organizations came together in the nation's capital to continue to raise public awareness about the moral wrong of racial segregation and to pressure the government into action. Standing at the Lincoln Memorial, Dr. Martin Luther King, Jr., delivered his famous "I Have a Dream" speech. Other speakers stressed the need for justice, jobs, and the desire for full access to the American Dream. After the march, civil rights leaders met with President John F. Kennedy in the White House to discuss civil rights legislation.

"Massive resistance" among White southerners attempted to block the desegregation efforts of the national government. For example, at Little Rock Central High School in 1957, an angry mob of White students prevented Black students, including Elizabeth Eckford (pictured here), from entering the school.

Selma-to-Montgomery Marches (1965) Even after significant inroads were made via Supreme Court cases and congressional legislation, some southern states still denied Black people the right to vote. In an effort to raise awareness and pressure Congress for additional voting legislation, Alabama activists organized a series of marches during 1965. Nonviolent participants were to walk along the 54-mile road from Selma to the state capitol in Montgomery. However, the first attempt on March 7 was violently interrupted by Alabama state troopers, who teargassed and beat the marchers with batons and clubs at the Edmund Pettus Bridge. The public was shocked at the inhumane treatment of Black people who simply wanted the right to vote. Instead of deterring the protesters, the violence led to greater public support, and the march grew. Marchers set back out on March 21 with Martin Luther King, Jr. When they reached the state capitol on March 25, their ranks had swelled to 25,000.

The Civil Rights Acts

Steadily, the civil rights movement applied intense pressure on a reluctant federal government to take more assertive steps to defend the civil rights of Black people (see Table 5.1).

The most important of the government's actions was the **Civil Rights Act of 1964**, which

Civil Rights Act of 1964 landmark legislation that ended segregation in public spaces and prohibited discrimination on the basis of race, gender, religion, sex, and national origin

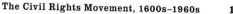

TABLE 5.1 | Cause and Effect in the Civil Rights Movement

Social movement action and government action worked in tandem to produce dramatic changes in American civil rights policies.

SOCIAL MOVEMENT ACTION	POLITICAL AND LEGAL ACTION
1930–54 NAACP legal campaign focused on segregated public education.	**1954** *Brown v. Board of Education*
1957 Little Rock Nine: NAACP recruited nine Black students to integrate Little Rock Central High School. Their efforts were met with violence.	**1957** Civil Rights Act created Civil Rights Commission; President Eisenhower sent 101st Airborne Division paratroops to Little Rock, Arkansas, to enforce integration of Central High School.
1960 The sit-in movement began and subsequently the Student Nonviolent Coordinating Committee formed. College students would walk into a segregated establishment, ask to be served, and then refuse to leave when denied service. In doing so, the students practiced the tactic of civil disobedience.	**1960** Many establishments in the South, including department store restaurants and lunch counters, were integrated.
1961 Freedom Rides: groups of White and Black civil rights activists rode together on buses through the South to protest segregated bus terminals. Freedom riders were met with violence but also garnered significant international media attention.	**1961** Interstate Commerce Commission ordered desegregation on all buses and trains and in terminals; President John F. Kennedy favored executive action over civil rights legislation.
1963 (April) Nonviolent demonstrations in Birmingham, Alabama, led to civil rights demonstrators facing police dogs and fire hoses. Martin Luther King, Jr., was arrested and wrote his "Letter from Birmingham Jail." (August) March on Washington was one of the greatest displays of mass civil rights protest that ever occurred in the United States.	**1963** President Kennedy shifted, indicating his support for a strong civil rights law; after JFK's assassination, President Johnson asserted strong support for civil rights.
1964 President Johnson met with civil rights leaders in the Oval Office.	**1964** Congress passed historic Civil Rights Act covering voting, employment, public accommodations, education.
1965 Selma-to-Montgomery marches took place: a series of marches organized in Alabama to raise attention to the continuing denial of voting rights to Black people.	**1965** Voting Rights Act was passed.

attacked discrimination in public accommodations, segregation in schools, and discrimination by employers in hiring, promoting, and laying off employees. Protections from discrimination against women were also included.

Public Accommodations After the 1964 Civil Rights Act was passed, public accommodations quickly removed some of the most blatant forms of racial discrimination, such as signs labeling "Colored" and "White" restrooms, water fountains, waiting rooms, and seating arrangements. In addition, the federal government filed more than 400 antidiscrimination suits in federal courts against hotels, restaurants, taverns, gas stations, and other establishments.

Education The 1964 Civil Rights Act also declared discrimination by state governments and their agencies (such as school boards) illegal and created administrative agencies to help the courts implement laws against it. Title IV of the act, for example, authorized the Justice Department to implement federal court orders for school desegregation without waiting for parents to bring complaints. Title VI of the act provided that federal grants-in-aid for education must be withheld from any school system practicing racial segregation.

Title VI became the most effective weapon for desegregating schools outside the South, because segregation in northern school districts was more subtle. To address this problem, the 1964 Civil Rights Act gave (1) the president, through the Justice Department's Office for Civil Rights, the power to withhold federal education grants[24] and (2) the attorney general of the United States the power to initiate suits (rather than having to await complaints) wherever there was a "pattern or practice" of discrimination.[25]

In 1971 the Supreme Court held that state-imposed desegregation could be accomplished by busing children across school districts.[26] Three years later, however, this principle was severely restricted when the Court determined that only districts found guilty of deliberate and de jure racial segregation would have to desegregate their schools,[27] effectively exempting most northern states and cities from busing. According to many studies, school segregation, mainly based upon residential patterns, continues today.[28]

Voting Rights The 1965 Voting Rights Act significantly strengthened voting rights protections. It barred literacy and other tests as a condition for voting, set criminal penalties for interference with efforts to vote, and provided for the replacement of local registrars with federally appointed ones in counties designated by the attorney general as significantly resistant to registering eligible Black people to vote. Of particular importance, Section 5 of the act required that counties with histories of voter discrimination seek "preclearance," or approval from the federal government, before changing their voting laws and procedures. The Section 5 oversight applied not just to states in the South but across the country. The right to vote was further strengthened in 1964 with ratification of the Twenty-Fourth Amendment, which abolished the poll tax, and in 1975 with legislation permanently outlawing literacy tests in all 50 states and mandating bilingual ballots or oral assistance for Spanish, Chinese, Japanese, and Korean speakers and for Native Americans and Alaska natives.

The progress in Black political participation produced by these acts has altered American politics. In 1965, in the seven states of the old Confederacy covered by the Voting Rights Act, 29.3 percent of eligible Black residents were registered to vote, compared with 73.4 percent of White residents. By 1972 the racial gap in registration was only 11.2 points. And today, more Black people hold public office in the states of the Deep South than in the North.

While the Voting Rights Act has protected racial and ethnic groups since 1965, there have been numerous attempts to weaken its protections. A significant blow to voting rights came in the 2013 case *Shelby County v. Holder*, when the Supreme Court declared that Section 4 of the Voting Rights Act, which Section 5 preclearance relied on, was unconstitutional.[29] As a result, states and counties with a history of discriminatory voting practices no longer have to seek approval from the government to change their voting rules. In the aftermath of *Shelby*, states that were previously covered by Section 5 (Texas, Mississippi, and Alabama) swiftly changed their laws. More recently, in 2022, state legislatures introduced over 250 bills with provisions that would restrict voting access in at least 27 states.[30] The proposed changes to voting registration and access included limiting same-day voter registration, new voter ID laws, shorter hours for voting, and curtailing voting by absentee ballot. These types of voting laws have been shown to disproportionately impact people in racial and ethnic minority groups, students, the elderly, and people with disabilities.[31] Supporters of these proposed voting bills argue they protect the integrity of the voting process and guard against voter fraud.

Employment The federal courts and the Justice Department entered the arena of economic equality through Title VII of the Civil Rights Act of 1964, which outlawed job discrimination by all private and public employers, including governmental agencies (such as fire and police departments) with more than 15 workers. Title VII makes it unlawful to discriminate in employment on the basis of color, religion, sex, national origin, and race.

Title VII delegated powers to enforce fair-employment practices to the Justice Department's Civil Rights Division and to the Equal Employment Opportunity Commission (EEOC). By executive order, these agencies now had the power to revoke or prohibit federal contracts for goods and services with any private company that could not guarantee that its rules for hiring, promotion, and firing were nondiscriminatory.

One problem with Title VII was that the accusing party (the plaintiff) had to show that deliberate discrimination was the cause of the failure to get a job or training opportunity. The courts have since allowed plaintiffs to make their case if they can show that an employer's hiring practices had the *effect* of exclusion.

Housing In 1968 Congress passed the Fair Housing Act specifically to prohibit housing discrimination. It eventually covered the sale or rental of nearly all the nation's housing. Housing was among the most controversial discrimination issues because of entrenched patterns of residential segregation nationwide. Besides the lingering effects of restrictive covenants, local authorities had deliberately segregated public housing, and federal guidelines had allowed discrimination in Federal Housing Administration mortgage lending, effectively preventing Black people from joining the movement to the suburbs in the 1950s and '60s.

The procedures for proving discrimination remained challenging until Congress passed the Fair Housing Amendments Act in 1988. This law put more teeth in the enforcement mechanisms and allowed the Department of Housing and Urban Development (HUD) to initiate legal action in cases of discrimination.[32]

Marriage In 1967 the Supreme Court ruled in *Loving v. Virginia* that any state laws outlawing interracial marriage were unconstitutional. At the time, 16 states outlawed interracial marriage. The case concerned a Virginia couple—Richard Loving, a White man, and Mildred Loving, a biracial woman who was Black and Native American—who married in Washington, D.C., where such unions were legal. After moving back to Virginia, they were charged with violating the state's law against interracial marriage; they returned to Washington and challenged the Virginia law. In striking such laws down, the Court declared marriage "one of the 'basic civil rights of man,' fundamental to our very existence and survival."[33] Over 50 years later, *Loving* served as precedent in the LGBTQ movement to argue for the right for same-sex couples to marry.

Check your understanding

3. What was the effect of the Supreme Court's landmark ruling in *Brown v. Board of Education?*

   a) Racial segregation in schools was immediately ended since *Brown* overruled the "separate but equal" rule.

   b) Although the "separate but equal" rule had been struck down, it took some time for desegregation to occur since some states failed to enforce the decision until sued and de facto segregation still existed.

   c) The effect of the *Brown* ruling was extensive, because it ended racial segregation and discrimination in schools, housing, and public accommodations.

   d) The effect of *Brown* was extensive, because it immediately was applied to end discrimination against other groups as well, including Native Americans, LGBTQ individuals, Asian Americans, and immigrants.

4. Which of the following statements about the development of the civil rights movement is true?

   a) Protests organized by civil rights groups proved ineffective in swaying public opinion and getting civil rights issues onto the government's agenda.

   b) Gains achieved in extending the civil rights of African Americans always resulted in propelling those rights even further in subsequent years.

   c) Social movements tended to stick with one strategy — bringing litigation to the courts — to advance civil rights.

   d) Social movements organized protests across the South, raising public awareness and shifting public opinion to get government officials to address civil rights for African Americans.

Civil Rights Have Been Extended to Other Groups

Explain how different social movements have expanded civil rights

While the civil rights movement is central to understanding the development of civil rights, many other groups have engaged in collective struggles and secured greater civil rights. Many participants in these social movements organized alongside the civil rights movement in the 1950s and '60s, building on established strategies and helping to secure expanded civil rights.[34]

The Women's Rights Movement

Through the nineteenth century, American women were denied rights that most people take for granted today. In numerous states, women did not have the right to vote, and the doctrine of "coverture," applied by many state courts, gave the husband control over his wife's property. Lacking political and property rights, women in the United States were effectively second-class citizens.

Property Ownership and Voting Rights In 1848 the quiet upstate New York town of Seneca Falls played host to a convention that began the modern women's movement. The centerpiece of the convention, organized by Elizabeth Cady Stanton and Lucretia Mott, was adoption of a Declaration of Sentiments and Resolutions patterned after the Declaration of Independence. The most controversial provision of the declaration, nearly rejected as too radical, was the call for the right to vote for women.

The climactic movement toward women's suffrage was formally launched in 1878 with the introduction of a proposed constitutional amendment in Congress. For women, electoral politics was a decidedly masculine world. Yet their exclusion did not prevent them from organizing. Of particular importance were suffrage organizations such as the National American Woman Suffrage Association (NAWSA), formed in 1890, which claimed 2 million members by 1917 and staged mass meetings, parades, petitions, and protests. When the **Nineteenth Amendment** was ratified in 1920, all American women were finally guaranteed the right to vote. However, the right to vote for Black women in the South would take many more decades to secure.

Nineteenth Amendment
amendment that guaranteed the right to vote to women

Ending Gender Discrimination In many ways, Title VII of the Civil Rights Act of 1964 fostered the growth of the women's movement in the 1960s and '70s. Beginning in the 1970s the Supreme Court helped establish gender discrimination as a major civil rights issue. While refusing to treat it as the equivalent of racial discrimination,[35] the Court did make it easier for plaintiffs to file and win gender-discrimination suits.[36] In doing so, the Court determined gender was a protected class and that a greater burden was placed on government to show that any laws which discriminate on the basis of gender served an important interest or purpose. Nevertheless, as discussed next, some forms of gender discrimination persist today.

Equality in Education and Employment Title IX of the 1972 Education Act outlawed gender discrimination in education. It led to few lawsuits until the Supreme Court ruled in 1992 that monetary damages could be awarded for gender discrimination.[37] In the two years after this case, complaints to the Education Department's Office for Civil Rights about unequal treatment of women's athletic programs nearly tripled. In several high-profile legal cases, prominent universities were ordered to create more women's sports programs, prompting many other schools to follow suit to avoid potential litigation.[38]

Women have also pressed for civil rights in employment through raising public awareness and by litigating court cases. In particular, they have fought against pay discrimination—paying a male employee more than a female employee of equal qualifications in the same job. After the Equal Pay Act of 1963 made such discrimination illegal, women's pay slowly approached the level of men's, although it remains about 20 percent less. And the pay difference is greater for Black women and Latinas, indicating both a race *and* a gender pay gap.

Sexual Harassment and the #MeToo Movement Largely through interpretation of Title VII of the 1964 Civil Rights Act, during the late 1970s courts began to find sexual harassment to be a form of sex discrimination. In 1986 the Supreme Court recognized two forms of sexual harassment: (1) "quid pro quo" harassment, an explicit or strongly implied threat that submission is a condition of continued employment, and (2) harassment that creates offensive or intimidating working conditions amounting to a "hostile environment."[39]

In two 1998 cases, the Court strengthened the law, saying that whether or not harassment causes economic harm to the employee, the employer is financially liable if someone with authority over the employee committed it—a supervisor, for example. But the Court also said that an employer may defend itself by showing that a sexual harassment prevention and grievance policy was in effect.[40]

In 2011 the Department of Education's Office of Civil Rights (OCR) issued a letter to the more than 7,000 colleges and universities receiving federal money, advising them, under the authority of Title IX, to adopt strict procedures to address charges of sexual assault and harassment on campus. OCR advised shifting the burden of proof from the accuser toward the accused in such cases, allowing accusers to appeal not-guilty findings (contrary to the Fifth Amendment's ban on double jeopardy), and not allowing accused persons to cross-examine their accusers (contrary to the Sixth Amendment). Some feared these procedures lacked due process and would lead to unfair proceedings. In 2018, Education Secretary Betsy DeVos rescinded the Obama-era guidelines and announced new rules that strengthened protections for those accused of sexual misconduct on college campuses. In May 2022, the Biden administration announced it would overhaul many Trump-era guidelines and extend federal protections to safeguard transgender students.

Recently, the #MeToo movement has encouraged women to demand justice for sexual crimes committed against them. The activist Tarana Burke started the #MeToo movement to raise awareness about sexual harassment. In 2017 the hashtag exploded on social media as women shared their experiences of sexual harassment in the workplace, in school, and in their community. As a result, some workplaces instituted changes, and several prominent men, including television star Bill Cosby and film producer Harvey Weinstein, were convicted of sexual misconduct.

Latinos

The labels *Latino* and *Hispanic* encompass a wide range of groups with diverse national origins, cultural identities, and experiences. As a result, civil rights issues for Latinos have varied considerably by group and by place.

For example, the early political experiences of Mexican Americans were shaped by race and by region. In 1848, under the Treaty of Guadalupe Hidalgo, the Texas border was extended to the Rio Grande and Mexico ceded to the United States the territory that now comprises Arizona, California, New Mexico, and parts of Colorado, Nevada, and Utah. Although the treaty guaranteed full civil rights to residents of these territories, Mexican Americans experienced ongoing discrimination. Even after the courts in 1898 reconfirmed their formal political rights, including the right to vote, Mexican Americans were prevented from voting through various means in many places, especially in Texas.[41] They also had to attend separate schools in Texas and much of southern California, and in many neighborhoods restrictive covenants banned them from buying or renting houses.

Like the NAACP, Mexican American civil rights organizations pursued a legal strategy to eliminate the segregation of Mexican American students. In 1954, the League of United Latin American Citizens (LULAC) achieved a major victory in *Hernandez v. Texas*,[42] in which the Supreme Court affirmed that Mexican Americans and all other nationality groups were entitled to equal protection under the Fourteenth Amendment.

Latino political strategy has developed along three tracks. One, a traditional path of voter registration and voting along ethnic lines, was blazed by La Raza Unida, an organization that worked to register Mexican American voters in Texas and several other states. The second is a legal strategy using civil rights laws designed to ensure fair access to the political system: the Mexican American Legal Defense and Educational Fund (MALDEF), founded in 1968, has been key in pursuing a litigation strategy focused on defending Latinos' constitutional rights. The third strategy is mass mobilization. For example, in 2006 protests broke out against anti-immigrant legislation being considered in Congress. In a display of effective collective action, millions of mostly Latino immigrants took to the streets and effectively stopped the legislation from becoming a law.[43]

Asian Americans

Like *Latino*, the label *Asian American* encompasses a wide range of people from very different backgrounds who came to the United States, or whose ancestors came, at different points in history.

AMERICA | SIDE BY SIDE

Global Economic Gender Equality

One can use many measures when trying to determine whether there is economic gender parity in a country. The World Economic Forum uses participation in the labor force, wage equality, earned income, and representation in the managerial and technical professions. Countries at the top of the list are ones where women are most likely to have the same participation and opportunities as men, regardless of the level of income or skill level of that employment.

1. Does the United States' position, 30th out of 156 countries, surprise you? What do you think accounts for the countries ranking in the top 30? What might explain why 29 other countries ranked higher? Israel ranks 65th while its regional neighbor, Saudi Arabia, ranks 149th. What factors could explain why geographically close countries might differ on this kind of ranking?
2. The measurement used here prioritizes women's economic equality over the quality of their economic opportunities. What are the benefits to this approach? What might be gained if we looked instead at a ranking of countries by women's economic opportunities rather than their economic equality?

Economic Gender Gap in Selected Countries

RANK	COUNTRY	SCORE	RANK	COUNTRY	SCORE
1	Laos	0.915	38	Portugal	0.746
2	Bahamas	0.857	39	Switzerland	0.743
3	Burundi	0.855	40	Canada	0.741
4	Iceland	0.846	41	Bulgaria	0.738
5	Belarus	0.840	42	Denmark	0.736
11	Sweden	0.810	43	Ireland	0.733
12	Lithuania	0.808	44	Ukraine	0.732
13	Finland	0.806	55	United Kingdom	0.716
18	Philippines	0.795	58	France	0.710
20	Norway	0.792	59	Belgium	0.709
22	Thailand	0.787	62	Germany	0.706
25	Russian Federation	0.767	65	Israel	0.705
27	New Zealand	0.763	89	Brazil	0.665
30	United States	0.754	122	Mexico	0.590
33	Singapore	0.749	149	Saudi Arabia	0.390

SOURCE: World Economic Forum, "Economic Participation and Opportunity Subindex," *Global Gender Gap Report 2018*, www3.weforum.org/docs/WEF_GGGR_2018.pdf (accessed 7/26/19).

During World War II, many Japanese Americans were forced into unsanitary internment prisons on the grounds of "military necessity" after the Japanese government launched an attack on Pearl Harbor. Japanese Americans faced great losses both during and in the aftermath of internment.

The early Asian experience in the United States was shaped by anti-immigrant naturalization laws dating back to 1790; the first of these declared that only White immigrants were eligible for citizenship. Chinese immigrants began arriving in California in the 1850s, drawn by the gold rush, but many stayed because their manual labor was needed by the Central Pacific Railroad company. From 1863 to 1869, over 15,000 Chinese railroad workers—90 percent of the construction force—were pivotal in building America's first transcontinental railroad.[44]

Despite this tremendous contribution, Chinese people faced hostility and discrimination. In 1870, Congress declared Chinese immigrants ineligible for citizenship, and in 1882 the first Chinese Exclusion Act suspended the entry of Chinese laborers.

The earliest Japanese immigrants came to California in the 1880s and faced similar discrimination. Early in the twentieth century, California and several other western states passed laws denying them the right to own property. Denial of their

FOR CRITICAL ANALYSIS ⟶

1. What states or regions have the highest percentage of foreign-born people? Why might immigrants live in some regions of the country and not others?

2. Do the data in this graphic confirm or contradict what you have heard about immigrants in America? Do you think immigration to the United States should be easier or more restrictive? What other information would be helpful in making your decision?

WHO ARE AMERICANS?

Who Are America's Immigrants?

America has always called itself a nation of immigrants, but immigration has consistently been a controversial issue. In 1900, 1.3 million of New York City's 3.4 million people were foreign born. The immigrants at that time came mostly from mainland Europe, the UK, and Ireland. Who are today's immigrants?

Percentage of Foreign-Born Residents by State

- <5%
- 5–9.9%
- 10–14.9%
- 15–19.9%
- 20%+

What kind of education do immigrants get?

Bachelor's degree

Postgraduate degree

17.8%

13.4%

Where do immigrants come from?

Region	Percentage
Asia	28%
Mexico	25%
Europe and North America	13%
Caribbean	10%
Central America	8%
South America	7%
Sub-Saharan Africa	5%
Middle East and North Africa	4% -

What is the legal status of immigrants?

45%
23%
5%
27%

- Naturalized citizens
- Lawful permanent residents
- Temporary lawful
- Unauthorized

Do immigrants help the economy?

25% of new businesses are started by immigrants

20% of Fortune 500 CEOs are immigrants

10% of Americans work for a private company owned by an immigrant

OPEN

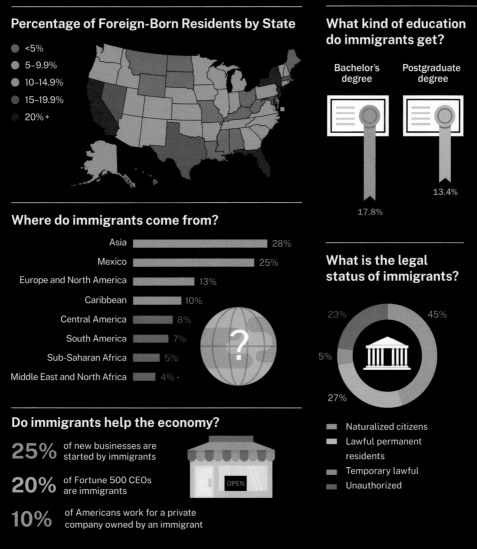

SOURCES: Jynnah Radford, "Key Findings about U.S. Immigrants," Pew Research Center, June 17, 2019; Jynnah Radford and Luis Noe-Bustamante, "Facts on U.S. Immigrants, 2017: Statistical Portrait of the Foreign-Born Population in the United States," Pew Research Center, June 3, 2019; U.S. Census Bureau, "American Community Survey," November 2018; Sari Pekkala Kerr and William R. Kerr, "2018 Immigrant Entrepreneurship in America: Evidence from the Survey of Business Owners 2007 & 2012," National Bureau of Economic Research, www.nber.org/papers/w24494.

civil rights culminated in President Franklin Roosevelt's decision during World War II, after the Japanese government attacked a U.S. naval base at Pearl Harbor, to forcibly confine 120,000 people of Japanese descent—including 90,000 American citizens—in internment prisons. These facilities were characterized by overcrowding, insufficient food, and primitive sanitary facilities. But the Supreme Court ruled that the internment was constitutional on the grounds of military necessity.[45]

Although in 1944 Roosevelt ended internment, many Japanese Americans never recovered from the property losses and health problems they had suffered from it. Fueled by the civil rights movement of the 1960s, they viewed internment as racial oppression and formed a movement centered on securing an apology and monetary reparations. Their work culminated in the **Civil Liberties Act of 1988**, historic legislation in which the federal government acknowledged their internment as a "grave injustice" that had been "motivated largely by racial prejudice, wartime hysteria, and a failure of political leadership." The act also provided reparations of $20,000 to each surviving Japanese American.[46]

Civil Liberties Act of 1988 a historic piece of legislation in which the federal government formally acknowledged the forced removal and internment of Japanese people as an injustice that had been motivated largely by racial prejudice

In addition to anti-immigrant legislation passed by Congress, the Supreme Court created legal obstacles for Asian Americans in the early twentieth century. In *Ozawa v. United States* (1922)[47] it ruled that because people of Japanese descent were not White, they were "ineligible for citizenship." One year later, it delivered a similar ruling concerning a Sikh immigrant from India. In *United States v. Bhagat Singh Thind* (1923),[48] the Court ruled that because Thind was of Indian descent he was ineligible for naturalization and could not become an American citizen. And the Supreme Court upheld Japanese internment in *Korematsu v. United States* (1944). These cases contributed to growing anti-Asian discrimination in the United States.[49]

Despite these political and legal barriers, Asian Americans have been active participants in expanding civil rights. Activists such as Yuri Kochiyama and Grace Lee Boggs participated in the civil rights movement and saw the importance of group solidarity and collective struggle. After the 1960s, a new sense of group solidarity among Asian immigrant groups developed as they pursued new political demands.

Native Americans

Since Native peoples inhabited the North American continent before European settlers arrived, land became a focus of struggle as the United States developed. In the early 1800s the courts had defined each Indian tribe as a nation and thus declared them noncitizens of the United States. In fact, in 1823, the Supreme Court declared that Native Americans did not actually own the land upon which they lived.[50] Subsequently, the 1830 Indian Removal Act forced many Native tribes and nations to give up their lands east of the Mississippi River and forcibly removed them to tribal "reservations" on less desirable lands west of the

Mississippi. During this process of forced removal, thousands of Native Americans lost their lives.

In 1924, Congress passed the Indian Citizenship Act and granted citizenship to all Native peoples born in the United States. Yet their history of citizenship is complicated: the Citizenship Act is part of a longer history of the federal government's attempts to coerce Native peoples into giving up sovereignty as members of independent nations and assimilating. Though Native Americans were now citizens, it was unclear whether the government viewed them as individuals or as members of Native tribes and nations. Several pieces of legislation enacted in the nineteenth century, including the Dawes Act (1887), sought to break up the various tribes by encouraging individuals to leave their tribal groups and strike out on their own. The 1934 Wheeler-Howard Law, however, renewed tribal rights and tribal self-government, though individuals were still free to leave their tribal lands.

Despite the problems associated with tribal reservations, strengthened tribal sovereignty gave Native Americans an instrument through which to achieve a measure of political influence. In the 1960s, they used tribes and nations as vehicles for militant protest and court litigation to improve their situation. Calling their movement "Red Power," Native activists sought to raise public awareness about issues such as the need to reclaim sovereignty, ongoing police brutality, and a long list of broken treaties. Applying the strategy of collective action, organizations such as the American Indian Movement and the National Indian Youth Council demanded the federal government honor its treaty obligations and do more to protect the civil rights of Native Americans. As a result of mobilization through the Red Power movement, new federal laws were passed. The federal government responded with the Indian Self-Determination and Education Assistance Act, which began to provide Native Americans more control over land.[51]

Native nations' sovereign status has also seen gains. Most significant in economic terms was a 1987 Supreme Court decision that freed Native nations from most state regulations prohibiting gambling. The establishment of casino gambling on tribal lands has brought a substantial flow of needed income to reservations.

Disabled Americans

The concept of rights for disabled people emerged in the 1970s from a little-noticed provision (Section 504) of the 1973 Rehabilitation Act, which outlawed discrimination against individuals on the basis of disabilities. As it did with many other groups, the law helped give rise to the movement demanding rights.[52] Inspired by the NAACP's use of a legal defense fund, the disability movement founded the Disability Rights Education and Defense Fund to press its legal claims.

The movement's greatest success has been passage of the Americans with Disabilities Act (ADA) of 1990, which guarantees disabled people access to public spaces and prohibits discrimination in employment, housing, and health care.[53] The law's impact has been far-reaching, as businesses and public facilities have installed ramps, elevators, and other devices to meet its requirements.[54]

LGBTQ Americans

In recent decades, the lesbian, gay, bisexual, transgender, and queer (LGBTQ) movement has become one of the largest civil rights movements in America. For most of American history, any sexual orientation other than heterosexuality was considered "deviant," and many states criminalized sexual acts considered "unnatural." People who identified as LGBTQ were usually afraid to reveal their sexual orientation for fear of the consequences, including being fired from their jobs, and police in many cities raided bars and other establishments where they gathered. While their political participation was not formally restricted, they faced the likelihood of discrimination, prosecution, and even violence.[55]

The contemporary LGBTQ movement began in earnest in the 1960s. In 1962, Illinois became the first state to repeal its sodomy laws. And the movement drew national attention in 1969 after patrons at the Stonewall Inn, a gay bar in New York City, rioted when police attempted to raid the establishment. In an effort to raise public awareness, the first march for gay rights was held in New York the following year to mark the anniversary of the Stonewall riots, and gay pride parades now take place annually in dozens of cities nationwide.

No Supreme Court ruling or national legislation explicitly protected gay and lesbian people from discrimination until 1996. After losing the first gay rights case decided by the Court, *Bowers v. Hardwick* (see Chapter 4), the LGBTQ movement brought test cases challenging local ordinances restricting the right to marry and allowing discrimination in employment, adoption, and parental rights.

In 2015 the Supreme Court legalized same-sex marriage nationwide with its decision in *Obergefell v. Hodges*. Supporters outside the Supreme Court and across the country celebrated the landmark decision.

In 1996 the Supreme Court, in *Romer v. Evans*, explicitly extended civil rights protections to gay and lesbian people by declaring unconstitutional a 1992 amendment to the Colorado state constitution that prohibited local governments from passing ordinances to protect gay rights.[56] Then in 2003, in *Lawrence v. Texas*, the Court overturned *Bowers* and extended the right to privacy to sexual minorities. In 2015, the Supreme Court's decision in **Obergefell v. Hodges** guaranteed same-sex couples the right to marry in all states and required states to recognize same-sex marriages performed in other jurisdictions.[57]

Obergefell v. Hodges court decision that guaranteed the right to marry to same-sex couples

Check your understanding

5. Which of the following statements concerning women's equality is correct?

   a) With the ratification of the Nineteenth Amendment in 1920, all barriers were removed, enabling all women in the United States to vote.

   b) The Equal Rights Amendment (ERA), which states that "equality of rights under the law shall not be denied or abridged by the United States or by any State on account of sex," was ratified in 1982.

   c) The Seneca Falls Convention in 1848 began the modern women's movement, with the adoption of a Declaration of Sentiments and Resolutions.

   d) According to Title IX, college and university procedures concerning sexual harassment and assault on campus must first and foremost ensure that the accused receive due process and the burden of proof be placed on the accuser.

6. How have Supreme Court decisions over the past few decades shaped LGBTQ rights?

   a) Over time, Supreme Court rulings have taken a narrower view of the constitutional right to privacy, resulting in fewer LGBTQ rights and protections now.

   b) Over time, the LGBTQ movement has had important wins from the Supreme Court in challenging local ordinances restricting the right to marry, allowing workplace discrimination, and restricting adoption and parental rights.

   c) The Supreme Court has nearly always ruled that state governments have the ultimate authority concerning LGBTQ rights, producing wide disparities in the treatment of LGBTQ people.

   d) While LGBTQ rights in the workplace have been expanded through recent court rulings, there have been no gains in marriage and parental rights.

Civil Rights Today

Describe key issues of civil rights that continue to impact American politics

Despite considerable progress, the struggle for civil rights continues. Today, in a resurgence of civil rights activism, new social movements are applying past strategies but are updating them in important ways, including using social media as a tool in shifting public opinion.

Affirmative Action

Beginning in the 1960s, the relatively narrow goal of equalizing educational and economic opportunity by eliminating discriminatory barriers evolved into the broader goal of **affirmative action**—policies designed to compensate for disadvantages due to past discrimination and to encourage greater diversity. Such policies address race, gender, or some other status in order to provide greater opportunities to historically disadvantaged groups. For example, in 1965, President Lyndon Johnson issued executive orders promoting minority employment in the federal civil service and in companies doing business with the government.

affirmative action government policies or programs that seek to redress past injustices against specified groups by making special efforts to provide members of those groups with access to educational and employment opportunities

Affirmative action also involved efforts by the Department of Health, Education, and Welfare to shift the focus of "desegregation" efforts to "integration."[58] These agencies, sometimes using court orders, required school districts to present plans for busing children across district lines, for closing certain schools, and for redistributing faculties as well as students. These efforts, enforced by threats of ending federal grants-in-aid, dramatically increased the number of children attending integrated classes.

Efforts by the government to shape affirmative action today generally center on one key issue: What is the appropriate level of judicial scrutiny in affirmative action cases? That is, on whom should the burden of proof be placed: the person or organization seeking to show that discrimination has not occurred, or the individual attempting to show that discrimination has occurred?

This question is difficult because the cases in which the Court scrutinized and struck down racially discriminatory laws—cases like *Brown* and *Loving*—all involved discrimination against historically disadvantaged racial groups. The Court concluded that these laws were motivated by racial hostility, which is not a valid government purpose, and that the disadvantaged groups were effectively unable to use the political process to challenge laws that harmed them.

Instead of being motivated by racial hostility, the new laws were enacted with the objective of assisting victims of past injustice. And instead of harming minority groups, they disadvantaged members of the dominant majority racial group. Yet critics argued that discriminating against *any* individual because of race violated the equal protection clause.

The Supreme Court directly addressed this question in 1978 in the case of Allan Bakke. Bakke, a White male, sued the medical school of the University of California at Davis on the grounds that in denying him admission, the school had discriminated against him on the basis of his race. That year, the school had reserved 16 of 100 admission slots for minority applicants.

Although the Court ruled in Bakke's favor and ordered him admitted to the medical school, it stopped short of declaring affirmative action unconstitutional. It accepted the school's argument that achieving "a diverse student body" was a "compelling public purpose" but found that using a rigid quota of admission slots assigned on the basis of race violated the Fourteenth Amendment's equal protection clause. Thus, the Court permitted universities (and other schools and businesses) to continue to consider minority status but limited the use of quotas to situations in which (1) previous discrimination had been shown and (2) the quotas served more as a guideline than as a precisely defined ratio.[59]

The status of affirmative action remained ambiguous in 2003, when the Court decided two cases involving the University of Michigan. The first alleged that by automatically adding 20 points (out of a maximum of 150) to the ratings of Black, Latino, and Native American applicants, the undergraduate admissions office discriminated unconstitutionally against White students. The Court agreed, saying that the policy amounted to a quota because it lacked the necessary "individualized consideration" and instead used a "mechanical one," based too much on the extra minority points.[60]

In the second case, Michigan's law school was sued on the grounds that its admissions policy discriminated against White applicants with equal or superior grades and scores on law board exams. The Supreme Court sided with the law school; applying strict scrutiny, they found that it was tailored to a compelling state interest in diversity because it gave a "highly individualized, holistic review of each applicant's file" in which race counted but was not used in a "mechanical" way.[61] This ruling—that diversity in education is a compelling state interest and that racial categories can be used to serve that interest—put affirmative action on stronger constitutional ground.[62] In 2022, the Court announced it would hear two new challenges to affirmative action, this time involving Harvard College and the University of North Carolina.[63] Activists on both sides have mobilized because these cases represent a significant challenge to the future of affirmative action.

Immigration

Despite the diversity of immigrants in the United States, the issue of immigration is contentious—especially as it relates to rights and eligibility for public services. In particular, the debate has heated up around the status of unauthorized immigrants as lawmakers have weighed economic, national security, and humanitarian concerns. The Supreme Court has ruled that unauthorized immigrants are eligible for education and emergency medical care but can be denied other government benefits.[64]

One priority for immigration advocacy groups has been the status of undocumented immigrants who were brought to the United States as children and have no real ties to their nation of birth. The DREAM Act was introduced in Congress in 2001 with the aim of allowing such individuals to become permanent legal residents through military service or college attendance. It has been defeated every year since, however, on the grounds that it would encourage unauthorized immigration.

Deferred Action for Childhood Arrivals (DACA) a government program intended to allow undocumented immigrants who were brought to the United States as minors to legally remain in the country to study or work

Absent legislation, the Department of Homeland Security instituted its own policy, **Deferred Action for Childhood Arrivals (DACA)**, instructing immigration officials to take no action to deport law-abiding people who as children entered the United States unauthorized. DACA is a temporary shield for a specific period (often two years) from removal proceedings. During this time, a person may obtain a work permit or attend school but does not have formal legal status. Legal experts and politicians are divided over the constitutionality of DACA. In 2021 a federal judge in Texas ruled that DACA was unlawful but allowed it to continue for current recipients. In response to continuing legal challenges, the Biden administration moved to provide more formal protections to DACA by issuing a rule that codified DACA as a federal regulation.

Another issue is federal cooperation with local and state law-enforcement agencies to enforce federal immigration laws. Several cities and states have declared themselves "sanctuaries" and declined to cooperate with federal immigration agents. The administration responded by threatening to cut off federal funding from local governments that failed to help federal authorities.

Immigration was a very divisive topic during the 2016 presidential election campaign. Seeking the Republican nomination, Donald Trump promised to build a wall along the U.S. border with Mexico, institute a temporary ban on Muslims traveling to the United States, and greatly reduce the Obama administration's resettlement program for refugees.[65] After taking office, he promptly began implementing these campaign promises. Numerous immigration rights groups such as United We Dream and Mijente mobilized to protest these restrictive policies and were instrumental in limiting their impact. As a result of organized protest around immigration, when Joe Biden took office in 2021 he immediately signed executive

Immigration is one of today's most controversial issues. Supporters of immigration advocate for the rights of undocumented people and believe they should have a path to American citizenship.

orders to begin dismantling the Trump administration's most restrictive immigration policies.

Arab, Middle Eastern, and Muslim Americans

After the terrorist attacks on 9/11, the United States launched a War on Terror and deployed troops abroad to Afghanistan and Iraq. At the same time, Americans who were perceived to be Arab, Middle Eastern, and/or Muslim faced increasing violence and discrimination as part of a wave of anti-Muslim backlash.[66] Some of those perceived to be Muslim had their homes burned, were threatened, and were even killed. According to the FBI, hate crimes against Muslims rose 1,617 percent from 2000 to 2001.[67]

As a result of this increase, the problem of Islamophobia received greater attention. **Islamophobia** involves fear of and discrimination against Islam or people who practice Islam. Studies have revealed that negative news portrayals of Muslims increase hostility toward Muslim Americans and increase support for stringent policies targeting them.[68] Pervasive Islamophobia has negatively impacted the civil liberties and civil rights of Arab and Muslim Americans.[69]

Islamophobia the fear of and discrimination against Islam or people who practice Islam

To push back against increasing discrimination and violence, organizations such as the Council on American-Islamic Relations and the Center for Constitutional Rights have sought greater protection of Arab and/or Muslim rights at

Supportive groups used outside strategies to protest the Trump administration's so-called Muslim travel ban that barred people from certain countries from entering the United States.

the local, state, and national levels—largely through inside strategies working within the political system. Outside strategies came into play when President Trump banned travel to and from Muslim countries: millions of Americans flooded airports and streets in a massive protest that raised awareness and galvanized public opinion.

The Criminal Justice System

More than 2.1 million Americans are currently incarcerated, most in state prisons and local jails. Some have argued that the criminal justice system—including policing, mass incarceration, parole, and the disenfranchisement of formerly incarcerated people—is a key civil rights area in need of reform.

The tremendous size of the incarcerated population means the United States is the world's leading jailer.[70] Yet its size does not reflect rising crime rates but, rather, a shift in criminal justice policy and practice that occurred in the 1980s and 1990s. In particular, the greater discretionary power given to prosecutors, and the War on Drugs with mandatory-minimum sentencing, fueled a growing incarcerated population and longer sentences.[71] Moreover, research shows that the criminal justice system has substantially negative effects not only on those who are incarcerated but also, significantly, on those who are stopped, frisked, fined, and surveilled.[72]

In addition, there are pronounced racial and ethnic disparities in criminal justice contact and involvement. Black people account for approximately one-third of prisoners but only about 12 percent of the U.S. population. About 20 percent of inmates convicted of minor drug offenses have received harsh mandatory sentences. Another 20 percent are awaiting trial and are too poor to post bail. Black people make up a substantial percentage of this group as well. As a result, large numbers of Black people—mainly but not exclusively men—are in prison awaiting trial for relatively minor offenses.

The problems connected to the criminal justice system have not escaped the attention of politicians. Over the last 10 years, there has been a growing bipartisan coalition of members of Congress focused on criminal justice reform. A significant victory came in the form of the First Step Act, a bipartisan criminal justice bill passed in 2018 that focused on reducing mandatory minimum sentencing and on improving conditions in federal prisons.[73]

As we read at the beginning of this chapter, in some states former prisoners lose their voting rights. Since many are poor and members of racial or ethnic groups, different organizations (such as the Florida Rights Restoration Coalition) have mobilized into a movement and pushed for restoration of voting rights to former prisoners—despite the resistance of numerous political elites. In addition, other campaigns pursuing inside strategies are focused on mandating body cameras on police, decreasing time prisoners spend in solitary confinement, and instituting bail reform.

The Racial Justice Movement

Claims of unequal treatment in the criminal justice system fueled the growth of the Black Lives Matter (BLM) movement. Formed in 2013 after the hashtag #blacklivesmatter went viral on social media, the movement became a means of affirming

Sparked by the 2013 killing of Trayvon Martin by George Zimmerman, a member of the neighborhood watch in Sanford, Florida, the Black Lives Matter movement has continued to organize to end police brutality and protect the rights of Black people. Intense protests also emerged after the 2020 police murder of George Floyd in Minneapolis. These were just two of many incidents targeted for protest by the Black Lives Matter movement.

Black people's humanity and calling attention to persistent forms of racism in the United States, including in policing, housing, and education. In 2020 frustration and rage exploded after the killing of George Floyd by a Minneapolis police officer. In particular, the viral video of murder in broad daylight displayed the vulnerability of Black lives and illuminated the continued need to fight for greater civil rights protections. BLM activists charged that Floyd's killing was not an isolated incident but reflected a longer pattern of racialized violence that was connected to the criminal justice system.

The BLM movement's significance is often attributed to its ability to mobilize collective action and to the scale of its public demonstrations: an estimated 20 to 26 million people participated during spring 2020, making it the largest mass movement in U.S. history.[74] As we have seen, changing public opinion is an important goal for social movements, and during the BLM protests in 2020 public opinion concerning race relations and policing dramatically shifted. One survey reported that 67 percent of Americans across racial groups supported the Black Lives Matter movement and that Americans' views on policing became less positive between 2016 and 2020.[75]

But there are ways to measure the significance of social movements beyond size and public opinion. One of BLM's most enduring contributions is its role in transforming the public conversation about race and democracy.[76] BLM made clear that the fight for a multiracial democracy was at stake. In doing so, the movement pushed the nation to confront the continuing struggles of different (and sometimes interconnected) groups, including LGBTQ people, Latino people, Asian Americans, Native Americans, and women. Indeed, intertwined with demands to protect Black lives were calls to protect the lives of transgender people, to address anti-Asian racism, and to return land to Native communities.

The 2020 phase of the racial justice movement also transformed people's understanding of the work that still lay ahead. The fight for civil rights in the

United States has made significant strides forward but it is an unfinished project. There is still much work that needs to be done to protect the future of a truly inclusive multiracial democracy. As we have seen throughout the chapter, one does not have to be a powerful politician to enact change—many of the most remarkable civil rights victories have come from the efforts of ordinary people (often students) who wanted to do something about injustice and worked together to achieve a common goal. As the racial justice movement churns forward, people will continue to draw on the outside and inside strategies of past movements and will innovate new strategies to address the challenges of today.

Check your understanding

7. What is the Supreme Court's position on affirmative action?

a) The Supreme Court has ruled that government does have a compelling interest in promoting diversity and that institutions can consider race as one of many factors in a holistic application process.

b) The Supreme Court has ruled that all affirmative action policies violate the equal protection clause and therefore are unconstitutional.

c) The Supreme Court has allowed the use of quotas in hiring and admissions decisions since it promotes greater diversity.

d) The Supreme Court has upheld affirmative action based on gender but not for race.

8. Which of the following statements about immigrants' rights is true?

a) Congress has passed Deferred Action for Childhood Arrivals (DACA) to allow minors brought to the United States to legally remain for work and to study.

b) Over time, the Supreme Court has expanded undocumented immigrant rights to include access to all public benefits, arguing that they are entitled to the services since they pay taxes.

c) The Supreme Court struck down the Secure Communities program, which initially targeted major drug offenders, violent criminals, and those already in prison, for violations of immigrants' equal protection through racial profiling.

d) The Supreme Court has ruled that unauthorized immigrants are eligible for education and emergency medical care but can be denied other government benefits.

WHAT DO YOU THINK?

CIVIL RIGHTS

Different groups have engaged in collective action and formed social movements that have transformed the civil rights and political and social landscape. As our nation becomes more and more diverse, equal protection of the laws will become more and more important if our society is to succeed and prosper. The tumultuous history of civil rights in America demonstrates that exclusion is a recipe for national calamity. It also demonstrates that struggles for civil rights take time, beginning with political action by a small group of committed individuals, such as Desmond Meade, and often ending with legislation and legal decisions from the highest court in the country.

- Knowing what you know now, do you support the kinds of actions Desmond Meade took in trying to secure civil rights for himself and others? Do you feel that civil rights are absolute, or are there situations in which curtailing them is justified? Explain your response.

- Have you—or people you know—experienced civil rights violations? What was the issue? Was there a remedy—and if so, what did achieving it involve?

- How does a country based on the democratic principle of majority rule ensure that the civil rights of racial and ethnic minority groups are protected? What can and should be done to remedy past wrongs that have continuing consequences (for example, discrimination that caused a racial or ethnic minority group to become an economic underclass)? How would Desmond Meade answer that question? What do you think?

Use 🤘 **INQUIZITIVE** *to help you study and master this material.*

6

WHAT GOVERNMENT DOES & WHY IT MATTERS

In 1991, Suzanna Hupp was eating lunch in a Texas restaurant when a man drove his truck through the window and began shooting. The gunman killed 23 people, including her parents. Suzanna had often carried a handgun in her purse, but had recently taken it out because at the time Texas did not allow carrying a concealed handgun, and she was afraid she would lose her license as a chiropractor if caught.

"Could I have hit the guy? He was fifteen feet from me. . . . Could I have missed? Yeah, it's possible. But the one thing nobody can argue with is that it would have changed the odds," Suzanna maintains. She has since become a strong proponent of gun rights: "One of my bugaboos is gun laws. Anytime we list a place where you can't carry guns, to me, that's like a shopping list for a madman."[1]

Fifteen-year-old Justin Gruber also survived a mass shooting, in his case at the Marjory Stoneman Douglas High School in Parkland, Florida, in 2018. The incident left 17 students and teachers dead but led Justin

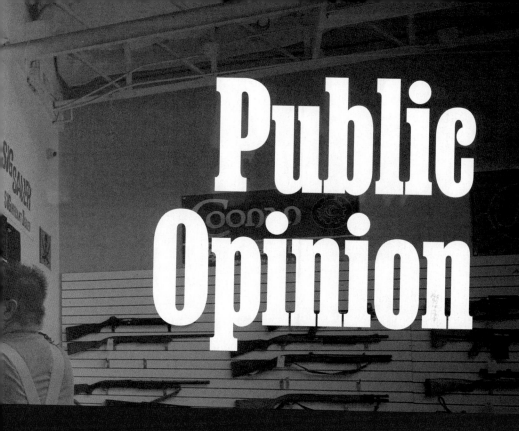

Public Opinion

and many of his schoolmates to the opposite view from Suzanna Hupp's: support for stronger gun control measures such as assault weapon bans and increased age limits for purchase. Objecting to one suggestion raised after the shooting, Justin said that arming teachers is a "terrible idea. . . . Adding guns to solve a gun problem will increase the possible negative outcomes."[2] Some students formed a group, Never Again MSD, known by the hashtag #NeverAgain, to advocate for tighter gun control.

After mass shootings, public support for stronger gun control measures tends to increase. The percentage of Americans telling the Gallup Organization that they wanted stricter gun-sale laws increased 5 points after the 2017 mass shooting in Las Vegas and 7 more points after the Parkland shooting five months later, to 67 percent overall.[3] At the same time, gun sales often increase after mass shootings as gun supporters fear tighter controls.[4] Soon after an incident, however, public outcry tends to fade, and elected officials seem to take no action. In these cases, are politicians following public opinion, or are they ignoring it?

We expect government to pay attention to the people. But whose opinion gets represented in public policy, particularly on issues such as gun control, where there are strong divides among the public? How influential is public opinion relative to other political forces, such as organized interest groups? How well informed are people, and by what

▲ Suzanna Hupp (left) and Justin Gruber (right) were both present during episodes of gun violence. These events pushed Suzanna to advocate for more gun rights, and Justin to speak out for more restrictive gun laws.

channels can individuals make their voices heard? As we will see in this chapter, research shows that public opinion does indeed have a significant impact on public policy. But scholars continue to debate whether the public is sufficiently informed about politics, as well as whether elected officials represent the interests of all Americans or only some.

CHAPTER GOALS

Describe Americans' core political values and ideologies (pp. 163–70)

Describe the major forces that shape public opinion (pp. 170–79)

Explain the relationship between public opinion and government policy (pp. 179–81)

Explain how surveys and big data can accurately measure public opinion (pp. 182–88)

Public Opinion Is Defined by Basic Values and Beliefs

Describe Americans' core political values and ideologies

The term **public opinion** refers to the collective attitudes or opinions that people have about policy issues, political events, and elected officials. Because democratic governments are designed to represent the will of the people, understanding public opinion is critical to understanding American politics. It is also useful to distinguish between values and beliefs, on the one hand, and attitudes and opinions, on the other. **Values (or beliefs)** make up a person's basic orientation to politics and include guiding principles. Values are not limited to the political arena; they include deep-rooted morals, ethics, aspirations, and ideals that shape an individual's perceptions of society, government, and the economy. **Liberty** (freedom), **justice** (fairness or equal treatment), and **equality of opportunity**, for example, are basic political values held by most Americans.

Another useful term for understanding public opinion is *ideology*. **Political ideology** refers to a set of beliefs and values that form a general framework about government. For example, many Americans believe that governmental solutions to problems are inherently inferior to solutions offered by the private sector and free markets. Such a philosophy may predispose them to view specific government programs negatively even before they know much about them.

Attitudes (or opinions) are views about particular issues, persons, or events. The attitude may have emerged from firsthand experience with dilapidated roads or natural disasters, a broad belief about climate change or about the role of government in society, or the political ideology of conservatism or liberalism, but the opinion itself is very specific. Some attitudes may be short-lived and can change based on changing circumstances or new information; others may change over a few years, and still others may not change over a lifetime.

When we think of public opinion, we often think in terms of differences of opinion. The media are fond of reporting political differences between Republicans and Democrats, rural and urban residents, Black people and White people, Hispanics and non-Hispanics, women and men, young and old people, more versus less educated people, people of different religions, and so on.

public opinion citizens' attitudes about political issues, leaders, institutions, and events

values (or beliefs) basic principles that shape a person's opinions about political issues and events

liberty freedom from governmental control

justice the fairness of how rewards and punishments are delivered, especially by governments and courts, but also in society

equality of opportunity a widely shared American ideal that all people should have the freedom to use whatever talents and wealth they have to reach their fullest potential

political ideology a cohesive set of beliefs that forms a general philosophy about the role of government

attitude (or opinion) a specific preference on a particular issue

Political Values

Most Americans share a common set of values, including a belief in the principles of a democracy: liberty, equality, and justice. The United States was founded on the principle of individual liberty, or freedom, and Americans have always voiced strong support for that principle and usually also for the idea that government interference with individuals' lives and property should be kept to a minimum.

Americans have strong views about the importance of freedom of expression. Support for freedom of speech, a free internet, and a free press is higher in the United States than in most other countries: 71 percent of Americans believe it is very important that "people can say what they want without state or government censorship," compared to a global average of 56 percent.[5] Eighty-five percent of Americans believe "the rights and freedoms of all people are respected" is "very important" for our country.[6]

Similarly, equality of opportunity has always been an important value in American society. More than 8 in 10 Americans say it is very important to our country that "everyone has an equal opportunity to succeed." Moreover, most believe that such success should be the result of individual effort and ability, rather than family connections or other forms of special privilege.

Most Americans also believe in democracy, the rule of law, and justice. They believe that all citizens should have the opportunity to take part in the nation's elections and policy-making processes.[7] Figure 6.1 shows there is consensus among Americans on fundamental democratic values, including the importance of free and fair elections, checks and balances of power among the branches of the federal government, the rule of law, and justice—even for elected officials.

Sometimes the political values that Americans espouse are not put into practice. For 200 years, Americans proclaimed the principles of equality of opportunity and individual liberty while denying them in practice to generations of African Americans. Ultimately, however, slavery and, later, segregation were largely defeated in the arena of public opinion because these practices differed so sharply from the fundamental principles accepted by most Americans.

Political Ideology

Americans share many fundamental political values, but the application of these values to specific policies and political candidates varies. As noted earlier, a set of underlying ideas and beliefs through which people understand and interpret politics is called a *political ideology*. In the United States the definitions of the two most common political ideologies—liberalism and conservatism—have changed over time. To some extent, contemporary liberalism and conservatism can be seen as differences in emphasis with regard to the fundamental American political values of liberty and equality.

Liberalism In classical political theory, a liberal was someone who favored individual entrepreneurship and was suspicious of government and its ability

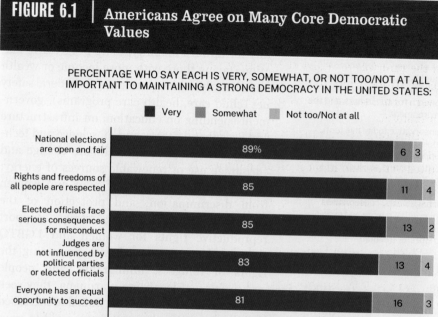

FIGURE 6.1 | Americans Agree on Many Core Democratic Values

PERCENTAGE WHO SAY EACH IS VERY, SOMEWHAT, OR NOT TOO/NOT AT ALL IMPORTANT TO MAINTAINING A STRONG DEMOCRACY IN THE UNITED STATES:

■ Very   ■ Somewhat   ■ Not too/Not at all

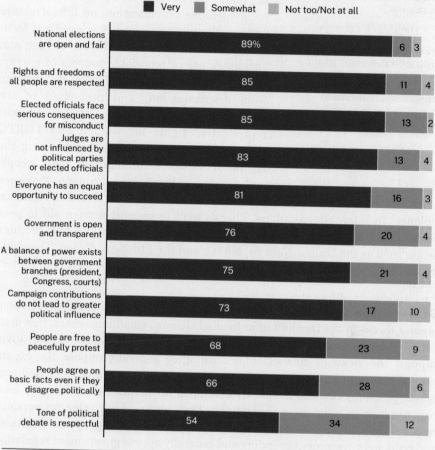

	Very	Somewhat	Not too/Not at all
National elections are open and fair	89%	6	3
Rights and freedoms of all people are respected	85	11	4
Elected officials face serious consequences for misconduct	85	13	2
Judges are not influenced by political parties or elected officials	83	13	4
Everyone has an equal opportunity to succeed	81	16	3
Government is open and transparent	76	20	4
A balance of power exists between government branches (president, Congress, courts)	75	21	4
Campaign contributions do not lead to greater political influence	73	17	10
People are free to peacefully protest	68	23	9
People agree on basic facts even if they disagree politically	66	28	6
Tone of political debate is respectful	54	34	12

SOURCE: Pew Research Center, "In Views of U.S. Democracy, Widening Partisan Divides over Freedom to Peacefully Protest," September 2, 2020, www.pewresearch.org (accessed 11/9/21).

to manage economic and social affairs—a definition akin to that of today's libertarian and many conservatives. The proponents of a larger and more active government called themselves "progressives." In the early twentieth century, however, many liberals and progressives united in support of "social liberalism," the belief that government action (laws and policies) are often needed to preserve individual liberty and promote equality. Today's liberals are social liberals rather than classical liberals. Many conservatives today are classical liberals.

In contemporary politics, being a **liberal** has come to mean supporting government policies to create a fairer economic system and opportunity for upward mobility; more progressive taxation (taxing those with more income or wealth more heavily); the expansion of the federal safety net (child care, health care programs); government spending on education, on infrastructure and broadband access, and on science and technology; measures to fight climate change and encourage use of renewable sources of energy; efforts to protect people of color and women from discrimination; and protection of the environment. Liberals generally support reproductive rights for women and LGBTQ rights and are concerned with protecting the rights of refugees, immigrants, and people accused of crimes. While they are in favor of legalizing marijuana, they seek more regulation of guns and assault weapons that have been linked to increased violence. In international affairs, liberals tend to support foreign aid to poor nations, arms control, free trade, and international organizations that promote peace, such as the United Nations, NATO, and the European Union. They tend to oppose U.S. military interventions in other countries, unless it is to protect an ally.

Conservatism By contrast, **conservatives** believe that a large government poses a threat to the freedom of individual citizens, small businesses, free markets, economic growth, and even democracy. Ironically, today's conservatives support the views of classical liberalism: they generally oppose the expansion of governmental activity, believing that solutions to many social and economic problems can and should be developed in the private sector or by local communities or religious organizations. They place a high value on personal responsibility to solve societal problems. Conservatives support cutting taxes and reducing government spending and generally oppose government regulation of business, including environmental policies that interfere with private business or individual choice.

FOR CRITICAL ANALYSIS

1. In what categories do you see the greatest differences between liberals and conservatives? Why do you think there are greater differences in these categories versus others?

2. How would you describe your own political ideology? Looking at the data here, does your ideology fit with, or differ from, the people who are most like you?

WHO ARE AMERICANS?

Who Are Conservatives? Who Are Liberals?

Political ideology refers to a set of beliefs and values that form a general framework about government. We categorize people as either liberal, conservative, or moderate, but the distinctions are not always clear. Some people have a mix of liberal and conservative opinions. There are significant differences in political ideology across gender, age, education, income, race/ethnicity, and geography, but the largest differences are between Democrats, who are more likely to be liberal, and Republicans who identify as conservative.

Percentage of each group who describe themselves as . . .

● Very liberal   ● Liberal   ● Moderate   ● Conservative   ● Very conservative   ● Not sure

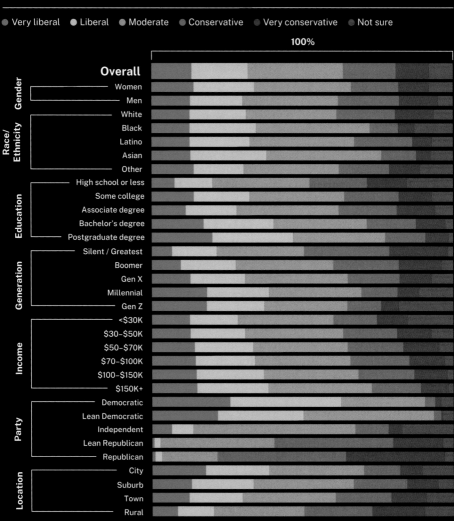

SOURCE: 2020 Cooperative Election Study of 61,000 American adults, https://cces.gov.harvard.edu/.

In social policy, conservatives generally support traditional family arrangements and often oppose legalized abortion and same-sex marriage. Many conservatives prefer stricter criminal justice laws and oppose recreational drug legalization. They favor increased government spending for police, the military, and emergency/first responders. On issues such as immigration, international trade, and the fairness of the U.S. economic system, conservatives are often deeply divided. On foreign trade, business-oriented conservatives favor free trade while social/populist conservatives (such as those aligning with former president Trump) prefer tariffs that reduce trade with foreign countries, including Mexico and China. Business-oriented conservatives often support a legal path to citizenship for immigrants, but social/populist conservatives want to lower legal and illegal immigration and build a wall between the United States and Mexico. In foreign policy, conservatives are also divided. Traditional conservatives support a strong military abroad to protect international free trade and the maintenance of American military power, while social or populist conservatives favor a more isolationist approach. (Who Are Americans? shows how people of different groups describe their political ideology.)

libertarian someone who emphasizes freedom and believes in voluntary association with small government

socialist someone who generally believes in social ownership, strong government, free markets, and a reduction in economic inequality

Libertarianism Other political ideologies also influence American politics. **Libertarians** argue that government policies can interfere with freedom of expression, free markets, and society, and so should be involved as little as possible in both the economy and society. They most closely align with classical liberalism. Libertarians come in many degrees but often oppose business- and environmental-regulation measures and gun control and support legalization of drugs and other policies that reduce government interference in private decisions.

Democratic Socialism While libertarians believe in less government across the board, **socialists** argue that more government is necessary to promote justice and to reduce economic and social inequality. In 2016 and 2020, Vermont senator Bernie Sanders, who calls himself a "democratic socialist," gained support from progressive and liberal Democrats, especially Millennials and members of Generation Z, in the party's presidential primaries. Like Social Democratic parties in Europe, Sanders and House of Representatives member Alexandria Ocasio-Cortez (D-N.Y.), along with the Congressional Progressive Caucus, support market capitalism but favor an expanded government social safety net to ensure more equality of opportunity. This includes free public college, free universal child care, single-payer health care, monthly payments to poor families with children, higher taxes on wealthy people, and protection of workers' rights and unions.

Americans' Ideologies Today Most Americans describe themselves as either liberals, conservatives, or moderates. Figure 6.2 shows that the percentages of Americans calling themselves moderates, liberals, or conservatives have remained relatively constant for the past two decades, though liberals have recently been

FIGURE 6.2 | American Ideology

More Americans identify themselves as "conservatives" than "liberals." During the period shown in this figure, however, Americans have had Democratic and Republican presidents. What might account for this apparent discrepancy? What role do moderates play in the electorate?

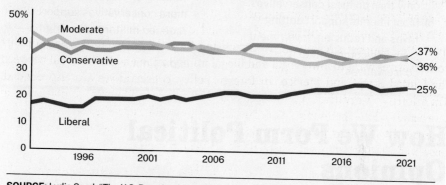

SOURCE: Lydia Saad, "The U.S. Remained Center-Right, Ideologically, in 2019," Gallup, January 9, 2020, https://news.gallup.com/poll/275792/remained-center-right-ideologically-2019.aspx (accessed 5/13/22).

gaining modestly. Gallup surveys indicate that as of 2022, 36 percent of Americans considered themselves conservatives, 37 percent moderates, and 25 percent liberals.[8] Political ideology and partisanship often overlap, but they are different. While liberals make up the largest share of Democratic voters, there is a lot of diversity in the party. Just under half of Democrats identify as liberal or very liberal, while nearly 40 percent identify as moderates and 14 percent identify as conservative.[9] Some moderates tend to hold middle-ground opinions on issues across the board, while others are economically liberal but socially conservative or vice versa.

Check your understanding

1. How do values or beliefs differ from political attitudes or opinions?

   a) Values or beliefs come from an individual's religion, while opinions or attitudes generally come from family or peers.

   b) Values or beliefs are more malleable and can be changed much more easily than opinions or attitudes.

   c) Values or beliefs make up a person's basic orientation to politics and are not limited to the political arena, while attitudes or opinions are views about particular issues, persons, or events.

   d) Values are determined by one's political ideology, whereas opinions or attitudes are not closely related to political ideology.

2. How does liberal political ideology differ from conservative political ideology?

a) Most liberals support greater government intervention in the economy than do most conservatives.

b) Most liberals support cutting taxes and reducing government spending compared to most conservatives.

c) Most liberals support a greater role for religion in government and politics compared to most conservatives.

d) Most liberals support greater funding of the military, while more conservatives support reduced military spending and a more expansive social safety net.

How We Form Political Opinions

Describe the major forces that shape public opinion

As noted before, broad ideologies do not necessarily determine every political opinion a person holds. How are political opinions formed? When and how do political opinions change?

Political Socialization

People's attitudes about political issues and elected officials tend to be shaped by their underlying political beliefs and values. For example, someone who dislikes government regulation of the economy would probably be predisposed to oppose the development of new health care programs. Similarly, someone who values environmental protection is likely to support government policy to address climate change by encouraging use of alternative energy (solar, wind, nuclear). The processes through which these underlying political beliefs and values are formed are called **political socialization.**

political socialization the induction of individuals into the political culture; learning the underlying beliefs and values on which the political system is based

agents of socialization social institutions, including families and schools, that help to shape individuals' basic political beliefs and values

Probably no nation, and certainly no democracy, could survive if its citizens did not share some fundamental beliefs. In contemporary America, the **agents of socialization** that promote differences in political opinions include family and friends, membership in social groups, religion, party affiliation, economic factors like income, and political environment such as region and the media. Other agents, such as public education, promote similarities in Americans' political opinions.

In addition to the factors that are important for everyone, experiences and influences that are unique to each person play a role in shaping political orientation. These may include an important mentor, such as a teacher, coach, or religious leader. A major political event such as the terrorist attacks of September 11, 2001, the surprising 2016 presidential election, or the coronavirus pandemic can leave an indelible mark on a person's political consciousness.

The family is one of the largest influences on a person's political views. Children raised in conservative or liberal families usually, but not always, hold those same views later in life.

Family and Friends Most people acquire their initial orientation to politics from their families. Differences in family background tend to produce divergent political perspectives. Although relatively few parents spend significant time directly teaching their children about politics, conversations about politics occur in many households, and children tend to absorb the views of parents and other caregivers, often without realizing it. Studies find, for example, that party preferences are initially acquired at home, even in households that don't explicitly talk about politics. Children raised in households in which both primary caregivers are Democrats or Republicans tend to become Democrats or Republicans, respectively.[10] Of course, not all children absorb their parents' political views.

Since the divisive 2016 presidential election, some surveys report young people are less likely to date people from opposing political parties, a measure of affective polarization (see Chapter 8), and that marriages between Republicans and Democrats are declining.[11] Research finds that partisans are increasingly avoiding members of the other party in their choice of neighborhood, social networks, and even their partners. Three in ten U.S. couples have mismatched partners in terms of partisanship.[12] Growing up in mixed partisan households may increase political tolerance and affect other opinions.

In addition to family members, our social networks—friends, coworkers, and neighbors—are an important source of political orientation for nearly everyone. One study argues that people are "social citizens" whose political opinions and behavior are significantly influenced by their social networks.[13] When members of a social network express a particular opinion, others notice and conform, particularly if their conformity is likely to be highly visible. The conclusion is that political behavior is surprisingly subject to social pressures. Social networks online may increase the role of peers in shaping public opinion as well.

Education Governments use public education to try to teach children a common set of civic values; it is mainly in school that Americans acquire their basic understanding of democracy and their beliefs in liberty, equality, and justice. At the same time, however, differences in formal education are strongly associated with differences in political opinion. In particular, those who attend college are often exposed to ways of thinking that will distinguish them from their friends and neighbors who do not attend. Education is one of the most important factors in predicting who engages in civic and political activities, such as regularly following the news and voting, as well as in predicting how much an individual will earn over a lifetime—itself another important factor in political beliefs.[14]

Social Groups and Public Opinion

The social groups to which individuals belong are another important influence on political values. Social groups include those that individuals haven't chosen (gender, age, and racial groups, for example) and those they have (political parties, labor unions, the military, and religious, environmental, and occupational groups).

Race Race plays an important role in shaping political attitudes.[15] The experiences of Black people and Asian Americans, for example, can differ significantly. Black people have been victims of persecution and discrimination throughout American history; while many Asians are relatively recent immigrants to the United States, they too can face discrimination. Black people and non-Black people also have different occupational opportunities and often live in segregated communities and attend separate schools. Such differences tend to produce distinctive political views. Many Black Americans perceive other Black people as members of a group with a common identity and a shared political interest in overcoming persistent racial and economic inequality. Political scientists refer to this phenomenon as "linked fate": Black people see their fate as linked to that of other Black people.[16] This linked fate acts as a sort of filter through which Black Americans evaluate information and determine their own opinions and policy preferences.

Even with highly charged issues of race, events and circumstances can cause opinions to change. In 2009, 80 percent of African Americans said Black people and other racial and ethnic minorities do not get equal treatment under the law; the number of non-Hispanic White people giving this response was 40 percent.[17] More recently, widely publicized incidents of excessive use of police force against Black people have caused a shift in public opinion on this issue (see Figure 6.3). Nationwide protests condemning police brutality erupted in May and June 2020 when George Floyd, an unarmed Black man, was arrested and killed by police. The Black Lives Matter (BLM) protests saw millions of people marching in the nation's cities to draw attention to the racial disparities not only in police treatment but in American society at large.

Support for the Black Lives Matter movement is particularly strong among Black Americans. In 2021, 83 percent supported the movement and 58 percent strongly supported it. Majorities of Asian Americans (68 percent) and Latinos (60 percent) also expressed at least some support for it, compared to 47 percent of non-Hispanic White people. There are also large differences by political party, with 85 percent of Democrats and independents leaning Democrat expressing support for the BLM movement compared to 19 percent of Republicans and independents leaning Republican.[18]

FIGURE 6.3 | Perception of Fair Treatment across Racial Groups

In the United States, racial groups may not perceive race relations in precisely the same way. According to the data in this figure, are Black or White people more likely to think that race relations are good? What factors help to account for these differences in perception?

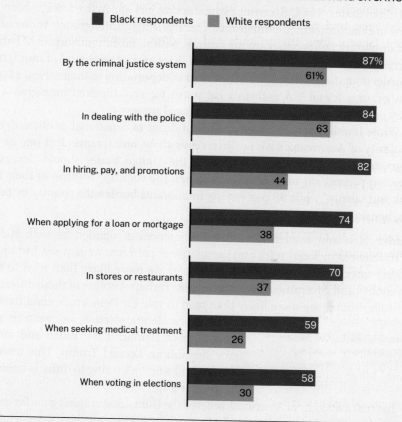

PERCENTAGE OF PEOPLE SAYING BLACK PEOPLE ARE TREATED LESS FAIRLY THAN WHITE PEOPLE IN EACH OF THE FOLLOWING SITUATIONS

- Black respondents
- White respondents

Situation	Black	White
By the criminal justice system	87%	61%
In dealing with the police	84	63
In hiring, pay, and promotions	82	44
When applying for a loan or mortgage	74	38
In stores or restaurants	70	37
When seeking medical treatment	59	26
When voting in elections	58	30

SOURCE: Juliana Menasce Horowitz, Anna Brown, and Kiana Cox, "Race in America, 2019," Pew Research Center, pewresearch.org (accessed 7/15/20).

Ethnicity Ethnicity also affects political attitudes separately from race. Latinos, who make up 19 percent of the total population, are the largest and fastest-growing racial and ethnic group in the United States at 62 million people in 2020. Between 2010 and 2020 this group accounted for half of the country's total population growth. While most Latinos are racially White, their shared ethnic and linguistic background contributes to a group consciousness that shapes opinions. The U.S. Latino population is diverse, comprising people of Mexican, Puerto Rican, Cuban, Central American, and South American descent and people from other Spanish-speaking countries whose backgrounds and circumstances are often quite different.[19] Cubans are more likely to vote Republican, while people from Mexico and Puerto Rico are more likely to vote Democrat. In spite of the differences, however, the Latino population has a growing sense of immigrant linked fate.[20] Generations living in the United States are important for Latino identity.

Nationwide, foreign-born citizens accounted for 13.7 percent of the U.S. population (44.8 million) in 2020, near the century high record set in the late 1800s and early 1900s with immigrants from Europe.[21] Mexico is the top origin country of U.S. immigrants; more than 10 million first-generation immigrants from Mexico live in the United States. The U.S. census estimates that just one in five foreign-born residents are undocumented immigrants. Unsurprisingly, immigration is one of the most important policy issues among Latinos, with significant majorities of Latinos concerned about restrictive immigration policies, unjust treatment of immigrants in border detention facilities, and the threat of deportation to themselves, a family member, or a friend.[22] A path to legal status for unauthorized immigrants is a policy priority for Latinos according to national surveys.[23]

While immigration has been at the forefront of a national political debate, a majority of Americans have positive views about immigrants. Just one in four Americans believe legal immigration to the United States should decrease.[24] Sixty-two percent say immigrants strengthen the country "because of their hard work and talents," while 28 percent say immigrants burden the country by taking jobs, housing, and health care.

Gender Men and women often have differences of opinion as well. Reflecting differences in social roles and occupational patterns, women tend to oppose military intervention more than men do and are more likely than men to favor gun control and government social programs. Perhaps because of these differences on issues, women are more likely than men to vote for Democratic candidates. In the 2020 presidential election, women were more likely to favor Democrat Joe Biden and men to favor Republican Donald Trump. This tendency of men's and women's voting to differ is known as the **gender gap**.

gender gap a distinctive pattern of voting behavior reflecting the differences in views between women and men

In 2020 a majority of Americans believed the United States hasn't gone far enough when it comes to giving women equal rights with men. However, there were significant differences by gender—64 percent of women agreed with the statement, compared to 49 percent of men. Women are also more likely than men to believe there are major obstacles to gender equality, specifically in women's positions of political power.[25]

Religion Religious affiliation, frequency of church attendance, and the belief that religion and prayer are important in one's life are important predictors of opinion on a range of issues. The United States is diverse in terms of religion, including individuals who are Buddhist, Catholic, Hindu, Jewish, Mormon, Muslim, Protestant, and secular (do not follow a religion). Nearly 3 in 10 Americans are secular.[26] Protestants make up the largest religion in the United States. White evangelical Protestants and weekly churchgoers are much more likely to hold conservative views and be Republican, while those without any religious affiliation (just under one-third of Americans) are more likely to hold liberal views and favor the Democratic Party.[27] Religious affiliation shapes opinions on policy. Just over 30 percent of evangelical Protestants believe abortion should always be permitted, compared to 75 percent of those without religious affiliation. Attitudes about LGBTQ rights also show similarly sharp differences.[28] Religion also helps explain opinions on teaching evolution in public schools, environmental policy, immigration, and other issues.

Party Affiliation Political party membership is one of the most important factors affecting political attitudes. We can think of partisanship as red- (Republican) or blue- (Democratic) tinted glasses that color opinion on how we "see" a vast array of issues. Self-identified partisans (individuals affiliating with the Republican or Democratic party) tend to rely on party leaders and the media for cues on the appropriate positions to take on major political issues.[29]

In recent years, political polarization has become a defining feature of Congress, many state legislatures, and the general public. As a result, the leadership of the Republican Party has become increasingly conservative, whereas that of the Democratic Party has become more liberal. These shifts have been reflected in public opinion. Geographic sorting—with liberals choosing to live in neighborhoods, cities, counties, and states that are more liberal, while conservatives move to areas whose populations hold more conservative views—also contributes to political polarization. A recent study based on all 180 million U.S. registered voters found evidence of extensive partisan segregation nationwide.[30] A large proportion of Americans live with virtually no exposure to people from the other party in their residential area, and this partisan isolation is found in both high-density (urban) and low-density (rural) places. Even Democrats and Republicans living in the same city, or the same neighborhood, are segregated by party.

Economic Class Another way that membership in groups can affect political beliefs is through economic self-interest. On many issues, for example, the interests of rich people and people in poverty differ significantly. Today, 61 percent of Americans say there is too much income inequality in the United States, including 41 percent of Republicans and 78 percent of Democrats. But while there might be agreement on the problem, there are huge disagreements about the solution.

Generation Natural group differences in interest also exist between generations. Millennials (born 1981–96) and Generation Z (born 1997 and later), for example, are much more accepting of legalization of marijuana and of LGBTQ rights than are older-age cohorts, and they are also more concerned about social injustice and criminal justice policies, the cost of a college education and housing, climate change, and privacy and security online (government surveillance). Older citizens, on the other hand, are more concerned than younger citizens with protecting Social Security, prescription drug prices, and Medicare benefits.

Region U.S. regions have distinct political histories that shape how people understand current events and policy issues. If you live in the South, you are more likely to be exposed to others with conservative viewpoints, while the reverse is true for the Northeast and Northwest. More people describe themselves as moderates in the Midwest and West.[31] Regions and geography affect how people understand their world, including climate change, which some contend has contributed to an increase in weather-related disasters. Americans living in regions the hardest hit by extreme weather are more likely to say global warming should be a high priority for the next president or Congress. This includes people living in coastal areas, near the southern border, and in the mountain West.

Political Leaders

All government leaders try to influence or manage public opinion. But the extent to which citizen attitudes are affected by government public relations can be limited. Often, claims made by political leaders are disputed by the media, interest groups, and the opposing political party.

These challenges haven't stopped modern presidents and congressional leaders from focusing a great deal of attention on shaping public opinion to support their policy agendas. Franklin Delano Roosevelt did so through his famous "fireside chat" radio broadcasts. Barack Obama's White House was the first to use digital and social media to promote the president's policy agenda, especially national health care reform.

Though Obama was the first president to use social media, Donald Trump was the nation's first Twitter president. Trump communicated his sentiments on politics like no other president in modern history, although his tweets often contradicted his own staff—and sometimes even himself. He used Twitter for proposing policies, making announcements, attacking his enemies, defending himself, promoting his party and his policies, and just plain venting. Laced with emotion and frequent typos, his tweets projected authenticity, even if they were not always factually correct.

Political Knowledge

The underlying factors that shape individuals' political attitudes remain relatively constant through time: one's level of education, for example, is generally set by early adulthood. However, individuals also encounter new information from political leaders, personal experience, and the media throughout their lives.

Presidents have used a variety of methods over the years to help shape public opinion in support of their policies. President Franklin D. Roosevelt held "fireside chats," or radio broadcasts that highlighted his policy goals. President Trump frequently tweeted about policies and other politicians to promote his agenda.

Donald J. Trump
@realDonaldTrump

I am SUBSTANTIALLY LOWERING MEDICARE PREMIUMS. Have instituted Favored Nations Clause and Rebates on Drug Companies. Never been done before. Drug companies are hitting me with Fake Ads, just like sleepy Joe. Be careful! Drug prices will be reduced massively, and soon.

8:03 AM · Sep 17, 2020 · Twitter for iPhone

AMERICA | SIDE BY SIDE

Comparative Trust in Government

A well-functioning government should generate confidence in its citizens. When citizens in various countries are asked about their level of trust in their government, we see a large disparity in the responses. In the most recent data from the Organization for Economic Co-operation and Development, confidence in national governments runs from the very low — less than 20% in Chile — to over 80% in countries such as Switzerland and Norway. The United States falls in the middle of this selected group of economically developed countries.

1. What factors do you think might explain why the population in some countries have more confidence in their national government than in others? What is different about the Dutch and German governments than, say, the Belgian or British governments that might lead to such differences in survey responses? What are the consequences of having either a high or a low level of trust in one's government?

2. In surveys of Americans in recent years, responses about trust in government have correlated strongly with partisan identification; Democrats trust the national government more when the president is Democratic, and Republicans do so when the White House is controlled by a Republican. Do you believe the country can rebuild a broader base of trust in the government that transcends partisan polarization? If so, how? If not, what do you believe are the implications of this for American democracy?

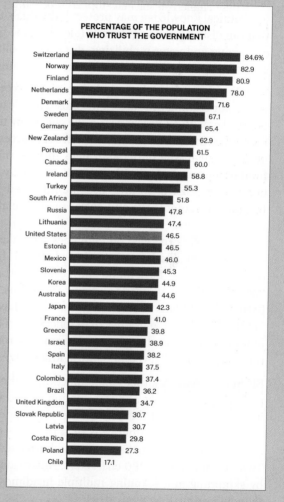

PERCENTAGE OF THE POPULATION WHO TRUST THE GOVERNMENT

Country	Percentage
Switzerland	84.6%
Norway	82.9
Finland	80.9
Netherlands	78.0
Denmark	71.6
Sweden	67.1
Germany	65.4
New Zealand	62.9
Portugal	61.5
Canada	60.0
Ireland	58.8
Turkey	55.3
South Africa	51.8
Russia	47.8
Lithuania	47.4
United States	46.5
Estonia	46.5
Mexico	46.0
Slovenia	45.3
Korea	44.9
Australia	44.6
Japan	42.3
France	41.0
Greece	39.8
Israel	38.9
Spain	38.2
Italy	37.5
Colombia	37.4
Brazil	36.2
United Kingdom	34.7
Slovak Republic	30.7
Latvia	30.7
Costa Rica	29.8
Poland	27.3
Chile	17.1

SOURCE: "Trust in Government," Organization for Economic Co-operation and Development, https://data.oecd.org/gga/trust-in-government.htm (accessed 10/29/21).

In general, knowledgeable citizens are better able to evaluate new information and determine whether it is relevant to and consistent with their beliefs and opinions; they are also more likely to be partisans and to have an ideology (such as liberal or conservative).[32] As a result, better-informed individuals can recognize their political interests and act consistently to further those interests.[33] Researchers found that the average American has little formal knowledge of policy debates or of political institutions, processes, or leaders. Many Americans cannot name their member of Congress and do not know that U.S. senators serve six-year terms.[34] Researchers also found that people who have more education and higher incomes are more likely to be informed about politics. As a result, people with more income and education have a disproportionate influence in politics and are better able to get what they want from government.

Political knowledge may protect individuals from exposure to misinformation that can distort public opinion. While social media have created new platforms for organizing and voter mobilizing, discussing politics, and creating networks, they have also been associated with increased misinformation (see Chapter 7).

Shortcuts and Cues Because being informed requires an investment of time and energy for reading the daily news, most Americans try to get political information and make political decisions "on the cheap" by using shortcuts. Researchers have found that individuals rely on cues from sources they trust—party elites, interest groups, and media outlets—to help them form their attitudes.[35] Today, tweets from trusted elected officials are an increasingly important source of information. Other "inexpensive" ways to become informed involve taking cues from trusted friends, social networks and social media, relatives, colleagues, and sometimes religious leaders.

The public's reliance on elite cues has taken on new significance in today's era of political polarization. As elected officials have become increasingly divided, political scientists have found stark evidence that this new environment changes how citizens form opinions and make decisions. Notably, polarization means that party endorsements of an issue or candidate have a larger impact on public opinion than they used to. Rather than reflecting on an issue, people are more likely to jump to conclusions based on endorsements from party leaders. Polarization may thus reduce overall levels of political knowledge.[36]

Skim and Scan Another factor affecting political knowledge is the *form* in which people consume news and information. The transformation of media in the digital era has changed the way the news is reported and how citizens learn about politics. Today most Americans read the news online. Recent research also indicates a trend in journalism toward shorter articles and flashier headlines, and Twitter limits text to 280 characters. Americans today are likely to read the news by skimming and scanning multiple headlines online, in bits and bytes, rather than by reading long news articles.[37]

Costs to Democracy Low levels of political knowledge pose problems for democratic governments. People who lack political knowledge cannot effectively defend their interests, rights, and freedoms and can easily become losers in political struggles and government policy. The presence of large numbers of misinformed citizens means that people can more easily be manipulated by political elites, the media, foreign governments, and special interests that seek to shape public opinion.

The public response to the coronavirus outbreak in 2020 shows that lack of political knowledge can sometimes have dire consequences. Early in the outbreak, lack of knowledge of the seriousness of the pandemic hindered public health efforts encouraging wearing face masks and, later, vaccinations to prevent the spread of the disease.

Check your understanding

3. Which of the following statements about the major forces shaping public opinion is true?

   a) Family and friends used to have a major influence over one's attitudes and opinions; however, in the age of social media, this is no longer the case.

   b) With increasing mobility within the United States, there is little regional variation in political attitudes and ideology.

   c) Social group memberships, like race, gender, and ethnicity, exert less influence on public opinion than in the past.

   d) White evangelical Protestants are more likely to hold conservative views, while those without any religious affiliation are more likely to hold liberal views.

4. How do political parties influence political attitudes and opinions?

   a) Most Americans filter their opinions and attitudes through their partisanship.

   b) The parties in Congress are more polarized than ever.

   c) Political parties generally have little influence over people's attitudes and opinions except on matters of the economy.

   d) Political attitudes and opinions tend to influence individuals' partisanship, while partisanship rarely influences political attitudes and opinions.

Public Opinion Can Shape Government Policy

Explain the relationship between public opinion and government policy

Given generally only moderate levels of political knowledge among voters, it's little wonder that politicians are sometimes unwilling to act solely on the basis of public opinion. But one could argue that consulting public opinion is a duty of elected officials in a democracy. Is government policy responsive to public opinion?

Government Responsiveness to Public Opinion

Many studies find that elected officials are influenced by the preferences of the public. Several have found that shifts in public opinion on particular issues do in fact tend to lead to changes in public policy.[38] This is especially true when there are wide swings in opinion on particularly high-profile issues that are relatively simple, such as requiring all Americans to have health insurance, and government aid for those unable to afford it.

Not all political scientists agree.[39] Some argue that voters—even those who are well informed and politically engaged—mostly elect candidates on the basis of social identities and partisan loyalties, not based on reasoned opinions on policy issues. Citizens also change their views on policy issues to match those loyalties. Despite extensive data measuring public opinion, proponents of this perspective argue that citizens and voters rarely influence government policy, even indirectly.

Despite these conflicting views of whether government responds to public opinion, there is reason to believe that the relationship between government policy and public opinion is dynamic, with policy responding to opinion but also opinions shifting based on new government policies.[40] Studies have found that government policy can cause changes in public opinion in areas such as environmental protection, public health, immigration enforcement and criminal justice, welfare reform, the death penalty, and smoking bans.[41] For example, in states that adopted smoking bans, public opinion then shifted to become more critical of cigarette smoking than in states without such bans.[42]

Of course, public opinion and policy often do not align.[43] Sometimes public officials act on their own preferences if they believe doing so will benefit government, businesses, or society, and lawmakers typically do use their own judgment when making policy choices.[44] When elected officials pursue policies not aligned with public opinion, it is often because they view particular groups of the electorate as more important than others. This has been called "winner-take-all politics."[45] Groups or individuals that regularly vote for or contribute financially to a candidate have their interests more closely represented than the general public does.[46]

To what extent do political leaders listen to the opinions of their constituents? To what extent should they listen? Is Calvin's father right that leaders should do what they believe is right, not what the public wants?

HERE'S THE LATEST POLL ON YOUR PERFORMANCE AS DAD. YOUR APPROVAL RATING IS PRETTY LOW, I'M AFRAID.

THAT'S BECAUSE THERE'S NOT NECESSARILY ANY CONNECTION BETWEEN WHAT'S GOOD AND WHAT'S POPULAR. I DO WHAT'S RIGHT, NOT WHAT GETS APPROVAL.

YOU'LL NEVER KEEP THE JOB WITH *THAT* ATTITUDE.

IF SOMEONE ELSE OFFERS TO DO IT, LET ME KNOW.

© 1994 Watterson/Dist. by Universal Press Syndicate

Does Everyone's Opinion Count Equally?

In a democracy, where each person has one vote, it is hoped that elected representatives will implement the policies favored by the majority of the people, and in a general sense this happens in the United States. But when policy issues are more complicated (such as taxation or foreign policy regarding trade and tariffs), the public is likely to have less of a voice. Further, citizens who are more affluent and more educated have a disproportionate influence over politics and public policy decisions. How do more affluent and educated citizens manage to exert outsize influence over policy makers? One way is obvious: they vote at higher rates and are more likely to express their political views and to contribute money to political campaigns.

Research has found that both Republican and Democratic senators are less likely to respond to the opinions of low-income constituents than higher-income ones.[47] Senate votes on such varied issues as the minimum wage, civil rights, and abortion are all more likely to reflect the opinions of the rich. Their influence may explain government policies such as failure to increase the federal minimum wage and the 2017 tax cuts that significantly reduced corporate taxes and reduced taxes paid by the wealthiest citizens, policies that contribute to growing income inequality.[48]

Check your understanding

5. Which of the following statements about government responsiveness to public opinion is correct?

   a) Many studies find that government is responsive to public opinion, especially on high-profile issues.

   b) Government is only responsive to the public during times of national security threats or economic recessions.

   c) While public opinion can influence public policies, public policies do not influence public opinion.

   d) Government responsiveness to public opinion only occurs on foreign policy issues.

6. Why do more affluent and educated Americans typically exert greater influence over government officials and public policy?

   a) Affluent people generally have more popular issue positions, so politicians will generally adopt those to win elections.

   b) More affluent and educated Americans are usually leaders within the political parties.

   c) More affluent and educated people are more likely to vote and engage in other political activities, such as donating to campaigns, which gives them sway over elected officials.

   d) Affluent and educated Americans follow government decision-making closely and form political action committees for each issue to apply pressure on members.

Measuring Public Opinion Is Crucial to Understanding It

Explain how surveys and big data can accurately measure public opinion

Public officials and political campaigns make extensive use of data analytics and **public-opinion polls** to help them decide whether to run for office, how to raise campaign funds, what policies to support, how to vote on legislation, and what types of appeals to make to voters. Understanding how public opinion is measured can help us evaluate claims and arguments made by politicians and political commentators.

public-opinion polls scientific instruments for measuring public opinion

Measuring Public Opinion from Surveys

It is not feasible to interview all 330 million–plus residents of the United States on their opinions of who should be the next president or how the government should improve the economy and create jobs. Instead, pollsters take a **sample** of the population and use it to make inferences (predictions and educated guesses) about the preferences of the population as a whole. For a political survey to be an accurate representation of the population, it must meet certain requirements, including an appropriate sampling method (choosing respondents randomly), a sufficiently large sample size, and the avoidance of selection bias.[49] Random sample surveys are used extensively in business and marketing as well as politics; they ensure that the samples are accurate and reliable predictions of the underlying population. Websites such as RealClearPolitics.com list the results of most political surveys released each day; during elections, this can be dozens of surveys.

sample a small group selected by researchers to represent the most important characteristics of an entire population

simple random sample (or probability sample) a method used by pollsters to select a representative sample in which every individual in the population has an equal probability of being selected as a respondent

Representative Samples One way to obtain a representative sample is what statisticians call a **simple random sample (or probability sample)**. To take such a sample, one would need a complete list of all the people in the United States, and individuals would be randomly selected from that list. Imagine that everyone's name was entered into a lottery, with names then drawn blindly from an enormous box. If everyone had an equal chance of selection, the result would be a random sample.

Since there is no complete list of all Americans, pollsters use census data, lists of telephone numbers, or national commercial voter-roll files (which, despite the name, include all U.S. adults—registered and nonregistered) to draw samples of people to interview. If respondents are chosen randomly and everyone has an equal chance of being selected, then the results can be used to predict behavior for the overall population. If randomization is not used or some people are excluded from the chance to be selected, then the sample will be biased and cannot be used to generalize to the population accurately. The timing of surveys is important; surveys conducted two months before an election may produce different results than those the week before an election, because public opinion may change during this time as one candidate gains momentum over the other.

Another method of drawing a random sample is a technique called **random digit dialing**. A computer random-number generator is used to produce a list of 10-digit telephone numbers. Given that 95 percent of Americans have telephones (cell phones or landlines), this technique usually results in a random national sample because almost every citizen has a chance of being selected for the survey. Telephone and text message surveys can be accurate, cost-effective, and flexible in the type of questions that can be asked, but many people refuse to answer political ones, and response rates—the percentage of those called who actually answer the survey—have been falling steadily, now averaging less than 10 percent.[50] This can lead to biased results.

> **random digit dialing** a polling method in which respondents are selected at random from a list of 10-digit telephone numbers, with every effort made to avoid bias in the construction of the sample

Sample Size A sample must be large enough to provide an accurate representation of the population. Surprisingly, the size of the population being measured doesn't matter, only the size of the sample. A survey of 1,000 people is almost as effective for measuring the opinions of all Texans (29.5 million residents) as the opinions of all Americans (over 330 million residents).

Flipping a coin shows how sample sizes work. After you toss a coin 10 times, the number of heads may not be close to 5. After 100 tosses of the coin, though, the number of heads should be close to 50, and after 1,000 tosses, very close to 500. In fact, after 1,000 tosses, there is a 95 percent chance that the percentage of heads will be somewhere between 46.9 and 53.1.

This 3.1 percent variation from 50 percent is called the **sampling error (or margin of error)**: the chance that a sample used does not accurately represent the population from which it is drawn. In this case, 3.1 percent is the amount of uncertainty we can expect with a typical 1,000-person survey. If we conduct a national survey and find candidate A leads candidate B 52 to 47 percent with a margin of error of 3 percent, it means the likely support for candidate A is anywhere from 55 to 49 percent and the likely support for candidate B is anywhere from 50 to 44 percent. Thus, in this scenario, the margin of error tells us that despite seeming to trail by 5 percent, B could actually be leading the election (50 to 49 percent)!

> **sampling error (or margin of error)** polling error that arises based on the small size of the sample

Normally, samples of 1,000 people are considered sufficient for accurately measuring public opinion through the use of surveys. Larger sample sizes can yield even more accurate predictions, but there is a trade-off in terms of cost since it is more expensive to survey more people. The consensus among statisticians and pollsters is that the optimal trade-off point—the "gold standard"—is 1,000. Today many surveys conducted online include sometimes hundreds of thousands of respondents, making their predictions potentially even more accurate. But if the sample is biased or does not reflect the electorate, even very large surveys can be wrong.

Survey Design and Question Wording Even with a good sample design, surveys may fail to reflect the true distribution of opinion in a population. One frequent source of measurement error is the wording of survey questions. The words used in a question can have an enormous impact on the answers it elicits. Survey results can be adversely affected by poor question wording (such as giving respondents only yes-or-no choices when many of them favor a third or middle-ground option), the ordering of questions (such as earlier questions encouraging certain responses to later ones), ambiguous questions, awkward questions, or questions with built-in biases (questions that prime answers in some way or another).

Differences in the wording of a question can convey different meanings to respondents and thus produce quite different response patterns. For example, for many years the University of Chicago's National Opinion Research Center has asked respondents whether they think the federal government is spending too much, too little, or about the right amount of money on "assistance for the poor." Answering the question posed this way, about two-thirds of all respondents seem to believe that the government is spending too little. However, the same survey also asks whether the government spends too much, too little, or about the right amount for welfare. When the word *welfare* is substituted for "assistance for the poor," about half of all respondents indicate that too much is being spent.[51]

Online Surveys Today, pollsters are increasingly turning to the use of online surveys, often using techniques similar to those of telephone surveys. Online surveys can be more efficient, less costly, and more accurate than standard phone surveys, and they include much larger samples of young people and provide more accurate results within age cohorts. A lot of polling is now hybrid, combining telephone and online surveys.

When Polls Are Wrong

The history of polling and data analytics over the past century contains many instances of getting results wrong and learning valuable lessons in the process. Opinion polls are best understood as best guesses about the real world but not as predictions of fact. The 2016 election provides a recent example. The vast majority of national public-opinion polls leading up to the election predicted that Hillary Clinton would win the presidency, but in fact she lost.

The failure of opinion polls was repeated in 2020 when they predicted Biden would win the presidency on average by 8.4 percentage points, but he ended up only winning by roughly 4 percent. In some states, like Wisconsin, the polls were off by nearly 10 percentage points. Despite generally predicting the winner of the election, national polls in 2020 saw the highest error rates since 1980.[52] At the state level, presidential polls understated Trump's support by about 3.3 percentage points on average, while overstating Joe Biden's support by about 1 point. Research suggests the most likely cause was that the polls were undersampling Trump supporters, either because they weren't reached by pollsters or they opted out of the surveys.

Social Desirability Effects Survey results can sometimes be inaccurate because the surveys include questions about sensitive issues for which individuals do not wish to share their true preferences. For example, respondents tend to overreport voting in elections and the frequency of attending church because these activities are considered socially appropriate. Political scientists call this **social desirability bias**: respondents report what they think is the socially acceptable response, rather than what they actually believe or know to be true.[53] On other topics, such as their income or alcohol use, people may feel self-conscious and choose not to answer the questions.

> **social desirability bias** the effect that results when respondents in a survey answer questions in a way that will be viewed favorably by others; can lead to overreporting good behavior or socially acceptable answers, or underreporting socially undesirable behavior or answers

Social desirability makes it difficult to learn voters' true opinions about some subjects because people hide their preferences from the interviewer for fear of social retribution (against what might be deemed "politically incorrect" opinions). However, surveys using experiments can be designed to tap respondents' latent or hidden feelings about sensitive issues without directly asking them to express their opinions.

Selection Bias Some polls prove to be inaccurate because of **selection bias**— when the sample is not representative of the population being studied. Selection bias came into play in preelection polls in the 2012 presidential election, when Gallup significantly overestimated Latino support for the Republican candidate, Mitt Romney, suggesting a close race between him and the Democratic candidate, Barack Obama. The Gallup numbers were incorrect because of selection bias.[54]

> **selection bias** polling error that arises when the sample is not representative of the population being studied, which creates errors in overrepresenting or underrepresenting some opinions

In the 2016 presidential election, although most polls predicted the direction of the popular vote correctly in Hillary Clinton's favor, they failed to predict the election outcome. Possible explanations for the polling inaccuracies in 2016 and 2020 included relying too heavily on interviewing only likely voters. This underrepresented some groups that ended up voting at higher-than-usual rates, such as rural, non-college-educated, blue-collar voters, who supported Trump in large numbers.

In recent years, the issue of selection bias has been complicated by the growing number of individuals who refuse to answer surveys or who use voice mail or caller ID to screen unwanted callers. Pew Research Center estimates that response rates for their telephone surveys have dropped to just 6 percent.

The Bandwagon Effect Public-opinion polls can influence elections. In fact, sometimes polling can even create its own reality. The so-called **bandwagon effect** occurs when polling results convince people to support a candidate identified as the probable victor.

> **bandwagon effect** a shift in electoral support to the candidate whom public-opinion polls report as the front-runner

HOW TO

Evaluate a Poll

NEIL NEWHOUSE, PARTNER AND COFOUNDER OF PUBLIC OPINION STRATEGIES, A LEADING REPUBLICAN POLLING FIRM

One of the main ways in which elected officials, other policy makers, the media, and members of the public know what Americans think about government, politics, and policy is the public-opinion poll. How can you know which poll results are credible and worthy of your attention?

We spoke to Neil Newhouse, partner and cofounder of Public Opinion Strategies, a leading Republican polling firm. He gave us these tips for evaluating surveys:

1 **Who did they interview?** Did the pollsters interview adults? Registered voters? Likely voters? Different topics require different interviewees. If you are interested in which candidate is ahead in an electoral contest, for example, you want a poll of likely voters, because they're who are going to make that decision. A poll of adults would be misleading because only a subset of adults turn out to vote.

2 **How did they interview their subjects?** Surveys should strive for a random sample of the target population, meaning all members of the target population had an equal chance of being interviewed. Polls where people opt in to be interviewed do not have random samples and will be misleading.

3 **How many did they interview?** A random sample allows pollsters to draw accurate conclusions about the attitudes of the underlying population. Surveying just 800 people nationwide can provide an estimate of an attitude such as presidential approval. It's just like the doctor's office. The doctor takes a sample of your blood rather than draining your entire body.

4 **What confidence do we have in the results?** Pollsters typically report a "point estimate," for example, "43 percent of likely voters approve of the president's performance." Random sampling also allows calculation of the "confidence interval," how confident we are in the results; larger samples provide more certainty. A confidence interval of plus or minus 3 points means true presidential approval is probably between 40 and 46 percent. A smaller sample might have a confidence interval of plus or minus 5 points, meaning the true answer is probably between 38 and 48 percent.

5 **Over what length of time?** The ideal poll is a "snapshot in time," conducted over three to five days, particularly for outcomes like election preferences.

6 **What survey mode was used?** Was it a live phone call, an automated call ("press 1 for candidate Smith, 2 for candidate Jones"), or on the internet? Each survey mode has a bias. Online polls result in more male and younger respondents. Landline phone surveys yield more older individuals, while cell phone surveys yield more young people. Often it is better to have a live phone call than an automated call, but a live interviewer can introduce bias as well. For example, Donald Trump's support before the 2016 presidential election was 3 percentage points higher in automated polls than in live phone polls, since some people were reluctant to tell pollsters that they were planning to vote for him.

7 **In what order were questions asked, and with what question wording?** To assess trends, it is best to ask the same questions in the same order over time so that you can compare apples to apples. Question wording also matters; quality polls use appropriate wording that doesn't go begging for an answer.

8 **Who conducted the poll?** Look for a name brand, a pollster that surveys on an ongoing basis, not just occasionally. If you never heard of the outfit or it seems obscure, it may not be the most reliable source of poll data.

Go to the aggregators, such as RealClearPolitics.com or FiveThirtyEight.com. They have made some judgments about quality and only include credible polls. And even if some lower-quality polls are included, you can see many poll results at once and triangulate the overall picture.

Not all pollsters are created equal. Here, FiveThirtyEight, an online source that rates and aggregates polls, grades pollsters on a scale from A to F based on how reliably the pollster gathers data and assesses it.

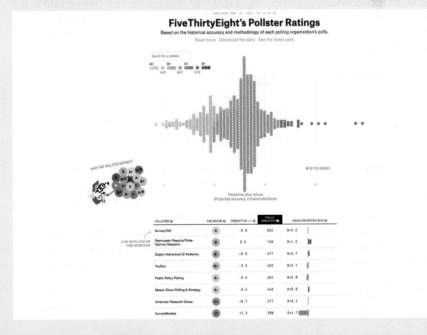

Public opinion is not always easy to interpret, and polls often fail to predict how Americans will vote. In 1948 election-night polls showed Thomas Dewey defeating Harry S. Truman for the presidency, which caused the *Chicago Daily Tribune* to print a banner incorrectly announcing Dewey's win. In 2016 polls considerably favored Hillary Clinton over Donald Trump, causing many to doubt the possibility of Trump winning the election.

This effect is especially likely in the presidential nomination process, where multiple candidates are often vying to be a party's nominee. Researchers found that the change in the amount of national media coverage received by a candidate before and after the Iowa caucuses, the first nominating event, was a major predictor of how well the candidate would do in later presidential primaries nationwide.[55] A candidate who has "momentum"—that is, one leading or rising in the polls—usually also finds it considerably easier to raise campaign funds than a candidate whose poll standing is poor. In 2020, Biden may have benefited from the national and statewide polls showing a wide advantage for the Democrats in a bandwagon effect.

Check your understanding

7. Public-opinion polls sometimes do not reflect the general population due to

   a) simple random sampling.
   b) random-digit dialing.
   c) social desirability effects.
   d) sampling.

8. How can public-opinion polls influence elections?

   a) Polls convince voters to change their partisanship, which can swing elections.

   b) Poll results can create a bandwagon effect in which people are convinced to support a candidate identified as the probable victor.

   c) Polls often cause candidates to adopt more extreme issue positions.

   d) Public-opinion polls often help combat misinformation and fake news among voters, leading to higher turnout.

WHAT DO YOU THINK?

PUBLIC OPINION

In theory, public opinion plays a major role in American politics. After all, a central purpose of democratic government, with its participatory procedures and representative institutions, is to ensure that political leaders will heed the public will.

- It is not always clear what the public will is. How do you think Suzanna Hupp and Justin Gruber, featured at the start of this chapter, would characterize public preferences regarding gun policy?

- Whose preferences should prevail when attitudes differ among groups? Or when they differ between the public and elites? Or between affluent people and people in poverty?

- What are the methods elected politicians use to understand what the public wants? And what do they do when they hear conflicting messages?

- The media are an important source of political information for the public, and the amount and diversity of that information has only grown as politics has migrated online. Do you think the greater availability of information increases the accuracy of public opinion?

Use ▣ **INQUIZITIVE** *to help you study and master this material.*

7

WHAT GOVERNMENT DOES & WHY IT MATTERS

Alexis Wray was the editor-in-chief of *The A&T Register*, the student newspaper of North Carolina A&T State University, the largest historically Black university in the United States, when she noticed something curious about local media coverage. Both television news broadcasts and newspapers had a tendency to use the university as a locator for describing crime events in Greensboro, even when the crimes had nothing to do with the campus or its students. Alexis knew that the media, an essential component of American democracy, have a widespread effect on politics—such as helping set the agenda of topics that Americans think about and discuss, and shaping public opinion on political issues. She worried that headlines such as "Person Shot in Leg at Convenience Store near NC A&T" or "Man, Woman Killed in Shooting near North Carolina A&T State University Campus" fed into stereotypes associating Black Americans with crime and implying that the university was a dangerous institution that local residents might want to avoid. As someone who had planned to pursue journalism professionally, she noted, "The result is a

The Media & Political Information

student body that's made to feel criminal simply for existing. That's not a media landscape I wanted to join."[1]

To study the biases in coverage, Alexis and her newspaper staff worked on a yearlong project supported by the Poynter Institute, a nonprofit organization that trains journalists and supports "fact-based" and "responsible" news.[2] They uncovered similar examples from news coverage near other HBCUs (historically Black colleges and universities) around the country. And they explored the sources of such biases. Alexis notes, "Once I understood that this coverage was built on cognitive bias (at best, in our most generous analysis) or racist tropes (at worst), I realized my role in this project had to change from investigator to problem-solver and solution-maker." Alexis invited local media professionals to join a roundtable discussion on the A&T campus. Her staff shared the results of their study as well as suggestions from a student survey that media include more stories on students' academic accomplishments.

Some of the participants expressed reluctance to change their coverage, noting that using "NC A&T" as a locator was easy and something "they have always done." But after the roundtable, Alexis and her staff did a follow-up study and found that headlines had changed. Stories that might have used the university's name now used other locators. "Just because we've always done something a certain way doesn't mean we can't reassess our processes to see where we might be able to improve them," Alexis said.[3]

▲ Alexis Wray (front right) and the staff at *The A&T Register*, the student newspaper of North Carolina A&T State University, analyzed and worked to change what they saw as biased coverage of HBCUs in the media.

The sharing of information is so central to governance and citizen participation that the Constitution's First Amendment guarantees freedom of the press, and most Americans believe that a free press is an essential condition for both liberty (freedom) and democratic politics. But the media emphasize some issues over others, influencing which issues people believe are important, and frame issues in one way or another, shaping how people think about those issues. As the media have evolved from print newspapers and magazines, television, and radio to today's digital media, questions about their role in government and politics have grown ever more complex. These include issues of emphasis and bias, as in the A&T example, as well as concerns about misinformation—especially in the digital realm, where it can be difficult to tell real news from fake stories. As the nature of the media evolves, a full understanding of America's dynamic media landscape may be more important than ever.

CHAPTER GOALS

Describe the key roles the media play in American political life (pp. 193–204)

Identify the sources of political news and how the news is delivered (pp. 204–13)

Assess why citizens have different levels of trust in the media (pp. 213–20)

The Media Are Indispensable to American Democracy

Describe the key roles the media play in American political life

Freedom of the press is protected under the First Amendment along with the most cherished individual rights in American democracy, including freedom of speech and religion. Political speech is especially protected. In the United States, individuals, groups, private organizations, and companies have the right to publish news, information, and opinion without government censorship and with few government restrictions. In many authoritarian countries, however, there is no freedom of the press, and governments control news and political information through state-sponsored media.

Why would our nation's Founders care so much about the rights of the media to report the news without interference from government? Under British rule, before the American Revolution, freedom of speech and the press did not exist in the American colonies. Criticizing the British king was a crime punishable, in some cases, by death. Today the same thing happens in some nondemocratic countries.

When the colonists won their independence, they wanted to be able to express their political opinions freely without fear of retaliation. The first of 10 amendments to the U.S. Constitution adopted during the Founding period states, "Congress shall make no law respecting an establishment of religion, or prohibiting the free exercise thereof; or abridging the freedom of speech, or of the press; or the right of the people peaceably to assemble, and to petition the Government for a redress of grievances." Even today, most Americans believe that freedom of the press is very important for maintaining a strong democracy.

Key Roles of the Media

Americans generally believe that the **media** should: (1) inform the public about current political issues and events; (2) provide a forum for candidates, politicians, and the public to debate policies and issues; and (3) act as a watchdog on the actions of politicians and government. In the first of these roles, the media serve as a type of public square where citizens become informed about their government, political leaders, societal problems, and possible solutions—a forum where information necessary for democracy is exchanged. After all, information presented by the media helps citizens form opinions about policy issues and make decisions in elections. And part of informing the public involves providing a variety of perspectives and fact-checking sources to ensure unbiased coverage of current events.

> **media** print and digital forms of communication—including television, newspapers, radio, the internet, and social media sites—that convey information to large audiences

The media's role as a watchdog includes investigating political scandals and possible corruption. The *New York Times* has done extensive investigative journalism into Donald Trump's finances and tax avoidance strategies. This reporting sparked lawsuits in New York against the Trump business.

The news media help level the playing field between political elites who have high levels of political knowledge and "the people"—thus giving citizens a more powerful voice in society. Without the news media, the public would not know as much about the actions of political leaders, corporations, or foreign governments and would have less opportunity to challenge them in the face of corruption. Journalists (people trained to report the news) give ordinary people information, and in their hands this information ultimately becomes power.

In their third role, the media serve as a watchdog for the public, scrutinizing the actions of elected officials on behalf of citizens—most of whom do not closely follow the actions of politicians and government. In this role the media notify the public of government actions that may affect them and about what policy issues are at stake in terms of changes in laws and regulations. They reveal which individuals and groups are exerting power in politics, what their goals and strategies are, and what arguments they are using. The media often expose ties between financial interests and political leaders, or corruption or scandalous behavior on the part of elected officials. By reporting the news in the public interest, the media continuously monitor the actions of public officials and strive to protect citizens from government overreach and corruption by serving as a check on political power.

Journalism

Most journalists are trained in schools of journalism and mass communication. They are guided by standards in reporting the news in the public interest, known as the principles of journalism. Above all, journalists seek to report the truth by fact-checking information, using unpaid sources, verifying sources as legitimate and credible, engaging in investigative journalism conducted lawfully and ethically, and vetting content before it is published to avoid libel laws (explained later in this chapter).

principled journalism reporting that involves being as accurate, fair, and balanced as possible, relying on original sources, being transparent about citing sources, and presenting multiple viewpoints

The traditional news media aim to balance coverage of current events by providing factual reporting that carefully avoids including the personal views of reporters or editors. **Principled journalism** involves being as accurate as possible, relying on original sources whenever possible, being transparent about citing sources, and presenting multiple viewpoints. While complete objectivity—reporting the news without bias—is impossible (all individuals have biases that influence how they understand and describe events), it remains a journalistic ideal.

Adversarial Journalism The political power of the news media greatly increased through the growing prominence of **adversarial journalism**, a form of watchdog reporting in which the media adopt a skeptical or even hostile posture toward the government and public officials. This type of

> **adversarial journalism** a form of reporting in which the media adopt a skeptical or hostile posture toward the government and public officials

journalism is a legacy of late-1800s reform-minded efforts to expose corruption, scandal, and other wrongdoing in politics and the corporate sphere.

On the presidential level, the growth of adversarial journalism in the 1960s and '70s represented a reversal of the more cordial relationship between presidents and the media that had developed through much of the twentieth century. Early in the 1900s, by communicating directly to the electorate through newspapers and magazines, presidents Theodore Roosevelt and Woodrow Wilson established political constituencies for themselves, independent of political parties, and thereby strengthened their own power relative to that of Congress. In the 1930s and 1940s, President Franklin Delano Roosevelt used the radio, most notably in his famous fireside chats, to reach out to voters throughout the nation and to make himself the center of American political life. As subsequent presidents used the news media to enhance their popularity, establishing friendly relationships with journalists became a key strategy of presidential administrations.

The Vietnam War (1954–75) shattered this relationship between the press and the presidency. During the early stages of U.S. involvement, American officials in Vietnam who disapproved of the way the war was being conducted leaked to reporters information critical of administrative policy. As the war dragged on, adverse media coverage fanned antiwar sentiment among the public and in Congress. In turn, these shifts in opinion emboldened journalists and publishers to continue to present news reports critical of the war.

The media were also central figures in the Watergate affair, the cluster of scandals that ultimately forced President Richard Nixon to resign from office in 1974. A series of investigations led by the *Washington Post* uncovered various crimes of which Nixon was guilty, leading to threats of impeachment and his subsequent resignation. Thereafter, a generation of journalists developed a commitment to adversarial journalism.

Adversarial journalism continues today. During Donald Trump's presidency, journalists revealed Trump's tax avoidance strategies, including failure to pay federal income taxes over many years. During the Biden administration, journalists focused on high inflation and an uneven economic recovery post-pandemic.

Political journalists sometimes rely on *leaks*, the disclosure of confidential government information to the news media. Leaks may originate from a variety of sources. These include "whistleblowers," lower-level officials who hope to publicize what they view as their bosses' or the government's improper activities. In 1971, for example, during the controversial Vietnam War, Daniel Ellsberg, a Defense

Department staffer, sought to discredit official justifications for America's military involvement in Vietnam by leaking top-secret documents to the press. The Pentagon Papers—the Defense Department's own secret history of the war—were published by the *New York Times* and the *Washington Post* after the U.S. Supreme Court ruled that the government could not block their release.[4] This led to erosion of public support for the war. Most leaks, though, originate not with low-level whistleblowers but rather with senior government officials, prominent politicians, and political activists.

The mass media exposed possible misconduct by President Trump in a July 2019 phone call between President Trump and Ukrainian president Volodymyr Zelensky. A government whistleblower alleged that Trump had pressured the Ukrainian president to open a corruption investigation against 2020 Democratic presidential candidate and former vice president Joe Biden—threatening to withhold $400 million in U.S. military aid if Zelensky didn't comply. The *Wall Street Journal* was one of the first to report that the military aid to Ukraine had been deliberately held up by the Trump administration in the weeks before the phone call. While Trump denied any bribery, the House of Representatives opened an impeachment inquiry of the president. The House voted to impeach Trump in December 2019 on charges of abuse of power and obstruction of Congress. Trump was later acquitted by the Republican-controlled Senate on both counts in February 2020.

As these examples show, without rigorous investigative and adversarial journalism, citizens would not have the means (and information) necessary to hold their elected representatives accountable. Adversarial journalism is a critical part of what makes democratic governments work.

Citizen Journalism Citizen journalism includes news reporting and political commentary by ordinary citizens and bystanders, advocacy groups, and even crisis coverage from eyewitnesses on the scene, thus involving a wider range of voices in gathering news and interpreting political events. Cameras on cell phones give people the capacity to photograph or record events, thus providing eyewitness accounts. At the same time, social media permit users to upload videos that can be viewed by hundreds of thousands of subscribers or relayed by the mainstream media for even wider dissemination.

citizen journalism news reporting and political commentary by ordinary citizens and bystanders, advocacy groups, and eyewitnesses to crises, often using cell phone images or video and distributed via social media

Teenager Darnella Frazier is a vivid example of a citizen journalist. Using her cell phone, Frazier filmed the May 2020 murder of George Floyd, a Black man killed by a Minneapolis police officer during a routine arrest. The officer, Derek Chauvin, pinned Floyd's neck to the ground for 9 minutes and 29 seconds, as Floyd said, "I can't breathe." Frazier uploaded her video to *TMZ*, an online tabloid specializing in entertainment gossip (and one of Frazier's primary news sources), and she eventually won a Pulitzer Prize in the category of Citizen Journalism for her film.

Citizen journalism enriches the diversity of media coverage and provides a key alternative to mainstream news, filling in gaps, exposing corruption or injustice, and even uncovering major factual errors in mainstream media reports. But because citizen journalism is not regulated or professionally edited, these reports may unintentionally spread distorted or false information.

Opinion-Driven Journalism Traditional print newspapers—and today's digital news websites and apps—have separate sections for news reporting and opinion pieces. But as the news media have diversified and gone online, the distinction between reporting and opinion has become blurred. Digital media have given rise to a massive increase in political commentators (also called pundits) and opinion-driven journalists who provide their own perspective on topics of the day, rather than doing original reporting, citing sources, and fact-checking content. A report from the American Press Institute found that more than half of internet users reported that they could not easily tell the difference between news reporting and opinions about the news, particularly on social media.[5] And nearly half of Americans have difficulty identifying whether news sources conduct their own reporting.[6]

The rise of **opinion-driven journalism** in the digital era began with blogs and talk radio where personal commentary entered, and often took over, debates about politics. On these sites and shows, a highly opinionated pundit—not an impartial journalist—offers commentary that may include conversations between reporters and guests. These formats often engage in a form of reporting called the **journalism of assertion**—publishing or broadcasting information and opinion as quickly as possible, with minimal concern for vetting the information prior to its release.[7] This is often paired with **journalism of affirmation**—putting forth opinion and information that is consistent with the consumer's preexisting beliefs.

opinion-driven journalism political blogs and talk shows where the writer or host provides highly opinionated personal commentary, usually through conversations with guests; these formats blur the boundaries between objective journalism and subjective reporting

journalism of assertion the publishing or broadcasting of information or opinion as quickly as possible, with minimal fact-checking

journalism of affirmation the putting forth of opinion and information that is consistent with the consumer's preexisting beliefs

While pundits and opinion-driven journalists draw viewers and listeners' attention to political debates, in these formats providing entertainment often takes precedence over conveying factual information. And this can lead to confusion among consumers. Consider, for example, the birther conspiracy alleging that former president Barack Obama was not born in the United States.[8] The claim was amplified on conservative radio host Rush Limbaugh's show and then became a major conspiracy theory that was eventually proven false[9] when Obama released his birth certificate from Hawaii.

The Profit Motive

Americans expect the media to provide a check on the power of government and political leaders. But who checks or controls the media? In the United States the media are not part of government and not subject to checks and balances

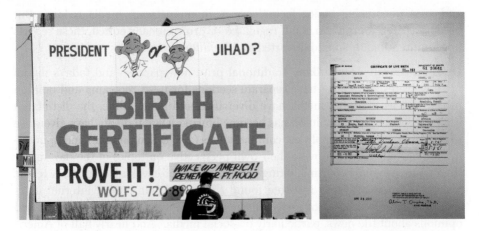

Without traditional media's commitment to fact-checking, digital media sometimes spread inaccurate information and rumors. In 2008 the false claim that President Obama was not a natural-born citizen spread rapidly online and remained a top story even after Obama released his official long-form birth certificate.

like Congress, the presidency, and the courts. Instead, most media in the United States are privately owned for-profit companies, like Verizon, the New York Times Company, Meta/Facebook, Fox Corporation, CNN, or Apple. Therefore, the profit motive is an important factor in how—and how well—the media deliver the news.

Public broadcasting refers to television, radio, and digital media that receive partial funding from license fees and government subsidies. In most other democratic countries public broadcasting plays a major role in informing the public about politics and current events, such as the British Broadcasting Company (BBC). In contrast, public broadcasting in the United States—such as National Public Radio (NPR) or the Public Broadcasting Service (PBS)—plays a relatively small role in the nation's media system and receives very little funding from the government. Public broadcasting in the United States has just 2 percent of market share, compared to 35 percent in France, 40 percent in Germany, and 65 percent in Denmark.[10] According to evidence from cross-national surveys, U.S. citizens have lower levels of political knowledge than those in European democracies, who consume more public broadcasting.[11] Also, other surveys also find that in the United States, levels of political knowledge are higher for people who rely frequently on public broadcasting outlets like NPR.[12]

U.S. media companies earn most of their revenue from advertising, although revenue from subscriptions has been increasing. They are, therefore, motivated by what audiences want, because higher ratings generate more advertising revenue. Because of the need to reach wide audiences to sell advertisements, the U.S. media are more focused on "soft news," such as entertainment, sports, and celebrity news, than are European media, which provide more "hard news" coverage of politics and government. This may help explain why political knowledge is higher in some European countries than in the United States.[13]

AMERICA | SIDE BY SIDE

Global Freedom of the Press

While freedom of the press is a cornerstone of American civil liberties, it is neither as firmly enshrined in law nor as respected as a matter of practice in other countries. This map looks specifically at how "free and independent" the media are in each country. The freedom of the media scale shown here is based on the degree to which media and artists are subject to censorship, self-censorship, and legal and/or physical harassment, among other factors.

1. Where is the press most free and independent? Where is it less so? Are there regions of the world that are better at respecting freedom of the press than others? How does the United States fare in comparison to other countries on this measure?

2. Why might a government want to impose constraints on media operating in its borders? On the other hand, what do governments gain by allowing, or even encouraging, the functioning of a free and independent press?

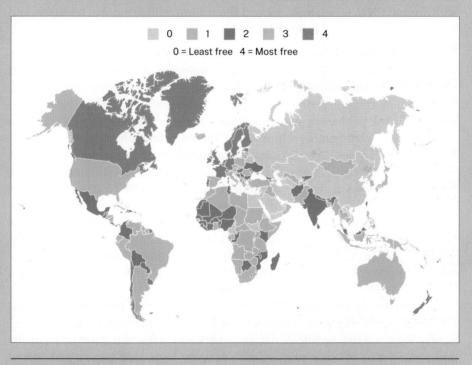

SOURCE: Freedom House, *Freedom in the World 2021,* Report, subcategory scores for question D1: "Are there free and independent media?" https://freedomhouse.org/report/freedom-world/2021/democracy-under-siege (accessed 10/21/21).

And when it comes to political news, American media tend to focus increasingly on more dramatic, highly conflictual events and issues. Sensational stories of scandals, corruption, or candidates' attacks often generate more interest—and thus revenue—than the stories of everyday governing and details of public policy. Nonetheless, objectivity is still the goal, and standard practice is that news, opinion, and ads should be separate and distinct; that is why the opinions of editors and writers are reserved for opinion pages.

The profit motive of the news industry contributed to greater exposure of Donald Trump's presidential campaign, and thus may have helped him win the 2016 election. Due to the novelty of a television celebrity running for president without any previous political experience, Trump's unusual campaign was a financial boon for the media industry. His candidacy received double the media coverage of his Democratic opponent, Hillary Clinton, an established political leader and U.S. senator from New York. The former head of CBS, Les Moonves, said the Trump phenomenon "may not be good for America, but it's damn good for CBS."[14] Throughout the election campaign and Trump's first year in office, cable news channels profited from higher ratings because of the public's fascination with Trump; CNN, for example, earned about $100 million more in television and advertising revenue than expected in 2016.[15]

Mass Media Ownership One noteworthy feature of the traditional media in the United States is the concentration of their ownership. A small number of giant, global corporations control a wide swath of media, including television networks, movie studios, streaming video, record companies, cable channels and local cable providers, book publishers, magazines, newspapers, and online and digital media outlets.[16] The overwhelming influence of **media monopolies**, such as AT&T/Time Warner, Disney, Comcast, and Fox Corporation, has prompted questions about whether enough competition exists among traditional media to produce a truly diverse set of views on political matters.[17] As major newspapers, television stations, and radio networks fall into fewer hands, the risk increases that politicians and citizens who express less popular viewpoints will have difficulty finding a public forum.

media monopolies giant, often global, corporations that control a wide array of media, including television networks, movie studios, record companies, cable channels, book and newspaper publishers, and digital media outlets

Despite the appearance of substantial diversity overall, the number of traditional news-gathering sources operating nationally is actually quite small—several wire services, a dozen broadcast television networks, a few elite print newspapers, and a smattering of other sources, such as a few large local papers and several small, independent radio networks. More than three-fourths of the daily print newspapers in the United States are owned by large media conglomerates such as the Hearst Communications, McClatchy, and Gannett corporations. Much of the national news that is published by local newspapers is provided by one wire service, the Associated Press.[18] Sinclair Broadcasting Group and Nexstar are the two largest local broadcast television station owners in the United States that carry local evening news programs, with 191 and 197 stations respectively.[19]

How the Media Shape News and Information

The content and character of news programming—what the media choose to present and how they present it—can have far-reaching consequences in setting the political agenda for the nation. The media can shape and modify, if not fully form, the public's perception of events, issues, institutions, and individuals. At the same time, the media are influenced by the individuals or groups who are subjects of the news. The president in particular has the power to set the news agenda through speeches, actions, and tweets. And all politicians seek to shape their media images by cultivating good relations with reporters and by leaking news and staging news events.

In American political history, the media have played a central role in many major events. For example, in the civil rights movement of the 1950s and '60s, television images showing peaceful demonstrators attacked by club-swinging police helped to generate sympathy among northern White people for the civil rights struggle and greatly increased the pressure on Congress to end legalized racial segregation.[20] The media were also instrumental in compelling the Nixon administration to negotiate an end to American involvement in the Vietnam War by portraying the war as misguided and unwinnable.[21] In 2020 media coverage of the Black Lives Matter protests on social media helped mobilize people to participate in protests and marches in thousands of U.S. cities and towns.[22]

Clearly, the media influence American politics in a number of important ways. As we'll discuss next, the power of all media lies in their ability to shape what issues Americans think about (through agenda setting or gatekeeping) and what opinions Americans hold about those issues (through framing and priming).[23]

Agenda Setting A key source of media power in politics is **agenda setting**, or gatekeeping: designating some issues, events, or people as important, and others not. The mass media act as a gatekeeper with the power to bring public attention to particular issues and problems. Groups or politicians that wish to generate support for policy proposals must secure media coverage. If the media are persuaded that an idea is newsworthy, such as climate change or inflation, then they may declare it an "issue" that must be confronted or a "problem" to be solved, thus helping it clear the first hurdle in the policy-making process.

> **agenda setting** the media's designation of some issues, events, or people as important and others not

Some stories—such as those about wars, fires and floods, presidential impeachment, political scandal, major health crises, mass political protests, and terrorist attacks—have such overwhelming significance that the main concern of political leaders is not whether a story will receive attention but whether they themselves will figure prominently and positively in media accounts about it. At the same time, many important issues—such as solar and wind power as alternative energy sources, homelessness, impacts of artificial intelligence on low-skill jobs, or election reform laws—don't often appear on mainstream media organizations' agendas. When policy issues are not on the media's agenda, they often receive relatively little attention from politicians.

During the 1960s, civil rights protesters learned a variety of techniques designed to elicit sympathetic media coverage. Television images of police brutality in Alabama led directly to the enactment of the 1965 Civil Rights Act.

Political scientists have shown that the media have two "modes": an "alarm mode" for breaking stories and a "patrol mode" for covering them in greater depth.[24] The incentive to reach a wider audience often sets off the alarm mode around a story, after which news outlets go into patrol mode to monitor what effect (if any) the story has on government policy—until the next big story alarm goes off. This pattern results in skewed coverage of political issues, with a few issues receiving the majority of media attention while others receive none at all.

Political candidates also need the media's agenda-setting role to win elections. Candidates who receive positive news coverage gain momentum: they pick up political endorsements, attract campaign contributions, and win more support from voters.[25] In the 2020 Democratic primaries for president, Joe Biden exceeded the media's expectations with his early win in South Carolina and strong support among African Americans. Biden's victory early in the process earned him increased press attention and led him to win the Democratic nomination.[26]

What the mainstream media decide to report on or highlight and what they ignore or downplay have important implications. For example, federal tax cuts of 2001 and 2003, which were extended in 2010, dramatically increased the federal budget deficit and widened the income gap between the super-rich and most other Americans by significantly lowering taxes for the wealthiest Americans. But the media provided little coverage of this major policy change; the result was that 40 percent of Americans had no opinion on whether they favored the 2001 cuts.[27] Without rigorous adversarial, investigative, and citizen journalism, the people will remain uninformed and unable to participate effectively in politics.

Framing The process of presenting information from a certain perspective to shape the audience's understanding of that information is called **framing**. Each issue or event can be presented through many possible frames, each with a slightly different spin (or slant) in describing the problem and possible solutions. Because the media have the power to include or exclude information, they can influence how events, issues, and people's actions are interpreted and understood. Frames, which political leaders and groups also help to develop, shape the meaning that individuals perceive from words or phrases, photographs, or video.[28]

> **framing** the process of presenting information from a certain perspective in order to shape the audience's understanding of that information

When the Russian military attacked Ukraine in 2022, for example, liberal-leaning media like CNN framed President Biden as a strong leader for swiftly enacting U.S. sanctions on Russian banks and its financial sector. This framing provided favorable coverage of the U.S. response to the international crisis. Conservative media, like Fox News, framed President Biden as a weak leader for not enacting strong enough sanctions targeting Russia's major export of oil and gas; they provided more negative coverage of the U.S. response.

Priming Another important way the media can shape the public's understanding of political events is by **priming**, which involves calling attention to some issues, and not others, when reporting on political events and officials.[29] Through priming, the media have power to alter how voters make choices. While agenda setting is about gatekeeping and what issues the media cover, framing and priming involve filtering the news and providing cues to the public for how to interpret those issues. As with agenda setting and framing, news media are not alone in priming; elected officials, interest groups, and other political players apply all three strategies in hopes of influencing public opinion.

> **priming** the process of calling attention to some issues, and not others, when reporting on political events and officials

Media priming can occur when an issue becomes important in evaluating political candidates. In these cases, the public is likely to judge a politician according to the media's attention to one issue, event, or policy over another. For example, in the lead-up to the 2020 election, the coronavirus pandemic was in the national media spotlight. The public health crisis and the accompanying economic crisis became the most important lens through which the public evaluated the presidential candidates, which ultimately benefited Joe Biden and hurt Donald Trump.

Check your understanding

1. Which of the following statements about the media is correct?

   a) Whereas European media provide more soft news coverage, U.S. media are more focused on hard news coverage of politics and government.

   b) U.S. media companies earn most of their revenue from subscriptions, although revenue from advertising has been increasing.

   c) There is a consolidation of print media ownership, with a majority of the daily print newspapers in the United States owned by a few large media conglomerates.

   d) In the United States, public broadcasting like National Public Radio (NPR) or the Public Broadcasting Service (PBS) represents the largest media share because it has government funding.

2. How do the media influence American politics?

   a) The media serve the government by highlighting the president's accomplishments, which influences how citizens evaluate government.

   b) The media's primary role is working with campaigns to help broadcast candidates' messages.

   c) The media mainly filter inaccurate and ideologically extreme information so that it is unavailable for public consumption.

   d) The media influence what issues Americans think about through gatekeeping and agenda-setting and how Americans think about the issues through priming and framing of news coverage.

There Are Many Sources of Political News

Identify the sources of political news and how the news is delivered

To understand the role of the media in American democracy, we need to understand who creates the news and how they deliver it. These factors greatly affect how people understand and interpret political events.

Sources of Political News

We live in a time when political news and information is literally at our fingertips. With a few taps on a smartphone, we can read Google News headlines, stream television news, or scroll through social media looking for updates on current events. But who produces the news we see? And do these sources fulfill the roles we expect from media in American democracy?

Mainstream News Organizations Mainstream **news organizations** adhere to the principles of journalism as discussed at the beginning of this chapter—they do original reporting, verify sources as credible, and fact-check content. They use unpaid sources, engage in investigative journalism, conduct lawful and ethical interviews, and vet content before it is published to comply with libel laws and avoid defamation lawsuits (defamation is the oral or written communication of a false statement about another person that unjustly harms their reputation and is a crime). To serve the public interest, they aim for balanced and factual reporting that avoids expressing any personal bias on the part of reporters or editors.

> **mainstream news organizations** organizations that adhere to the principles of journalism by doing original, balanced, factual reporting; using unpaid, credible sources; conducting interviews ethically; and avoiding personal bias by editors or reporters

But even scholars of journalism and the media don't agree on which sources of news fall into the mainstream. In 2021, Pew Research Center conducted a large survey of the American public to uncover what most Americans think is the mainstream media, so it can be more concretely defined. The survey found that a majority of Americans consider seven news outlets to be part of the mainstream (see Figure 7.1).[30] Remarkably, both Republicans and Democrats widely agree on these assessments. When asked to name their main source for political news, about two-thirds of Americans (53 percent of Republicans and 78 percent of Democrats) cite mainstream news sources.

Partisan Media In contrast to the mainstream media, some news organizations appeal to users who are strongly ideologically liberal or conservative. **Partisan media** do not prioritize balance with factual reporting to the same extent as the mainstream media, and instead mix in opinion-driven journalism. Partisan media can also be identified by ideological agenda setting and priming and by framing. Conservative media, for example, tend to paint the actions of Democratic president Joe Biden negatively, while liberal media provide negative coverage of Republicans, including former president Trump. In the Pew survey discussed above, news sources not categorized as mainstream were often partisan. BuzzFeed and HuffPost, for example, are read mostly by liberal audiences, while conservatives turn to the Sean Hannity Show, Newsmax, and Breitbart.

> **partisan media** news organizations that mix opinion-driven journalism with factual reporting in order to appeal to consumers who are ideologically liberal or conservative; often characterized by ideological agenda setting, priming, and framing

How the News Is Delivered

As we've just seen, *who* delivers the news is an important factor that influences the news we see. Another important factor is *how* we consume the news—what platforms we use to view, read, or listen to political news and information. Traditionally TV and radio are referred to as **broadcast media**.

> **broadcast media** communication methods such as television and radio; they tend to take the form of one publisher (e.g., a television station) to many (viewers)

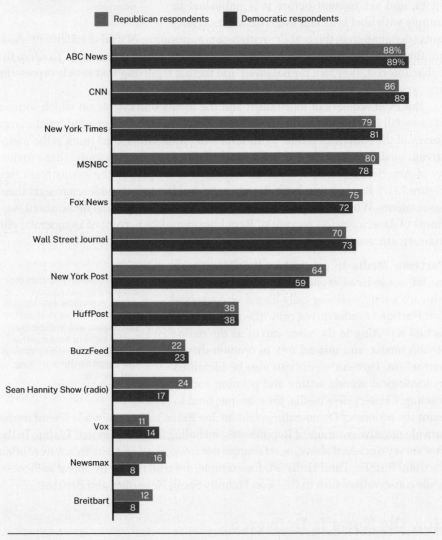

FIGURE 7.1 | What Are the Mainstream Media? Republicans and Democrats Agree

While Republicans and Democrats may, on average, tune in to different news sources, they do agree on what media outlets are mainstream.

PERCENTAGE OF U.S. ADULTS WHO SAY EACH SOURCE IS PART OF THE MAINSTREAM NEWS MEDIA

■ Republican respondents   ■ Democratic respondents

Source	Republican	Democratic
ABC News	88%	89%
CNN	86	89
New York Times	79	81
MSNBC	80	78
Fox News	75	72
Wall Street Journal	70	73
New York Post	64	59
HuffPost	38	38
BuzzFeed	22	23
Sean Hannity Show (radio)	24	17
Vox	11	14
Newsmax	16	8
Breitbart	12	8

SOURCE: Elisa Shearer and Amy Mitchell, "Broad Agreement in U.S.—Even among Partisans—on Which News Outlets Are Part of the 'Mainstream Media,'" Pew Research Center, May 7, 2021, www .pewresearch.org/fact-tank/2021/05/07/broad-agreement-in-u-s-even-among-partisans-on-which -news-outlets-are-part-of-the-mainstream-media/ (accessed 5/17/22).

But now, in the digital age, news and information can be communicated and shared in many ways, by many people and organizations. Political scientists have worked to understand the ways in which *how* people get their news affects their level of political knowledge and the quality of the news they receive.

News Websites Today, around 86 percent of Americans get their news digitally. Two-thirds get their news at least sometimes from news websites.[31] **News websites** deliver content similar to that in print newspapers, in that the layout of stories is similar for users regardless of their geographic location, demographic characteristics, partisanship, or friend networks. The most popular news websites are NYTimes.com, Washington-Post.com, and CNN.com. Leading news websites like these have millions of viewers daily.[32] And these leading online newspapers are especially influential because they help set the political agenda for the nation by providing in-depth news coverage and original investigative reporting.

> **news websites** digital sites that are owned and managed by newspapers, follow the principles of journalism, and deliver content like that of print newspapers, with similar story layout for all users regardless of location, demographic characteristics, partisanship, or friend networks

The digital delivery of news is a relatively recent occurrence. Twenty years ago, most Americans said that after television, print newspapers were their main source for news, and under 20 percent read the news online.[33] As the media and news have moved online, so has revenue generated from advertising. Today nearly two-thirds of all ad revenue in the United States is from digital advertising.[34] This is important, because the news media are mostly privately owned, for-profit companies that need to make revenue to survive. If customers are going online, then the news and revenue-generating ad content need to be delivered online as well.

And after years of worry that digital delivery would undermine the revenue streams of major newspapers, the model may be changing. Traditionally, U.S. newspapers made more revenue from advertising than from circulating (selling subscriptions), but in 2020, for the first time, newspapers made more money from circulation than from ad revenue. This change was largely driven by paywalls, which allow a certain number of free visits to a news site before requiring users to pay for content. Paywalls have become the norm for reading digital newspapers, and they appear to be a viable business model. In recent years, some major U.S. newspapers like the *New York Times* and the *Washington Post* have reported large increases in digital subscriptions.[35] Digital ad revenue continues to be strong, accounting for nearly 40 percent of all revenue to newspapers in 2021.[36]

The *Washington Post* has been a model for making the news media profitable. While revenues for most newspapers continued to decline or remain constant, the *Post* experienced double-digit revenue growth over multiple years. Along with providing a viable financial model, it has emerged as a leader in investigative reporting, data analytics, and marketing. Amazon CEO Jeff Bezos rebuilt the *Post* into a media technology company, producing over 1,000 articles, graphics, or videos per day, including staff-produced articles and wire stories written by others. The paper has high digital readership. It distributes news content using social media and offers discounts to Amazon Prime members. The *Post* also tracks how different headlines and story framings affect readership of each story.[37]

News Aggregators Websites that pull together content from a wide range of online sources, thus providing a very broad perspective, are known as **news aggregators**. Aggregators organize content from diverse digital-only news organizations, including mainstream media, partisan media, political groups, governments, candidates, nonprofit organizations, corporations, and professional media organizations. Stories that appear at the top of news aggregators are those that have been the most read or watched. Aggregators deliver thousands of news stories each day, as well as the latest public-opinion polls and their own synthesis of the headline news.

> **news aggregators** websites that pull together news from a wide range of online sources and make them available on one platform or page; news aggregators can be a way to avoid partisan or filtered news, providing a broad overview of the news of the day from many sources

Two-thirds of Americans get their news at least sometimes from news aggregators, with Google News being the most popular.[38] Other news aggregators, such as Reddit (which also has aspects of a social media site; see the next section) and RealClearPolitics, generally compile and repackage stories created by other sources, and then deliver them online to consumers in convenient formats.

Using news aggregators can be a way to avoid partisan or filtered media because they provide an overview of the news of the day from many sources. They are particularly effective for learning about American politics and the world from an international perspective.

Social Media Social media sites are diverse, interactive, and convenient for obtaining breaking news 24 hours a day. While social media regularly serve up mainstream news stories, they also deliver posts from friends (about politics, sports, or anything else), opinion pieces, citizen journalism, and almost any other content you can think of. One's social media feed might thus reflect a blend of objective reporting and factual information with opinion-driven and personal commentary.

Using social media for political information is evident across all demographic groups. As of 2020, 36 percent of U.S. adults sometimes got news from Facebook and 23 percent from YouTube and Twitter.[39] About 70 percent of Reddit, Twitter, and Facebook users get news on those sites. Users rely on Twitter for breaking news, and 70 percent of Twitter news consumers say they use the platform to follow live news events.[40]

> **algorithms** software programs that analyze the viewing, liking, and commenting data of all of a platform's users, as well as individual users' prior data, to present users with additional content tailored to their individual interests instead of ordering posts based on the most recently published (as broadcast media do)

Although consumers of television, radio, and print media and most news websites see or hear roughly similar content regardless of their geographic location or individual demographics, that is not the case for social media and some news websites. Social media differ from traditional broadcast media in their extensive use of computer **algorithms** to personalize individual user content. Instead of ordering news stories based on which were most recently published, as traditional broadcast media do, algorithms analyze "engagement data" to present each user with a unique set of additional news stories and other content tailored to the user's preferences. Such data may include information on which posts and videos have been generating the most likes, comments, and views from all users as well as what types of posts the individual user has watched or liked before. Thus, what the audience is saying and sharing plays a significant role in shaping the political content that social media present.[41] Unfortunately, this dynamic has the potential to spread misinformation that can have dangerous consequences (see later in this chapter).

Television Despite the rise of digital media, television news still commands larger audiences than most other news sources. According to Pew survey data, just over two-thirds of Americans get their news from watching television "at least sometimes," and 40 percent get their news from TV "often."[42] Most Americans have a television, and millions watch national and local news programs every day. The major broadcasting companies are NBC, CBS, and ABC; in addition, cable TV (CNN, Fox News, and MSNBC) has become an important source of information for many Americans. Local TV news programs collectively attract 25 million nightly viewers, far more than national cable programs such as Fox News and MSNBC.[43]

Television news serves the important function of alerting viewers to issues and events—headline news—via brief quotes and short characterizations of the day's events. It generally covers fewer topics and provides less depth of coverage than newspapers and news websites, because written text can present more detailed and complete information. Furthermore, television stations don't do as much of their own reporting, instead relying on leading newspapers or digital media to set their news agenda. Because politicians and others are aware of the character of television news coverage, they often seek to manipulate the news by providing interviews and sound bites that will dominate this coverage. Twenty-four-hour cable news stations such as MSNBC, CNN, and Fox News offer more detail and commentary than the half-hour evening news shows on ABC, NBC, and CBS. During the 2020 presidential election, cable TV was the most relied-on platform for election night news, according to Pew, with news websites and apps second and network TV third.[44]

Local TV continues to be a major source of news, especially for older Americans, Black people, and people without a college degree.[45] However, its importance is declining overall, especially among younger people.[46] In general, though, Americans' reliance on television as a news source is likely to continue.[47]

Radio and Podcasts Radio is a less common source of news, compared with television, social media, and news websites. According to the Pew Research Center, 16 percent of people use radio for news "often" and 32 percent use it "sometimes."[48] The audio news sector in the United States is divided by delivery formats: traditional terrestrial (AM/FM) radio, and digital—including online audio and podcasting. Nationwide, nearly one-quarter of Americans prefer to get the news by listening to it on radio or from podcasts.[49]

In the 1990s, talk radio became an important source of political commentary as well as entertainment. Conservative radio hosts such as Rush Limbaugh and Sean Hannity gained huge audiences and helped to mobilize support for conservative political causes and candidates, but today it is conservative radio podcasts that bring in large audiences (e.g., Joe Rogan and Ben Shapiro).

Although public broadcasting, as noted earlier, has a much smaller share of the total media market in the United States than in many other countries, NPR—in the political center—is an important source for in-depth political reporting and in the top 10 mainstream news outlets. In fact, listeners of public radio have been found to have higher levels of political knowledge than consumers of other media sources.[50] Hundreds of local and regional radio and television stations also make up the U.S. public broadcasting sector.

While traditional AM/FM radio reaches almost all Americans and remains steady, podcasting has seen a dramatic increase. In 2021, 41 percent of Americans over age 12 had listened to a podcast in the last month, up from just 9 percent in 2008.[51]

Newspapers Newspapers are the oldest medium for dissemination of the news, though today most Americans read digital rather than print versions, as previously discussed. Just 5 percent of Americans frequently read print newspapers now, while two-thirds read newspapers online.[52]

Beginning in the late nineteenth century, the emergence of newspapers (and later of radio and television networks) as mass-audience businesses operated primarily for profit significantly shaped politics in the United States. In fact, the development of standardized reporting and writing practices emphasizing objectivity in political news coverage was motivated largely by financial factors. The owners of large newspaper companies determined that the best way to make a profit was to appeal to as broad an audience as possible, which meant not alienating potential readers who held strongly liberal or conservative views. This goal, in turn, required training and "disciplining" reporters to produce a standardized, seemingly neutral news product.

This approach proved successful in attracting readers, and for a long time most cities and towns in the country had their own newspaper, and often more than one. However, for most traditional newspapers, recent decades have been financially challenging. Competition from broadcast media and new online content sources has resulted in declines in advertising revenue and circulation levels, thus changing the traditional business model of newspapers, as we previously discussed.[53]

The Rise of Media Technology Companies

In recent years, big technology companies like Apple, Amazon, Alphabet (owner of Google and YouTube), Microsoft, and Meta/Facebook (owner of Instagram and WhatsApp) have become major players in the business of journalism, creating media technology companies. This has changed many aspects of the production, packaging, and delivery of the news. Using computer algorithms and market research, they push specific news alerts to specific people based on those individuals' interests and

FOR CRITICAL ANALYSIS ⟶

1. Who are the people most likely to use social media for political news and information? What does this mean for the future of other platforms?

2. Do you think that users of certain platforms (social media, print publications, TV, etc.) are more politically knowledgeable than others? Why or why not?

WHO ARE AMERICANS?

How Do Americans Get Their Political News?

How people consume political news and information can have a profound effect on the news and information they see. The vast majority of American adults consume news on their smartphones, computers, or tablets. With the rise of sophisticated algorithms on social media apps, this likely means that people are being exposed to news that fits with their preexisting beliefs or is popular among their social networks. These dynamics raise important questions about the future of the news media and the quality of political news and information.

Percentage of U.S. adults who often or sometimes get news from . . .

■ Often
■ Sometimes

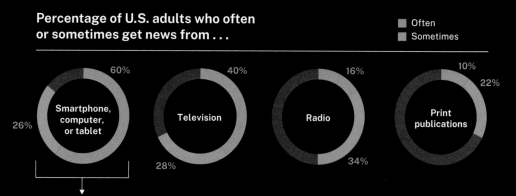

Smartphone, computer, or tablet — 60%, 26%
Television — 40%, 28%
Radio — 16%, 34%
Print publications — 10%, 22%

What digital platform people use to consume news and information

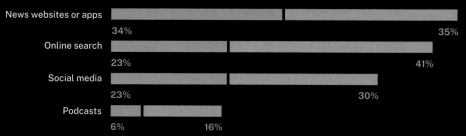

News websites or apps — 34%, 35%
Online search — 23%, 41%
Social media — 23%, 30%
Podcasts — 6%, 16%

How people consume news, by age

■ 18–29
■ 30–49
■ 50–64
■ 65+

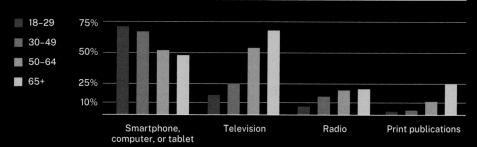

Smartphone, computer, or tablet / Television / Radio / Print publications

SOURCE: Pew Research Center, www.pewresearch.org/fact-tank/2021/01/12/more-than-eight-in-ten-americans -get-news-from-digital-devices/ (accessed 10/20/21).

preferences, often through social media. Editors choose stories and titles based on consumer interests. Digital ad revenue has become one of the most important forms of advertising. Nearly $356 billion was spent on digital advertising in 2020.[54] In that year, 54 percent of all advertising revenue in the United States was for digital ads.

The Effect of Big Tech on the Media The interdependence of technology and media companies continues to grow, and it's a phenomenon that has both positive and negative consequences. In one of the latest trends, technology companies and their CEOs are developing or buying major news media companies, such as eBay founder Pierre Omidyar creating The Intercept, Disney buying FiveThirtyEight, and Amazon CEO Jeff Bezos purchasing the *Washington Post*. Both The Intercept and the *Washington Post* have a reputation for forceful investigative journalism, while FiveThirtyEight is a premier website focused on data journalism. Elon Musk, the richest man in the world and owner of SpaceX and Tesla, purchased Twitter for $44 billion in 2022. In an unusual move for the CEO of a social media platform, Musk used the platform to tweet his endorsement of Republicans for Congress in the 2022 midterm elections and Florida governor Ron DeSantis for president in 2024.

Beyond making some news outlets profitable again, these high-tech collaborations are changing how Americans learn about current events in the United States and globally.[55] This is evident in the growing number of Americans who read or watch the news using social media platforms.[56]

Facebook's CEO Mark Zuckerberg came under fire for allowing politicians to lie in 2020 political campaign ads, highlighting how corporate decisions can shape the news and politics. While Facebook cracked down on made-up news flooding its platforms after the 2016 presidential election, with fact-checking software to stop everyday users from sharing viral misinformation, politicians were exempt.

The algorithms used in social media have a profound effect on what constitutes the news and political information. In 2021, Frances Haugen, a former Facebook employee, revealed to the world that the company's software engineers used algorithms with an internal scoring system in which news articles and posts likely to make readers angry (with inflammatory, controversial information) were scored 5 points. Those likely to make readers happy were scored with a 1. This 5-to-1 formula, embedded in the software, was intended to drive traffic and thereby earn revenue for the company's shareholders. But it meant the news on the top of readers' social media feeds had the negative effect of fostering anger, divisiveness, and polarization. Why did the company allow this to continue? "Anger and hate is the easiest way to grow on Facebook," Haugen said. These negative emotions are used for engagement data, getting people to come back to the platform, since anger is a core human emotion.

When Facebook undid this policy after negative feedback, users began to get less misinformation and graphic violence in their news feeds. Surprisingly, levels of user activity on the platform didn't change.

Social media companies finally took a stance against the dangers of misinformation on their platforms following the January 6, 2021, attack on the U.S. Capitol. When Congress was certifying the 2020 election, Trump—who had a history of promoting misinformation via Twitter during his presidency—held a rally in Washington,

D.C., where he called for the election result to be overturned. He urged his supporters to "take back our country" by marching to the Capitol to "fight like hell." After his speech ended, the large mob broke into the Capitol building, destroying property and injuring many. Five people died, including a police officer. During the violence, Trump posted mixed messages on Twitter and Facebook calling the mob "great patriots" and eventually tweeting to his supporters to "go home with love & in peace."

Following this event, Trump was banned from Facebook, Instagram, Twitter, and other platforms for instigating the mob violence. (Later, Facebook extended the ban until 2023.) After the attack, Congress reconvened and confirmed President Biden's victory. Significantly, after Trump's ban from several social media sites, online misinformation about election fraud dropped 73 percent.[57]

The January 6, 2021, attack underscores the powerful role technology companies play in deciding what information can run on their platforms—i.e., what is news. Today misinformation and sometimes outright lies about politics are widespread online. For example, after the FBI searched Mar-a-Lago, former president Trump's Florida home, for missing confidential government documents in summer 2022, viral information online claimed the FBI had instead planted the documents at Trump's residence to frame him.

Check your understanding

3. Where do most Americans receive their news?

   a) radio stations
   b) public broadcasting, such as NPR or PBS
   c) news aggregators, like Google News
   d) print newspapers

4. What effect has "Big Tech" had on news media?

   a) Transforming media from news organizations to digital and citizen journalism has led to less rigorous fact-checking.

   b) Transforming media from news organizations to digital and citizen journalism has led to more rigorous fact-checking.

   c) Media are now much less profit driven, which has led to more in-depth coverage of politics and government.

   d) There has been a significant reduction in "fake news" stories as tech companies typically vet every story on their websites.

The Quality of Political News

Assess why citizens have different levels of trust in the media

While digital media hold promise for improving access to political information citizens need, the shift toward online media has also given rise to several major concerns. These include the accuracy and depth of news content, the rise in misinformation, growing gaps in political knowledge between the informed and the uninformed,[58] the prominence of partisan media, and the negative effects of these factors on civic engagement and people's tolerance of each other.

What Americans Think of the Media

Views about the influence of the media in American politics have shifted dramatically since Joe Biden was elected president. In 2020 the nation faced a highly competitive presidential election, violent conflict in certifying the election (the January 6 U.S. Capitol attack), a public health crisis (the Covid-19 pandemic), and nationwide protests for racial justice. In each case Americans turned to the news for information.

Today 41 percent of Americans believe news organizations are gaining influence in the United States, while 33 percent believe their influence is declining.[59] This is a stark contrast to a year before, when nearly half of Americans (48 percent) said news organizations were less important and just over 30 percent said their influence was growing. These patterns are found for Republicans and Democrats alike, but overall Republicans are more likely to say the news media are losing their influence.[60]

Trust in the news media is linked to views about its influence. People who have greater trust in national news organizations tend to be more likely to see the news media as gaining influence, while those with low levels of trust are generally more likely to see it waning.

Before the pandemic, just one in five American adults had a lot of trust in "information from national news organizations," and half had some trust, while 30 percent had not much/none at all.[61] During the coronavirus pandemic, however, public trust in media rose, as most people believed the media were providing needed information.[62] Yet there are partisan differences in trust when it comes to the news media's watchdog role and perceived fairness in political coverage; Democrats, for example, are much more likely than Republicans to think information from national news organizations is trustworthy (see Figure 7.2). Distrust in the mainstream media increased with the Trump presidency, during which Trump waged an unprecedented war on the American media, frequently referring to major newspapers and traditional broadcast media as "fake news." (Yet these mainstream sources do not produce fabricated news.) In a tweet shortly after Trump's inauguration in 2016, he even called the press "the enemy of the American people."[63]

Polarized Information Environments and Media Bias

Contributing to low trust in the news media, today many news sources are perceived as distinctly left- or right-leaning. People tend to select sources that conform with their political beliefs due to the phenomenon of motivated reasoning:[64] individuals will seek out information in favor of the conclusions they want to believe (e.g., "Covid-19 vaccines are harmful") and reject arguments they don't want to believe (e.g., "Covid-19 vaccines are safe"). This can lead people to cling to false beliefs despite substantial scientific evidence and accumulation of fact to the contrary. Motivated reasoning is related to **confirmation bias**,

confirmation bias the tendency to favor information that confirms a person's existing beliefs; it involves discounting evidence that could disprove or challenge those beliefs

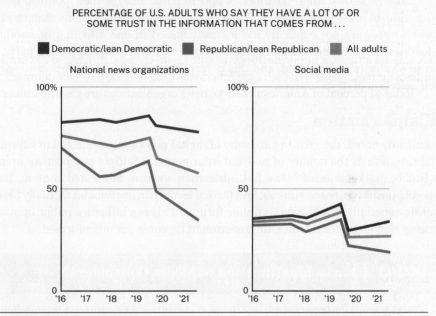

FIGURE 7.2 | Trust in Media

Trust in media has declined in recent years. The steepest drop has come in Republicans' trust of national news organizations. What factors do you think have led to these changes?

PERCENTAGE OF U.S. ADULTS WHO SAY THEY HAVE A LOT OF OR
SOME TRUST IN THE INFORMATION THAT COMES FROM . . .

■ Democratic/lean Democratic   ■ Republican/lean Republican   ■ All adults

National news organizations   Social media

SOURCE: "Wider Partisan Gaps Emerge in Trust of National and Local News Organizations, Social Media," Pew Research Center, August 27, 2021, www.pewresearch.org (accessed 5/17/22).

in which people search for, or give more credibility to, information or evidence that confirms a preexisting belief than they do to information or evidence that challenges a preexisting belief. Both motivated reasoning and confirmation bias contribute to the creation of partisan news bubbles.

A **filter bubble** is an online environment in which platform users are exposed primarily to opinions and information that conform to and reinforce their existing beliefs; this is a result of algorithms that personalize each individual's online experience. In a **media echo chamber**, by contrast, users' beliefs are amplified or reinforced through repetition inside a closed system of communication. By participating in an echo chamber, people can seek out information that reinforces their existing views without encountering opposing views.

How many Americans live in partisan news bubbles? Earlier studies suggested this was very common, but the consensus is now that a minority

filter bubbles partisan media environments in which users are exposed primarily to opinions and information that conform to their existing beliefs; constructed by algorithms that analyze and then personalize each user's online experience

media echo chambers closed communication systems in which individual beliefs are amplified or reinforced by repetition; they may increase social and political polarization because users do not encounter opposing views

get information only from partisan sources: 25 percent of Democrats choose only news outlets with left-leaning audiences most of the time, and 24 percent of Republicans consistently turn only to sources with right-leaning audiences.[65] The vast majority of Americans get information from sources that reflect moderate and/or diverse political viewpoints.[66]

Table 7.1 shows where Democrats and Republicans get their political news. According to one recent study, with the exception of Fox News, many mainstream news sources are not explicitly ideologically biased in one direction or another. Most have been found to be centrist.[67] Of course, many people perceive particular news stories to be biased, and this perception may be what drives ideological self-selection of news sources.

Misinformation

As already noted, the growing diversity of digital news sources has led to substantial variation in the quality of political information. Multiple perspectives create a livelier marketplace of ideas, but misleading content, fabricated content, hate speech, unsubstantiated rumors, and factual errors can overwhelm factually based voices, especially in anonymous online forums. This can influence public opinion, posing challenges for democratic government if people are misinformed.

TABLE 7.1 | Party Identification of Media Consumers

This table shows the percentage of people who got political and election news recently from each source. Which sources have the largest gap between Democrats and Republicans? Which have the smallest?

	ALL U.S. ADULTS	DEMOCRATIC/LEAN DEMOCRATIC	REPUBLICAN/LEAN REPUBLICAN
Fox News	39%	23%	60%
ABC News	33	37	30
CBS News	30	33	26
NBC News	34	40	28
CNN	39	53	24
NPR	20	30	11
New York Times	20	31	9
Washington Post	17	26	8

SOURCE: Mark Jurkowitz et al., "Americans Are Divided by Party in the Sources They Turn to for Political News," Pew Research Center, January 24, 2020, www.pewresearch.org (accessed 5/18/22).

Misinformation is a common problem, as fake news and other untrue or false content, such as conspiracy theories, can substitute for real news online.[68] Political candidates and leaders are particularly susceptible to online attacks because negative stories about them can easily go viral, spreading quickly without being fact-checked. The posting or publication of false stories circulated to benefit one candidate or party over another, or just to generate ad revenue, is a serious problem. In the 2016 presidential election, for example, circulation of the top 10 fake news stories on Facebook was more widespread than the top real news stories about the election. A study published by Stanford University found that fake news stories on social media about the election disproportionately favored Trump (the most widely publicized was the false story that the pope had endorsed him).[69] The Republican Senate Intelligence Committee and Special Counsel Robert Mueller both released reports that the Russian government was involved in generating many of the fake news stories to discredit Hillary Clinton and her campaign.[70] Social media platforms clamped down on misinformation in the 2020 election, but it was still widespread. Misinformation continued online before and during the 2022 election, especially regarding the assault of Paul Pelosi, husband of Speaker of the House Nancy Pelosi, two weeks before the election. Fake news claimed the attack never occurred even though it was videotaped and occurred in front of police who arrived at the house after a 911 call.

> **misinformation** false, inaccurate, or misleading information in the media, especially social media; often targeting political candidates and leaders, misinformation can include manipulated or fabricated content, satire, and parody content to the public via airwaves on electromagnetic frequencies

According to the Pew Research Center, 4 in 10 Americans say they "often" "come across made-up news and information," and another half say they "sometimes" do. In response, people have changed their news and technology habits. Nearly 80 percent of Americans say they now "regularly" check the facts in news stories themselves, 63 percent have stopped getting news from a particular outlet, and 43 percent have reduced their overall news intake on social media.[71] A number of websites, such as FactCheck.org, Snopes.com, and PolitiFact.com, are devoted exclusively to checking the truthfulness of political claims.

Misinformation on social media was especially concerning during the coronavirus pandemic. As the virus spread again among the unvaccinated U.S. population in summer 2021, President Biden said Facebook was "killing people" by spreading misinformation about the coronavirus vaccines.[72] That day Facebook released an independently conducted study showing that more users of the platform (85 percent) were vaccinated than the general public (at the time roughly 60 percent). Facebook's data analytics showed that 12 people were responsible for 65 percent of the Covid-19 misinformation on Facebook and that the platform had removed 18 million pieces of Covid-19 misinformation since the start of the pandemic.[73] Critics countered Facebook's response by noting that what mattered most was how many false pages were uploaded to the site or how many people saw the misinformation, not how many pages were removed.

As this example illustrates, the problem of misinformation on social media has less to do with what gets said by individual users than with what gets amplified

HOW TO

Evaluate a News Source

MIKE CAULFIELD, RESEARCH SCIENTIST AT THE CENTER FOR AN INFORMED PUBLIC AT THE UNIVERSITY OF WASHINGTON, shared "four moves" for assessing digital content, an approach he calls "SIFT." These moves help us to recognize clickbait and misinformation, to sort "truth from fiction from everything in between," and to amplify better treatments of issues.

1 **Stop.** When viewing a claim on the internet, Mike says we should stop and ask ourselves first, "Hey, do I know what I'm looking at?" That's especially true if we have "some sort of emotional reaction or surprise." It's a "subtle point," Mike says, "but when we do personal fact-checking, what we're really investigating is our reaction to what we looked at.

2 **Investigate the source.** If the source is highly trusted — for example, a media source that engages in fact-checking and adheres to the norms of professional journalism — you can stop there.

3 **Find better coverage.** If you do not know the source, try to find better coverage from a reputable outlet. Open up a search tab and type in the event or news story and pull up better and more complete stories.

4 **Trace claims, quotes, and media** back to the original context. If there is a link, click through to the original story or study, or do a fresh search with relevant key words.

In taking the SIFT steps, "what we're really doing is recontextualizing," Mike says, investigating the claim and seeing its full context. "The vast majority of what we see is something that has a kernel of truth at the center but whose context has been hacked, changed in such a way to significantly alter the meaning." By being skeptical and by investigating sources and claims, you can be a better consumer of the internet.

by platforms' algorithms. Researchers have called for greater government focus on algorithms and software design choices by social media companies rather than decisions about what content to allow or prohibit. Critics argue that government policy should focus on creating incentives for social media companies to promote reliable and truthful information, just as traditional media do.

Government Regulation of the Media

In the United States, print and online media are essentially free from government regulation, whereas broadcast radio and television are regulated by the Federal Communications Commission (FCC). Radio and TV stations must have FCC licenses, which must be renewed every five years. Through regulations prohibiting obscenity, indecency, and profanity, the FCC has sought to prohibit radio and television stations from airing explicit sexual and excretory references between 6 A.M. and 10 P.M., the hours when the audience is most likely to include children. Generally speaking, FCC regulation applies only to the over-the-air broadcast media and not to cable television, the internet, or satellite radio.

When Congress passed the Telecommunications Act of 1996, a broad effort to end most regulation of business practices and mergers, it allowed the formation of media tech giants and media conglomerates. The legislation loosened restrictions on media ownership and allowed telephone companies, cable television providers, and broadcasters to compete with one another to provide telecommunication services. Following the passage of this act, mergers between telephone and cable companies and different entertainment media produced a greater concentration of media ownership than had been possible previously. In radio, for example, a 40-station ownership cap was lifted, leading to an unprecedented consolidation. ClearChannel Communications (rebranded as iHeartMedia in 2014) grew from 40 to 1,200 stations.

Although the government's ability to regulate the content of the internet is limited, the FCC has used its licensing power to impose several regulations that can affect the political content of radio and TV broadcasts. The first of these is the **equal time rule**, under which broadcasters must provide candidates for the same political office with equal opportunities to communicate their messages to the public. Under the terms of the Telecommunications Act of 1996, during the 45 days before an election, broadcasters are required to make time available to candidates at the lowest rate charged for that time slot. The second regulation affecting the content of broadcasts is the **right of rebuttal**, which requires that individuals be given the opportunity to respond to personal attacks.

equal time rule the requirement that broadcasters provide candidates for the same political office with equal opportunities to communicate their messages to the public

right of rebuttal a Federal Communications Commission regulation giving individuals the right to respond to personal attacks made on a radio or television broadcast

Effects on Knowledge and Tolerance

Perhaps the greatest concern about politics in the digital age is that the very diversity of digital media may *lower* tolerance for social, religious, and political diversity, leading to more partisan polarization and societal conflict. Fully 85 percent of Americans believe that the tone and nature of political debate in the United States has become more negative in recent years—as well as less respectful, less fact based, and less focused on policy issues.[74] This is partly attributable to the fact that digital media often do not abide by traditional media's principle of objective journalism. Some liberals and conservatives alike can self-select media that are consistent with their beliefs and avoid exposure to information that might challenge these.[75] Moreover, as search engines and social media algorithms cater to our individual preferences, it becomes increasingly easy to select news that conforms with our own beliefs. As discussed above, motivated reasoning, confirmation bias, or self-selected news can filter out information that might broaden our worldview.[76]

Despite the dramatic rise in available political information, average levels of political knowledge in the population have not increased.[77] The failure of digital media to promote higher levels of knowledge is not driven by partisan news per se, but is a reflection of information environments having shifted to be more entertaining and less informative. If digital media are to create a more informed democratic process, they must produce more substantive political information and citizens must have "information literacy"—the ability to find and evaluate that information.[78] Today's greater access to all types of information online means that education and critical thinking among citizens are more important than ever before.

Check your understanding

5. Which of these statements regarding Americans' trust in the media is true?

   a) Those with greater trust in national news organizations tend to be more likely to see the news media as gaining influence, while those with low levels of trust tend to see it waning.

   b) During the coronavirus pandemic, public trust in media significantly declined, as most people believed the media were providing misinformation.

   c) There are no significant differences between Democrats and Republicans when it comes to trust in the media.

   d) Americans' perceptions of partisan slant in news media have produced an increase in the public's trust in the media.

6. How has partisan polarization affected the media?

   a) An overwhelming majority of Democrats and Republicans only use news outlets that align with their views politically, which further reinforces partisan polarization.

   b) Many mainstream news sources are not explicitly ideologically biased in one direction or another. Rather, most are centrist.

   c) Motivated reasoning is one way to combat partisan polarization and produce less biased news.

   d) Partisan polarization has produced more hard news coverage and reduced the amount of soft news stories.

WHAT DO YOU THINK?

THE MEDIA

The freedom of the press is essential to democratic government. Ordinary citizens depend on the media to investigate wrongdoing, publicize and explain governmental policy, evaluate politicians, and bring to light matters that might otherwise be known to only a handful of governmental insiders. Without free and active media, democratic government would be virtually impossible. Citizens would have few means through which to know or assess the government's actions — other than the claims or pronouncements of the government itself. Moreover, without active (indeed, aggressive) media, citizens would be hard-pressed to make informed choices among competing candidates at the polls. But the rise of digital media has fundamentally changed how political information is gathered and distributed. News today is participatory and involves citizens as well as professional journalists. New platforms raise new questions about who should decide what content is disseminated.

- How widely do your friends and family seek out information? Do they tend to rely on a small number of sources, or reach out more broadly? What about your media habits?

- What media sources do you see playing the role of "watchdog" over government and politics? What kinds of stories do they publish? Do you see these sources as biased or unbiased? What would Alexis Wray and her colleagues at *The A&T Register,* featured at the beginning of this chapter, say?

- Knowing what you know now, what do you think of investigations into online content and the debates over the responsibilities and liabilities of digital media companies such as Facebook and Twitter? Should they monitor and edit content and users? Should they be legally responsible for content that users post?

Use 📖 **INQUIZITIVE** *to help you study and master this material.*

8

WHAT GOVERNMENT DOES & WHY IT MATTERS

In 2021 Congress debated two large bills: a $1.2 trillion infrastructure package and a $3.5 trillion social safety net and climate package. With so much at stake, business interest groups used the full arsenal of their advocacy weapons to shape the final legislation and help determine whether each passed into law. They lobbied members of Congress, advertised to support or oppose the plans, and threatened to withhold campaign contributions from lawmakers with differing views. The pharmaceutical industry spent millions to defeat a proposal to reduce prescription drug costs. The American Petroleum Institute lobbied against a fee on methane emissions. The American Bankers Association opposed a proposal requiring them to report tax information to the federal government to reduce cheating by high-income taxpayers.[1]

What about ordinary Americans who might benefit from the legislation? During the pandemic, the American Rescue Plan increased the value of the Child Tax Credit and expanded eligibility to most families, but just for

Political Parties & Interest Groups

2021. The second, larger package Congress debated would make the expansion permanent. Nikki Wells, who runs a child-care business in her home in the Appalachian region of Ohio, noted that the pandemic put huge stress on families, especially those that make too much to qualify for Medicaid or food assistance but too little to meet their expenses. With the Child Tax Credit, these families could afford the child care that enables them to work. And policy advocates argued that the credit could reduce child poverty by 40 percent.[2]

But some interests in American politics are better organized than others. The businesses and associations that swung into action on the infrastructure and safety net packages are well-resourced and have permanent lobbying operations. Ordinary people like Nikki Wells and the families that relied on the increased Child Tax Credit have fewer organizations representing their interests in Washington, D.C., or in statehouses. Many worry that despite the array of interest groups in American politics, not all interests are represented equally, and the results of competition among various interests are not always consistent with the common good.

Moreover, although both interest groups and parties link individuals and groups to government using democratic mechanisms to change or shape government policy, they also differ. Parties organize to nominate

▲ Groups representing business and labor can have a big influence over government policies, like the allocation of stimulus money during the pandemic. But who represents the interests of people like Nikki Wells and the families who use her child-care center, who rely on tax credits and other benefits in times of crisis?

candidates and to win elected office; interest groups do not, although interest groups often engage in political campaigns to help candidates and parties favorable to their policy goals win elections. In other words, parties tend to concern themselves with the *personnel* of government, while interest groups tend to focus on the *policies* of government. Ultimately, elected officials determine the direction of government, often with party considerations in mind. Some Republicans in the House and Senate voted for the infrastructure bill, but only after it was pared back in keeping with their partisan preferences for smaller government. And no Republicans supported the social policy and climate package, which stalled in the Senate. In this chapter we will examine the nature and consequences of political parties and interest groups in the United States.

CHAPTER GOALS

Explain how and why political parties form and change (pp. 225–33)

Explain how parties organize to win elections and influence policy making in government (pp. 234–37)

Identify the reasons for, and sources of, party identification and increased polarization (pp. 238–45)

Describe the major types of interest groups and whom they represent (pp. 245–53)

Explain how interest groups try to influence government and policy (pp. 253–60)

What Are Political Parties?

Explain how and why political parties form and change

Political parties are coalitions of people who form a united front to win control of government and implement policy.[3] A party seeks to control the government by nominating candidates, electing them to public office, and winning elections. Once in office, parties organize government lawmaking and seek to change government policy. Interest groups do not seek to control the operation of government or win elections but, rather, try to influence specific policies, often by lobbying elected officials and contributing to political campaigns. Political parties are not part of government but are private organizations governed by their own rules.

political parties coalitions of people who form a united front to win control of government and implement policy

partisanship identification with or support of a particular party or cause

Although the Founders were generally opposed to parties, the first national parties emerged with the writing of the U.S. Constitution, and parties quickly became a core feature of the American political system. Over centuries the names of American parties have changed, but their core function has not. Parties and **partisanship** organize the political world and simplify complex policy debates for citizens and elected officials. Parties also play central roles in mobilizing citizens to vote in elections—for example, by informing the public about government policies.

Today the Democratic and Republican parties are two broad coalitions strategically bringing together many diverse interests, organizations, and millions of Americans. When we talk about political party coalitions, we mean not only the formal Republican and Democratic party organizations but also media, interest groups, think tanks, donors, and Super PACs affiliated with the parties. American political parties are best understood as broad teams, not just politicians and formal organizations.

Because parties are coalitions, their members do not necessarily agree on all issues. For example, the Democratic Party includes many pro-environment groups who favor electric vehicles and alternative energy such as wind and solar, but it also includes labor unions who favor protection of the auto industry, which mostly makes cars that rely on fossil fuels. The Republican Party includes libertarians who want to reduce government interference with personal decisions, such as abortion or drug use, but it also contains religious conservatives who want government to pass laws restricting these same personal decisions.[4] Despite differing goals and perspectives, party members set aside some disagreements to focus on the common goal of electing party candidates. Once a party controls government, they must negotiate and compromise to pass policy that will benefit the party members.

Parties and Democracy

Without political parties, democracy as we know it would be difficult to achieve. In the United States, citizens take for granted that the people elect leaders to public office, that there is competition among candidates, that citizens will be able to learn about policy issues from candidate campaigns and cast their ballots in fair elections, and that once in office, political leaders will work to adopt policy and govern. Each of these tasks is complex, however, and would be more so if political parties did not exist. Parties mobilize people to vote, offer choices to voters in elections, and provide officeholders with organization for running government.[5]

Since the Founding, an enduring question has been whether parties hinder or enhance democracy. In the early Republic, parties were seen as threats to the stability of the new democratic government and were referred to as "factions." In his 1796 Farewell Address, President George Washington warned his countrymen to shun partisan politics, and in *Federalist* 10 James Madison, writing under the name Publius, focused on the evils of "factions," or parties.[6] A faction could be any group of people who intensely advocate for their own interest, whether defined by region, religion, race, or any other characteristic. For Madison, factions did not present a problem if their supporters consisted of only a slim minority of the nation's population, whose ideas could be easily defeated in elections and with majority voting in the legislature. Madison feared that if a faction had the support of a majority, it could take over government, tyrannize the rights of an unpopular minority, and destroy democracy. Madison believed that in a country like the United States, the strong, diverse interests of the large population would cancel each other out, preventing any one faction from dominating government.

Today there remains considerable debate about whether the two major parties are beneficial or harmful. Many people believe that parties and political leaders today are too divided along liberal and conservative lines (what is called party or political polarization). Parties once helped smooth over social divisions by grouping different sorts of people under the same umbrella, but now they reinforce those divisions.[7] Today the parties are increasingly divided along lines of race, ethnicity, religion, education, region, and ideology. This has made members of one party increasingly dislike members of the other, so much so that some even see members of the other party as a threat to the country.

Others believe the parties are controlled more by interest groups, especially big business and wealthy campaign donors, than by the people. Some argue the United States is simply too large and diverse to be represented by only two political parties. Others believe our election system needs reform so that there are more than two major parties to better represent citizens' views.[8]

Despite these concerns, political parties are essential to democracy.[9] We can see this in the way parties mobilize voters to participate in elections. For example, in 2020 the Democratic Party's coalition showed record-breaking turnout increases for many groups, including young people, Latinos, Asians, and Black Americans. The Republican Party was especially effective in mobilizing non-college-educated voters.

Why the United States Has a Two-Party System Most democratic countries use a **proportional representation** system for elections to their national legislature or parliament. Under this system, some or all seats are allocated to political parties based on their share of the total votes cast in the election. For example, if a party wins 40 percent of the votes in an election, it controls 40 percent of the seats in the legislature. In contrast, most elections in the United States use a **plurality system**. Under these voting rules, the candidate with the most votes wins, no matter if that candidate received 40 percent, 51 percent, or 80 percent of the overall vote. Other countries require the winning candidate to win a majority (50 percent plus one), not just a simple plurality. Plurality voting rules combined with geographic single-member districts produce a winner-take-all election system.[10]

Election rules largely determine how many political parties there are in a country. **Duverger's law** holds that plurality voting rules with single-member districts (just one candidate wins each legislative seat, as in the United States) will result in a **two-party system**. Why? Under U.S. election rules, voters have an incentive not to vote for small- or minor-party candidates for fear of "wasting" their vote, because only one party's candidate (usually a Republican or Democrat) can win the election for each office. In contrast, the proportional voting rules used in many other countries tend to result in multiple parties in government. Some political analysts suggest that switching to such a system would decrease polarization in the United States.

proportional representation a multimember district system that allows each political party representation in proportion to its percentage of the total vote

plurality system a type of electoral system in which, to win a seat in the parliament or other representative body, a candidate need only receive the most votes in the election, not necessarily a majority of the votes cast

Duverger's law a law that holds that plurality-rule elections, where the winner has the most votes but not necessarily a majority within single-member geographic districts, tend to result in a two-party system, whereas proportional representation tends to result in a multiparty system

two-party system a political system in which only two parties have a realistic opportunity to compete effectively for control

How Political Parties Form and Change

Historically, parties form in one of two ways. The first occurs when societal conflict leads political elites and competing coalitions within government to mobilize popular support. The second occurs when groups outside of government organize popular support to win control of government. We see these dynamics in the evolution of the United States' party systems.

Despite the deep partisan divides we see today, political parties are not static. History shows that parties can change significantly as they respond to important events and are influenced by charismatic leaders. Historians often refer to the set of parties that are important at any given time as a nation's *party system*. The term encompasses not only the number of parties competing for power but also the main issues that divide the parties and which regional, occupational, and demographic groups support them. Over the course of American history, changes in political alignments have produced multiple party systems. While the United

States has had a two-party system for most of its history, it has not consisted of the same two parties (see Figure 8.1). Factions within the parties and different coalitions of groups in society can lead to change.

Early Party Systems The first party system emerged with the adoption of the U.S. Constitution in the 1790s and pitted the Federalists, who favored a strong national government and president, against the Antifederalists (also known as Jeffersonian Republicans), who favored a weaker national government, with the states retaining protections for individuals from government interference. The Federalist coalition included New England merchants who supported protective tariffs (taxes on imports) to encourage domestic (i.e., U.S.) manufacturing, forgiveness of states' Revolutionary War debts, creation of a national bank, commercial ties with Britain, and a strong national government. The Antifederalist coalition included southern agricultural interests, who favored free trade (and opposed tariffs), continuation of the practice of slavery, alliance with France, and states' rights. In the election of 1800, Thomas Jefferson defeated the incumbent Federalist president, John Adams, and over the following years the Federalists gradually weakened. The party disappeared after the pro-British sympathies of some Federalist leaders during the War of 1812 led to charges of treason against the party.

Subsequently the United States had only one political party until 1830—the Jeffersonian Republicans, which gradually came to be known as the Democrats. At this time the party experienced intense internal conflict, particularly between the supporters and opponents of President Andrew Jackson, a hero of the War of 1812 between the United States and the United Kingdom. Jackson had a wide base of support but was controversial. In 1830, Jackson signed the Indian Removal Act, which forcibly removed most members of major Native American tribes of the Southeast to Indian territory along what is known as the Trail of Tears, resulting in widespread death and disease. At the same time, Jackson was a populist who fought to give more political rights to common working people. He gave regular party members more say in picking presidents through the emergence of the national party conventions.

During the 1830s, groups opposing Jackson united to form the Whig Party, giving rise to the second party system. The Whigs were the successors of the Federalists, with strong support in the Northeast among merchants and less support in the South and West among farmers. Both the Democrats and the Whigs built national party coalitions and tried to enlarge their bases of support by eliminating the requirement of property ownership for voting.

As mentioned previously, parties can change when groups outside of government (factions) organize popular support to take control of government. This is what happened during the late 1840s and early 1850s, when conflicts over slavery produced sharp divisions within both the Whig and the Democratic parties. During the 1850s a group of state civic and community leaders who opposed slavery built what became the Republican Party by constructing party organizations in the Northeast and West.

By 1856 the Whig Party had all but dissolved under the strain. Many Whig politicians and voters, along with antislavery Democrats, joined the new

FIGURE 8.1 | How the Party System Evolved

During the nineteenth century, the Democrats and Republicans emerged as the two dominant parties in American politics. As the American party system evolved, many minor parties emerged, but few of them remained in existence for very long.

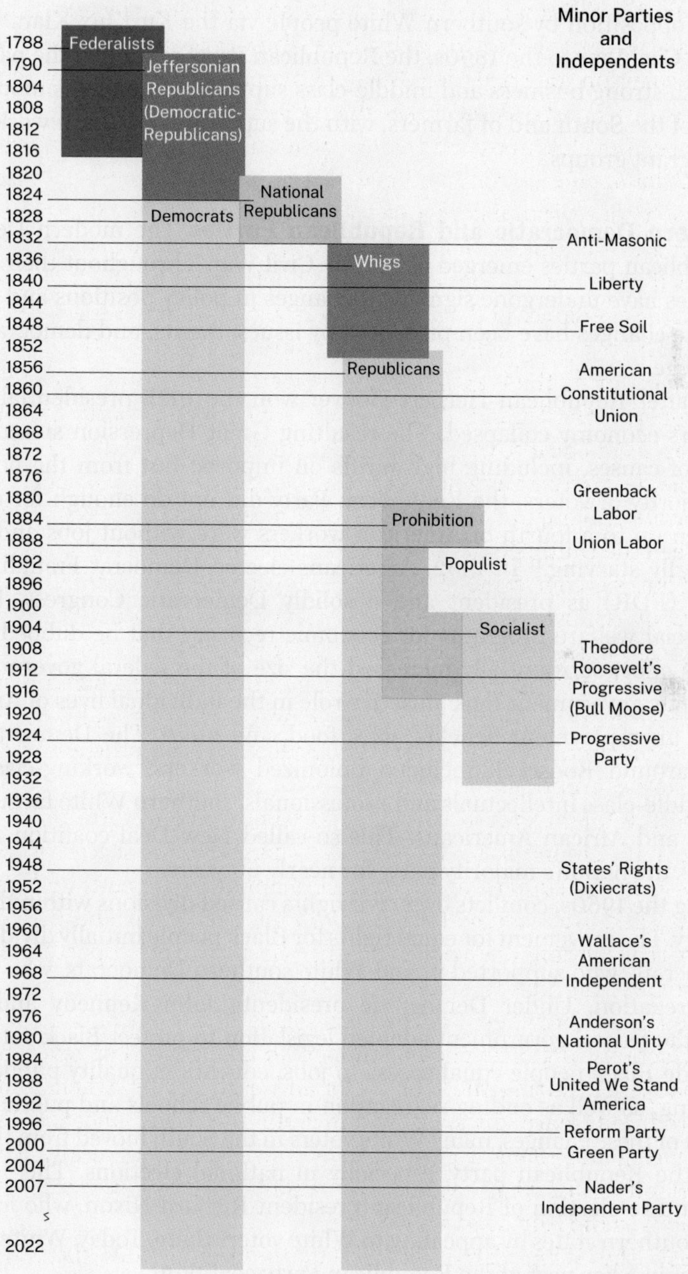

		Minor Parties and Independents
1788	Federalists	
1790	Jeffersonian	
1804	Republicans	
1808	(Democratic-	
1812	Republicans)	
1816		
1820		
1824	National	
1828	Democrats Republicans	
1832		Anti-Masonic
1836	Whigs	
1840		Liberty
1844		
1848		Free Soil
1852		
1856	Republicans	American
1860		Constitutional
1864		Union
1868		
1872		
1876		
1880		Greenback
1884	Prohibition	Labor
1888		Union Labor
1892		Populist
1896		
1900		
1904		Socialist
1908		Theodore
1912		Roosevelt's
1916		Progressive
1920		(Bull Moose)
1924		Progressive
1928		Party
1932		
1936		
1940		
1944		
1948		States' Rights
1952		(Dixiecrats)
1956		
1960		Wallace's
1964		American
1968		Independent
1972		
1976		Anderson's
1980		National Unity
1984		Perot's
1988		United We Stand
1992		America
1996		Reform Party
2000		Green Party
2004		
2007		Nader's
		Independent Party
2022		

Republican Party, which pledged to ban slavery from the western territories. In 1860 the Republicans nominated Abraham Lincoln for the presidency. Lincoln's victory in a four-way candidate race, with less than 40 percent of the popular vote, strengthened southern calls for secession from the Union and soon led to the Civil War. With the defeat of the Confederacy in 1865, Republicans granted the right to vote to formerly enslaved men, thus creating a large pro-Republican voting bloc. Voting rights for Black men ultimately met resistance, however, because of violent opposition by southern White people via the Ku Klux Klan. From the end of the Civil War to the 1890s, the Republican Party remained the party of the North, with strong business and middle-class support, while the Democrats were the party of the South and of farmers, with the support of northern working-class and immigrant groups.

The Modern Democratic and Republican Parties The modern Democratic and Republican parties emerged out of the Civil War. Throughout their histories, both parties have undergone significant changes in policy positions and membership. These changes have been prompted by issues, events, and demographic and social change.

Soon after Republican Herbert Hoover won the 1928 presidential election, the nation's economy collapsed. The resulting Great Depression stemmed from a variety of causes, including high tariffs on imports; but from the perspective of the majority of voters, the Republican Party did not do enough for economic relief when up to a fourth of American workers were without jobs and millions were actually starving.[11] In 1932, Americans elected Democrat Franklin Delano Roosevelt (FDR) as president and a solidly Democratic Congress. Roosevelt created social welfare programs for economic recovery that he dubbed the New Deal. This effort substantially increased the size of the federal government. For the first time, government took an active role in the individual lives of Americans, providing unemployment benefits, jobs, food, and more. The Democratic Party coalition around Roosevelt included unionized workers, working-class voters, upper-middle-class intellectuals and professionals, southern White farmers, Jews, Catholics, and African Americans. This so-called New Deal coalition made the Democrats the nation's majority party for nearly 60 years.

During the 1960s, conflicts over civil rights caused divisions within the Democratic Party. The movement for equal rights for Black people initially divided northern Democrats, who supported it, and White southern Democrats, who defended racial segregation. Under Democratic presidents John Kennedy and Lyndon Johnson, the federal government adopted legislation to protect Black voting rights and provide Black people equal access to jobs, education, quality public schools, and housing, as well as ending segregation in public schools and public facilities. In the face of these changes, many White voters in the South moved from the Democratic to the Republican party, especially in national elections. This led to the election and re-election of Republican president Richard Nixon, who focused on winning southern states by appealing to White voters there. Today, White southern voters remain a key part of the Republican Party coalition.

Richard Nixon's "southern strategy" helped broaden the Republican Party's base in the late 1960s and the 1970s by appealing to White southerners. Here, Nixon meets supporters in Georgia in 1968.

During the 1980s, the Republican Party coalesced around President Ronald Reagan, adding religious conservatives who were opposed to abortion and felt the Democrats were not protecting traditional family and religious values. The coalition also added working-class White voters (southern and northern), who were drawn to Reagan's tough approach to foreign policy, opposition to affirmative action, and promise of economic prosperity through low taxes and free trade. Many Republicans consider Reagan's presidency a "golden era" that saw deregulation of key industries (airlines, railroads, mail), a reduction of government intervention in the economy, and robust economic growth.

In the 1980s and 1990s, the Democratic Party maintained its support among a majority of unionized workers, the working class, upper-middle-class professionals, and racial and ethnic minority groups. The Democrats appealed to Americans concerned with economic fairness and inequality, women's rights, the environment, and other social causes.

In 2008, as the United States was experiencing the worst financial crisis since the 1930s, Democrat Barack Obama was elected the nation's first Black president. He was re-elected in 2012, winning large popular majorities both times. The Obama coalition united racial and ethnic groups, including Black, Latino, and Asian Americans, with young voters, White liberals and moderates, and voters from the Northeast, Midwest, and West. Obama helped the nation recover from global economic recession; adopted national health care; and promoted clean energy and environmental protections, labor policies, and LGBTQ rights. He was deeply unpopular with Republicans, who objected to what they saw as overreach by the federal government. Reflecting this unease, Republicans won control the House of Representatives in 2010 and the Senate in 2014.

Factions Reemerge: The Tea Party and Donald Trump Beginning in 2009, the Tea Party movement formed to oppose President Obama's agenda, especially national health care.[12] The Tea Party was a powerful insurgent faction within the Republican Party, not a spontaneous nonpartisan movement, as some have described it.[13] Tea Party members used the Republican Party's organizational networks to fund more conservative challengers to mainstream Republicans in primary elections. The Tea Party hoped that their candidates would be less willing than mainstream Republicans to compromise conservative principles. In total, the Tea Party succeeded in electing about 32 percent of its candidates in 2010—a strong showing for a newly organized group.

Tea Party Republicans coalesced around Donald Trump as their candidate for the Republican Party's nomination and presidency in 2016. Once in office, Trump delivered on the policy priorities the Tea Party movement wanted most. Despite public opposition, congressional Republicans passed a major tax cut for corporations and wealthy citizens. Trump also successfully appointed a record three of nine Supreme Court justices to lifetime appointments, and the majority-conservative Supreme Court ended federal protection for abortion—another Tea Party policy goal.

Party Polarization of Congress

A distinguishing feature of the contemporary party system is **political polarization,** where the two major political parties and their supporters are divided on

political polarization the division between the two major parties on most policy issues, with members of each party unified around their party's positions with little crossover

many issues. Today's parties have become ever more politically distant from one another, and voters and members of Congress increasingly vote along party lines. Levels of polarization in Congress today are very high, with members of Congress voting over 90 percent of the time in agreement with the majority of their party.[14]

The extent of party polarization in Congress was exemplified by party-line voting in 2017 for the most significant overhaul of the U.S. tax code in three decades.[15] The bill reduced taxes temporarily for some Americans but provided major financial gains to affluent taxpayers and a massive tax cut to corporations. Through concessions, threats, and extended negotiations, Republican leaders secured votes of support from all but 12 Republican members of the House, and every Senate Republican except one. Democrats in the House and Senate unanimously opposed the bill.

Party polarization in Congress may result from how members of the House are elected. Every 10 years, in states with more than one House member, congressional district boundaries are redrawn so that each district has roughly the same population. Partisan-controlled state legislatures draw district lines so that each district has a clear majority of either Republicans or Democrats. The lines favor the party controlling the legislature. With most lawmakers now elected from these "safe" districts, incumbents have little chance of losing in the next election; on average, they win 70 percent of the vote to challengers' 30 percent.[16] Facing little competition during general elections, those elected to Congress can be strong partisans. Today lawmakers face the greatest risk during their own party's primary elections, which often favor ideologically extreme candidates.

Some scholars argue that party polarization has occurred not because of how congressional districts are drawn but because people choose to live in liberal or conservative geographic areas.[17] This tendency is known as self-sorting. Increased geographical separation between Democrats and Republicans means lawmakers in safe districts have less incentive to compromise; thus, such districts add to party polarization.[18]

Check your understanding

1. What are political parties?

   a) Political parties are coalitions of individuals that organize the political world, recruit candidates, mobilize the public, and link the public to government.

   b) Political parties are organizations that seek to influence government officials on a narrow set of policy issues.

   c) Political parties are formal entities that constrain elected officials in their actions.

   d) Political parties are organizations that form solely to raise money for advertisements to advocate for or against particular issues.

2. Which of the following statements about the evolution of the two-party system is true?

   a) With growing electoral competition, the two-party system in the United States has produced more moderate parties that lack distinct positions due to candidates trying to appeal to moderate swing voters.

   b) Although the United States has had a two-party system since the 1780s, the nature of the parties has changed over time with various issues and events producing fluctuations in the parties' members and positions.

   c) The Democratic Party has remained static in its membership and policy positions, while the Republican Party grew more conservative after the Tea Party Movement took hold after 2009.

   d) The two-party system has undergone significant changes since the civil rights movement due to third parties successfully challenging major party candidates, resulting in both major parties taking more liberal positions on racial equality issues.

Parties in Elections and Government

Explain how parties organize to win elections and influence policy making in government

Political parties speak on behalf of citizens who individually have little voice but collectively, acting through the parties, can have a loud voice. Parties have been the chief points of contact between government officials, on the one side, and individual citizens and interest groups, on the other. Parties succeed when they win elections; but how exactly do they do that? And how do parties organize governmental activities?

Recruiting Candidates

Each election year, candidates run for thousands of state and local offices and congressional seats. One of the most important party activities is recruiting candidates. For "open" seats, where no incumbent is running for re-election, party leaders attempt to identify strong candidates and encourage them to run.

An ideal candidate has experience holding public office and the capacity to raise enough money to mount a serious campaign, especially if that candidate will face an incumbent or a well-funded opponent in the general election. Candidate recruitment is challenging in an era when politicians must assume that their personal lives will be intensely scrutinized on social media, in the press, and in negative campaign ads run by their opponents.[19]

Party Rules and Organizations Define How Parties Operate

In the United States, **party organizations** exist at every level of government. State law and party rules dictate how such party committees are created. Usually, members are elected at local party business meetings, called caucuses, or as part of primary elections. The best-known examples of these committees are at the national level: the Democratic National Committee (DNC) and the Republican National Committee (RNC).

The DNC and RNC are made up of party elites and act as gatekeepers for their respective parties, influencing which candidates have a chance to win the primaries by giving candidates money for their campaigns. They seek to minimize disputes within the party, work to enhance its media image, and set the rules for primary elections and caucuses, national debates, party conventions, and more.

party organization the formal structure of a political party, including its leadership, election committees, active members, and paid staff

political action committee (PAC) a private group that raises and distributes funds for use in election campaigns

Money for campaigns is critical to winning elections. The DNC and RNC have each established Super PACs (**political action committees**)

as critical fundraising organizations. Super PACs promote and publicize political issues by airing campaign ads. As nonprofit political advocacy groups, they can claim tax-exempt status under Section 527 of the Internal Revenue Code. They can raise and spend unlimited amounts of money as long as their activities are not coordinated with those of formal party organizations or candidates.

Parties Seek to Control Government

When the campaign and election are over, does it matter which party has won? Yes. The party with the majority of seats in the House or the Senate controls party leadership positions and sets the policy-making agenda.

Parties in Congress Parties form the basic organization for running Congress and every state legislature except Nebraska's, which has a nonpartisan legislature. In Congress, the Speaker of the House is a party office. All the members of the House take part in the election of the Speaker, but the actual selection is made by the **majority party**—the party that holds a majority of seats in the House. (The other party is the **minority party**.) Today party leaders in both the House and the Senate wield more power, and there is more unity when important votes are held on policy issues. As Congress has become increasingly divided, members have given more power to their party leaders, who have changed the rules in Congress so that the majority party can control the legislative process more easily, further intensifying polarization. The ability to debate legislation on the floor of the House has been restricted, and individual members have less personal choice about how to vote. (See Chapter 10.)

majority party the party that holds the majority of legislative seats in either the House or the Senate

minority party the party that holds the minority of legislative seats in either the House or the Senate

Each party also has House and Senate campaign committees made up of members of Congress who are expected to raise money from small and large donors, including corporations. These committees direct funds to competitive House and Senate races during each election cycle.

Parties and Policy For decades, one of the most familiar complaints about American politics was that the two major parties tried to be all things to all people and were therefore indistinguishable from each other. But since the 1980s fundamental differences have emerged between the positions of Democratic and Republican party leaders on many key issues.

For example, the national leadership of the Republican Party supports reducing spending on social and health care programs, cutting taxes on corporations and the wealthy, protecting rights of gun owners, reducing immigration to the United States, maintaining or increasing military spending, preserving traditional family structures, and opposing abortion. The Republican Party also opposes government regulation of businesses, including environmental laws.

AMERICA | SIDE BY SIDE

Comparing Party Systems

While the American political system features two competitive major political parties, many countries have either only one dominant party or more than two competitive parties. The number varies depending on several factors, especially the electoral rules in place. This map shows whether a country has either a strict one-party system, a dominant one-party system, a two-party system, or a multiparty system. Many authoritarian countries still maintain the trappings of democracy, including the presence of a dominant political party. Having two or more competitive political parties is therefore often considered a necessary feature of a free and fair democracy.

1. Which kind of party system seems most common? Why might it be the case that a dominant party system, one in which only one party has a realistic chance of winning elections, would not be considered fully democratic? When considering the party systems that are likely to occur in a democracy (two-party and multiparty), do you see any geographic or regional patterns to where such systems exist?

2. What do you think might be the advantages and the disadvantages to having a two-party system versus a multiparty system? What are the trade-offs involved in each of those arrangements? If you were designing a new democracy, which would you prefer and why?

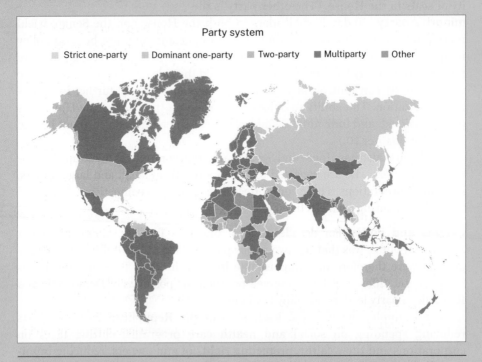

Party system

■ Strict one-party   ■ Dominant one-party   ■ Two-party   ■ Multiparty   ■ Other

SOURCES: Thomas Poguntke, Susan E. Scarrow, and Paul D. Webb, Political Party Database, www.politicalpartydb.org/ (accessed 10/27/21); CIA World Factbook, www.cia.gov/the-world-factbook/countries/ (accessed 10/27/21).

The Democratic Party, on the other hand, supports expanded funding for public education and social services, a national health insurance system, increased regulation of business to address climate change, higher taxes on the wealthy and corporations to reduce economic inequality, restrictions on gun ownership, and consumer protection programs. Democrats also support legalized abortion and protecting the rights of racial, ethnic, religious, and sexual minorities and undocumented immigrants.

Partisan conflict has intensified in recent years. Americans believe there are stronger conflicts in U.S. society today between Democrats and Republicans than between Black people and White people, rich people and people in poverty, and other demographic groups. In 2020, 91 percent of Americans said conflicts between Democrats and Republicans are either strong or very strong.[20]

Check your understanding

3. What role do political parties play in elections?

   a) Parties are the gatekeepers that determine who wins office; without the party's support, no candidate can win.

   b) Parties finance and administer all elections.

   c) Parties play no role in elections, as their role is restricted to the policy-making process.

   d) Parties recruit and nominate candidates for office, coordinate campaigns, mobilize voters, and raise money for campaigns and advertisements.

4. What are the key policy differences between the Democratic and Republican parties?

   a) The Republican Party supports renewable energies, stricter environmental regulations, and increased spending on social programs, while the Democratic Party supports reducing regulations on corporations, cutting taxes on the wealthy, and reducing spending on social programs.

   b) The Republican Party supports reducing spending on social programs, cutting taxes on corporations, and protecting gun ownership, while the Democratic Party supports expanding funding for public education and social services, higher taxes on corporations, and gun control.

   c) The Republican Party is socially liberal and fiscally conservative, while the Democratic Party is socially conservative and fiscally liberal.

   d) Both the Republican Party and the Democratic Party support more government control over health care, but Republicans support subsidies to help people buy private insurance plans while Democrats support expanding Medicare coverage.

Party Identification and Polarization Guide Voters

Identify the reasons for, and sources of, party identification and increased polarization

Party identification has been likened to wearing blue- or red-tinted glasses: they color voters' understanding of politics in general and are the most important cue in how to vote in elections. The vast majority of Republicans vote for Republican candidates, and the vast majority of Democrats vote for Democrats. On any general-election ballot, there are a number of candidates about whom the average voter has little information. In those cases, most voters fall back on their party identification to make their voting choice.

party identification an individual voter's psychological ties to one party or another

As we saw in Chapter 6, once these attachments are formed, usually in youth, they are likely to persist and even be handed down to children, unless some strong factors convince individuals that their party is no longer serving their interests.[21]

Partisanship as a reflection of party identification has both an ideological or policy component and an emotional component. Some have argued that partisanship reflects a person's rational evaluations: people choose parties that are closest to their own preferences across a wide range of issues and policies—and today, the gaps between Republicans and Democrats on issues are often extreme.[22] Others have argued that partisanship is more like a "running tally" of performance evaluations, an expectation of the future based on experiences in the past. The "running tally" is consistent with the idea of **retrospective voting**. People vote retrospectively when they reward or punish the incumbent party for its past performance, such as a weak or strong economy, handling of the pandemic, or high inflation. Voters may use considerations based on personal experience (especially about the state of the economy and their financial situation), or they may combine personal experience with evaluations from the media and other political actors. The party performing better in people's running tally wins their vote.

retrospective voting voting based on the past performance of a candidate or political party

Most people also understand partisanship as an emotional attachment.[23] According to this view, parties are so important that people tend to change their policy preferences on the issues to match their party. For example, before President Trump's administration, Republicans staunchly supported free trade and opposed tariffs on products made in other countries. But after Trump waged a trade war with China and Mexico, many Republicans switched to favoring tariffs on many imported goods and opposing unrestricted free trade to protect U.S.-made goods. When attachment to the party shapes opinions on policy, party

FIGURE 8.2 | Trends in Party Identification, 1970–2022

In the last fifty years, Democrats have lost strength as more Americans identified themselves as Republicans and independents. Today more than 40 percent of Americans reject both parties and identify as independents, an all-time high. Why do you think this is?

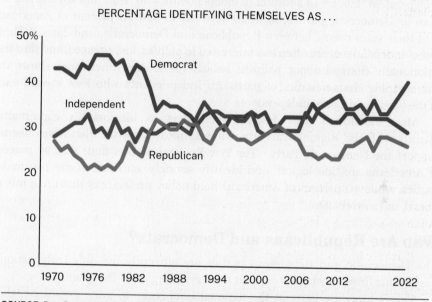

PERCENTAGE IDENTIFYING THEMSELVES AS . . .

SOURCE: Pew Research Center, "Democratic Edge in Party Identification Narrows Slightly," June 2, 2020, www.pewresearch.org/politics/2020/06/02/democratic-edge-in-party-identification-narrows-slightly/ (accessed 8/7/20); Roper Center for Public Opinion Research, https://ropercenter.cornell.edu/ (accessed 11/10/22).

identification is more like other social group identities, such as religious affiliation or being a fan of a certain sports team.[24]

Party identification gives citizens a stake in election outcomes that goes beyond the particular race at hand. This is why strong party identifiers are more likely to vote, to be contacted by campaigns, and to become activists for their party. **Party activists** are those who not only vote but also actively contribute their time, money, and effort to party affairs, organizations, and elections, thus giving them an outsize role in the party. They also tend to be less moderate and more ideological than the average person in the party.

Party Identification Today

Roughly equal numbers of people identify as Democrats and Republicans today, but more people identify as **independents**, an all-time high (see Figure 8.2).[25] Young people are more likely to be independents. Independents

party activists partisans who contribute time, energy, and effort to support their party and its candidates

independents people not formally aligned with a political party; also called unaffiliated

distrust the political system, dislike the parties and contentious politics, may prefer to keep their political opinions private, and often favor reforms to allow for multiple parties.[26]

Most independents vote consistently with either the Democratic or Republican party.[27] Some call these people "hidden partisans" because they privately hold policy opinions similar to partisans but reject the party labels and prefer the "independent" label.[28] In addition to independents who "lean" toward the Republican or Democratic parties, in 2020 between 15 and 20 percent of Americans split their votes evenly between Republican and Democratic candidates.[29] These "pure" independents are often less interested in politics, less engaged, and thus less emotionally charged about political issues.[30] Who Are Americans? shows the demographic characteristics of partisans, independents who lean toward each of the parties, and pure independents.

Most individuals who describe themselves as ideologically conservative identify with the Republican Party, whereas most who call themselves liberals support the Democratic Party. The Pew Research Center finds that 60 percent of Americans are "ideological" and identify strongly with one of the two major parties, while 40 percent of Americans hold policy preferences that are a mix of liberal and conservative.[31]

Who Are Republicans and Democrats?

The Democratic and Republican parties are currently the only truly national parties that draw substantial support from every region of the country.

The Democratic Party at the national level seeks to unite organized labor, people in poverty and working-class people, professionals, people with college degrees and graduate degrees, members of racial and ethnic groups, the young, the nonreligious, and civilian government workers. The Republicans, by contrast, appeal largely to non-Hispanic White people, a growing segment of Latino Americans, people without college degrees, business and wealthy people, the elderly, military families, and religious conservatives. Women overall are somewhat more likely to affiliate with the Democrats than the Republicans, but majorities of White women and women without a college degree vote Republican. People from rural areas tend to vote for Republicans, while people from urban areas tend to vote for Democrats. The suburbs, where the majority of Americans live, are a swing region. Suburban voters were evenly split when Democrats took control of the Congress in 2018, but suburban voters favored Republicans by 6 percentage points in 2022.

FOR CRITICAL ANALYSIS ⟶

1. What categories are the best predictors of party identification?
2. Do you think of yourself as a Democrat, Republican, or independent? Are other Americans of your gender, age, race, and income level likely to share your preferences?

WHO ARE AMERICANS?

Who Identifies with Which Party?

Party identification varies by gender, age, race and ethnicity, level of education, and income. For example, as these statistics show, Americans with higher incomes are more supportive of the Republican Party than are Americans with lower incomes. Women are more likely to identify with the Democratic rather than the Republican Party. Younger men have a greater tendency to identify as independents.

Legend: Democratic · Lean Democratic · Independent · Lean Republican · Republican

Gender
- Women
- Men

Age
- 18–29
- 30–49
- 50–64
- 65+

Race/Ethnicity
- White non-Hispanic
- Black
- Hispanic
- Asian
- Other

Education
- Postgraduate
- College graduate
- Some college
- High school diploma or less

Income
- <$20K
- $20–40K
- $40–80K
- $80K+

NOTE: Percentages do not add to 100 because the category "other/don't know" is omitted for some. ANES does not include rural/urban/suburban data.

SOURCE: Brian Schaffner, Stephen Ansolabehere, and Sam Luks, 2021, "Cooperative Election Study Common Content, 2020," https://doi.org/10.7910/DVN/E9N6PH, Harvard Dataverse, V3.

Members of racial and ethnic minority groups tend to favor Democratic candidates. In 2020, Joe Biden gained strong support from Black people.

Race and Ethnicity The United States' racial and ethnic composition is reflected both in changing partisanship among racial and ethnic groups and in growing divisions between the two major parties in their racial and ethnic makeup. One group whose partisan allegiance remains largely unchanged is African Americans. Approximately 92 percent of Black people describe themselves as Democrats and support Democratic candidates in national, state, and local elections.[32] One in five Americans are Latino and, as voters, are less monolithic than Black people; 4 in 10 Latinos voted Republican and 6 in 10 for Democrats in 2020.[33] Cuban Americans, for example, generally vote Republican, whereas Mexican Americans have favored Democrats. Asian Americans were also politically divided until recent years, but now tend to favor Democratic candidates. Figure 8.3 shows the racial and ethnic groups that made up the Democratic and Republican party coalitions in the 2020 election.

Region Since the 2000 election, maps showing the regional distribution of the vote have given rise to the idea of America being divided between "blue" and "red" states. Democrats, usually represented as blue, tend to be clustered on the coasts, in the upper Midwest, across the northern states, and in urban areas nationwide. Republicans, usually represented as red, tend to be concentrated in the Mountain West, the Great Plains, and the South, and in rural areas.[34] Some states that used to be solidly red or blue are now turning "purple" as Republicans and Democrats battle to win elections.

Age Today young people are much more likely to be Democrats and older voters are likely to be Republicans. Individuals from the same age cohort are likely to have experienced a similar set of events during the period when their party loyalties were formed. Millennials, for example, who came of age during the Great Recession and experienced growing economic inequality, reacted against the Republican Party as a result. In the 2020 elections, support for Republicans among the elderly

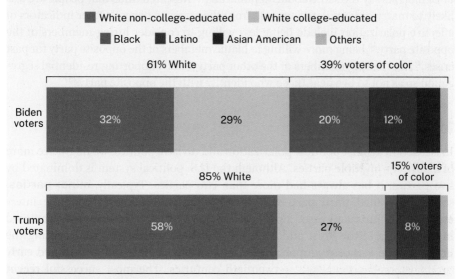

FIGURE 8.3 | Racial and Ethnic Composition of Biden and Trump Coalitions, 2020

The 2020 presidential election showed how race can be a powerful though not perfect predictor of vote choice. Thirty-nine percent of Biden voters, and only 15 percent of Trump voters, were people of color. Do you think these coalitions predict more wins for Democrats or Republicans in the future?

■ White non-college-educated   ■ White college-educated

■ Black   ■ Latino   ■ Asian American   ■ Others

61% White   39% voters of color

Biden voters: 32% | 29% | 20% | 12%

85% White   15% voters of color

Trump voters: 58% | 27% | 8%

SOURCE: Yair Ghitza and Jonathan Robinson, "What Happened in 2020," Catalist, https://catalist.us/wh-national/ (accessed 7/5/22).

decreased in part because older voters were concerned about the coronavirus pandemic. There is also a growing number of young people who identify as independent. Nonetheless, in 2020, roughly 6 in 10 people ages 18 to 29 voted for Democrat Joe Biden.[35]

Affective Polarization

For the last two decades, divisions between people who affiliate with the Republican and Democratic parties have been growing. Negative feelings among partisans toward members of the opposing party have intensified. This emotional disliking of members of the other party is called **affective polarization**. It is rooted in partisanship as a group identity, and widespread use of partisan media encourages it (see Chapter 7). Using national survey data spanning 1948 to 2008, research finds that Americans' feelings toward their own party have been stable, while heightened negative feelings toward the other party account for increasing polarization.[36] This reflects **negative partisanship**, a situation in which

affective polarization the emotional dislike of members of the other party

negative partisanship a phenomenon in which people form strong opinions against a political party rather than in support of one

which people form their opinions against a political party, rather than in support of one.[37]

Though Democrats and Republicans remain far apart on many policy issues, political divisions have moved beyond disagreements about policy and become more personal. For example, Republicans and Democrats think members of the other party are unpatriotic compared to other Americans. Fifty percent of Republicans say Democrats are more immoral compared to other Americans, and a similar number of Democrats say the same about Republicans.[38] Research finds that people are less likely to marry or even date someone from the opposite party.[39] Other indicators of affective polarization include being less willing to consider hiring members of the opposite party,[40] being more willing to blame members of the opposite party for past crises,[41] not trusting members of the other party,[42] and supporting residential segregation so as not to live near those who identify with the opposite party.[43]

Minor Parties

In a reaction against political polarization and divisive politics, we might see more of a push for multiple parties. Although the U.S. political system is dominated by two parties, it has always had more than two parties. Typically, **minor parties**, sometimes called third parties, have represented social and economic interests that were not addressed by the two major parties.[44] The Populists, centered in rural areas of the West and Midwest, and the Progressives, representing the urban middle class, are important examples from the late nineteenth and early twentieth centuries. The most successful recent minor-party presidential candidate, H. Ross Perot, who ran in 1992 as an independent and in 1996 as the Reform Party's nominee, won the votes of almost one in five Americans in 1992.

minor parties parties that organize to compete against the two major American political parties

Minor parties exist mainly as protest movements against the two major parties or to promote specific policies. Minor parties can be sources of new ideas and can profoundly affect elections, taking votes from one of the major parties and enabling the other party to win. In the extremely close 2000 presidential election, for example, minor-party candidate Ralph Nader won just 3 percent of the popular vote, but that split the Democratic vote enough to swing the election to Republican George W. Bush. In the 2016 election, neither major-party candidate won a majority of the popular vote because minor parties took 5 percent of it. In addition, minor parties have at times enjoyed an influence far beyond their electoral size because large parts of their platform were adopted by one or both of the major parties, which wanted to appeal to the voters mobilized by the new party and thus expand their own electoral strength.

One election reform that may promote the development of multiple parties is ranked choice voting (RCV). RCV is currently in use in 250 local elections and statewide in Maine and Alaska. The idea is to give voters more choice: rather than casting a single vote for one's preferred candidate, a voter ranks multiple candidates (usually three) from most preferred (first choice) to least preferred (third choice). If a candidate wins a majority of first-choice votes, that candidate is declared the winner, and second- and third-choice votes are not counted. But if no candidate receives a majority, the candidate with the fewest first-choice votes is eliminated, and those voters' ballots are redistributed to their second-choice candidates. Then the ballots are recounted; if any candidate now has a majority, a winner is declared. The process is repeated until one candidate has a majority. Ranked choice voting eliminates the possibility that votes for a minor-party candidate will be wasted.

Check your understanding

5. What causes people to identify as Democratic or Republican?

   a) People form partisan attachments because they agree with one party more than the other on policy issues; partisanship can also be an emotional attachment that can cause people to form their issue positions to match their party.

   b) People usually choose their partisanship based on which party controls their state government, since state government usually has a high public approval rating.

   c) Partisanship is always determined by charismatic leaders in government, since the public does not follow politics closely.

   d) Partisanship fluctuates according to the performance of the economy; people switch parties to the one in power if the economy is doing well.

6. What has caused the rise in partisan polarization in U.S. politics?

   a) The rise of partisan polarization was caused entirely by partisan gerrymandering, which creates safe partisan districts for congresspeople.

   b) The rise of partisan polarization is caused by the shift to primary elections where extreme voters turn out and support candidates at the extreme ideological ends of the spectrum.

   c) Democrats and Republicans have not only grown apart on policy issues but also are more negative in their feelings toward the other party, which has eroded trust of those in the other party.

   d) Democrats and Republicans have become more polarized because campaign donors tend to favor ideologically extreme candidates, and this gives them an electoral advantage.

There Are Many Types of Interest Groups

Describe the major types of interest groups and whom they represent

An **interest group** is an organized group of people or institutions that uses various forms of advocacy to influence public policy. This definition includes membership organizations of ordinary individuals as well as business organizations and

interest group an organized group of people or institutions that uses various forms of advocacy to influence public policy

trade associations, labor unions, university associations, professional groups for particular occupations, and even government groups such as the National League of Cities or National Governors Association that lobby other levels of government. Individuals and other entities form groups to increase the chance that their views will be heard and their interests treated favorably by the government. Unlike political parties, which represent the people, interest groups represent narrow, often economic, interests.

Interest groups are sometimes referred to negatively as "lobbies," "special interests," or "pressure groups," or discussed positively as "advocacy organizations" or, in some cases, "citizen groups." They are also sometimes confused with political action committees (PACs), which are groups that raise and distribute money for use in election campaigns. Many interest groups do create PACs in their name to be the money-giving arm of the interest group. For example, the NRA Political Victory Fund donates money to political candidates and officeholders on behalf of the NRA, which represents the interests of gun owners.

Interest groups also differ from social movements (although sometimes movements become interest groups). Both types of groups try to influence government, but interest groups tend to be more formalized and try to influence policy through political channels, while social movements may also engage in collective action such as protests, boycotts, and civil disobedience. Examples of social movements include Black Lives Matter, environmentalism, the gay rights movement, the pro-life movement, and the Tea Party.

Interest groups serve important functions in American democracy, interacting with nearly all of the players in the governmental system. Millions of Americans are members of one or more interest groups, at least to the extent of paying dues, attending an occasional meeting, following a group on social media, reading its newsletter or website, or being on its email list. Organized groups use these means to educate their members on policy issues and mobilize them for elections. Interest groups of businesses, professionals, governments, and other entities similarly conduct research and provide information to the members about relevant policy matters. Both types of groups furnish information to and lobby members of Congress during the lawmaking process. They provide information to the executive branch and participate in administrative rule making and the design of regulations. They also monitor government programs and regulations to ensure these do not adversely affect their members. Additionally, they use the judicial system to engage in litigation. Through these means, organized interest groups represent their members' interests and help promote democratic politics. But as we will see, not all interests are represented equally in society, nor are all organized groups equally successful.

Types of Interest Groups

Interest groups range from corporate associations to groups organizing ordinary people. All hope to influence policy outcomes.

Corporate Groups and Trade Associations One powerful set of interest groups has a direct economic interest in governmental policy: businesses. Corporations commonly form trade associations with other businesses in their economic sector, such as the American Beverage Association or the American Fuel and Petrochemical Manufacturers. They may join broader groups as well, such as the U.S. Chamber of Commerce, which represents many types of businesses, and the National Federation of Independent Business, which represents small businesses. As government regulation increased in the 1970s, many individual firms began hiring their own lobbyists to try to persuade government officials and influence policy outcomes.[45]

Groups working on behalf of businesses and industry far outweigh citizen groups and unions in the number of registered lobbyists in Washington, D.C., and state capitals, and in terms of money spent. Corporations and trade associations constitute nearly half of all entries in the *Washington Representatives* directory, the "phone book" of organizations with a lobbying presence in the nation's capital.[46] Their financial resources are even more disproportionate. In 2021, labor organizations spent $49 million on lobbying, and "ideology/single issue" groups—the label used by the Center for Responsive Politics for citizen groups—spent $177 million. But those amounts are eclipsed by lobbying expenditures by businesses and business and trade associations. The health sector alone spent $589 million.[47] Altogether, corporations, trade associations, and business associations spend $34 on lobbying to every $1 spent by citizen groups and labor unions combined.[48]

Labor Groups Labor organizations are also active in lobbying government. Unions such as the United Auto Workers, the United Mine Workers, and the Teamsters lobby on behalf of organized labor in the private sector, while the American Federation of State, County and Municipal Employees (AFSCME) and the American Federation of Teachers (AFT) are examples of public-sector unions that represent members who work in government and public education. Some labor unions, such as the Service Employees International Union (SEIU), organize workers in both the private and public sectors.

Unions constitute less than 1 percent of the organized interests in Washington.[49] Despite declining membership, especially in the private sector, where union membership fell from 35 percent of workers in the 1950s to 6.1 percent in 2021,[50] and despite having fewer resources than business groups, labor unions continue to exercise influence in Washington and state capitals. Union members vote at high rates and often work on campaigns.[51]

Professional Associations Professional associations represent the interests of individuals who work in specific occupations (as opposed to trade associations, which are composed of business firms in a given sector) and constitute 5.4 percent of the organized groups in Washington.[52] Physicians, lawyers, accountants, real estate agents, dentists, and even college faculty have professional associations. Many individuals may not think of themselves as participants in the interest group system but nonetheless have professional associations working on their behalf. Some professional lobbies such as the American Bar Association, the American Medical Association, and the National Realtors Association have been particularly successful.

Although public schoolteachers are a minority of the total population, the unions that represent them are an influential interest group in many states because they are highly informed and act as a group in support of issues related to their profession, including teachers' salaries.

Professional associations are active at the state level as well, in part because states are responsible for licensing many occupations, from physicians to beauticians.

Citizen Groups Citizen groups are open to ordinary citizens and represent a wide variety of interests, with groups organized on issues from the environment to abortion, to gun policy, to disability rights. The largest citizen group is AARP (formerly the American Association for Retired People), which has around 40 million members—anyone age 50 and older can join—and represents the interests of older Americans. Other citizen groups include the National Rifle Association, the Sierra Club, and Mothers Against Drunk Driving (MADD). The wide variety of citizen groups makes for some confusing terminology. Some citizen groups are referred to as "public interest groups" if they purport to lobby for the general good rather than their own economic interests.[53] Some citizen groups are also referred to as "ideological groups," organized in support of a particular political or philosophical perspective. Examples include the Christian Coalition, the National Taxpayers Union, and NARAL Pro-Choice America. Citizen groups make up only about 14 percent of the groups with lobbying offices in Washington.[54]

pluralism the theory that all interests are and should be free to compete for influence in the government; the outcome of this competition is compromise and moderation

Why Do Interest Groups Form?

Pluralism, the theory that most interests are and should be free to compete for influence in the government, was long the dominant view of the U.S. political system. Early pluralist thinkers held that interest groups would naturally arise in response to a "disturbance in society."[55] The large number of interest groups in the United States seems to suggest such spontaneity is common. But there are significant barriers to group formation, such as the need for resources and the difficulty of motivating potential members.

Indeed, one prominent critique of pluralism has pointed out the difficulties of attracting and maintaining group membership.[56] Suppose there is a community where polluted air threatens the health of thousands or even millions of residents. Each resident wants to breathe clean air. But no single individual has an incentive to join an environmental group—and pay membership dues or volunteer—as the group works to reduce pollution. Why join the group and spend your precious time and money on this when you are going to benefit from the **collective goods** of reduced pollution anyway (collective goods being benefits sought by groups that are broadly available and cannot be denied to nonmembers)? Each of the inactive residents would be a **free rider** on the efforts of the residents who joined the group and worked to reduce pollution, enjoying the benefits of collective goods without having worked toward acquiring them. The collective action problem is that if all individuals follow the same logic, then no one would join environmental groups, and pollution would continue.

collective goods benefits sought by groups that are broadly available and cannot be denied to nonmembers

free riders those who enjoy the benefits of collective goods but did not participate in acquiring or providing them

The challenge for interest groups is to overcome the free-rider problem. To do so, groups offer "selective benefits," available only to group members, to induce people to join. Table 8.1 gives some examples of the range of such benefits.

TABLE 8.1	Selective Benefits of Interest Group Membership
CATEGORY	**BENEFITS**
Informational benefits	Conferences Professional contacts Publications Coordination among organizations Research Legal help Professional codes Collective bargaining
Material benefits	Travel packages Insurance Discounts on consumer goods
Solidary benefits	Friendship Networking opportunities
Purposive benefits	Advocacy Representation before government Participation in public affairs

SOURCE: Adapted from Jack Walker, Jr., *Mobilizing Interest Groups in America: Patrons, Professions, and Social Movements* (Ann Arbor: University of Michigan Press, 1991), 86.

HOW TO

Start an Advocacy Group

SHANNON WATTS, THE FOUNDER OF MOMS DEMAND ACTION FOR GUN SENSE IN AMERICA

Do you ever think, "Hey, that's not right. Somebody should do something about that"? That somebody could be you. Shannon Watts was a stay-at-home mom of five who "wasn't political at all" when the shooting at Sandy Hook Elementary School in Newtown, Connecticut, occurred in December 2012. She decided to mobilize "mothers and others" around gun safety, and her grassroots network now has chapters in all 50 states. Here is Shannon's advice for starting an advocacy group:

1 **Figure out what you're passionate about and get educated about the issue.** Don't be afraid to call people for their wisdom. You don't have to take every piece of advice — some people may even advise you not to start an organization. But seek out any input and issue information that will help.

2 **Decide on the scope of the goal and the objective that you are trying to accomplish.** Are you trying to create change in your neighborhood, your community, your state, your region, even nationwide? What policy change do you seek?

3 **Think about the people you need around you.** Start with your personal networks to find volunteers willing to help out. Seek help from experts for website development or pro bono legal work or other organizing help. Recruit in person, online — use every mode that works. I started with just 75 Facebook friends, and I was able to tap into the power of perfect strangers because of social media.

4 **Figure out your group's branding: the group's look and feel, including name, logo, font, and colors.** A successful brand brings people together, empowers them, and bonds them. Our organization (Moms Demand Action) uses the color red, which makes the mom members feel like they have superhero capes.

5 **Keep going even when you face defeats.** Regroup, learn from the loss, and take advantage of the positives that emerge even from setbacks. It's important to emphasize to your volunteers that you may have created new relationships with lawmakers; you may have made relationships with the media; you may have grown your organization.

6 **Realize that change typically comes in small steps.** I think young people are particularly frustrated with incrementalism, but that's how our democracy is set up. Change doesn't happen overnight. I always say, incrementalism is what leads to revolution.

Each generation and each segment of the population has very specific levers of power that are available to them, and they have to figure out what those are. Our members' special power is motherhood and love for their children. What's your group's special power?

informational benefits special newsletters, periodicals, training programs, conferences, and other information provided to members of groups to entice others to join

material benefits special goods, services, or money provided to members of groups to entice others to join

solidary benefits selective benefits of group membership that emphasize friendship, networking, and consciousness-raising

purposive benefits selective benefits of group membership that emphasize the purpose and accomplishments of the group

Informational benefits, the most widespread and important category of selective benefits, are provided through online communication such as email, conferences, training programs, and newsletters and other periodicals sent automatically to those who have paid membership dues.

Material benefits include anything that can be measured monetarily, such as gifts like tote bags and mugs; discounts on travel (provided by AARP), gun club memberships (offered by the NRA), and other purchases; and health and retirement insurance (offered by many professional associations).

Solidary benefits include the friendship and networking opportunities that membership provides as well as the satisfaction of working toward a common goal with like-minded individuals. The Sierra Club, for example, offers "Sierra Singles" programming by which single people can participate in hikes, picnics, and cultural outings with others interested in environmental issues and meet new friends or perhaps a life partner at the same time.[57] Members of associations based on ethnicity, race, or religion also derive solidary benefits from interacting with individuals they perceive as sharing their own backgrounds, values, and perspectives.

A fourth type of benefit involves the appeal of the purpose of an interest group. An example of these **purposive benefits** is businesses joining trade associations to further their economic interests. Similarly, individuals join consumer, environmental, or other civic groups to pursue goals important to them. Many of the most successful interest groups of the past 30 years have been organized largely around shared ideological goals, including government reform, civil rights, economic equality, "family values," and even opposition to government itself.

What Interests Are Not Represented?

A second critique of pluralism is that not all interests are equally represented in debates over government and policy. As the political scientist E. E. Schattschneider put it, "The flaw in the pluralist heaven is that the heavenly chorus sings with a strong upper-class accent."[58] His point was that interest group politics is heavily skewed in favor of corporate, business, and upper-class groups, leaving those with lower socioeconomic status less able to participate in and influence government. The central reason for this skew is that people with higher incomes, more education, and managerial or professional occupations are much more likely to have the time, money, and skills needed to play a role in a group or contribute financially to it.[59]

A recent study examining the advocacy efforts of over 2,600 interest groups finds considerable diversity of views but also confirms that trade and business associations, corporations, and occupational associations have more conservative preferences than unions, public interest groups, and identity groups—and that lobbying expenditures and campaign expenditures are greater among more conservative groups.[60] The result is that interest groups and their members are not as economically or racially diverse as the U.S. population. And even for marginalized groups that do organize, group leadership is often more privileged and may have different policy priorities than the group's members.[61] Because organized interests skew toward more privileged groups, many policy issues critical to working- and middle-class people may be ignored by government, while issues of importance to the upper class and to business receive priority.

Check your understanding

7. Washington, D.C.-based interest groups that have the most financial resources and lobbyists tend to represent which of the following?

   a) professional associations
   b) corporate groups and trade associations
   c) citizen groups
   d) labor groups

8. To win over free riders who enjoy the benefits provided by a group without participating in acquiring them, interest groups offer

   a) cash benefits.
   b) collective goods.
   c) selective benefits.
   d) collective action.

What Do Interest Groups Do?

Explain how interest groups try to influence government and policy

Interest groups work to improve the likelihood that their policy interests will be heard and treated favorably by the government. The quest for political influence or power takes many forms. "Inside strategies" include gaining access to key decision makers, lobbying, conducting executive branch oversight, and litigating cases in courts. "Outside strategies" include using electoral politics and going public (see Figure 8.4). These strategies do not exhaust all the possibilities, but they paint a broad picture of ways that groups use their resources in the competition for influence.

FIGURE 8.4 | How Interest Groups Influence Congress

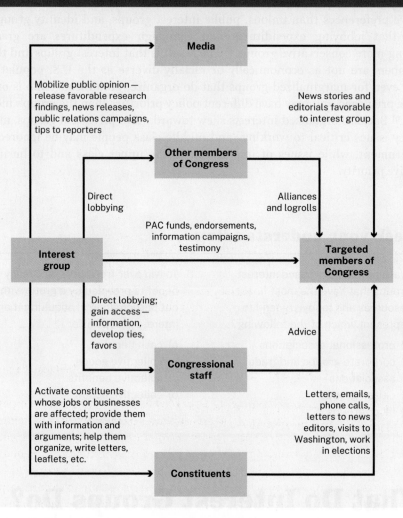

Interest Groups Influence Congress through Lobbying

Lobbying is an attempt by a group to influence the policy process through the strategic sharing of information, building relationships with policy makers across government.[62] Traditionally, the term *lobbyist* referred to those seeking to influ-

lobbying a strategy by which organized interests seek to influence the passage of legislation by exerting direct pressure on government officials

ence the passage of legislation in Congress. The First Amendment provides for the right to "petition the Government for a redress of grievances." As early as the 1870s, *lobbying* became the common term for petitioning: since petitioning cannot take place on the floor of the House or

Business owners are often able to gain access to elected officials. Here, President Biden meets with business and labor leaders to discuss improving America's infrastructure.

Senate, petitioners must confront members of Congress in the lobbies of the two chambers.

The 1946 Federal Regulation of Lobbying Act defines a lobbyist as "any person who shall engage himself for pay or any consideration for the purpose of attempting to influence the passage or defeat of any legislation of the Congress of the United States." Some lobbyists are directly employed by a particular interest group or a specific business corporation, while others work for lobbying firms that can be hired by any group seeking representation and lobbying services. All organizations employing lobbyists are required to register with Congress and to disclose whom they represent, whom they lobby, what they are looking for, and how much they are paid.

Approximately 11,700 lobbyists are currently registered, down from a high of over 14,000 in 2007.[63] The decline in the number of registered lobbyists may not be nearly as large as these numbers suggest.[64] Critics allege that recent changes in lobbyist registration requirements merely reduce the number of official lobbying registrations while the true amount of lobbying remains undiminished, and that disclosure laws have significant loopholes.[65]

Lobbyists attempt to influence the policy process in a variety of ways,[66] the most important being providing information to lawmakers, administrators, and committee staff about their interests and the legislation and regulations that they seek to promote, amend, or defeat. In addition, they often testify on behalf of their clients at congressional committee and agency hearings, talk to reporters, place ads in newspapers, and organize letter-writing, phone-call, email, and social media campaigns. Many lobbying efforts occur in private meetings with lawmakers and campaign leaders. Lobbyists also play an important role in fundraising, helping to direct clients' contributions to certain members of Congress and presidential candidates.

Congress has become more dependent on lobbyists. Over time, Congress has cut funding for its own research and support staff; the combined staffs of the Congressional Research Service, Government Accountability Office, and Congressional Budget Office fell by 45 percent between 1975 and 2015.[67] Also, the total number of congressional staff working directly for representatives and senators in Washington has fallen since the late 1970s, as lawmakers have sent more staff to home districts and states to help constituents. These D.C. staff members are stretched thin and work across many issue areas even as public policy has become more complex.[68] As a result, lobbyists have the ability to fill the information and expertise void to the benefit of those they lobby for.

Lobbying and Overseeing the Executive Branch Even when an interest group is successful at getting its bill passed by Congress and signed by the president, full implementation of that law is up to executive branch agencies, and participation in their rule-making process is a key activity for many interest groups. Just like lawmakers and their staffs, executive branch bureaucrats undertaking rule making need information and expertise, which lobbyists readily provide. Interest groups also monitor policy implementation, engaging in executive branch oversight.

How Interest Groups Make Policy: Iron Triangles and Issue Networks
Many government policies are the product of a so-called **iron triangle**, which has one point in an executive branch program (bureaucratic agency), another point in a Senate or House committee or subcommittee, and a third point in some well-organized interest group. In policy areas such as agriculture, energy, or veterans' affairs, interest groups, government agencies, and congressional committees routinely work together for mutual benefit. The interest group provides campaign contributions for members of Congress, lobbies for larger budgets for the agency, and provides policy expertise to lawmakers. The agency, in turn, provides government contracts for the interest group and constituency services for friendly members of Congress. The congressional committee or subcommittee, meanwhile, supports the agency's budgetary requests and the programs the interest group favors. Together the three points in an iron triangle create a mutually supportive relationship. Figure 8.5 illustrates the iron triangle of the defense industry.

iron triangle the stable, cooperative relationship that often develops among a congressional committee, an administrative agency, and one or more supportive interest groups; not all of these relationships are triangular, but the iron triangle is the most typical

issue network a loose network of elected leaders, public officials, activists, and interest groups drawn together by a specific policy issue

Policy development in a number of important areas, such as the environment, taxes, and immigration, is controlled not by highly structured and unified iron triangles but by broader **issue networks**. These consist of like-minded politicians, consultants,

FIGURE 8.5 | The Iron Triangle in the Defense Sector

Defense contractors are powerful actors in shaping defense policy; they act in concert with defense committees and subcommittees in Congress and executive agencies concerned with defense.

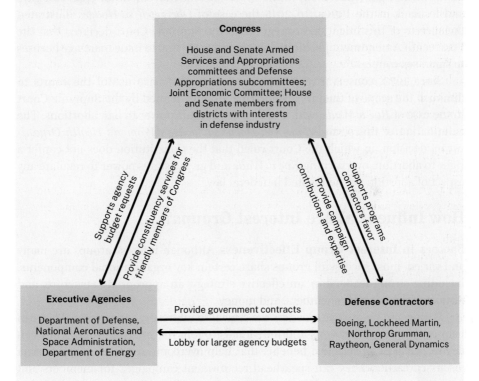

Congress

House and Senate Armed Services and Appropriations committees and Defense Appropriations subcommittees; Joint Economic Committee; House and Senate members from districts with interests in defense industry

Supports agency budget requests

Provide constituency services for friendly members of Congress

Provide campaign contributions and expertise

Supports programs contractors favor

Executive Agencies

Department of Defense, National Aeronautics and Space Administration, Department of Energy

Provide government contracts →

← Lobby for larger agency budgets

Defense Contractors

Boeing, Lockheed Martin, Northrop Grumman, Raytheon, General Dynamics

activists, and interest groups who care about the issue in question. Issue networks are more fluid than iron triangles, coming together when an issue appears on the agenda and then dissolving until the next round of policy making. The two concepts can coexist: some issue networks have iron triangles at their core. For example, there are iron triangles at the center of many areas of energy policy, but sometimes a high-profile proposal, such as a new interstate oil and gas pipeline, activates a broader issue network including landowners, environmentalists, state officials, and so on.

Using the Courts

Interest groups sometimes turn to litigation when they lack access or feel they have insufficient influence to change a policy. A group can use the courts to affect public policy in at least three ways: (1) by bringing suit directly on behalf of the group itself, (2) by financing suits brought by individuals, or (3) by filing a companion brief as an *amicus curiae* (literally "friend of the court") to an existing court case.

Among the best-known examples of using the courts for political influence is the litigation by the National Association for the Advancement of Colored People (NAACP) that led to *Brown v. Board of Education of Topeka, Kansas* (1954), in which the U.S. Supreme Court held that legal segregation of public schools was unconstitutional (see Chapter 5).[69] Later, extensive litigation accompanied the women's rights movement in the 1960s and the movement for rights for gays and lesbians in the 1990s. In 2015 the case of *Obergefell v. Hodges* illustrated the success of this litigation strategy when the Supreme Court declared that the Fourteenth Amendment prohibited states from refusing to issue marriage licenses to same-sex couples.[70]

Since 1973, conservative groups have made extensive use of the courts to diminish the scope of the privacy doctrine initially defined by the Supreme Court in the case of *Roe v. Wade*, which took away a state's power to ban abortions. The culmination of this strategy was the *Dobbs v. Jackson Women's Health Organization* decision, in which the Court ruled that the Constitution does not confer a right to abortion, overturning *Roe v. Wade* and giving states power to regulate any aspect of abortion not delineated in federal law.[71]

How Influential Are Interest Groups?

Factors in Interest Group Effectiveness Although interest groups are many and varied, most successful groups share certain key organizational components, including strong leadership, an effective strategy, an appropriate structure, and resources such as staff, members, and money.

Strong and charismatic leaders are crucial to interest group success. They can help convince organizations and individuals to join the interest group. They can devise packages of selective benefits that help overcome the free-rider dilemma discussed earlier. They can spearhead recruitment campaigns for members and media campaigns to spread the group's message. And they can engage in lobbying and the other activities of group influence.

Resources are also a factor in group effectiveness. The sheer number of members can be a resource that leaders cite in their interactions with government officials. The fact that AARP has nearly 40 million members—about half the U.S. population age 50 and over—can make lawmakers hesitate to adopt policies that older Americans view as harmful to their interests.[72]

Staff members are another type of group resource—their numbers and their talent for recruiting members, publicizing the group's activities through media, conducting research, monitoring government activity, and lobbying. And money is perhaps the ultimate resource. It funds membership drives and it is necessary for conducting media campaigns aimed both at the public and at policy makers. Having more money means a group can hire more and better-connected lobbyists who can access more government decision makers. Money helps interest groups engage in all of their activities, but studies show that more money doesn't always lead to more interest group success.

Measuring Interest Group Influence

How influential are interest groups? Some people are concerned that interest groups are *too* effective—that their lobbying is too convincing or that their campaign contributions can buy lawmakers' votes on legislation. Indeed, some scholars characterize American politics as less about electoral politics than about "organized combat" among high-resource interest groups fighting over issues far from ordinary Americans' concerns.[73] Yet others argue that much interest group activity does not change policy outcomes and that there is little relationship between spending on lobbying and policy wins.[74] For analysts, the dilemma is trying to measure the effectiveness of interest groups. We are pretty sure they have an influence on government and policy, but how much? And what is the nature of that influence?

As noted earlier, the most important way lobbyists win influence is not by persuading their opponents to change their policy views but by providing information to their allies in Congress and the bureaucracy, which helps them do their jobs.[75] Those groups with demonstrated technical expertise have been shown to have more access to lawmakers.[76] Similarly, executive branch officials engaged in rule making are most responsive to the side of an issue that participates the most.[77] The groups with the most expertise and that participate the most tend to be corporate and professional groups.

Regulating Lobbying

The role that lobbyists play in policy making raises concerns, and periodically Congress tries to address abuses. Sometimes the actions of lobbyists are outside of the law. In 2005 a prominent Washington lobbyist, Jack Abramoff, was convicted of fraud and violations of federal lobbying laws. Abramoff had collected tens of millions of dollars from several Native American tribes that operated lucrative gambling casinos. Much of this money found its way into the campaign war chests of Abramoff's friends in Congress, including former House majority leader Tom DeLay (R-Tex.). In exchange for these campaign funds, key Republican members of Congress helped Abramoff's clients shut down rival casino operators. Thus, through a well-connected lobbyist, money had effectively purchased access and influence. Abramoff and several of his associates pleaded guilty to federal bribery and fraud charges, and Abramoff was sentenced to five years in prison.

Because lobbyists are so influential in Washington, D.C., Congress has tried periodically to limit their role by adopting stricter guidelines. For example, businesses may no longer deduct lobbying costs as a business expense. Trade associations must report to members the proportion of their dues that goes toward lobbying, and that proportion may not be reported as a business expense. Congress also passed legislation limiting the size of gifts its members could accept from interest groups, and members cannot accept honoraria for speeches.[78]

Check your understanding

9. Which of the following statements explains why so-called iron triangles are important to policy making?

   a) Iron triangles establish the Super PACs that get members of Congress elected.

   b) Iron triangles serve as watchdogs of Congress, alerting committees to wasteful spending and malfeasance.

   c) Members of iron triangles hold authority over their policy domain and establish policies that mutually benefit one another.

   d) Members of iron triangles help draw media attention to certain issues and hold considerable sway over public opinion.

10. Which of the following statements regarding interest groups' electoral activity is true?

   a) Ballot measures by business groups are more likely to pass than those sponsored by citizen groups.

   b) Interest groups invest more resources overall on lobbying than on electoral politics.

   c) Interest groups' spending has remained constant over time.

   d) Reforms to campaign finance laws in the 1970s have significantly reduced interest groups' influence in elections.

WHAT DO YOU THINK?

POLITICAL PARTIES AND INTEREST GROUPS

We would like to think that government policies are products of legislators representing the public interest. But in truth few programs and policies ever reach the public agenda without the vigorous efforts of the political parties and key interest groups, which help to crystallize a world of possible government actions into a set of distinct choices. The activity of parties and interest groups is of critical importance, although some interests are better represented than others, as the demise of the Child Tax Credit expansion showed.

- James Madison wrote that "liberty is to faction as air is to fire."[79] By this he meant that the organization and proliferation of political parties and interests are inevitable in a free society. In what ways do political parties and organized interests enhance liberty? In what ways do they limit it?

- Is the two-party system ideal for American politics, or would electoral reforms encourage more parties to form and thereby promote more choice for voters?

- Is party polarization likely to remain high in the near future? Is this a problem? What rules or processes, if any, could reduce party polarization?

- What do you think of competition among different interests — is it free, open, and vigorous, or are some types of interests more likely to organize? What are the implications for government and politics? What would Nikki Wells, the day-care teacher featured at the beginning of this chapter, say?

Use 🐰 **INQUIZITIVE** *to help you study and master this material.*

9

WHAT GOVERNMENT DOES & WHY IT MATTERS
Elections are the core of any democracy. In a democratic system like the United States, citizens self-govern by choosing among candidates and electing leaders to represent them in government. Meet two of the nation's youngest elected politicians, who became interested in government early in life and decided to take the next step—launching campaigns for office.

When Democrat David Morales was sworn in to the Rhode Island House of Representatives in January 2021, he was only 22 years old, one of the youngest Latino lawmakers in the country. Born to Mexican immigrants in rural California, David worked hard to make his mom proud, knowing that she had sometimes worked three jobs to support him and his sister. Because he took college courses during high school, he earned his bachelor's degree in two years, followed by a public affairs master's degree from Brown University, the program's youngest graduate ever at age 20. His campaign for state legislator emphasized issues of housing, education, and health care and mobilized not just "super voters" who regularly

Participation, Campaigns & Elections

turn out for primary elections but also "working people, poor people, young people, and people of color who ended up voting for the first time," David said. During his campaign, he would appear at community events in a Spider-Man costume. "To me, Peter Parker represents the working class. If you follow the comic, he's usually poor and struggling. The average person can relate to him, and that's what makes his story so beautiful," David said. His efforts to champion working-class issues and mobilize voters paid off: David beat a six-year incumbent by more than 20 points.[1]

After knocking on many doors like David Morales, Republican Caleb Hanna won office by a commanding margin too, in his case to West Virginia's state legislature. Caleb was a 19-year-old college freshman when he was elected in 2018 and remains one of the youngest legislators in the United States and the youngest Black person ever to be elected to a state legislature. He first became interested in politics in third grade, inspired by Barack Obama: "Here was this charismatic Black man who rose to be president of the United States. I thought, 'I can do that.'" But Caleb also blamed Obama's environmental policies when his adoptive father, a coal miner, was laid off, and he decided to register to vote as a Republican when he turned 18. During his campaign he worked hard to contact every registered Republican in the district and made sure all of his eligible classmates from high school were registered

▲ In 2020, Democrat David Morales (left) and Republican Caleb Hanna (right) became two of the country's youngest elected officials.

to vote. Caleb is an active member of a Christian youth organization, and a strong defender of Second Amendment rights and the rights of the unborn. Like David Morales, Caleb too champions education as an issue, in his case technical education: "There are a lot of good-paying, high-skill jobs out there that don't require a four-year degree. We need to focus more on teaching kids about the opportunities in those fields."[2] Having won unlikely campaigns through their commitment and hard work, both David and Caleb began sponsoring legislation to pursue their policy goals immediately upon assuming office.

In this chapter, we will learn about how elections work in the United States and how electoral rules and other considerations influence campaign strategy and turnout. We will see how election laws, the candidates' campaigns, and voters' choices shape the outcome of elections, determining who represents the American people in government.

CHAPTER GOALS

Describe the patterns of participation among major demographic groups (pp. 265–73)

Describe the major rules and types of elections in the United States (pp. 273–82)

Explain strategies campaigns use to win elections (pp. 282–91)

Identify the major factors that influence voters' decisions (pp. 291–92)

Analyze the strategies, issues, and outcomes of the 2022 elections (pp. 292–306)

Who Participates and How?

Describe the patterns of participation among major demographic groups

---

Political participation refers to a wide range of activities in politics. Participation in politics includes not only voting in elections but also attending campaign events, rallies, and fundraisers; contributing money to campaigns, candidates, and parties; contacting elected officials; working on behalf of candidates and campaigns, such as canvassing voters; displaying campaign signs; and signing political petitions. Protests, demonstrations, and strikes, too, are age-old forms of participatory politics. Participation also includes publicly expressing support for or opposition to candidates or campaigns on social media, and organizing campaign events. The expansive world of digital politics includes not only the exchange of information but also new forms of fundraising and voter mobilization.

Riots and Protests

If there is any natural or spontaneous form of popular political participation, it is not the election but the protest or riot. In fact, for much of American history, fewer Americans exercised their right to vote than participated in urban riots and rural uprisings, because voting for a long time was limited to White, male, landowning citizens.

January 6, 2021, was a riot but also an **insurrection**, defined as a violent attack on government. The rioters were Trump supporters who attacked the U.S. Capitol building as Congress was certifying President Biden's 2020 election victory.[3] Their aim was to prevent the counting of the electoral college votes from the 50 states and stop Biden from becoming president. Most Americans polled viewed the rioters as "extremists," "domestic terrorists," or "anti-democratic." But a third of survey respondents called them "protesters," 20 percent "looters," and 10 percent "patriots," or someone vigorously supporting their country.

As this example illustrates, the vast majority of Americans today reject rioting or other violence for political ends, but peaceful **protest** is protected by the First Amendment and generally recognized as a legitimate and important form of political activity. During the height of the civil rights movement in the 1960s, hundreds of thousands of Americans took part in peaceful protests to demand social and political rights for Black people. Peaceful marches and demonstrations have since been employed by a host of groups across the ideological spectrum. In recent years, even before the protests following George Floyd's death in May 2020, growing concern over excessive use of police force against Black people had led to hundreds of protests across the nation. The Black Lives Matter movement prompted national discussion and political action around racial inequity in the criminal justice system and reform,

insurrection a violent attack on government; the act of revolting against civic authority or an established government

protest participation that involves assembling crowds to confront a government or other official organization

although critics argued that continued instances of excessive force, such as George Floyd's death in police custody, showed continued need for reform.

Political Participation in Elections

For most people, voting in elections is the most common form of participation in politics. When asked what makes a good citizen, the top reason mentioned by 75 percent of Americans is voting.[4]

By contributing to political campaigns, publicly expressing support for candidates, contacting political officials, attending campaign events and rallies, or volunteering to work on a campaign, citizens can communicate much more detailed information to public officials than they can by voting, thus making these other political activities often more satisfying.[5] But these forms of political action generally require more time, effort, and/or money than voting. As a result, the percentage of the population that participates in ways other than voting is relatively low (see Figure 9.1).

Voting For most Americans, voting is the single most important political act. The right to vote gives ordinary Americans an equal voice in politics, since each vote within the same district or state has the same value. Voting is especially important because it selects the officials who make the laws that the American people must follow.

During early periods of American history, the right to vote, called **suffrage**, was usually restricted to White males over the age of 21. Many states further limited voting to those who owned property or paid more than a specified amount of annual tax. Until the early 1900s, state legislatures elected U.S. senators, and there were no direct elections for members of the electoral college (who in turn elect the president). As a result, elections for the U.S. House as well as for state legislatures and local offices were how eligible citizens could participate in government. Voter **turnout** as a percentage of the adult U.S. population during this period was relatively low.

suffrage the right to vote; also called *franchise*

turnout the percentage of eligible individuals who actually vote

During the nineteenth and early twentieth centuries, states often further restricted voting rights, initially through poll taxes (fees charged to vote) and literacy (reading) tests designed to limit immigrant voting in northern cities. These strategies were later imported into the southern states to prevent Black people and poor White people from voting during the Jim Crow era—the period after the Civil War when African Americans were legally granted the right to vote and before the passage of the 1965 Voting Rights Act (see Chapter 5). Before the 1960s civil rights movement, voting rights often varied greatly from state to state, with many southern states using an array of laws to prevent participation in politics, including all-White primaries and requiring that voters own property in order to be able to vote.[6]

Given the variation in voting rights across states, over the past two centuries of American history many federal statutes, court decisions, and

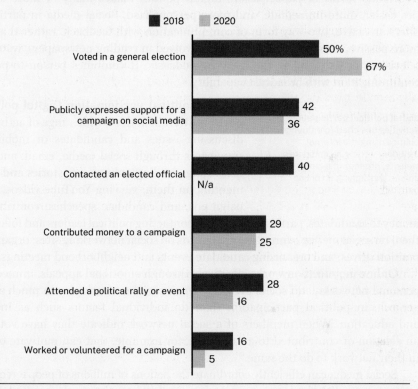

FIGURE 9.1 | Political Participation

Political activities such as volunteering generally take more time and effort than voting. When asked about various forms of political participation, over 40 percent of respondents said they expressed support for a campaign on social media.

PERCENTAGE OF PEOPLE WHO REPORT PARTICIPATING IN EACH ACTIVITY

■ 2018   ▨ 2020

Activity	2018	2020
Voted in a general election	50%	67%
Publicly expressed support for a campaign on social media	42	36
Contacted an elected official	40	N/a
Contributed money to a campaign	29	25
Attended a political rally or event	28	16
Worked or volunteered for a campaign	16	5

SOURCE: Based on a sample made up primarily of registered voters; "Political Engagement, Knowledge, and the Midterms," Pew Research Center, April 26, 2018, www.people-press.org/2018/04/26/10-political -engagement-knowledge-and-the-midterms/ (accessed 10/12/18); Andrew Daniller and Hannah Gilberstadt, "Key Findings about Voter Engagement in the 2020 Election," Pew Research Center, www .pewresearch.org/fact-tank/2020/12/14/key-findings-about-voter-engagement-in-the-2020-election/ (accessed 6/20/22).

constitutional amendments have been designed to override state voting laws and expand suffrage.[7]

Women nationwide won the right to vote in 1920 through the adoption of the Nineteenth Amendment. The women's suffrage movement had held rallies, demonstrations, and protest marches for more than half a century before achieving this goal. Before the Nineteenth Amendment, numerous states and territories adopted women's suffrage, paving the way for women to earn the right to vote nationally.

The most recent expansion of the right to vote, the Twenty-Sixth Amendment, lowered the voting age from 21 to 18. Ratified during the Vietnam War, in 1971, it was intended to channel the disruptive student protests against the war into peaceful participation at the ballot box.

Online Political Participation

Digital media give citizens greater access to information about candidates and campaigns and a greater role in politics than ever before. While building on traditional forms of participation, digital politics makes many of those activities easier, more immediate, and more personalized. Social media in particular offers an active, two-way form of communication with feedback, rather than the more passive, one-way communication involved in reading newspapers, watching television, or listening to the radio or podcasts. It combines person-to-person communication with broadcast capability.

digital political participation
activities designed to influence politics using the internet, including visiting a candidate's website, organizing events online, and signing an online petition

Digital political participation Digital political participation includes a wide range of activities: discussing issues and candidates or mobilizing supporters through social media, email, and text messaging; reading online news stories and commenting on them; viewing YouTube videos, campaign ads, and candidate speeches; contributing money to candidates, parties, and groups; contacting political leaders and following them on social media; running campaign ads on social networking sites; organizing petition drives; and organizing candidate events and neighborhood meetings.

Online mobilization works effectively through emotional appeals, immediacy, personal networks, and social pressure. One's social network plays a much stronger role in political participation than do individual factors such as income and education. When members of a social network indicate they have voted in an election or contributed to a candidate, for example, that can motivate others in their network to do the same.[8]

Social media can efficiently coordinate the actions of millions of people required for running political campaigns and winning elections. One in three social media users has encouraged others to vote, and roughly the same percentage have shared their own thoughts on politics or government online.[9] Social media make possible tiny acts of political participation—sharing, following a candidate or organization, liking a post, commenting—that can scale up to dramatic changes, leading to real-world political protests, voter-mobilization drives, and the election of candidates and parties to government.[10] Such acts give those who are uninterested in or rarely engaged by politics an easy way of getting involved, which can then encourage them to do more.

Some have dismissed political activity on social media as *clicktivism*—forms of participation that require little effort and may not convert to offline acts of participation in politics. Others argue that so-called clicktivism is the building block for sustained participation in politics. Donald Trump's extensive use of Twitter is evidence that audience-building on social media matters for political leadership and winning votes. The clicks of millions of Americans can and do add up.

AMERICA | SIDE BY SIDE

Voter Turnout in Comparison

Many factors influence whether or not an individual decides to vote. Governments can take several steps to try to increase voter turnout. These include making registration automatic upon reaching voting age, scheduling elections on weekends or a national holiday, conducting elections by mail-in ballot, or even making voting compulsory with the potential for imposing a fine if one does not have a valid excuse.

1. Which of the government policies seem to have the greatest effect on voter turnout? How does each of these policies make voting easier? Why might even countries with compulsory voting fail to achieve high turnout? How difficult might it be to enforce such a law?

2. What are the downsides to each of these policies? How can a country balance the desire for electoral participation against the desire to protect the right of its citizens to choose to abstain from politics? Why do you think America has lower voter turnout than some other countries on this list? Which of the previously mentioned policies do you think would be most likely to improve voter turnout in the United States?

COUNTRY	TURNOUT AS PERCENT OF VOTING AGE POPULATION	COMPULSORY VOTING	WEEKEND OR HOLIDAY VOTING	AUTOMATIC OR COMPULSORY REGISTRATION
Australia	81	Yes	Yes	Yes
Brazil	77	Yes	Yes	Yes
Germany	69	-	Yes	Yes
India	69	-	Yes	Yes
United Kingdom	62	-	-	Yes
United States	62	-	-	-
Canada	55	-	-	-
Mexico	55	Yes	Yes	Yes
Japan	52	-	Yes	Yes
Tunisia	47	-	-	-
South Africa	47	-	Yes	-
Switzerland	36	-	Yes	Yes

SOURCES: International Institute for Democracy and Electoral Assistance (IDEA) Voter Turnout Database, www.idea.int/data-tools/data/voter-turnout; ACE Electoral Knowledge Network, http://aceproject.org/epic-en/CDTable?view=country&question=VR008 (accessed 10/26/21).

Socioeconomic Status

Americans with some college or a college degree, more income, and professional occupations—what social scientists call higher **socioeconomic status**—participate much more in politics than do those with less education and less income.[11] Education is the single most important factor in predicting whether someone will not only vote but also participate in most other ways, such as by encouraging other people to vote or supporting an issue and donating to a candidate or cause. In the 2020 presidential election, 78 percent of people with a bachelor's degree voted, compared to 56 percent of people with a high school degree.[12]

socioeconomic status status in society based on level of education, income, and occupational prestige

Unsurprisingly, income is another important factor when it comes to making contributions, as well as voting. Eighty-one percent of people with high incomes ($100,000–$150,000) voted in 2020 compared to 64 percent of people whose income was $30,000–$40,000.[13] Individuals higher on the socioeconomic scale also tend to have higher levels of interest in politics.[14]

Age

Older people have much higher rates of participation than do young people, in part because they are more likely to own homes and pay property taxes, which makes them more aware of the importance of government.

The pattern of older people voting more was evident in 2020, with citizens 65 years and older reporting the highest turnout (74 percent), followed by those age 35–64 (69 percent), according to the Census Bureau. Turnout for young people age 18–34 rose from 49 percent in 2016 to 57 percent in 2020.[15] In midterm elections, youth turnout has historically been extremely low, but it is growing rapidly. Among the youngest age cohort, voter turnout went from 20 percent in 2014 to 36 percent in 2018. In 2022 early estimates showed that turnout among 18- to 29-year-olds was 27 percent, the second highest turnout for younger voters in midterm elections in almost three decades.

Even though much time and effort is spent mobilizing young voters, people who actually vote tend to be older than the average American.

Race and Ethnicity

Changes in the nation's demographic composition are rapidly changing U.S. politics. In general, members of racial and ethnic minority groups are more likely to vote Democratic, while non-Hispanic White people are more likely to vote Republican. The 2016 and 2020 electorates were the country's most racially and ethnically diverse ever; combined, Black, Latino, and Asian Americans accounted for 3 in 10 votes cast, while non-Hispanic White people accounted for just over 7 in 10 votes.

Black Voters As we mentioned earlier, during much of the twentieth century, the widespread use of the poll tax, literacy tests, and other measures deprived Black people in the South of the right to vote and meant that they had few avenues for participating in politics. Through a combination of protest, legal action, and political pressure, however, the victories of the civil rights movement made Black people full citizens and stimulated a tremendous growth in voter turnout. The movement drew a network rooted in Black churches, the National Association for the Advancement of Colored People (NAACP), and historically Black colleges and universities. Because they tended to vote largely as a cohesive bloc, Black voters began to wield considerable political power, and the number of Black elected officials grew significantly. Today, however, some state voting laws have created new impediments that tend to have a disproportionate impact on voters of color in some states.

Racial segregation remains a fact of life in the United States, along with proportionally higher levels of poverty among Black people.[16] Participation in politics for all racial and ethnic groups is highly correlated with more income, higher education, and higher-level occupations. Nevertheless, Black people are somewhat more likely to vote than non-Hispanic White people of similar socioeconomic status.[17]

White Voters Non-Hispanic White people accounted for 7 in 10 voters in 2020 and have generally high voter turnout. A majority of this group has tended to vote Republican; 59 percent voted for Mitt Romney in 2012, 57 percent for Trump in 2016, and 55 percent for Trump in 2020.[18] But White voters are a diverse racial group with big partisan differences based on educational attainment, age, income, geography, and region. A majority of this group with a college degree support Democratic candidates and turn out at higher rates, for example, while those without a college degree are more likely to support Republicans and are less likely to vote.

In 2016, Donald Trump helped mobilize less-educated and lower-income White voters with a populist campaign promising to "Make America Great Again" and bring back manufacturing jobs. White voters without a college degree were critical to Trump's victory; he won nearly two-thirds of this group. In 2020, Biden won back many blue-collar workers, with Biden and Trump almost evenly split among non-college-educated voters. Biden won 20 percent more White non-college-educated men in 2020 than Hillary Clinton had in 2016.

Latino Voters While 95 percent of Latinos identify racially as White, they are a separate ethnic identity, connected to a shared linguistic heritage. Between 2010 and 2020, the population grew by 23 percent; more than half (51 percent) of the total U.S. population growth in the past decade came from growth in the Latino population. For many years, political analysts called the Latino vote "the sleeping giant" because Latinos, while accounting for a large portion of the U.S. population, as a group had relatively low levels of political participation. For instance, 54 percent of Latinos voted in the 2020 presidential election, compared with 71 percent of non-Hispanic White people.[19] Compared with non-Hispanic White people and Black people, more Latinos are recent immigrants and thus have fewer opportunities, such as access to a quality education. Therefore, they are more likely to lack resources for participation in politics, such as education, time away from family and work, and language skills.[20] Although voter registration and turnout are lower among Latinos than among non-Hispanic White people, these rates have been increasing.

Asian American Voters Asian Americans are a smaller group than White people, Latinos, or Black people, making up roughly 6 percent of the population, or 21 million citizens. In some states, such as California, home to a third of the nation's Asian American population, the group has become an important political presence. Asian Americans have education and income levels closer to those of non-Hispanic White people than of Latinos or Black people, but until recently they were less likely to participate in politics. No one national group dominates among the Asian American population, and this diversity has impeded the development of group-based political power.

Gender

Women register to vote at rates similar to those of men but are more likely to vote. In the high-turnout 2018 midterm election, 55 percent of women voted compared with 52 percent of men, a 3-percentage-point gap. The ongoing significance of gender issues in American politics is best exemplified by the **gender gap**—a distinctive pattern of male and female voting decisions—in electoral politics. Women tend to vote in higher numbers for Democratic candidates, whereas men tend to vote in higher numbers for Republicans. Though the gender gap generally runs around 10 percentage points in presidential elections, the 2016 presidential election saw the first female major-party candidate and a significantly larger gender gap, with 54 percent of women supporting Hillary Clinton compared to 41 percent of men.[21] Looking at women as a whole, women prefer Democrats, but among non-Hispanic White women with lower education and income, support for Trump in 2016 and 2020 was high. In presidential elections from 1952 to 2020, a majority of White women supported a Democratic candidate for president only twice.

gender gap a distinctive pattern of voting behavior reflecting the differences in views between women and men

Religion

For many Americans, religious groups provide an infrastructure for political participation. Black churches, for example, were instrumental in the civil rights movement, and Black religious leaders continue to play important roles in national and local politics. Jews have also been active as a group in politics, but less through religious bodies than through a variety of social action agencies, including the Anti-Defamation League. Some of the most divisive conflicts in politics today, such as those over abortion, contraceptives, and LGBTQ rights, hinge on differences over religious beliefs.

Check your understanding

1. Political participation
   a) has been used in the same manner and at a similar rate by members of all groups to pursue their political interests throughout the course of American history.
   b) refers to a wide range of activities, including voting, contacting an elected official, protesting, or signing a petition, that are designed to influence government, politics, and public policy.
   c) is a right enshrined in the U.S. Constitution that prohibits any restrictions or limitations.
   d) is among the highest in the United States compared to other developed countries.

2. Which Americans are more likely to participate in politics?
   a) Younger working-class Americans have the highest levels of voting and political participation.
   b) Less educated, blue-collar working Americans have the highest levels of voting and political participation.
   c) More educated, wealthier, white-collar professional Americans have the highest levels of voting and political participation.
   d) Younger, middle-class, highly educated Americans have the highest levels of voting and political participation.

State Electoral Laws Regulate Most Voting

Describe the major rules and types of elections in the United States

Presidential elections take place every four years and congressional elections every two years, both on the first Tuesday after the first Monday in November. Congressional elections that do not coincide with a presidential election are called **midterm elections** and generally have lower voter turnout (see Figure 9.2). Localities and states can choose when to hold their elections. Most Americans have the opportunity to vote in several elections each year. Voting in elections is the most common form of participation in American politics, and elections are central to democratic government.

In the American federal system (where power is shared between the states and the federal government), the responsibility for running elections

> **midterm elections** congressional elections that do not coincide with a presidential election; also called *off-year elections*

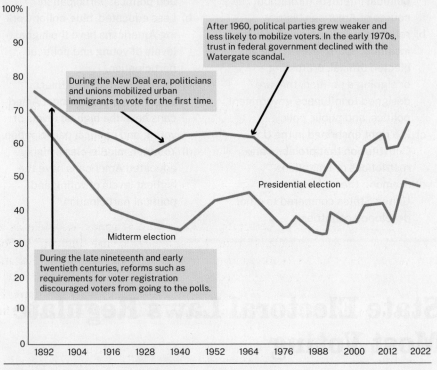

FIGURE 9.2 | Voter Turnout* in Presidential and Midterm Elections, 1892–2022

Though voter turnout has fluctuated over time, one pattern is consistent: more Americans tend to vote in presidential election years than in years when only congressional and local elections are held. What are some of the reasons that participation rose and fell during the last century and then rose again in 2020?

During the New Deal era, politicians and unions mobilized urban immigrants to vote for the first time.

After 1960, political parties grew weaker and less likely to mobilize voters. In the early 1970s, trust in federal government declined with the Watergate scandal.

Presidential election

Midterm election

During the late nineteenth and early twentieth centuries, reforms such as requirements for voter registration discouraged voters from going to the polls.

*Percentage of voting-eligible population.

SOURCES: Erik Austin and Jerome Clubb, *Political Facts of the United States since 1789* (New York: Columbia University Press, 1986); United States Election Project, www.electproject.org (accessed 11/10/22).

is decentralized, resting largely with state and local governments. Elections are administered by state, county, and city election boards, which are responsible for establishing and staffing polling places, processing mail-in ballots, and verifying the eligibility of voters (voter registration). State laws influence who may vote, how they vote, and where they vote. For example, states decide whether to require photo identification to vote and whether to allow residents to vote by mail, to vote in person before Election Day, and to register to vote and then vote on the same day.

primary elections elections held to select a party's candidate for the general election

Election season begins with **primary elections**, which in most states are held to select each party's candidates for the **general election**. Used for offices at the national, state, and often local levels, primary elections are usually races where

Elections are the most important way that Americans participate in politics. Some of the rules of elections have changed over time. (Left) African Americans vote for the first time in Wilcox County, Alabama, after the passage of the Voting Rights Act in 1965. (Right) An 18-year-old registers to vote in Illinois after the Twenty-Sixth Amendment in 1971 lowered the nationwide voting age from 21 to 18.

Democrats compete against Democrats and Republicans against Republicans. A few states, including California, Washington, and Alaska, have "top two" or "top four" primaries in which candidates from all parties run against one another and then the two who get the most votes face each other in the general election.

The United States is one of the few nations to hold primary elections. In most countries, selection of candidates is controlled completely by party officials, as they once were in the United States. Primary elections were introduced at the turn of the twentieth century by Progressive Era reformers who hoped to weaken the power of party leaders by enabling voters to pick candidates directly. In states with **closed primaries**, only registered members of a political party may vote in a primary election to select that party's candidates, and independents do not get to participate. States with **open primaries** allow all registered voters, including independents, to choose which party's primary they will participate in. Today, some argue that party primaries are the most consequential elections in American politics: as general congressional elections have become less and less competitive, primaries have come to matter more. With congressional districts dominated by one party or the other, the only real choices for voters are in party

general election a regularly scheduled election involving most districts in the nation or state, in which voters select officeholders; in the United States, general elections for national office and most state and local offices are held on the first Tuesday after the first Monday in November in even-numbered years (every four years for presidential elections)

closed primary an election in which voters select candidates but only of the party in which they are enrolled

open primary a primary election in which the voter can wait until the day of the primary to choose which party to enroll in to select candidates for the general election

primaries. Primary elections often have low voter turnout and can lead to surprising results for both parties.

As stipulated by the Constitution, the states, not the federal government, control voter registration and voting itself. This creates wide variation in the laws governing elections and voting, which affects participation in politics.[22] Voter turnout in presidential elections in the last decade ranges from a high of nearly 80 percent of eligible voters in Minnesota to a low of 55 percent in Oklahoma. State electoral laws can make voting easier or harder.

Registration Requirements

One of the most common reasons people in the United States give for not voting is that they are not registered. Young people especially are less likely to register to vote than are older Americans, in part because they tend to change residences more often. Other groups with lower registration rates include people with lower incomes and education, who also tend to change residences more frequently. Once individuals become interested in an election and learn about the candidates, it may be too late for them to register.

In most democratic countries, residents are automatically registered to vote in elections at adult age. In most states (except North Dakota, which doesn't require voter registration), individuals who are eligible to vote must take the initiative to register with the state election board before they are actually allowed to vote—sometimes 30 days beforehand.

same-day registration the option in some states to register on the day of the election, at the polling place, rather than in advance of the election

early voting the option in some states to cast a vote at a polling place or by mail before the election

In 2016 Oregon instituted automatic voter registration (AVR) and, as of 2022, 22 states and the District of Columbia have approved AVR.[23] Automatically registering residents to vote is related to another state election reform, **same-day registration**. As of 2021, 21 states plus Washington, D.C., had enacted same-day registration laws, allowing individuals to register to vote and cast a ballot on the same day (including Election Day).[24] Not only is voter turnout in these states higher than the national average, but younger and less educated voters are also more likely to participate. Research shows that same-day registration is one of the most effective laws to boost turnout.[25] In addition, as of 2021, 34 states have either no-excuse absentee or all-mail voting, where a ballot is mailed to the voter's home and the voter completes the ballot and mails it back or drops off the ballot at a drop box.

Another reform that has been adopted by many states is **early voting**, which allows registered voters to cast a ballot at their regular polling place during a designated period before Election Day. Almost two-thirds of votes cast in the 2020 election were cast early, either in person or via mail. As of 2021, 44 states allowed early voting, up from 38 in 2020.[26]

Claiming that these reforms have opened elections to fraud, many states have introduced and passed laws purporting to make voting more secure, but the changes may make voting more difficult. In 2021, 440 bills with provisions to restrict voting access were introduced in 49 states; 19 states passed laws restricting access to voting.[27] This includes laws that shorten the time period to apply for or deliver a mail ballot, reduce the number of days for early voting, limit the number or location of mail drop boxes, make it harder to obtain an absentee mail ballot or register to vote, or make voter identification laws more rigorous.

Voter Identification Requirements

Another barrier to voting is the requirement that voters provide proof of identity. Recent adoption of voter ID laws in many states has reduced turnout rates, especially for racial and ethnic minorities and people with low income or disabilities—all of whom disproportionately lack government ID. By 2020 more than 35 states had laws requesting or requiring voters to show some form of identification at the polls (the most common are strict identification laws or photo ID), and 7 of them have strict laws that require a government-issued photo.[28] The remaining 15 states use other methods to verify identity, such as a signature checked against the information on file. National surveys find three in four Americans favor government photo identification to vote.[29]

The research is mixed as to whether identification laws reduce voter turnout. A highly cited study found that more stringent forms of these laws lower voter turnout and especially participation for Black and Latino voters.[30] Others find that while voter identification laws reduce overall turnout rates, they do not uniquely affect the participation of racial or ethnic minorities.[31] New research using the national voter file of millions of Americans finds identification laws do not reduce turnout, while other research finds some forms of identification laws reduce turnout for young people.[32] Latinos are more likely to be asked to show identification to vote, and an innovative study from Texas finds these laws are more likely to prevent Black people and Latinos from voting.[33]

The Ballot

In the United States, it is the state and county governments, not the federal government, that run elections and create ballots. Some counties still use paper ballots, but most now use computerized electronic voting systems. The controversial 2000 presidential election led to a closer look at different ballot forms and voting systems used across the 3,000 U.S. counties. In 2000 the margin of victory for Republican George W. Bush over Democrat Al Gore in Florida was so small that the state ordered a recount. Careful examination of the results revealed that the punch card voting

Convenience voting, such as early voting and voting by mail, removes the need to stand in a potentially long line to cast a vote and may result in increased voter turnout.

HOW TO

Register . . . and Vote

MAGGIE BUSH, PROGRAMS AND OUTREACH DIRECTOR FOR THE LEAGUE OF WOMEN VOTERS OF THE UNITED STATES

The League of Women Voters emerged from the fight for women's suffrage in the early twentieth century. Its primary goal today is to help Americans of all descriptions understand and navigate the voting process. Maggie Bush, Programs and Outreach Director for the League of Women Voters of the United States, says, "In most elections, only 50 percent of 18-year-olds are registered to vote, which means that older voters are making decisions that affect all of us. We need to be part of the process. Elections are how we determine how safe our streets are, what kind of health care we have, how community college decisions are made and resources allocated. The first step to participating in these democratic decisions is voting." Here are Maggie's tips for registering to vote and going to the polls:

Registering to Vote

1 **How do I know how to register?** Consult a website such as Vote411.org, run by the League of Women Voters. Registration procedures and rules vary from state to state. From your state's site at Vote411.org, you can register online (in over 30 states) or print and fill out a paper form. Note that the registration deadline can be up to 30 days prior to the election.

2 **What information do I need to provide?** On the voter-registration form, you will provide your name and address and will certify that you are eligible — that you are a U.S. citizen and of the appropriate age. The voting age is 18, but some states allow preregistration or primary-election voting at younger ages. You may also need an identification number such as a driver's license, state ID, or the last four digits of your Social Security number, depending on your state.

3 **Which address should I use?** It is up to students where they want to vote. You can use your school address or be registered and vote absentee from your home address if it differs.

Am I required to register with a political party? In most states, you will be asked to declare an affiliation with a political party or to remain an independent or unaffiliated voter. In many states, if you do not specify a party, you will not be able to vote in primary elections, which parties use to choose their candidates for general elections. Some states have "open primaries," which do not require voters to have a party affiliation.

After you submit your registration electronically or by mail to your local election officials, they will follow up, usually by mail, to confirm that you are eligible to vote in the next election. If your address changes—even if you switch apartments in the same building—you need to update your registration. You can update at Vote411.org.

Voting

Where can you vote? At Vote411.org you can enter your address of residency to find your polling place, its hours of operation, and any early voting options. Many states offer early voting in the evenings and on weekends in the weeks before elections to facilitate voting by busy people such as students.

What's on the ballot? You can check Vote411.org to see a list of candidates and ballot initiatives for your location. When you go to vote you can take a sample ballot or notes on your phone or on paper with your selections, though some states prohibit taking a selfie with your ballot.

What will happen at the polling place? You will check in with a poll worker, who will locate your name on the registration list and may check your identification, depending on state rules. You will then be directed to a voting machine or given a paper ballot. Voters have the right to privacy while they vote and the right to accommodations for disabilities. After you vote, you submit your ballot electronically or insert it into a ballot box.

What happens if you have a problem voting? The first step is to ask a poll worker on-site for help. Another resource is the 866-OUR-VOTE hotline run by volunteers with a legal support staff to make sure people's votes are being counted properly.

That's it. At many polling places you will receive an "I Voted" sticker so you can proudly display your democratic participation.

machines and "butterfly ballot" used in Florida had led to many voting and counting errors.

In the wake of this election, Congress adopted the Help America Vote Act (HAVA) in 2003, requiring the states to use computerized voter-registration databases. Critics of HAVA feared that such systems might be vulnerable to unauthorized use, or hacking. In 2016, 21 states experienced intrusion by Russian hackers into their computerized election systems, although to date there is no evidence that ballots were changed.[34] In the past, computerized voting machines generally worked well and significantly updated America's election system, but all computerized systems have vulnerabilities. Protecting state and county election systems from hackers is a priority.

Presidential Elections

Presidential elections follow unique rules because the president and vice president are the only public officials elected by all American voters (though they are technically elected by the electoral college).

Presidential Primaries and Caucuses Before the presidential election every four years, the major parties start the process of selecting their presidential candidates by holding primary elections (where people show up and vote for their preferred candidate) and caucuses (which are party business meetings and thus are more influenced by party leaders and engaged members). Most states hold primaries. State primaries are run by state and local governments with a secret ballot. In an open primary or caucus, people can vote for a candidate of any political party. During a closed primary or caucus, only voters registered with that party can take part and vote.

Primaries and caucuses begin in January or February of a presidential election year and end in June, with state elections roughly every two weeks. Traditionally, Iowa, New Hampshire, Nevada, and South Carolina have had a disproportionate role in picking presidential candidates because they are the first states to cast votes. Early voting states in the primaries are important because they can help candidates gain momentum by securing national media attention, campaign contributions, and higher ratings in public-opinion polls, as well as name recognition. Candidates who perform well send signals to voters in later voting states that they are viable (can win the nomination) and electable (can win the general election).[35] A candidate who fares poorly in these early voting states may be written off as a loser and drop out of the race. In general, states seek to move their presidential primaries earlier in the calendar, a dynamic known as **frontloading**, so their citizens have more say in which candidates are chosen.

frontloading the moving up of presidential primaries by states to provide those states greater influence on the selection of candidates

delegate (in political parties) a representative to national party conventions who votes according to the preferences of voters in caucus and primary elections

The result of each state's primary election or caucuses determines how its **delegates** will vote at their party's national convention.

Party Conventions By the time the two party conventions convene in the summer, the candidates usually arrive at the convention knowing who has enough delegate support for victory in the first round of balloting. If one candidate does not win a majority in the first round, a second ballot occurs, and delegates can vote for a different candidate. The Democratic Party designates a number of party leaders and elected officials as so-called **superdelegates**—just under 15 percent of all delegates—who can vote as they wish, but only if no candidate wins a majority of regular delegates in the first round of convention voting.

The national party conventions also make the rules for delegate selection and future presidential primary elections. During the convention the party drafts its **party platform**, a statement of principles and pledges around which the delegates can unite. Most important, the convention allows the party to showcase its candidates in anticipation of the general election. Presidential candidates select a vice president shortly before or at the convention. Before a large national audience, the presidential and vice-presidential nominees deliver acceptance speeches that begin their formal general-election campaign and provide them an opportunity to make a positive impression on voters.

superdelegate (in the Democratic Party) an unelected party member/leader who is free to support any candidate for the presidential nomination at the party's national convention. They are only allowed to vote if no candidate has a majority after the first round of voting

party platform a party document, written at a national convention, that contains party philosophy, principles, and positions on issues

electoral college the presidential electors from each state who meet after the general election to cast ballots for president and vice president

The Electoral College In most U.S. elections, candidates are elected directly by popular vote. But the president and vice president are not elected directly by voters. Instead, they are chosen by electors through a process called the **electoral college**. Each state's political parties choose their own slate of potential electors, and when people vote for president and vice president they are technically choosing between each party's slate of electors, who are almost always loyal to the party's nominee and go on to vote for that candidate. No other country in the world uses an electoral college to pick its president.

Electors are allocated to each state based on the size of its congressional delegation (House and Senate); there are currently 538 electors in total. Wyoming, for example, has 3 votes in the electoral college (based on its 2 senators plus 1 representative), while California has 54 (2 senators plus 52 representatives). Each elector in Wyoming (a state with roughly 577,000 people) represents roughly 192,000 people, while each elector in California (39.5 million people) represents 731,000. Because of this, the electoral college, like the U.S. Senate, is biased against large-population states and overrepresents small-population states. Under this system, one vote in California is worth about a quarter of a vote in Wyoming.

The president of the United States is the winner of the electoral college—the candidate who wins at least 270 of the college's 538 votes—and not necessarily the candidate with the most popular votes, or votes from the people. This is in part because the electoral college and most elections in the United States are governed by plurality, winner-take-all rules. With only two exceptions, each state awards *all* of its electors to the candidate who receives the most votes in the state.[36] Thus, in 2020, Biden received all 16 of Michigan's electoral votes, though he won only 50.6 percent of the votes in the state.

There have been four times when the winner of the electoral college did not win the popular vote. Most recently, in 2016, Donald Trump won the majority in the electoral college even though Hillary Clinton won almost 3 million more votes nationwide.

Check your understanding

3. Which of the following statements concerning elections in the United States is true?

   a) The United States differs from most nations worldwide because it only holds closed primary elections.

   b) Some argue that primary elections are perhaps more consequential than general elections, because general congressional elections have become less competitive over time.

   c) Voter identification requirements always increase voter turnout, because citizens have more trust in the election results.

   d) Laws that allow voters to register on Election Day do not have any effect on voter turnout.

4. Electing the United States president through the electoral college means that

   a) a candidate can win without receiving the most popular votes.

   b) candidates will spend all of their time in large states like California or New York because they have more electoral votes.

   c) voters will be more satisfied with the outcome, because there is overwhelming support for the electoral college.

   d) large states are overrepresented, while small states are underrepresented.

Election Campaigns

Explain strategies campaigns use to win elections

campaign an effort by political candidates and their supporters to win the backing of donors, political activists, and voters in their quest for political office

Because of the complexity of the campaign process and the amount of money that candidates must raise, presidential campaigns often begin almost two years before the November election, and congressional campaigns, a year in advance. The **campaign** for any office consists of a number of steps. Candidates often form an exploratory committee consisting of supporters who will help them raise funds and bring their names to the attention of the media, potential donors, and voters. **Incumbents** have an advantage in

these areas over the candidates challenging them. They usually are already well known and have little difficulty attracting supporters and contributors—unless, of course, they have been subject to damaging publicity while in office.

Campaign Consultants and Volunteers

A formal organization and professional campaign managers are critical for campaign success. For a local campaign, candidates generally need hundreds of volunteers and a few paid professionals. State-level campaigns call for thousands of volunteers, and presidential campaigns require tens of thousands of volunteers and hundreds of paid staff nationwide. Virtually all serious contenders for national and statewide office retain the services of professional campaign consultants, including a campaign manager, media consultants, pollsters and a data analytics team, financial advisers, a press spokesperson, and staff directors to coordinate the activities of volunteer and paid workers. Consultants offer candidates the expertise necessary to craft campaign messages, conduct opinion polls, produce television and social media ads, organize direct-mail campaigns, open field offices, and make use of information about their constituents from digital voter files, text messaging, email, political donations, and more.

Fundraising

Candidates generally begin raising funds long before an election, and many politicians spend more time on it than on any other campaign activity.[37] Serious fundraising efforts involve appealing to both small and large donors. High levels of campaign spending on U.S. politics continued in 2022. Combined spending on congressional races by federal candidates and political committees was more than $8.9 billion, a new record, swamping the $7.1 billion spent four years earlier, and even higher than the $8.7 billion in the 2020 presidential election.

Once elected to office, members of Congress find it much easier to raise funds and are thus able to outspend their challengers.[38] Incumbents out-raise their opponents by significant amounts because most donations from businesses, interest groups, and political action committees (PACs) go to incumbents. These donors seek a voice in government from their investment; thus, they want to invest in the candidate most likely to win, and incumbents win most of the time.[39]

Modern high-profile campaigns require a great deal of money. But candidates with the most campaign dollars often, but don't always, win. Barack Obama and Joe Biden raised more than their opponents and won. In 2016, though Hillary Clinton spent more than her opponent, Donald Trump, she did not win. In 2020, Democrat Jaime Harrison spent a record $160 million on his campaign for Senate in South Carolina—considerably more than his opponent—and still lost.

Campaigns spend a huge amount of time raising the necessary funds, which are obtained from at least seven possible sources: individual donors, **political action committees (PACs)**, **527 committees**, **Super PACs**, **dark money groups or 501(c)(4) committees**, public funding, and the candidate's own funds. Each of these sources has rules for contribution limits and how (or if) donors have to be disclosed. Table 9.1 lists the sources of campaign funds and the major federal laws or court decisions that created these forms of spending.

The most important decisions were the pair of 2010 federal court cases, *Citizens United* and *SpeechNow*, which allowed unlimited spending by corporations, unions, wealthy donors, and interest groups by way of "outside groups," or groups not directly coordinated with a candidate campaign (they are often called independent expenditure groups). Outside spending by Super PACs and dark money groups or 501(c)(4) committees have played a critical role in all recent presidential and midterm elections, as these groups ran extensive television and digital ads. Super PACs on both sides relied on very large contributions. Outside spending more than doubled in the 2020 election compared to 2016 and 2018. A growing concern is that elections in the United States can be bought with big money from corporations and wealthy donors, who will then hold significant influence when their candidate is elected.

Campaign Strategy

To take office, candidates who win their party's nomination must win the general election. There are essentially two types of general-election campaigns in the United States today: **grassroots campaigns** and mass media campaigns. Grassroots campaigns, which include local and many congressional elections, are organizationally driven and labor intensive. Candidates make many public appearances and recruit volunteers to make phone calls, knock on doors, hand out leaflets, and organize rallies and other public events. Such extensive grassroots outreach and mobilization are designed to increase candidate visibility. Statewide campaigns, some congressional races, and the presidential election are mass media campaigns: media driven and money intensive.

TABLE 9.1 | Sources of Campaign Funds

SOURCE	LIMITS AND RULES (2021–22 ELECTIONS)	RELEVANT COURT CASES AND LAWS
Individuals	$2,900 per candidate per election $5,000 per federal PAC per calendar year $35,500 per national party committee per calendar year $10,000 to state and local committees per calendar year	*McCutcheon et al. v. Federal Election Commission* (2014) allowed individuals to contribute to an unlimited number of candidates and PACs. *Buckley v. Valeo* (1976) established the idea that political donations to campaigns are an expression of First Amendment rights.
Political Action Committees (PACs) organizations established by corporations, labor unions, or interest groups to channel money into political campaigns.	$5,000 to a candidate per election (primary and general) $15,000 to a political party per year $5,000 to another PAC per year	The Federal Election Campaign Act (1971) is the basis of all modern campaign finance regulations (amended 1974, 1976, 1979, and 2002). The law requires full disclosure of federal campaign contributions.
Super PACs or "independent expenditure-only" committees are a type of political action committee but cannot donate money directly to candidates.	Unlimited Prohibited from coordinating their expenditures with those of a candidate's campaign, Super PACs can raise and spend unlimited sums of money to advocate for or against a political candidate, including paying for campaign ads. Required to disclose their donors to the Federal Election Commission.	*Buckley v. Valeo* (1976) struck down limits on "independent expenditures." *Citizens United v. Federal Election Commission* (2010) was a landmark Supreme Court case that allows 527 committees to raise unlimited funds. *SpeechNow.org v. FEC* (2010), an extension of *Citizens United* (2010), created Super PACs.
527 committee a group established for the purpose of political advocacy and required to report its sources of funding to the IRS.	Unlimited, except for PACs All political committees, including state, local, and federal candidate committees, traditional political action committees (PACs), Super PACs, and political parties are 527s. The money can be used to buy campaign ads, send mail, or otherwise advocate for the election or defeat of specific candidates.	*Citizens United v. Federal Election Commission* (2010) was a landmark Supreme Court case that allows 527 committees to raise unlimited funds.
Candidate's own money	Unlimited	*Buckley v. Valeo* (1976) struck down, as violating free speech, limits on contributions by candidates to their own campaigns.

Continued

TABLE 9.1 | Sources of Campaign Funds—cont'd

SOURCE	LIMITS AND RULES (2021–22 ELECTIONS)	RELEVANT COURT CASES AND LAWS
Public funding	Candidates running in the major-party presidential primaries are eligible for public funds by raising at least $5,000 in individual contributions of $250 or less. Candidates who reach this threshold may apply for federal funds to match, on a dollar-for-dollar basis, all contributions of $250 or less. By accepting matching funds candidates agree to spend no more than $48.07 million in their presidential primary campaign, including their personal funds and funds from private donors.	*Buckley v. Valeo* (1976) struck down, as violating free speech, limits on campaign spending (unless the candidate accepts public financing).
Dark money groups or 501(c)(4) committees a nonprofit social welfare group that also engages in political advocacy but may not spend more than half its revenue for political purposes.	Unlimited These nonprofits can spend unlimited amounts on political campaigns and not disclose their donors as long as their activities are not coordinated with the candidate campaigns and political activities are not their primary purpose. The group's campaign ads must omit the "magic words" (see column at right). Common practice for wealthy and corporate donors, as well as foreigners, is to route campaign contributions through a 501(c)(4) to avoid the legal limits on contributions.	*Buckley v. Valeo* (1976) defined express advocacy as communication that advocates the election or defeat of a federal candidate and is identifiable by eight "magic words." The words (and phrases) include "vote for," "elect," "cast your ballot for," and "reject." Any political ad using any one of these words would be considered "express advocacy," and subject to federal campaign regulations.

All campaigns must decide on a strategy: What will their main message be? How will they allocate their resources (to television, social media, face-to-face mobilization)? Which voters will they target? The electoral college is one election rule that influences the campaign strategy of presidential candidates by forcing them to campaign heavily in a small number of battleground, or swing, states—those whose populations are divided roughly evenly between Democrats and Republicans—while often ignoring the rest of the country. In 2020, 96 percent of the presidential campaign events occurred in 12 battleground states.[40]

Residents of battleground states are smothered with attention from the candidates and media as presidential candidates vie for those states' votes, while the millions of residents of states considered safe for Republicans (West Virginia, Utah) or Democrats (New York, Illinois, California) are often ignored (see Who Are Americans?).

The Media Contemporary political campaigns rely on a number of communication tools to reach the voters they want to target for support, including television, radio, social media/digital advertising, massive computerized databases, and micro-targeting. Digital media are especially important in mobilizing people to vote.

Extensive use of television advertising is central to modern political campaigns. Television ads are used to establish candidate name recognition, create a favorable image of the candidate and a negative image of the opponent, link the candidate with desirable groups in the community, and communicate the candidate's stands on selected issues. Often, in the later stages of a campaign, candidates and the political advocacy groups that support them will "go negative," airing ads that criticize their opponents' policy positions, qualifications, or character.

Voters consistently say they reject so-called negative campaigning, but negative ads can benefit voters more than positive ones in some cases.[41] Negative ads are more likely to address important policy differences and provide supporting evidence, while positive ads tend to focus on candidates' personal characteristics. Interestingly, when negative ads are misleading or even patently false, they are effective in that voters remember more from them than from positive ads, possibly because they are designed to elicit emotional responses, such as fear, anxiety, or anger.

A growing percentage of negative campaign ads are sponsored by political action committees and dark money groups, not candidates. The 2010 *Citizens United* Supreme Court decision allowed corporations, unions, and interest groups to form Super PACs that can spend unlimited amounts to advocate for or against candidates, as long as the Super PACs are "independent" of the candidate's campaign.

Candidates also benefit from *free media*, where the cost of advertising is borne by the television and print media themselves when they cover the candidates' statements and activities as news. In 2016, Donald Trump benefited from much free media coverage, largely due to his many controversial statements and tweets.[42]

Social media have become another major weapon in modern political campaigns as more Americans go online for news. Today, every campaign for presidential, congressional, and major state offices develops a social media strategy for fundraising, mobilizing supporters, and getting out the vote. One reason digital media are so effective at organizing presidential campaigns is cost: digital platforms enable inexpensive tools to help organize volunteers and offer more opportunities for free advertising, when supporters share their support for candidates on social media.

Micro-Targeting and Polling The media and televised debates allow candidates to communicate their policy goals and promises to a broad range of voters, but this is also a blunt instrument; different voters care about different issues, after all. The idea behind **micro-targeting** is to send different campaign ads or messages to different demographic and ideological groups of voters and potential voters. Suburban "soccer moms," for instance, would be targeted with ads different from those targeting rural "cowboy dads."

> **micro-targeting** a campaign strategy that uses data and demographics to identify the interests of small groups of like-minded individuals and deliver tailored ads or messages designed to influence their voting behavior
>
> **mobilization** the process by which large numbers of people are organized for a political activity

Micro-targeting was first used effectively by Republican president George W. Bush in 2000 and 2004.[43] It became more sophisticated during the 2008 presidential campaign as Democrats built an extensive organization to contact and turn out voters. The Obama campaign made use of an unprecedented volume of survey data, conducting thousands of interviews each week to gauge voters' preferences. Statistical algorithms looked for patterns in the data the campaign had assembled for voters based on massive state voter-registration files, consumer data, and past campaign contacts. The campaign used extensive quantitative data to generate different, carefully targeted messages for different demographic, regional, and ideological groups to persuade them to turn out and vote for Obama.[44]

Mobilization "People power" remains critical in modern political campaigns, since research suggests that direct mail and robocalls are less effective than face-to-face and in-person phone contacts.[45] Candidates continue to use the services of tens of thousands of volunteers, especially for get-out-the-vote drives. People become much more likely to participate when someone—a candidate campaign, a political party, or (especially) someone they know—asks them to get involved. Research on political **mobilization** has shown that face-to-face interaction with a canvasser greatly increased the chances that the person contacted would go to the polls, boosting overall voter turnout by almost 10 percent. The impact of direct mail was much smaller, increasing turnout by just 0.5 percent.[46] "Robocalls" (prerecorded phone calls) had no measurable effect on turnout, while in-person telephone calls were found to have a modest positive effect.

As means of mobilization, social media and instant messaging can mimic face-to-face communication. In a study involving 61 million users of Facebook, political scientists found that election appeals from Facebook friends were responsible

FOR CRITICAL ANALYSIS ⟶

1. Which 10 states had the highest total presidential campaign spending per capita? What explains why the campaigns spent more in these states than in others?

2. Are the states where the candidates spent the most money representative of the nation overall? Does this matter?

WHO ARE AMERICANS?

Are Presidential Battleground States Representative of the Country?

Spending on campaign advertising, per capita

Representative States Index*

- $20+
- $15–$19.99
- $10–14.99
- $5–$9.99
- Under $5

.000

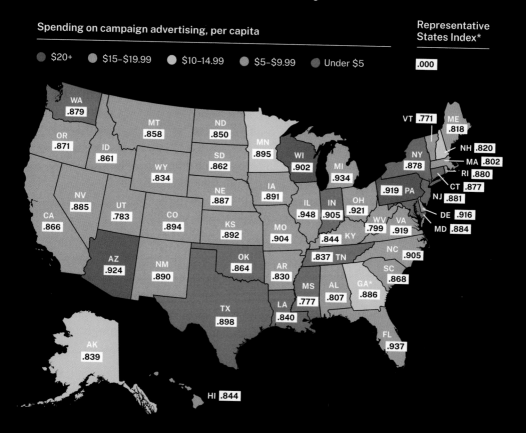

WA .879
OR .871
MT .858
ND .850
MN .895
VT .771
ME .818
ID .861
SD .862
WI .902
NY .878
NH .820
WY .834
MI .934
MA .802
RI .880
NV .885
NE .887
IA .891
PA .919
CT .877
CA .866
UT .783
CO .894
IL .948
IN .905
OH .921
NJ .881
DE .916
KS .892
MO .904
WV .799
VA .919
MD .884
AZ .924
NM .890
OK .864
KY .844
NC .905
TN .837
AR .830
SC .868
MS .777
AL .807
GA* .886
TX .898
LA .840
FL .937
AK .839
HI .844

The electoral college forces presidential candidates to campaign heavily in a small number of battleground states — those that have roughly even numbers of Democrats and Republicans — in order to win. In 2020, the total campaign spending on advertising was $23 per person in Arizona and Wisconsin and $17 in Florida — all battleground states. It was just $4 per person in Texas and New York. How representative are the battleground states of the nation overall?

* Representative States Index measures how closely each state matches U.S. averages on 31 metrics across 5 dimensions: (1) socio-demographics, (2) economy, (3) education, (4) religion, and (5) public opinion. For each metric, the researchers calculated the absolute difference between the value for each state and the U.S. average value.

SOURCES: Wesleyan Media Project, https://mediaproject.wesleyan.edu/releases-102920/#table4; OpenSecrets, www.opensecrets.org/online-ads/map/google; www.opensecrets.org/online-ads/map/facebook.

People are more likely to turn out to vote if someone asks them face-to-face. Direct mail and impersonal phone calls are less likely to have an effect on turnout.

for increasing turnout by 340,000 people (who otherwise would not have voted). Users' closest connections ("friends" on the network) had the most influence in getting them to vote.[47]

Since 2000, competitive presidential and congressional elections have motivated both parties to build strong grassroots organizations to reach voters and turn them out on Election Day. In 2004, Republicans were more successful in this effort, training more than 1.4 million volunteers to make calls, go door-to-door to register voters, write letters in favor of President Bush, create pro-Bush blogs, and phone local radio call-in shows.

In 2008, Barack Obama's campaign made mobilization a centerpiece of its strategy, organizing a base of volunteers to go door-to-door seeking support for their candidate. Many of Obama's crucial primary victories relied on direct voter mobilization. The campaign created a nationwide organization, opening more than 700 field offices. Obama campaigned in all 50 states, rather than focusing solely on battleground states as his predecessors had done. By mobilizing support in places where Democrats had not seriously contended in the past, the Obama campaign expanded the party's electoral map. For the first time in decades, turnout rates were comparable to those in 1960. In the 2016 and 2020 elections, political campaigns shifted to social media and text messages as a primary way to mobilize voters and directly provide their supporters with election updates.[48]

Check your understanding

5. How do political action committees (PACs) differ from Super PACs?

   a) PACs must disclose all contributors to the Federal Election Commission, while Super PACs are not required to disclose their contributors to the Federal Election Commission.

   b) PACs are forbidden from coordinating with campaigns, while Super PACs may freely coordinate their campaign activities with campaigns.

   c) PACs may only raise money from U.S. citizens, while foreign money comes into U.S. elections through Super PACs since they do not disclose their donors to the Federal Election Commission.

   d) While PACs have limits on how much they can contribute to candidates, parties, or other PACs, Super PACs can raise and spend unlimited sums to advocate for or against a candidate.

6. Which campaign strategy tends to be most effective in mobilizing voters?
   a) phone calls from campaigns
   b) television advertisements
   c) personal contact from friends and family
   d) direct mailers from campaigns

How Voters Decide

Identify the major factors that influence voters' decisions

Even if well-funded groups and powerful individuals influence the electoral process, it is the millions of individual voter decisions that ultimately determine election outcomes. Three factors influence voters' choices: partisan loyalty, issues and policy preferences, and candidate characteristics.

Partisan Loyalty

Most voters feel a sense of identification with the Democratic or Republican party, predisposing them to favor their party's candidates and oppose those of the other party. Partisanship is the most reliable indicator of which candidates people will vote for. While issues and candidate personalities may get attention in a campaign, they often have very little impact on how partisans vote.

Once formed, voters' partisan loyalties seldom change unless some crisis causes them to reexamine their loyalties. For example, at the beginning of the New Deal era, between 1932 and 1936, millions of former Republicans traumatized by the Great Depression transferred their allegiance to President Franklin Roosevelt and the Democrats.

Issues and Policy Preferences

Policy preferences are a second factor influencing voters' choices. Voters may cast their ballots for the candidate whose position on economic issues, climate change, abortion, funding college education, or any issue they believe to be closest to their own, or the one they believe has the best experience in foreign policy. Though candidates for the presidency or Congress are often judged on the basis of their economic policies or promises, other issues vary in importance depending on the election.

The Economy Election outcomes are affected by a variety of forces that candidates cannot control. Among the most important of these is the condition of the economy at the time of the election. If voters are satisfied with their economic conditions, they tend to support the party in power, while concern about the economy tends to favor the opposition. This was true in 2022, when people concerned with high levels of inflation tended to vote against Democrats, who controlled Congress and the presidency.

Candidate Characteristics

Candidates' personal attributes are a third factor influencing voters' decisions, with the more important being race, ethnicity, religion, gender, geography, and socioeconomic background. Voters may be proud to see someone similar to themselves in a position of leadership and may presume that such candidates are likely to have perspectives and opinions closer to their own.

Voters also pay attention to candidates' personality characteristics, such as "authenticity," "decisiveness," and "honesty." In recent years, "integrity" has become a key election issue.

Check your understanding

7. Which of the following statements concerning the factors affecting voters' decisions is true?

   a) Partisanship is the most reliable indicator of which candidate a voter will support.

   b) The role of partisanship on voters' decisions has declined, with issues like foreign policy playing a more significant role.

   c) The economy plays very little role in voters' decisions.

   d) Candidate characteristics play the most important role in voters' decisions, with charisma and confidence being the best predictors of support for a candidate.

8. How does the economy influence voting decisions?

   a) The economy is not a major factor for voters, since it is a complex issue.

   b) When voters are satisfied with their economic conditions, they tend to support the party in power, while concern about the economy tends to favor the opposition.

   c) The economy and economic conditions always benefit the incumbent.

   d) The economy and economic conditions always favor the challenger.

The 2022 National Elections: A Contest between Two Candidates Not on the Ballot?

Analyze the strategies, issues, and outcomes of the 2022 elections

Midterm elections are influenced by a mix of national and local factors. They provide voters an opportunity to register their approval or disapproval of the political party controlling the presidency as well as to cast their ballots for the senatorial, congressional, and statewide candidates and ballot issues that best reflect their own views and identities. Though midterm elections still serve both these purposes, in today's political world electoral politics has become more nationalized and organized around the presidency than focused on local matters, even when the president's name is not on the ballot.[49]

When Americans vote in presidential years, many, though not all, voters cast ballots for the same political party whose presidential candidate they have decided to support. This "presidentialization" of congressional elections carries over into off-year congressional elections as well. More than 60 percent of those voting in the 2018 midterm elections characterized their choice of a member of Congress as a vote for or against President Trump, though Trump's name obviously did not appear on the ballot.[50]

After months of campaign hoopla and more than $9 billion in campaign spending, the 2022 elections gave Republicans a razor-thin majority in the House, a closely divided Senate under Democratic control, and Donald Trump poised to announce his 2024 presidential candidacy. In this section, we review these events, examine President Biden's first two years in office, discuss the policy issues that were important to voters in 2022, and analyze the results of the 2022 election itself. We conclude by reflecting on the implications of the 2022 race for the 2024 presidential contest and the future of American politics.

The Backdrop: A Divided Nation

Polarization Americans today are sharply divided politically and ideologically. Indeed, millions of Americans view events through partisan and ideological lenses, only believing news reports and commentary consistent with their existing party and ideological commitments. This tunnel vision is encouraged by the partisan media and by political activists who often hold extreme positions on national issues.[51] Many local party organizations responsible for organizing voter mobilization on both sides have been taken over by ideological activists inclined to demonize the opposition.[52] Democratic politicians and activists declare that Republicans are racist, sexist, homophobic, and a threat to American democracy. Republican activists tell their voters that the Democrats are hostile to America and indifferent to the nation's values and traditions. More than half the adherents of each party have developed highly negative views of the other party's supporters.[53]

The violent events of January 6, 2021, provided a polarizing backdrop for the 2022 elections, with many Republican voters hoping for a return to Trump-style Republican control of Congress and Democrats fearing a drastic turn away from Biden's Democratic agenda.

"Rejectionism" At one time, Americans accepted and trusted the verdict of the polls. Today, however, America's deep partisan and ideological divisions have contributed to the rise of "rejectionism," in which some partisans refuse to accept the validity and legitimacy of a defeat at the polls. Rejectionism gained a foothold during the Obama years when many Republicans, including future president Donald Trump, claimed to be "birthers," professing to believe the false claim that former president Obama had been born in Kenya and so was not eligible to serve as president (Obama was born in Hawaii and is a U.S. citizen).

In 2016, when Trump surprised most pundits by defeating Hillary Clinton, the result was immediately challenged by Clinton's supporters. First, Green Party candidate Jill Stein spearheaded recount efforts in Wisconsin, Michigan, and Pennsylvania, states that Trump had carried by narrow margins. While Clinton declined to be formally associated with the recount effort, many Clinton backers encouraged Stein, hoping that Trump might yet be kept out of the White House. When the recount effort failed, about 80 percent of Democrats surveyed said they fully believed charges that Trump had conspired with the Russians to steal the election. This percentage remained steady even after the Mueller report found no credible evidence to support such claims.

In 2020, Donald Trump became the first president in American history who threatened to refuse to cede power after suffering a defeat at the polls. Despite his angry and unsubstantiated claims of widespread voting fraud, Trump had lost his bid for re-election and would soon be forced to leave the White House after Congress confirmed the electoral vote for Biden to become president. Foiled at the polls, Trump turned to more direct action. Encouraged by the outgoing president, hundreds of Trump's riotous supporters descended upon the Capitol on January 6, 2021, as Congress was meeting to formally count the electoral votes. Some rioters came to protest and stop the counting of the votes; many were content to proudly snap selfies that would later help the authorities identify and arrest them; a small number, including several military veterans carrying weapons and zip tie restraints, seemed to have more sinister motives. By the end of the day, the rioters had been dispersed by the police, though not without casualties on both sides. On January 7, Congress reconvened to count the electoral votes and Joe Biden was formally declared the winner. The counting of the electoral votes, however, did not completely end the matter. Millions of Americans remained convinced that Trump had actually won the election. Since the 2020 election, Trump has continued to challenge the outcome of the presidential contest, and more than 300 Republican candidates in 2022, including a number of congressional candidates, claimed to believe that Democrats had stolen the 2020 presidential election.[54]

Crises of the Biden Presidency It was in this toxic atmosphere of division and rejectionism that Joe Biden took office. The first two years of the Biden presidency were filled with domestic tumult and controversy, international crises, and the continuing claims of Donald Trump and his supporters that the 2020 election had been stolen from him. At the same time, Republicans blamed Biden for the largest spike in inflation in several decades, including a substantial increase in food and fuel costs. Democrats responded by asserting that the Russian invasion of Ukraine and attendant interruptions in natural gas and oil supplies were largely responsible for inflationary pressures, which would soon abate.

To add to the administration's problems, in February 2022 Russia invaded its neighbor, Ukraine (a democratic country), claiming, rather improbably, that it wanted to liberate Ukraine from Nazis. A more likely explanation for the Russian invasion is that Russia feared Ukraine's growing ties to the West and coveted Ukraine's enormous natural resources. The Biden administration was initially cautious in its support for Ukraine, but when it seemed clear that the Ukrainian army was willing and able to defend its country, the United States and its NATO allies sent billions of dollars in weapons to the Ukrainians, allowing them to blunt the Russian attack and launch their own counteroffensive to reclaim territory that had been seized by Russia. From America's perspective, the situation was complicated. The United States sought to help Ukraine without triggering a full-scale war with Russia and the possible use of nuclear weapons. Republicans declared that it was Biden's perceived weakness that encouraged the Russians to launch their invasion in the first place. Former president Trump was fond of declaring that Russian leader Vladimir Putin would never have dared invade Ukraine if Trump had remained in office.

A Referendum on Joe Biden? Many argue that "midterms are always a referendum on the president,"[55] and Biden is an unpopular president. Since World War II, his job approval rating (43 percent on the eve of the 2022 election) is ahead of only two other presidents: Ronald Reagan and Donald Trump. Republicans in Congress lost 26 House seats in Reagan's first midterm and 40 in Trump's. This pattern—the party of the president losing seats in Congress in the midterm election—is well known.

Notable are the demographic groups that have more negative than positive opinions of Biden's job performance. Among Latinos and Asians, two groups that historically have voted Democrat, 50 percent disapprove of Biden's job performance compared to 46 percent of Latinos and 48 percent of Asians who approve. This appears to be largely due to the nation's poor economy that disproportionately affects these groups. While a majority of young people have voted for Democrats in recent elections, there is widespread disapproval of Biden's presidency across age groups, including 56 percent among ages 18–29, 59 percent among ages 30–64, and 60 percent among people age 65 plus.[56] These numbers posed a challenge for the Democrats in 2022. In the end, youth voter turnout ended up significantly helping Democrats.

A Referendum on Donald Trump? Though his name was not on the ballot, for many voters Trump was an important factor in their 2022 vote. Trump is among the most polarizing figures in modern American history. After he left office, 37 percent of Republicans thought Trump had been a great president and most of the rest approved of his policies. Seventy-two percent of Democrats, on the other hand, thought Trump had been a terrible president, with another 17 percent thinking he was merely poor.

Even within the Republican Party, opinion on Trump, particularly his future role in the GOP, is divided. While few Republicans publicly criticize him, many wish Trump would retire from the political arena and make room for less divisive figures. Millions of Republicans, particularly White working-class conservatives, support Trump, but many moderate upper-middle-class Republicans are offended by Trump's combative rhetoric, his divisive comments about race, immigrants, and white nationalism, and his extensive legal problems, as well as his willingness to ignore the rule of law when to do so serves his own interests (for example, his attempts to overturn the 2020 election results). And, while they recognize that Trump has many diehard supporters, the GOP's more moderate leaders fear that Trump's liabilities outweigh his political strengths and undermine Republican prospects in national elections.

The Campaign

The 2022 elections took place in this context of deep polarization and profound economic and foreign policy challenges. And the stakes of the 2022 election were high: if the Republicans could take control of both the House of Representatives and the Senate, the agenda of Biden and the Democrats would be stopped in its tracks. The Democrats, facing the conventional wisdom that midterm elections go against the president's party, were hoping they could at least hold on to the Senate, which would allow Biden's appointees to the federal courts to continue to be approved.

Many Republicans had hoped that Trump would at least remain on the sidelines during the 2022 elections and allow them to craft a strategy based on inflation, crime, and Joe Biden's fitness for office. But Trump seemed incapable of retreating to the political margins. This soon became apparent during the primaries. During the 2022 Republican primaries Trump sought to demonstrate his power in the party by holding numerous rallies and endorsing candidates who supported him, while he attacked Republicans like Congresswoman Liz Cheney of Wyoming, who dared to oppose him. In August 2022, Cheney was overwhelmingly defeated by a pro-Trump candidate in the Wyoming Republican congressional primary. Many of Trump's other endorsees, such as GOP Senate candidates Dr. Mehmet Oz in Pennsylvania and former football star Herschel Walker in Georgia, also won Republican primaries, though quite a few seemed too radical or inexperienced to have a good chance in the general election. In some instances, Democratic political action committees provided financial support to Trump endorsees in the GOP primaries, believing that they would be easier to defeat in the general election. In the end, a number of Trump-endorsed candidates were successful, but several high-profile Trump endorsees, including Dr. Oz, went down to defeat in the general election. Walker's fate remained to be decided in a December runoff election.

In 2022 several Republican critics of Donald Trump, like Liz Cheney (R-Wyo.), lost re-election.

The Issues

The Economy The economy was a major factor in the 2022 election, helping the Republicans take control of the House of Representatives. When Pew Research asked a nationally representative sample of Americans to rate the national economy in late October, 8 in 10 said the economy was very important in deciding who to vote for in the 2022 election. Public opinion was overwhelmingly negative about the economy, with 82 percent of adults saying that economic conditions today are poor or only fair. Among those who rated the economy as "poor," only 20 percent planned to vote for Democratic candidates (the party in power) versus 61 percent who planned to vote Republican.[57] Similarly, national exit polls conducted by Edison Research found a third of voters said inflation was the issue that mattered most in deciding how they voted for House candidates. Of those, 7 in 10 opted for Republicans.[58]

Pew also reported that over 70 percent of Americans were concerned with rising prices, especially prices for food, consumer goods, and gasoline, while 60 percent were concerned about housing costs. Concerns about inflation were shared across demographic (age, race, education, gender) and income groups.[59]

Crime Nearly all voters agreed that the economy was an important concern. When it came to other matters, however, Republican and Democratic voters appeared to have different priorities. For Republican voters, violent crime and illegal immigration were major worries. Indeed, three-quarters of Republican voters said immigration and violent crime were important to their vote choices in 2022. By contrast, only one-third of Democrats mentioned immigration and less than half said violent crime was a key issue. Republicans campaigned heavily against Democratic candidates for being "soft on crime." Overall, 6 in 10 registered voters said violent crime was very important when making their decision on how to vote in 2022, but the issue was more important to Republican (75 percent) than Democratic voters (50 percent).[60]

Abortion For Democratic voters, abortion was one of the most important issues and key reasons to vote. Abortion became a key issue in the election after the Supreme Court decision in *Dobbs v. Jackson Women's Health Organization* overturned *Roe v. Wade* and many states instituted complete abortion bans. Between March and October 2022, the percentage of registered voters who said abortion was very important in the election increased 13 points, from 43 to 56 percent.[61] According to national exit polls more than a quarter of voters in 2022 said abortion was the most important factor determining their choice at the polls. About 6 in 10 said they were unhappy with the Supreme Court's decision to overturn *Roe v. Wade*, and, among those, 7 in 10 backed

After the Supreme Court overturned *Roe v. Wade*, abortion became a critical issue in the 2022 elections. In states where abortion rights measures were on the ballot, Democrats generally supported them, while Republicans generally opposed.

Democrats for Congress.[62] The issue of abortion became even more salient in the several states, including California, Vermont, and Michigan, where state constitutional amendments protecting abortion appeared on referendum ballots. These referenda helped to remind voters of the significance of the issue.

Threats to Democracy Throughout the campaign Democrats argued that Donald Trump and his followers represented a threat to American democracy. As we noted, Democrats emphasized Trump's links to the January 6, 2021, attack on the U.S. Capitol. The fact, moreover, that a number of Republicans continued to deny the validity of the 2020 election gave Democrats an opportunity to paint their opponents as enemies of democratic processes. On the eve of the 2022 elections, President Biden warned voters that democracy itself was at stake. Biden's warning was, in effect, a reminder to voters to come to the polls and support Democratic candidates. The threat-to-democracy issue was an important one for Democrats. A sizable majority of voters (70 percent) said the "future of democracy in the country" was a very important issue in the election. Among this group, 46 percent supported Democratic candidates, while 40 percent favored Republicans. Thus, the future of democracy is important to both Democrats and Republicans.[63]

The Results

On the eve of the 2022 elections, Republicans had hoped for a "red wave" that would give the GOP control of both houses of Congress as well as many state-level positions. However, the election produced neither a red wave nor a blue wave. Instead it was a return to divided government, and, according to some, a call for political moderation. The outcome was mixed. Republicans won a slim majority in the House, but President Biden appeared to have had the best midterms in 20 years, since his party lost so few seats in the House. Democrats maintained control of the Senate, the first time a sitting president's party has held the Senate in 20 years. (Additionally, a highly contested runoff election was set to take place in Georgia between Republican Herschel Walker and Democrat Raphael Warnock, where the Democrats could further boost their numbers in the Senate.) Democrats also won 9 of the 12 contested state gubernatorial races. Democrats performed well in state legislative contests, so that in 18 states Democrats now control the governor's office and both houses of the state legislature—a slight gain from 2020.

Numerous referenda appeared on state ballots. Several states passed ballot measures to protect legalized abortion. These included California, Michigan, and Vermont. Iowans voted to protect a constitutional right to bear arms. Maryland and Missouri legalized recreational use of marijuana, while voters in Arkansas, North Dakota, and South Dakota voted against legalization.

Who Voted? Overall, voter turnout in the 2022 midterm was above average (almost 47 percent), but lower than the record high set in 2018.[64] In states with especially contested races, turnout was up, including in Pennsylvania, where turnout was about 5 percentage points above 2018, and Michigan, where 6 in 10 eligible people voted.[65] Youth turnout (people under 30) was the second highest in three decades for a midterm and appears to have been important in giving Democrats control of the Senate.[66]

While Democrats secured key victories in Senate races in 2022, like John Fetterman's (left) win in Pennsylvania, Republicans were able to win control of the House of Representatives. Mike Lawler (right) was able to oust Democratic incumbent Sean Patrick Maloney in a hotly contested race in New York.

Because midterm elections generally have lower turnout than presidential elections, the 2022 electorate overall was skewed toward older Americans: just 13 percent of all voters were under age 30, while 29 percent were age 65 or older. It was split about evenly between people who generally identify as Democrats (33 percent) and those who generally identify as Republicans (36 percent), with the remainder consisting of political independents and members of other parties. In 2018, Democrats made up a larger share of the electorate. Among the one-third of the electorate who identify as independent, 42 percent favored Democrats for Congress and 38 percent favored Republicans, similar to four years earlier. White voters without a college degree (4 in 10 voters) favored Republican candidates by about a 2-to-1 margin over Democrats, according to exit polls. White voters with a college degree (32 percent of the electorate) were about evenly split in their support for Democratic and Republican candidates. A majority of nonwhite voters (28 percent of electorate) favored Democratic candidates regardless of a college degree.[67] These patterns are consistent with past trends.

In some swing states youth turnout was high. The youth vote was critical in helping to flip Pennsylvania's Senate race, where Democrat John Fetterman won the open seat over Trump-endorsed Republican Dr. Mehmet Oz. National exit polls show the youth vote for House candidates was 63 percent for Democrats, 35 percent for Republicans.[68] Nevertheless, voter turnout of people age 30 and under was only 27 percent; if that number doubled, election outcomes would be different nationwide.

The 2022 Elections and the Future of American Politics

The immediate result of the 2022 national election will be a return to divided government. Republican control of the U.S. House almost guarantees that President Biden will be unable to secure congressional passage of significant policy proposals. Biden, like his predecessors, will likely turn to greater use of executive orders and other unilateral instruments of presidential power (see Chapter 11). Given America's deep partisan divisions, the chance of bipartisanship in the coming two years seems low.

But what of the larger implications of the 2022 contest? Many Republicans fear that Trump's candidacy in 2024 will ensure a GOP defeat and hope that a new Republican standard bearer, perhaps Governor DeSantis of Florida, will emerge. In 2022, the American national electorate seemed to want to move beyond Trump, as a number of his endorsees lost. One victorious Trump endorsee, senator-elect J. D. Vance of Ohio, sought to distance himself from Trump by failing to mention the former president in his victory speech. This seemed to be a clear indication that at least some Republicans believe, or at least hope, that Trump's star is in decline.

Check your understanding

9. Although neither person was on the ballot, how were the 2022 midterm elections influenced by President Joe Biden and former president Donald Trump?

   a) Since President Biden has the highest approval rating of any modern president, this election saw record Democratic turnout and a "blue wave," with Democrats substantially extending their majorities in the House and Senate.

   b) Electoral politics has become more nationalized over time and focused on the president (or former presidents) rather than local candidates and issues.

   c) With an overwhelming majority of voters rating the current economic conditions as poor, all the Republican candidates endorsed by former president Trump capitalized on these concerns, winning office by large margins.

   d) Although candidates tried to tie their opponents to these unpopular figures, voters cited competence and likability of the congressional candidates, not feelings toward Biden or Trump, as the primary factors influencing their vote choice.

10. With growing polarization between the parties, what issues shaped the decisions of Democratic and Republican voters during the 2022 elections?

    a) Democratic and Republican voters were equally concerned about illegal immigration, economic inequality, and nuclear proliferation.

    b) While both Democrats and Republicans cited threats to American democracy as a concern, Republicans were most concerned with Russia's invasion of Ukraine, and Democrats were most concerned about economic inequality.

    c) Republican voters cited rising crime, economic inflation, and illegal immigration as major concerns, and for Democratic voters, abortion was a key issue after the Supreme Court overturned *Roe v. Wade,* as well as the future of American democracy.

    d) Republican voters were primarily concerned with government corruption and the growing federal deficit, while Democratic voters were primarily concerned with college affordability and access to health care.

WHAT DO YOU THINK?

PARTICIPATION, CAMPAIGNS, AND ELECTIONS

The American political community has expanded over the course of history, with new groups winning and asserting political rights. But for much of the twentieth century, the electoral system in the United States failed to mobilize an active citizenry, giving rise to an uneven pattern of political participation that gives some people more voice in politics than others. Since 2000 a series of highly competitive presidential elections has spurred political campaigns to pay more attention to drawing greater numbers of voters into the political process; even so, many Americans still do not participate in politics. Unequal participation has consequences: one important study found that elected officials respond more to the preferences of voters than nonvoters, confirming long-held assumptions that affluent, more educated, and older citizens have more voice in politics and public policy.[54]

- What barriers to participation do you observe among your friends and family? What reforms would help? What would it take to increase political engagement among citizens of all backgrounds?

- Will moneyed interests continue to play a large role in the election process? What new laws may be needed to make the rules of the game fair?

- How might you be involved in campaigns and elections in the future? Do you feel that your voice is heard? What changes would increase electoral participation among young people? What do you think David Morales and Caleb Hanna, featured at the beginning of this chapter, would say?

Use 📖 **INQUIZITIVE** *to help you study and master this material.*

10

WHAT GOVERNMENT DOES & WHY IT MATTERS

In October 2021, former Facebook product manager Frances Haugen startled members of Congress with testimony that Facebook knowingly created products that "harm children, stoke division and weaken our democracy." She testified before the Senate Commerce Subcommittee on Consumer Protection that the social media giant designed its algorithms to amplify information to keep people using their sites longer, allegations supported by thousands of internal documents she leaked to the media. She said that the company knew that vulnerable people were particularly susceptible to harmful content—for example, teens exposed to information that made them feel bad about their bodies, and isolated adults (the widowed, the divorced, new arrivals in a city) targeted with misinformation. The company, she said, had adopted practices that eased the sharing of misinformation, amplified hate speech, and made users angrier. Despite earlier media exposés and internal research on how to reduce such harms, the company had declined to do so.

Congress

In 1996, Congress passed a law, Section 230 of the Communications Decency Act, that protects internet companies from legal liability for content posted by its users. Essentially, technology companies cannot be sued over third-party content. Congress considered revising the liability shield many times in the subsequent decades, but reforms were never passed, even as social media use rose from 5 percent of American adults in 2005 to 72 percent in 2021 and as alarm over the effects of misinformation and other harms increased. Frances urged lawmakers to revise Section 230 to make Facebook responsible for its algorithms. She said that "Facebook should not get a free pass on choices it makes to prioritize growth, virality, and reactiveness over public safety."[1]

In a rare show of bipartisanship, both Republican and Democratic members of Congress reacted with outrage to the evidence Frances provided. But would Congress pass new laws to force Facebook to address these concerns? Senator Richard Blumenthal (D-Conn.), who chaired the subcommittee holding the hearings, noted, "Parents across America are deeply disturbed" by the reports that Facebook knew that Instagram could harm children's mental health.[2] Senator Roger Wicker (R-Miss.) said, "The tech gods have been demystified. The children of America are hooked on their product. There is cynical knowledge on behalf of these big tech companies that this is true."[3] But Facebook and other tech

▲ In 2021, Congress called Frances Haugen, a former Facebook employee, to testify about what she said were the company's damaging business practices.

companies had blocked reform in the past. Senator Amy Klobuchar (D-Minn.) noted, "There are lobbyists around every single corner of this building that have been hired by the tech industry. Facebook and other tech companies are throwing a bunch of money around this town and people are listening to them."[4] The question remained whether this time would be different.

Congress has vast authority over many aspects of American life. Laws related to federal spending, taxing, regulation, and judicial appointments all pass through Congress. While the debates over these laws may seem hard to follow because they are often complex and technical or because heated, partisan struggles distract from the substance of the issue, it is important for the American people to learn about what Congress is doing. As the examples of Section 230 of the Communications Decency Act and the recent investigation of Facebook show, actions taken—or not taken—in Congress affect the everyday experiences we sometimes take for granted.

CHAPTER GOALS

Describe how Congress fulfills its role as a representative institution (pp. 305–18)

Describe the factors that structure congressional activity (pp. 318–23)

Describe the regular order and "unorthodox" processes of how a bill becomes a law (pp. 323–33)

Identify the factors that influence which bills Congress passes (pp. 333–37)

Describe the powers that Congress uses to influence other branches of government (pp. 338–41)

Congress Represents the American People

Describe how Congress fulfills its role as a representative institution

Congress is the most important representative institution in American government. In theory, members' primary responsibility is to the people in their district or state—their **constituency**—not to the congressional leadership, a party, or even Congress itself. Yet views about what constitutes fair and effective representation differ, and different constituents may have very different expectations of their representatives. Members of Congress must consider these diverse views and expectations as they represent their constituencies.

It is also important to understand that Congress is among the world's most powerful legislative bodies. In most countries, executives govern and legislatures can do little more than reject or approve bills they write. The U.S. Congress does a great deal of the work involved in writing and shaping legislation and exercises substantial power over the nation's budget. In recent decades, though, the power of Congress has declined relative to that of the presidency (see Chapter 11).

House and Senate: Differences in Representation

The framers of the Constitution provided for a **bicameral legislature**—that is, a legislative body consisting of two chambers. As we saw in Chapter 2, the framers intended each of these chambers, the House of Representatives and the Senate, to serve a different constituency. Members of the Senate, appointed by state legislatures for six-year terms, were to represent the states, while members of the House were to represent the people of the United States. (Today, members of both the House and the Senate are elected directly by the people.) The 435 members of the House are elected from districts apportioned according to population; the 100 members of the Senate are elected in statewide votes, with two senators from each state. Senators continue to have much longer terms in office and usually represent much larger and more diverse constituencies than do their counterparts in the House (see Table 10.1).

The House and Senate play different roles in the legislative process. Traditionally, the Senate is the more deliberative of the two bodies—the forum in which any and all ideas that senators raise can receive a thorough public airing. The House is the more centralized and organized of the two bodies. In part, this difference stems from the different rules governing the two bodies. These rules give House leaders more control over the legislative process and allow House members to specialize in certain legislative areas. The rules of the much smaller Senate give its leadership less power and discourage specialization.

constituency the residents in the area from which an official is elected

bicameral legislature a legislative assembly composed of two chambers or houses

TABLE 10.1 | Differences between the House and the Senate

	HOUSE	SENATE
Minimum age of member	25 years	30 years
U.S. citizenship	At least 7 years	At least 9 years
Length of term	2 years	6 years
Number representing each state	1–52 per state (depends on population)	2 per state
Constituency	Local	Statewide

Other factors also contribute to differences between the two chambers. Differences in the length of terms and the requirements for holding office, specified by the Constitution, generate differences in how members of each body serve their constituencies and exercise their powers of office. For the House, the relatively small size and uniform nature of their constituencies and the need to seek re-election every two years make members more attuned to the immediate legislative needs of local interest groups. The result is that the constituents they most effectively and frequently serve are well-organized local interests with specific legislative agendas—for instance, used-car dealers seeking relief from regulation, labor unions seeking more favorable workplace laws, or farmers looking for higher subsidies. Senators, on the other hand, serve larger and more diverse constituencies and seek re-election every six years. As a result, they are somewhat more insulated from the pressures of individual, narrow, and immediate interests.

Trustee versus Delegate Representation

Members of Congress can interpret their jobs as representatives in two different ways: as a **delegate**, acting on the express preferences of their constituents, or as a **trustee**, more loosely tied to constituents and empowered to make the decisions they think best.

The delegate role requires representatives to stay in constant touch with constituents and their wishes. But most constituents do not do this. Many pay little attention and are too busy to become well informed even on issues they care about. Thus, the delegate form of representation runs the risk that the voices of only a few active and informed constituents get heard.

delegate (member of Congress role) a representative who votes according to the preferences of their constituency

trustee a representative who votes based on what they think is best for their constituency

When congressional members act as trustees, on the other hand, they may not pay sufficient attention to the wishes of their constituents, often making decisions based on their own judgment. In this scenario, the only way the public can exercise influence is by voting every two years for representatives and every six years for senators. In fact, most members of Congress take this

To more effectively promote a legislative agenda addressing issues that disproportionately affect racial and ethnic minority groups, members of Congress from those groups have formed caucuses. Here, Representative Judy Chu (D-Calif.), chair of the Congressional Asian Pacific American Caucus, speaks at a press conference on the Covid-19 Hate Crimes Act.

electoral check very seriously. They try to anticipate the wishes of their constituents, because they know that unpopular decisions can be used against them in the coming election.

Descriptive versus Substantive Representation

A representative claims to act or speak for some other person or group. But how can one person be trusted to speak for another? How do we know that those who call themselves our representatives are actually speaking on our behalf, rather than simply pursuing their own interests?[5]

There are two circumstances under which one person reasonably might be trusted to speak for another. The first occurs if the two individuals are so similar in background, character, interests, and perspectives that anything said by one would very likely reflect the views of the other as well. This principle is at the heart of what is called **descriptive representation**—the sort that takes place when representatives have the same racial, gender, age, social class, ethnic, religious, or educational backgrounds as their constituents. If

descriptive representation a type of representation in which representatives have the same racial, gender, ethnic, religious, or educational backgrounds as their constituents; it is based on the principle that if two individuals are similar in background, character, interests, and perspectives, then one can correctly represent the other's views

demographic or sociological similarity helps to promote good representation, then the sociological composition of a representative assembly like Congress should mirror the composition of society.

The second circumstance under which one person might be trusted to speak for another occurs if the representatives are in some way formally accountable to those they are supposed to represent. Because they may fear defeat at the polls, or simply because they believe in serving their constituents, representatives may work to serve their constituents' interests even if their own personal backgrounds, views, and interests differ from the backgrounds of those they represent. This principle is called **substantive representation**. Both descriptive and substantive representation play a role in the relationship between members of Congress and their constituencies.

The Social Composition of the U.S. Congress The extent to which the U.S. Congress is representative of the American people in a sociological sense can be seen by examining social characteristics of the House and Senate today. Women, African Americans, Latinos, and Asian Americans have increased their congressional representation in the past two decades (see Figure 10.1). But the representation of women and people of color in Congress is still not comparable to their increasing proportions in the general population (see Who Are Americans?).

The occupational backgrounds of members of Congress have always been a matter of interest because many issues split along lines relevant to occupations and industries. The legal profession is the most common career of members prior to their election, and public service or politics is also a frequent background. In addition, many members have important ties to business and industry. Moreover, members of Congress are much more highly educated than most Americans. More than 9 in 10 have college degrees, and more than one-third have law degrees.[6]

Can Congress legislate fairly or take account of a diversity of views and interests if it is not a sociologically representative assembly? Representatives can serve as the agents of their constituents even if they do not precisely mirror their sociological attributes. Yet descriptive representation is important. At the least, the social composition of a representative assembly is important for symbolic purposes: to demonstrate to groups in the population that the government takes them

FOR CRITICAL ANALYSIS ⟶

1. Does it matter whether the backgrounds of members of Congress reflect the population as a whole? Can members represent their constituents effectively if they do not come from similar backgrounds?

2. Visit www.house.gov and www.senate.gov to identify your representatives in Congress and visit their web pages. How similar are their backgrounds to yours?

WHO ARE AMERICANS?

Who Are the Members of Congress?

Although the number of women, Black people, and Latinos in Congress has increased in recent decades, Congress is still much less diverse than the American population. Members of Congress are predominantly male, White, and Protestant, and a large percentage hold a law degree. These data compare the 117th Congress, which took office in 2021, with the U.S. population as a whole.

Gender

	Senate	House	U.S. pop.
Women	24%	29%	51%
Men	76%	71%	49%

Party

	Senate	House	U.S. pop.*
Republican	50%	49%	27%
Democratic	48%	51%	29%
Independent	2%	0%	42%

Key

U.S. population

Senate

House of Representatives

Race

	Senate	House	U.S. pop.*
White	88%	71%	59%
Black	3%	13%	14%
Latino	7%	10%	19%
Asian	2%	4%	6%
Native American	0%	1%	1%

Religion

	Senate	House	U.S. pop.
Protestant	58%	55%	42%
Catholic	24%	33%	24%
Jewish	9%	5%	1%
Mormon	3%	1%	2%
All others	1%	1%	32%

Foreign birth

Senate	1%
House	7%
U.S. population	14%

Military service

Senate	16%
House	17%
U.S. population	5%

Holds a law degree

Senate	50%
House	33%
U.S. population	0.4%

Average age   Senate 64.3   House 58.4   U.S. population 38

* Numbers may not add up to 100 percent due to rounding.

SOURCES: U.S. Census Bureau, "QuickFacts: United States," www.census.gov/quickfacts/fact/table/US/PST045221; "Self-Described Religious Identification of the Adult Population in the United States in 2021," Statista, www.statista.com /statistics/183817/religious-identification-of-adult-population; "Number of Lawyers in the United States from 2007 to 2021," Statista, www.statista.com/statistics/740222/number-of-lawyers-us.; Jeffrey M. Jones, "U.S. Political Party Preferences Shifted Greatly During 2021," Gallup, January 17, 2022 (accessed 7/27/22).

FIGURE 10.1 | Diversity in Congress, 1971–2021

Congress has become much more socially diverse since the 1970s. After a gradual increase from 1971 to 1990, the number of female and Black members grew quickly during the first half of the 1990s. Despite the increased representation of women and minorities in Congress, most members of Congress are White men. Do you think these numbers will rise in the future? Why or why not?

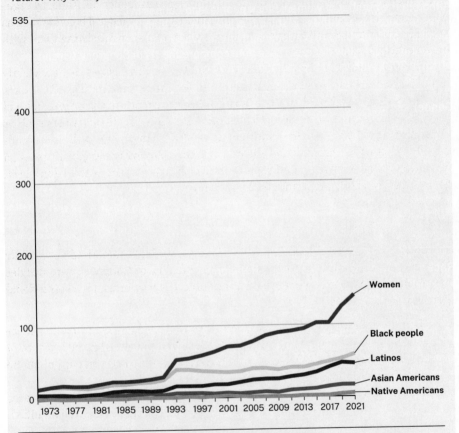

SOURCES: Vital Statistics, "Demographics of Members of Congress," Tables 1-16, 1-17, 1-18, 1-19, www .brookings.edu/multi-chapter-report/vital-statistics-on-congress/; Jennifer E. Manning, *Membership of the 116th Congress: A Profile* (Washington, DC: Congressional Research Service, March 31, 2020), https://fas. org/sgp/crs/misc/R45583.pdf (accessed 4/8/20); authors' updates; Katherine Schaeffer, "Racial, Ethnic Diversity Increases Yet Again with the 117th Congress," Pew Research Center, January 28, 2021, www .pewresearch.org/fact-tank/2021/01/28/racial-ethnic-diversity-increases-yet-again-with-the-117th-congress/.

seriously. If Congress is not representative symbolically, then its own authority, and indeed that of the entire government, is reduced.[7]

Representatives as Agents A good deal of evidence indicates that whether or not members of Congress share their constituents' sociological characteristics, they *do* work hard to speak for their constituents' views and to serve their constituents' interests. Indeed, we expect that representatives will seek to discover the interests of their constituencies and take those interests into account as they govern. Whether members of Congress always represent the interests of their constituents is another matter, as we will see later in this chapter.[8]

One important aspect of congressional representation is constituency service, also called "casework." Both senators and House members assign numerous staffers to their district offices to deal with constituent concerns.[9] The service that these offices provide includes talking to constituents; providing them with minor services; presenting special bills for them; attempting to influence decisions by regulatory commissions on their behalf; helping them apply for federal benefits such as Social Security and Small Business Administration loans; and assisting them with immigration cases.

In many districts and states there are often two or three issues that are clearly top priorities for constituents and, therefore, for the representatives. For example, representatives from districts where the insurance industry is prominent will likely give legislation on these subjects great attention. In oil-rich states such as Oklahoma and Texas, senators and members of the House are likely to be leading advocates of oil interests. On the other hand, on many issues constituents do not have very strong views, and representatives are free to act as they think best. Foreign policy issues often fall into this category.

Congressional Elections

Elections have an enormous impact on Congress. Three factors are especially important in understanding who serves as a member of Congress: who decides to run for office, the incumbency advantage, and the way in which congressional district lines are drawn.

Who Runs for Congress In the past, decisions about who would run for a particular elected office were made by local party officials. A person who had a record of service to the party, who was owed a favor, or whose "turn" had come up might be nominated by party leaders.

Today, few party organizations have the power to slate candidates in this way. Instead, parties try to ensure that their congressional candidates are well qualified. Even so, the decision to run for Congress is a personal one, and one of the most important factors determining who runs for office is an individual's political ambition.[10] Potential candidates may also assess whether they can raise enough money to mount a credible campaign. Fundraising ability depends on connections with other politicians, interest groups, and national party organizations.

Incumbency The role of **incumbency** is central in shaping the American electoral system and the kind of representation citizens get in Washington. Once in office, members of Congress gain access to an array of tools they can use to stack the deck in favor of their re-election. Their success in doing so is evident in the high rates of re-election for congressional incumbents. In most elections, roughly 90 percent of House and Senate incumbents seeking re-election are successful, with most

incumbency holding the political office for which one is running

winning by comfortable margins.[11] The electoral success of incumbents does not mean that Congress never changes, though. Over the course of a decade, it is likely that nearly half the members of Congress will be replaced.[12]

Incumbents have a number of advantages. To begin with, members of Congress and their staffs are in a position to provide many individual services to constituents—the casework described earlier. Also, under a law enacted in 1789, members of Congress may send mail free of charge to their constituents informing them of governmental business and public affairs. Most senators and representatives send regular newsletters to all constituent households highlighting the many efforts and initiatives the incumbent has undertaken on behalf of the community.

Members of Congress lose no opportunity to garner local publicity and advertise their efforts on the constituency's behalf. Events that are ignored by the national media may nevertheless be of considerable significance to local voters. Senators and representatives seek to associate themselves with these events and send out press releases highlighting their involvement. For example, a press release issued by the office of Congressman Eric Swalwell of California's 15th District honored the managers and employees of a new sanitation facility in his district. In fact, at the ribbon-cutting ceremony for the new plant, a staffer from Swalwell's office presented the facility's general manager with a "Certificate of Special Congressional Recognition" for the facility's "commitment and dedication to renewable energy."[13] Thousands of these certificates, suitable for framing, are awarded by members of Congress every year. Generally, the recipients are grateful and the event is covered by local television and newspapers and promoted on social media.

Unlike challengers, who can offer only promises, incumbents have a chance to promote legislation favored by important groups and interests in their districts. If the constituency includes a major industry, representatives will almost always promote legislation that will please the workers and managers of that industry. The late senator Henry M. Jackson of Washington took pleasure in being known as the Senator from Boeing (a large aerospace manufacturer then based in Seattle). Such **pork barrel** efforts provide tangible benefits and achievements for which they can claim credit and which can be crucial to their re-election.[14]

pork barrel (or pork) appropriations made by legislative bodies for local projects that are often not needed but that are created so that local representatives can win re-election in their home districts

Often, representatives find it useful to strongly support essentially symbolic legislation that will please constituency groups. For example, members with large numbers of Black constituents were eager to support recognition of Dr. Martin Luther King, Jr.'s birthday as a national holiday. These symbolic gestures are one form of what is sometimes called "position taking."[15]

Another important electoral advantage for incumbents is superior access to campaign funds. Incumbents are usually far more able than challengers to raise money. For most senators and representatives, fundraising is a year-round activity. Incumbents hope not only to outspend challengers but to deter prospective challengers from even undertaking the race knowing they probably face an insurmountable fundraising disadvantage.

AMERICA | SIDE BY SIDE

Women's Legislative Representation

While the percentage of women in the U.S. House of Representatives is currently at an all-time high of 27.6 percent, the United States still lags behind much of the rest of the world in this area.

1. Which parts of the world have the highest proportion of women in their legislatures? What do you think may account for certain areas having higher levels of elected women officeholders than others? Are there areas of the world where the percentage of women in the legislature surprises you?

2. How much should a legislature reflect the demographic makeup of its citizens? Should a country create legal requirements, or change its electoral rules, to encourage the election of underrepresented groups?

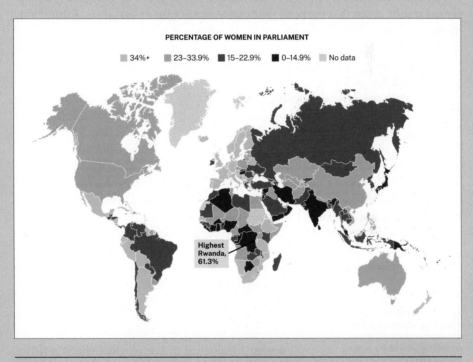

PERCENTAGE OF WOMEN IN PARLIAMENT

34%+ · 23–33.9% · 15–22.9% · 0–14.9% · No data

Highest
Rwanda,
61.3%

SOURCE: Inter-Parliamentary Union, "Women in National Parliaments," IPU Parline, October 1, 2021, https://data.ipu.org/women-ranking?month=10&year=2021 (accessed 11/2/21).

The electoral success of congressional incumbents is often cast in a negative light as though it was undeserved or a result of improper activities. It is worth noting, however, that incumbents are re-elected, at least in part, because of the vigorous efforts they make on behalf of their constituents. Incumbents undertake constituency casework, try to make certain that the flow of funds from the federal pork barrel favors their own districts, and work to identify legislative responses to their constituents' concerns.

Apportionment and Redistricting The drawing of congressional district lines also has a major impact on election outcomes. Districting, of course, affects only the House of Representatives. (Senators are chosen from states, and these boundaries do not change.) At least every 10 years, and sometimes more frequently, state legislatures redistrict, or redraw the borders of their state's districts. Decennial redistricting is required by the Constitution to reflect population changes in accordance with the federal census.

Because the number of House seats has been fixed by law at 435 since 1929, the census results mean that every 10 years some states gain or lose seats. **Apportionment**, the redistribution of seats among the states, is a zero-sum process: for one state to gain a seat, another must lose one. So some states with population growth over the previous decade gain additional seats; some with population decline or lower growth lose seats.

Over the past several decades, the shift of the American population to the South and the West has greatly increased the size of the congressional delegations from those regions. This trend continued in the 2020 census (see Figure 10.2). Texas gained two seats (it gained four after 2010), and Florida gained one. States in the Northeast and the upper Midwest Rust Belt lost seats. Proportionally, Latino voters are nearly three times as numerous in states that gained seats compared with states that lost seats, suggesting that the growth of the Latino population is a major factor in the American political landscape.[16]

In most states, **redistricting** is controlled by the state legislature and is a highly political process to create an advantage for the party with a majority in the legislature. For example, redistricting can put two incumbents of the opposing party into the same district, ensuring that one of them will lose, while creating an open seat that favors the redistricting party. Redistricting can also give an advantage to one party by clustering voters with similar ideological or sociological characteristics in a single district or by separating those voters into two or more districts. The manipulation of electoral districts to serve the interests of a particular group is known as **gerrymandering**.

Concern about partisan gerrymandering has led some states to take redistricting power away from state legislatures and give it to independent bipartisan commissions that try to develop congressional district maps that do not give an unfair advantage to either party.[17]

apportionment the process, occurring after every decennial census, that allocates congressional seats among the 50 states

redistricting the process of redrawing election districts and redistributing legislative representatives; this happens every 10 years, to reflect shifts in population

gerrymandering drawing legislative districts in such a way as to give unfair advantage to a political party or one racial or ethnic group

FIGURE 10.2 | Congressional Reapportionment, 2020

States in the South and the West were the big winners in the reapportionment of House seats following the 2020 census. The old manufacturing states in the Midwest and Mid-Atlantic regions were the biggest losers. Is this shift likely to favor Democrats or Republicans?

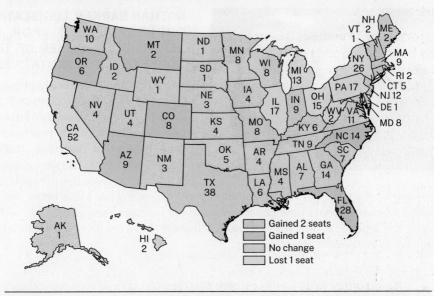

SOURCE: "Apportionment of the U.S. House of Representatives Based on the 2020 Census," www2
.census.gov/programs-surveys/decennial/2020/data/apportionment/apportionment-2020-map01.pdf
(accessed 9/9/22).

The federal courts have often intervened in cases involving partisan gerrymandering. In 2019, however, the Supreme Court ruled that gerrymandering was a "political question" beyond the reach of the federal judiciary,[18] though the Court's decision left open the possibility that state courts might continue to intervene in gerrymandering cases. And the decision applied only to partisan gerrymandering, not to claims of racial gerrymandering. Since 2019, state courts in such states as North Carolina, New York, and Maryland have declared apportionment plans developed by state legislatures to be efforts at partisan gerrymandering.

Since the passage of the 1982 amendments to the Voting Rights Act of 1965, race has become a major, and controversial, consideration in drawing voting districts. The Voting Rights Act, which encouraged the creation of districts in which people of color have decisive majorities, has greatly increased the number of representatives of color in Congress. An important case affecting minority voting was *Shelby County v. Holder*.[19] In its decision, the Court struck down a portion of the 1965 Voting Rights Act that had required states and localities with a history of racially biased election laws to obtain federal preclearance before adopting any new voting rules. Critics charge that the elimination of preclearance has encouraged racial gerrymandering and other restrictions on minority voting.

HOW TO

Contact Your Member of Congress

NATHAN BARKER, LEGISLATIVE CORRESPONDENT FOR A REPUBLICAN MEMBER OF THE HOUSE OF REPRESENTATIVES

Let's say you feel strongly about an issue, and you want to contact those in power who can make a difference. One important way is to reach out to your member of Congress. Nathan Barker, who is a legislative correspondent for a southern Republican member of the House of Representatives, says, "I love my job. I love being able to connect people, connect the constituent and the member each and every day because this republic of ours wouldn't work without it." Here are his tips for contacting legislators in the most effective way:

1. It's important to do some research first. You can convey your opinion about a general issue area, but it's even better to refer to a specific piece of legislation by title or the House H.R. number or the Senate S. number. At congress.gov you can search by key word or member name and follow bills through the process. Also make sure you're contacting about a federal issue, not a state legislative bill.

2. If you want to voice your opinion about an issue or piece of legislation, contact your representative or senator's Washington, D.C., office, because that's "where the experts on policy issues are," Nathan says. If you need casework assistance — help with a federal agency, for example — contact the member's local office.

3. Should you write, email, or call? If you want a response, a letter or email is best (keep in mind that a response may take a couple of weeks due to volume). If you simply want to register your opinion, a phone call is good. Leave a voice mail with your full name, your city or town, your subject, and a short message, and staff will log your call.

4 Always contact your own representative or senator. They very much want to hear from their constituents. Contacting officials from other districts or states, who have no obligation to respond, or every single Republican or Democrat, or those in leadership, is not an effective use of your time. Better to contact your own member and urge them to speak with leadership or other members of the congressional delegation about your issue.

5 Nathan says there is no single script to follow, but always state your name, your location, your background ("I'm a veteran" or "I'm a teacher," which provides a helpful frame of reference), and your opinion or call for action. It's important to be specific and succinct ("I'm a student worried about student loans, and I support bill H.R. ___ for ___ reason"). If you're calling about a specific piece of legislation, better to call and voice support or opposition *before* it comes up for a vote. And feel free to contact again. "The status quo is always shifting, and new bills are constantly coming up," Nathan says.

6 To follow up, Nathan suggests signing up for legislators' newsletters to keep informed about their activities, legislation under consideration, and upcoming events such as town hall meetings or coffee meet-ups. Most have Facebook and Twitter accounts as well. You may even be able to set up a one-on-one meeting, especially with a House member. It helps to be informed about your issue and persistent but also kind and respectful in interacting with the office — hard-working staff members really appreciate that (and they are often student interns, an opportunity you might pursue).

"There is nothing that should stop a student in college from contacting a member about an issue they find important," Nathan says. "If you're passionate about an issue, just do it."

Check your understanding

1. How do differences between the U.S. House of Representatives and the U.S. Senate influence representation?

   a) The relatively small size and uniform nature of their constituencies and two-year terms make U.S. representatives more responsive to local interest groups compared to U.S. senators.

   b) U.S. senators are more insulated from elections, and therefore senators do not represent their constituents, while U.S. representatives always adhere to constituency opinion.

   c) Because U.S. senators serve a larger constituency, they are better able to represent constituents compared to U.S. representatives, who serve a narrower constituency.

   d) Because the U.S. Senate is typically more deliberative than the U.S. House, senators are able to respond more quickly to changes in public opinion.

2. Which of the following statements regarding congressional representation is true?

   a) Congress members acting as delegates may not pay sufficient attention to the wishes of their constituents, while those acting as trustees closely adhere to their constituents' views.

   b) While Congress is descriptively representative of society, Congress members rarely engage in substantive representation.

   c) Members of Congress tend to prioritize issues that are highly important to their constituents.

   d) Members of Congress place little value on constituency service and instead focus the vast majority of their attention on sponsoring bills.

Congressional Organization Determines Power

Describe the factors that structure congressional activity

The building blocks of congressional organization include the political parties, the committee system, and congressional staff. Each of these factors plays a key role in the organization of Congress and in the process through which Congress formulates and enacts laws.

Party Leadership

Political parties are not mentioned in the Constitution, but soon after the nation's Founding, a party system developed in the Congress. Much of the actual work of Congress is controlled by the parties, which write most of the rules of congressional procedure and select the leaders who direct the flow of congressional business. Without party leadership and party organization, Congress could not function as a lawmaking body.

Every two years, at the beginning of a new Congress, the members of each party gather to elect their House leaders. House Republicans call their gathering the **conference**. House Democrats call theirs the **caucus**. The elected leader of the majority party is later proposed to the whole House and is automatically elected to the position of **Speaker of the House**, with voting along straight party lines. The House majority conference or caucus then also elects a **majority leader**. The minority party goes through the same process and selects a **minority leader**. Each party also elects a **whip** to line up party members on important votes and to relay voting information to the leaders.

At one time, party leaders strictly controlled committee assignments, using them to enforce party discipline. Today, in principle, representatives receive the assignments they want. But often too many individuals seek assignments to the most important committees, which gives the leadership an opportunity to curry favor with their members when it resolves conflicting requests.

Generally, representatives seek assignments that will allow them to influence decisions of special importance to their districts. Representatives from farm districts, for example, often request seats on the Agriculture Committee.[20] Especially popular seats are those on powerful committees such as Ways and Means, which is responsible for tax legislation, and Appropriations.

Within the Senate, the majority party designates the member with the greatest seniority to serve as president pro tempore, a position of primarily ceremonial leadership. Real power is in the hands of the majority leader and minority leader, who together control the Senate's calendar, or agenda for legislation.

conference a gathering of House Republicans every two years to elect their House leaders; Democrats call their gathering the "caucus"

caucus (political) a normally closed political party business meeting of citizens or lawmakers to select candidates, elect officers, plan strategy, or make decisions regarding legislative matters

Speaker of the House the chief presiding officer of the House of Representatives; the Speaker is the most important party and House leader and can influence the legislative agenda, the fate of individual pieces of legislation, and members' positions within the House

majority leader the elected leader of the majority party in the House of Representatives or in the Senate; in the House, the majority leader is subordinate in the party hierarchy to the Speaker of the House

minority leader the elected leader of the minority party in the House or Senate

whip a party member in the House or Senate responsible for coordinating the party's legislative strategy, building support for key issues, and counting votes

The Committee System

The committee system is a prominent feature of Congress. At each stage of the legislative process, Congress makes use of committees and subcommittees to sort through alternatives, secure information, and write legislation. There are several different kinds of congressional committees: standing committees, select committees, joint committees, and conference committees.

The most important arenas of congressional policy making are **standing committees**. These committees remain in existence from one session of Congress to the next; they have the power to propose and write legislation. The jurisdiction of each one covers a particular subject matter, which in most cases parallels a major department or agency in the executive branch.

Among the most important standing committees are those in charge of finances. The House Ways and Means Committee and the Senate Finance Committee are powerful because of their jurisdiction over taxes, trade, and expensive entitlement programs such as Social Security and Medicare. The Senate and House Appropriations committees also play important roles because they decide how much funding various programs will actually receive and exactly how the money will be spent.

Except for the House Rules Committee, all standing committees receive numerous legislative proposals. The House Rules Committee decides the order in which bills come up for a vote on the House floor and determines the specific rules that govern the length of debate and opportunity for amendments. The Senate Rules and Administration Committee has far less power than its House counterpart.

Most standing committees are broken into subcommittees that specialize in particular aspects of the committee's work. For example, the Senate Committee on Foreign Relations has seven subcommittees, each specializing in a different geographic region. When a bill is referred to committee, the committee leadership will determine which subcommittee is most appropriate for the matter in question. Subcommittee jurisdictions are loosely defined and committee chairs have considerable discretion in assigning bills. Much of the hard work of deliberating, holding hearings, and going through "**markup**," as the process of amending and rewriting a bill is called, takes place in the subcommittees, though further markup may occur in the full committee after the amended bill leaves the subcommittee.

One important power of the standing committees is the power to conduct hearings and launch investigations. There are two types of legislative hearings: legislative and oversight. Legislative hearings are conducted to address specific bills. In a legislative hearing, experts and stakeholders are invited to offer information and testimony relevant to the bill being considered. Oversight hearings are investigative in nature. Executive branch officials or other relevant individuals are brought before the committee and questioned on their conduct or the causes of some problem.

Select committees are usually not permanent and usually do not have the power to present legislation to the full Congress. (The House and Senate Select Intelligence committees are exceptions.) These committees hold hearings and serve as focal points for the issues they are charged with considering. Congressional leaders form select committees when they want to take up issues that fall outside the jurisdictions of existing committees, to highlight an issue, or to investigate a particular problem.

standing committee a permanent committee with the power to propose and write legislation that covers a particular subject, such as finance or agriculture

markup the session in which a congressional committee rewrites legislation to incorporate changes discussed during hearings on a bill

select committees (usually) temporary legislative committees set up to highlight or investigate a particular issue or address an issue not within the jurisdiction of existing committees

For example, in 2021 the House created a select committee to investigate the January 6, 2021, attack on the Capitol by Trump supporters who believed that Joe Biden had stolen the election. The committee issued subpoenas to Trump aides in an effort to determine whether the mob had formed spontaneously or had been organized by Trump and his associates. Some former Trump aides testified before the committee while others refused and faced legal repercussions. A good deal of testimony linked Trump directly to the January 6 riot, but it remained to be seen whether Trump would be held accountable for his role. Democrats hoped that the committee's findings would, at the very least, discredit pro-Trump Republicans in the 2022 national elections and prevent Trump himself from ever regaining the White House.

Joint committees involve members from both the Senate and the House. There are four such committees—economic, taxation, library, and printing; they are permanent, but do not have the power to present legislation. The Joint Economic Committee and the Joint Taxation Committee have often played important roles in collecting information and holding hearings on economic and financial issues.

Conference committees are temporary committees whose members are appointed by the Speaker of the House and the presiding officer of the Senate. These committees are charged with reaching a compromise on legislation once it has been passed by the House and the Senate. Conference committees can play an important role in determining the laws that are actually passed because they must reconcile any differences in the legislation passed by the House and Senate. Today, however, House and Senate leaders often prefer to bypass conference committees in favor of sending a bill back and forth until agreement is achieved.

joint committees legislative committees formed of members of both the House and Senate

conference committees joint committees created to work out a compromise on House and Senate versions of a piece of legislation

seniority the ranking given to an individual on the basis of length of continuous service on a committee in Congress

Politics and the Organization of Committees Within each committee, leadership is partly based on **seniority**, determined by years of continuous service on that particular committee. In general, each committee is chaired by the most senior member, or at least a senior member, of the majority party. But the principle of seniority is not absolute. When the Republicans took over the House in 1995, they disregarded it in the selection of key committee chairs.

Since then, Republicans have continued to depart from the seniority principle, often choosing committee chairs on the basis of loyalty to the party leadership's legislative priorities or the member's fundraising abilities rather than seniority. In 2007, Democrats returned to a modified seniority principle for selecting committee chairs, appointing from among the most senior members.

Over the years, Congress has reformed its organizational structure and operating procedures. Most changes have been made to improve efficiency, but some reforms have also been a response to political considerations. For example, the Republican leadership of the 104th Congress (1995–97), seeking to concentrate its authority, reduced the number of subcommittees and limited the time committee chairs could serve to three terms. They made good on this limit in 2001, when they replaced 13 committee chairs.

As a consequence of these changes, while remaining important for deliberation and generating legislative ideas, committees no longer have as central a role as they once held in policy making. Furthermore, sharp partisan divisions have made it difficult for committees to deliberate and bring bipartisan expertise to bear on policy making as in the past. Today they typically do not deliberate for very long or call witnesses, and it has become more common in recent years for party-driven legislation to go directly to the floor, bypassing committees altogether.[21] Nonetheless, committees continue to play a role in the legislative process, especially on issues that are not sharply partisan.[22]

The Staff System

Another important congressional institution is the staff system. Every member of Congress employs many staff members, whose tasks include handling constituent requests and dealing with legislative details. Staffers often bear the primary responsibility for formulating and drafting proposals, organizing hearings, dealing with administrative agencies, and negotiating with lobbyists. Indeed, legislators typically deal with one another through staff rather than through direct personal contact. Representatives and senators together employ roughly 11,500 staffers—about half in each chamber—in their Washington and home offices.

In addition, Congress employs more than 2,000 committee staffers.[23] These make up the permanent staff that stays attached to every House and Senate committee regardless of turnover in Congress and that is responsible for organizing and administering the committee's work, including doing research, scheduling, organizing hearings, and drafting legislation. Committee staffers can play key roles in the legislative process.

Not only does Congress employ personal and committee staff, but it has also established **staff agencies** designed to provide the legislative branch with resources and expertise independent of the executive branch. These agencies include the Congressional Research Service, which performs research for legislators who wish to know the facts and competing arguments relevant to policy proposals or other legislative business; the Government Accountability Office, through which Congress can investigate the financial and administrative affairs of any government agency or program; and the Congressional Budget Office, which assesses the economic implications and likely costs of proposed federal programs.

staff agencies legislative support agencies responsible for policy analysis

Check your understanding

3. How does leadership in the U.S. House differ from leadership in the U.S. Senate?

   a) While the U.S. House of Representatives organizes its leadership by political partisanship, leadership in the U.S. Senate is only organized based on seniority.

   b) The Speaker holds the most power in the U.S. House of Representatives, while the majority party leader holds the most power in the U.S. Senate.

c) The U.S. Senate has more leadership positions compared to the U.S. House of Representatives.
d) Senate leaders determine the calendar; the House leadership does not have control over the calendar.

4. Congressional committees, which were once considered central to policy making, have much less power in the contemporary Congress due to

a) the elimination of dedicated committee staff.
b) seniority determining leadership of committees.
c) less need for technical expertise on issues in the internet age.
d) sharp partisan divisions lessening the role of deliberation and bipartisan expertise in policy making.

How a Bill Becomes a Law

Describe the regular order and "unorthodox" processes of how a bill becomes a law

Article 1, Section 1, of the U.S. Constitution assigns the legislative power, the power to make the law, to the Congress of the United States. The framers viewed the legislative power as the fundamental power of government and believed that it should belong to a representative assembly, not to the executive or the courts. Any member of the House or Senate may propose a law. These legislative proposals are usually called **bills** and must be passed by a majority vote in both houses of Congress and signed by the president before they can become law. Members of Congress may also propose *resolutions,* which, with one exception, are essentially expressions of congressional opinion and do not have the force of law. The exception is the *joint resolution,* most often used for emergency appropriations, to propose constitutional amendments, or to declare war.

Each year many bills are introduced in Congress, but very few are actually enacted into law. In fact, only 2 to 3 percent of the total number of bills introduced each year become laws. The framers feared constant change in the law and, hence, thought it should not be easy to enact laws. This is one reason they devised a legislative process that required many steps.

In high school civics classes students are usually taught a version of the congressional process that, on Capitol Hill, is known as "regular order." As explained in more detail in this section, regular order is the basic "textbook" version of how a bill becomes a law (see Figure 10.3). Under the terms of regular order, a member introduces legislation and the Rules Committee refers the bill to the appropriate subject matter committee. In the committee the

> **bill** a proposed law that has been sponsored by a member of Congress and submitted to the clerk of the House or Senate

FIGURE 10.3 | How a Bill Becomes a Law: The Regular Order

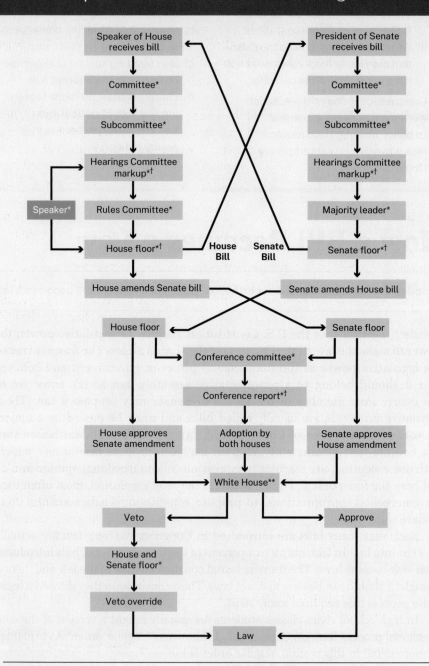

*Points at which a bill can be amended.

**If the president neither signs nor vetoes a bill within 10 days, it automatically becomes law.

†Points at which a bill can die by vote.

bill is debated and hearings are held before a final draft of the proposed legislation is reported out and then voted on by the full chamber.

The congressional process, though, has changed in recent decades. What some call "unorthodox lawmaking" reduces the power of congressional committees and undermines deliberation, but still can produce legislation, especially when Congress and the president are of the same party.

Regular Order

Introducing a Bill Any member of the House or Senate can introduce a bill. Bills are usually drafted by members and their staff, sometimes with the help of interest groups and outside experts. The member of Congress who introduces a bill becomes the bill's sponsor. Members usually sponsor bills of interest to themselves and their constituents. In some cases, members do not expect their bill to be passed. They introduce legislation to satisfy important constituencies or to make symbolic points. This is known as position taking (as discussed earlier). Often enough, though, members are prepared to fight hard to see their bill enacted. Sponsors will often seek cosponsors to broaden the base of support for their bill. Cosponsors will be able to claim credit with relevant constituencies as though the bill was their own idea.

In the House, a bill clerk assigns the bill a number that begins with "H.R." (This stands for "House Resolution," and there are various types.) In the Senate, a bill clerk assigns a bill number that begins with "S." Once this happens the bill's title will be read on the floor. This is called the "first reading of the bill." After the first reading, the bill is referred by the majority party leadership to a committee for the next stage of legislative action. Once the bill is introduced, an electronic copy is sent to the Library of Congress and its status will be entered on Congress.gov. In the House, the Rules Committee will determine the rules under which the bill will be considered by the committee and on the floor, if and when the chamber votes on it. The Senate has a tradition of open debate, and its Rules Committee does not have the power to set the terms under which a bill will be considered.

In the House, the majority party controls the Rules Committee, with nine majority and four minority party members. The House Speaker will almost always appoint their closest allies to the Rules Committee. Accordingly, the Rules Committee is known as "the Speaker's Committee," and the House majority leadership works through the committee to advance the party's legislative agenda.

There are generally four types of rules:

1. *Open rules* allow any member to offer an amendment that complies with the standing parliamentary rules of the House (and also the Budget Act, as discussed later).
2. *Modified open rules* allow only amendments that have been preprinted in the Congressional Record, or may put a time limit on consideration of amendments, or may put both of these types of restrictions in place.
3. *Structured rules* limit amendments offered to a bill to only those designated in a special rule.
4. *Closed rules* prohibit any amendments being offered other than those recommended by the committee reporting out the bill.

The choice of rules by the leadership of the House is extremely important. Closed and structured rules reflect and reinforce the power of the majority party leadership and will be applied to important pieces of legislation when the leadership is fairly confident of being able to enforce its will. Closed rules also limit the influence of the minority party. Open rules, on the other hand, will generally be applied when the leadership faces considerable dissent in its own party and thinks it can only build consensus by allowing members an opportunity to voice their views. Open rules also allow members of the minority party to exert some influence over legislation.

Committee Action and Markup When a bill is referred to a committee, it is placed on the committee's calendar and on that date the committee begins debate on the bill, schedules hearings, and may rewrite some or all of its provisions. This stage of the legislative process is called the markup of a bill. In the past, members of the committee would literally sit together around a conference table and mark up the bill with handwritten edits. Typically, the majority committee members reach agreement on changes before even showing the committee's minority party members the proposed legislative text. This pre-markup is called the "Chairman's Mark." Once the markup is complete, the committee votes to accept or reject changes made to the bill during the markup session. Any amendments offered by the minority are usually rejected, although sometimes token amendments are accepted if they are considered harmless, such as calling for research on the topic at hand. Sometimes the committee decides to introduce a new "clean bill" with a new number, if many changes or amendments to the bill have been made. In this entire process, committee chairs exercise considerable power. Chairs generally control the committee's staff and may instruct staffers to give priority to a bill or to ignore it. The chair has the power of recognition and, during markup, may recognize members who share the chair's views. The chair influences the selection of witnesses and can instruct the staff to stack the witness list with individuals who will support a particular point of view.

In some instances, with little or no apparent consideration, a committee may "table" or stop action on a bill because it decides it is not necessary or desirable to act upon it. If the bill is not tabled it will usually be sent to a subcommittee that deals with the bill's particular subject matter. Once a bill is placed on the subcommittee's calendar it is reviewed and studied by subcommittee members and staffers. If subcommittee leaders favor the proposal, they will schedule hearings. At these hearings, witnesses will be called to speak for and against the bill and testimony will be heard from interested parties. Representatives of interest groups favoring or opposing the bill, private citizens, academics, and agency experts with experience in the matter at hand are the types of individuals who are called to testify at congressional hearings.

A subcommittee can also table a bill it decides it does not want to advance. If the subcommittee wishes to move the bill forward, hearings are followed by markup in which both majority and minority members participate, and members then vote to accept or reject the changes. If a marked-up version of the bill is approved, it is sent back to the full committee for approval or rejection. At this point, the full committee may table the bill or hold additional hearings and undertake its own markup. If the full committee passes the bill, it is "reported out," which means it is released along with a report explaining the provisions of the bill. Committee reports become part of the legislative history of the bill. If the bill becomes a law the committee report can be important if there are any legal challenges to it and the courts need to determine "legislative intent." The bill now is put on the chamber's calendar.

Floor Debate and Vote The bill will then be brought to the floor for a vote by the chamber as a whole, but this can happen in a variety of ways. The usual way for important bills in the House is through a parliamentary device known as the "committee of the whole," in which the House is considered a single large committee. The rules of the committee of the whole speed up floor action and debate and require a smaller quorum (100 members) than is normally required for floor action in the House. The rules of the House require that all revenue and appropriations bills be considered, first, by the committee of the whole and then by the House itself. This requirement is intended to ensure appropriate deliberation. Other bills are not required to follow this process, but most do.

As previously noted, the members debate bills according to rules set by the Rules Committee, so under an open, modified open, structured, or closed rule or some other form of special rules. The Rules Committee also determines the order in which bills will be brought to the floor. If the committee favors a bill, it may give it precedence over the House's regular order of business. If the Rules Committee (and its chair) opposes a bill, it will find reason to delay floor action. After the bill has been granted a rule, it will be assigned a date on the House calendar. For minor pieces of legislation, the House leadership may move to suspend the rules and quickly pass the bill. Suspension requires approval of two-thirds of those present and so is not likely to be allowed in the cases of important bills.

After the floor debate, a second reading of the bill section by section occurs and, if the bill is being considered under an **open rule**, amendments can be offered by members at this time. If a **closed rule** is in effect, only amendments recommended by the reporting committee can be considered. In the House, proposed amendments must be "germane" to the subject matter of the bill. In the Senate, amendments may be proposed that seem unrelated to the matter at hand. Such unrelated amendments are known as "riders." Senators will seek to attach riders to bills likely to pass, such as military appropriations bills.

open rule a provision by the House Rules Committee that permits floor debate and the addition of new amendments to a bill

closed rule a provision by the House Rules Committee limiting or prohibiting the introduction of amendments during debate

In the Senate, the majority leader directs the floor activity for a bill in coordination with the committee chairs and minority party leaders. The majority and minority parties have some incentive to work together to bring legislation to the floor because this is typically done by a procedure called "unanimous consent," a process used to expedite proceedings. Unanimous consent means all senators present agree that the bill may be discussed. If even one senator objects, the request is rejected and a time-consuming vote must be taken on a "motion to proceed." A request for unanimous consent to vote on a bill is generally not made until the senators supporting the proposed legislation have negotiated with their colleagues and can inform the majority leader and minority leader that the Senate is ready to proceed.

In the Senate, as required by the Constitution, a quorum is needed for the body to act. A quorum is defined as a majority, currently 51 senators. A quorum is presumed to be in place unless a senator requests a quorum call by "suggesting the absence of a quorum," which triggers the Senate clerk to call the roll of the senators and note which are present. In most cases, senators request quorum calls to delay action without having to call for the adjournment of a session. Typically, a senator may be seeking a delay to gain more time for a compromise to be worked out with colleagues off the floor or to give colleagues time to return to the chamber to make speeches.

During the debate on a bill the first senator to stand up to speak must be recognized by the presiding officer (although the majority leader and minority leader are given priority even if another senator rises first). According to the Standing Rules of the United States Senate, speeches may be of any length, although only two may be given by the same senator on the same legislative day. Sometimes time limits for speeches are adopted through unanimous consent agreements; in the case of the budget they are imposed by statute.

filibuster a tactic used by members of the Senate to prevent action on legislation they oppose by continuously holding the floor and speaking until the majority backs down; once given the floor, senators have unlimited time to speak, and it requires a vote of three-fifths of the Senate to end a filibuster

cloture a rule or process in a legislative body aimed at ending debate on a given bill; in the U.S. Senate, 60 senators (three-fifths) must agree in order to impose a time limit and end debate

Other times the **filibuster** is used to prolong debate on a bill or motion or defeat it. A filibuster is a parliamentary procedure that allows debate over legislation to be extended and is an obstructionist tactic in which one or more senators speak to "talk out a bill" or "talk it to death." The filibuster may involve offering amendments or additional motions along with long speeches. The late Senator Strom Thurmond (D-S.C.; later R-S.C.) holds the record for the longest filibuster. Thurmond held the floor for more than 24 hours when he tried unsuccessfully to block passage of the Civil Rights Act of 1957. **Cloture** is the procedure that can be used to end a filibuster. It is rarely used because it requires bipartisan support to achieve a three-fifths supermajority of 60 senators to stop the filibuster. In 2021 many Democrats called for the elimination of the filibuster to facilitate the enactment of major bills in President Biden's agenda.

A third reading of the bill takes place after debate on the amendments has ended. The floor debate is recorded for the Congressional Record and also sent to Congress.gov, which is updated based on the latest actions on the bill. The bill is then put to a vote and members in attendance vote electronically to pass or not to pass the bill in the House and cast votes nonelectronically in the Senate. In the House, voting is generally held open for only 15 minutes to discourage last-minute deal making. In the Senate, the presiding officer has the discretion to decide when to close the voting, but the voting must be open for at least 15 minutes.

In the House, for many votes a tally is taken, but the identities of voters are not recorded—the equivalent of a secret ballot. In the Senate, this is called a voice vote, in which senators shout "aye!" (for a "yes" vote) or "no!" when against a measure. **Roll-call votes**, in which members' individual votes are recorded, can occur in either chamber. The Constitution requires that a roll-call vote be held if it is demanded by one-fifth of a quorum. Since a quorum is defined by the Senate as 51 senators, one-fifth of a quorum equals 11 senators. In the House, a minimum of 144 members is necessary to require a roll-call vote. Members will call for a roll-call vote whenever they want to create a public record of how each member voted on the measure. Constituents or any members of the public can find out a member's voting record for all roll-call votes. Members cast a vote of "yea" for approval, "nay" for disapproval, or "present" to record that they are present for the vote but choose not to vote on the bill. If the majority of the members in the chamber passes the bill, then it is recorded as passed legislation and is referred to the other chamber to go through a similar process of approval.

roll-call vote a vote in which each legislator's yes or no vote is recorded as the clerk calls the names of the members alphabetically

veto the president's constitutional power to turn down acts of Congress; a presidential veto may be overridden by a two-thirds vote of each house of Congress

pocket veto a presidential veto that is automatically triggered if the president does not act on a given piece of legislation passed during the final 10 days of a legislative session

Bill Referral to the Other Chamber and the Conference Committee When it receives a bill that's passed, the chamber receiving the bill may send it to committee for study or markup or it may ignore the bill passed by its colleagues and, instead, work on its own bill dealing with the same issue. When the matter is one that party leaders deem to be of national importance, the House and Senate typically work on legislation simultaneously. If a bill or similar bill is passed by the other chamber, a conference committee is convened to consider and reconcile differences between the bills. According to the Constitution, before a bill can be sent to the president it must be passed in identical language by both houses of Congress. The conference committee is composed of members of both the House and the Senate. Once differences are worked through and the bill is agreed upon by the conference committee, it is sent to the president for signature.

Presidential Action: Law, No Law, and Veto Override The president may sign the bill and it becomes law. Or, the president can decide to **veto** or reject the bill. The president may also employ what is called a **pocket veto**. A pocket veto occurs when the president does nothing and Congress adjourns while the bill remains in the president's "pocket." If this happens, the bill dies and does not become a law. If, however, the president does nothing and Congress remains in session, the bill automatically becomes law after 10 days. If the president vetoes the bill, they will issue a veto statement noting the reasons for objecting to the bill. When a bill is vetoed it returns to the chamber from which it originated. The presidential veto can be debated on the floor of each chamber and a vote taken to override it if there are the votes for that; otherwise the bill does not become a law. A two-thirds vote is needed in both chambers to override the president's veto. On the rare occasions when the president's veto is overridden, the bill becomes a law without the approval of the chief executive.

Unorthodox Lawmaking

The foregoing discussion summarizes regular order in Congress. Regular order guarantees that a bill's journey to becoming a law will be long and arduous. Indeed, for a bill's proponents, the process can be maddeningly slow. Though slow and cumbersome, regular order ensures a deliberative process in which many voices are heard and both the majority and minority parties play a role. For better or worse, however, today regular order is often abandoned in favor of procedures designed to move bills along more quickly, or with fewer layers of review, trading deliberation for speed.

Today, instead of regular order, bills tend to follow a set of paths that are often called "**unorthodox lawmaking**."[24] Regular order enhanced the power of committees and subcommittees. Unorthodox lawmaking reflects the strengthening of partisanship and the power of party leaders, in particular the Speaker and the majority leader, but also leaves room for individual action by the members of Congress. One thing unorthodox lawmaking does not emphasize is deliberation. Instead, it allows party leaders to push the president's agenda if the president is of their own party or to do battle with the president if the president is of the opposite party. We can call this "follow-the-leader" lawmaking. These leaders use various tactics to achieve their legislative goals and move legislation more quickly than regular order would allow.

Closed Rules The first element of follow-the-leader lawmaking is the frequent use of closed rules to prevent rank-and-file members—and the minority party—from amending legislation approved by the leadership. Closed rules, which some critics call "gag rules," prohibit most floor amendments and often limit debate to a short period of time. Debate on a complex measure may be limited to one hour—hardly enough time to begin to read, much less debate, a bill that may be more than 1,000 pages long.

For many years, tax bills have been considered under closed rules because most members have agreed that tax provisions are too complex and the provisions too intertwined to be amended from the floor.[25] What once was limited mainly to tax bills has now become the "new normal."[26] Whether Congress is controlled by the Democrats or the Republicans, party leaders use closed rules and strict time limits on debate to enhance their own power, compel the rank and file to follow the leader, and restrict the influence of the other party on legislation.

unorthodox lawmaking a set of legislative procedures that deviates from regular order; reflects a greater level of control from party leaders and less deliberation from members

multiple referral the practice of referring a bill to more than one committee for consideration

Multiple Referral A second element of follow-the-leader lawmaking is **multiple referral**. In the House multiple referral was introduced by a rule change in 1975 and has since become commonplace. Used more often in the House than the Senate, multiple referral means that bills are sent to several committees rather than just one for consideration and markup. Multiple referral often works to expand the power of party leaders and reduce the power of committees by preventing any one committee from blocking a piece of legislation. Leaders can even assign a bill to committees sequentially, so if they don't like what one committee does with a bill, they take their chances with another.

Ping-ponging A third element of follow-the-leader lawmaking is the declining use of the conference committee. Conference committees can expand the number of voices heard in discussions of a piece of legislation. However, the effort to create a conference committee, particularly in the case of a controversial bill, gives the Senate minority, in particular, many opportunities to block enactment of the bill. Under Senate rules, the minority party has opportunities to filibuster several steps in the process, to propose amendments, and to move to instruct its conferees to insist upon provisions known to be unacceptable to the House. The House minority also has procedural weapons with which it might derail a conference. To deal with these problems, House and Senate leaders have developed procedures for **ping-ponging** amendments back and forth between the relevant House and Senate committees to reconcile differences between bills or major measures without convening a conference committee at all. The ping-pong approach to legislating strengthens the House and Senate leadership and further marginalizes the role of the minority parties.[27]

Catching the Omnibus: Unorthodox Budget Process A key element of follow-the-leader lawmaking is the use of the omnibus budget bill. The U.S. Congress is one of the few legislatures in the world to have the primary role in its government's budgetary process. This "power of the purse" derives directly from Article I, Section 8, of the Constitution, which asserts that Congress "shall have the Power to lay and collect Taxes, Duties, Imposts, and Excises [and] To borrow Money on the credit of the United States." According to Article I, Section 9, moreover, "no Money shall be drawn from the Treasury, but in Consequence of Appropriations made by Law." The Constitution also specifies that revenue measures must originate in the House. By tradition, **appropriations** bills also originate in the House

While giving Congress the power of the purse, the Constitution does not prescribe the procedures to be used for actually drafting the government's budget. Over the years Congress has enacted legislation specifying budgetary procedures and has developed a "regular order" for appropriations bills. Every federal program requires both an authorization and an appropriation. Authorization bills, which might cover multiple years, must be passed by Congress to grant the actual legal authority for government agencies to spend budget money. Appropriations bills are the funding mechanisms that specify how much money will be given to different government agencies and programs.

ping-ponging sending amendments sent back and forth between the relevant House and Senate committees to reconcile differences between bills or major measures without convening a conference committee at all

appropriations the amounts of money approved by Congress in statutes (bills) that each unit or agency of government can spend

If a program is authorized but no money is appropriated, the program cannot be implemented. In principle, authorizing bills set policies and appropriations bills pay for them. In practice, the line is sometimes not so clear. Appropriations committees sometimes attach limitation riders to the appropriations bill, prohibiting funds from being spent for particular purposes. Republicans, for example, have sought to use limitation riders to prevent federal dollars from being spent on abortions.

As is true for much of the rest of contemporary congressional policy making, the "regular order" of the budget process, as set out by the 1974 Congressional Budget and Impoundment Act, is not typically followed in Congress today. Partisan division and struggles between Congress and the White House have made it difficult to secure the enactment of the 12 separate appropriations bills reported by the 12 House and Senate Appropriations committees. In 2016, for example, congressional Republicans and Democrats agreed in January to cooperate in passing the 12 regular spending bills. By mid-year, though, failed appropriations bills had "piled up in the Senate like a multicar crash on the highway."[28] Similar problems in 2019 led to a brief government shutdown. Republicans were especially outraged that Senate Democrats filibustered the defense appropriations bill. Republicans said Democrats were willing to compromise national security for partisan reasons. Democrats said it was the GOP that demonstrated indifference to the nation's real security needs. Indeed, since 1999, the "regular" budget process has failed to produce a budget as often as it has succeeded.

Departing from regular order, Congress has come to rely on the **omnibus appropriations bill** crafted by party leaders, usually in consultation with the chairs and ranking members of the House and Senate Appropriations committees and the White House. The omnibus bill combines all or many of the smaller appropriations bills into a single package that can be passed with one vote in each house of Congress. For the most part, the legislative minority is excluded from the process, though in some instances the support of minority party members can be garnered by giving them influence over the omnibus process.

omnibus appropriations bill a bill that deals with a number of unrelated topics

In sum, the omnibus bill is the budgetary component of unorthodox lawmaking. Omnibus bills discourage deliberation because of their sheer size. Members may have only a couple of days to digest a bill that can be 2,000 pages long and include many complex funding provisions. Rather than read, members seek to make sure that their own favored programs are included in the omnibus spending bill. Like harried commuters throughout the nation's capital, members must run to "catch the omnibus." The idea of deliberation is lost in the rush.

Taken together, closed rules, multiple referrals, ping-ponging, and omnibus bills strengthen party leader power in Congress, reduce the power of the committees and subcommittees, and compel members to follow the leader. Though there have been pleas from current and former members of Congress to return to regular order, it appears unlikely that party leaders will be willing to give up control over the legislative process.

Check your understanding

5. How does regular order lawmaking differ from unorthodox lawmaking?

   a) Unorthodox lawmaking is more deliberative compared to lawmaking under regular order.
   b) Committees and subcommittees are more powerful under regular order than unorthodox lawmaking.
   c) Party leaders play a much greater role in policy making under regular order compared to that of unorthodox lawmaking.
   d) Passing policies is much more difficult under unorthodox lawmaking compared to regular order because of the increased number of steps in the policy-making process.

6. What strategies do party leaders use to strengthen their power under follow-the-leader lawmaking?

   a) Party leaders use open rules, which allow more members to amend legislation, to curry favor among rank-and-file party members.
   b) Party leaders have relied less on multiple referral, which refers to sending bills to multiple committees for consideration, instead relying on a single committee to mark up legislation.
   c) Party leaders rely less on large omnibus appropriations bills, since that would provide influence to many more members.
   d) House and Senate leaders rely much less on conference committees to reconcile chamber differences on bills, instead ping-ponging amendments between the chambers to work out differences.

Who Influences Congressional Decision-Making?

Identify the factors that influence which bills Congress passes

The process of creating a legislative agenda, drawing up a list of possible measures, and deciding among them is a very complex one, in which a variety of influences from inside and outside government play important roles. External influences include a legislator's constituency and various interest groups. Influences from inside government include party leadership, congressional colleagues, and the president.

Representatives spend a lot of time meeting with constituents in their districts to explain how they have helped their district and learn what issues their constituents care about. Such meetings are often informal events where constituents can ask questions. Here, Representative Alexandria Ocasio-Cortez (D-N.Y.) speaks with constituents in Queens, New York.

Constituency

Because members of Congress, for the most part, want to be re-elected, we would expect the views of their constituents to be a primary influence on the decisions that they make. In fact, most constituents pay little attention to politics and often do not even know what policies their representatives support. Nonetheless, members of Congress spend a lot of time worrying about what their constituents think because they realize that the choices they make may be used as ammunition by an opposing candidate in a future election.[29]

For example, in 2022, despite intense lobbying by President Biden, only one Republican senator supported the so-called John Lewis Voting Rights Act to reimpose federal oversight of election procedures in states that had historically engaged in discriminatory voting practices. The bill was quite unpopular among rank-and-file Republicans.

Interest Groups

Interest groups are another important influence on congressional policies. Members of Congress pay close attention to interest groups for a number of reasons: they can mobilize constituents, serve as watchdogs on congressional action, and supply candidates with information and money.

Many interest groups also use legislative "scorecards" that rate how members of Congress vote on issues of importance to that group, often posting them on their websites for members and the public to see. A high or low rating by an important interest group may provide a potent weapon in the next election.

Interest groups also have substantial influence in setting the legislative agenda and, working with members and staffers of congressional committees, in helping to craft specific language in legislation. Today, lobbyists representing such groups provide information about policies, as well as campaign contributions, to busy members of Congress. The $1.1 trillion end-of-year spending bill passed at the end of 2014 included an amendment exempting many financial transactions from federal regulation under the Dodd-Frank Act, which governs many of the activities of the financial industry. The amendment language was taken from a bill originally written by Citigroup lobbyists, with 70 of 85 lines of the bill directly copying Citigroup's language.[30] After further lobbying by the banking industry, legislation enacted in 2018 loosened a number of other Dodd-Frank rules.

Close financial ties between members of Congress and interest group lobbyists often raise concerns that interest groups get favored treatment in exchange for political donations. Interest groups are influential in Congress, but the character of their influence is often misunderstood. Interest groups seldom "buy" votes in the sense of pressuring members of Congress to radically change their positions on issues. Their main effect is to encourage members already inclined to agree with them to work harder on behalf of the group's goals.

Party

In both the House and the Senate, party leaders have a good deal of influence over the behavior of their party members. This influence, sometimes called "party discipline," is today at an all-time high.

A vote in which half or more of the members of one party take one position while at least half of the members of the other party take the opposing position is called a **party unity vote**. At the beginning of the twentieth century, nearly half of all roll-call votes in the House of Representatives were party unity votes. For much of the twentieth century, the number of party unity votes declined as bipartisan legislation became more common. The 1990s, however, witnessed a return to strong party discipline as partisan polarization increased between Democrats and Republicans, and congressional party leaders aggressively used their powers to keep their members in line. That high level of party discipline continues today.

Party unity has been on the rise in recent years because the divisions between the parties have deepened on many high-profile issues such as abortion, health care, and financial reform (see Figure 10.4). Party unity also rises when congressional leaders try to put a partisan stamp on legislation. Typically, party unity is greater in the House than in the Senate. House rules grant

party unity vote a roll-call vote in the House or Senate in which at least 50 percent of the members of one party take a particular position and are opposed by at least 50 percent of the members of the other party

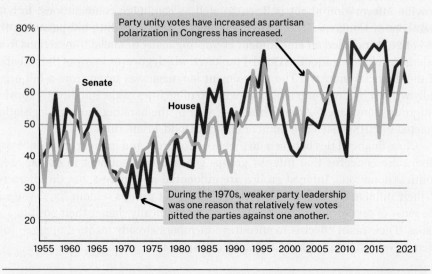

FIGURE 10.4 | Party Unity Votes in Congress

Party unity votes are roll-call votes in which a majority of one party lines up against a majority of the other party. Party unity votes increase when the parties are polarized and when the party leadership can enforce discipline. Why did the percentage of party unity votes decline in the 1970s? Why has it risen in recent years?

Party unity votes have increased as partisan polarization in Congress has increased.

During the 1970s, weaker party leadership was one reason that relatively few votes pitted the parties against one another.

SOURCE: Niels Lesniewski and Ryan Kelly, "Party Unity Vote Studies Underscore Polarized State of the Union," Roll Call, March 1, 2022, https://rollcall.com/2022/03/01/party-unity-vote-studies-underscore-polarized-state-of-the-union/ (accessed 11/13/22).

greater procedural control of business to the majority party leaders, which gives them more influence over House members.

To some extent, party unity is based on ideology and background. In the House, Republican members of the House are more likely to have been elected by rural or suburban districts and Democrats by urban ones; in both houses, Democrats are more liberal on economic and social questions than their Republican colleagues. The extent of partisan division in the contemporary Congress was underscored when almost all Democrats and almost no Republicans condemned former president Trump's efforts to reverse the results of the 2020 election, including Trump's refusal to condemn the actions of the mob that stormed the Capitol on January 6, 2021. Of course, partisan polarization in Congress reflects a divided America. Congress is, after all, a representative institution.

When Congress Has Trouble Deciding

Though the 116th Congress (2019–20) passed several important pieces of legislation, simply in terms of the number of bills passed it was the least productive in modern history, enacting only 163 pieces of legislation. As of September 15, 2022, the 117th Congress (2021–22) had passed only 85 bills. This number, however, is somewhat deceptive, since many matters were combined in the 2021 budget reconciliation bill.[31]

polarization the deep ideological distance between the two parties

Many critics charge that Congress is too slow and cumbersome to deal with crises. Yet, when faced with emergencies, Congress can act quickly. Witness Congress's ability to enact major funding programs in March 2020 in response to the coronavirus pandemic and resulting financial collapse. Some pundits became impatient as Congress debated, but argument, debate, and partisanship are part of democracy. Self-government is never smooth, but it can be effective.

Congressional Polarization Congress's sometime inability to decide reflects **polarization**, the deep ideological distance between the two parties. Republicans and Democrats have been diverging sharply since the mid-1970s and are now more polarized than at any time in the last century. Democrats have become more liberal and Republicans have become more conservative.[32]

Moreover, because congressional districts are increasingly unified in their ideology—due in part to gerrymandering but mainly to natural clustering of the population—most members of Congress are in safe seats. Their constituents will not punish them for failing to compromise. In addition, organizations on the right, such as the National Rifle Association (NRA), often punish Republican members of Congress who do support compromises by recruiting and financing alternative candidates to challenge members who vote against the organization's positions.[33]

Check your understanding

7. Which of the following statements regarding congressional decision-making is true?

   a) Because constituents lack political knowledge, members of Congress rarely take constituents' opinions into account in decision-making.

   b) Interest groups exercise significant influence by providing information to lawmakers and often helping to craft specific language in legislation.

   c) Bipartisanship in lawmaking has increased over the past decade, allowing for swift decision-making.

   d) Members of Congress often change their positions on important bills due to receiving campaign donations from interest groups.

8. What effect has partisan polarization had on bill passage in Congress?

   a) Congress has been unable to pass important legislation to address crises such as the coronavirus pandemic due to partisan polarization.

   b) Although partisan polarization has been on the rise, Congress has been able to pass legislation to address important crises like the coronavirus pandemic.

   c) Although party polarization is on the rise, party unity votes are on the decline since constituents punish legislators for not compromising.

   d) Interest groups have counteracted the role of partisan polarization on congressional decision-making.

Congress Does More Than Make Laws

Describe the powers that Congress uses to influence other branches of government

In addition to the power to make the law, Congress has a number of other ways to influence the process of government. The Constitution gives the Senate the power to approve treaties and appointments. And Congress has a number of other powers through which it can help administer laws.

Oversight

Oversight, as applied to Congress, usually refers to the effort to oversee or supervise how the executive branch carries out legislation. Sometimes committees can look into the actions of private firms, as exemplified by recent hearings into Facebook's privacy policies and business practices. Oversight is carried out by committees or subcommittees of the Senate or the House, which conduct hearings and investigations to analyze and evaluate bureaucratic agencies and the effectiveness of their programs. Their purpose may be to locate inefficiencies or abuses of power, to explore the relationship between what an agency does and what a law intends, or to change or abolish a program. Most programs and agencies are subject to some oversight every year during the course of hearings on appropriations, the funding of agencies and government programs.

oversight the effort by Congress, through hearings, investigations, and other techniques, to exercise control over the activities of executive agencies

Committees or subcommittees have the power to subpoena witnesses, administer oaths, cross-examine, compel testimony, and bring criminal charges for contempt (refusing to cooperate) and perjury (lying under oath). Hearings and investigations are similar in many ways, but a hearing is usually held on a specific bill, and the questions asked are usually intended to build a record with regard to that bill.

In recent years, congressional oversight power has increasingly been used as a tool of partisan politics. Almost as soon as Donald Trump took office in 2017, Democrats called for investigations into allegations that his campaign had colluded with Russian operatives to help Trump win the 2016 election. House and Senate committees, chaired by Republicans, failed to find evidence of presidential wrongdoing. Democrats, however, demanded the appointment of a special counsel after President Trump's firing of FBI director James Comey. Over the course of the investigation, the special counsel, Robert Mueller, indicted several close Trump aides for improper contacts with Russian officials.

Another high-profile congressional investigation came in 2021, when the House of Representatives established the Select Committee to Investigate the

January 6th Attack on the United States Capitol. The committee, consisting of seven Democrats and two anti-Trump Republicans, held hearings seeking to link former president Trump and his close advisers to the January 6, 2021, assault on the U.S. Capitol by a mob of Trump supporters claiming the presidential election had been stolen by the Democrats. Several former Trump aides were indicted or cited for criminal contempt for refusing to cooperate with the committee.

Advice and Consent: Special Senate Powers

The Constitution says the president has the power to make treaties and to appoint top executive officers, ambassadors, and federal judges—but only "with the Advice and Consent of the Senate" (Article II, Section 2). For treaties, two-thirds of senators present must consent; for appointments, a simple majority is required.

The power to approve or reject presidential requests includes the power to set conditions. In fact, the Senate only occasionally exercises its power to reject treaties and appointments, and, despite recent debate surrounding judicial nominees, during the past century only a small number of them have been rejected by the Senate or withdrawn by the president to avoid rejection, whereas hundreds have been approved.

Impeachment

The Constitution also grants Congress the power of **impeachment**, which means formally charging a federal official with "Treason, Bribery, or other high Crimes and Misdemeanors"; officials found guilty are removed from office. Impeachment is thus like a criminal indictment in which the House of Representatives acts like a grand jury, voting (by simple majority) on whether the accused ought to be impeached. If the House votes to impeach, the Senate then acts like a trial jury, voting on whether to convict and remove the official (which requires a two-thirds majority of the Senate).

impeachment the formal charge by the House of Representatives that a government official has committed "Treason, Bribery, or other high Crimes and Misdemeanors"

The impeachment power is the power of Congress to remove the president and is a safeguard against the executive tyranny so greatly feared by the framers of the Constitution. The House has initiated impeachment proceedings more than 60 times in U.S. history. Fewer than 20 officials were ultimately impeached, however, and only 8—all federal judges—were convicted by the Senate and removed from office.[34]

Controversy over Congress's impeachment power has arisen over the grounds for impeachment, especially the meaning of "high Crimes and Misdemeanors." An impeachable offense could be a crime but is not necessarily one, as the phrase also covers a noncriminal offense that is an abuse of the powers of office. Yet the vagueness of the term also means that impeachment is political, too, sometimes defined as "whatever the majority of the House of Representatives considers it to be at a given moment in history."[35]

The House possesses the power to impeach federal officials. In American history, three presidents have been impeached. In 2019–20 the House impeached Donald Trump for abuse of power and obstruction of Congress after aid to Ukraine was allegedly withheld, though he was acquitted in February 2020. Trump was impeached and acquitted again in 2021, this time on the charge of inciting an insurrection.

In 2019, House Democrats voted to impeach President Trump on charges that he had sought to pressure the Ukrainian government to investigate Joe Biden and Biden's son, Hunter, for their business activities in Ukraine. Democrats asserted that Trump had threatened the Ukrainians with a cutoff of military aid if they did not help him undermine a major political foe. Despite a leaked phone call that seemed to support the allegation, Trump denied the charge and averred that the Democrats and liberal media were conspiring against him. After a short Senate trial, Trump was acquitted, with all but one GOP senator (Mitt Romney) choosing to support the president. Most Republican voters agreed that the charges against the president did not merit his removal from office. In January 2021, Trump became the only president in American history to be impeached a second time. The president was charged with inciting an insurrection for his alleged role in the January 6, 2021, attack on the Capital by a mob of Trump supporters. In a Senate vote in February the former president's opponents failed to obtain the two-thirds majority needed for conviction. By the time of the vote, Trump's term had expired and he had already left office, but a conviction might have resulted in Trump being disqualified from future office. With his acquittal, Trump is free to run for president again.

Check your understanding

9. How does Congress exercise influence over other branches of government?

   a) Congress can fail to enforce a president's executive orders.

   b) Congress can fail to enforce the Supreme Court's rulings.

   c) Congress can intervene in challenges to federal laws, intercepting them before the Supreme Court grants the cases certiorari.

   d) Congress can exercise oversight over the executive branch with hearings investigating effectiveness of programs, inefficiencies, and abuses of power.

10. What power does Congress have to check the president?

    a) Congress can impeach the president for "high Crimes and Misdemeanors."

    b) Congress can deem executive orders issued by the president as unconstitutional.

    c) Congress can unilaterally appoint the president's Cabinet.

    d) While the president is commander in chief, the Constitution grants Congress all other authority in matters concerning the military.

WHAT DO YOU THINK?

CONGRESS

Much of this chapter has described the major institutional components of Congress and has shown how they work as Congress makes policy. But what do these institutional features mean for how Congress represents the American public?

- Does the organization of Congress promote the equal representation of all Americans? Or are there institutional features of Congress that allow some interests more access and influence than others? What might Facebook whistleblower Frances Haugen say?

- What areas of public policy might suffer if Congress continues its inability to decide?

- What types of institutional changes would make Congress work better? Some suggest the appointment of citizen commissions to draw district lines in order to elect more moderate candidates and make compromise in Congress easier. Others argue for eliminating the filibuster in the Senate to reduce gridlock. What do you think the effects would be?

- Will continued partisan gridlock hurt Congress as an institution?

Use 🐰 **INQUIZITIVE** *to help you study and master this material.*

11

WHAT GOVERNMENT DOES & WHY IT MATTERS

In the American constitutional system, the president typically works with other branches of government to create law. But when they are frustrated by congressional inaction or when the law allows, presidents sometimes act unilaterally. In 1906, Congress passed the Antiquities Act, which allows presidents to enlarge or designate new national monuments without having to consult Congress. All but four presidents have done so, starting with Theodore Roosevelt, who used the law to set aside the Grand Canyon as a national monument (later it became a national park). Barack Obama used the act to establish the Bears Ears National Monument in Utah. The monument was the culmination of years of work by a coalition of five sovereign nations in the area—the Navajo, Hopi, Ute, Zuni, and Ute Mountain Ute—who mapped the area and compiled oral histories on the use and location of medicinal herbs, religious shrines, traditional hunting grounds, and other important cultural and historical sites. The monument Obama set aside included over 100,000 Native American sites such as petroglyphs and burial grounds.

The Presidency

President Donald Trump issued a proclamation in late 2017 reducing the size of Bears Ears by 85 percent, becoming the first president to use the Antiquities Act to reduce the size of a national monument. The reduction was advocated by fossil fuel companies, Republican lawmakers, and state officials, who had long argued for greater state control of federal land. For Native Americans Trump's move was an enormous blow. Russell Begaye, president of the Navajo Nation, said, "We will stand and fight all the way," and that the United States government has already taken "millions of acres of my people's land."[1]

Executive orders and proclamations allow presidents to change policy on their own, but these changes can be easily altered by subsequent presidents. Sure enough, on his first day in office, President Joe Biden ordered a review of the boundaries of Bears Ears and other national monuments. In her report, Interior secretary Debra Haaland, the first Native American cabinet secretary in U.S. history, recommended restoration of the borders, which Biden carried out in an October 2021 executive order. Lauding the policy change, Shaun Chapoose, chairman of the Ute Indian Tribe, said, "It was important that we protect our cultural identity."[2] Utah governor Spencer Cox vowed to fight Biden's unilateral action in federal court, arguing that Congress should handle the land's status.

In this chapter, we examine the foundations of the American presidency and assess presidential power. Presidents are empowered by

▲ The fate of Bears Ears National Monument has been caught between differing presidential actions, but Shaun Chapoose, chairperson of the Ute Tribe, believes the land is an important part of the identity and cultural heritage of Native nations.

democratic political processes and, increasingly, by their ability to control and expand the institutional resources of the office. They sit atop the executive branch, a large bureaucracy of departments and agencies. They influence policy with their appointments to the Cabinet, the White House staff, and the Executive Office of the President, choosing officials who are sympathetic to their policy goals. They use regulatory review and executive orders and proclamations to make policy, as the Obama, Trump, and Biden orders on the Bears Ears monument show. They set the tone for government as the sole elected official representing the entire country. But, as we will see, presidential power is not without limit. America's Constitution emphasizes checks and balances among the branches of government, not unlimited power. The framers thought a powerful and energetic president would make America's government more effective but knew that presidential power needed to be subject to constraints to prevent it from becoming a threat to citizens' liberties.

CHAPTER GOALS

Identify the expressed, implied, delegated, and inherent powers of the presidency (pp. 345–56)

Describe the institutional resources presidents have to help them exercise their powers (pp. 357–62)

Explain how modern presidents have become even more powerful (pp. 363–70)

Presidential Power Is Rooted in the Constitution

Identify the expressed, implied, delegated, and inherent powers of the presidency

The presidency was established by Article II of the Constitution, which begins: "The executive power shall be vested in a President of the United States of America." This language is known as the Constitution's "vesting clause." The president's executive power is underscored in Section 3 of Article II, which confers upon the president the duty to "take care that the laws be faithfully executed." The president's oath of office in Section 1, moreover, obligates—and thus empowers—the chief executive to "preserve, protect and defend the Constitution of the United States."

This language seems to require the president to take action, without specifying any limits to that action, if constitutional government is threatened. In 1861, during the Civil War, President Abraham Lincoln cited his oath of office as justification for suspending the writ of habeas corpus, which protects against arbitrary government detention of individuals. He declared that his oath would be broken if the government were overthrown and that suspension of habeas corpus was necessary to prevent that calamity from taking place.

Abraham Lincoln, like many other presidents, cited the presidential oath of office as providing the president the authority to take all the necessary actions to protect the nation.

On the basis of Article II, presidents have three types of powers: expressed powers, implied powers, and delegated powers. A fourth type of power claimed by presidents does not appear in Article II. This is called the inherent power of the office.

Expressed Powers

The **expressed powers** of the presidency are those specifically established by the language of the Constitution. These fall into several categories:

1. *Military.* Article II, Section 2, provides for the power as "Commander in Chief of the Army and Navy of the United States, and of the Militia of the several States, when called in to the actual Service of the United States."

2. *Judicial.* Article II, Section 2, also provides the power to "grant Reprieves and Pardons for Offences against the United States, except in Cases of Impeachment."

3. *Diplomatic.* Article II, Section 2, further provides the power "by and with the Advice and Consent of the Senate to make Treaties." Article II, Section 3, provides the power to "receive Ambassadors and other public Ministers."

4. *Executive.* Article II, Section 3, authorizes the president to see to it that all the laws are faithfully executed; Section 2 gives the power to appoint, remove, and supervise all executive officers and to appoint all federal judges.

5. *Legislative.* Article I, Section 7, and Article II, Section 3, give the president the power to participate authoritatively in the legislative process.

Military Power The president's military powers are among the most important. The position of **commander in chief** makes the president the highest military authority in the United States, with control of the entire defense establishment. The president is also head of the nation's intelligence network, which includes the Central Intelligence Agency (CIA), the National Security Council (NSC), the National Security Agency (NSA), the Federal Bureau of Investigation (FBI), and a host of less well-known but very powerful international and domestic security agencies. As we will see later in the chapter, Congress sought to limit presidential military powers with the 1973 War Powers Resolution, but this effort had little impact.

The president's military powers extend into the domestic sphere as well. Article IV, Section 4, provides that the "United States shall [protect] every State . . . against . . . Invasion . . . and . . . domestic Violence." Congress has made this an explicit presidential power through statutes directing the president as commander in chief to discharge these obligations.[3] The Constitution authorizes state governments to request that the president deploy federal troops to maintain public order, but presidents can act without such a request. Under the terms of the 1807 Insurrection Act, the president may deploy troops without a

expressed powers specific powers granted by the Constitution to Congress (Article I, Section 8) and to the president (Article II)

commander in chief the role of the president as commander of the national military and the state National Guard units (when called into service)

One of the president's responsibilities is the maintenance of public order in times of crisis. In 1951, President Eisenhower used this to justify sending the troops to Little Rock to enforce racial integration of public schools (left). During the coronavirus crisis of 2020, President Trump sent the USNS *Mercy*, a navy hospital ship, to Los Angeles to treat patients suffering from Covid-19 as hospitals became overwhelmed (right).

specific request from the state legislature or governor if the president considers them necessary to keep order, maintain an essential national service during an emergency, enforce a federal judicial order, or protect federally guaranteed civil rights.[4]

A historic example of the unilateral use of presidential emergency power is the decision by President Dwight D. Eisenhower in 1957 to send troops into Little Rock, Arkansas, against the wishes of the Arkansas government, to enforce court orders to integrate Little Rock's Central High School. The state's governor, Orval Faubus, had posted the Arkansas National Guard at the school entrance to prevent the court-ordered admission of nine Black students. After an effort to negotiate with Governor Faubus failed, President Eisenhower reluctantly sent 1,000 paratroopers from the U.S. Army's 101st Airborne Division to Little Rock; they stood watch while the Black students took their places in the previously all-White classrooms.

In most instances of domestic disorder, whether from human or natural causes, presidents tend to exercise unilateral power by declaring a "state of emergency." President Trump did so in response to three hurricanes in 2017, thereby making available federal grants, insurance, and direct aid. In 2019, President Trump ordered federal troops to America's southern border after declaring that illegal immigration constituted a national emergency. President Trump also declared states of emergency in all 50 states to free federal funds for use in 2020 during the coronavirus pandemic. In February 2021, President Biden declared a state of emergency in Texas after a severe winter storm closed highways and triggered a statewide power and water crisis.

Judicial Power The president has power to grant reprieves, pardons, and amnesty. Presidents may use this power on behalf of a particular individual, as did Gerald Ford when he pardoned Richard Nixon in 1974 "for all offenses against the United States which he . . . has committed or may have committed." Or they may use it on a large scale, as did President Andrew Johnson in 1868, when he gave full amnesty to all southerners who had participated in the Civil War.

In some instances, presidents use the pardon power to make a political point. For example, before leaving office, President Obama commuted the sentences of several hundred nonviolent drug offenders. The president had long opposed the harsh sentences often meted out to such offenders and used his pardon power to underscore his view that such sentences were not warranted.

Diplomatic Power The president is America's chief representative in dealings with other nations, having the power to make treaties for the United States (with the advice and consent of the Senate) as well as the power to "recognize" the governments of other countries. Diplomatic recognition means that the United States acknowledges a government's legitimacy—that is, its claim to be the legal and rightful government of the country.

In recent years, presidents have expanded the practice of using executive agreements instead of treaties to establish contracts with other countries.[5] An **executive agreement** is exactly like a treaty except that it does not require approval by two-thirds of the Senate. The courts have held that executive agreements have the force of law, as though they were formal treaties.

> **executive agreement** an agreement, made between the president and another country, that has the force of a treaty but does not require the Senate's "advice and consent"

Executive Power The Constitution focuses executive power and legal responsibility on the president. The most important constitutional

As the head of state, the president is America's chief representative in dealings with other countries. Here, President Biden meets with French president Emmanuel Macron.

basis of the president's power as chief executive is found in Article II, Section 3, which stipulates that the president must see that all the laws are faithfully executed, and Section 2, which provides that the president will appoint and supervise all executive officers and appoint all federal judges (with Senate approval). The power to appoint the principal executive officers and to require each of them to report to the president on subjects relating to the duties of their departments makes the president the true chief executive officer (CEO) of the nation.

Another component of the president's power as chief executive is **executive privilege**, the claim that confidential communications between a president and close advisers should not be revealed without presidential consent. Presidents have made this claim ever since George Washington refused a request from the House of Representatives to deliver documents concerning negotiations of an important treaty. Washington refused (successfully) on the grounds that, first, the House was not constitutionally part of the treaty-making process and, second, diplomatic negotiations required secrecy.

> **executive privilege** the claim that confidential communications between a president and close advisers should not be revealed without the consent of the president

Although many presidents have claimed executive privilege, the concept was not tested in the courts until the "Watergate" affair of the early 1970s, when President Richard Nixon refused congressional demands that he turn over secret White House tapes that congressional investigators suspected would establish his involvement in illegal activities. In *United States v. Nixon* (1974), the Supreme Court ordered Nixon to turn over the tapes.[6] The president complied with the order and was eventually forced to resign from office as a result.

In *United States v. Nixon* the Court ruling recognized for the first time the legal validity of executive privilege, though noting that it was not absolute and could be set aside in the face of a criminal inquiry. An executive privilege claim would be much stronger if it involved national security. Subsequent presidents have cited the case in support of executive privilege claims. In 2019, President Trump asserted executive privilege to block the release of portions of the Mueller report on Russian meddling in the 2016 election and again to prevent the release of certain documents relating to the Census Bureau's deliberations over the proposed addition of a citizenship question to the 2020 census.

In 2021, after the end of his term in office, Trump asserted a claim of executive privilege to prevent documents from his administration from being turned over to a congressional committee investigating the January 6, 2020, Capitol Hill insurrection (see Chapter 12). Trump asserted that former presidents could assert executive privilege to protect their administrations' sensitive communications. A federal judge disagreed, reminding Trump that Joe Biden was now president and executive privilege was his to invoke or not. In September 2022, the powers and privileges of former presidents once again became an issue when FBI agents raided Trump's Florida residence, Mar-a-Lago. The FBI said it was searching for classified documents Trump removed from the White House when he left office. By law, Trump was required to return any classified documents in his possession at the end of his presidency, and he did return many. For reasons that remained unclear, however,

Trump chose to keep roughly 100 documents marked as classified. Among other claims, Trump said he had given verbal orders to declassify these documents and so could keep them if he wished. The Mar-a-Lago raid is certain to be the subject of litigation regarding executive power and the prerogatives of former presidents.

Legislative Power—Agenda Setting Two constitutional provisions are the primary sources of the president's power in the legislative process. The first of these, in Article II, Section 3, provides that the president "shall from time to time give to the Congress Information of the State of the Union, and recommend to their Consideration such Measures as he shall judge necessary and expedient." Delivering a "State of the Union" address may at first appear to be little more than the president's obligation to make recommendations for Congress's consideration. But in the twentieth century, as political and social conditions began to favor an increasingly prominent presidential role, each president, especially since Franklin Roosevelt, increasingly relied on this provision to become the primary initiator of proposals for legislative action in Congress and the most important single participant in legislative decision-making. The address has also become the principal source for public awareness of national issues.[7]

With some important exceptions, Congress depends on the president to set the agenda of public policy. For example, under the terms of the 1921 Budget and Accounting Act, the president is required to submit a budget to Congress. This gives presidents the power to set the terms of debate about budgetary matters. Presidents also often set the country's policy agenda, beyond the budget. During the weeks immediately following the September 11, 2001, terrorist attacks, President George W. Bush took many presidential initiatives to Congress, and each was given almost unanimous support. President Obama made health care his chief domestic priority and negotiated with divided congressional Democrats to bring about the enactment of the Affordable Care Act (ACA), known as "Obamacare." Congress enacted President Trump's proposals for a sweeping tax reform bill and a budget that substantially increased spending on military programs. President Biden's infrastructure and domestic spending plans set the agenda for much of the work of the 117th Congress.

Legislative Power—the Veto The second of the president's constitutionally authorized legislative powers is the **veto** power to reject acts of Congress (see Figure 11.1), which is provided in Article I, Section 7.[8] This power effectively makes the president the most important single legislative leader,[9] since no vetoed bill can become law unless both the House and Senate override the veto by a two-thirds vote. In the case of a **pocket veto**, as explained in Chapter 10, Congress does not even have the chance to override the veto but must pass the bill again in its next session.

veto the president's constitutional power to turn down acts of Congress; a presidential veto may be overridden by a two-thirds vote of each house of Congress

pocket veto a presidential veto that is automatically triggered if the president does not act on a given piece of legislation passed during the final 10 days of a legislative session

Use of the veto varies according to the political situation each president confronts. During his last two years in office, when Democrats had control of both houses of Congress, Republican president George W. Bush vetoed 10 bills, including legislation

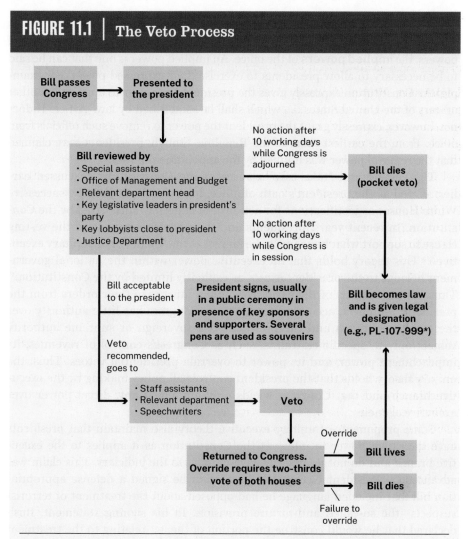

FIGURE 11.1 | The Veto Process

Bill passes Congress → Presented to the president

↓

Bill reviewed by
- Special assistants
- Office of Management and Budget
- Relevant department head
- Key legislative leaders in president's party
- Key lobbyists close to president
- Justice Department

No action after 10 working days while Congress is adjourned → **Bill dies (pocket veto)**

No action after 10 working days while Congress is in session → **Bill becomes law and is given legal designation (e.g., PL-107-999*)**

Bill acceptable to the president → **President signs, usually in a public ceremony in presence of key sponsors and supporters. Several pens are used as souvenirs**

Veto recommended, goes to
- Staff assistants
- Relevant department
- Speechwriters
→ **Veto**

↓

Returned to Congress. Override requires two-thirds vote of both houses

Override → **Bill lives**

Failure to override → **Bill dies**

*PL — public law; 107 — number of Congress (107th was 2001–02); 999 — number of the law.

designed to prohibit the use of harsh interrogation tactics, saying it "would take away one of the most valuable tools in the war on terror."[10] Similarly, 10 of President Obama's 12 vetoes occurred during his last two years in office, when Republicans held the majority in both houses. Among the most significant was his 2015 veto of a bill authorizing construction of the Keystone XL pipeline, which would have carried oil from Canada to U.S. refineries but was opposed by environmentalists.

Since the time of George Washington, presidents have used their veto power more than 2,500 times, and on only 111 occasions has Congress overridden them. During his four years in office, President Trump issued 10 vetoes, including a veto of a House resolution seeking to terminate the state of national emergency that the president had declared along America's southern border. During his first two years in office, President Biden did not use the veto power.

Implied Powers

Each expressed power has become the foundation of a second set of presidential powers, the **implied powers** of the office. An implied power is one that can be said to be necessary to allow presidents to exercise their expressed power. For example, the Constitution expressly gives the president the power to appoint "all other officers of the United States . . . which shall be established by law." Article II does not, however, expressly grant the president the power to remove such officials from office. From the earliest years of the Republic, though, presidents have claimed that the removal power was implied by the appointment power.

The vesting and "take care" clauses of the Constitution, discussed earlier, as well as the president's oath of office, have also been cited by successive White Houses as justifications for actions not expressly authorized by the Constitution. In recent years, presidents and their advisers have used the vesting clause to support what has come to be known as the "theory of the unitary executive."[11] This theory holds that all executive power within the national government belongs to the president except as explicitly limited by the Constitution.[12] Thus, all the officials of the executive branch must take their orders from the president. Moreover, according to this view, Congress has little authority over the executive branch and the president is a sovereign or supreme authority subject only to specific restraints, such as Congress's control of revenues, its impeachment power, and its power to override presidential vetoes. Thus, the unitary theory holds that the president controls all policy making by the executive branch and that Congress wields only limited, if any, direct power over executive agencies.

Some proponents of unitary executive theory also maintain that presidents have their own power to interpret the Constitution as it applies to the executive branch and do not necessarily have to defer to the judiciary. This claim was advanced by President George W. Bush when he signed a defense appropriation bill that included language he had opposed about the treatment of terrorist suspects—the so-called anti-torture provision. In his signing statement, Bush declared that he would construe the portion of the act relating to the treatment of detainees "in a manner consistent with the constitutional authority of the President to supervise the unitary executive branch and as Commander in Chief and consistent with the constitutional limitations on the judicial power."[13] The president was claiming, in other words, that, particularly in the military realm, he possessed the authority to execute acts of Congress according to his own understanding of the law and the nation's interests. He also seemed to be claiming that the authority of the courts to interfere with his actions was limited.

implied powers powers derived from the necessary and proper clause of Article I, Section 8, of the Constitution; such powers are not specifically expressed but are implied through the expansive interpretation of delegated powers

Critics of unitary executive theory, however, argue that the principle of constitutional checks and balances provides Congress with powers over executive agencies through "congressional oversight" of the executive branch. Article I of the Constitution gives Congress a number of powers,

AMERICA | SIDE BY SIDE

Comparative Constitutional Executive Authority

The American president is the face of the federal government. While the role has become much more powerful since the Founding, the role of the president as outlined in the Constitution is quite weak compared to the constitutional powers of peer executives in other countries. While most countries have constitutions that outline the powers of the executive, in practice executives often claim powers beyond what is explicitly granted to them. The figure below shows the countries with the most and least powerful executives. It is based on an index compiled by the Comparative Constitutions Project, which measures whether constitutions give executives explicit powers to do things such as dissolving the legislature, or the power to initiate legislation or constitutional amendments.

1. What are the benefits of having a strong executive in a country? Do you think the office of the president in the American system has too much power? Not enough? Does seeing the data in this graphic change your opinion? If you wanted to study how much power presidents actually have — versus how much power the Constitution gives them as seen in the chart — how might you go about doing so?

2. What might be an argument for giving an executive the ability to dissolve the legislature or declare a state of emergency? How do you put checks on such a strong executive while still granting them some powers?

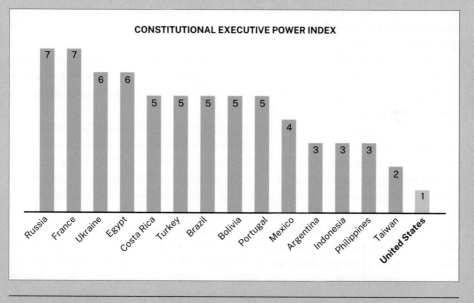

SOURCE: Comparative Constitutions Project, http://comparativeconstitutionsproject.org/ccp-rankings/ (accessed 11/8/21).

including the power to appropriate funds, to raise and support armies and navies, to regulate interstate commerce, and to impeach officials of the executive branch. Article I also gives Congress the authority "to make all laws which shall be necessary and proper for carrying into execution the foregoing powers."

Congressional oversight, which includes hearings, investigations, studies, and reports, is arguably implied by this language. If Congress is to carry out its constitutional responsibilities, it must be able to obtain information about the activities of executive branch agencies and officials. Thus, the stage is set for conflict between the implied powers of Congress and those of the president.

Delegated Powers

Many of the powers exercised by the president and the executive branch are not found in the Constitution but are **delegated powers**, the products of congressional statutes and resolutions. Over the past century, Congress has voluntarily delegated a great deal of its own legislative authority to the executive branch. To some extent, this delegation of power has been an almost inescapable consequence of the expansion of government activity in the United States since the New Deal.

In the nineteenth century, the federal government was small and had relatively few domestic responsibilities, so Congress could pay close attention to details. Given the vast range of the federal government's responsibilities today, however, Congress cannot possibly execute all federal laws and administer all of the thousands of federal programs. Inevitably, it must turn more and more to the hundreds of departments and agencies in the executive branch or, when necessary, create new agencies to implement its goals. Thus, for example, in 2002, to strengthen protection against terrorist attacks, it established the Department of Homeland Security, with broad powers in the realms of law enforcement, public health, and immigration.

As they implement congressional legislation, federal agencies collectively develop thousands of rules and regulations and issue thousands of orders and findings every year. Agencies interpret Congress's intent, publish rules aimed at implementing that intent, and issue orders to individuals, firms, and organizations to compel them to conform to the law. Such administrative rules have the effect of law; the courts treat them like congressional statutes.

Since the New Deal of the 1930s, Congress has tended to draft legislation that defines a broad goal for agencies but offers few clear standards or guidelines for how that goal is to be achieved. The 1972 Consumer Product Safety Act, for example, authorizes the Consumer Product Safety Commission to reduce "unreasonable" risks of injury from household products but offers no suggestions about what constitutes reasonable and unreasonable risks or how the latter are to be reduced.[14] As a result, the executive branch, under the president's direction, has wide discretion to make rules that impact American citizens and businesses.

delegated powers constitutional powers that are assigned to one governmental agency but are exercised by another agency with the express permission of the first

Inherent Powers

Presidents have also claimed a set of powers not specified in the Constitution but said to stem from the rights, duties, and obligations of the presidency. These are referred to as **inherent powers** and are most often asserted by presidents in time of war or national emergency. Presidents Roosevelt (World War II), Truman (Korean War), and both Presidents Bush (Persian Gulf and Middle East wars) claimed inherent powers to defend the nation.

> **inherent powers** powers claimed by a president that are not expressed in the Constitution but are inferred from it

Since the Korean War, presidents have used their claim of inherent powers along with their constitutional power as commander in chief to bypass the constitutional provision giving Congress the power to declare war. Congress declared war after the Japanese attack on Pearl Harbor on December 7, 1941. Since that time, American forces have been sent to fight foreign wars on more than 100 occasions, but not once was Congress asked for a declaration of war. In 1973, Congress passed the War Powers Resolution, designed to restore its role in military policy. Presidents, however, have regarded the resolution as an improper limitation on their inherent powers and have sometimes ignored its provisions.

The difference between inherent and implied powers is often subtle, and the two are frequently jointly claimed in support of presidential action. Implied powers can be traced to the powers expressed in the actual language of the Constitution.[15] Inherent powers, on the other hand, derive from national sovereignty. Under international law and custom, sovereign states possess a number of inherent rights and powers, the most important being the rights to engage in relations with other nations, to defend themselves against attacks from other states, and to curb internal violence and unrest.

No president has acted so frequently on the basis of inherent powers as President George W. Bush. He claimed that they authorized him to create military commissions; designate U.S. citizens as enemy combatants; engage in "extraordinary renditions" of captured suspects, who would be moved to unknown facilities in unnamed countries for interrogation; and order the NSA to monitor phone conversations between the United States and other nations.[16] When challenged, some but not all of these actions were overturned by the courts.

President Obama continued to rely on the concept of inherent power in ordering drone strikes against suspected terrorists and ordering American air strikes in Libya. Testifying before Congress in 2014, Attorney General Eric Holder defended the president's unilateral actions, saying, "Given what the president's responsibility is in running the executive branch, I think there is an inherent power there for him to act in the way that he has."[17]

In 2017, President Trump's order banning travelers from several Muslim countries was based mainly on a claim that the president had the inherent power to bar any class of immigrants he thought to be a threat to the United States. In 2018, the Supreme Court overruled lower-court decisions that had sought to block Trump's travel ban, saying that the president was entitled to deference in judging whether a particular group of immigrants represented a threat to the United States.[18]

In 2020, President Trump asserted that he had the inherent power to determine whether businesses could reopen or must remain closed in the face of the coronavirus threat.

Congress has tried to place some limits on powers that presidents claim to be inherent. For example, although presidents believe they have the inherent power to deal with emergencies, Congress has passed legislation to restrict and guide the use of this power. Under the 1976 National Emergencies Act, the president is authorized to declare a national emergency in the event of major threats to America's national security or economy.[19] An emergency declaration relating to foreign threats allows the president to embargo trade, seize foreign assets, and prohibit transactions with whatever foreign nations are involved. The 1976 act provided, however, that an emergency declaration does not remain in force indefinitely but expires in one year unless renewed by the president. Congress may also terminate a state of emergency by a joint resolution of the two houses. Nevertheless, several declarations have been renewed for quite some time.[20]

Check your understanding

1. Which of the following statements regarding presidential powers is correct?

a) While President Clinton relied on inherent powers to carry out much of his agenda, presidents since then have relied much less on inherent powers.

b) The executive branch is constrained to exercise only those powers found in the Constitution, which places it at a disadvantage relative to the other branches of government.

c) Congress routinely delegates authority not explicitly granted by the Constitution to the executive branch to implement policies it passes.

d) The U.S. Supreme Court has upheld every instance in which presidents have invoked executive privilege, illustrating how expansive executive privilege is.

2. What is the significance of the unitary executive theory?

a) Unitary executive theory holds that the president can only derive authority from the Constitution, and thus it greatly restricts executive power.

b) Unitary executive theory holds that the president controls all policy making by the executive branch and that Congress wields only limited direct power over executive agencies.

c) Unitary executive theory holds that the president has absolute power over state governments.

d) Unitary executive theory holds that the president must seek congressional approval for all military actions.

Presidents Claim Many Institutional Powers

Describe the institutional resources presidents have to help them exercise their powers

Since the ratification of the Constitution, the president has been joined by thousands of officials and staffers who work for, assist, or advise the chief executive (see Figure 11.2). Collectively, these individuals could be said to make up the institutional presidency and to give the president a capacity for action that no single individual could duplicate. The first component of the institutional presidency is the president's Cabinet.

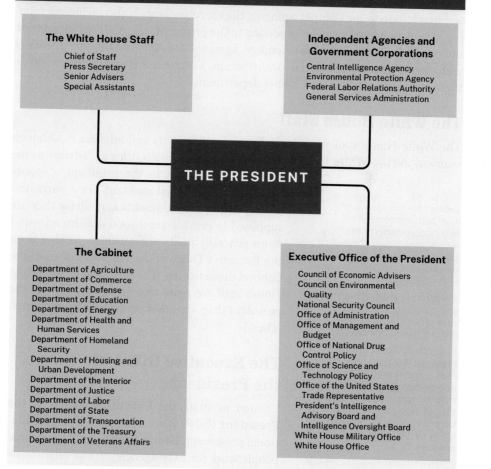

FIGURE 11.2 | The Institutional Presidency

The White House Staff
Chief of Staff
Press Secretary
Senior Advisers
Special Assistants

Independent Agencies and Government Corporations
Central Intelligence Agency
Environmental Protection Agency
Federal Labor Relations Authority
General Services Administration

THE PRESIDENT

The Cabinet
Department of Agriculture
Department of Commerce
Department of Defense
Department of Education
Department of Energy
Department of Health and
  Human Services
Department of Homeland
  Security
Department of Housing and
  Urban Development
Department of the Interior
Department of Justice
Department of Labor
Department of State
Department of Transportation
Department of the Treasury
Department of Veterans Affairs

Executive Office of the President
Council of Economic Advisers
Council on Environmental
  Quality
National Security Council
Office of Administration
Office of Management and
  Budget
Office of National Drug
  Control Policy
Office of Science and
  Technology Policy
Office of the United States
  Trade Representative
President's Intelligence
  Advisory Board and
  Intelligence Oversight Board
White House Military Office
White House Office

The Cabinet

In the American system of government, the **Cabinet** is the traditional but informal designation for the heads of all the major federal government departments. The Cabinet has no constitutional status. Unlike in Great Britain and many other parliamentary countries, where the cabinet *is* the government, the American Cabinet is not a formal organized body. It meets but makes no decisions as a group. Each appointment to it must be approved by the Senate, but Cabinet members are not responsible to the Senate or to Congress at large. However, Cabinet secretaries and their deputies frequently testify before congressional committees to justify budgets and policy objectives, or to explain policies or recent major events or issues.

Each of the 15 government departments is led by a secretary, who is a member of the president's Cabinet. Reporting to the secretary is a deputy secretary, while individual offices and activities are led by undersecretaries and assistant secretaries. Government departments range in size from the Department of Education, which employs about 4,200 people, to the Department of Defense (DoD), which oversees some 700,000 civilian employees and 1.3 million military personnel and is also responsible for maintaining the military readiness of 1.1 million reserve and National Guard troops.

In addition to the Cabinet agencies, the executive branch also includes a number of "independent" agencies reporting to the president. Like Cabinet secretaries, the chief executives of the independent agencies are appointed by the president and usually require senatorial confirmation. Congress engages in oversight of these agencies as it does the Cabinet departments.

The White House Staff

The White House staff is composed mainly of analysts and advisers.[21] Although many of the top **White House staff** members hold such titles as "adviser to the president," "assistant to the president," "deputy assistant," and "special assistant" for a particular task or sector, the judgments and advice they are supposed to provide are a good deal broader and more generally political than those coming from the Executive Office of the President or from the Cabinet departments. The members of the White House staff are more closely associated with the president than are other presidentially appointed officials.

Cabinet the secretaries, or chief administrators, of the major departments of the federal government; Cabinet secretaries are appointed by the president with the consent of the Senate

White House staff analysts and advisers to the president, each of whom is often given the title "special assistant"

Executive Office of the President (EOP) the permanent agencies that perform defined management tasks for the president; created in 1939, the EOP includes OMB, the Council of Economic Advisers (CEA), the NSC, and other agencies

The Executive Office of the President

Created in 1939, the **Executive Office of the President (EOP)** is a major part of the institutional presidency. Nearly 4,000 highly specialized people work for EOP agencies.[22] The importance of each agency in the EOP varies according to the personal orientation of each president.

The most important and the largest EOP agency is the Office of Management and Budget (OMB). This agency takes the lead role in preparing the nation's budget and helping presidents to define their programs and objectives. OMB is also the government's "watchdog," auditing the agencies of the executive branch and making sure their regulatory proposals are consistent with the president's plans. OMB exercises great power, and its director is therefore one of the most powerful officials in Washington. At one time the process of budgeting was a "bottom-up" one, with expenditure and program requests passing from the lowest bureaus through the departments to "clearance" in OMB and then to Congress, where each agency could be called in to explain what its "original request" was before OMB revised it. Now the budgeting process is "top-down": OMB sets the terms of discourse for agencies as well as for Congress.

> **National Security Council (NSC)** a presidential foreign policy advisory council composed of the president, the vice president, the secretary of state, the secretary of defense, and other officials invited by the president

The **National Security Council (NSC)** is composed of designated Cabinet officials who meet regularly with the president to give advice on national security. The staff of the NSC assimilates and analyzes data from all intelligence-gathering agencies (such as the CIA and NSA). In some administrations, the head of the NSC, the president's national security adviser, has played a more important role in foreign and military policy than the Cabinet secretaries in these domains.

The Vice Presidency

The Constitution specifies only two official responsibilities for the vice president: to succeed the president in case of death, resignation, or incapacity, and to preside over the Senate, casting a tie-breaking vote when necessary.[23] There are informal roles, however, that can make vice presidents key political allies.

Typically, presidential candidates choose running mates who they feel can win the support of at least one state that may not otherwise support the ticket or running mates who provide some regional, gender, ideological, or ethnic balance to the ticket.

During the course of American history, eight vice presidents have had to replace presidents who died in office, and one, Gerald Ford, became president when his predecessor resigned. Until the ratification of the Twenty-Fifth Amendment in 1965, the succession of the vice president to the presidency was merely a tradition, launched by John Tyler when he assumed the presidency after William Henry Harrison's death in 1841. The Twenty-Fifth Amendment codified this tradition by providing that the vice president would assume the presidency in the event of the chief executive's death or incapacity and setting forth the procedures that would be followed. The amendment also provides that if the vice presidency becomes vacant, the president is to nominate an individual who must be confirmed by a majority vote of both houses of Congress. In the event that both the president and vice president have died, the Presidential Succession Act of 1947

Kamala Harris served as a U.S. senator from California and was the first woman and person of color ever elected to the vice presidency.

establishes an order of succession, beginning with the Speaker of the House and continuing with the president pro tempore of the Senate and the Cabinet secretaries.

The President's Party

Presidents have another tool: their own political party. Most presidents have sought to use their own party to implement their legislative agenda. For example, in 2009–10, President Obama ultimately had to rely on congressional Democrats to pass the Affordable Care Act (ACA, or "Obamacare") when it was clear that there was virtually unanimous Republican opposition to the bills. In 2021 enactment of major portions of President Biden's agenda depended upon the nearly unanimous support of congressional Democrats. In 2021, President Biden's "Build Back Better" Plan was blocked in the evenly divided Senate when one Democratic senator, Joe Manchin of West Virginia, announced that he would not support it and Republicans unanimously opposed the plan. Although the party is valuable, it has not been a fully reliable presidential tool.

Moreover, in America's system of separated powers, the president's party may be in the minority in Congress and unable to do much to advance the president's agenda. When the 2018 elections gave Democrats control of the House of Representatives, very few of Trump's policy initiatives could be enacted even with full GOP support. In 2022, Republicans won control of the House. This made it extremely difficult for President Biden to secure congressional enactment of any of his policy initiatives.

The First Spouse

The president serves as both chief executive and head of state—the equivalent of Great Britain's prime minister and monarch rolled into one, simultaneously leading the government and representing the nation at official ceremonies and functions. Presidential spouses, because they are traditionally associated with the head-of-state aspect of the presidency, are usually not subject to the

FOR CRITICAL ANALYSIS ————————————————————→

1. Why do you think all presidents have been men and all but one have been White? Do you think this is likely to change in coming years?

2. Why do you think so many presidents have come from the South and the East? What electoral or historical factors may have produced this trend?

WHO ARE AMERICANS?

Who Are America's Presidents?

American presidents have all been men. Until the election of Barack Obama in 2008, they had all been White. As the data show, a majority of presidents have come from the eastern United States, with Virginia producing the most American presidents, especially in the nation's first decades.

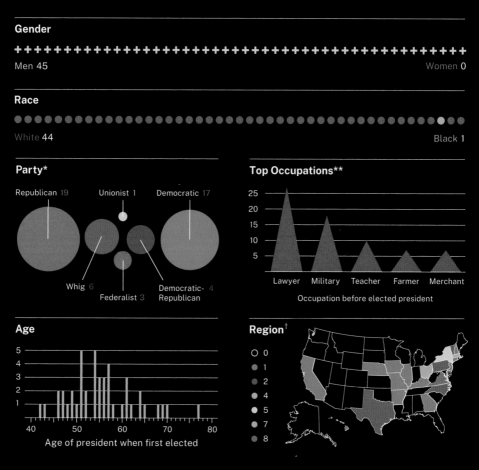

Gender

+++

Men 45   Women 0

Race

●●●○●●

White 44   Black 1

Party*

Republican 19   Unionist 1   Democratic 17

Whig 6   Federalist 3   Democratic- 4
                                 Republican

Top Occupations**

25
20
15
10
5

Lawyer   Military   Teacher   Farmer   Merchant

Occupation before elected president

Age

5
4
3
2
1

40   50   60   70   80

Age of president when first elected

Region†

○ 0
● 1
● 2
● 4
● 5
● 7
● 8

NOTE: Grover Cleveland served as America's 22nd and 24th presidents. He is counted only once in the demographic data here, thus the total number of people who have served as U.S. president is 45.

* Some presidents switched parties during their political careers, thus the numbers sum to more than 45.

** This chart reflects the top nonpolitical careers of U.S. presidents. (All presidents except George Washington and Donald Trump had previous political and/or public service experience.) Presidents may have had more than one occupation, and some occupations do not appear on this list, thus the numbers do not sum to 45.

† Andrew Jackson was born in the Waxhaw area, on the North Carolina–South Carolina border.

SOURCES: Roper Center, www.ropercenter.uconn.edu/elections/common/pop_vote.html; David Leip, http://uselectionatlas.org/RESULTS/; the American Presidency Project, www.presidency.ucsb.edu/showelection.php?year=1840; Miller Center, University of Virginia, http://millercenter.org/president (accessed 3/17/14).

same sort of media scrutiny or partisan attack as that aimed at the president. Historically, most first spouses have limited their activities to the ceremonial portion of the presidency: greeting foreign dignitaries, visiting other countries, and attending important national ceremonies. Some take up causes and advocate for them—in 2021, Jill Biden acted as an advocate for education and supported the idea of free community college tuition. President Biden initially proposed, but later dropped, free community college from his legislative agenda.

Some first spouses, however, have had considerable influence over policy. Franklin Roosevelt's wife, Eleanor, was widely popular but also widely criticized for her active role in many elements of her husband's presidency. During the 1992 campaign, Bill Clinton often implied that his wife would be active in the administration; he joked that voters would get "two for the price of one." After the election, Hillary Clinton took a leading role in many policy areas, most notably health care reform. She also became the first presidential spouse to seek public office on her own, winning a seat in the U.S. Senate from New York in 2000 and then running for president in 2008 and 2016, having served in between as President Obama's secretary of state.

Check your understanding

3. How do White House staff members differ from those in the Executive Office of the President?

   a) The White House staff performs work and gives advice that is generally broader and more political in nature.
   b) The White House staff gives more technical advice on complex issues such as the budget and macroeconomics.
   c) The White House staff is more formal and structured in nature compared to the Executive Office of the President.
   d) The White House staff stays consistent in size, but presidents frequently grow or reduce the Executive Office of the President based on personal preference.

4. Which of the following statements about the Cabinet is true?

   a) Cabinet members must be approved by the U.S. Senate.
   b) Cabinet members are directly accountable to the Senate.
   c) The Cabinet must meet yearly to approve the budget before it is sent to Congress.
   d) The Cabinet is established in Article II of the Constitution.

Presidential Power Grew in the Twentieth Century

Explain how modern presidents have become even more powerful

During the nineteenth century, Congress was America's dominant institution of government, and its members sometimes treated the president with disdain. Today, however, presidents seek to dominate the policy-making process and claim the power to lead the nation in time of war. The expansion of presidential power over the course of the past century has come about as the result of an ongoing effort by successive presidents to enlarge the powers of the office. Generally, presidents can expand their power in two primary ways: by "going public,"[24] and by taking steps to reduce their dependence on Congress and to give themselves a more independent governing and policy-making capability.

Going Public

In the nineteenth century, it was considered inappropriate for presidents to engage in personal campaigning on their own behalf or in support of programs and policies. In the twentieth century, though, popular mobilization became a favored weapon in the political arsenals of most presidents. The first to make systematic use of appeals to the public were Theodore Roosevelt and Woodrow Wilson, but the president who used them most effectively was Franklin Delano Roosevelt (FDR). In particular, he made effective use of a relatively new medium, the radio, to reach millions of Americans. In his famous "fireside chats," Roosevelt's voice could be heard in almost every living room in the country, discussing programs and policies, assuring Americans that he was aware of their difficulties and working diligently toward solutions.

Roosevelt was also an innovator in press relations. When he entered the White House, he faced a press mainly controlled by conservative members of the business establishment.[25] To bypass these generally hostile editors and publishers, the president worked to cultivate the reporters who covered the White House. FDR made himself available for biweekly press conferences, where he offered candid answers to reporters' questions and made important policy announcements that would provide the reporters with significant stories for their papers.[26]

Every president since FDR has sought to craft a public-relations strategy that would emphasize their strengths and maximize their popular appeal. For John F. Kennedy, who was handsome and quick-witted, the televised press conference was an excellent public-relations vehicle. Both Bill Clinton and Barack Obama held televised town hall meetings—carefully staged events that let these presidents appear to consult with rank-and-file citizens about their goals and policies without having to face pointed questions from reporters.

An innovation introduced by Clinton and continued by his successors was to make the White House Communications Office an important institution within the EOP. The Communications Office became responsible not only for responding to reporters' queries but also for developing and implementing a coordinated communications strategy—promoting the president's policy goals, developing responses to adverse news stories, and making certain that a favorable image of the president would, insofar as possible, dominate the news.

Going Public Online President Obama was the first chief executive to make full use of the internet as a communication medium. Drawing on the interactive tools of the web, Obama's 2008 and 2012 campaigns changed the way politicians organize supporters, advertise to voters, defend against attacks, and communicate with their constituents.[27]

In the 2016 presidential campaign, candidates Hillary Clinton and especially Donald Trump made particular use of Twitter to communicate with millions of voters, bypassing traditional media. Trump usually tweeted many times a day, often making outrageous claims that guaranteed that he would dominate media coverage as reporters rushed to analyze and criticize his assertions. While Trump may have pioneered the social media campaign, by 2020 the Democrats followed suit and both campaigns made extensive use of social media, including YouTube, Twitter, Facebook, and Instagram. In August 2020, the major social media platforms announced a partnership to guard against misinformation and foreign efforts to use American social media to influence the outcome of the election.

The internet has changed not only the way modern presidents campaign but also how they govern. Circumventing television and other older media, it allows them to broadcast their policy ideas directly to citizens. Whitehouse.gov keeps constituents abreast of the president's policy agenda with weekly streaming video addresses by the president, press briefings, speeches and remarks, a daily blog, photos of the president, the White House schedule, and other information.

The Limits of Going Public Some presidents have been able to make effective use of popular appeals to overcome congressional opposition. Popular support, though, has not been a firm foundation for presidential power. President George W. Bush maintained an approval rating of over 70 percent for more than a year following the September 11, 2001, terrorist attacks. By the end of 2005, however, Bush's approval rating had dropped to 39 percent as a result of the growing unpopularity of the Iraq War, the administration's handling of hurricane relief, and a number of White House scandals.

President Obama's public approval ranged from a high of 76 percent in 2009 to a low of 36 percent in 2014.[28] By the end of his term in 2016, Obama's popularity had recovered to about 56 percent. Declines in popular approval during a president's term in office are nearly inevitable and follow a predictable pattern.[29] Both before and after they are elected, presidents generate popular support by promising to undertake important programs that will contribute directly to the well-being of large numbers of Americans. Almost without exception, presidential performance falls short of promises and popular expectations, leading to a decline in public support and the ensuing weakening of presidential influence.[30] It is a rare American president, such as Bill Clinton, who exits the White House more popular than when he went in.[31]

The Administrative Strategy

Contemporary presidents have increased the administrative capabilities of their office in three ways. First, they have enhanced the reach and power of the EOP. Second, they have increased White House control over the federal bureaucracy. Third, they have expanded the role of executive orders and other instruments of direct presidential governance. Taken together, these three components of what might be called the White House "administrative strategy" have given presidents a capacity to achieve their policy goals even when they are unable to secure congressional approval. Indeed, some recent presidents have been able to accomplish a great deal with remarkably little congressional, partisan, or even public support.

The Growth of the EOP The EOP has grown from six administrative assistants in 1939 to several hundred employees today, along with some 4,000 individuals staffing the several EOP divisions. The White House staff has given the president enormous capacity to gather information, plan programs and strategies, communicate with constituencies, and exercise supervision over the executive branch. The staff multiplies the president's eyes, ears, and arms, becoming a critical instrument of presidential power.[32]

In particular, the Office of Management and Budget serves as a potential instrument of presidential control over federal spending and hence as a mechanism through which the White House has greatly expanded its power. OMB has the capacity to analyze and approve all legislative proposals, not only budgetary requests, emanating from all federal agencies before they are submitted to Congress. This procedure, now a matter of routine, greatly enhances the president's control over the entire executive branch. All legislation originating in the White House and all executive orders also go through OMB.[33] Thus, through one White House agency, the president has the means to exert major influence over the flow of money and the shape and content of national legislation.

Regulatory Review A second instrument that presidents have used to increase their power and reach is an agency within OMB called the Office of Information and Regulatory Affairs (OIRA), which supervises the process of regulatory review. Whenever Congress enacts a law, implementing it requires the promulgation of hundreds of rules by the agency charged with administering the law and giving effect to what Congress intended. For example, if Congress wishes to improve air quality, it must delegate to an agency—say, the Environmental Protection Agency (EPA)—the power to establish numerous regulations governing actions by businesses, individuals, and government agencies (including the EPA itself) that may affect the atmosphere.

The agency rule-making process is governed by a number of statutory requirements concerning public notice (the most important being publication in the *Federal Register*), hearings, and appeals. Once completed and published in the massive *Code of Federal Regulations*, administrative rules have the effect of law and will be enforced by the federal courts.

Beginning with little fanfare during the Nixon administration, recent presidents gradually have tried to take control of the rule-making process and to use it in effect to make laws without the interference of the legislature. For example, in his final two years in office, Obama sought new regulations governing power plant emissions, overtime pay for workers, the educational practices of career (for-profit) colleges, and a host of other matters.

President Trump moved aggressively to reverse these and other Obama directives. In the four years of his presidency, for example, Trump eliminated or began the process of rescinding 99 environmental regulations.[34] The administration also proposed new rules that would rewrite the nation's asylum rules, blocking asylum in most new cases and likely foreclosing asylum to the more than 300,000 individuals whose cases have already been filed.

When he took office, President Biden did away with several Trump-era rules. Under Biden's direction, federal agencies reversed Trump's rollback of fuel efficiency and vehicle emission rules and reinstated water efficiency rules for plumbing fixtures. In addition, President Biden issued a memorandum modifying the regulatory review process. The Biden memo declared that the regulatory review process should take account of goals including "racial justice, environmental stewardship, human dignity, equity, and the interests of future generations." It remains to be seen how these criteria will affect the rule-making process.

Governing by Decree: Executive Orders and Memoranda A third mechanism through which contemporary presidents have sought to enhance their power to govern unilaterally is the use of executive orders and other forms of presidential decrees.

An **executive order** is a presidential directive to the bureaucracy to undertake some action. Executive orders have a long history in the United States and have been the means for imposing a number of important policies, including the purchase of the Louisiana Territory, the annexation of Texas, the emancipation of enslaved people, the wartime internment of Japanese Americans, the desegregation of the military, the initiation of affirmative action, and the creation of federal agencies, including the Environmental Protection Agency, the Food and Drug Administration, and the Peace Corps (although the creation of these agencies was later approved by Congress).[35] Historically, executive orders were most often used during times of war or national emergency. In recent years, though, executive orders have become routine instruments of presidential governance (see Figure 11.3).

executive order a rule or regulation issued by the president that has the effect and formal status of legislation

President Obama issued executive orders halting the deportation of undocumented immigrants who had come to the United States as children, prohibiting federal agencies and contractors from discriminating against transgender employees, and declaring more than 700,000 square miles of the central Pacific Ocean off-limits to fishing. By the end of his term, President Trump had issued 219 executive orders on such matters as the Covid-19 pandemic and other health care issues, regulatory reform, cybersecurity, freedom of speech at colleges and universities, and the imposition of new sanctions on Iran. Trump's orders included several that rescinded some of former president Obama's orders; for example, he invalidated several environmental protections and limits on gun purchases. During his first months in office, President Biden issued a number of orders, in many cases reversing actions taken by Trump. Biden rejoined the Paris climate agreement, which Trump

FIGURE 11.3 | Presidential Executive Orders*

Executive orders are a tool presidents have for influencing policy. Their use has varied considerably over time. Each bar in the graph shows the average number of executive orders each president issued per year in office. Which presidents issued the most executive orders? What events in U.S. history were occurring when those presidents were in office?

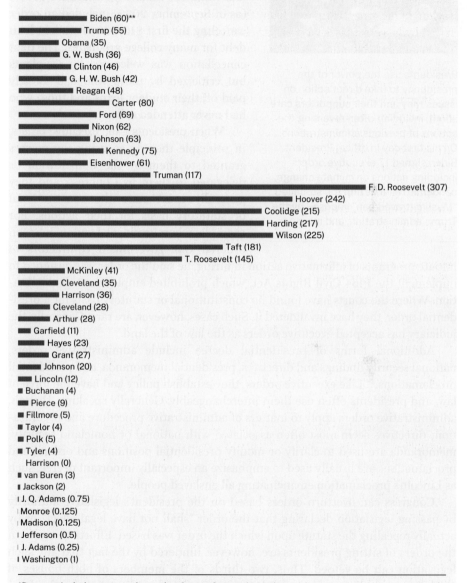

Biden (60)**
Trump (55)
Obama (35)
G. W. Bush (36)
Clinton (46)
G. H. W. Bush (42)
Reagan (48)
Carter (80)
Ford (69)
Nixon (62)
Johnson (63)
Kennedy (75)
Eisenhower (61)
Truman (117)
F. D. Roosevelt (307)
Hoover (242)
Coolidge (215)
Harding (217)
Wilson (225)
Taft (181)
T. Roosevelt (145)
McKinley (41)
Cleveland (35)
Harrison (36)
Cleveland (28)
Arthur (28)
Garfield (11)
Hayes (23)
Grant (27)
Johnson (20)
Lincoln (12)
Buchanan (4)
Pierce (9)
Fillmore (5)
Taylor (4)
Polk (5)
Tyler (4)
Harrison (0)
van Buren (3)
Jackson (2)
J. Q. Adams (0.75)
Monroe (0.125)
Madison (0.125)
Jefferson (0.5)
J. Adams (0.25)
Washington (1)

*Does not include memoranda or other forms of executive action.

**As of September 2022.

SOURCE: The American Presidency Project, "Executive Orders," September 20, 2022, www.presidency.ucsb.edu (accessed 9/20/22).

Presidents use the power of the presidency to take direct action on issues they and their supporters care about, including often reversing the actions of previous administrations. On his first day in office, President Biden signed 17 executive orders, including actions on climate change, pandemic relief, lifting the so-called "Muslim [travel] ban" imposed by the Trump administration, and more.

had abandoned; he revoked the permit granted by Trump for construction of a major natural gas pipeline; he stopped construction on the border wall begun by a Trump order; and he lifted the travel ban targeting Muslim countries that Trump had initiated. Biden's 99 executive orders (as of September 2022) included an order canceling the first $10,000 of student loan debt for many college graduates. The debt cancellation was welcomed by recipients but criticized by those who had already paid off their student loans and those who had never attended college.

When presidents issue executive orders, in principle they do so using the powers granted to them by the Constitution or delegated to them by Congress, and they generally must state the constitutional or statutory basis for their actions. For example, when President Lyndon Johnson ordered U.S. government contractors to initiate programs of affirmative action in hiring, he said the order was designed to implement the 1964 Civil Rights Act, which prohibited employment discrimination. Where the courts have found no constitutional or statutory basis for a presidential order, they have invalidated it. Such cases, however, are rare. Generally, the judiciary has accepted executive orders as the law of the land.

Additional forms of presidential decree include administrative orders, national security findings and directives, presidential memoranda, and presidential proclamations.[36] Like executive orders, they establish policy and have the force of law, and presidents often use them interchangeably. Generally speaking, though, administrative orders apply to matters of administrative procedure and organization; directives seem most often associated with national or homeland security; memoranda are used to clarify or modify presidential positions and orders; and proclamations are usually used to emphasize an especially important decree, such as Lincoln's proclamation emancipating all enslaved people.

Congress can overturn orders based on the president's legislative authority by passing legislation declaring that the order "shall not have legal effect" or by actually repealing the statute upon which the order was based. Efforts to overturn the orders of sitting presidents are, however, hindered by the fact that any such legislation can be vetoed. Thus, two-thirds of the members of both houses of Congress would have to agree to the move. One study indicates that only about 4 percent of all presidential orders have ever been rescinded by legislation.[37] Failure by Congress to act strengthens the legal validity of a presidential order. The Supreme Court has held that congressional inaction tends to validate an order by indicating congressional "acquiescence" to the president's decision.[38]

Signing Statements Recent presidents have also increasingly found ways other than vetoes to negate congressional actions to which they objected. In particular, they have made frequent and calculated use of presidential **signing statements**.[39] The signing statement is an announcement made

signing statements announcements made by the president when signing bills into law, often presenting the president's interpretation of the law

by the president, at the time of signing a bill into law, that offers the president's interpretation of the law and usually innocuous remarks predicting the many benefits the new law will bring to the nation.

Occasionally, however, presidents have used signing statements to point to sections of the law they consider improper or even unconstitutional, and to instruct executive branch agencies in how to execute the law.[40] In 2018, for example, when President Trump signed the 2019 National Defense Authorization Act, he issued a signing statement declaring "constitutional concerns" with more than 50 of the act's provisions. The president said he would interpret these provisions in a manner consistent with his authority as president rather than simply accepting the law as written.

Presidential Nonenforcement of Laws A final instrument of direct presidential governance is nonenforcement of statutes. Congress may make the law, but if the president decides that a particular law is not to their liking and refuses to enforce it, Congress may find that its intent is stymied. President Obama, for example, suspended enforcement of portions of the Affordable Care Act when its rollout produced public confusion and inefficient implementation. President Trump, in an effort to undercut the ACA, effectively ordered the IRS to not enforce a provision of it that required taxpayers to indicate on their tax returns that they had health insurance—a major blow to the law's mandate.

The Advantages of the Administrative Strategy Because presidents can act on their own, the unilateral administrative powers of the office are tempting as means of achieving their policy goals. In recent decades, the expansion of the Executive Office of the President, the development of regulatory review, and the use of executive orders and signing statements have allowed presidents to achieve significant policy results despite congressional opposition to their legislative agendas.

In principle, Congress could respond more vigorously to unilateral policy making by the president than it has. But the president has significant advantages in such struggles. In battles over presidential directives and orders, Congress is on the defensive. When the president issues a decree, Congress must respond through the cumbersome and time-consuming lawmaking process, overcome internal divisions, and enact legislation that the president may ultimately veto.

The Limits of Presidential Power: Checks and Balances

While the framers of the Constitution wanted an energetic executive, they were also concerned that executive power could be abused and might stifle citizens' liberties. To guard against this possibility, the framers contrived a number of checks on executive power. The president's term is limited to four years, though with the possibility of re-election. Congress is empowered to impeach and remove the president, to reject presidential appointments and refuse to ratify treaties, to refuse to enact laws requested by the president, to deny funding for the president's programs, and to override presidential vetoes of legislation. And only Congress can enact legislation, levy taxes, and appropriate funds. Despite fears that the executive would be too weak and the potential energy of executive power lost, presidential power has grown significantly beyond the framers' vision.

Although the requirement that the Senate consent to presidential appointments was seen by the framers as another important check on executive power, in recent years severe partisan disagreements have often led presidents to resort to—and the Senate to resist—"recess appointments." These are authorized by Article II, Section 2, which states, "The President shall have power to fill up all Vacancies that may happen during the Recess of the Senate, by granting Commissions which shall expire at the End of their next Session."

Until recent years, recess appointments were made only when the Senate was between sessions or when a regular session of the Senate was adjourned for holidays or other lengthy periods. However, presidents have sometimes sought to make recess appointments even when the Senate was only briefly recessed. The Senate has responded with a strategy also sometimes used to prevent pocket vetoes. During periods when the Senate is recessed, one senator is assigned the task of calling the chamber to order for a few moments every day for a pro forma session so that the president cannot claim the Senate was actually in recess. Presidents have viewed this procedure as nothing more than a subterfuge, since the Senate is incapable of actually conducting business during these periods. The Supreme Court, however, has supported the Senate's strategy.[41]

Check your understanding

5. Which of the following statements about the power of modern presidents is true?

a) Presidents in the nineteenth century had much more power than modern presidents.

b) Presidents have decreased the size of the Executive Office of the President so it can be more focused on the president's policy agenda.

c) In recent years, executive orders are generally only issued by presidents during wartime.

d) Presidents have increased their power through the use of regulatory review, which gives the president authority over the implementation of laws.

6. To guard against abuse of power, the framers placed checks on executive power. Which of the following is a check on presidential power?

a) The White House staff must be confirmed by the Senate.

b) Presidents may not enter into any agreement with foreign governments without the approval of the Senate.

c) The Constitution provides that a president may be impeached for "high Crimes and Misdemeanors."

d) The president is restricted from being involved in the rule-making process.

WHAT DO YOU THINK?

THE PRESIDENCY

The framers of the Constitution created a system of government in which the Congress and the executive branch were to share power. At least since the New Deal, however, the powers of Congress have waned, whereas those of the presidency have expanded dramatically. Congress continues to be able to confront presidents and even, on occasion, hand the White House a sharp rebuff. In the larger view, however, presidents' occasional defeats, however dramatic, have to be seen as temporary setbacks in a gradual but decisive shift toward increased presidential power.

A powerful presidency, a weak Congress, and a partially apathetic electorate make for a dangerous mix. Who we vote into the office of the president matters, as the example of the back-and-forth on the Bears Ears monument demonstrates. Presidents have increasingly asserted the right to act unilaterally. Presidential power, to be sure, can be a force for good. It was President Lyndon Johnson, more than Congress or the judiciary, who helped smash America's racial apartheid system. Yet, as the framers knew, unchecked power — whether executive or legislative — is always dangerous. The framers of the Constitution believed that liberty required checks and balances.

- Presidential strength works both ways. The growth of executive power means that policies and individual favors can more easily become the law of the land, because Congress works slowly while the president can work quickly. But for those who oppose a particular policy, the stroke of the presidential pen might seem hasty and autocratic. What if the president fails to act? What would Shaun Chapoose, Russell Begaye, and Utah governor Spencer Cox have to say about presidential power?

- How have the checks and balances between branches of government changed in practice over the decades? Are there some issue areas — or certain conditions — in which presidential rather than congressional policy making is necessary?

- Have you been affected by a presidential decision? Do you think the policy outcome would have been different if Congress had been more involved?

Use 📙 **INQUIZITIVE** *to help you study and master this material.*

12

WHAT GOVERNMENT DOES & WHY IT MATTERS

Hope Grosse and Joanne Stanton grew up near military bases in the Philadelphia suburbs, watching the Blue Angels when they were in town as well as the weekly drills when Navy personnel set planes on fire and doused them with foam. "We would run up the street as the sirens went off and sit with our fingers in the fence," said Hope. "It was fun. I don't think we were worried about anything."

But the firefighting foam contained PFAS, a family of chemicals also used in nonstick cookware, food packaging, furniture, cosmetics, and paint. Scientists call them "forever chemicals"—chemicals that accumulate in soil, air, water, and the human body and which do not break down for thousands of years. They are associated with many adverse health conditions, including various cancers, thyroid disease, liver damage, immune dysfunction, and preeclampsia during pregnancy.[1] Groundwater tests near the military bases where Hope and Joanne had grown up found PFAS contamination. They immediately thought of the conditions that had hit their own families: Hope was diagnosed with melanoma; her father died from cancer; her daughter was born without

The Bureaucracy

a set of adult teeth; Joanne's son was diagnosed with a brain tumor at age six. "You can't tell us that we drank contaminated water for 50 years and that it did nothing, that it didn't have a health impact," said Joanne.[2]

Unlike substances such as arsenic, benzene, and uranium, PFAS chemicals are not regulated under the Safe Drinking Water Act, and federal law does not require local water utilities to test for them.[3] For years, environmentalists and citizens had been urging the Environmental Protection Agency (EPA), the federal agency tasked with protecting human health and the environment, to regulate the chemicals. In 2019, Congress considered but later dropped legislation requiring the Department of Defense to clean up contaminated sites. In 2021, during the Biden administration, the EPA finally took action, announcing a plan to regulate the chemicals, with new limits on their presence in drinking water and new requirements on manufacturers to report use of PFAS. The Department of Defense also committed to clean up 700 sites where PFAS were used.

One of the people who pushed for increased regulation of PFAS was Michael Regan, EPA administrator under President Biden. In fact, in his previous position as North Carolina's top environmental official, Michael had led negotiations to clean up a river contaminated with PFAS. "PFAS contamination has been devastating communities for decades now, even before we knew how dangerous these chemicals were," Michael said.[4]

◄ Hope Grosse stands above a creek in Warminster, Pennsylvania. The water there was contaminated by harmful chemicals unregulated by the EPA.

PFAS contamination is a tragic example of bureaucratic failure. Americans depend on public bureaucracies to provide services they use both every day and in emergencies. On a typical day, a college student might check the weather forecast, drive on an interstate highway, mail the rent check, attend a class, go online, and meet a relative at the airport. Each of these activities is possible because of the work of a government bureaucracy: the National Weather Service, the U.S. Department of Transportation, the U.S. Postal Service, student loan programs of the U.S. Department of Education, the Advanced Research Projects Agency (which developed the internet in the 1960s), and the Federal Aviation Administration. Without the ongoing work of these agencies, many of these common activities would be impossible, unreliable, more expensive, or even unsafe. And in the face of emergencies bureaucracies can mobilize in crucial ways, as when Operation Warp Speed, a collaboration between the Department of Health and Human Services (HHS) and the Department of Defense during the Trump administration, helped accelerate the development and manufacture of Covid-19 vaccines.[5]

Though Operation Warp Speed was incredibly high-profile, when bureaucracies work well, we usually barely notice. But when bureaucracies fail, the results can be truly alarming, like PFAS contamination; or lack of clarity from the Centers for Disease Control and Prevention (CDC) during the Covid-19 pandemic; or the September 11, 2001, terror attacks, widely viewed as a failure of the national security bureaucracy.[6] These examples raise a number of questions: Should the bureaucracy be smaller or larger? How can it become more efficient and effective? How can the bureaucracy be made more responsive to the needs of the American people?

CHAPTER GOALS

Describe the characteristics and roles of bureaucrats and bureaucracies (pp. 375–88)

Explain civil service hiring, political appointments, and the use of federal contracting (pp. 388–92)

Explain how the president, Congress, and the judiciary try to manage the bureaucracy (pp. 392–400)

What Is the Federal Bureaucracy?

Describe the characteristics and roles of bureaucrats and bureaucracies

Bureaucracy is the complex structure of offices, tasks, rules, and principles that organize all large-scale institutions to coordinate the work of their personnel. The bureaucracy of the federal executive branch plays a crucial role in administering national policy on the ground. Bureaucrats carry out the policies that Congress and the president have passed and that the court system may have weighed in on. The teachers you had in (public) elementary school, the Social Security officer who approved your grandmother's retirement pension, the air traffic controller who guided the plane on your last vacation, the engineers who designed the roads that carried you to class, and the inspector who approved the meat in this morning's breakfast sausage are all bureaucrats. The focus in this chapter is on the federal bureaucracy, but state and local governments also employ many bureaucrats (like the public school teachers mentioned) who carry out policy at those levels of government.

> **bureaucracy** the complex structure of offices, tasks, rules, and principles of organization that is employed by all large-scale institutions to coordinate the work of their personnel

At its best, bureaucracy ensures fair, accountable administration performed by expert professionals. To provide services, government bureaucracies employ specialists such as meteorologists, doctors, and scientists. To do their jobs effectively, these specialists require resources and tools (ranging from paper to complex computer software). They must coordinate their work with others (for example, traffic engineers must communicate with construction engineers). And they must effectively reach out to the public (for example, people must be made aware of health warnings). Bureaucracy is a means of coordinating the many different parts that must work together for the government to provide useful services.

When bureaucracy runs well, it can be virtually invisible. When it fails, the results can be spectacularly public (and even tragic), as when Hurricane Katrina breached levies built by the Army Corps of Engineers in 2005 and the Federal Emergency Management Agency (FEMA) reacted ineffectually, or when the Department of Veterans Affairs was criticized in 2014 for long waiting lists for veterans seeking medical care and was even blamed for veteran deaths in Phoenix.[7] Or when Food and Drug Administration (FDA) and CDC missteps delayed coronavirus testing as the pandemic swept across the nation. How bureaucrats carry out their responsibilities shapes individuals' experiences of government in profound ways.

What Bureaucrats Do

Bureaucrats execute and implement laws. They determine who is eligible for Medicare, for example, or study whether a new medicine is safe and effective. They deliver mail, tell national park campers that they can build a fire *here* but not *there*, and calculate how long it would take a spacecraft to reach the edge of the solar system. They gather data and conduct research. Some, like customs officials, are "street-level bureaucrats" who regularly interact with the public. Yet others, like researchers at the National Institutes of Health, work in specialized facilities with other experts. As bureaucrats carry out their responsibilities, implementing and enforcing laws, making rules, and innovating, they exercise discretion and help define how public policy gets expressed.

> **implementation** the efforts of departments and agencies to translate laws into specific bureaucratic rules and actions

Bureaucrats Implement Laws Congress is responsible for making the laws, but the federal bureaucracy is responsible for putting laws into effect. In most cases legislation sets only the broad parameters for government action. Bureaucracies are responsible for filling in the details by determining how the laws should be implemented. This requires bureaucracies to draw up detailed rules that guide the process of **implementation** and to play a key role in enforcing the laws. For example, during the coronavirus pandemic, while Congress appropriated funds for direct payments to individuals and for economic relief for small businesses, these programs were implemented by the Internal Revenue Service (part of the Treasury Department) and the Small Business Administration, an independent agency of the federal government. Congress also increased unemployment insurance benefits and broadened eligibility, but had to rely on the state-level bureaucracies that run the program, which were overwhelmed by the enormous rise in jobless claims. If the federal student loan forgiveness plan that President Biden announced in 2022 withstands legal challenges, the Department of Education will implement it, beginning with creating an application for those seeking relief. Administrative capacity is an important factor in bureaucracies' ability to implement laws effectively. Congress increased IRS funding in 2022, for example, to boost taxpayer services and the enforcement of federal tax laws.

Bureaucrats Make Rules One of the most important activities that government agencies do is issue rules that provide more detailed and specific indications of what a given congressional policy will actually mean. For example, the Clean Air Act empowers the EPA to implement pollution control programs that set wastewater standards for industry and water quality standards for surface waters.

Once Congress passes a new law, the relevant agency studies the legislation and proposes a set of rules to guide implementation. These proposed rules are submitted to the White House Office of Management and Budget (OMB) for review. If OMB approves, the proposed rule is published in the *Federal Register*, a daily publication of the federal government, which anyone can read and where they can leave comments, which are also published. After reviewing public comments and making changes, the agency proposes a final rule, which goes back to OMB for clearance, upon which it is published in the *Federal Register*. The agency's rules have the force of law.

Although bureaucratic rule making has the force of law, it is easier to change than laws passed by Congress.[8] If Congress passes a new law, changing it usually requires another congressional action, while rules made by the bureaucracy in one administration can be easily reversed by the next. For example, during the Obama

Bureaucratic rules can affect Americans both positively and negatively. In 2021 the Department of the Interior filed an agreement on the operation of federal dams on the Columbia River to try to balance concerns of environmentalists and the Nez Perce Tribe on salmon passage with the need for hydroelectric power generation.

administration, the EPA imposed new emission standards for automobiles that raised the average fuel economy for new vehicles to 35.5 miles per gallon starting in 2016, a standard later boosted to 54.4 miles per gallon by 2025.[9] Under President Trump the EPA rolled back the standard to 40 miles per gallon by 2026. Then under President Biden, the EPA proposed increasing the standard again, to 52 miles per gallon by 2026.[10]

Bureaucrats Enforce Laws In addition to rule making, bureaucracies play an essential role in enforcing the laws, thus exercising considerable power over private actors. In 2015 the EPA charged Volkswagen with cheating on emissions tests of its diesel vehicles. For over seven years, the company had installed software that showed emissions at legal levels during testing conditions, but once the cars were on the road emissions were actually 10 to 40 percent higher. After the EPA threatened to bar the company from selling some of its 2016 cars in the United States, Volkswagen admitted that it had cheated and agreed to a $14.7 billion settlement that required it to buy back the faulty vehicles and compensate owners and to fund several clean-air programs.[11]

Bureaucrats Innovate A good case study of the important role agencies can play is the story of how ordinary federal bureaucrats created the internet. It's true: what became the internet was developed largely by the U.S. Department of Defense, and defense considerations still shape the basic structure of the internet. In 1957, immediately following the profound American embarrassment over the Soviet Union's launching of Sputnik, the first satellite to orbit the earth, Congress authorized the establishment of the Advanced Research Projects Agency (ARPA) to develop, among other things, a means of maintaining communications in the event of a strategic attack on the existing telecommunications network (the telephone system). Since the telephone network was highly centralized and therefore could have been completely disabled by a single attack, ARPA developed a decentralized, highly redundant network with an improved probability of functioning after an attack. The full design, called ARPANET, took almost a decade to create. By 1971 around 20 universities were connected to the ARPANET. The forerunner to the internet was born.[12]

Key Characteristics of Bureaucracies In the United States, bureaucracies are typically defined by mission statements, which lay out each agency's role and responsibilities. For example, the mission of the Department of Health and Human Services (HHS) is to "enhance the health and well-being of all Americans, by providing for effective health and human services and by fostering sound, sustained advances in the sciences underlying medicine, public health, and social services."

Another key characteristic is expertise. Bureaucracies are populated by policy-specific experts who are deeply knowledgeable about the issue areas they oversee. Expertise is one of the main resources and distinguishing characteristics of the federal bureaucracy. Bureaucrats often have specialized training, such as advanced degrees, and may spend their careers working on a given set of issues, developing deep knowledge.

Bureaucracies are also characterized by hierarchical structures with clear lines of authority and standardized procedures governed by rules. These structures are intended to foster equal treatment of citizens. In the United States, the bureaucracy is supposed to be insulated from politics as well. The long length of employment of many career civil servants—whose service may persist through many presidencies and congressional terms—is one form of protection. There are also merit systems in place for hiring and promotion, meant to maximize the political neutrality of the bureaucracy regardless of which party controls the presidency or Congress. In addition, the nonpartisan nature of the bureaucracy is underscored by the 1939 Hatch Act and its amendments, which prevent federal employees from engaging in certain types of political activities, such as wearing political buttons while on duty or using their official authority to interfere with an election.

The Decision to Delegate Federal bureaucrats greatly shape the nation's public policy, and we might wonder why Congress writes laws but then delegates such significant policy-making responsibility to the bureaucracy. One reason is that bureaucracies employ people who have much more specialized expertise in specific policy areas than do members of Congress. Decisions about how to achieve many policy goals—from managing the national parks to regulating air quality to ensuring a sound economy—rest on the judgment of specialized experts. A second reason is that updating legislation can take many years, and bureaucratic flexibility can ensure that laws are administered in ways that take new conditions into account more quickly. Finally, members of Congress often prefer to delegate politically difficult decision-making to bureaucrats, thus avoiding having to deal with controversial issues that might anger constituents or interest groups and threaten their chances for re-election. For example, when Congress wrote the Affordable Care Act, it required health insurance plans to cover "essential health benefits" but did not define what those benefits are. Instead, lawmakers provided some general guidelines and instructed the bureaucracy—the Department of Health and Human Services—to specify which benefits must be covered.[13]

Delegation comes with risks. In delegating, Congress gives agencies discretion to use their expertise as they implement laws and create rules. But such discretion can lead to the **principal-agent problem**, which occurs when one entity (the principal) gives decision-making authority to another (the agent), but the agent makes decisions that are different from what the principal may have wanted. In 2020 funds ran out before numerous small businesses could secure loans because many banks accepted applications from their existing business customers or larger businesses first. Congress responded with a new round of relief with tighter rules and pressured larger companies like AutoNation to return the program funds they had received.[14]

principal-agent problem a conflict in priorities between an actor and the representative authorized to act on the actor's behalf

executive departments the 15 departments in the executive branch headed by Cabinet secretaries and constituting the majority of the federal bureaucracy

independent regulatory commission a government agency outside the executive department usually headed by commissioners

A 2022 Supreme Court ruling may limit the bureaucracy's regulatory authority on major matters. In *West Virginia v. EPA*, the Court ruled that in the Clean Air Act, Congress gave the EPA authority to regulate individual power plants only, not to set pollution caps for states as proposed during the Obama administration. "A decision of such magnitude and consequence rests with Congress itself" or requires "clear delegation," the Court wrote. Some observers believe this "major questions" doctrine will open the way for other legal challenges to agencies' policy expertise.[15]

How the Bureaucracy Is Organized

Currently there are 15 **executive departments** in the federal government. The first 4 were established in 1789 under President George Washington: State, Treasury, Defense, and Justice. Others were added over time: Interior, Agriculture, Commerce, Labor, Health and Human Services, Housing and Urban Development, Transportation, Energy, Education, Veterans Affairs, and most recently, in 2002, Homeland Security. These 15 executive departments employ over 80 percent of the federal civilian workforce, with Defense, Veterans Affairs, and Homeland Security having the most employees.[16] The rest work in agencies in the Executive Office of the President (for example, the Council of Economic Advisers or the Office of the United States Trade Representative) or in agencies outside of the executive departments (for example, the Central Intelligence Agency [CIA] or the National Aeronautics and Space Administration [NASA]). At the top of each department is an official who is called the secretary of the department (though the head of the Justice Department is the attorney general). The executive department secretaries, along with the vice president and attorney general, make up the president's "Cabinet." Presidents can also confer Cabinet-level status on additional agencies.

The federal bureaucracy also consists of independent agencies that are not part of executive departments but have independent authority to implement policy and design regulations in their particular area. Some are called administrations, including the National Aeronautics and Space Administration (NASA), the Small Business Administration, and the Social Security Administration. There are also **independent regulatory commissions** such as the Federal Trade Commission (FTC), Federal Communications Commission (FCC), and Securities and Exchange Commission (SEC).

AMERICA | SIDE BY SIDE

Bureaucracy in Comparison

As the third-largest country by area, with over 330 million residents, the United States has a sizable bureaucracy to run government programs and services. As a percentage of the labor force, however, the number of government employees in the United States is not especially high compared to other nations. We can also see differences in whether most government employees work at the national level or the subnational (state and local) level in each country.

1. What factors might lead a country like Norway or Japan to have a significantly larger or smaller government workforce as a percentage of its population? Would you expect these percentages to be going up or down over time? How might you expect them to change during times of economic growth versus during recessions?

2. What might explain the differences in how some countries have most of their government employment at the national level whereas others focus their employment at the subnational level? How does America's federal structure influence its bureaucratic hiring?

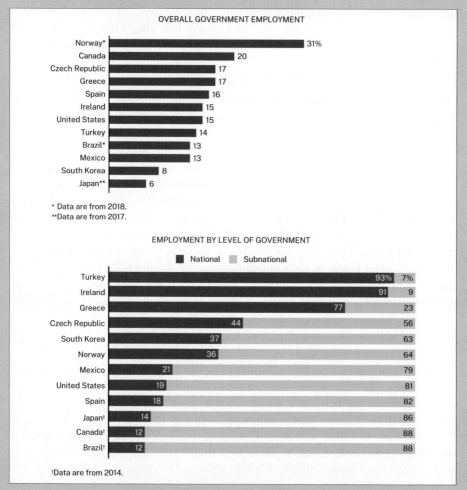

OVERALL GOVERNMENT EMPLOYMENT

* Data are from 2018.
**Data are from 2017.

EMPLOYMENT BY LEVEL OF GOVERNMENT

■ National　■ Subnational

†Data are from 2014.

SOURCE: OECD, "Public Employment and Pay," Government at a Glance, 2017, www.stats.oecd.org (accessed 10/31/21).

The National Aeronautics and Space Administration (NASA), an independent agency of the federal government, was established by President Eisenhower in 1958. Its mission is "To reach for new heights and reveal the unknown so that what we do and learn will benefit all humankind." Here, NASA public affairs officer Dwayne Brown announces the presence of water on Mars.

These commissions are typically run by a small number of commissioners appointed by the president for fixed terms. And there are **government corporations**, which receive federal funding and are subject to federal control but function like private businesses in charging for a service, such as transporting railroad passengers (Amtrak) or delivering the mail (United States Postal Service).

government corporation a government agency that performs a market-oriented public service and raises revenues to fund its activities

For simplicity we will call all of these bureaucratic entities "agencies." As Figure 12.1 shows, the federal bureaucracy handles a vast number of important functions. Some agencies work to promote national security, such as the State Department, whose primary mission is diplomacy, sending foreign-service officers and ambassadors to other countries where they work to promote American perspectives and interests in the world; and the Defense Department, one of the largest bureaucracies in the world. Headquartered at the Pentagon, across the Potomac River from Washington, D.C., the Department of Defense includes the Office of the Secretary of Defense, which provides civilian oversight of the military; the Joint Chiefs of Staff, which includes the five military service chiefs; the six regional Unified Combatant Commands, which execute military operations in different parts of the world; and a number of additional agencies that supply and service the military.

FIGURE 12.1 | The Executive Branch of the Federal Government

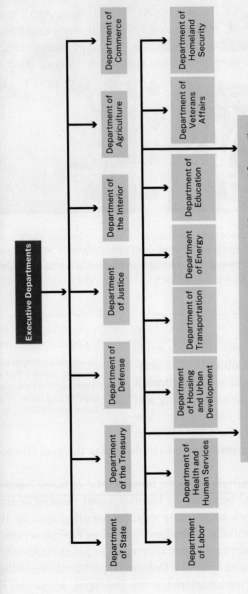

Executive Departments

Department of State

Department of the Treasury

Department of Defense

Department of Justice

Department of the Interior

Department of Agriculture

Department of Commerce

Department of Labor

Department of Health and Human Services

Department of Housing and Urban Development

Department of Transportation

Department of Energy

Department of Education

Department of Veterans Affairs

Department of Homeland Security

Selected Independent Administrations, Commissions, and Government Corporations

Amtrak
Central Intelligence Agency
Consumer Financial Protection Bureau
Consumer Product Safety Commission
Environmental Protection Agency
Equal Employment Opportunity Commission
Federal Communications Commission
Federal Deposit Insurance Corporation
Federal Election Commission

Federal Maritime Commission
Federal Reserve System
Federal Trade Commission
General Services Administration
National Aeronautics and Space Administration
National Endowment for the Arts
National Labor Relations Board
Office of Personnel Management

Office of the Director of National Intelligence
Peace Corps
Postal Regulatory Commission
Securities and Exchange Commission
Small Business Administration
Social Security Administration
Tennessee Valley Authority
U.S. Agency for International Development
U.S. Postal Service

While the State and Defense Departments confront threats from outside the nation, the Department of Homeland Security (DHS) has responsibility for maintaining domestic security, and was created after the September 11, 2001, terrorist attacks to reorganize existing agencies and expand their mission from fighting crime to preventing terrorism as well. The antiterrorism mandate requires the DHS to integrate information from intelligence agencies and law enforcement to protect the nation. The DHS is also responsible for securing the nation's borders; administering and enforcing its immigration laws; addressing cybersecurity and energy security issues; running the Secret Service, which protects federal officials; administering disaster relief through FEMA; and any number of other responsibilities, from running the national flood insurance program to coordinating the national health security response to infectious-disease outbreaks and natural disasters with HHS.[17] Little wonder that the Government Accountability Office (GAO)—an agency that works for Congress as a "watchdog" over executive branch functions, as we will see later—has issued hundreds of recommendations for managerial improvements over the DHS's two-decade history.[18]

Yet other federal agencies work to maintain a strong economy. The Treasury Department collects taxes through the Internal Revenue Service (IRS), manages the national debt, prints currency, and performs economic policy analysis. The Federal Reserve System (called the Fed) is the nation's key monetary agency and is headed by the Federal Reserve Board. The Fed has authority over the interest rates and lending activities of the nation's most important banks. It was established by Congress in

The president regularly meets with the Cabinet to discuss the affairs of each department or agency. Here, President Biden delivers remarks before beginning a Cabinet meeting.

HOW TO

Apply for a Federal Job

ANTHONY MARUCCI, DIRECTOR OF COMMUNICATIONS AT THE OFFICE OF PERSONNEL MANAGEMENT

The federal government employs a couple of million people, mostly outside of Washington, D.C. Now that you see the wide variety of responsibilities the federal government carries out, perhaps you would like to apply your skills and knowledge to an issue that you care about and that the federal government tackles. Anthony Marucci gave us these tips for getting a job in the federal government:

1 **Where can I look for a job in the federal government?** Look at USAJobs (www.usajobs.gov), the official federal government portal. You can also look at the "employment" or "careers" section of any government agency website.

2 **Can I find a job in the federal government outside of Washington, D.C.?** Yes. You should set up a profile on USAJobs, where you can add work preferences such as desired work location. This and other preferences you include on your profile will refine and improve your results when searching for jobs on USAJobs.

3 **How can I tell if I'm qualified?** Read the entire job announcement and focus on the "critical information" in three key sections: Duties and Qualifications, How to Apply, and How You Will Be Evaluated. You will be able to see the level and amount of experience, education, and training needed.

4 **What should I include on my résumé?** Show how your skills and experiences meet the qualifications and requirements listed in the job announcement in order to be considered. List your experiences, beginning with the most recent, and include dates, hours, level of experience, and examples of your activities and accomplishments. The best examples use numbers to highlight your accomplishments, such as "Managed a student organization budget of more than $7,000" or "Wrote 25 news releases in a three-week period under daily deadlines." Also, provide greater detail for experiences that are relevant to the job for which you are applying. And be sure to use the key terms in the job listing: if the qualifications section says you need experience with MS Project you need to use the words "MS Project" in your résumé. You should customize your résumé for each job to which you apply.

5 **Will I have to take a civil service exam?** Federal government hiring in the civil service positions in the executive branch, with some exceptions, must be done through a competitive process. This typically means an evaluation of the individual's education and experience, and/or an evaluation of other attributes necessary for successful performance in the position to be filled. In some cases the process may also consist of a written test.

6 **Can I apply for more than one position?** Yes, you can apply for multiple jobs at USAJobs, but note that you must apply for each under the specific job announcement. One key thing to remember (and this is likely true for any job to which you apply): hiring agencies often receive dozens or even hundreds of résumés for certain positions, so you want to look at your résumé and ask, "Can a hiring manager see my main credentials within 10 to 15 seconds? Does critical information jump off the page? Do I effectively sell myself on the top quarter of the first page?" Working for the federal government can be rewarding. As with pursuing any job, it can take time. So if you do apply, be patient and persistent. Best of luck!

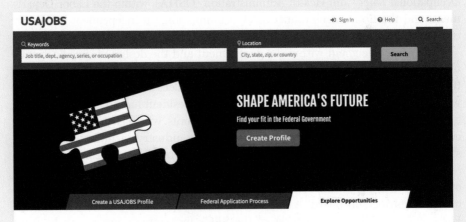

1913 as a clearinghouse for adjusting the supply of money and credit to the needs of commerce and industry in different parts of the country. Many other agencies work to strengthen other parts of the economy, for example the Agriculture Department, which disseminates information on effective farming practices; the Transportation Department, which promotes economic growth by overseeing the nation's highway and air traffic systems; and the Commerce Department, whose Small Business Administration provides loans and technical assistance to small businesses across the country.

Another set of agencies promotes citizen well-being. The Department of Health and Human Services includes the National Institutes of Health (NIH), which conducts cutting-edge biomedical research; the FDA, which monitors the safety and efficacy of human and veterinary drugs, cosmetics, and the nation's food supply; the CDC, which protects public health and safety; and the Medicaid and Medicare programs, which provide health insurance to low-income and elderly Americans. The Department of Agriculture's Food and Nutrition Service administers the federal school-lunch program and Supplemental Nutrition Assistance Program (SNAP, formerly known as food stamps). The Interior Department's National Park Service maintains natural areas for the public to enjoy. Yet other agencies, such as the FDA, within HHS; the Occupational Safety and Health Administration (OSHA), within the Labor Department; and the Consumer Product Safety Commission, an independent regulatory commission, make rules to protect the public's health and welfare.

Agencies' placement within the government and the design of specific agency functions often reflect politicians' attempts to shape agency behavior and jurisdiction. Most agencies are created by Congress, which decides whether to locate them within the executive branch or outside of it. The president has greater control over organizations contained within executive departments, whereas independent agencies, such as the SEC, which oversees the security industry, including the nation's stock exchanges, have more freedom from both the president and Congress.

In creating agencies, Congress also decides whether they will be headed by one person (who reports to the president, if the agency is in the executive branch) or by a multiperson board. A board structure allows for bipartisan leadership. For example, no more than three of the SEC's five commissioners can be from the same political party. Boards may also have members with staggered terms of office, which reduces the power of any one president to name the entire agency leadership. Other structural features can increase independence as well, for example the fact that the president appoints SEC commissioners but cannot fire them. Independent agencies and regulatory commissions are meant to be relatively insulated from politics, hence their location outside of the executive departments, but

WHO ARE AMERICANS?

Who Are Bureaucrats?

Bureaucrats are often stereotyped as being more concerned with procedure and forms than with helping people. But the reality is that the millions of executive branch employees that work in agencies in D.C. and around the country are essential to keeping America running smoothly. Bureaucrats manage everything from national security and veterans' services to providing help for needy families and ensuring that Americans have clean and safe drinking water. But who are bureaucrats? How is the bureaucracy similar to the American population? How is it different?

Executive Branch Employees, 2019

Gender
- Women
- Men

U.S. population: 51% / 49%
Executive branch: 43% / 57%

Race/Ethnicity
- White
- Black
- Latino
- Asian

U.S. population: 60% / 13% / 19% / 6%
Executive branch: 62% / 19% / 9% / 6%

Education
- Less than high school
- High school degree
- Some college
- College degree
- Postgraduate degree

U.S. population: 11% / 27% / 29% / 20% / 13%
Executive branch: 1% / 24% / 19% / 28% / 28%

Military service
- Yes
- No

U.S. population: 7% / 93%
Executive branch: 31% / 69%

Location of executive branch employees, 2019

Washington, D.C., area
279,092
15%

Other
1,872,141
85%

SOURCE: American Community Survey 1-Year Estimates, www.census.gov/programs-surveys/acs (accessed 11/11/21); Office of Personnel Management, www.opm.gov (accessed 11/11/21).

escaping politics entirely is impossible. Since presidents appoint agency heads or commissioners, they may do so on the basis of party loyalty. Also, the budgets of most such agencies are proposed by the president and approved by Congress, and agencies must therefore be responsive to congressional oversight.

Check your understanding

1. How do bureaucrats exercise influence over public policies?

   a) Bureaucrats use fire alarm oversight to evaluate the effectiveness of new laws and propose modifications when needed.

   b) Bureaucrats formally make amendments to laws under consideration before Congress.

   c) Bureaucrats make rules and implement laws, filling in details of legislation passed by Congress.

   d) Bureaucrats use the regulatory capture process in which an agency lobbies Congress for more funding.

2. Which of the following statements about the political control of bureaucratic agencies is correct?

   a) All bureaucratic agencies are completely insulated from politics since employees cannot be removed without cause.

   b) All bureaucratic agencies are subject to the same political pressures since they are all appointed and controlled by the president.

   c) Agencies that are headed by a board face greater political pressures of the president and Congress since there are multiple constituencies they must serve, compared to agencies with a single head who can more readily resist political pressures.

   d) Agencies within the executive are subject to control by the president and Congress, whereas independent agencies that require bipartisan commissioners who cannot be fired by the president are more insulated.

Who Are Federal Bureaucrats?

Explain civil service hiring, political appointments, and the use of federal contracting

The federal government is most effective when well-qualified individuals fill the roles in the federal workforce. (This was the goal of reforms to the civil service implemented several times in American history.) The bureaucracy is also charged with fulfilling the president's agenda, hence the placement of political appointees with presidential or party ties in executive branch leadership positions. But because Americans tend to be sensitive to the size of government, presidents have met increasing demands on the federal government by contracting some government responsibilities to private companies.

Populating the Bureaucracy

The vast majority of bureaucrats are members of the "civil service" and work under the **merit system** created by the Pendleton Civil Service Reform Act of 1883. With this act, the federal government required bureaucratic personnel to be qualified for the jobs to which they were hired. The goal was to end the "spoils system" that dominated federal hiring during the 1800s and awarded government jobs based on political connections and support for the political party in office. The Pendleton Act replaced such patronage with a system of competitive examinations through which the very best candidates were to be hired for every job.

As a further safeguard against political interference, merit-system employees were given legal protection against being fired without a show of cause. The objective of this job protection was to shield bureaucracy from political interference while upgrading performance. The 1883 civil service reform was updated by the Civil Service Reform Act of 1978, which set up new processes to ensure that the recruitment and promotion of civil servants remained merit based rather than political. The 1978 act created the Merit Systems Protection Board to defend competitive and merit-based recruitment and promotion of civil servants from efforts to make these personnel policies more political. The Federal Labor Relations Authority was set up to administer collective bargaining and to address individual personnel grievances. A third new agency, the Office of Personnel Management, was created to manage the recruiting, testing, and training of federal employees, as well as their retirement system.[19]

At the higher levels of government agencies are several thousand **political appointees**, who fill posts as Cabinet secretaries and assistant secretaries and who are not part of the civil service. Of the 4,000-plus political appointees, just over 1,000 require Senate confirmation. Many political appointees have ties to the president or the president's party—they may have worked on or donated to the president's campaign, for example—and serve to advance the president's agenda through agency action. Some critics see appointees as a modern form of patronage and believe there are too many, while others view them as an important part of the transition from campaigning to governance.[20] Presidents also often use Cabinet secretary nominations—the handful of appointed positions at the very top of the bureaucracy, which are the most visible to the public—to make political statements or to send messages about their style of management or expectations for government. For example, President Obama, the nation's first Black president,

merit system a product of civil service reform, in which appointees to positions in public bureaucracies must objectively be deemed qualified for those positions

political appointees the presidentially appointed layer of the bureaucracy on top of the civil service

nominated 7 women and 10 people of color to his first Cabinet. Both President George W. Bush (the first president with an MBA) and President Trump came from business backgrounds and nominated many business leaders to their Cabinets.

In addition to political appointees, in many agencies there are top executives who are members of the **Senior Executive Service (SES)**, a top management rank for career civil servants—and sometimes individuals from outside of government. The SES was created by the 1978 civil service reform and intended to foster "public management" as a profession. For career bureaucrats, moving to the SES means losing their civil service protections, but it also provides an opportunity to pursue a top position. The SES also provides the president with an additional layer of high-level managers to select beyond the political appointees.

Size of the Bureaucracy

The size of the federal service has been a subject of political contention for decades. Particularly in the post-Watergate era of low trust in government, politicians from both parties, from Reagan to Clinton, have asserted that the federal government is too big. Bill Clinton's vice president, Al Gore, headed a National Performance Review during the 1990s, which sought to reduce paperwork, improve communications across agencies, streamline government purchasing procedures, and cut the federal workforce; by 2000 the number of federal jobs had fallen by more than 400,000.[21] President Barack Obama struck a different note in his first inaugural address, saying, "The question we ask today is not whether our government is too big or too small, but whether it works."[22] President Trump's first budget proposed major decreases in federal departments outside of Defense and Homeland Security. Under President Trump, some agencies were reorganized or had positions relocated, such as the relocation of two Department of Agriculture research groups from Washington, D.C., to Kansas City, which reduced the workforce when over half of the researchers declined to move.[23]

Despite fears of bureaucratic growth getting out of hand—or perhaps because of such fears—the federal service has shrunk in size both absolutely and relative to the total population. The number of civil federal employees has fallen from its postwar peak of just over 3 million in the late 1980s to 2.8 million in 2019, while the number of military personnel has fallen from 3.6 million to 1.3 million over the same period.[24] As a percentage of the total workforce, federal employment has declined since the 1950s, as Figure 12.2 indicates.

While the federal bureaucracy has decreased in size, both state and local government employment and government contracting have grown. State and local civil service employment has increased from about 6.5 percent of the country's workforce in 1950 to nearly 13 percent in 2020.[25] Federal employment, in contrast, exceeded 6 percent of the workforce only during World War II, and almost all of that temporary growth was military.

Since the 1950s, the ratio of federal employment to the total workforce has gradually declined. Today, federal employees make up less than 2 percent of the total workforce in the United States. Even at the federal bureaucracy's height, federal employees made up less than 5 percent. What do these numbers suggest about the size of the federal government today?

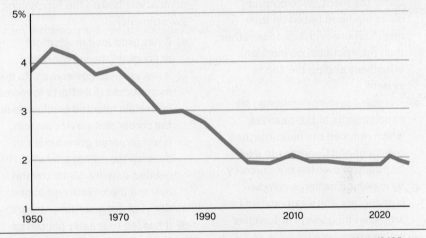

SOURCES: Office of Personnel Management, "Executive Branch Civilian Employment since 1940," www .opm.gov (accessed 4/24/20); United States Postal Service, "Number of Postal Employees since 1926," https://about.usps.com/who-we-are/postal-history/employees-since-1926.pdf (accessed 4/24/20).

Private Contracting

The number of federal contractors has also grown and exceeds the number of federal employees. Private contractors of all types provide an enormous range of goods and services, from nonprofit firms that run Head Start day-care centers, to military contractors that build fighter jets, to universities that conduct government-funded basic science research. **Privatization** downsizes the government in that the workers providing the service are no longer counted as part of the government bureaucracy—and pointing to a small federal government has appealed to both Republican and Democratic elected officials over the past several decades. Contracting may or may not lead to reduced costs, depending on the performance of the contractors and the competitiveness of the bidding process. And while contracting reduces the size of the federal workforce, it also requires a new role for government, to manage and oversee the private companies carrying out government work.[26] Critics of contracting worry that oversight and accountability are insufficient and that the emphasis on contracting has detracted from efforts to recruit and retain talented employees in the career civil service itself.[27]

privatization the process by which a formerly public service becomes a service provided by a private company but paid for by the government

Check your understanding

3. How did the merit system established by the Pendleton Civil Service Reform Act change the federal bureaucracy?

   a) Using the merit system, candidates are hired based on their qualifications and expertise rather than their political connections, effectively ending the spoils system.

   b) The merit system eliminated all appointments of bureaucrats, which reduced the ability of the president and Congress to exercise control over the bureaucracy.

   c) By making it easier to remove bureaucrats, the merit system has produced high levels of turnover within agencies.

   d) The merit system has concentrated most of the workforce of the federal bureaucracy in Washington, D.C.

4. What effect has the rise in private contractors had on the functioning of government?

   a) It has produced much more accountability and oversight.

   b) It has enabled government to make more successful efforts to recruit and retain talented employees in the career civil service system.

   c) It has required government to develop the managerial expertise needed to write contracts and oversee the private companies carrying out government work.

   d) It has led to greater perceived legitimacy of government.

Managing the Bureaucracy

Explain how the president, Congress, and the judiciary try to manage the bureaucracy

By their very nature, bureaucracies pose challenges to democratic governance. Although they provide the expertise needed to implement the public will, they can also become entrenched organizations that serve their own interests. The challenge is to take advantage of the bureaucracy's strengths while making it accountable to the demands of democratic politics and representative government, including the president and Congress.

The word *bureaucracy* does not appear in the Constitution, but the bureaucracy has constitutional roots nonetheless. Article II, Section 2, gives the president the power to nominate with the "Advice and Consent of the Senate" the officers of the United States. It also tells the president to "require the Opinion, in writing, of the principal Officer in each of the executive Departments, upon any subject relating to the duties of their respective Offices." These sections establish the existence of executive departments whose heads are nominated by the president and confirmed by the Senate and which are tasked with giving the president advice. Article II, Section 3, then gives the president broad executive powers to "take Care that the

Laws be faithfully executed," making the president the administrator in chief. The Constitution thus lays the groundwork for a federal bureaucracy that carries out the duties of government under the president with congressional oversight.

This structure raises two ongoing questions for American governance. One concerns whether the amount of control the democratically elected president and Congress have over the unelected bureaucracy is sufficient. The other concerns relations between the president and Congress: both have levers of control over the bureaucracy—one of the many ways in which the Constitution creates what political scientist Richard Neustadt termed "separated institutions sharing powers"[28]—and this framework ensures that the president and Congress will disagree at times about bureaucratic action. Much of the controversy that we observe in federal government is a result of the push-and-pull between the president and Congress that the constitutional framework makes inevitable.

The President as Chief Executive

The Constitution charges the president with seeing that the laws are faithfully executed. The president heads the federal government, which is the largest employer in the country and the largest purchaser of goods and services in the world.[29] As the CEO of this enormous organization, the president may have goals associated with both management (striving for efficiency) and control (shaping policy outcomes). Presidents have several tools at their disposal.

One major tool of bureaucratic control that presidents possess is appointment power over the political appointees atop the career civil service. Presidents have an incentive to appoint officials who are loyal to them and who they believe are likely to pursue their policy agendas. And such appointments require Senate approval, as the Constitution gives both the president and the Congress mechanisms for controlling the bureaucracy. The Senate rarely rejects nominees; more commonly, if it is clear that Senate support is weak, a president will withdraw a nominee before the confirmation vote. For example, Neera Tanden withdrew her nomination to lead President Biden's Office of Management and Budget after several senators

Presidential appointments can be controversial. Neera Tanden (left), President Biden's nominee for director of the Office of Management and Budget (OMB), had to withdraw her nomination because some senators objected to tweets she made about President Trump. Biden then named Shalanda Young (right, with hand raised) as acting director of OMB.

objected to tweets she issued while head of the Center for American Progress, an economic think tank, criticizing President Trump and some members of Congress.[30]

Another instrument of presidential control over the bureaucracy is the Executive Office of the President (EOP). The EOP was established during the presidency of Franklin Roosevelt, when the rapid growth of the national government led a Committee on Administrative Management to note in 1937, "The president needs help." The EOP includes key staffs reporting directly to the president on budgetary, military, and economic policies, such as the National Security Council and the Council of Economic Advisers. The EOP is usually considered the component of the bureaucracy most responsive to the presidency because it has the highest share of political appointees and because Congress gives the president greater control over its structure.[31]

One of the most important EOP agencies is the **Office of Management and Budget (OMB)**. All federal rules go through OMB. OMB also collects the budgets for all government agencies, allowing presidents to emphasize their own priorities and policy goals in the federal budget submitted annually to Congress. The centralization of these regulatory and budgetary functions is another indicator of increased presidential power relative to Congress.

In addition to making political appointments at the top of the bureaucracy, presidents may also appoint "policy czars"—or task forces—with responsibilities for addressing a specific policy need, often working across agencies. President Roosevelt was the first to appoint policy czars; Presidents G. W. Bush and Obama each had dozens in their administrations. President Trump appointed a coronavirus pandemic task force in late January 2020, while President Biden created task forces on Covid-19 health equity and supply chain disruptions, climate, artificial intelligence research, and other topics.[32] Presidents often appoint czars to signal responsiveness to some acute policy problem. There have been multiple illicit-drug czars, several AIDS czars, a car czar (who managed the auto industry bailout during the Great Recession), an Ebola czar (who managed the response to an outbreak in 2014), an Asian carp czar, cybersecurity czars, and so on. These advisers report directly to the president and do not require Senate confirmation, but they also lack budget authority and have to rely on the formal departments and agencies to act.[33]

Although the president is ostensibly in charge of the federal bureaucracy and has the tools of control just discussed, influence over the bureaucracy remains a challenge. Sometimes department secretaries pursue their own agendas, or become advocates for the agency itself rather than the president's agenda. Sometimes presidential appointees turn out to be poor managers, and their agency is unable to execute its duties optimally.[34] Interest groups also have ongoing relationships with agencies and may try to shape agency agendas, interfering with presidential preferences (some critics say, for example, that the pharmaceutical industry has too much influence over its regulatory agency, the FDA).[35] One reason that bureaucratic action may seem inefficient is that the bureaucracy answers to many players, such as Congress, not just to the president.

Congressional Control

The Constitution gives Congress several tools of control over the bureaucracy as it interprets and implements the laws Congress has passed. Most important, Congress approves agencies' annual funding. At hearings on appropriations, members of Congress can evaluate agency performance and may reduce funding if they are not satisfied. Agencies wish to avoid this fate and so take congressional opinion—and by extension public opinion—into account as they implement programs. In addition, the Senate approves presidential nominations to the top levels of the executive agencies.

Like the president, Congress can change the location or structure of agencies, creating new ones or reorganizing policy responsibilities across existing agencies in an effort to shape agency behavior or to reduce presidential control. For example, Congress may choose to place a regulatory body or commission outside of the 15 executive departments. Or it can designate a multimember board rather than a single person to head an agency, which limits presidential control by allowing for a partisan-balance requirement (members have to come from both parties, not just the president's), or staggered terms of office (so that a president cannot replace all board members at once). Fixed terms of office, especially long ones, also diminish presidential control (members of the Board of Governors of the Federal Reserve serve 14-year terms, for example, far longer than a president). And one of the most important ways Congress can check presidential control of the bureaucracy is by limiting the president's ability to *remove* agency officials. In many instances the congressional statutes creating or reorganizing agencies do not allow presidents to remove officials except "for cause," such as neglect of duty or wrongdoing, not merely for policy disagreements.

Congress can also make political or policy statements with its organizational choices. For example, Congress first created the Department of Health, Education, and Welfare in 1953. Then, 25 years later, during the Carter administration, Congress divided the agency into the Department of Health and Human Services and the Department of Education to underscore the federal role in education. When Congress placed the Transportation Security Administration (TSA), in charge of airport security, in the Department of Homeland Security rather than the Department of Transportation, it signaled that domestic security concerns were to be a more central aspect of the administration's mission than facilitating transportation, as those who have stood in long TSA lines at airports can attest.[36]

Congress can also hold the bureaucracy accountable through **oversight**. Congressional committees and subcommittees have jurisdictions roughly parallel to the departments and agencies in the executive branch, and members of Congress who sit on these committees can develop expertise in these policy areas. For example, both the House and the Senate have Agriculture Committees and subcommittees that oversee the Department of Agriculture.

The most visible indication of Congress's oversight efforts is the use of public hearings, before which bureaucrats and other witnesses are summoned to discuss and defend agency budgets and decisions. Congress can also pass laws requiring agencies to submit regular reports on their

oversight the effort by Congress, through hearings, investigations, and other techniques, to exercise control over the activities of executive agencies activities and can create advisory committees to make recommendations to agencies and to help Congress oversee them. For example, the FDA has several dozen advisory committees consisting of physicians, scientists, statisticians, pharmaceutical industry representatives, and members of the public, including an FDA Patient Representative, who provide independent advice on scientific and policy questions concerning the safety and effectiveness of new medical and drug therapies.[37]

In recent years, there appears to be less **"police patrol" oversight**—regular or even anticipatory hearings on agency operations—and more **"fire alarm" oversight** prompted by media attention or advocacy group complaints. For example, in early 2021, media reports of studies showing far higher Covid-19 death rates in nursing homes with large shares of nonwhite residents, compared to those with more White residents, prompted hearings by the Senate Finance Committee to investigate both the practices of nursing home operators and the adequacy of regulatory efforts by the Centers for Medicare and Medicaid Services, the federal agency that oversees these facilities.[38]

As a result, Congress has created additional sources of oversight. The Inspector General Act of 1978 established **inspectors general (IGs)**, which are nonpartisan, independent organizations now located in most agencies, which investigate agency activities on Congress's behalf. IGs audit agency operations to uncover cases of waste, fraud, or misconduct. They alert agency heads to any severe problems, and the agency head must then send the IG's report, along with comments and corrective plans, to Congress. Inspectors general of the Cabinet-level agencies are appointed by the president and approved by the Senate, another example of shared control over the bureaucracy; in other federal agencies, the agency head appoints the IG. In both cases, agency heads cannot interfere with IG audits or investigations. On several occasions, President Trump exerted control over inspectors general. For example, during the coronavirus pandemic, he replaced a deputy inspector general in HHS whose report revealed extensive supply shortages at hospitals, and he blocked a Defense Department inspector general from heading a new Pandemic Response Accountability Committee to oversee the government's coronavirus relief spending. Critics alleged that while the president did have the authority to remove these officials, he did so in an effort to avoid transparency and congressional oversight.[39]

Another source of oversight involves the three large agencies Congress created for itself to research the executive branch: the Government Accountability Office (GAO), the Congressional Research Service (CRS), and the Congressional Budget Office (CBO). These organizations provide information independent from what Congress gets from the executive branch. The GAO is the nation's "supreme audit institution," providing Congress with information about how tax dollars are spent and how the government could be made more efficient.[40] The CRS, part of the Library of Congress, provides expert analysis to congressional committees and members of Congress on policy issues. The CRS responds to inquiries from individual congresspeople; creates tailored memos, briefings, and consultations; runs seminars and workshops; and provides congressional testimony.[41] And the CBO provides independent analyses of budgetary and economic issues to assist Congress in its budget process, for example estimating the cost of proposed legislation.[42]

Presidential–Congressional Struggle for Bureaucratic Control: A Case Study

A look at the birth of a new agency, the Consumer Financial Protection Bureau (CFPB), helps illustrate the struggle between the president and Congress over the bureaucracy. The financial crisis that began in 2007 had its roots in the collapse of the housing market. Many borrowers had taken on home mortgages that were difficult to understand and unaffordable, and when they could no longer pay, they lost their homes to foreclosure, which in turn caused their neighbors' home values to fall. Critics of this system believed there were insufficient consumer protections in place and proposed creating the CFPB. This new agency would address consumer complaints and regulate banks, credit unions, payday lenders, debt collectors, and other firms that provide consumer financial products and services such as mortgages, credit cards, and student loans. In 2010, Congress passed the Dodd-Frank Wall Street Reform and Consumer Protection Act, which imposed new banking regulations and also created the CFPB.[43]

President Obama and congressional Republicans disagreed about the structure, funding, and location of the CFPB. The 2010 legislation made the CFPB an independent agency located inside the Federal Reserve System, with automatic funding based on a fixed percentage of the Fed's operating expenses and with a

The Consumer Financial Protection Bureau is an agency created by President Obama under the Department of the Treasury. Here, President Obama, with Timothy Geithner, Treasury secretary at the time, nominates Elizabeth Warren as its head (although congressional Republicans later blocked the nomination).

single director appointed by the president with the consent of the Senate. Congressional Republicans argued that the CFPB's funding should be annually appropriated by Congress instead, obviously increasing Congress's influence over the agency, and that it should be headed by a multimember board rather than a single person, diminishing any president's influence over the agency's leadership. Proponents argued that the automatic funding and the location inside the Fed, which is already an independent institution, were necessary to give the CFPB independence from political forces and the muscle it needed to help consumers confronting powerful financial institutions. They felt Senate consent for the director was a sufficient check on the president's influence.

Disagreements over the CFPB's design have continued ever since. The idea for the agency came from Massachusetts senator and 2020 Democratic presidential candidate Elizabeth Warren, back when she was a law professor studying bankruptcy. President Obama had planned to appoint her the first head of the agency but, in the face of Republican opposition, selected former Ohio attorney general and treasurer Richard Cordray. But that nomination was held up by Senate Republicans, who continued to urge a multimember board structure. (Cordray became head in a recess appointment.) Later, President Trump appointed Mick Mulvaney as the acting head of the agency. As a member of Congress, Mulvaney had proposed legislation eliminating the CFPB. After some members of the CFPB's consumer advisory board criticized him in 2018, Mulvaney had the entire 25-member board removed. Controversy over the CFPB's structure and role continues.

Judicial Oversight

The third branch of government serves an important role as well. The bureaucracy's decisions are subject to judicial review; the *Marbury v. Madison* decision in 1803 posited that the Supreme Court has final authority to judge the constitutionality of executive actions, whether taken by the president or the bureaucracy. The courts also settle disputes between Congress and executive agencies about the interpretations of laws. In addition, they monitor the implementation of laws by creating an arena in which individuals or groups who are negatively affected by a regulation or program can bring lawsuits.

Whistleblowing

Sometimes a form of control comes from within bureaucratic agencies themselves. **Whistleblowers** are employees who report wrongdoing within public or private organizations, including federal agencies. Congress passed the Whistleblower Protection Act in 1989 to protect federal employees reporting mismanagement or corruption from punishment by their colleagues or superiors. In 2019 a whistleblower from the U.S. intelligence community filed a complaint about a phone call between President Trump and the president of Ukraine in which the whistleblower feared that the president was "using the power of his office to solicit interference from a foreign country in the 2020 U.S. election," including "pressuring a foreign country

whistleblowers employees who report wrongdoing in public or private organizations, including federal agencies

to investigate one of the president's main domestic political rivals," Joe Biden and his son Hunter Biden.[44] The whistleblower complaint prompted an impeachment investigation by the House Democrats that began in fall 2019.

Citizen Oversight

The Freedom of Information Act of 1966 (FOIA) provides ordinary citizens and journalists the right to request records from any federal agency. Congress's intent in passing the law was to increase bureaucratic transparency and executive branch oversight.[45] Agencies must comply with the requests unless they fall under one of nine exemptions, which concern issues such as personal privacy, national security, or law enforcement, or unless disclosure of the information is prohibited by another federal law. Agencies are required by law to produce records within 20 days, but frequently there are backlogs. Agencies can also disclose portions rather than entire records.

FOIA requests sometimes prompt congressional oversight and investigation when agency misbehavior is revealed. In 2017, a *USA Today* story revealed that the CDC, an agency within the Department of Health and Human Services that conducts research and provides information to protect people from health threats, had tried to keep secret a series of accidents from 2013 to 2015 involving dangerous pathogens such as anthrax and Ebola. The article was based on heavily redacted lab incident reports that a reporter had obtained through a FOIA request. After the article was published, the House Committee on Energy and Commerce sent a letter to the director of the CDC stating that "the details in the article seem to indicate that most, if not all, of these incidents were not disclosed to the Committee," and demanding that the CDC turn over the unredacted reports.[46]

The Difficulties of Bureaucratic Control

Controlling the bureaucracy is difficult. On the one hand, having a federal branch populated by experts who implement laws and issue regulations in an impartial, uniform manner, with minimal political interference, is necessary to make the government operate as efficiently and responsibly as possible. On the other hand, bureaucrats may pursue their own goals rather than those of the president, who oversees the bureaucracy, or Congress, which writes the laws the bureaucracy implements. The tools of control are imperfect.

In addition, there are sometimes outright bureaucratic failures. In 2014 a waiting-list scandal rocked the Veterans Health Administration (VHA), the organization within the Veterans Administration (VA) that provides health care to military veterans. Some VHA hospitals that had not met the target of providing appointments for veterans within 14 days had created unofficial lists to make their waiting times look better. A VA audit and FBI investigation found that over 120,000 veterans were left waiting or never got appointments. In response, VA secretary Eric Shinseki resigned, and Congress passed and President Obama signed legislation that added funding, allowed some veterans to get private health care at government expense, and gave the VA secretary increased authority to fire poorly performing managers.[47]

Bureaucracies can also be subject to **regulatory capture**. This occurs when an agency, rather than acting in the public interest, becomes too favorable toward

regulatory capture a form of government failure in which regulatory agencies become too sympathetic to interests or businesses they are supposed to regulate

the organized interests or corporations it is supposed to be regulating. Critics point to two 737 Max airliner crashes in 2018 and 2019, which killed nearly 400 people, as a classic example of regulatory capture, in which the Federal Aviation Administration (FAA) allowed the Boeing Corporation to handle key aspects of safety assessments needed to get the new airliner model approved for commercial service. The FAA approved Boeing's safety analysis, which was later revealed to have critical lapses.[48]

Many presidents have proposed or enacted broad-based reorganization schemes to enhance their control, increase bureaucratic efficiency, or to respond to bureaucratic failures. The September 11, 2001, terrorist attacks not only prompted the creation of the Department of Homeland Security in 2002, as we have seen, but also the creation of the Office of the Director of National Intelligence (DNI) in 2004. With that reform, the DNI became the head of the intelligence community, a role previously played by the director of the CIA. Similarly, both the savings-and-loan crisis of the 1980s and the financial crisis of 2007–09 prompted reorganized or new entities regulating the financial industry.[49]

Check your understanding

5. While the bureaucracy's important role in rule making and implementation of public policies often raises concerns of accountability, how do Congress and the president exercise control over the bureaucracy?

   a) by using their sole appointment and removal power over all agencies
   b) through the appointment and confirmation of high-level bureaucrats, the congressional oversight process, and the budgetary process
   c) by closing the open comment sessions to the public
   d) through the removal of inspectors general from agencies

6. Ideally, agencies implement laws and issue regulations in an impartial and uniform manner, but sometimes agencies become too favorable toward the organized interests or corporations they are charged with regulating (known as regulatory capture). How can Congress and the president address issues like regulatory capture or other types of failures of bureaucratic agencies?

   a) Presidents and Congress can fire agency heads and replace agency employees hired through the civil service system with political appointees to regain control.
   b) Presidents and Congress can ban organized interests from lobbying federal agencies to ensure they do not receive special treatment.
   c) Presidents and Congress can turn over the regulatory authority to industries instead of relying on bureaucratic agencies.
   d) Presidents and Congress can propose extensive reorganization to increase their control or to increase bureaucratic efficiency.

WHAT DO YOU THINK?

THE BUREAUCRACY

Americans' views about the federal government bureaucracy present something of a paradox. On the one hand, the public expresses dislike for "big government," exemplified by bureaucracy. From this perspective, the federal government is too large, inherently wasteful, and at odds with individual freedom. On the other hand, Americans support many government programs and have high expectations for government. Bureaucracies try to balance these competing imperatives but may undermine one benefit for citizens in trying to maximize another. PFAS chemicals help with firefighting, furniture manufacturing, food packaging, and many other processes. Yet we now know they are also carcinogenic. Bureaucracies may lack the information they need to carry out their missions, or, with information in hand, can lack the statutory permission to take the actions they deem necessary to protect the public.

- Some argue that Americans' liberties are threatened when the bureaucracy grows too large, while others contend that a bureaucracy with too few resources is the real threat. What do you think Hope Grosse and Joanne Stanton, featured at the beginning of this chapter, would say?

- Are there ways in which you have benefited from bureaucratic action, or been harmed by it? What types of bureaucratic activity are most noticeable to you, and what types are most hidden?

- What kinds of reforms would make the bureaucracy more accountable to the public? What reforms do you think Hope Grosse and Joanne Stanton would advocate?

Use 🐰 **INQUIZITIVE** *to help you study and master this material.*

13

WHAT GOVERNMENT DOES & WHY IT MATTERS

Karina Pichardo's 11-year-old daughter Miranda "loves going to school." In the beginning of 2021, Miranda's school district in Houston, Texas, adopted a mask requirement because of the coronavirus pandemic. Karina was relieved. Because Miranda has Down syndrome and is at higher risk for Covid-19, the mask mandate allowed her to attend school safely.[1]

In July 2021, however, Texas governor Greg Abbott issued an executive order banning local officials, including school authorities, from requiring face masks. When they returned at the end of the summer, students would "not be forced by government or by schools to wear masks in school," Abbott said. "They can by parental choice wear a mask, but there will be no government mandate requiring masks."

Although in the governor's view, mask mandates were a violation of "parental rights," for the Pichardo family the executive order meant quite the opposite. When Miranda's school stopped requiring masks, "we had to keep our daughter home so she would be safe,"

The Federal Courts

her mother said. With the help of an advocacy group, Disability Rights Texas, the Pichardos and six other families challenged the ban on mask mandates in court, arguing that it discriminated against students with disabilities by forcing them to stay home from school or risk exposure to the coronavirus. Because the families felt that the governor's ban on school mask mandates violated a 1990 federal law, the Americans with Disabilities Act (ADA), they filed their suit in federal court.

In November 2021, a federal judge ruled in the families' favor. In his decision, he wrote that "the spread of Covid-19 poses an even greater risk for children with special health needs." Because such students "are being denied the benefits of in-person learning on an equal basis as their peers without disabilities" he determined that the ban violates the ADA. Kym Davis Rogers, an attorney for Disability Rights Texas, said, "No student should be forced to make the choice of forfeiting their education or risking their health, and now they won't have to."

The governor vowed to appeal the ruling through the federal court system. The Disability Rights Texas case was decided in the United States District Court for the Western District of Texas, one of 94 federal district courts. Governor Abbott's appeal would next go to the Fifth Circuit Court of Appeals, which covers Texas, Louisiana, and Mississippi. If the case continued, it could be heard by the Supreme Court.

▲ Concerned with the safety of their daughter during the coronavirus pandemic, the Pichardo family, with the help of a disability rights group, went to federal court to challenge Texas's removal of its public school mask mandate.

Every year, approximately 25 million cases are tried in American courts. Sometimes these cases center around intense and controversial issues like mask mandates and the health and safety of children, but often they tackle more mundane questions. Cases can arise from disputes between citizens, from efforts by government agencies to punish wrongdoing, from citizens' efforts to prove that government action—or inaction—has infringed on their rights, and from efforts by interest groups to promote their agendas. Given the contentious issues often in front of them, who sits on the federal courts, and what power the courts wield in the American political system, has become hotly debated.

CHAPTER GOALS

Identify the general types of cases and types of courts in America's legal system (pp. 405–11)

Describe the different levels of federal courts, the expansion of federal court power, and the process of appointing federal judges (pp. 411–18)

Explain the Supreme Court's judicial review of national law (pp. 418–24)

Describe the process by which cases are considered and decided by the Supreme Court (pp. 424–31)

Describe the factors that influence Court decisions (pp. 432–36)

The Legal System Settles Disputes

Identify the general types of cases and types of courts in America's legal system

Originally, a "court" was the place where a monarch ruled. Settling disputes between one's subjects was part of governing. In modern democracies, courts made up of judges and juries have taken over the power to settle conflicts, which they do by hearing the facts on both sides of a case and applying the relevant law or constitutional principle to the facts to decide which side has the stronger argument. Courts have been given the authority to settle disputes not only between citizens but also between citizens and the government itself, where judges and juries must maintain the same impartiality as they do in disputes involving two citizens. This is the essence of the "rule of law": that "the state" and its officials must be judged by the same laws as the citizenry.

Cases and the Law

Court cases in the United States proceed under two broad categories of law: criminal law and civil law.

Cases of **criminal law** are those in which the government charges an individual with violating a statute enacted to protect public health, safety, morals, or welfare. In criminal cases, the government is always the **plaintiff** (the party that brings charges) and alleges that a criminal violation has been committed by a named **defendant**. Most criminal cases arise in state and municipal courts and involve matters ranging from traffic offenses to robbery and murder. However, a large and growing body of federal criminal law deals with matters ranging from tax evasion and mail fraud to acts of terrorism and the sale of narcotics. Defendants found guilty of criminal violations may be fined or sent to jail or prison.

Cases of **civil law** involve disputes among individuals, groups, corporations, and other private entities, or between such litigants and the government, in which no criminal violation is charged. Unlike in criminal cases, the losers in civil cases cannot be incarcerated, although they may be required to pay monetary damages to the winners.

The two most common types of civil cases involve contracts and torts. In a typical contract case, one party—an individual or corporation—charges that it has suffered because of another's violation of an agreement between the two.

criminal law the branch of law that regulates the conduct of individuals, defines crimes, and specifies punishment for proscribed conduct

plaintiff the individual or organization that brings a complaint in court

defendant the one against whom a complaint is brought in a criminal or civil case

civil law the branch of law that deals with disputes that do not involve criminal penalties

In criminal cases, the government charges an individual with violating a statute protecting health, safety, morals, or welfare. Most such cases arise in state and municipal courts. Here, an Illinois county court hears testimony in a murder case.

For example, the Smith Manufacturing Corporation may charge that Jones Distributors failed to honor an agreement to deliver raw materials at a specified time, causing Smith to lose business. Smith asks the court to order Jones to compensate it for the damage it allegedly suffered. In a typical tort case, one individual charges suffering an injury caused by another's negligence or bad conduct.

Another important area of civil law is administrative law, which involves disputes over the jurisdiction, procedures, or authority of administrative agencies. A plaintiff may assert, for example, that an agency did not follow proper procedures when issuing new rules and regulations. A court will then examine the agency's conduct in light of the Administrative Procedure Act, the legislation that governs agency rule making.

In deciding cases, courts apply statutes (laws) and legal **precedents** (prior decisions). Jones Distributors might argue that it was not obliged to fulfill its contract with the Smith Manufacturing Corporation because actions by Smith, such as the failure to make promised payments, constituted fraud under state law. Precedents established in previous cases also guide courts' decisions in new cases. Attorneys for a physician being sued for malpractice might search for prior instances in which courts ruled that actions similar to those of their client did not constitute negligence.

precedent a prior case whose principles are used by judges as the basis for their decision in a present case

If a case involves the actions of the federal government or a state government, a court may also be asked to examine whether the government's conduct was consistent with the Constitution. In a criminal case, for example, defendants might assert that their constitutional rights were violated when the police searched their property. Similarly, in a civil case involving federal or state restrictions on land development, plaintiffs might assert that government actions violated the Fifth Amendment's prohibition against taking private property without just compensation. Thus, both civil and criminal cases may raise questions of constitutional law.

Types of Courts

In the United States, systems of courts have been established both by the federal government and by the governments of the individual states. Both systems have several levels, as shown in Figure 13.1. More than 97 percent of all court cases

FIGURE 13.1 | The U.S. Court System

The state and federal court systems both include several types of courts. The Supreme Court hears appeals from both systems.

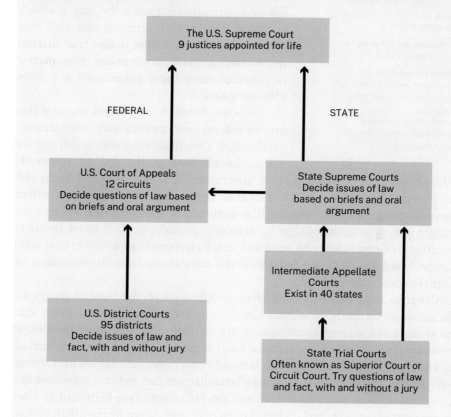

The U.S. Supreme Court
9 justices appointed for life

FEDERAL

STATE

U.S. Court of Appeals
12 circuits
Decide questions of law based
on briefs and oral argument

State Supreme Courts
Decide issues of law
based on briefs and oral
argument

Intermediate Appellate
Courts
Exist in 40 states

U.S. District Courts
95 districts
Decide issues of law and
fact, with and without jury

State Trial Courts
Often known as Superior Court or
Circuit Court. Try questions of law
and fact, with and without a jury

in the United States are heard in state courts. The overwhelming majority of criminal cases, for example, involve violations of state laws prohibiting such actions as murder, robbery, fraud, theft, and assault. If such a case is brought to trial, it will be heard at a state **trial court**, in front of a judge and sometimes a jury, who will determine whether the defendant violated state law. A defendant who is convicted may appeal the conviction to a higher court, such as a state **court of appeals**, and

> **trial court** the first court to hear a criminal or civil case
>
> **court of appeals** a court that hears appeals of trial court decisions
>
> **supreme court** the highest court in a particular state or in the United States; this court primarily serves an appellate function

from there to a court of last resort, usually called the state's **supreme court**. The government is not entitled to appeal if the defendant is found not guilty.

The party filing an appeal, known as an *appellant*, usually must show that the trial court made a legal error in deciding the case. Appeals courts do not

plea bargain a negotiated agreement in a criminal case in which a defendant agrees to plead guilty in return for the state's agreement to reduce the severity of the criminal charge or prison sentence the defendant is facing

jurisdiction the sphere of a court's power and authority

original jurisdiction the authority to initially consider a case; distinguished from appellate jurisdiction, which is the authority to hear appeals from a lower court's decision

hear witnesses or examine additional evidence and will consider new facts only under unusual circumstances. Thus, for example, a physician who loses a malpractice case might appeal on the basis that the trial court misapplied the relevant law or incorrectly instructed the jury. It should be noted that in both criminal and civil matters most cases are settled before trial through negotiated agreements between the parties. In criminal cases these agreements are called **plea bargains**.

Cases are heard in the federal courts if they involve federal laws, treaties with other nations, or the U.S. Constitution; these areas are the official **jurisdiction** of the federal courts. In addition, any case in which the U.S. government is a party is heard in the federal courts. If, for example, an individual is charged with violating a federal criminal statute, such as evading the payment of income taxes, charges are brought before a federal judge by a federal prosecutor. Civil cases involving the citizens of more than one state and in which more than $75,000 is at stake may be heard in either the federal or the state courts, usually depending on the preference of the plaintiff.

Congress has assigned federal court jurisdictions on the basis of geography. The nation is currently, by statute, divided into 94 judicial districts. Every state has at least one district court, and in states with more than one, the district courts are divided by geographic area. Each of the 94 U.S. district courts, including one court for each of three U.S. territories, exercises jurisdiction over federal cases arising within its district. The judicial districts are, in turn, organized into 11 regional circuits, 1 federal circuit, and the D.C. circuit (see Figure 13.2). Each circuit court exercises appellate jurisdiction over cases heard by the district courts within its region.

Article III of the Constitution gives the Supreme Court **original jurisdiction** in a limited variety of cases, including (1) cases between the United States and one of the states, (2) cases between two or more states, (3) cases involving foreign ambassadors or other ministers, and (4) cases brought by one state against citizens of another state or against a foreign country. Courts of original jurisdiction discover the facts in a controversy and create the record on which a judgment is based. In all other federal cases, Article III assigns original jurisdiction to the lower courts that Congress was authorized to establish. The Constitution gives the Supreme Court appellate jurisdiction in all federal cases, but the Constitution also grants Congress the power to regulate this jurisdiction. Almost all cases heard by the Supreme Court today are appealed from lower courts. In courts that have appellate jurisdiction, judges receive cases after the factual record is established by the trial court. Ordinarily, new facts cannot be presented before appellate courts.

FIGURE 13.2 | Federal Appellate Court Circuits

The 94 federal district courts are organized into 12 regional circuits: the 11 shown here, plus the District of Columbia, which has its own circuit. Each circuit court hears appeals from lower federal courts within the circuit. A thirteenth federal circuit court, the U.S. Court of Appeals for the Federal Circuit, hears appeals from a number of specialized courts, such as the U.S. Court of Federal Claims.

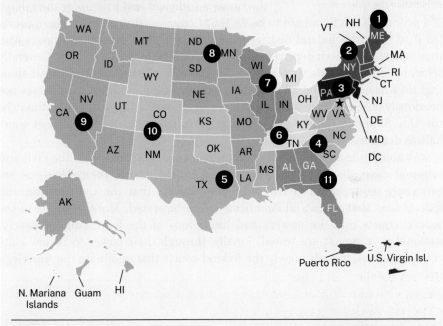

SOURCE: "Federal Court Finder," www.uscourts.gov/court_locator.aspx (accessed 7/27/10).

Congress has also established several specialized courts that have nationwide original jurisdiction in certain types of cases, such as the U.S. Court of International Trade, created to deal with trade and customs issues, and the U.S. Court of Federal Claims, which handles damage suits against the United States. Congress has also established a court with nationwide appellate jurisdiction, the U.S. Court of Appeals for the Federal Circuit, which hears appeals involving patent law and those arising from the decisions of the trade and claims courts.

The appellate jurisdiction of the federal courts extends to cases originating in the state courts. In both civil and criminal cases, a decision of the highest state court can be appealed to the U.S. Supreme Court by raising a federal issue. Defendants who appeal a state court decision in federal court might assert, for example, that they were denied the right to counsel or were otherwise deprived of the **due process of law** guaranteed by the federal Constitution or that important issues of federal law were at stake in the case.

due process of law the right of every individual against arbitrary action by national or state governments

habeas corpus a court order that the individual in custody be brought into court and shown the cause for detention; habeas corpus is guaranteed by the Constitution and can be suspended only in cases of rebellion or invasion

In addition, in criminal cases, defendants who have been convicted in a state court may request a writ of **habeas corpus** from a federal district court. Sometimes known as the "Great Writ," habeas corpus is a court order to the authorities to show cause for a prisoner's incarceration. The court will then evaluate whether the cause is sufficient and may order the release of a prisoner if it is found not to be. In 1867 Congress's distrust of southern courts led it to authorize federal district judges to issue such writs to prisoners who they believed had been deprived of constitutional rights in state court. Generally speaking, state defendants seeking a federal writ of habeas corpus must show that they have exhausted all available state remedies and must raise issues not previously raised in their state appeals. Federal courts of appeals and, ultimately, the U.S. Supreme Court have appellate jurisdiction for federal district court habeas decisions.

Although the federal courts hear only a small fraction of all the civil and criminal cases decided each year in the United States, their decisions are extremely important. It is in the federal courts that the Constitution and federal laws that govern all Americans are interpreted. Moreover, it is in the federal courts that the powers and limitations of the increasingly powerful national government are tested. Finally, through their power to review state court decisions, it is ultimately the federal courts that dominate the American judicial system.

Check your understanding

1. How do criminal cases differ from civil cases?

   a) In civil cases, the government charges an individual with violating a statute enacted to protect public health, safety, morals, or welfare; criminal cases involve disputes among people or businesses over money or some injury to personal rights.

   b) In criminal cases, the government charges an individual with violating a statute enacted to protect public health, safety, morals, or welfare; civil cases involve disputes among people or businesses over money or some injury to personal rights.

   c) Whereas the two most common types of criminal cases involve contracts and torts, civil cases originate in state and municipal courts and range from tax evasion and mail fraud to acts of terrorism and the sale of narcotics.

   d) Criminal cases do not involve money, and civil cases do involve money.

2. How do courts of original jurisdiction differ from appellate courts?

a) Courts of original jurisdiction hear all cases involving matters of criminal law, while courts of appellate jurisdiction hear all cases involving matters of civil law.

b) In appellate courts, judges hear cases involving disputes of more than $10,000, while in courts of original jurisdiction, cases must involve disputes totaling no more than $10,000.

c) In courts of original jurisdiction, all judges are elected by and accountable to the people, and in appellate courts, judges are appointed initially and at the end of their term subject to a retention election.

d) Courts of original jurisdiction are responsible for discovering the facts in a controversy and creating the record on which a judgment is based, while new facts are not presented before appellate courts.

Federal Courts Hear a Small Percentage of All Cases

Describe the different levels of federal courts, the expansion of federal court power, and the process of appointing federal judges

During the year ending in September 2021, federal district courts (the lowest federal level) received 344,567 cases. Though large, this number is less than 1 percent of the number of cases heard by state courts. The federal courts of appeal had a caseload of 44,546 during the same period. Generally, about 15 percent of the verdicts rendered by these courts are appealed to the U.S. Supreme Court.

Most of the 5,307 cases filed with the Supreme Court are dismissed without a ruling on their merits. The Court has broad latitude to decide what cases it will hear and generally listens to only those it believes raise the most important issues and those where different federal courts have issued conflicting decisions. In recent years, fewer than 100 cases per year have received full-dress Supreme Court reviews.[2]

Federal Trial Courts

Most federal cases begin in the lowest courts—the 94 federal district courts. Congress has authorized the appointment of 678 federal district judges to staff these courts. District judges are assigned to district courts according to the workload; the busiest courts may have as many as 28 judges. Only one judge is assigned to each case, except where statutes provide for three-judge courts to deal with special issues.

Federal Appellate Courts

Roughly 20 percent of all lower-court cases, along with appeals from some federal agency decisions, are subsequently reviewed by federal appeals courts. As noted earlier, the country is divided geographically into 11 regional circuits, each of which has a U.S. Court of Appeals. The twelfth appellate court, the D.C. Circuit, is a unique court that because of its geographical jurisdiction over D.C. hears a wide range of cases related to federal law. In the past, these have included cases pertaining to national security, gun safety, and election law. The D.C. Circuit is considered the most powerful of the Circuit Courts. A thirteenth appellate court, the U.S. Court of Appeals for the Federal Circuit, has a subject-matter jurisdiction, rather than a geographical one. Congress has authorized the appointment of 179 court-of-appeals judges.

Unlike federal trial court decisions, decisions by the appeals courts are final and considered binding precedent that all other courts in that circuit must follow. The only exceptions are cases selected for review by the Supreme Court. Because of this finality, certain safeguards have been built into the system. The most important is the provision of more than one judge for every appeals case. Each court of appeals has from 6 to 28 permanent judgeships, depending on the workload of the circuit. Normally three of these judges hear each case, and in some instances a larger number sit together "en banc."

Another safeguard is provided by the assignment of a Supreme Court justice as the circuit justice for each of the 12 circuits. The circuit justice deals with requests for special action by the Supreme Court. The most frequent and best-known action of circuit justices is that of reviewing requests for stays of execution when the full Court is unable to do so—primarily during the summer, when the Court is in recess.

The Supreme Court

Article III of the Constitution vests "the judicial power of the United States" in the Supreme Court, and this court is supreme in fact as well as name. The Supreme Court is the only federal court established by the Constitution. The lower federal courts were created by Congress and can be restructured or, presumably, even abolished. The Constitution does not specify the number of justices on the Supreme Court, so Congress has the authority to change its size. In the early nineteenth century, there were six justices; later there were seven. Congress set the number at nine in 1869, and the Court has remained that size ever since. In 2021, however, President Biden put together a commission to study expanding the number of seats on the Supreme Court and other changes, such as term limits for justices.

The Supreme Court is made up of the chief justice of the United States and eight associate justices. The **chief justice** presides over the Court's public sessions and conferences and is always the first to speak and vote when the justices deliberate. In deliberations and decisions, however, the chief justice has no more authority than the other justices. Each justice casts one vote. A chief justice who has voted with the majority decides which of the justices will write the formal opinion for the Court. The character of the opinion can be an important means of influencing the evolution of the law beyond the mere affirmation or denial of the appeal on hand. To some extent, the influence of the chief justice is a function of the justice's own leadership ability. Some chief justices, such as the late Earl Warren, have been able to lead the Court in a new direction.

> **chief justice** justice on the Supreme Court who presides over the Court's public sessions and whose official title is "chief justice of the United States"

Traditional Limitations on the Federal Courts

While federal courts have amassed a considerable amount of influence today, for much of American history the power of the federal courts was subject to a number of limitations.[3] First, unlike other governmental institutions, the courts cannot exercise power on their own initiative. Judges must wait until a case is brought to them before they can make authoritative decisions.

Second, courts were traditionally limited in the kind of remedies they could provide to those who won cases. In general, courts acted to offer relief or assistance only to individuals and not to broad social classes.

Third, courts lacked enforcement powers and had to rely on executive or state agencies to ensure compliance with their rulings. If the executive or state agencies were unwilling to do so, judicial decisions could go unheeded, as when President Andrew Jackson declined to enforce Chief Justice John Marshall's 1832 order that the state of Georgia release two missionaries it had arrested on Cherokee lands. Marshall asserted that the state had no right to enter the lands without the Cherokees' assent.[4] Jackson is reputed to have said, "John Marshall has made his decision, now let him enforce it."

Finally, Congress has the power to change both the size and the jurisdiction of the Supreme Court and other federal courts. In many areas, federal courts obtain their jurisdiction not from the Constitution but from congressional statutes.

Federal Court Expansion

Since the Second World War, however, the role of the federal judiciary has been strengthened and expanded as a result of two "judicial revolutions." The first and more visible of these were substantive innovations in judicial policy. As we saw earlier in Chapters 4 and 5, in many policy areas, including school desegregation, legislative apportionment, and criminal procedure, and in obscenity, abortion, and voting rights, the Supreme Court was at the forefront of a series of sweeping changes in the role of the U.S. government and, ultimately, the character of American society.[5]

At the same time, the courts were also bringing about a second, less visible revolution. During the 1960s and '70s the Supreme Court and other federal courts instituted a series of changes in judicial procedures that fundamentally expanded the power of the courts in the United States.

First, the federal courts liberalized the concept of standing (see p. 424) to permit almost any group that wishes to challenge the actions of an administrative agency to bring a federal court case. Second, the federal courts broadened the scope of remedies they could provide by permitting suits on behalf of broad categories or classes of persons in "class-action" cases, rather than just on behalf of individuals.[6] A **class-action suit** permits large numbers of individuals with common interests to join together to bring or defend a lawsuit.

class-action suit a legal action by which a group or class of individuals with common interests can file a suit on behalf of everyone who shares that interest

A third procedural expansion of the power of the federal courts came when they began to use so-called structural remedies, in effect retaining jurisdiction over a case until the court's ruling had actually been implemented to its satisfaction.[7] The best known of these remedies was the effort of federal judge W. Arthur Garrity, Jr., to operate the Boston school system from his courtroom in order to ensure its desegregation.

Through these three procedural mechanisms, the federal courts paved the way for an unprecedented expansion of national judicial power. In essence, liberalization of the rules of standing and expansion of the scope of judicial relief drew the federal courts into alliances with important social interests and classes, such as civil rights, consumer, environmental, and feminist groups, while the introduction of structural remedies enhanced the courts' ability to serve these constituencies.

How Judges Are Appointed

As the power of federal courts has expanded, there has been increased focus on who federal judges are and the process of their appointment and confirmation. Federal judges are nominated by the president and must be confirmed by the Senate. They are generally selected from among the more prominent or politically active members of the legal profession, and many previously served as state court judges or state or local prosecutors. However, there are no formal qualifications for service as a federal judge. In general, presidents try to appoint judges whose partisan and ideological views are similar to their own.

Once the president has formally nominated someone, the nominee must be considered by the Senate Judiciary Committee and confirmed by a majority vote in the full Senate. In recent years, the partisan conflict around judicial appointments has intensified. Senate Democrats have sought to prevent

The Trump administration was able to nominate three conservative Supreme Court justices to the bench, including Brett M. Kavanaugh (left) and Amy Coney Barrett (center). The Biden administration was able to nominate Ketanji Brown Jackson (right), the first Black female justice on the Court.

Republican presidents from appointing conservative judges, while Senate Republicans have worked to prevent Democratic presidents from appointing liberal judges.

During the early months of the Obama administration, Republicans were able to slow the judicial appointment process through filibusters and other procedural maneuvers so that only 3 of the president's 23 nominees were confirmed by the Senate.[8] Some of Obama's allies urged the president to take a more aggressive stance because he risked allowing Republicans to block what had been considered a key Democratic priority. In 2013 the Senate voted to end the use of the filibuster against all executive branch and judicial nominees except those to the Supreme Court, allowing President Obama to quickly secure the appointment of more than 300 new district court judges and 55 new appeals court judges. In 2017, Republicans turned the tables and extended these rule changes to include Supreme Court nominees, thus blocking Democratic efforts to prevent President Trump from appointing Neil Gorsuch to the Court.

Partisanship and Supreme Court Nominations Political factors are decisive when it comes to Supreme Court appointments. Because the high court has so much influence over American law and politics, virtually all presidents have made an effort to select justices who share their political philosophies.

Six of the nine current justices were appointed by Republican presidents (see Table 13.1). With the exception of the months between the death of Antonin Scalia in February 2016 and the confirmation of Gorsuch in April 2017, the Court has had a conservative majority for over 50 years, most recently consisting of Chief Justice John Roberts and justices Samuel Alito, Clarence Thomas, Neil Gorsuch, Brett Kavanaugh, and Amy Coney Barrett.[9] This majority propelled the Court in a more conservative direction in a variety of areas, including civil rights and election law.

It may be surprising, but the intense partisan battles over Supreme Court appointments are a fairly recent phenomenon. In fact, many nominations sailed

TABLE 13.1 | Supreme Court Justices

NAME	YEAR OF BIRTH	LAW SCHOOL ATTENDED	PRIOR EXPERIENCE	APPOINTED BY	YEAR OF APPOINTMENT
Clarence Thomas	1948	Yale	Federal judge	G. H. W. Bush	1991
John Roberts, Jr. (Chief Justice)	1955	Harvard	Federal judge	G. W. Bush	2005
Samuel Alito	1950	Yale	Federal judge	G. W. Bush	2006
Sonia Sotomayor	1954	Yale	Federal judge	Obama	2009
Elena Kagan	1960	Harvard	Solicitor general	Obama	2010
Neil Gorsuch	1967	Harvard	Federal judge	Trump	2017
Brett Kavanaugh	1965	Yale	Federal judge	Trump	2018
Amy Coney Barrett	1972	Notre Dame	Federal judge	Trump	2020
Ketanji Brown Jackson	1970	Harvard	Federal judge	Biden	2022

through the Senate via unanimous vote. This all changed when President Ronald Reagan nominated Robert Bork in 1987. Bork had stellar credentials. However, he was a legal conservative and believed the Supreme Court had become too activist on cases involving civil rights and privacy rights. In response, Democrats in the Senate led an aggressive campaign to derail his confirmation, and Bork's nomination was defeated by a vote of 58 to 42—the largest margin of any failed Supreme Court nominee in history.

Since Bork, more attention has been focused on the nomination process and we have continued to see deep and lasting partisan divisions over court appointments. Typically, after the president has named a nominee, interest groups opposed to the nomination mobilize opposition in the media, among the public, and in the Senate. In 2016, Republicans refused to act on Obama's nomination of Merrick Garland. In 2017 newly elected President Trump secured the appointment of a conservative, Neil Gorsuch, and Republicans used their Senate majority to change the rules and prevent a Democratic filibuster.

In 2018, President Trump nominated the judge Brett Kavanaugh to replace retiring justice Anthony Kennedy. The Kavanaugh nomination touched off an intense political struggle when three women accused Kavanaugh of sexual impropriety in high school and college. Kavanaugh vehemently denied the allegations. Democrats argued that Kavanaugh was unfit to serve on the Court, while Republicans asserted that the charges against him had been invented for political reasons. Ultimately, Kavanaugh was confirmed, receiving the votes of all but one Republican and only one Democrat.[10]

After the death of Ruth Bader Ginsburg in September 2020, President Trump decided to move quickly to appoint a third Supreme Court justice. With only weeks remaining before the 2020 presidential election, Trump nominated former Notre Dame law professor and federal appeals court judge Amy Coney Barrett to replace Ginsburg. Republicans used their Senate majority to expedite the confirmation process and Justice Barrett was duly sworn in just days before the election. Her appointment solidified the Court's conservative majority.

In early 2022, Justice Stephen Breyer announced his retirement from the Supreme Court. To replace Breyer, President Biden nominated Ketanji Brown Jackson, a former public defender who was serving as a federal judge on the U.S. Court of Appeals. After a tense confirmation hearing in April 2022, Jackson was confirmed with the support of all Democratic senators and three Republicans.

Democracy and Supreme Court Appointments

While presidents attempt to entrench their political ideology on the court through the appointment of justices, does the Supreme Court represent the will of the people? Disgruntled citizens on both sides of the aisle have charged that the Court is undemocratic, particularly in the way judges are nominated and appointed: the people do not get to vote on Supreme Court nominations or on the confirmation of the justices, and Supreme Court justices (and federal judges) have lifetime appointments.

These concerns have been elevated by the vast racial, ethnic, and gender disparities in federal judges (see Who Are Americans?). While the federal bench has become more representative of the American population in terms of gender and race, it is still overwhelmingly male and White.

The Supreme Court trails the lower federal court on matters of diversity. Justices on the Supreme Court were all White until the appointment of Thurgood Marshall, a Black man, in August 1967, and it took until September 1981 to appoint the first woman justice, Sandra Day O'Connor. In August 2009, Sonia Sotomayor became the first Latina to serve on the Supreme Court. And in the summer of 2022, Ketanji Brown Jackson became the first Black woman to sit as a justice on the Supreme Court. These historic appointments have helped to make the Supreme Court more representative of the American people. (As of October 2022, the Court has four female justices and three justices of color.) Yet, many groups are still not represented, and questions remain about how Supreme Court justices should be selected, and how long they should serve, given their immense influence over American politics.

Check your understanding

3. Which of these factors has led to a vast expansion of the role of the federal judiciary since World War II?

a) The federal courts expanded the concept of standing so that nearly any group wishing to challenge the actions of an administrative agency could have access to the federal courts.

b) The federal courts eliminated filing fees to enable a more equitable system of justice.

c) State courts began restricting their dockets, so the federal judiciary were required to hear many more cases.

d) Federal appellate courts, including the U.S. Supreme Court, were told by Congress that they must hear all cases and no longer were given discretion.

4. Which of the following statements about the selection and composition of federal judges is true?

a) While political factors play an important role in the selection of Supreme Court appointments, such factors are not important for district and appellate court judges.

b) The U.S. Supreme Court currently has a liberal majority, with six of the nine appointments made by Democratic presidents.

c) The intense partisan battles over Supreme Court appointments are a fairly recent phenomenon.

d) The federal bench is representative of the racial, ethnic, and gender composition of the population they serve.

The Power of the Supreme Court Is Judicial Review

Explain the Supreme Court's judicial review of national law

The term judicial review refers to the power of the judiciary to examine actions undertaken by the legislative and executive branches and, if necessary, invalidate them if it finds them unconstitutional.

FOR CRITICAL ANALYSIS ⟶

1. Would you describe the federal judiciary as diverse? Does racial, ethnic, and gender diversity of federal judges matter? Why or why not?

2. What similarities and differences do you notice among the judicial appointments of the presidents shown? What might account for the differences in terms of the diversity of their appointees?

WHO ARE AMERICANS?

Who Are Federal Judges?

One factor among many that presidents may take into account when selecting judicial nominees is diversity. The number of Supreme Court justices is relatively small, so it is easy to count the number of Black people (2), women (4), Latinos (1), and White men (4). How diverse is the rest of the federal judiciary?

Federal Judges in 2020,* by Race and Gender

👤 = 10 federal judges

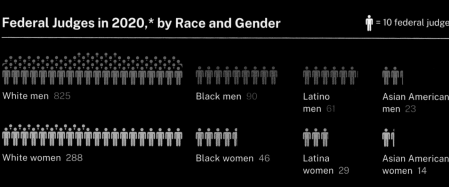

White men 825

Black men 90

Latino men 61

Asian American men 23

White women 288

Black women 46

Latina women 29

Asian American women 14

Appointments to Federal Courts, by Administration

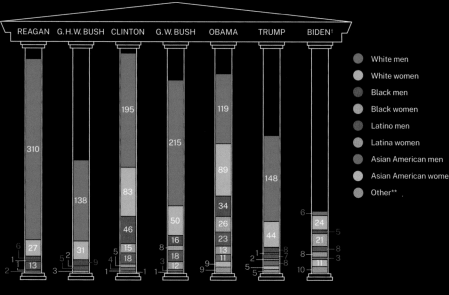

REAGAN | G.H.W. BUSH | CLINTON | G.W. BUSH | OBAMA | TRUMP | BIDEN‡

- ⬤ White men
- ⬤ White women
- ⬤ Black men
- ⬤ Black women
- ⬤ Latino men
- ⬤ Latina women
- ⬤ Asian American men
- ⬤ Asian American women
- ⬤ Other**

REAGAN: 310, 27, 6, 1, 13, 2

G.H.W. BUSH: 138, 31, 5, 2, 9, 3

CLINTON: 195, 83, 46, 15, 18, 5, 4, 1, 1

G.W. BUSH: 215, 50, 16, 18, 12, 8, 3, 1, 1

OBAMA: 119, 89, 34, 26, 23, 13, 11, 9, 5

TRUMP: 148, 44, 1, 2, 5, 8, 7, 8

BIDEN‡: 24, 21, 11, 6, 5, 8, 3, 10

Not including the Supreme Court.

"Other" includes women and men who identify as Native American or multiracial. Multiracial data only collected since 2000.

Biden data through August 5, 2022.

SOURCE: Federal Judicial Center, www.fjc.gov/history/judges/search/advanced-search (accessed 1/28/22).

Judicial Review of Acts of Congress

The Constitution does not explicitly give the Supreme Court the power of **judicial review** over congressional enactments, although the idea was discussed at the Constitutional Convention. Some delegates expected the courts to exercise this power, while others were "departmentalists," believing that each branch of the new government would interpret the Constitution as it applied to that branch's own actions, with the judiciary mainly ensuring that individuals did not suffer injustices.

judicial review the power of the courts to review actions of the legislative and executive branches and, if necessary, declare them invalid or unconstitutional; the Supreme Court asserted this power in *Marbury v. Madison* (1803)

Ambiguity over the framers' intentions was settled in 1803 in the case of *Marbury v. Madison*.[11] This case arose after Thomas Jefferson succeeded John Adams as president. Jefferson's secretary of state, James Madison, refused to deliver an official commission to William Marbury, who had been appointed to a minor office by Adams and approved by the Senate just before Adams left the presidency. Marbury petitioned the Supreme Court to order Madison to deliver the commission.

Jefferson and his allies did not believe that the Court had the power to issue such an order and might have resisted it. Chief Justice John Marshall was determined to assert the power of the judiciary but wanted to avoid a direct confrontation with the president. Accordingly, he turned down Marbury's petition but gave as his reason the unconstitutionality of the legislation upon which Marbury had based his claim. Thus, Marshall asserted the power of judicial review but did so in a way that would not provoke a battle with Jefferson. The Supreme Court's decision in this case established the power of judicial review.

The Court's legal power to review acts of Congress has not been seriously questioned since 1803. One reason for that is that the Supreme Court makes a self-conscious effort to give acts of Congress an interpretation that will make them constitutional. For example, in its 2012 decision upholding the constitutionality of the Affordable Care Act, the Court agreed with the many legal scholars who had argued that the Congress had no power under the Constitution's commerce clause to order Americans to purchase health insurance. But, rather than invalidate the act, the Court declared that the law's requirement that all Americans purchase insurance was actually a tax and, thus, represented a constitutionally acceptable use of Congress's power to levy taxes.[12] In more than two centuries, the Court has concluded that fewer than 160 acts of Congress directly violated the Constitution.[13]

Judicial Review of State Actions

supremacy clause Article VI of the Constitution, which states that laws passed by the national government and all treaties are the supreme law of the land and superior to all laws adopted by any state or any subdivision

The power of the Supreme Court to review state legislation or other state action to determine its constitutionality is also not explicitly granted by the Constitution. But the logic of the **supremacy clause** of Article VI, which declares the Constitution itself and laws made under its authority to be

The courts may be called on to review the actions of the president. After President Trump's "travel ban" was implemented in early 2017, many court cases challenged this policy, and eventually one case was tried before the Supreme Court. In a 5–4 decision, the Court upheld the travel ban, sparking outrage from Democratic lawmakers like Senator Cory Booker (N.J.).

the supreme law of the land, is very strong. Furthermore, in the Judiciary Act of 1789, Congress conferred on the Supreme Court the power to reverse state constitutions and laws whenever they are clearly in conflict with the U.S. Constitution, federal laws, or treaties.[14] This power gives the Supreme Court appellate jurisdiction over all the millions of cases that American courts handle each year.

The supremacy clause not only established the federal Constitution, statutes, and treaties as the "supreme Law of the Land" but also provided that "the Judges in every State shall be bound thereby, anything in the Constitution or Laws of the State to the Contrary notwithstanding." Under this authority, the Supreme Court has frequently overturned state constitutional provisions or statutes, state court decisions, and local ordinances it finds in violation of rights or privileges guaranteed under the federal Constitution or federal statutes.

One realm in which the Court constantly monitors state conduct is that of law enforcement. Over the years, the Supreme Court has developed a number of principles to ensure that police conduct does not violate constitutional liberties. These principles, however, must often be updated to keep pace with changes in technology. In a 2012 decision, the Supreme Court found that police use of a GPS tracker—a device invented more than 200 years after the adoption of the Bill of Rights—constituted a "search" as defined by the Fourth Amendment.[15] And in the 2014 case of *Riley v. California*, the Court held that the police could not undertake a warrantless search of the digital contents of a cell phone—another device hardly imagined by the framers.[16]

Judicial Review of Federal Agency Actions

Although Congress makes the law, to administer the thousands of programs it has enacted it must delegate power to the president and to a huge bureaucracy. For example, if Congress wishes to improve air quality, it cannot anticipate all the conditions that may arise with respect to that general goal. Inevitably, it must delegate to the executive substantial discretionary power to make judgments about the best ways to bring about improved air quality in the face of changing circumstances. Thus, almost any congressional program will result in thousands upon thousands of pages of administrative regulations developed by executive agencies.

Over the past two centuries, a number of court decisions have dealt with the scope of the delegation of power. Courts have also had to decide whether regulations adopted by federal agencies are consistent with Congress's express or implied intent.

Judicial Review and Presidential Power

The federal courts are also called on to review the actions of the president. On many occasions, members of Congress as well as individuals and groups have challenged presidential orders and actions in the federal courts. In recent years, the judiciary has usually upheld assertions of presidential power in such realms as foreign policy, war and emergency powers, legislative power, and administrative authority.[17] In 2004, however, in two of three cases involving President George W. Bush's antiterrorism initiatives, the Supreme Court appeared to place some limits on presidential authority.

One important case was *Hamdi v. Rumsfeld*.[18] Yaser Esam Hamdi, apparently a Taliban soldier, was captured by American forces in Afghanistan and brought to the United States. Hamdi was classified as an "enemy combatant" and denied civil rights, including the right to counsel, despite the fact that he was an American-born citizen. In 2004 the Supreme Court ruled that Hamdi was entitled to a lawyer and "a fair opportunity to rebut the government's factual assertions."

The Court asserted that it could review and place some constraints on the president's power, but it also affirmed that the president had unilateral power to declare individuals, including U.S. citizens, enemy combatants, who could be detained by federal authorities under adverse legal circumstances.

Judicial review of presidential actions is not limited to presidential war powers and the realm of terrorism. In 2014 the Supreme Court upheld a lower-court ruling that President Obama had violated the Constitution when he made so-called recess appointments to the National Labor Relations Board in order to avoid the need to secure Senate confirmation. Recess appointments are customarily used only when the Senate adjourns at the end of the year, but the president had made the appointments in question when the Senate had recessed for only three days. A recess of less than 10 days was "presumptively too short" to justify a recess appointment.[19]

In a 2018 decision, however, the Court upheld the use of presidential power.[20] Through an executive order, President Trump had prohibited travel into the United States by people from several Muslim-majority countries. The Court held that the president had broad authority, given by statute, to determine that certain travelers might pose a risk to the security of the United States.

AMERICA | SIDE BY SIDE

Courts in Comparison

Constitutional courts (courts with the power of judicial review) aim to preserve judicial independence, as they play an important role in checking executive and legislative overreach. Different countries have sought to balance the need for judicial independence with having a more responsive court. Here we see that countries have very diverse approaches to the selection and composition of their courts, including how many justices serve, how long they serve, and who is responsible for appointing them.

1. How does the United States compare with other countries when it comes to term limits for judges? What are the benefits and drawbacks to having term limits for judges?
2. Why might some countries choose to have larger courts than others?
3. We see a variety of systems for appointing judges, including some where only one branch appoints them, others where multiple branches each appoint some judges, and still others, such as the United States, where one branch nominates judges and a second branch confirms them. Which system do you prefer, and why?

NAME	TERM LIMITS (YEARS)	MANDATORY RETIREMENT AGE	SIZE	HOW SELECTED?
Chilean Constitutional Court	9	—	9	Each branch appoints some
French Constitutional Council	9	—	9	Each branch appoints some
German Constitutional Court	12	68	18	Legislature
High Court of Australia	Life	70	7	Executive
Indian Supreme Court	Life	65	28	Executive
South African Constitutional Court	12	70	11	Executive
South Korean Constitutional Court	6	65	9	Each branch appoints some
Supreme Court of Canada	Life	75	9	Executive
Supreme Federal Court of Brazil	Life	75	11	Executive with Legislative confirmation
United States Supreme Court	Life	—	9	Executive with Legislative confirmation

SOURCE: CIA World Factbook, www.cia.gov/index.html (accessed 11/1/21).

Check your understanding

5. Why was the Supreme Court's decision in *Marbury v. Madison* important?

a) It established the right to privacy through interpretation of the Sixth Amendment.

b) It led to the lifetime appointment of Supreme Court justices.

c) It established judicial review.

d) It applied the right to a jury trial to the state courts through selective incorporation.

6. On what basis can the U.S. Supreme Court review state actions?

a) the supremacy clause of the Constitution

b) tort law

c) the Tenth Amendment

d) the principle of original jurisdiction

Most Cases Reach the Supreme Court by Appeal

Describe the process by which cases are considered and decided by the Supreme Court

Given the millions of legal disputes that arise every year, the Supreme Court could not do its job if it were not able to control the flow of cases and its own caseload. Over the years, the Supreme Court has developed formal rules and informal criteria that govern which cases within their jurisdiction they will and will not hear.

Accessing the Court

Article III of the Constitution and Supreme Court decisions define judicial power as extending only to "cases and controversies." This means that the case before a court must be an actual controversy, not a hypothetical one, with two truly adversarial parties. The courts have interpreted this language to mean that they do not have the power to render advisory opinions to legislatures or agencies about the constitutionality of proposed laws or regulations. Furthermore, even after a law is enacted, the courts will generally refuse to consider its constitutionality until it is actually applied.

standing the right of an individual or organization to initiate a court case, on the basis of having a substantial stake in the outcome

Parties to a case must also have **standing**— that is, they must show that they have a substantial stake in the outcome of the case. The traditional requirement for standing has been to show injury to oneself. That injury can be personal, economic, or even aesthetic, such as a neighbor's building a high fence that blocks one's view of the ocean. In order for a group or class of people to have standing, each member must show specific injury. This means that a general interest in the environment, for instance, does not provide a group with sufficient basis for standing.

The Supreme Court also uses a third criterion in determining whether it will hear a case: that of **mootness**. In theory, this requirement disqualifies cases that are brought too late—after the relevant facts have changed or the problem has

> **mootness** a criterion used by courts to screen cases that no longer require resolution

been resolved by other means. The criterion of mootness, however, is subject to the discretion of the courts, which have begun to relax it, particularly in cases where a situation that has been resolved is likely to come up again. In the abortion case *Roe v. Wade*, for example, the Supreme Court rejected the lower court's argument that because the pregnancy in question had already come to term, the case was moot. The Court agreed to hear the case because no pregnancy was likely to outlast the lengthy appeals process.[21]

The Supreme Court is most likely to accept cases that involve conflicting decisions by the federal circuit courts, important questions of civil rights or civil liberties, or appeals by the federal government. Ultimately, however, the question of which cases to accept can come down to the preferences and priorities of the justices. If a group of justices believes that the Court should intervene in a particular area of policy or politics, the justices are likely to look for a case or cases that will serve as vehicles for doing so.

Writs Most cases reach the Supreme Court through a **writ of certiorari**, an order to a lower court to deliver the records of a particular case to be reviewed for legal errors. The term *certiorari* is sometimes shortened to *cert*, and cases deserving certiorari are referred to as "certworthy." An individual who loses in a lower federal court or state court and wants the Supreme Court to review the decision has 90 days to file a petition for a writ of certiorari with the clerk of the U.S. Supreme Court. Petitions for thousands of cases are filed with the Court every year (see Figure 13.3).

Since 1972 most of the justices have participated in a "certiorari pool" or "cert pool" in which their law clerks work together to evaluate the many petitions filed each year. Cases selected by the clerks are reviewed by the justices and may be placed on a "discuss list," which is circulated by the chief justice. If a case is not placed on the discuss list, it is automatically denied certiorari.

> **writ of certiorari** a court process to seek judicial review of a lower court or government agency; *certiorari* is Latin, meaning "to make more certain"

Cases placed on the discuss list are considered and voted on during the justices' closed-door conference. In the Supreme Court, four of the nine justices must vote to accept a case in what is called the **rule of four**. For certiorari to be granted, at

> **rule of four** a decision of at least four of the nine Supreme Court justices to review a decision of a lower court

FIGURE 13.3 | Cases Filed in the U.S. Supreme Court, 1938–2021 Terms*

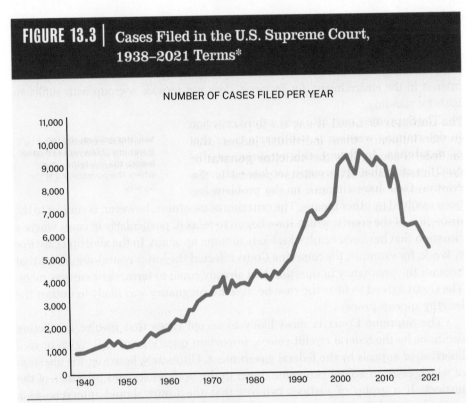

NUMBER OF CASES FILED PER YEAR

* Number of cases filed in term starting in year indicated.

SOURCES: *The United States Law Week* (Washington, DC: Bureau of National Affairs); U.S. Bureau of the Census, *Statistical Abstract of the United States*; Office of the Clerk, Supreme Court of the United States; Supreme Court of the United States, Cases on Docket, www.uscourts.gov; Supreme Court, "Chief Justice's Year-End Reports on the Federal Judiciary," www.supremecourt.gov/publicinfo/year-end/year-endreports.aspx (accessed 5/2/22).

least four justices must be convinced that the case satisfies rule 10 of the Rules of the Supreme Court of the United States, which states that certiorari is to be granted only when there are special and compelling reasons. These include conflicting decisions by two or more circuit courts, by circuit courts and state courts of last resort, or by two or more state courts of last resort; decisions by circuit courts on matters of federal law that should be settled by the Supreme Court; and a circuit court decision on an important question that conflicts with previous Supreme Court decisions.

Few cases are able to gain the support of four justices needed for certiorari. In recent sessions, the Court has granted it to barely more than 80 petitioners each year—about 1 percent of those seeking a Supreme Court review.

A handful of cases reach the Supreme Court through avenues other than certiorari. One of these is the writ of certification, which can be used when a U.S. Court of Appeals asks the Supreme Court for instructions on a point of law that has never been decided. A second alternative avenue is the writ of appeal, which is used to appeal the decision of a three-judge district court.

Beyond the Judges: Key Players in the Federal Court Process

In addition to the judges, other actors play important roles in how (and which) cases proceed through the federal courts: the solicitor general and federal law clerks.

The Solicitor General If any single person has greater influence than individual judges over the federal courts, it is the **solicitor general** of the United States. The solicitor general is the third-ranking official in the Justice Department (below the attorney general and the deputy attorney general) but is the top government lawyer in virtually all cases before the Supreme Court in which the government is a party. More than half the Supreme Court's total workload consists of cases under the direct charge of the solicitor general, whose actions are not reviewed by any higher authority in the executive branch.

> **solicitor general** the top government lawyer in all cases before the Supreme Court where the government is a party

The solicitor general exercises especially strong influence by screening cases that any federal agency wishes to appeal to the Supreme Court.[22] Agency heads may lobby the president or otherwise try to circumvent the solicitor general, and a few of the independent agencies have a statutory right to make direct appeals, but requests that lack the solicitor general's support are seldom accepted for review by the Court. Therefore, the solicitor general exercises substantial control over the flow of cases.

Law Clerks Every federal judge employs law clerks to research legal issues and assist with the preparation of opinions. Each Supreme Court justice is assigned four clerks, almost always graduates of the nation's top law schools. A clerkship with a Supreme Court justice is a great honor and generally indicates that the fortunate individual is likely to reach the very top of the legal profession. The work of the Supreme Court clerks is a closely guarded secret, but it is likely that some justices rely heavily on their clerks for advice in writing opinions and in deciding whether the Court should hear specific cases. A former law clerk to the late justice Harry Blackmun charged that Supreme Court justices yielded "excessive power to immature, ideologically driven clerks, who in turn use that power to manipulate their bosses."[23] In addition, historically law clerks have not been representative of the population; 85 percent of all justices' law clerks were White and 68 percent were male in 2019.[24]

Lobbying for Access: Interests and the Court

While the Court exercises discretion over which cases it will review, groups and forces in society try various ways to persuade the justices to listen to their grievances. Lawyers representing interest groups try to choose the proper client and the proper case so that the issues in question are most dramatically and appropriately portrayed. When possible, they also pick a court with a sympathetic judge in which to bring the case. Sometimes they even wait for a favorable political climate. They must also attempt to develop a proper record at the trial court level, one that includes some constitutional arguments and even, when possible, legal errors on the part of the trial court.

One of the most effective strategies in getting cases accepted for review by the Supreme Court is to bring the same type of suit in more than one circuit (that is, to develop a "pattern of cases") in the hope that inconsistent rulings will improve the chance of a review. The two most notable users of the pattern-of-cases strategy in recent years have been the National Association for the Advancement of Colored People Legal Defense Fund (NAACP-LDF) and the American Civil Liberties Union (ACLU).

Another way that interest groups attempt to influence Supreme Court decision-making is through writing an **amicus curiae** ("friend of the court") brief. A friend of the court is not a direct party to a case but has a vital interest in its outcome. Groups on opposing sides of an issue file amicus briefs to signal where they stand and to provide legal rationale why the justices should decide in a certain manner.

The Supreme Court's Procedures

The Supreme Court's decision to accept a case is the beginning of what can be a lengthy and complex process (see Figure 13.4). After a petition is filed and certiorari is granted, the Court considers the reasoning on both sides as presented in briefs and oral argument, the justices discuss the case in conference, and opinions are carefully drafted.

Briefs First, the attorneys on both sides must prepare **briefs**, written documents in which the attorneys explain why the Court should rule in favor of their client. Briefs are filled with references to precedents chosen to show that other courts have frequently ruled in the same way the attorneys are requesting that the Supreme Court rule. The attorneys for both sides muster the most compelling precedents they can in support of their arguments.

Oral Argument The next stage of a case is **oral argument**, in which an attorney for each side appears before the Court to present their position and answer the justices' questions. Each attorney has only a half hour to present a case, and this time includes interruptions for questions. Certain justices, such as the late Antonin Scalia, are known to interrupt attorneys dozens of times. Others, such as Clarence Thomas, seldom ask questions.

For an attorney, the opportunity to argue a case before the Supreme Court is an honor and a mark of professional distinction. It can also be harrowing, as when justices interrupt a carefully prepared presentation. Oral argument can be very important to the outcome of a case because it allows justices to understand better the heart of the case

FIGURE 13.4 | Timeline of a Supreme Court Case

This calendar of events in the case of *Matal v. Tam* (2016) illustrates the steps of the process a case goes through as it moves through the Supreme Court. The total time from petition to the Supreme Court to the decision is just over one year, although the initial case was filed years earlier in a lower court.

April 20, 2016

Petition for a writ of certiorari filed.

June 20, 2016

Filing of brief for respondent The Slants.

July 6, 2016

The case is distributed for conference.

July 12, 2016

Brief of petitioner, United States Patent and Trademark Office, filed.

September 29, 2016

The petition (certiorari) is granted.

December 5, 2016

Date for oral argument is set for January 18, 2017.

December 2016

Brief and amicus curiae briefs are filed on behalf of respondent.

January 2017

Brief filed on behalf of petitioner.

January 18, 2017

Oral argument of one hour

July 21, 2017

Decision

SOURCE: "Matal v. Tam," SCOTUSblog, www.scotusblog.com/case-files/cases/lee-v-tam/ (accessed 12/9/21).

and to raise questions that might not have been addressed in the opposing sides' briefs. It is not uncommon for justices to go beyond the strictly legal issues and ask opposing counsel to discuss the implications of the case for the Court and the nation at large.

The Conference Following oral argument, the Court discusses the case in its Wednesday or Friday conference, a strictly private meeting that no outsiders are permitted to attend. The chief justice presides over the conference and speaks first; the other justices follow in order of seniority. The justices discuss the case and eventually reach a decision on the basis of a majority vote. If the Court is divided, a number of votes may be taken before a final decision is reached. As the case is discussed, justices may try to influence or change one another's opinions, a process that may result in compromise decisions.

Opinion Writing After a decision has been reached, one of the members of the majority is assigned to write the **opinion**. This assignment, which is made by the chief justice or by the most senior justice in the majority if the chief justice is on the losing side, can make a significant difference to the interpretation of a decision. Every opinion of the Supreme Court sets a major precedent for future cases throughout the judicial system. Lawyers and judges in the lower courts will examine it carefully to determine the Supreme Court's intent, since differences in wording and emphasis can have important implications.

opinion the written explanation of the Supreme Court's decision in a particular case

One of the more dramatic instances of the importance of opinion assignment occurred in 1944, when Chief Justice Harlan F. Stone chose Justice Felix Frankfurter to write the opinion in the "White primary" case *Smith v. Allwright*.[25] The chief justice believed that this sensitive case, which overturned the southern practice of prohibiting Black participation in nominating primaries, required the efforts of the most brilliant and scholarly member of the Court. But the day after Stone made the assignment, Justice Robert H. Jackson wrote a letter to him urging a change of assignment on the grounds that Frankfurter, a foreign-born Jew from New England, would not win over the South with his opinion, regardless of its brilliance. Stone accepted the advice and substituted Justice Stanley Reed, an American-born Protestant from Kentucky.

Once the majority opinion is drafted, it is circulated to the other justices. Some members of the majority may wish to emphasize a particular point in the majority opinion. For that purpose, they draft a **concurring opinion**, called a *regular concurrence*. In other instances, one or more justices may agree with the majority decision but disagree with the rationale for it that is presented in the majority opinion. These justices may draft *special concurrences*, explaining their own rationale and how it differs from the majority's.

concurring opinion a written opinion by a judge agreeing with the majority opinion but giving different reasons for the decision

dissenting opinion a decision written by a justice in the minority in a particular case, in which the justice wishes to express the reasoning for dissenting in the case

Dissent Justices who disagree with the majority decision may choose to publicize the character of their disagreement in the form of a **dissenting opinion**, which is generally assigned by the senior justice among the dissenters. Dissents can be used to express opposition to an outcome or to signal to the losing side that its position is supported by at least some members of the Court. Because there is no need to please a majority, dissenting opinions can be more eloquent and less guarded than majority opinions. Dissenting justices will sometimes read their dissents aloud from the bench to dramatize their concerns.

Dissent plays a special role in the work and impact of the Court because it amounts to an appeal to lawyers all over the country to keep bringing similar cases. Ironically, a dependable way an individual justice can exercise influence on the Court is to write an effective dissent, which influences the future flow of cases through the Court and the arguments that lawyers will use in later cases. Even more important, dissent points out that the Court's ruling is the opinion only of the majority—and one day the majority might go the other way.

The Shadow Docket In recent years, the Supreme Court has made greater use of its "shadow docket," which refers to when the Court uses emergency orders and hands down short (one- or two-sentence) opinions on cases. Unlike the majority of cases that have been discussed in this chapter, cases on the shadow docket go through an accelerated decision-making process: full briefs are not filed, no oral arguments are heard, and justices do not provide lengthy opinions that describe their reasoning. Previously, the shadow docket was used sparingly—for uncontroversial petitions for certiorari and for emergencies such as federal death penalty cases. For example, during the period 2001–17, the Department of Justice filed eight applications for emergency relief. Yet the Trump administration filed 41 applications for emergency relief in four years. Post-Trump, the Supreme Court has continued to use the shadow docket to resolve controversial cases. Noting the increased use of the shadow docket, the House of Representatives held hearings in 2021 to better understand its present use and how it might be reformed.

Check your understanding

7. The U.S. Supreme Court considers a small number of cases each term. Which of the following is an important factor in the Supreme Court's decision to hear a case?

a) mootness
b) media attention to the issue
c) public opinion
d) experience of the lawyers involved

8. Which of the following statements regarding Supreme Court decision-making is true?

a) While the Court exercises discretion over which cases it will review, the Court is less likely to review a case with inconsistent outcomes among different circuit courts.

b) In recent years, the Supreme Court has made greater use of its "shadow docket," which affords an accelerated decision-making process, even on controversial cases.

c) The solicitor general has little role in federal cases, since only a few Supreme Court cases are under the solicitor general's direct charge.

d) While interest groups used to routinely file amicus curiae briefs in cases, amicus curiae briefs are generally no longer filed by interest groups, since judges typically vote along partisan lines.

Supreme Court Decisions Are Influenced by Activism and Ideology

Describe the factors that influence Court decisions

Like other actors in government, justices are influenced by institutional concerns, prior experience, and personal philosophy.

Influences on Supreme Court Decision-Making

The Supreme Court explains its decisions in terms of law and precedent. But it is the Court itself that decides what the laws actually mean and what importance the precedent will actually have. Throughout its history, the Court has shaped and reshaped the law.

In the late nineteenth and early twentieth centuries, for example, the Supreme Court held that the Constitution, law, and precedent permitted racial segregation in the United States. Beginning in the 1950s, however, the Court found that the Constitution prohibited segregation and that the use of racial categories in legislation was always suspect. By the 1970s and '80s the Court once again held that the Constitution permitted the use of racial categories—when they were needed to help members of racial and ethnic minority groups achieve full participation in American society. Since the 1990s the Court has retreated from this position, too, indicating that governmental efforts to provide extra help to people of color could represent an unconstitutional infringement on the rights of White people.

Constitutional Law As we have learned, there is not one formula that produces a Supreme Court opinion; the Court's decision-making depends on multiple factors. The most important factor is what the Constitution says; the Founders designed the Supreme Court to have the responsibility of interpreting the law. Thus, the justices read the briefs and listen to the oral arguments while applying legal principles to the issues laid out in a particular case. The overriding concern is making sure their decision-making is in line with the law.

To prevent arbitrary decision-making, the justices apply previous precedents; this process is known as **stare decisis**, a Latin phrase meaning "let the decision stand." The application of past rulings is instrumental to determining case outcomes. Yet there are rare times (historically 1–2 percent of previous cases) when the Supreme Court determines it ruled incorrectly in the past and reverses itself due to changing societal conditions. Such was the case in *Brown v. Board of Education* (1954), when the Court overruled itself

stare decisis deciding cases on the rules and principles set forth in previous court rulings; stare decisis is Latin, meaning "to let the decision stand"

and declared that segregation in the area of education was unconstitutional. Despite the low percentage of instances in which the Court reverses itself, applying constitutional law to modern-day issues, such as internet privacy, is not always clear and leaves lots of room for interpretation of what the law means.

Political Ideology and Partisanship While it is commonly assumed that Supreme Court justices make decisions solely on the law, most cases that reach the high court are complex and require a certain level of legal interpretation. However, interpretation of the law can be impacted by political ideology. This is because constitutional law can mean different things to different people. Take the Eighth Amendment protection from "cruel and unusual punishments," for example. What is cruel and unusual to one person may not be to another. Research on key landmark decisions suggests that the partisan ideological preferences of justices play a significant role in Supreme Court decision-making.[26] In other words: a Democrat-leaning Supreme Court would be more likely to produce more liberal decisions and a Republican-leaning Supreme Court would produce more conservative decisions.

Indeed, the overall trend of Supreme Court decisions for the last 70 years has revealed that ideology matters. From the 1950s to the 1970s the Supreme Court took a liberal role in such areas as civil rights, civil liberties, abortion, voting rights, and police procedures. It was more responsible than any other governmental institution for breaking down America's system of racial segregation. In the following decades, however, conservative justices appointed by presidents Ronald Reagan, George H. W. Bush, George W. Bush, and Donald Trump became the dominant bloc on the Court and moved the Court to the right on a number of issues, including affirmative action and abortion.

The political struggles of recent years illustrate the importance of ideology to judicial decision-making. Is abortion a fundamental right or a criminal activity? How much separation must there be between church and state? What protections do people accused of committing national security crimes have in court? The legal answers to these questions are often mediated by justices' values or personal policy preferences.

Activism and Restraint Given the importance of ideology on judicial decision-making, how far should justices go in promoting their ideological preferences? Should they overturn existing precedent? Put another way: Should the Supreme Court be a more active or more restrained institution? The answers to these questions reflect judicial philosophy. Over the years, some justices have believed that courts should interpret the Constitution according to the stated intentions of the Founders and defer to the views of Congress when interpreting federal statutes. Justice Felix Frankfurter, for example, advocated judicial deference to legislative bodies and avoidance of the "political thicket" in which the Court would entangle itself by deciding questions that were essentially political rather than legal in character. Some, but not all, advocates of **judicial restraint** are also called

> **judicial restraint** judicial philosophy whose adherents refuse to go beyond the clear words of the Constitution in interpreting the document's meaning

"originalists" because they look strictly to the words of the Constitution and the writings of the Founders in interpreting what was originally meant at the time the law was written.

Nevertheless, there are times in which the original meaning of the Constitution can seem too constraining to judges. Justice Stephen Breyer argued that the Founders wrote the Constitution in broad and flexible terms to create a "living" document. Therefore, justices should go beyond the words of the Constitution or a statute to consider the broader societal implications of its decisions.

judicial activism judicial philosophy that posits that the Court should go beyond the words of the Constitution or a statute to consider the broader societal implications of its decisions

The alternative to restraint is **judicial activism**, which advances the belief that judges should be more active in reviewing cases. Such judges sometimes strike out in new directions, putting forth new interpretations or formulating new legal and constitutional concepts when they believe these to be socially desirable. The accusation of being an "activist judge" is not the province of one particular political party; both liberal and conservative judges have been accused of activism at different times. During the 1950s–70s, liberal justices dominated the Supreme Court and were decried as being activist in cases that struck down laws related to segregation and in creating new ones around abortion. However, the tables turned from 1986 to 2005, when the Supreme Court was dominated by conservatives under Chief Justice William Rehnquist and was among the most activist in American history, particularly in such areas as federalism and election law.

The Roberts Court is continuing in the Rehnquist version of the active tradition. For example, in the 2014 case of *McCutcheon v. Federal Election Commission*, the Court struck down one of the major remaining elements of Congress's efforts to regulate campaign finance. The Court's five conservative justices said that limits on how much individuals could contribute in any given election were a restraint on free speech.[27] This decision could be described as "activist" because it broadens the interpretation of "speech" and overturns congressional legislation that has significant public support. As these examples illustrate, a judge may be philosophically conservative and believe in an originalist interpretation of the Constitution but also believe that the courts must play an active and energetic role in policy making, if necessary striking down acts of Congress to ensure that the intent of the framers is fulfilled.

Institutional Interests The Supreme Court's justices are aware of the Court's place in history, and their desire to protect its power and reputation for integrity can sometimes influence judicial thinking. During the 1935–36 term, for example, the Court struck down several of President Franklin Roosevelt's New Deal programs in a series of 5–4 votes. Furious, the president responded by proposing a reform plan that would have enlarged the Court to as many as 15 justices in what has been called his "court-packing" plan. Roosevelt hoped to pack the Court with his own appointees and, thus, win future cases over New Deal programs. Justice

Since the retirement of Justice Anthony Kennedy, Chief Justice John Roberts has some-times served as a swing vote on the Court to protect the precedents set by past decisions. He ruled with the liberal justices to reject the Trump administration's suit against DACA, a program that protects young undocumented immigrants from deportation.

Owen Roberts, one of the five justices who had been voting against the president's initiatives, then made a sudden reversal, voting in favor of an important New Deal policy he had been expected to oppose. The media dubbed Roberts's shift "the switch in time that saved nine."

More recently, Chief Justice John Roberts seemed to have institutional concerns in mind when he surprised fellow conservatives by casting the decid-ing vote in favor of the constitutionality of the Affordable Care Act in 2012 and again in 2015. The Court's conservative majority had come under increas-ing political fire for its positions on such matters as campaign finance and affirmative action. Roberts, according to one commentator, saw himself as "uniquely entrusted with the custodianship of the Court's legitimacy, reputa-tion, and stature" and was determined to show that the Court stood above mere political ideology.[28]

In 2020, Chief Justice Roberts once again demonstrated his concern for the reputation of the institution of the Court. He angered conservatives, and President Trump in particular, when he sided with the Court's liberals in supporting trans-gender rights, and in blocking the administration's efforts to proceed quickly with the deportation of young undocumented immigrants—the so-called DREAMers. In the immigration and abortion cases, Roberts cast the deciding fifth vote. How-ever, after Trump's successful nomination of Amy Coney Barrett in late 2020 after the death of Justice Ruth Bader Ginsburg, the balance of power on the Supreme Court shifted to a strong (6–3) conservative majority. Since he was no longer the deciding vote in controversial cases, Roberts wielded less power. This dynamic was on display in his concurring opinion in a 2022 Mississippi abortion case in which the Court's conservative majority ruled that the Constitution does not confer a right to abortion.[29]

In the end, however, the Supreme Court is a court of law and must pay heed to statutes and legal precedent. A decision that cannot be justified by law and precedent cannot be issued. To ignore the law would be to undermine the rule of law and to destroy the constitutional structure in which the Supreme Court occupies such a prominent place.

Check your understanding

9. Which of the following statements concerning court decisions is true?

   a) Since legal precedents constrain judges, partisanship and ideology play little to no role in deciding cases.

   b) Outside considerations like institutional interest and the legacy of the Supreme Court play no role in judges' decisions.

   c) Judges apply previous precedents, a process known as stare decisis, to prevent arbitrary decision-making.

   d) Only Democratic justices engage in judicial activism.

10. How do the philosophies of judicial restraint and judicial activism differ?

   a) Judicial restraint refers to the practice of only hearing cases in which all justices wish to grant a writ of certiorari, while judicial activism is the idea that the Court should take a more active role in cases.

   b) Judicial restraint refers to the philosophy that judges must use legal precedent when making decisions, while judicial activism refers to the philosophy that judges should rely solely on political ideology when making decisions.

   c) Judicial restraint refers to the philosophy that judges should avoid overly harsh sentences, while judicial activism refers to the belief that harsher sentences will deter crime.

   d) Judicial restraint refers to the philosophy that judges should strictly adhere to the Constitution when making decisions, while judicial activism is the philosophy that courts should go beyond the words of the Constitution to consider the broader societal implications of decisions.

WHAT DO YOU THINK?

THE FEDERAL COURTS

In their original conception, the framers intended the judiciary to be the institution that would protect individual liberty from the government. As we saw in Chapter 2, they believed that "tyranny of the majority" was a great threat to democracy, fearing that a popular majority, "united or actuated by some common impulse or passion," would "trample on the rules of justice."[30] For most of American history, the federal courts' most important decisions were those that protected the freedoms — to speak, worship, publish, vote, and attend school — of groups and individuals whose political views, religious beliefs, or racial or ethnic backgrounds made them unpopular. But today, Americans of all political persuasions seem to view the courts as useful instruments through which to pursue their policy goals. Conservatives want to ban abortion and help business maintain its profitability, whereas liberals want to enhance the power of workers in the workplace and reduce the role of private money in political campaigns.

- These may all be noble goals, but they also pose dilemmas and conflicts. For example, as government institutions, the courts protect the liberty of individuals. But whose liberty? The liberty of parents in general, or the liberty of the parents of disabled children? What would Texas governor Greg Abbott and Karina Pichardo say?

- Can you think of ways that federal court or Supreme Court decisions affect your life? For example, how might the Supreme Court's campaign-finance decisions affect who will govern the nation you inherit? How could its decisions on health care influence the type of care you receive and its cost? How will its decisions in the realm of immigration affect who will and will not be able to call themselves Americans?

- Given what you know now, do you view the Court as the "least dangerous branch" or an "imperial judiciary"? What evidence do you see for each characterization?

Use 🐰 INQUIZITIVE *to help you study and master this material.*

> **United States Treasury** 5-51 000
>
> Pay to the order of
>
> **AMERICAN PARENTS**
> **THREE HUNDRED AND 00/100 PER MO**
>
> **CHILD TAX CREDIT**
>
> Courtesy of President Bider
> & Congressional Democrat
>
> C000000 C

14

WHAT GOVERNMENT DOES & WHY IT MATTERS

For decades, the Child Tax Credit has provided taxpayers below an income limit with a lump sum credit for each child under 18. Congress doubled the credit to $2,000 per child under President Trump and increased it again, to $3,600, in 2021 pandemic relief legislation under President Biden. The latter change increased eligibility to most families, including those with higher incomes and those with incomes so low that they do not have to file federal tax returns, which previously prevented them from receiving the credit.

The expanded credit reduced child poverty by almost one-third.[1] It also helped Anna Lara and Jeremy Finley, a couple with two children, make ends meet. They had long lived "right on the edge of need." They were not in poverty, but were unable to save for emergencies, a situation that worsened when Anna lost her job during the pandemic and when rising child care costs made it difficult to return to work.[2] They used the money to fix the brakes on Anna's car and to buy new shoes and a car seat for their daughter. However, the tax credit's expansion was temporary, lasting just one year.[3]

Domestic Policy

Congress failed to pass President Biden's Build Back Better (BBB) legislation, which would have made the expanded tax credit permanent, and it reverted to its old parameters. Without the extra money, Anna said, "It's going to be hard next month. . . . Honestly, it's going to be scary. It's going to be hard going back to not having it."[4]

Senate Democrats could not pass the Build Back Better bill because they needed all 50 Democratic senators to support it, and Senator Joe Manchin of West Virginia, Anna and Jeremy's state, objected to the BBB package. He said that it was too expensive, fueling inflation, and that he couldn't support a continuation of the expanded Child Tax Credit without a work requirement attached. Public opinion was not that favorable either, which surprised some observers who thought it would be popular because most American families received it. But a December 2021 poll found opinion divided, with 47 percent of adults favoring an extension of the expanded credit and 42 percent opposing it.[5]

American social policy has three main goals. It addresses the risks that people might face in their everyday lives: illness, disability, loss of income due to aging or, as in Anna and Jeremy's case, financial insecurity. It provides opportunity, such as student loans to expand access to higher education. And it seeks to alleviate poverty, the most controversial goal. Social policy contributes to the government's larger goals in economic policy: ensuring economic stability and growth, promoting

▲ During the coronavirus pandemic, many families, like that of Anna Lara and Jeremy Finley, faced economic difficulties. The Biden administration responded by revising a government policy — temporarily expanding the size and availability of the Child Tax Credit.

business development, and protecting employees and consumers. However, as in other policy areas, Americans disagree about the role of government in social and economic policy. Some believe it should be as small as possible. Others prefer a more active role in shaping societal outcomes.

In this chapter, we will examine these two types of domestic public policy. Both social policy and economic policy have profound effects on societal resources and benefits: who gets what, and why. Here we try to answer: What factors go into deciding who gets what from economic and social policies? How do these choices reflect the viewpoints of politicians, interest groups, and various members of the public? Do the outcomes we see mirror or contradict American values of liberty and equality?

CHAPTER GOALS

Describe how the government uses fiscal, monetary, and regulatory policies to influence the economy (pp. 441–48)

Describe the arguments for and against government intervention into the economy (pp. 449–53)

Trace the history of government programs designed to promote economic security (pp. 453–58)

Describe how education, health, and housing policies try to advance equality of opportunity (pp. 458–65)

Explain how contributory, noncontributory, and tax expenditure programs benefit different groups of Americans (pp. 465–70)

The Government Shapes Economic Policy with Three Tools

Describe how the government uses fiscal, monetary, and regulatory policies to influence the economy

The U.S. economy is the result of specific policies that have expanded American markets and sustained massive economic growth. The Constitution provides that Congress shall have the power "to lay and collect Taxes . . . to pay the Debts and provide for the common Defence and general Welfare . . . To borrow Money . . . To coin Money [and] regulate the Value thereof." These clauses of Article I, Section 8, are the constitutional sources of the fiscal and monetary policies of the national government.

The Constitution says nothing, however, about *how* these powers can be used. As it works to meet the multiple goals of economic policy, the federal government relies on a broad set of tools that has evolved over time. Decisions about which tools to use are not simply technical; they are highly political and reflect conflicts over whether the government should act at all and, if so, how.

Fiscal Policies

Fiscal policy includes the government's taxing and spending powers. Fiscal policy shapes the economy and can be used to counteract the business cycle, which is the pattern of highs and lows that nations' economies experience over time. During economic slowdowns the government may decide to stimulate the economy by increasing spending, as it did during the coronavirus pandemic, or by reducing taxes. Conversely, if the economy is growing too fast, which might bring **inflation** (a consistent increase in prices), the government might cut back on spending or raise taxes. Through fiscal policy the government also influences the distribution of resources in the economy when it decides what programs to spend more or less on and which groups to tax at higher or lower rates.

Taxation During the nineteenth century, the scope of the federal government was quite modest, and most of its revenue came from **tariffs** on imported goods, and from excise taxes, which are taxes levied on specific products, such as tobacco and alcohol. As federal activities expanded in the twentieth century, the federal government added new sources of tax revenue, including the corporate income tax in 1909 and the individual income tax in 1913. At first only top earners paid the individual income tax; it became a tax that most households paid during World War II, when the government's revenue needs increased dramatically.

fiscal policy the government's use of taxing, monetary, and spending powers to manipulate the economy

inflation a consistent increase in the general level of prices

tariff a tax on imported goods

With the creation of the Social Security system in 1935, social insurance taxes became an additional source of federal revenue.

The largest share of federal revenue today comes from the individual income tax. It accounts for about half of federal revenues. At the same time, social insurance taxes have risen as a share of federal revenues while corporate income taxes have declined significantly (see Figure 14.1).

redistribution a policy whose objective is to tax or spend in such a way as to reduce the disparities of wealth between the lowest and the highest income brackets

progressive taxation taxation that hits upper-income brackets more heavily

The federal tax system has several goals, including raising revenue for government operations, achieving some income **redistribution** (reducing gaps between the lowest and highest income groups), and providing incentives for activities policy makers deem desirable, such as investment. One of the most important features of the individual income tax is that it is a "progressive," or "graduated," tax, with the heaviest burden carried by those most able to pay. A tax is called **progressive**

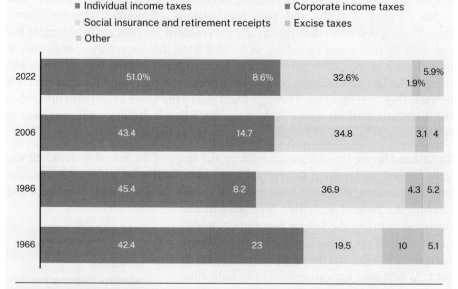

FIGURE 14.1 | Federal Revenues by Type of Tax

The federal government collects revenue from a variety of different taxes. Most important is the individual income tax, which has grown as a share of total federal revenue over the last 50 years to 51 percent. Revenues from corporate income tax have fallen considerably over this time period, from 23 percent in 1966 to 8.6 percent in 2022. In the same period, taxes for social insurance and retirement have grown substantially. Does the federal government draw more of its revenue from progressive taxes or regressive taxes?

■ Individual income taxes ■ Corporate income taxes
■ Social insurance and retirement receipts ■ Excise taxes
■ Other

Year	Individual income taxes	Corporate income taxes	Social insurance and retirement receipts	Excise taxes	Other
2022	51.0%	8.6%	32.6%	1.9%	5.9%
2006	43.4	14.7	34.8	3.1	4
1986	45.4	8.2	36.9	4.3	5.2
1966	42.4	23	19.5	10	5.1

NOTE: Data for 2022 are estimated.

SOURCE: Office of Management and Budget, "Table 2.2—Percentage Composition of Receipts by Source: 1934–2027," www.whitehouse.gov/omb/budget/historical-tables (accessed 9/22/22).

if people with higher incomes pay a greater share of their income in tax. A tax is **regressive** if people with higher incomes pay a smaller share of their income in tax. The individual income tax is progressive because taxable income is divided

regressive taxation taxation that hits lower-income brackets more heavily

into brackets, with higher tax rates imposed on higher brackets. For example, in 2022, a single person paid no tax on the first $12,950 of income. Then the next $10,275 was taxed at 10 percent, the next $31,500 at 12 percent, and so on through the top bracket, which taxed income above $539,900 at 37 percent.[6] In contrast, the Social Security tax is regressive. In 2022, Social Security law applied a tax of 6.2 percent on the first $147,000 of income for the retirement program.[7] This means that a person earning $147,000 pays $9,114 and a person making twice as much, $294,000, pays the same $9,114, a rate of 3.1 percent. And a CEO earning $5 million in income also pays the same $9,114, for a rate of 0.18 percent.

Over time the individual income tax and the corporate income tax have become less progressive. Tax cuts passed under President Reagan in the 1980s, President George W. Bush in the 2000s, and President Trump in 2017 reduced income taxes for most individuals and families, with the largest reductions going to the highest earners. The 2017 tax cut also lowered corporate and small business taxes substantially. Advocates of tax cuts directed toward high earners and businesses argue that such cuts will provide incentives for those individuals and companies to increase their investments in the economy and that the cuts will not harm federal revenues. Critics say such cuts will undermine the government's revenue-raising capacity and reduce redistribution.

Spending and Budgeting The federal government's power to spend is one of the most important tools of economic policy. Decisions about how much to spend affect the overall health of the economy. They also affect every aspect of American life, from the distribution of income to the availability of different modes of transportation to the level of education in society.

Government spending is sometimes used to counteract the effect of economic recessions, when the economy slows down and consumers and businesses spend less. Unlike state governments, most of which are required by the state constitution to balance their budgets from year to year, the federal government can run a **budget deficit**, which means that government spending exceeds revenues, with the federal government borrowing the difference by selling government bonds on which the government pays interest. The sum of all federal government borrowing is called the **national debt**. The government used deficit spending to stimulate the economy during both the Great Recession that began in 2007 and the coronavirus pandemic that began in 2020.

Government spending can also incentivize certain behaviors through subsidies and contracts. **Subsidies** are government grants of cash or other

budget deficit the amount by which government spending exceeds government revenue in a fiscal year

national debt the total amount of money the government has borrowed

subsidies government grants of cash or other valuable commodities, such as land, to an individual or an organization; used to promote activities desired by the government, reward political support, or buy off political opposition

AMERICA | SIDE BY SIDE

Global Tax Rates

Countries vary in how much and who they tax. For example, some countries set different income tax rates for married people and those with children, whereas other countries levy similar tax rates regardless of marital or family status. Income taxes are just one form of tax that governments collect; they also collect sales tax, property tax, and social security contributions.

1. Why might a country want to have a different tax rate for a single person without children versus a married couple with a single wage earner, raising two children? What kinds of policy goals might a country be trying to achieve with different tax rates? What might be an argument for having the same tax rate regardless of marital or family status?

2. Do you believe a government should favor lowering taxes or collecting revenue to provide services? How much does your answer change depending on the quality of the services the government is providing its residents for those dollars?

Average Income Tax and Social Security Contribution Rate on Average Wage, 2019–20

	SINGLE-PERSON, NO CHILD	ONE-EARNER MARRIED COUPLE, TWO CHILDREN	TAX REVENUE AS A PERCENTAGE OF GDP
Australia	24%	24%	29%*
France	27	21	46
Germany	40	20	39
Japan	22	21	32*
Mexico	11	11	17
Republic of Korea	15	13	28
Sweden	25	25	43
Turkey	29	27	23
United Kingdom	23	23	33
United States	24	13	25

* Data are from 2018.

SOURCES: OECD, "Average Rate of Income Tax and Employees' Social Security Contributions by Household Type," stats.oecd.org (accessed 11/3/21); OECD, "Revenue Statistics," 2020, stats.oecd.org (accessed 11/3/21).

valuable commodities, such as land. During the nineteenth century the federal government tried to persuade pioneers to settle the vast western lands by giving away plots of land contingent on improvements. Today, economic sectors receiving substantial subsidies include agriculture, energy,

> **contracting** the power of government to set conditions on companies seeking to sell goods or services to government agencies

transportation, health, and national defense. **Contracting** is also an important technique of policy. Like any corporation, a government agency must purchase goods and services by contract. Contracting can be used to encourage corporations to improve themselves, to build up whole sectors of the economy, and to promote certain desirable goals or behavior, such as equal employment opportunity. For example, the early airline industry of the 1930s was nurtured by the national government's lucrative contracts to carry airmail. More recently, President Biden required federal contractors to pay a minimum wage of $15 per hour even though the prevailing federal minimum wage set by Congress was (and still is) $7.25 per hour.

Decisions about spending are so important that both the president and Congress have created institutions to assert control over the budget process. The Office of Management and Budget (OMB) in the Executive Office of the President is responsible for preparing the president's budget, which contains the president's spending priorities and the estimated costs of the president's policy proposals. The president's budget may have little influence on the budget that Congress ultimately adopts, but the president's budget is viewed as the starting point for the annual budget debate.

Congress created the Congressional Budget Office (CBO) in 1974 so that it could have reliable information about the costs and economic impact of the policies it considers. At the same time, it set up a budget process designed to establish spending priorities and to consider individual expenditures in light of the entire budget. A key element of the process is the annual budget resolution, which designates broad targets for spending. By estimating the costs of policy proposals, Congress hoped to control spending and reduce deficits.

Monetary Policies

Monetary policies manipulate the growth of the entire economy by controlling the availability of money to banks. These policies are set chiefly by the nation's central bank, the Federal Reserve System (the Fed), which has a dual mandate to ensure price stability and maximum sustainable employment. The Fed also provides financial and payment systems to the nation's banks and the U.S. government.

Federal Reserve System With very few exceptions, banks in the United States are privately owned and locally operated. Many are chartered by states, which give banks permission to make loans, hold deposits, and make investments

> **monetary policies** efforts to regulate the economy through the manipulation of the supply of money and credit; America's most powerful institution in this area of monetary policy is the Federal Reserve Board

within that state. However, the most important banks are members of the federal banking system.

In 1913, Congress established an institution, the **Federal Reserve System**, to integrate private banks into a single national system.

The Federal Reserve System is composed of 12 Federal Reserve banks, each located in a major city. The Federal Reserve banks are not ordinary banks; they are bankers' banks that make loans to other banks, clear checks, and supply the economy with currency. They also play a regulatory role over the member banks. Every national bank must be a member of the Federal Reserve System and must follow national banking rules. State banks and savings-and-loan associations may also join if they accept national rules.

At the top of the system is the Federal Reserve Board comprising seven members appointed by the president (with Senate confirmation) for 14-year terms. The chair of the Fed is selected by the president from among the seven members for a 4-year term. In all other concerns, however, the Fed is an independent agency inasmuch as its members cannot be removed during their terms except "for cause," and the president's executive power does not extend to them or their policies.

Financial markets closely watch the statements of the Federal Reserve. Here, Fed chair Jerome Powell speaks about how income inequality is widening in the United States.

The major advantage that a bank gains from being in the Federal Reserve System is that it can borrow from the system. Borrowing enables banks to expand their loan operations continually, as long as there is demand for loans in the economy. On the other hand, it is this very access of member banks to the Federal Reserve System that gives the Fed its power: the ability to expand or contract the amount of credit available in the United States. During the coronavirus pandemic, the Fed under Chairman Jerome Powell used monetary policy to stimulate the economy, cutting interest rates and buying Treasury securities (the nation's debt) to keep credit markets functioning, then raised interest rates to combat inflation that emerged in 2022.

Regulation and Antitrust Policy

In addition to fiscal and monetary policy, another tool of economic policy making is regulation and antitrust policy. Federal economic regulation aims to protect the public against potential abuses by concentrated economic power in two ways. First, the federal government can establish rules for the operation of big businesses to ensure fair competition—for example, requiring businesses to make information about their activities and account books publicly available. Second, it can force a large business to break up into smaller companies if it finds that the business has established a **monopoly**. This is called **antitrust policy**. In addition to economic regulation, the federal government engages in social regulation, which establishes conditions on businesses to protect workers, the environment, and consumers.

monopoly a single firm in a market that controls all the goods and services of that market; absence of competition

antitrust policy government regulation of large businesses that have established monopolies

Federal regulatory policy has evolved, in part, as a reaction to public demands. In the nineteenth century, some companies grew so large that they were recognized as possessing "market power," dominant enough to eliminate competitors, collude on prices, and impose conditions on consumers rather than cater to consumer demand. Small businesses, laborers, farmers, and consumers all began to clamor for protective regulation. The Interstate Commerce Act of 1887 created the first national independent regulatory commission, the Interstate Commerce Commission (ICC), designed to control the monopolistic practices of the railroads. Regulatory power to cover all monopolistic practices was later extended by the Sherman Antitrust Act of 1890 and the Clayton Antitrust Act of 1914. The ICC was abolished in 1995, but the enforcement of antitrust law continues under the Federal Trade Commission, also created in 1914. Social regulation protecting consumers got a start when Upton Sinclair's best-seller about the meatpacking industry, *The Jungle*, led to the Federal Meat Inspection Act of 1906. In the late 1930s, the Food and Drug Administration was given broad powers to test and regulate products viewed as essential to public health.

Indeed, the modern era of national regulation began in the 1930s. Many agencies were established to regulate companies in a variety of economic sectors, including the securities, radio (and eventually television), banking, coal-mining, and agriculture industries. For example, the Securities and Exchange Commission (SEC), created after the stock market crash of 1929, requires companies to disclose information about the stocks and bonds they are selling, inform buyers of the investment risks, and protect investors against fraud. In this way the SEC helps maintain investor confidence and a strong supply of capital for American business.

Also during the 1930s and '40s, Congress set the basic framework of American labor regulation, including the rules for collective bargaining and the minimum wage. Regulation increased in the 1970s, with increased scope for agencies such as the Occupational Safety and Health Administration (OSHA), the Consumer Product Safety Commission, and the Environmental Protection Agency (EPA).

Despite occasional high-profile regulatory cases, the trend since the late 1970s has been against regulation. Over the years, businesses complained about the burden of the new regulations they confronted, and many economists began to argue that excessive regulation was hurting the economy. In the 1980s, Congress and the president responded with a wave of **deregulation**. For example, shortly after taking office, President Reagan gave OMB authority to review all executive branch proposals for new regulations, decreasing the total number of regulations issued by federal agencies and dropping the number of pages in the *Federal Register* from 74,000 in 1980 to 49,600 in 1987.[8] Similarly, President Trump signed an executive order within days of assuming office in 2017 requiring that two significant regulations be eliminated for every one added. How much government regulation is necessary remains a subject of considerable partisan disagreement.

deregulation a policy of reducing or eliminating regulatory restraints on the conduct of individuals or private institutions

Check your understanding

1. Fiscal policy seeks to influence the economy through

   a) taxing and spending.
   b) privatizing and nationalizing selected industries.
   c) controlling the availability of money and credit to banks.
   d) foreign exchange of currency.

2. Monetary policy seeks to influence the economy through

   a) taxing and spending.
   b) privatizing and nationalizing selected industries.
   c) controlling the availability of money and credit to banks.
   d) foreign exchange of currency.

Economic Policy Is Inherently Political

Describe the arguments for and against government intervention into the economy

The goal of maintaining a strong economy is extremely important to political leaders because the economy is usually a very important issue to voters. As was discovered by presidents from Herbert Hoover (who presided over the beginning of the Great Depression of the 1930s) to Jimmy Carter (who faced double-digit inflation in the 1970s) to Donald Trump (who faced the economic fallout of the coronavirus pandemic), voters punish politicians for poor economic conditions. Politicians of both parties strive to ensure a strong economy, but they differ over which goals and tools are appropriate. Indeed, disagreements about the role of the government in the economy are some of the defining differences between the political parties.

How Much Should the Government Intervene in the Economy?

Until 1929 most Americans believed that government should not actively manage the economy. The world was guided by the theory—called **laissez-faire capitalism**—that the economy, if left to its own devices, would produce full employment and maximum production. This traditional view crumbled beginning in 1929 before the stark reality of the Great Depression, when around 20 percent of the workforce lost their jobs. Many had no savings or family farm to fall back on, and when banks failed, those with savings were wiped out as well. Thousands of businesses closed, throwing middle-class Americans onto the breadlines alongside unemployed laborers and farmers who had lost their land. The Great Depression proved to Americans that the economic system was not, in fact, perfectly self-regulating. Demands grew for the federal government to act.

When President Franklin Delano Roosevelt took office in 1933, he energetically threw the federal government into the business of fighting the Depression. He proposed a variety of temporary relief and work programs, most of them financed by the federal government but administered by the states. Roosevelt also created several important federal programs designed to provide future economic security for Americans. Since that time, the public has held the government, and the president in particular, responsible for ensuring a healthy economy.

After World War II, Republicans and Democrats broadly agreed that Keynesian ideas, such as running deficits during periods of recession to stimulate demand, could best guide economic

laissez-faire capitalism an economic system in which the means of production and distribution are privately owned and operated for profit with minimal or no government interference

policy. By the 1960s, **Keynesians** believed that economic policy did not need to provoke political controversy because they could ensure ongoing prosperity by "fine-tuning" the economy. Democrats and Republicans often disagreed about how much the government should do to alleviate unemployment or inflation, but they shared a pragmatic view that government intervention could solve economic problems.

Partisan Divisions over the Role of Government in the Economy By the 1980s, a growing number of Republicans began to reject the idea that government could help ensure prosperity. Instead, they argued that freeing markets from government intervention would produce the best economic results. As Ronald Reagan put it in his first inaugural address, "Government is not the solution to our problem, government is the problem."[9] The ideas of laissez-faire capitalism began to make a comeback in American politics.

Although only a few politicians would entirely remove government from the economy, Republicans today draw on the ideas of laissez-faire economics as they argue for significant reductions in nonmilitary spending. Many Democrats, on the other hand, stress the important role of government in promoting a strong economy. This fundamental disagreement between the parties underlies the fierce contemporary political debates over taxes, government spending, and economic regulation. These debates reemerged in 2022 when Democrats urged more coronavirus pandemic rescue and preparedness spending after Congress had already passed the Families First and CARES acts and the American Rescue Plan in the previous two years, while Republicans hesitated to engage in more deficit spending.

Taxes As Republicans embraced the idea that reducing the role of government in the economy would promote investment and spur growth, they made tax cuts their highest priority. Rejecting Keynesian ideas, they adopted **supply-side economics**, the idea that lower tax rates create incentives for more productive and efficient use of resources. When individuals know they can keep more of their earnings, they are more likely to be productive workers and creative investors. This greater productivity, Republicans argue, ultimately produces more

FOR CRITICAL ANALYSIS ⟶

1. When federal, state, and local taxes are combined, there is a relatively small difference between the rates that the richest and poorest Americans pay. Why do you think that is?

2. The share of total taxes paid by each income group is similar to the share of total income they earn. Why do you assume that is?

WHO ARE AMERICANS?

Who Pays the Most in Taxes?

Governments need revenue to operate and fund the military, Social Security, Medicare, Medicaid, public schools, and much more. Individual income taxes are the federal government's single biggest source of revenue and are critical to most states. Federal income taxes are progressive, with higher-income people paying a higher tax rate than lower-income people. State and local taxes are regressive, with higher-income people paying a smaller share of their income than lower-income people.

Federal, State, and Local Taxes as a Percentage of Income

Federal taxes   State and local taxes

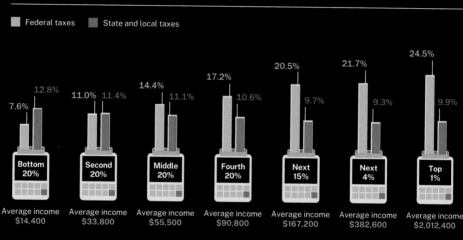

	Bottom 20%	Second 20%	Middle 20%	Fourth 20%	Next 15%	Next 4%	Top 1%
Federal taxes	7.6%	11.0%	14.4%	17.2%	20.5%	21.7%	24.5%
State and local taxes	12.8%	11.4%	11.1%	10.6%	9.7%	9.3%	9.9%
Average income	$14,400	$33,800	$55,500	$90,800	$167,200	$382,600	$2,012,400

Shares of Total Taxes Paid Compared to Shares of Total Income

Share of total income   Share of total taxes paid

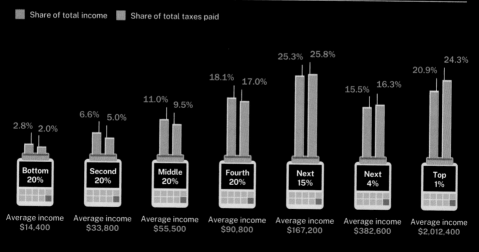

	Bottom 20%	Second 20%	Middle 20%	Fourth 20%	Next 15%	Next 4%	Top 1%
Share of total income	2.8%	6.6%	11.0%	18.1%	25.3%	15.5%	20.9%
Share of total taxes paid	2.0%	5.0%	9.5%	17.0%	25.8%	16.3%	24.3%
Average income	$14,400	$33,800	$55,500	$90,800	$167,200	$382,600	$2,012,400

SOURCES: Institute on Taxation and Economic Policy (ITEP), "Who Pays Taxes in America in 2019?," April 11, 2019, https://itep.org/who-pays-taxes-in-america-in-2019/.

revenue, and therefore more taxes. In this perspective, low taxes are not just a temporary measure to stimulate the economy; taxes should remain low at all times to ensure a growing economy.

Spending The two parties have long battled over government spending. Contending that the federal government has become too big, Republicans argue that government spending is excessive and creates deficits that harm the economy. It is not hard to convince Americans that government spending is wasteful, that government is too big, or that deficits are bad. When asked, a majority of Americans regularly say they would prefer a smaller government with fewer services (although during the pandemic in 2021, slightly more said they would prefer a bigger government with more services—50 percent, compared to 47 percent preferring smaller government).[10]

Yet polls reveal little support for cutting specific government programs.[11] In fact, the public shows the strongest support for the most expensive programs: Social Security and Medicare, which provide pensions and health insurance to elderly people. Only the most ardent spending foes among Republicans have argued for cutting these programs. Indeed, in 2003, Republicans agreed to a major expansion in Medicare spending by adding a prescription drug benefit to the program.

Because neither party wishes to cut big, expensive, popular programs and because tax increases have been so difficult to enact, budget deficits have grown periodically over the past four decades. Democratic critics and most economists point to rising deficits as proof that supply-side economics does not work; they argue that the economy would be better off without tax cuts. Some go further, arguing that Republicans deliberately reduced taxes in order to force spending cuts, a strategy called "starving the beast."[12]

Because raising taxes or reducing big-spending programs is politically difficult, most cuts have fallen on smaller programs, where spending has decreased substantially since 2010. Nondefense discretionary spending includes everything the government does outside of defense and mandatory programs such as Social Security and Medicare. For 2021 such spending was the smallest share of the economy ever recorded, with data going back to 1962.[13]

In response to the economic catastrophe caused by the coronavirus pandemic, Congress passed the Families First and CARES acts and the American Rescue Plan to provide cash payments to individuals, assistance to businesses, and expanded unemployment benefits.

Economic Regulation The federal government regulates business to promote economic stability, maintain workplace safety, set minimum wages and define overtime work, ensure consumer satisfaction, and protect the environment. However, regulation often attracts intense political conflict as businesses seek to limit the government role and other interests press for stronger government action. While Democrats usually favor regulation more than Republicans do, each party can point to public-opinion polls to support its position. Americans agree that government regulation of business does more harm than good on the whole but, as with spending, they often express strong support for maintaining or even strengthening current regulations.[14] One area of regulation that sharply divides the parties is the minimum wage, which has become a regular target of political conflict as Democrats aim to raise it to keep pace with inflation. In 2021, President Biden signed an executive order requiring federal contractors to pay a $15 per hour minimum wage.[15] However, opposition from Republican lawmakers has prevented Congress from considering the broader issue, perhaps because a 2021 poll found that while 87 percent of Democrats supported a $15-an-hour minimum wage, only 28 percent of Republicans agreed.[16] As of January 2022, 30 states and dozens of cities and counties had enacted minimum wages higher than the federal wage.[17]

Check your understanding

3. Which of the following economic perspectives argues that the government can stimulate economic growth by running deficits during periods of recession?

   a) Keynesianism
   b) laissez-faire
   c) libertarianism
   d) monetarism

4. Which of the following is an accurate statement about the debates on government intervention in the economy?

   a) Business groups have less influence than ordinary voters in shaping economic policy.

   b) Republicans often draw on the ideas of laissez-faire economics in support of their preferred policies, while Democrats stress the important role of government in promoting a strong economy.

   c) Majorities of Democrats and Republicans in Congress agree the federal minimum wage should be increased.

   d) Because of concerns about the federal budget deficit, Congress did not pass stimulus legislation during the Great Recession.

The Welfare State Was Created to Address Insecurity

Trace the history of government programs designed to promote economic security

For much of American history, the goal of social policy was to alleviate poverty, and local governments and private charities were in charge of caring for the poor. During the 1930s, when this system collapsed in the face of

welfare state the collection of policies a nation has to promote and protect the economic and social well-being of its citizens

widespread economic destitution, the federal government created the beginnings of an American **welfare state**, the term given to the collection of social policies a nation uses to address well-being. The idea of the welfare state was new; it meant that the national government would oversee programs designed to promote economic security for all Americans—not just the poor. Today, the American system of social welfare includes many different policies enacted over the years since the Great Depression. Some programs continue to be aimed at relieving poverty while others are available across income groups to offset risks such as old age and unemployment or to provide opportunity such as K–12 education. Some are run by the federal government and some jointly by federal and state governments. Because each program is governed by distinct rules, the type and level of assistance available vary widely.

Foundations of the Welfare State

The modern welfare state in the United States consists of three separate categories of social policy: contributory and noncontributory programs, many created by the Social Security Act of 1935, and the tax expenditure system, first established by the new federal income tax in 1913 and expanded over time.

Contributory Programs Contributory programs, also known as social insurance, are funded by taxes that are "earmarked," collected specifically for that

During the Great Depression, the government took a more active role in helping poor and struggling Americans. Here, people line up to receive free bread.

program. **Social Security**, the best-known **contributory program**, pays a monthly pension to retirees. Essentially a form of mandatory savings, Social Security applies to nearly all workers and is funded by an employer and an employee paying equal amounts. Their contributions in 2022 were 6.2 percent each on the first $147,000 of income.[18]

Social Security does not work like ordinary private insurance; workers' contributions do not accumulate in a personal account. The contributions are pooled across workers, and while one's benefits are based on one's earnings—the higher one's income, the higher one's retirement pension—the benefits formula is redistributive, providing lower-income workers with a higher proportion of their contributions than higher-income workers receive. This is because Social Security, a form of *social* insurance, is aimed at the twin goals of financial security and poverty alleviation in retirement.

Social Security a contributory welfare program into which working Americans contribute a percentage of their wages and from which they receive cash benefits after retirement or if they become disabled

contributory programs social programs financed in whole or in part by taxation or other mandatory contributions by their present or future recipients

indexing a periodic process of adjusting social benefits or wages to account for increases in the cost of living

cost-of-living adjustments (COLAs) changes made to the level of benefits of a government program based on the rate of inflation

Medicare a form of national health insurance for elderly people and disabled people

Senior citizens' purchasing power is protected by **indexing**, whereby benefits are raised annually by **cost-of-living adjustments (COLAs)** tied to the rate of inflation. The average payment for retired workers in 2022 was $1,657 each month; because of high inflation arising from supply chain problems and other pandemic-related issues, the 2022 increase was the largest in many years.[19] The program also plays a vital role for young people by providing survivor benefits to those whose parents die, retire, or become disabled, fulfilling the third goal of social policy: equality of opportunity. Surviving spouses also receive survivor benefits. In addition, in 1956, Social Security Disability Insurance (SSDI) was created to provide a monthly cash benefit to the permanently disabled.[20]

The biggest single expansion in contributory programs after 1935 was the establishment in 1965 of **Medicare**, which provides substantial medical services to elderly people and permanently disabled people. Employees and their employers pay a tax of 1.45 percent on all earnings for Medicare; households earning over $250,000 a year pay an extra 0.9 percent due to a provision in the Affordable Care Act (ACA).

Unemployment insurance, another contributory program, is funded by a combination of federal and state taxes. In most states, benefits last for a maximum of 26 weeks. In periods of high unemployment, Congress can authorize an additional 13 weeks, as it did in 2020 in response to the coronavirus pandemic; such extended benefits are generally funded by federal taxes. For most workers, unemployment benefits replace only half of their lost wages. Unemployment insurance is not as broad-ranging as Social Security or Medicare; because states impose criteria about how long people must work or how much they must earn to become eligible for unemployment insurance, only about half of workers who lose their jobs receive benefits.[21] Independent contractors, gig employees, and part-time workers are normally ineligible for unemployment benefits, but pandemic rescue legislation in 2020 and 2021 temporarily extended coverage to them.

Noncontributory Programs Programs to which beneficiaries do not have to contribute—**noncontributory programs**—are also known as "social assistance programs" or, more commonly, as "welfare." Eligibility is determined by **means testing**, which requires applicants to show a financial need for assistance. The 1935 Social Security Act created programs for cash assistance to low-income families with children (later known as Aid to Families with Dependent Children [AFDC]) and to poor elderly, blind, and disabled people (Old Age Assistance, later changed to Supplemental Security Income, or SSI). In the ensuing decades the government also created programs to provide housing assistance, food stamps, and school lunches. The largest expansion was the establishment in 1965 of **Medicaid**, which provides medical services to low-income Americans. The main goal of noncontributory social assistance programs is to offset poverty, although the benefits are typically not high enough to pull recipients above the federal poverty line.

Like contributory programs, the noncontributory ones also made their most significant advances during the 1960s and '70s. The creation of SSI in 1974 made benefits for elderly, blind, and disabled people uniform across the nation. The number of people receiving AFDC benefits expanded in the 1970s, in part because of the establishment in the 1960s of Medicaid and food stamps, later renamed the **Supplemental Nutrition Assistance Program (SNAP)**. These programs provide what are called **in-kind benefits**—noncash goods and services that would otherwise have to be paid for in cash by the beneficiary. At the time, AFDC recipients were automatically eligible for Medicaid and food stamps. After the mid-1970s, AFDC benefits fell because they were not indexed to inflation (unlike Social Security), and the number of recipients decreased after the 1996 welfare reform broke the linkages among Medicaid, food stamps, and cash welfare and replaced AFDC with Temporary Assistance for Needy Families (TANF).

State Variation in Welfare Benefits Some means-tested, noncontributory programs are run by the federal government, with uniform eligibility criteria and benefits nationwide, such as SNAP, the school lunch program, and SSI. However, many such programs are run jointly by the federal government and the states, as is

noncontributory programs social programs that provide assistance to people on the basis of demonstrated need rather than any contribution they have made

means testing a procedure by which potential beneficiaries of a social assistance program establish their eligibility by demonstrating a genuine need for the assistance

Medicaid a federally and state-financed, state-operated program providing medical services to low-income people

Supplemental Nutrition Assistance Program (SNAP) the largest antipoverty program, which provides recipients with a debit card for food at most grocery stores; formerly known as food stamps

in-kind benefits noncash goods and services provided to needy individuals and families by the federal government

FIGURE 14.2 | Maximum Monthly TANF Benefits

Spending on TANF benefits varies widely across the country. In 11 states, monthly benefits for a single-parent family of three are below $300; in 17 states and Washington, D.C., they are above $600. In which regions does spending on TANF benefits tend to be highest? In which regions is it generally lower?

SOURCE: Ali Safawi and Cindy Reyes, "States Must Continue Recent Momentum to Further Improve TANF Benefit Levels," Center on Budget and Policy Priorities, December 2, 2021, www.cbpp.org /research/family-income-support/states-must-continue-recent-momentum-to-further-improve -tanf-benefit (accessed 1/27/22).

unemployment insurance. Because states provide some of the funding and have considerable flexibility to set program criteria, benefits for means-tested programs can vary greatly by state.

For example, in 2021 states' maximum monthly TANF benefits for a family of three varied from $204 in Arkansas to $1,098 in New Hampshire, which passed legislation in 2017 to increase TANF benefits to 60 percent of the federal poverty level.[22] Most TANF payments are well below the federal poverty line for a family of three, which was $23,030 per year or $1,919 per month in 2022 (see Figure 14.2).[23] The share of poor families that receive TANF benefits also differs across states, from 70 percent in California to 4 percent in Louisiana (nationwide, just 23 percent of poor families receive TANF).[24]

Tax Expenditures In addition to contributory and noncontributory programs, the United States provides social welfare benefits through tax breaks—credits, deductions, and preferential tax rates that analysts call tax expenditures or the *shadow welfare state*. These include subsidies for benefits that employers may offer to their workers, such as medical insurance and retirement plans—both traditional pensions and 401(k)s. The federal government subsidizes such benefits by not taxing the payments that employers and employees make for them.

The shadow welfare state also includes tax breaks that individuals can file for when they prepare their federal tax returns. For example, taxpayers can deduct from their income the amount they paid in home mortgage interest and in state and local taxes (up to a limit). There are also tax deductions for out-of-pocket medical expenses, child care, charitable contributions, and so on. These tax breaks lower the effective cost of home ownership, health insurance, child-rearing, and other subsidized activities. But such benefits are concentrated among middle- and upper-income people who are most likely to have employer-provided benefits at work and to engage in subsidized activities such as buying a house.

People often do not think of these tax expenditures as part of social policy because they are not as visible as the programs that provide direct payments or services to beneficiaries.[25] But they cost the national treasury over $1 trillion in forgone revenue each year.[26]

Check your understanding

5. Which of the following characterizes noncontributory, means-tested programs?

a) Almost all Americans receive them.
b) They are funded by payroll taxes.
c) They are more controversial than contributory programs.
d) Benefits mainly go to high-income households.

6. Which of the following statements accurately describes the role of states in American social policy?

a) States run Social Security and Medicare.
b) States jointly run some programs with the federal government, especially means-tested policies.
c) States play no role; the federal government runs social policy.
d) States all set the same eligibility criteria and benefit levels for the social policies they run.

Social Policies Open Opportunity

Describe how education, health, and housing policies try to advance equality of opportunity

The welfare state aims at providing not only a measure of economic security but also **equality of opportunity**. Programs that provide opportunity keep people from falling into poverty and offer a hand up to those who are poor. Three types of policies are most significant in opening opportunity: education policies, health policies, and housing policies.

Education Policies

Although education policies are the most important single force in the distribution and redistribution of opportunity in America, they are largely set by state and local governments.

Elementary and Secondary Education (K–12) Embarrassment that the Soviet Union had beaten the United States into space with the launch of Sputnik, the world's first satellite, prompted national government involvement in K–12 education. In 1958 the National Defense Education Act set forth a federal policy of improving education in science and mathematics. Soon after, the federal government officially recognized the role of education in promoting equality of opportunity. In 1965 the Elementary and Secondary Education Act offered federal funds to school districts with substantial numbers of children whose parents were unemployed or had low income.

Today the federal government accounts for 10 percent of all spending on K–12 education; states and localities each account for 45 percent. Over time, however, federal education funds have become less targeted on low-income districts as Congress has failed to update the formula for allocating funds.[27]

The No Child Left Behind Act of 2001 (NCLB), enacted during the presidency of Republican George W. Bush with bipartisan support in Congress, combined the goals of higher standards and equality of opportunity. It aimed to improve standards through stronger federal requirements for testing and school accountability. Every child in grades 3 through 8 had to be tested yearly for proficiency in math and reading. The law quickly generated considerable controversy. Teachers objected that "teaching to the test" undermined the development of critical thinking. With little federal funding attached, many states deemed NCLB an unfunded mandate. Schools that failed to meet the new standards were required to provide new services such as tutoring, longer school days, and additional summer school; parents in failing schools could transfer their child to another school. Critics charged that NCLB actually undermined equality of opportunity because it punished underperforming schools—mostly those schools that bear the greatest burden for teaching the neediest students.[28]

Faced with these conflicts, the Obama administration overhauled NCLB, allowing states to get exemptions from its requirements in return for adopting a strong set of education standards and linking teacher evaluations to test results. Most states endorsed the Common Core State Standards, drawn up by representatives of the National Governors Association and the Council of Chief State School Officers in 2010, although some educators criticized the Common Core testing regime as a return to the failed policies of NCLB.[29]

In 2015, a bipartisan coalition in Congress enacted a major new education law entitled Every Student Succeeds. The new law returned control to the states by making them responsible for devising their own methods of ensuring accountability. Controversial federal requirements for teachers' evaluations and mandated standards were eliminated. Every Student Succeeds continues to require testing and the sorting of testing results by minority race and ethnicity, English learners, and disability. It also requires states to intervene to correct problems in the lowest-scoring 5 percent of schools but leaves the specific remedies up to the states.[30]

The Secretary of Education under Donald Trump, Betsy DeVos, strongly supported charter schools, publicly funded schools that can design their own curricula and that are free from school districts' usual bureaucratic rules, and vouchers, which allow students to use public funds to attend private schools. In 2020 the Supreme Court sided with voucher supporters in ruling that voucher-like private-school state scholarship programs cannot exclude religious schools.[31] As a former public school teacher, President Biden's education secretary, Miguel Cardona, brought a different perspective, once again reorienting federal policy toward closing gaps in education inequality. And despite the changes in federal policy, states and local governments continue their preeminent role in setting most education policies and providing most K–12 funding. One challenge is ensuring that all children, regardless of income or where they live, enjoy equality of opportunity.

Higher Education The federal government also plays an important role in helping to fund higher education, another important pathway toward opportunity. College graduates earn 75 percent more than high school graduates, and this "wage premium" has stabilized at around $30,000 since 2000.[32]

Most higher education has historically been funded by the states, not the federal government. However, federal programs have made a big difference in promoting equal access to higher education. The GI Bill of 1944 put higher education in reach of a whole generation of World War II veterans who had never thought they would attend college. In the 1950s and '60s, the federal government built on this role with the National Defense Education Act, which offered low-interest loans to college students, and the Higher Education Act, which supplied assistance directly to colleges and offered additional need-based grants allocated to students by universities. In 1972, Congress created the Pell Grant program, which offered grants directly to lower-income students.

Since the mid-1970s, however, as states have sharply reduced funding for higher education and college tuition has risen dramatically, these financial assistance programs have not kept pace. Whereas Pell Grants had initially provided enough to pay for tuition plus room and board at a four-year public college, by 2021–22, they covered only 62 percent of tuition and fees alone.[33] The growing costs of higher education have put college out of reach for many lower-income students and have left those who do attend with a heavy load of debt. The Biden administration announced a plan in 2022 to forgive $10,000 in debt ($20,000 for Pell Grant recipients) for individuals earning less than $125,000 per year ($250,000 per household).[34]

Health Policies

Until recent decades, no government in the United States (national, state, or local) concerned itself directly with individual health. But public responsibility was always accepted for *public* health. After New York City's newly created Board of

Health was credited with holding down a cholera epidemic in 1867, most states created statewide public-health agencies, recognizing that government can play an important role in preventing the spread of disease and reducing the likelihood of injury.

At the federal level, agencies committed to public health gained new visibility with the outbreak of the coronavirus pandemic in 2020. The U.S. Public Health Service, headed by the U.S. surgeon general, was established in 1798 and includes, among other agencies, the National Institutes of Health (NIH), dedicated to biomedical research, and the Centers for Disease Control and Prevention, which monitors outbreaks of disease and implements prevention measures and awareness campaigns about HIV/AIDS, Ebola, Zika, Covid-19, and other public-health threats. Additional federal commitments to the improvement of public health include the numerous laws aimed at cleaning up and defending the environment (including the creation in 1970 of the Environmental Protection Agency) and laws to improve the safety of consumer products (regulated by the Consumer Product Safety Commission, created in 1972).

Health policies aimed directly at people in poverty include nutritional programs, such as SNAP and the school lunch program, and Medicaid. Medicaid is the single largest medical insurance program in the United States. Together with the Children's Health Insurance Program (CHIP) for low-income children, it covers 83.6 million people, a number that rose by 46 percent after the ACA's expansion provisions were put into place.[35] Medicaid covers the poor and people who are disabled; it also assists elderly people in poverty who cannot pay Medicare premiums. Because there is no government provision for long-term care, Medicaid has become the de facto program financing nursing home residents when they have exhausted their savings. In fact, the disabled and elderly account for two-thirds of all Medicaid spending.[36]

Health Care Reform The United States is the only advanced industrial nation without universal access to health care. Opposition from the American Medical Association, the main lobbying organization of doctors, prevented President Franklin D. Roosevelt from proposing national health insurance during the 1930s, when other elements of the welfare state became law. In the following decades, the United States developed a patchwork system: older Americans were covered through Medicare, people in poverty and disabled people were assisted with Medicaid, and many working-age people and their families received health insurance through their employers.

The Affordable Care Act ("Obamacare") After the 2008 election, the Obama administration and the Democratic Congress implemented health care reform. The administration aimed to cover most Americans who lacked health insurance with a reform strategy that built on the existing system.

The plan that ultimately passed had three key features. The first was the creation of exchanges where individuals could buy health insurance, along with regulations prohibiting insurers from denying benefits for a variety of reasons, such as preexisting conditions. With a few exceptions, the legislation also made insurers

Some Americans opposed the 2010 Affordable Care Act because they were concerned that decisions previously left to patients and their doctors would be made by the government.

cover preventive care, such as vaccinations, mammograms, and other screenings, in full. The second key provision of the ACA, known as "the individual mandate," required uninsured individuals to purchase health insurance; those who did not would be subject to a fine (later revoked by Congress).

The third major provision of the ACA was a set of subsidies to help uninsured people and small businesses purchase insurance, as well as an expansion of Medicaid and CHIP. The Medicaid expansion made more people eligible for the program by opening it up to people with incomes up to 138 percent of the poverty level ($31,781 a year for a family of three in 2022).[37] The reform also allowed working-age adults without dependent children to qualify for the program for the first time.

The new health reform law faced challenges from state governments: 21 states filed lawsuits against it, arguing that the individual mandate was unconstitutional as were provisions stipulating that states would lose all federal Medicaid funds if they did not expand their Medicaid programs, even though the federal government initially paid for 100 percent of the expansion and starting in 2016 would cover 90 percent of new costs.

The Supreme Court ruled in 2012 that most of the act was constitutional, including the individual mandate.[38] Regarding Medicaid, the Court ruled that Congress did not have the power to take existing Medicaid funds away from states if they did not comply with the expansion requirements. Several governors

FIGURE 14.3 | Health Insurance Coverage, 1972–2021

The percentage of Americans under 65 without health insurance reached 17.7 percent in 2010, when the ACA was enacted. With implementation beginning in 2014, the uninsured rate fell to 10 percent in 2016. It began to rise in 2018 with reductions in the ACA enrollment period and advertising and the repeal of the individual mandate, effective 2019. During the pandemic, ACA outreach was restored and the uninsured rate declined.

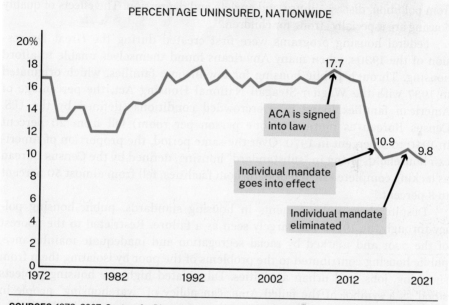

PERCENTAGE UNINSURED, NATIONWIDE

SOURCES: 1972–2007: Centers for Disease Control and Prevention, "Trends in Health Care Coverage and Insurance for 1968–2011," November 6, 2015, www.cdc.gov/nchs/health_policy/trends_hc_1968_2011 .htm (accessed 8/9/18); 2008–2018: U.S. Census Bureau, "Trends in Health Care Coverage Status and Type of Coverage by State — Persons under 65: 2008–2019," Table HIC-6, www.census.gov/data/tables /time-series/demo/health-insurance/historical-series/hic.html (accessed 1/27/22); Katherine Keisler-Starkey and Lisa N. Bunch, "Health Insurance Coverage in the United States: 2020," U.S. Census Bureau, September 2021, www.census.gov/content/dam/Census/library/publications/2021/demo/p60-274.pdf (accessed 7/30/22).

announced their intention to opt out of the expansion. Although some states later decided to expand, as of August 2022, 12 had not, leaving 2.3 million people who would have qualified for Medicaid without access to health care (see Figure 14.3).[39]

Health care reform remains a focus of partisan contention. By 2016 Republican members of the House of Representatives had voted 62 times to repeal the ACA.[40] After Republicans won control of the presidency and both houses of Congress in the 2016 election, they drafted a replacement bill that would have ended the Medicaid entitlement by turning the program into a block grant to the states, and would have effectively ended some regulatory protections for people with preexisting conditions. Though the bill failed in the Senate, the individual mandate was ultimately repealed with the 2017 Tax Cuts and Jobs Act. The number of

Americans enrolled in ACA health plans fell somewhat, but then reached a new record for 2022 after the American Rescue Plan temporarily increased eligibility and subsidies.[41]

Housing Policies

Economic opportunity is also closely connected to housing. Access to quality, affordable housing provides individuals and families with stability and protection from pollution, disease, injury, and anxiety and depression. The effects of quality housing are especially strong for children.[42]

Federal housing programs were first created during the Great Depression of the 1930s, when many Americans found themselves unable to afford housing. Through public housing for low-income families, which originated in 1937 with the Wagner-Steagall National Housing Act, the percentage of American families living in overcrowded conditions (defined by the U.S. Census Bureau as more than one person per room) fell from 20 percent in 1940 to 9 percent in 1970. Over the same period, the proportion of American households living in "substandard" housing, defined by the Census Bureau as lacking complete kitchen or bathroom facilities, fell from almost 50 percent to 8 percent.[43]

Despite these improvements in housing standards, public-housing policy through the 1970s was largely seen as a failure. Restricted to the poorest of the poor and marked by racial segregation and inadequate maintenance, public housing contributed to the problems of the poor by isolating them from shopping, jobs, and urban amenities. Dilapidated high-rise housing projects stood as a symbol of the failed American policy of "warehousing" people in poverty.

By the 1980s the orientation of housing policy changed. Federal housing assistance for low-income Americans shifted toward vouchers that provide recipients with support to rent in the private market. Most cities and suburbs have long waiting lists for vouchers; only one-quarter of eligible individuals and families receive them.[44] Another concern is that vouchers provide too little money to cover rental costs in very active housing markets. Overall, federal housing aid for low-income Americans is smaller in value than aid to higher-income homeowners in the form of tax deductions such as the home mortgage interest deduction.[45]

Other types of federal housing policy have had a discriminatory effect, worsening patterns of residential segregation by race. For decades the federal government permitted banks to engage in "redlining," refusing to issue mortgage loans or extend credit in predominantly minority neighborhoods. Federal programs that encouraged home ownership by providing insurance for loans made by private lenders (called underwriting) also discriminated against minority home buyers and contributed to segregation by allowing "restrictive covenants," which prevented owners from selling their houses to racial or religious minorities.[46] Such policies exacerbated vast Black–White differences in personal wealth that exist to this day.[47]

7. Which of the following correctly characterizes American education policy?

   a) K–12 schools are funded primarily by the federal government.
   b) Pell Grants enable students to attend four-year colleges and universities free of charge.
   c) Under No Child Left Behind, students had to pass national tests to advance from grade to grade.
   d) The federal government has periodically incentivized states to devise tests and report results for subgroups in order to measure and address educational inequalities.

8. Which of the following correctly characterizes American housing policy?

   a) The value of the home mortgage interest deduction and other tax deductions for housing exceeds spending on housing assistance for lower-income people.
   b) More people live in public housing than receive housing vouchers.
   c) Housing vouchers are available to all low-income households who qualify.
   d) Since the federal government became involved in housing policy in the 1930s, its policies have always prohibited practices that discriminate by race.

Who Gets What from Social Policy?

Explain how contributory, noncontributory, and tax expenditure programs benefit different groups of Americans

Elderly people and middle-class people receive the most benefits from the government's social policies, and children and people in poverty receive the fewest. In addition, America's social policies do little to change the fact that racial and ethnic minorities and women are more likely than White men to be poor.

Elderly People

Elderly people are the beneficiaries of the two strongest and most generous social policies: retirement pensions (Social Security) and health insurance for older Americans (Medicare). As these programs have grown, they have provided most elderly Americans with economic security and have dramatically reduced the poverty rate among elderly people. Social Security has been called the most effective antipoverty program in the United States: the elderly poverty rate fell from 35 percent in 1959, before many older people received social insurance benefits, to 10.3 percent in 2021.[48] This does not mean that elderly people are rich, however; in 2021 the median income of elderly households was $47,620, well below the median of $80,734 for those under age 65.[49]

Older Black people and Latinos are much more likely to be poor than are White seniors, with respective rates of 17.8, 18.7, and 8.0 percent in 2021.[50] The difference is due in part to the lower wages of these groups during their working years, since Social Security benefits are pegged to wages.

Social Security and Medicare are politically strong because they serve a constituency that has become quite powerful electorally. Elderly people are not only a very large group—in 2021, there were almost 55 million Americans over the age of 65, constituting 16.5 percent of the population—they also vote at higher rates than the rest of the population.[51] In addition, elderly people have developed strong and sophisticated lobbying organizations that can influence policy making and mobilize older Americans to defend these programs against proposals to cut them. The largest and most influential such organization, AARP, has 40 million members, amounting to one-quarter of all voters. It also has a lobbying organization in Washington that employs 58 lobbyists and more than 40 policy analysts.[52]

The Middle and Upper Classes

Americans don't usually think of the middle and upper classes as benefiting from social welfare policies, but government action promotes their welfare in a variety of ways. First, health insurance and pensions for elderly people, as well as Medicaid coverage of nursing home bills, help relieve the middle class of the burden of caring for elderly relatives. Before these programs existed, old people were more likely to live with and depend financially on their adult children.

Second, the middle and upper classes are the chief beneficiaries of the shadow welfare state of tax expenditures.[53] Beyond the Earned Income Tax Credit (EITC), which benefits the working poor, the great majority of tax expenditure benefits go to middle- and upper-income households. For example, while households with incomes under $30,000 receive 68 percent of the EITC, households with incomes over $200,000 claim 57 percent of the state and local tax deduction (the figure was 71 percent before the deduction was limited by the 2017 Tax Cuts and Jobs Act), 63 percent of the home-mortgage deduction, and 95 percent of the deduction for charitable contributions.[54]

The Working Poor

People who are working but are poor or just above the poverty line receive only limited assistance from government social programs. They typically hold jobs that do not provide pensions or health insurance; often, they are renters because they cannot afford to buy homes. This means they cannot benefit from the shadow welfare state that subsidizes the social benefits enjoyed by most middle-class Americans. Because the wages of less-educated workers have declined significantly since the 1980s and minimum wages have not kept pace with inflation, the problems of the working poor remain acute.

The Supplemental Nutrition Assistance Program (SNAP), formerly known as "food stamps," helps people in need buy food. Today recipients use a government-provided debit card that is accepted at most grocery stores. In 2022, 41 million Americans were enrolled in SNAP.

Government programs that assist the working poor include the EITC, SNAP, and the ACA. Implemented in 1976, the EITC refunds some or all of the Social Security and income taxes the working poor pay, particularly those with children, providing a modest wage supplement and allowing them to catch up on utility bills or pay for children's clothing. SNAP is available to households earning below 130 percent of the poverty line (about $29,929 a year for a three-person family in 2022). The average monthly benefit for a family of three is $520 a month; the benefit decreases with income.[55] Both the EITC and SNAP serve tens of millions of families because, unlike many social assistance programs like TANF and housing subsidies, they do not have waiting lists.

The ACA was intended in part to address lack of health insurance among the working poor. The law expanded Medicaid to cover workers who earn up to 138 percent of the poverty line ($31,781 for a family of three in 2022). However, as we saw earlier, the decision of 12 states to opt out of Medicaid expansion has left a gap in coverage in which 2.3 million people have incomes above the Medicaid eligibility limits in their states but below 100 percent of the federal poverty line, the income level at which subsidies for purchasing private insurance on the marketplaces begin. About half of Americans falling into this coverage gap and lacking insurance live in Texas or Florida. Latinos and Black people disproportionately fall into the coverage gap.[56]

Even though the working poor may be seen as deserving, they are not politically powerful because they are not organized. There is no equivalent to AARP for this group. Nonetheless, because work is highly valued in American society, these programs enjoy more support among politicians than those for the nonworking poor.

The Nonworking Poor

The only nonworking, able-bodied poor people who receive federal cash assistance are parents caring for children. The primary source of cash assistance for these families is the state-run TANF program; they also rely on SNAP and Medicaid. Able-bodied adults not caring for children are not eligible for federal assistance other than SNAP. Such individuals may receive small amounts of cash through "general assistance" in some states and Medicaid in the states that chose to expand the program under the ACA.

Restrictions have been added to many programs for the poor. Under TANF, states receive a fixed amount of federal funds, unadjusted for inflation, whether the welfare rolls rise or fall. Also, the term "nonworking poor" is a bit of a misnomer, because work requirements have been imposed on TANF since 1996 and on SNAP more recently.

Welfare recipients have little political power to resist cuts to their benefits. Because they are widely viewed as undeserving and are not politically organized, they have played little part in debates about welfare.

Racial and Ethnic Minorities, Women, and Children

Members of some ethnic and racial minorities, as well as women and children in general, are disproportionately poor. In 2021 the poverty rates for Black people and Latinos were 19.5 percent and 17.1 percent, more than double that for White people, 8.1 percent. Although poverty *rates* are higher among minority groups, the *composition* of those in poverty leans toward White people. White Americans make up 43 percent of the poor, a larger share than Black Americans, who constitute 23 percent of the poor, and Latinos, who make up 28 percent of the poor. Median household incomes were $48,297 for Black Americans, $57,981 for Latinos, and $77,999 for White Americans.[57]

Much of this economic inequality occurs because minority workers tend to have lower-wage jobs than White Americans—often without employer-provided benefits—and to become unemployed more often and for longer periods. Black people, for example, typically have experienced twice as much unemployment as other Americans. Scholars have argued that deep-seated patterns of structural racism affect the access of American racial and ethnic minorities not just to jobs but also to quality education, housing, and health care. As a result these groups are disproportionately vulnerable to financial insecurity, risk, poverty, and lack of opportunity.[58]

More than 30 years ago, policy analysts began to talk about the "feminization of poverty," or the fact that women are more likely than men to be poor. For example, single mothers are more than twice as likely to be poor as the average American (see Figure 14.4). When the Social Security Act was passed in 1935, lawmakers

FIGURE 14.4 | Poverty Levels in the United States, 1966–2021

Poverty rates in the U.S. population vary considerably. The rate of poverty among female-headed households declined significantly in the 1990s, increased again after 2000, and declined again after 2010. Which group has seen the greatest reduction in its poverty level since 1966? How were poverty levels affected by the coronavirus pandemic in 2020?

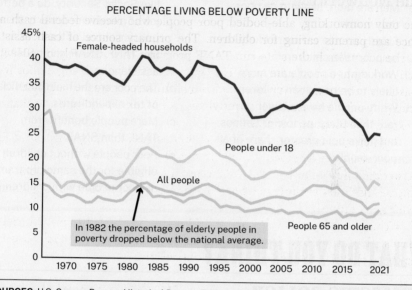

PERCENTAGE LIVING BELOW POVERTY LINE

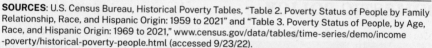

In 1982 the percentage of elderly people in poverty dropped below the national average.

SOURCES: U.S. Census Bureau, Historical Poverty Tables, "Table 2. Poverty Status of People by Family Relationship, Race, and Hispanic Origin: 1959 to 2021" and "Table 3. Poverty Status of People, by Age, Race, and Hispanic Origin: 1969 to 2021," www.census.gov/data/tables/time-series/demo/income-poverty/historical-poverty-people.html (accessed 9/23/22).

did not envision that so many single women would be heading families or that so many women with children would also be working. This combination of changes helped make AFDC more controversial. Many people asked why welfare recipients shouldn't work, if the majority of women not on welfare worked. Such questions led to the welfare reform of 1996, which created TANF.

One of the most troubling issues related to American social policy is the number of children who live in poverty. The rate of child poverty in 2021 was 15.3 percent—4 percentage points higher than that of the population as a whole—and the rates for Black children (27.3 percent) and Latino children (22.4 percent) were much higher than for White children (8.8 percent).[59] These high rates of poverty stem in part from the design of American social policies. Because these policies offer little help to poor adults, either working or nonworking, the children of these adults are likely to be poor as well.

As child poverty has grown, several lobbying groups have emerged to represent children's interests; the best known of these is the Children's Defense Fund. But even with a sophisticated lobbying operation on their behalf, and although their numbers are large, poor children do not vote and therefore cannot wield much political power.[60]

Check your understanding

9. Which of the following correctly characterizes poverty rates in the United States?

a) Men are more likely to be poor than women.

b) Elderly people are more likely to be poor than children.

c) Working-age people are more likely to be poor than children.

d) White people have a lower poverty rate than Black people or Latinos but make up a greater share of all poor people.

10. Which of the following statements is correct?

a) Social policies for elderly people, like Social Security, do a better job of alleviating poverty than policies aimed at the poor, like TANF, SNAP, and housing assistance.

b) The poor are the main beneficiaries of tax expenditures.

c) More people benefit from TANF than SNAP.

d) Poor people without children are eligible for the same programs as poor people with children.

WHAT DO YOU THINK?

DOMESTIC POLICY

Economic and social policies raise issues that cut to the core of Americans' lives and livelihoods. You may have frustrations with government economic policies that affect your life in areas such as college funding, wages, taxes, and transportation, or with social policies that help particular groups. Government policy affects your future job opportunities, what kinds of further education or training you can access, and where you may live. Yet changing policy in any of these areas means tough decisions: If more government funding is provided for, say, college financial aid, where does the money come from? Cuts to other programs? If so, which ones? Higher taxes, but on whom?

- Most Republicans have pressed for freer markets and less government, while most Democrats have defended the need for market regulation and more government intervention in the economy. Where do you stand on this debate?

- Do you tend to agree with liberals, who often argue that more generous social policies are needed if the United States is truly to ensure equality of opportunity? Or do you tend to agree with conservatives, who often argue that social policies that offer income support take the ideal of equality too far and do for individuals what those individuals should be doing for themselves?

- What do you think is the government's most effective tool in economic policy making: fiscal policy, monetary policy, or regulation?

- Look back at Anna Lara and Jeremy Finley's story at the beginning of the chapter. What views do you imagine they have about the role of government? Do you think the coronavirus pandemic will change people's views about social and economic policy? Why or why not?

- Which do you think the government should increase spending on (if any): social insurance, social assistance, or tax expenditures? Who would benefit most from your plan?

Use 🐰 **INQUIZITIVE** *to help you study and master this material.*

15

WHAT GOVERNMENT DOES & WHY IT MATTERS

Foreign policy involves issues ranging from warfare (the U.S. war in Afghanistan, 2001–21, which was the nation's longest) to homeland security (President Trump's 2017 travel ban on people from Iran, Iraq, Libya, Somalia, Sudan, Syria, and Yemen was contested but upheld in court). It includes responses to threats such as North Korea's and Iran's nuclear-weapon programs as well as international agreements such as the climate change pacts negotiated in Paris in 2015 and Glasgow in 2021.

Although government's strategy in dealing with other nations can feel distant and abstract, foreign policy can also be deeply personal. In 2021 record demand for consumer goods stretched supply chains and created transportation bottlenecks, with problems worsening just before the holiday shopping season. Among the causes: foreign policy. In 2018, President Trump imposed tariffs on a large number of goods from China, including chassis, the metal frames with wheels that carry shipping containers around ports, rail yards, and delivery locations. A group of U.S. chassis manufacturers had lobbied to have Chinese-source chassis added to

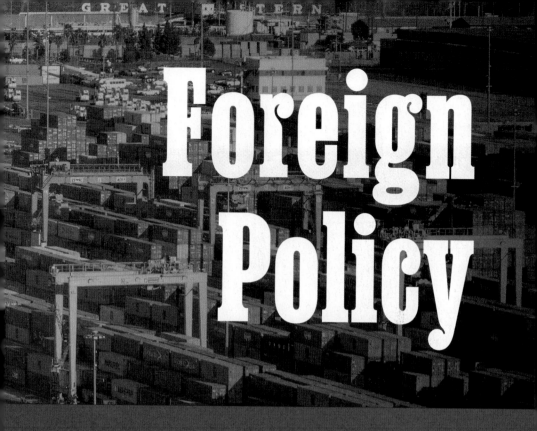

Foreign Policy

the tariff list, a practice the Biden administration continued in 2020. The tariffs greatly increased the price of Chinese chassis—from $10,000 to $35,000—protecting the domestic manufacturers.[1]

For Stoughton Trailers CEO Bob Wahlin, the tariffs were welcome. His Wisconsin-based company had ceased production of chassis in 2005 after Chinese manufacturers began selling entire chassis to U.S. companies for less than what Stoughton paid for steel alone. In his view, Chinese manufacturers had been "dumping" chassis at low cost, taking over the U.S. market. With the new tariffs in place, the company announced in 2021 that it would hire hundreds of employees for its Evansville, Wisconsin, plant as it restarted chassis production, improving the plant and raising wages twice to hire enough workers.

The heads of the nation's ports and trucking companies, however, were less enthusiastic about the chassis tariffs. Weston LaBar, executive director of the Harbor Trucking Association, which represents trucking companies that work the ports in Southern California, said that the tariffs created a shortfall of chassis. Together with a shortage of drivers and dock workers, the lack of chassis resulted in severe delays in getting goods out of ports. In his view, "the ITC [the U.S. International Trade Commission, the federal agency that approved the tariffs] really botched their decision, at a time when our industry is needing to inject more equipment, both for capacity and for folks trying to retire older

▲ Stoughton Trailers CEO Bob Wahlin (left) and Weston LaBar, executive director of the Harbor Trucking Association (right), disagree about the effects of tariffs imposed on Chinese goods by the Trump administration.

equipment. Now people have to stretch out the useful life of existing equipment, which isn't an ideal thing from a safety standpoint." He said that for Southern California, the Chinese chassis suppliers *were* the local provider, because U.S. manufacturers were so distant: "We have to pay thousands of dollars to transport chassis across the country—if we can get any."[2]

The chassis tariff case—an issue of foreign trade—illustrates what's at the heart of all foreign policy issues: complicated trade-offs, differing interests both within the United States and across allies, a constantly changing set of leaders around the world, and so on. Foreign policy is inherently complex, and the United States, like other nations, struggles to strike the right balance between competition and cooperation in the international arena.

CHAPTER GOALS

Explain how foreign policy is designed to promote security, prosperity, and humanitarian goals (pp. 475–82)

Describe the structure and roles of the major organizations and players in U.S. foreign-policy making (pp. 483–91)

Describe the means the United States uses to carry out foreign policy today (pp. 491–97)

Explain the foreign policy problems facing American policy makers today (pp. 497–502)

The Goals of Foreign Policy

Explain how foreign policy is designed to promote security, prosperity, and humanitarian goals

The term *foreign policy* refers to the programs and policies that determine America's relations with other nations and foreign entities. Foreign policy includes diplomacy, military and security policy, international human rights policy, and various
forms of economic policy, such as trade policy and international energy policy. In
fact, foreign policy and domestic policy are not completely separate categories but
are closely intertwined. As we will see, domestic politics affects foreign policy, and
foreign policy certainly affects domestic politics.

Although U.S. foreign policy has a number of purposes, two main goals stand
out: security and prosperity. Some Americans also favor a third goal—improving
the quality of life for all the world's people. Others say the United States should
remain focused on its own challenges and not get involved in solving the world's
problems. These foreign policy goals overlap with one another, and none can be
pursued fully in isolation.

Security

Though we might prefer to maintain peaceful and friendly relations with other
nations, the world can be dangerous. International rivalries and even wars are
commonplace as nations compete with one another for resources and influence.
Currently, the United States boasts the world's largest economy and most powerful military. Yet America's rivals, most notably China, hope to surpass the United
States on both of these dimensions, and still other nations, such as Russia and
Iran, challenge American influence in Europe and the Middle East.

Traditionally, the United States has been concerned about possible threats
from other nation states, such as Nazi Germany during the 1940s and then the
Soviet Union until the late 1980s. Today, American security policy is concerned
with the actions not only of other nations but also of terrorists and other hostile
groups and individuals, often called **non-state actors**.[3] To protect the nation's
security from foreign threats, the United States has built an enormous military
apparatus and a complex array of intelligence-gathering institutions, such as
the Central Intelligence Agency (CIA), charged with evaluating and anticipating
challenges from abroad.[4]

Security is, of course, a broad term. Policy makers must be concerned with
Americans' physical security. The September 11, 2001, terrorist attacks killed and
injured thousands, and new attacks could be even
more catastrophic. Policy makers must also be
concerned with such matters as the security of
food supplies, transportation infrastructure, and
energy supplies. Many American efforts in the
Middle East, for example, are aimed at ensuring

non-state actors groups other
than nation-states that attempt
to play a role in the international system; terrorist groups
are one type of non-state actor

continuing American access to vital oil fields, stopping America's foes from expanding their influence in the region, stabilizing energy markets, and preventing bitter ethnic and territorial rivalries in this volatile region from spilling over into other areas of the world.

In recent years, cyberspace has become an important security concern. The nation's dependence on digital communication and infrastructure means that the government must be alert to efforts by hostile governments, groups, or even individual "hackers" to damage computer networks or access sensitive or proprietary information. The U.S. government has often charged Chinese and Russian government and military agencies with stealing American secrets through cyber espionage. Recently, it appeared that a popular antivirus software marketed by a Russian company was being used by the Russian government to spy on American corporations and government agencies, and the United States has strongly discouraged the use of Chinese software for similar reasons. Of course, America has launched its own cyber campaigns aimed at acquiring foreign intelligence and disabling computer networks belonging to hostile powers.

During the eighteenth and nineteenth centuries, American security was based mainly on the geographic isolation of the United States. Separated by oceans from European and Asian powers, many Americans thought that the country's security would be best preserved by remaining aloof from international power struggles. This policy was known as **isolationism**. In his 1796 Farewell Address, President George Washington warned Americans to avoid permanent alliances with foreign powers, and in 1823, President James Monroe warned foreign powers not to meddle in the Western Hemisphere. Washington's warning and what came to be called the Monroe Doctrine were the cornerstones of U.S. foreign policy until the end of the nineteenth century. The United States saw itself as the dominant power in the Western Hemisphere and, indeed, believed that its "manifest destiny" was to expand from sea to sea. The rest of the world, however, should remain at arm's length.

isolationism avoidance of involvement in the affairs of other nations

Within its own sphere of influence, of course, the United States conducted an active foreign policy and aggressive military policy. During the nineteenth century, the United States defeated a number of Native American nations, which were forced to cede their land to American settlers. Through diplomacy, the United States assumed control of the remains of France's North American empire. The United States fought a war against Mexico and seized huge swaths of territory in the Southwest. The United States fought wars to drive European powers from Cuba, Puerto Rico, and the Philippines. And, of course, the United States fought a brutal civil war to block the secession of the southern states. American foreign policy was isolationist with regard to Europe but quite activist nearer home.

In the twentieth century, technology made oceans less of a barrier to foreign threats, and the world's growing economic interdependence meant that the nation could no longer ignore events abroad. The United States entered World War I in 1917 on the side of Great Britain and France when President Woodrow Wilson concluded that a German victory would adversely affect U.S. economic and security interests. In 1941 the United States was drawn into World War II when Japan, hoping to become the dominant power in the Pacific, attacked the U.S. Pacific naval fleet anchored at Pearl Harbor, Hawaii. Even before the attack, President Franklin Roosevelt had concluded that the United States must act to prevent a victory by the German–Japanese–Italian Axis alliance. The attack proved that the Pacific Ocean could not protect the United States from foreign foes and effectively discredited isolationism as a security policy.

Following World War II, the United States developed a new security policy known as **containment** to check or "contain" the growing power of the Soviet Union, which by the end of the 1940s had built a huge empire and enormous military forces. Some Americans wanted a more aggressive policy and argued that the United States should attack the Soviets before it was too late, a policy known as **preventive war**. Others said that we should show our peaceful intentions and attempt to placate the Soviets, a policy called **appeasement**. The disastrous results of the British effort to prevent World War II by appeasing Nazi Germany, however, had left most Americans with little confidence in appeasement as a policy.

containment a policy designed to curtail the political and military expansion of a hostile power

preventive war a policy of striking first when a nation fears that a foreign foe is contemplating hostile action

appeasement the effort to forestall war by giving in to the demands of a hostile power

deterrence an effort to prevent hostile action by promising to retaliate forcefully against an attacker

Cold War the period of struggle between the United States and the former Soviet Union lasting from the late 1940s to about 1990

The policies that the United States actually adopted, **deterrence** and containment, could be seen as midway between preventive war and appeasement. Deterrence signals, on the one hand, peaceful intentions but also, on the other hand, a willingness and ability to fight if attacked. Thus, during the era of confrontation with the Soviet Union, known as the **Cold War**, the United States frequently asserted that it had no intention of attacking the Soviet Union but also built a huge military force, including an arsenal of over 1,500 nuclear warheads, and frequently asserted that it had the ability and will to respond to a Soviet attack with overwhelming force. The Soviet Union, which had also built powerful nuclear and conventional military forces, announced that its nuclear weapons were also intended for deterrent purposes.

Eventually, the two sides possessed such enormous arsenals of nuclear missiles that each had the ability to destroy the other many times over. This heavily armed standoff came to be called a posture of "mutually assured destruction," which discouraged either side from attacking the other. Eventually, this situation led to a period of "détente," in which a number of arms control agreements were signed and the threat of war was reduced. The Soviet Union collapsed in 1991, and the new Russia, though still a formidable power, at the time seemed to pose less of a threat to the United States.

A policy of deterrence requires that a nation not only possess large military forces but also convince potential adversaries with *certainty* that it is willing to fight if attacked. Thus, during the Cold War the United States engaged in wars in Korea and Vietnam, where it had no particular interests, because American

During the Cold War, the United States and the Soviet Union engaged in an arms race, each acquiring nuclear weapons to deter the other from attacking.

policy makers believed that if it did not, the Soviets would be emboldened to pursue an expansionist policy elsewhere, thinking that the Americans would not respond.

This arrangement may not be valid or relevant in the context of some contemporary security threats. The September 11, 2001, terrorist attacks, for example, demonstrated the threat that non-state actors and so-called rogue states might acquire significant military capabilities, including nuclear weapons, and would not be affected by America's deterrent capabilities. Unlike **nation-states**, which are countries with governments and fixed borders, terrorist groups have no fixed geographic location that can be attacked. Terrorists may believe they can attack and melt away, leaving the United States with no one against whom to retaliate. Hence, the threat of massive retaliation does not deter them. Rogue states are nations with often unstable and erratic leaders who seem to pursue policies driven by ideological or religious fervor rather than careful consideration of economic or human costs. The United States considers North Korea and Iran to be rogue states, though most academic analysts see both nations' leaders as behaving belligerently but not necessarily irrationally.

To counter these new security threats, the George W. Bush administration shifted from a policy of deterrence to one of preventive war—the willingness to strike first in order to prevent an attack, particularly by enemies that might be armed with weapons of mass destruction. The United States declared that, if necessary, it would take action to disable terrorist groups and rogue states before they could develop the capacity to harm the United States.[5] The Bush administration's "global war on terror" was an expression of prevention, as was the U.S. invasion of Iraq in 2003. The United States also refused to rule out the possibility that it would attack North Korea or Iran if it deemed those nations' nuclear programs to be imminent threats to American security. Accompanying this shift in military doctrines was an enormous increase in overall U.S. military spending (see Figure 15.1).

President Obama took a less aggressive line, saying that the United States would rely on diplomacy and economic sanctions. President Trump, however, said that the United States was prepared to use overwhelming force against its adversaries. Trump, moreover, declared that the United States would pursue its

FIGURE 15.1 | U.S. Spending on National Defense since 2000*

During the 1990s the budget for national defense declined as the country was generally at peace following the conclusion of the Cold War. After the attacks of September 11, 2001, and the commencement of the war on terrorism, however, national defense spending rose steadily; in a decade, spending increased by 70 percent. Defense spending then fell, but after a lifting of spending caps in the 2018 budget agreement, spending rose and was predicted to continue rising.

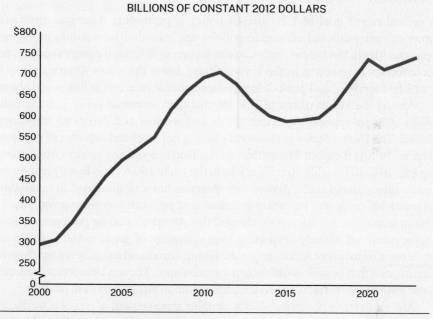

BILLIONS OF CONSTANT 2012 DOLLARS

*Data for 2021, 2022, and 2023 are estimated.

SOURCE: Office of Management and Budget, "Table 3.1—Outlays by Superfunction and Function: 1940–2025," www.whitehouse.gov/omb/historical-tables/ (accessed 3/7/22).

own interests without paying much attention to the views of its allies. Indeed, Trump declared that America's European allies were not doing enough to defend themselves and were relying on American weapons and money when they should bolster their own military capabilities.

Trump's aggressive posture and unilateral policies were criticized by Democrats, and after taking office in 2021, President Biden vowed to improve relations with America's allies and to rely on diplomacy rather than force in international affairs. During his first two years in office, however, Biden faced a number of serious foreign policy challenges that threatened these goals. In 2021, for example, America's European allies were furious when the United States precipitously withdrew its forces from Afghanistan without giving much notice to allied governments. And in 2022 diplomacy did not prevent Russia from invading Ukraine. In the wake of the invasion, Biden made an effort to work through the North American Treaty Organization (NATO) to counter the Russian challenge, joining the United States' NATO allies in sending military equipment to Ukraine and deploying more American forces to Europe to deter Russian action on the continent. In Asia, Biden has worked to bolster a security alliance that includes Japan, Australia, India, and South Korea as a counter to growing Chinese power. President Biden has also visited Saudi Arabia in an effort to improve relations with that country. Biden urged the Saudis to increase oil production in order to lower oil prices and reduce Western dependence on Russian energy exports.

Economic Prosperity

A second major goal of U.S. foreign policy is promoting American prosperity. America's international economic policies are intended to expand employment opportunities in the United States, maintain access to foreign energy supplies, promote foreign investment in the United States, lower the prices Americans pay for goods and services, and protect American economic interests at home and abroad.

Among the key elements of U.S. international economic policy is trade policy, which seeks to promote American goods and services and American investments abroad. The United States is the world's largest importer and exporter of goods and services. In 2017 it exported more than $2.3 trillion in goods and services while importing $2.9 trillion. Roughly 40 million jobs in the United States are directly or indirectly tied to international trade. Accordingly, America has a vital interest in maintaining international trade and monetary practices that promote American prosperity. The Trump administration frequently charged that America's trading partners, especially China, competed unfairly—exporting huge quantities of goods to the United States while refusing to accept American goods. Trump introduced a number of tariffs on foreign imports that he said would redress the imbalance. Though Democrats denounced these restrictions on trade, the Biden administration has kept most in place.

American trade policy involves a complex arrangement of treaties, tariffs, and other mechanisms of policy formation. Trade policy is always complicated because Americans have a complicated relationship to trade. Most Americans benefit from a policy of free trade, which tends to reduce the cost of goods and services. Consumer electronics such as televisions and smartphones, for example, would be far more expensive if they were not imported from all over the world. However, many American industries and their employees are hurt by free trade if it results in factories and jobs moving abroad. Hence, as we saw in the story at the beginning of the chapter, trade policy always produces fierce political battles between those who stand to benefit and those who stand to lose from particular policies.

World Trade Organization (WTO) an international organization promoting free trade that grew out of the General Agreement on Tariffs and Trade

United States–Mexico–Canada Agreement (USMCA) a trade treaty between the United States, Canada, and Mexico to lower and eliminate tariffs among the three countries

The United States is a member of the most important international organization for promoting trade, the **World Trade Organization (WTO)**, as well as a number of regional arrangements designed to reduce trade barriers. These include the **United States–Mexico–Canada Agreement (USMCA)**, formerly known as NAFTA, a trade treaty among the United States, Canada, and Mexico that the Trump administration renegotiated in 2018. Under the terms of the new agreement, the United States was able to obtain better access to the Canadian dairy market and obtained concessions from Mexico on auto imports.

The U.S. government also works to protect American investments abroad. Today, it tries to protect the intellectual property of American firms against foreign cyber attacks and protect against efforts by others, including the European Union, to reduce the local market power of American firms.

Promoting U.S. Ideals Overseas

Many Americans believe that the United States has an obligation to protect human rights, promote democracy, and provide humanitarian assistance throughout the world. Other Americans say we should spend our resources at home and let other nations look after their own people. Still a third group of Americans view human rights and humanitarian policies as a form of "soft power," serving American interests and winning friends by demonstrating our concern for the oppressed and less fortunate throughout the world. This third group has generally been dominant within the American foreign policy community.

The United States has a long-standing commitment to human rights and is a party to most major international human rights agreements. This commitment has a lower priority in American foreign policy than security concerns and economic interests, however; thus, the United States is likely to overlook human rights violations by its major trading partners, such as China, and such allies as Saudi Arabia. Nevertheless, human rights concerns do play a role in American foreign policy. For example, beginning in 2007 the United States has annually made available several million dollars in small grants to pay medical and legal expenses of individuals who have been the victims of retaliation in their own countries for working against their governments' repressive practices. In this small way, the United States is backing its often-asserted principles.

As the world's wealthiest nation, the United States also recognizes an obligation to assist nations facing emergencies. In 2020, for example, the United States provided assistance to Pacific Island nations that suffered millions of dollars in damage from Tropical Cyclone Harold and to the people of war-torn Yemen. In 2021 the United States assisted the people of Malawi after floods devastated the southern tip of the nation.

In many ways, the coronavirus pandemic revealed the limits on international cooperation in the face of global emergencies. Every nation, including the United States, worked to secure medical supplies and future supplies of potential vaccines for its own people with little concern for the interests of others. Eventually, however, these countries realized that so long as the virus raged and mutated in poorer nations, no country would be safe. Today, along with other wealthy states, the United States is donating hundreds of millions of dollars in vaccines to countries that could not afford to purchase the vaccines themselves.

As to the promotion of democracy, the United States generally favors demo-cratically elected governments and opposes regimes that fail to honor electoral outcomes. In 2021, for example, the United States condemned the coup in Myanmar that led to the arrest of many government officials and civil society leaders. However, the United States generally does not allow its pro-democracy stance to override what it sees as national interests. Thus, America supports autocratic regimes in Egypt, Saudi Arabia, and elsewhere that are friendly to the United States.

Check your understanding

1. Which of the following statements regarding U.S. foreign policy is true?

   a) Since the Cold War, the United States has taken an isolationist approach to foreign policy with the view that security is best served by leaving foreigners to their own devices.

   b) Whereas President Obama took an aggressive stance on foreign policy with threats of force against adversaries, President Trump took a less adversarial approach, relying on diplomacy and economic sanctions instead.

   c) While the United States used to be isolationist, technology and growing economic inter-dependence have led to the con-struction of an enormous military apparatus and a complex array of intelligence-gathering institu-tions charged with evaluating and anticipating challenges from abroad.

   d) Since the September 11 terrorist attacks, the United States has shifted from a policy of preventive war toward one of deterrence, focusing primarily on nation-states rather than non-state actors.

2. How is the foreign policy of the United States designed to promote prosperity?

   a) Since the 1970s, the United States has adopted a protection-ist approach in foreign policy involving tariffs and import quotas to protect the manufacturing industry.

   b) The United States has adopted international economic policies aimed at expanding employment opportunities in the United States, promoting foreign investment in the country, and protecting American economic interests at home and abroad.

   c) The United States ended its trade agreement with Mexico and has substantially reduced its exports.

   d) During the Trump administration, the United States entered into many trade agreements and reduced tariffs to promote free trade; however, the Biden administration has taken a different approach by ending trade agreements and introducing tariffs to protect U.S. workers.

American Foreign Policy Is Shaped by Government and Nongovernment Actors

Describe the structure and roles of the major organizations and players in U.S. foreign-policy making

As we have seen, domestic policies are made by governmental institutions and influenced by a variety of interest groups, political movements, and even the mass media. The same is true in the realm of foreign policy. The president and the chief advisers are the principal architects of U.S. foreign policy. However, Congress, the bureaucracy, the courts, political parties, interest groups, and trade associations also play important roles.

More than other policy arenas, foreign policy is the domain of elites. There is very little economic or racial and ethnic diversity within the American foreign policy establishment, and, for most Americans, foreign policy is a mystery. Except in times of war, Americans do not see foreign policy as being clearly linked to their daily lives.[6] And even during wartime, foreign policy can seem distant to most Americans. Since the 1970s, America's wars have been fought by all-volunteer professional military forces. This has helped to insulate elites from popular opposition to their policies and increased the extent to which foreign policy is driven by elite rather than popular opinion.

The President and the Executive Branch

The president is the leading figure in the conduct of American foreign policy. The president's foreign policy powers today, particularly in the military realm, are far greater than the Constitution's framers had thought wise. The framers gave the power to declare war to Congress and made the president the nation's top military commander when Congress chose to go to war. Today, presidents both command the troops and decide when to go to war.

Among America's 15 presidents during the past century only 5—Hoover, Eisenhower, Nixon, George H. W. Bush, and Joe Biden—had any extensive foreign policy experience before taking office.[7]

All recent presidents, like most of their predecessors, were nevertheless faced with momentous challenges to American security and to America's international interests. George W. Bush, in particular, was compelled to develop a response to the September 11, 2001, terror attacks. In a 2002 speech at West Point, the president announced a policy of unilateral action and preemptive war—what came to be called the **Bush Doctrine**. Bush said, "Our security will require all Americans . . . to be ready for preemptive action when necessary to defend our liberty and to defend our lives."

Bush Doctrine foreign policy based on the idea that the United States should take preemptive action against threats to its national security

In his own West Point speech in 2014, President Obama articulated a different policy when he said the United States must reduce its reliance on military force and make more use of diplomacy. But even though he expressed reservations about unilateral preemption, during his administration the United States continued to launch many attacks against suspected terrorists before they were able to strike.

President Trump rattled America's allies by declaring an "America first" foreign policy and adopting a confrontational posture toward North Korea and Iran. President Biden hoped to reduce international tensions but found himself facing a Russian invasion of Ukraine and the possibility that China would attack Taiwan. These problems forced Biden to focus his efforts on rallying America's allies, accelerating American arms transfers to Ukraine, and demonstrating American resolve in the Pacific through naval exercises and other warnings to China.

As the dominant figure in American foreign and military policy, the president is in a position to decide with whom, when, and how the United States will interact in the international arena. Since World War II, American military forces have fought in many parts of the world. The decision to commit troops to battle was generally made by the president, often without much consultation with the Congress. When President Obama ordered special operations soldiers to attack Osama bin Laden's compound in Pakistan, members of Congress learned of the operation and bin Laden's death from news broadcasts—just like other Americans. And it is the president and his representatives who conduct negotiations with other nations to deal with international problems and crises.

Presidents can also make use of **executive agreements** to partially bypass congressional power in foreign relations. Executive agreements are agreements made by the president with other countries that have the force of a treaty but do not require Senate ratification. Thus, the importance of the Senate's constitutional power to block treaties has sharply diminished. Since 1947 the United States has entered into more than 17,000 different agreements with other nations and international entities. Of these, only 6 percent were submitted to the Senate for approval.[8]

executive agreement an agreement, made between the president and another country, that has the force of a treaty but does not require the Senate's "advice and consent"

Beyond the president, several government agencies within the executive branch play important roles in shaping and executing American foreign policy.

The National Security Council The National Security Council (NSC) was created in 1947 as an entity within the Executive Office of the President (EOP) to oversee America's foreign policy institutions, synthesize information coming from the bureaucracy, and help the president develop foreign policy.[9] The NSC is a "subcabinet" made up of the president, the vice president, and the secretaries of defense, state, and homeland security, plus other presidential appointees, including the director of the CIA and the director of national intelligence. The heart of the NSC is its staff, consisting of about 200 foreign policy experts capable of evaluating political, economic, and military issues throughout the world. The head of the NSC staff is the president's national security adviser.[10] Some national security

AMERICA | SIDE BY SIDE

Foreign Aid in Comparison

Many Americans overestimate both the amount that the government spends on foreign aid and the percent of gross national income (GNI), a measure of the overall size of the economy, spent on foreign aid. In these figures we see that the United States is the clear global leader if one looks at the dollars spent on foreign aid. However, if we take account of the size and wealth of a country's economy, the United States falls much further down the rankings.

1. Why would a country choose to spend money on foreign aid? What factors would limit the amount a country was willing or able to spend on such aid?
2. Do the data in these figures imply that America is less generous with aid than other nations are? What other explanations are there for the differences across countries? America also spends substantially more than those other countries on its military and on overseas defense. How should that be factored into considerations of the value that America provides its allies?

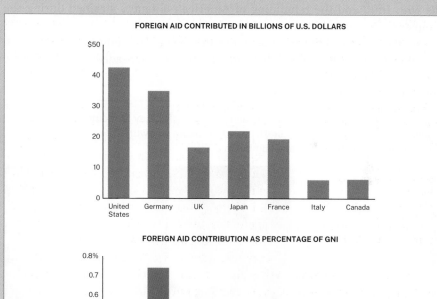

FOREIGN AID CONTRIBUTED IN BILLIONS OF U.S. DOLLARS

FOREIGN AID CONTRIBUTION AS PERCENTAGE OF GNI

SOURCE: Organization for Economic Cooperation and Development, "Development Cooperation Report 2021," www.oecd.org (accessed 6/3/22).

advisers have been close presidential confidants and have exercised considerable power because they had the president's ear and trust.

The State Department Routine matters of international diplomacy come under the authority of the Department of State, the first federal agency created by the first Congress in 1789. The State Department is headed by the secretary of state, a member of the president's Cabinet and, nominally, the most important foreign policy official after the president. The secretary's actual importance varies with their relationship to the president. Franklin Delano Roosevelt, for example, was barely aware that Cordell Hull existed, relegating the secretary to observer of the diplomatic scene. On the other end of the spectrum, George W. Bush worked very closely with Condoleezza Rice, who served as his chief foreign policy adviser. In some instances, presidents use their secretaries less as advisers and more as roving ambassadors, like John Kerry in the Obama administration.

Joe Biden appointed Antony Blinken, a career diplomat, to the post of secretary of state. Blinken has played important roles in the formulation of Biden's policies toward Russia and China, Biden's decision to resume nuclear talks with Iran, and the rebuilding of American alliances strained during the Trump era.

The State Department oversees more than 300 U.S. embassies, consulates, and diplomatic missions around the world. Embassies are headed by ambassadors.

The president meets with many foreign leaders, often after key agreements have been hammered out by the president's staff. President Biden met with Mexican president Andrés Manuel López Obrador at a summit in 2021.

While most embassy staff members are officers of the U.S. Foreign Service, the State Department's professional diplomatic corps, a number of ambassadors have no diplomatic expertise and are, instead, political appointees being rewarded for their campaign contributions to the president.

The United States "recognizes" and maintains diplomatic relations with 195 countries. It does not officially recognize Iran or North Korea. Recognition means that the United States accepts the nation's government as lawful, will engage in routine trade and diplomatic exchanges with it, and will accept its citizens' passports for travel into the United States. At the various embassies and missions, State Department officials monitor American treaty and trade relations with the host country, assist American business interests and tourists, and deal with foreign nationals attempting to emigrate to or visit the United States.

Department of Defense Since its creation in 1947, the Defense Department (DOD) has played a major role in the making of American foreign policy. DOD employs more than 2 million military and civilian personnel and is a huge and complex bureaucratic entity.[11] Each of the military services—the army, navy, air force, marines, and National Guard—is led by a chief of staff, and collectively these leaders constitute the Joint Chiefs of Staff (JCS), led by the chairperson of the Joint Chiefs, a presidential appointee who serves as the nation's top military commander. The chairperson reports directly to the secretary of defense, who, in turn, answers to the president. Each of the three main services—army, navy, and air force—possesses its own civilian and military bureaucracies to administer and support its combat forces.

In recent years, American ambassadors have complained that they have been relegated to secondary status as the White House has looked to military commanders for information, advice, and policy implementation. For every region of the world, the U.S. military has assigned a "combatant commander," a senior general or admiral, to take charge of operations in that area. In many instances, these combatant commanders, who control troops, equipment, and intelligence capabilities, have become the real eyes, ears, and voices for American foreign policy in their designated regions. The combatant commanders report to the JCS.

Intelligence Agencies America's intelligence community consists of some 18 agencies. The most prominent of these is the Central Intelligence Agency (CIA).

President Biden nominated army four-star general Lloyd Austin to be secretary of defense. Austin is the first Black person to head the Department of Defense.

The CIA is the United States' chief civilian intelligence agency, collecting information throughout the world, preparing analyses, and launching covert operations if the president wishes to use force but is unwilling to publicly acknowledge America's involvement. CIA operators also pilot many of the drones used to attack and kill suspected terrorists. Although the CIA and DOD were created by the same piece of legislation, the CIA director and secretary of defense have generally viewed one another as rivals in the intelligence field.

In 2005, Congress created the position of director of national intelligence (DNI) to coordinate intelligence activities and prepare the president's daily intelligence summary—a responsibility previously held by the CIA's director. This change came about because Congress concluded that the intelligence community's failure to anticipate the September 11, 2001, attacks was the result of a lack of coordination among the various agencies. Both the CIA and DOD resented the creation of the DNI, however, and put aside their mutual suspicions to join forces against the new position. Both agencies generally refuse to share information with the DNI, who, having no operational capabilities, has been left in the dark on many intelligence matters. National intelligence agencies seem generally to regard one another as rivals.[12]

The National Security Agency The National Security Agency (NSA) is a highly influential, and controversial, intelligence agency. Though housed within DOD, the NSA effectively reports directly to the president, providing the results of its worldwide electronic surveillance efforts. Surveillance of electronic communication has a long history in the United States, going back to a World War I government effort to read suspicious telegrams.[13] During the 1970s, however, Congress became concerned about secret White House surveillance efforts and, in 1978, enacted the Foreign Intelligence Surveillance Act (FISA), designed to regulate electronic surveillance by government agencies.

Congress

Through its general legislative powers, Congress can exercise broad influence over foreign policy. Congress may, for example, refuse to appropriate funds for presidential actions it finds unwise or inappropriate. This power of the purse also extends to military action. Not only does Congress have the constitutional power to declare war, but under its general legislative powers it must appropriate the funds needed to support military activities. In *Federalist* 69, Hamilton argues that Congress's power of the purse provides it with an ultimate check on the president's power as commander in chief.[14]

Presidents, as we saw, control several enormous bureaucracies through which to develop and implement foreign and security policies. Congress has far less bureaucratic capacity of its own, but it has committees that can influence the nation's international and military programs. Chief among these are the House and Senate committees charged with overseeing foreign policy, military affairs, and the collection and analysis of intelligence.

Key Congressional Committees in Foreign Policy In the Senate, the most influential committee dealing with foreign policy is the U.S. Senate Committee on Foreign Relations. Established in 1816 as one of the original 10 standing committees of the Senate, it oversees the State Department, other foreign policy agencies, and executive branch compliance with several statutes, including the War Powers Resolution. Each of its seven subcommittees has jurisdiction over a specific region or subject matter.

Throughout its history, the Foreign Relations Committee has viewed its role as the guardian of congressional power in the foreign policy realm. Its power stems from its responsibility to confirm State Department officials and the requirement that it review treaties proposed by the executive branch before they can be referred to the full Senate for a vote on ratification. In recent years, the committee's efforts to influence presidential foreign policy initiatives have become less successful because presidents, as we noted previously, have made use of executive agreements (not requiring senatorial approval) rather than treaties. Nevertheless, the committee occasionally asserts itself.

Paralleling the jurisdiction of the Senate Foreign Relations Committee is the House Committee on Foreign Affairs. The House committee is considerably less influential than its Senate counterpart, however, because it is involved neither in appointments nor in the ratification of treaties. For the most part, its hearings focus on symbolic questions.

In both houses of Congress, standing subcommittees of the Appropriations Committees are responsible for funding the State Department, foreign aid programs, and other matters in the foreign policy realm. Through these subcommittees as well as through the Foreign Relations and Foreign Affairs Committees, the Senate and House can indicate their displeasure with presidential programs by cutting or withholding funds. In 2020, for example, the Senate Appropriations Committee restored a 20 percent cut in funding for the State Department and foreign operations that had been mandated by the Trump administration.

Armed Services and Intelligence The House and Senate Armed Services Committees oversee the Department of Defense and the Department of Energy (which houses America's nuclear weapons programs). In both houses of Congress, other standing committees are responsible for such matters as veterans' affairs. Defense appropriations are the domains of the House and Senate Defense Appropriations Subcommittees.

Generally, the House and Senate Armed Services Committees are friendly to the military and the defense contractors who provide support and equipment for America's military services. Sometimes, however, they make use of their staff resources and contacts in the military community to advocate for military programs not currently in the Pentagon's plans. In 2022, for example, the House and Senate armed services committees sought to add programs costing $37 billion to the $773 billion in military spending proposed by the president.

The House and Senate Intelligence Committees were established during the 1970s to oversee America's growing intelligence bureaucracies and to review their activities at home and abroad. These committees have focused on such matters as American intelligence failures (notably the failure to predict and prevent the September 11, 2001, terrorist attacks), the use of private military contractors in missions organized by the CIA, clandestine CIA missions in other nations, and the use of drones to carry out military and intelligence missions in other nations. In 2019 the House Intelligence Committee reviewed allegations that President Trump had behaved improperly in dealing with Ukraine. Information reviewed by the Intelligence Committee helped to persuade congressional Democrats to support the president's impeachment.

Interest Groups

Although the president, the executive branch bureaucracy, and Congress are the true makers of foreign policy, the "foreign policy establishment" is a much larger arena. Many unofficial players exert varying degrees of influence on foreign policy, depending on their prestige and socioeconomic standing and, most important, the party and ideology that are dominant at a given moment.

The most important unofficial players are interest groups. Economic groups are reputed to wield the most influence, but in fact it varies enormously from issue to issue and year to year. Some business groups represent industries dependent on exports, and others represent ones threatened by imports. Hence, "business" has more than one view on trade policy.

Another type of interest group with significant foreign policy influence comprises people who strongly identify with a particular country. For example, many Jewish Americans and evangelical Protestants possess strong emotional ties to Israel. In 2015 many, though not all, Jewish and evangelical groups lobbied heavily but ultimately unsuccessfully against the Obama administration's agreement with Iran, which they argued posed a threat to both the United States and Israel. Similarly, Cuban Americans, most recently represented by two powerful senators, Marco Rubio and Ted Cruz, have long been a strong voice in support of maintaining sanctions against the former Castro regime in Cuba. Their influence helps explain why U.S. relations with Cuba were not normalized until 2015 and remain tenuous today.

A third type of interest group, more prominent in recent decades, is devoted to human rights or other global causes such as protection of the environment. An example is Amnesty International, whose exposés of human rights abuses have led to reforms in some countries. Environmental groups often depend more on demonstrations than on lobbying and electoral politics. Demonstrations in strategically located areas can have significant influence on American foreign policy. In recent years environmental activists have staged major protests, including at the 2015 Paris environmental summit that led to the signing of a series of international accords aimed at limiting the production of greenhouse gases. Environmental groups were furious when the Trump administration announced in 2017 that the United States would withdraw from the Paris Agreement.

Check your understanding

3. Which of the following statements best describes the major governmental players in foreign policy?

   a) Congress and the president have a co-equal role in foreign policy, with other executive agencies and legislative committees serving in an advisory role.

   b) Congress has the leading role on foreign policy, with the president serving in an advisory role.

   c) An executive committee of military generals has the leading role in foreign policy, with Congress and the president implementing their policies.

   d) The president is the leading figure in foreign policy but has a network of advisers such as the National Security Council, the State Department, the Department of Defense, and the National Security Agency.

4. Which outside groups or organizations exercise the most influence over foreign policy?

   a) interest groups
   b) the public
   c) state governors
   d) churches

Tools of American Foreign Policy: Diplomacy, Money, and Force

Describe the means the United States uses to carry out foreign policy today

Governments possess a variety of instruments, or tools, to implement foreign policy. We examine those instruments of American foreign policy most important today: diplomacy, the United Nations, the international monetary structure, economic aid and sanctions, collective security, military force, soft power, and arbitration.

Diplomacy

Diplomacy is a national government's representation of itself to foreign governments. Its purpose is to promote national values or interests by peaceful means. As mentioned earlier, the United States maintains diplomatic missions throughout

> **diplomacy** the representation of a government to other governments

the world. American ambassadors are tasked with maintaining good relations with foreign governments, promoting a positive view of the United States abroad, and securing information about foreign governments that might be helpful to the United States in its international dealings. When it comes to major diplomatic initiatives, however, such as new international agreements, presidents or their personal representatives usually take charge.

The United Nations

The **United Nations (UN)** is a very large and unwieldy institution with few powers, no standing armed forces of its own to implement its rules and resolutions, and little organization to make it an effective decision-making body. However, the usefulness of the UN to the United States as an instrument of foreign policy can be too easily underestimated. Its defenders maintain that although it lacks armed forces, it relies on the power of world opinion—and this is not to be taken lightly. The UN can serve as a useful forum for international discussions and as an instrument for multilateral action. Most peacekeeping efforts to which the United States contributes, for example, are undertaken under UN auspices.

United Nations (UN) an organization of nations founded in 1945 to be a channel for negotiation and a means of settling international disputes peaceably

The United Nations' supreme body is the UN General Assembly, comprising one representative of each of the 193 member states; each member representative has one vote, regardless of the size of the country. Important issues require a two-thirds majority vote, and the annual session of the General Assembly runs only from September to December (although it can call extra sessions). The powers of the UN belong mainly to its "executive committee," the UN Security Council, which alone has the real power to make decisions that member states are obligated by the UN Charter to implement. The Security Council may be called into session at any time, and the representative of each member (or a designated alternate) must be present at UN headquarters in New York at all times.

The Security Council is composed of 15 members: 5 are permanent (China, France, Russia, the United Kingdom, and the United States—the major countries on the winning side in World War II), and 10 are elected by the General Assembly for two-year terms. Each of the 15 members has only one vote, and a 9-vote majority is required on all substantive matters. But each of the 5 permanent members also has a negative vote, a "veto," and one veto is sufficient to reject any substantive proposal.

The International Monetary Structure

Fear of a repeat of the economic devastation that had followed World War I brought the United States together with its World War II allies (except the Soviet Union) to Bretton Woods, New Hampshire, in 1944 to create a new international economic structure for the postwar world. One major goal was to prevent economic instability that might lead to political instability and war, like the economic collapse in

Germany that had opened the way for Nazism. At the same time, the new structure would give the United States and its allies greater leverage in the economic and political affairs of developing countries.

The Bretton Woods conference resulted in two institutions: the International Bank for Reconstruction and Development, commonly called the World Bank, and the **International Monetary Fund (IMF)**. The World Bank's chief mission is development aid to poor countries through long-term capital investments. The IMF was set up to provide for the short-term flow of money. After the war, the U.S. dollar replaced gold as the chief means by which the currency of one country would be "changed into" the currency of another country for purposes of making international transactions. To permit debtor countries with no international credit to make purchases and investments, the IMF was prepared to lend them dollars or other appropriate currencies to help them overcome temporary trade deficits.

International Monetary Fund (IMF) an institution established in 1944 that provides loans and facilitates international monetary exchange

During the 1990s the importance of the IMF increased through its efforts to reform some of the largest debtor nations and formerly communist countries to bring them more fully into the global capitalist economy. Today, IMF loans total nearly $200 billion to 35 countries, including 16 in sub-Saharan Africa, where drought and war have undermined local economies.

Economic Aid and Sanctions

Every year, the United States, acting on its own, provides nearly $50 billion in economic and military assistance to other nations. Some aid has a humanitarian purpose, such as health care, shelter for refugees, or famine relief. A good deal of it, however, is designed to promote American security interests or economic concerns. For example, the United States provides military assistance to a number of its allies in the form of advanced weapons or loans to help them purchase such weapons. These loans generally stipulate that the weapons must be purchased from American firms. In this way, the United States hopes to bolster its security and economic interests with one grant. The two largest recipients of American military assistance are Israel and Egypt, American allies that fought two wars against each other. The United States believes that its military assistance allows both countries to feel sufficiently secure to remain at peace with each other.

Aid is an economic carrot (an incentive or reward). Sanctions are an economic stick (a punishment). Economic sanctions that the United States employs against other nations include trade embargoes, bans on investment, and efforts to prevent the World Bank or other international institutions from extending credit. Sanctions are most often imposed when the United States wants to weaken what it considers a hostile regime, to compel some particular action, or to advance its international humanitarian and human rights policy goals. U.S. sanctions are currently in place against a number of governments with records of serious violations of civil and political rights.[15]

Collective Security

Collective security refers to the development of alliances and agreements among a group of nations that pledge to aid one another in fending off or confronting security threats. In the aftermath of World War II, the United States' first collective security agreement was the Rio Treaty (1947), which created the Organization of American States. This was the model for all later collective security treaties, providing that an armed attack against any of its members "shall be considered as an attack against all the American [Western Hemisphere] States," including the United States. It was followed by the North Atlantic Treaty (signed in 1949), which created NATO, joining the United States, Canada, and western European nations. The Australian, New Zealand, United States Security (ANZUS) Treaty was signed in 1951. Three years later, the Southeast Asia Treaty created the Southeast Asia Treaty Organization (SEATO).

Since 1998, NATO has expanded to include formerly communist eastern European states such as the Czech Republic, Hungary, and Poland. After the collapse of the Soviet Union, the importance of NATO as a military alliance seemed to diminish. However, since 2014 the resurgence of Russia as a military power has forced NATO members to look to one another for support. In 2014, Russia seized the Crimean Peninsula from Ukraine and appeared to pose a threat to the Baltic states and other portions of the old Soviet empire. Russia has also sent military forces to support the Assad regime in Syria. In 2019, Russia sought to take advantage of President Trump's decision to withdraw most American forces from Syria by expanding its own power in the region. And, in 2021–22, Russia invaded Ukraine to deal with what it claimed were threats to its own security emanating from NATO's support for the Ukrainian regime. Making good use of weapons supplied by the United States and NATO allies, Ukraine was able to inflict considerable damage on the Russian army and prevent Russia from overrunning the country. By September 2022, the Ukrainians were able to launch major counterattacks that drove the Russians out of much of the territory they had seized. NATO's period of relative quiet seemed to be ending. And, in response to Russian aggression in Ukraine, NATO is set to expand by accepting Finland and Sweden into the alliance.

Military Force

The most visible instrument of foreign policy is, of course, military force. The United States has built the world's most imposing military, with units stationed in virtually every corner of the globe, and accounts for one-third of the world's total military expenditures. The Prussian military strategist Carl von Clausewitz famously called war "politics by other means." By this he meant that force or the threat of it is a tool nations must sometimes use to achieve their foreign policy goals. Military force may be needed not only to protect a nation's security and economic interests but also, ironically, to achieve humanitarian goals. For example, in 2014 and 2015, international military force was required to protect tens of thousands of Yazidi refugees threatened by ISIS forces in Iraq. Without the use of military force, humanitarian assistance to the Yazidis would have been irrelevant.[16]

Military force is generally considered a last resort and is avoided if possible, for several reasons. First, its use is extremely costly in both human and financial terms. Over the past 50 years, tens of thousands of Americans have been killed and hundreds of billions of dollars spent in America's military operations. Before they use military force to achieve national goals, policy makers must be certain that achieving those goals is essential and that other means are unlikely to succeed.

Second, the use of military force is inherently extremely risky. However carefully policy makers and generals plan, variables ranging from the weather to opponents' unexpected weapons and tactics may turn calculated operations into chaotic disasters, or operations expected to be quick and decisive into long, drawn-out, expensive struggles. In 2003, American policy makers expected to defeat the Iraqi army quickly and easily—and they did. They did not anticipate, however, that American forces would still be struggling years later to defeat the insurgency that arose in the war's aftermath.

Finally, in a democracy any government that addresses policy problems through military means is almost certain to encounter political difficulties. Generally speaking, the American public will support relatively short and decisive military engagements. If, however, a conflict drags on, producing casualties and expenses with no clear outcome, the public loses patience, and opposition politicians point to the government's lies and ineptitude. The wars in Korea, Vietnam, and Iraq are all examples of protracted conflicts whose domestic political repercussions became serious liabilities for the governments that launched them.

Soft Power

The term *soft power* refers to efforts by one nation to influence the people and governments of other nations by persuasion rather than coercion. The instruments of soft power include development aid, cultural diplomacy, student-exchange

---

Often, military efforts abroad do not turn out as the government or the public expected. Though most Americans were in favor of U.S. involvement in Afghanistan following September 11, 2001, public opinion on the issue shifted.

programs, and other mechanisms designed to shape perceptions. Cultural programs that send American actors, athletes, and musicians around the world are thought to offer a positive view of the United States that will encourage foreign governments and their citizens to see America as the "good guy" in international disputes. The Peace Corps sends young Americans to poor countries to help with projects and programs and to build friendships between Americans and the citizens of those countries. Exchange programs that bring foreign students to the United States serve a similar purpose. Although the effects of soft power are difficult to measure, the United States promotes its "brand" of freedom and democracy throughout the world.

Arbitration

The final foreign policy tool to be considered is dispute arbitration. *Arbitration* means referring an international disagreement to a neutral third party for resolution. Arbitration is itself sometimes seen as a form of soft power, as distinguished from military force, economic sanctions, and other coercive foreign policy instruments. The United States occasionally turns to international tribunals to resolve disputes with other countries—in 2008 it asked the International Court of Justice to resolve a long-standing dispute with Italy over American property confiscated by the Italian government more than 40 years earlier. The Trump administration generally rejected the authority of international bodies that it saw as limitations on American sovereignty.

The United States continues to rely heavily on the work of arbitral panels to maintain the flow of international trade on which the U.S. economy depends. U.S. firms would be reluctant to do business abroad if they could not be certain that their property and contractual rights would be honored by other nations. Arbitration helps produce that certainty. Almost every international contract contains an arbitration clause requiring that disputes between the parties be resolved not by their governments but by impartial arbitral panels accepted by both sides.

Check your understanding

5. The United States relies on different tools to achieve its goals internationally. Sometimes these involve soft powers, while in other cases states may rely on hard powers. How do soft powers and hard powers differ?

   a) Hard powers refer to those authorized by the United Nations Security Council, while soft powers are those within the authority of the North Atlantic Treaty Organization.

   b) Hard powers include coercive foreign policy instruments like military force or economic sanctions, while soft powers refer to efforts to influence other nations through persuasion, including development aid, student-exchange programs, arbitration, or cultural diplomacy.

c) Hard powers refer to those that must involve the military, while soft powers do not generally involve the military.

d) Hard powers are tools implemented by the United States that have a duration for at least one year, while soft powers are short-term tools that typically only last three months.

6. What function have alliances played in foreign policy since World War II?

a) Alliances have had a mostly symbolic function since World War II as nation-states, including the United States, have taken an isolationist approach to foreign policy.

b) Alliances have served only a diplomatic function with limited role in fending off security threats.

c) Alliances, such as the North Atlantic Treaty Organization (NATO), have advanced members' collective interests, such as fending off or confronting security threats by combining capabilities.

d) Alliances have declined in importance since the War on Terror.

Daunting Foreign Policy Issues Face the United States

Explain the foreign policy problems facing American policy makers today

The United States currently faces many foreign policy problems, but this section will examine only a few major issues that stand out: relations with China and Russia, relations with Iran and North Korea, international trade policy, and the global environment. Each reveals how the key players in foreign policy use the tools at their disposal to achieve their policy goals.

A Powerful China and a Resurgent Russia

After the United States, China and Russia are the world's greatest military powers. China is an economic power as well, with an economy that in some respects already outpaces America's and continues to grow. China seems determined to expand its military capabilities and to replace the United States as the dominant power in Asia. The United States has no desire to engage in a military conflict with China but, at the same time, would prefer to blunt Chinese ambitions.

The relationship between the United States and China represents a growing concern for American policy makers, who have worked to strengthen U.S. alliances with other Asian nations, including India, Japan, and Vietnam, in order to increase American power in the region and prevent the rise of China. President Trump sought to use trade policy, especially tariff barriers and stricter efforts to prevent China from acquiring American intellectual property, to forestall the rise of Chinese power.

While relations with China are a long-term problem, those with Russia present a more immediate set of issues. Once the center of a global superpower that was America's chief rival, Russia remains heavily armed but economically weak. Under its current leader, Vladimir Putin, Russia has challenged the United States in Europe and in the Middle East, and has even meddled in American politics.[17]

The first in this series of direct Russian challenges to the United States came in 2014, when Russian forces seized control of the Crimean Peninsula, an area that had been part of Ukraine and that was important to Russia because of its strategic location on the Black Sea, giving Russia a significant naval base. Russian troops next massed along other portions of the Ukrainian border. The Obama administration urged the Russians to withdraw, announced a program of economic sanctions, and encouraged NATO allies to impose sanctions as well.

The result illustrated the difficulties inherent in collective action and the use of sanctions. Many of the United States' European allies depend on Russian energy supplies and engage in a good deal of trade with the Russians. As a result, while all agreed in principle that Russia should withdraw from Crimea, none were prepared to follow the American lead of imposing sanctions. Later in 2014, Russia formally annexed Crimea, though the action was not officially recognized by the United States. Subsequently, Russian forces supported separatist groups in several other parts of Ukraine.

In 2022, Russia invaded Ukraine, hoping to topple the pro-Western government and replace it with a regime more friendly to Moscow. The Ukrainians resisted fiercely, and with billions of dollars in arms from the United States and other NATO countries, Ukraine was able to stop the Russians. The United States and its allies feared that Ukraine would be just the first step in a Russian effort to dominate Europe and were determined to thwart Russia's plans.

Both the Chinese and the Russians have made use of extensive electronic hacking to break into the computer systems of American government agencies and American firms and, in the case of Russia, interfere in U.S. elections.[18] Both countries deny these allegations—as does the United States when accused of hacking into Russian and Chinese systems.[19]

To complicate America's problems, China and Russia have found common ground in their rivalry with the United States in recent years. The two countries have developed significant trade relations and support one another in international affairs. What some call the "alliance of autocrats" poses a major challenge to the United States.

Nuclear Proliferation in Iran and North Korea

Unlike China and Russia, Iran and North Korea are not great powers, but both present challenges to the United States, especially in the realm of nuclear proliferation. Though it is a nuclear power, the United States has generally seen nuclear proliferation as leading to a more dangerous world and has done what it can to prevent more countries from developing nuclear weapons.

Iran and the United States have been adversaries since 1979, when Iranians overthrew an unpopular U.S.-backed leader, Shah Reza Pahlavi. For years the United States has worried that Iran is working toward obtaining nuclear weapons with which it could threaten Saudi Arabia and Israel—both close U.S. allies—and bring Middle Eastern oil fields under its control. To prevent Iran from obtaining nuclear weapons, U.S. presidents have used a mix of carrots (in the form of diplomacy) and sticks (in the form of sanctions). Sanctions made it more difficult for Iran to sell its oil, its major export, hurting its economy. In this case, U.S. allies mostly cooperated with the sanctions.

In 2015 the United States and Iran signed an agreement in which the Iranians pledged not to build nuclear weapons in exchange for a lifting of the economic sanctions. Critics of the agreement charged it would not deter the Iranians from continuing with their nuclear program, and during his presidential campaign Donald Trump promised to abandon the agreement. In 2018, Trump withdrew from the agreement. In 2019, Iran resumed parts of its nuclear program.

As for North Korea, U.S. efforts to undermine its regime have been difficult because China, North Korea's major backer and trading partner, will not cooperate. China regards North Korea as a useful pawn on the geopolitical chessboard, preventing the United States and two of its allies, Japan and South Korea, from dominating the Sea of Japan. As a result, the North Koreans have continued to build nuclear warheads and to test missiles capable of carrying them.

Trade Policy

Trade is one of the most contentious issues in contemporary international relations. The United States persistently imports more than it exports, producing a substantial trade deficit with the rest of the world. The United States has accused China and other nations of unfair trade practices that limit the sale of imported goods in their markets while they export billions of dollars in goods to the United States. Trade also affects job growth in the United States. Populist politicians like Donald Trump charge that this is the result of trade policies that allowed American jobs to be exported to Asia and Mexico, where labor is cheaper. Trade, as we saw previously, supports many millions of jobs in the United States. However, U.S. workers whose jobs were lost when industries moved abroad call for tariffs and other remedies they hope might bring their jobs back to the United States.

Many workers voted for Trump, who during his 2016 campaign promised to bring these jobs back. One of Trump's first acts in office was to withdraw from the Trans-Pacific Partnership (TPP), a free-trade agreement between the United States and 11 Pacific Rim nations. Trump said the TPP would allow foreign countries to profit at America's expense.

Trade disputes have especially complicated America's relationship with China. President Trump declared that the Chinese act unfairly and promised to change the rules in America's favor—a move that increased Chinese hostility toward the

United States. In 2018 he announced the imposition of $50 billion in tariffs on Chinese steel, aluminum, and electronic goods sold to the United States, and China quickly announced that it would retaliate with tariffs on U.S. farm products, seafoods, and autos sold in China. These moves raised the prospect of an all-out trade war between the world's two largest economies. In January 2020, however, the United States and China signed a new trade agreement that reduced some U.S. tariffs in exchange for a Chinese agreement to purchase more American agricultural goods.

Global Environmental Policy

Another trouble spot for American policy makers is international environmental policy. The environment is a global matter, since pollutants produced in one country affect all others, and America, along with other industrial nations like China, is a major producer of pollution. Generally speaking, the United States supports various international efforts to protect the environment. These include the United Nations Framework Convention on Climate Change, an international agreement to study and ameliorate harmful changes in the global environment, and the Montreal Protocol, an agreement by over 150 countries to limit the production of substances potentially harmful to the world's ozone layer.

Other nations have criticized the United States for withdrawing from the 1997 Kyoto Protocol, an agreement setting limits on industrial countries' emissions of greenhouse gases. The United States asserted that the limits would harm American economic interests. The Kyoto Protocol expired in 2012, but 37 of the original signatories signed the Doha Amendment to renew their commitment to reduce greenhouse gas emissions. The United States refrained from signing this new agreement as well.

In 2015, however, the United States did agree to the Paris Agreement to reduce greenhouse gas emissions. Each country agreed to reduce emissions but would determine its own contribution to the effort. Many Republicans, including Donald Trump, opposed the agreement, and, as president, Trump ended U.S. participation in it, stating that strict environmental controls would undermine American manufacturing interests and cause more jobs to leave the United States to the benefit of developing nations without such standards. America's western European allies, on the other hand, remain committed to the Paris Agreement and view the American decision as uninformed and reckless.[20] Soon after taking office, President Biden issued executive orders restoring American participation in the Paris Agreement.

FOR CRITICAL ANALYSIS

1. Which states would you expect to benefit the most from international trade? Why?
2. The United States' top trading partners are Canada and Mexico. What impact does this have on our relationship with those two countries?

WHO ARE AMERICANS?

Who Benefits from International Trade?

International trade is crucial to both the American economy and the global economy. In fact, 18.3 percent of revenue in the United States comes from trade. Certain U.S. states engage in more international trade than others, but all participate. Which states engage in the most international trade, and with whom?

Trade Revenue as a Percentage of Total State Revenue, 2019

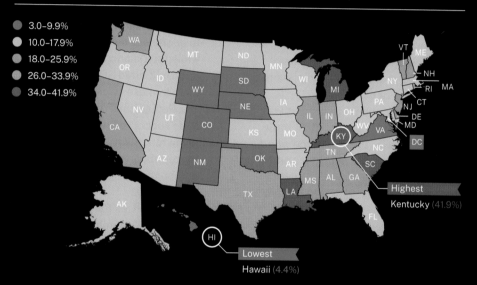

- 3.0–9.9%
- 10.0–17.9%
- 18.0–25.9%
- 26.0–33.9%
- 34.0–41.9%

Highest
Kentucky (41.9%)

Lowest
Hawaii (4.4%)

Top Exported Goods and Trading Partners by State, 2019

States with highest percent of revenue from trade	Top trading partner	Top exported products
1 Kentucky	Canada	Civilian aircraft parts
2 Michigan	Canada	Motor vehicles
3 Louisiana	Mexico	Oil/petroleum
4 South Carolina	China	Civilian aircraft parts
5 Texas	Mexico	Oil/petroleum
6 Tennessee	Canada	Medical instruments
7 Indiana	Canada	Medicine
8 New Jersey	Canada	Minerals
9 Illinois	Canada	Oil/petroleum
10 Mississippi	Canada	Oil/petroleum

SOURCE: Bureau of Economic Analysis, "Regional Data, GDP," www.bea.gov; U.S. Census Bureau, "Foreign Trade," www.census.gov (accessed 9/15/20).

Check your understanding

7. Which of the following statements regarding contemporary foreign policy issues is true?

   a) Although Iran was an adversary, the agreement that the United States signed with Iran in 2015 resulted in Iran abandoning its nuclear weapons program and the two countries forming an alliance.

   b) The United States has worked to strengthen its alliances with Asian nations, including India, Japan, and Vietnam, to increase American power in the region and prevent the rise of China.

   c) Although the United States was operating at a substantial trade deficit with the rest of the world, it implemented policies to address unfair trade practices by China, enabling the United States to now export more than it imports.

   d) The United States has been a leader in the efforts to reduce greenhouse gas emissions to address climate change; it is among the strongest supporters of the Paris Agreement.

8. Which of the following statements regarding partisan divisions over foreign policy is true?

   a) Republicans are unified in their support for free trade, while Democrats are unified in opposition to free trade, arguing that it harms American workers.

   b) The Republican Party supports the United States taking an active role in the global efforts to address climate change, while the Democratic Party has resisted United States involvement in these efforts.

   c) The Republican Party is unified in its support of increasing immigration, while the Democratic Party supports restricting the number of immigrants entering the country.

   d) The Republican Party is supported by America's defense industry and supports high levels of military spending, while the Democratic Party favors decreased military spending and greater spending on social programs.

WHAT DO YOU THINK?

FOREIGN POLICY

The foreign policy areas discussed in this chapter are only a few of the problems facing America in the world. Policy makers must constantly monitor, assess, and determine a response to these and other challenges facing the nation.

- America's history and ideals hold that U.S. foreign policies should have a higher purpose than the pursuit of self-interest and that the United States should use force only as a last resort. In what ways do American responses to various security, trade, and humanitarian challenges reflect these historic ideals, and in what ways do they sometimes clash?

- Greater trade reduces the price of many products for American and international consumers. Yet globalization also creates economic winners and losers. What can U.S. leaders do in the future to make sure that globalization is a positive force that promotes U.S. security and prosperity? What do you think Bob Wahlin and Weston LaBar, featured at the beginning of this chapter, would say?

- Under what conditions do you think it is appropriate for the United States to use military force? Under what conditions do you think diplomacy is the appropriate channel?

Use 📖 **INQUIZITIVE** *to help you study and master this material.*

Appendix

The Declaration of Independence

In Congress, July 4, 1776

The unanimous Declaration of the thirteen united States of America,

When in the Course of human events, it becomes necessary for one people to dissolve the political bands which have connected them with another, and to assume among the powers of the earth, the separate and equal station to which the Laws of Nature and of Nature's God entitle them, a decent respect to the opinions of mankind requires that they should declare the causes which impel them to the separation.

We hold these truths to be self-evident, that all men are created equal, that they are endowed by their Creator with certain unalienable Rights, that among these are Life, Liberty and the pursuit of Happiness.—That to secure these rights, Governments are instituted among Men, deriving their just powers from the consent of the governed.—That whenever any Form of Government becomes destructive of these ends, it is the Right of the People to alter or to abolish it, and to institute new Government, laying its foundation on such principles and organizing its powers in such form, as to them shall seem most likely to effect their Safety and Happiness. Prudence, indeed, will dictate that Governments long established should not be changed for light and transient causes; and accordingly all experience hath shewn, that mankind are more disposed to suffer, while evils are sufferable, than to right themselves by abolishing the forms to which they are accustomed. But when a long train of abuses and usurpations, pursuing invariably the same Object evinces a design to reduce them under absolute Despotism, it is their right, it is their duty, to throw off such Government, and to provide new Guards for their future security.—Such has been the patient sufferance of these Colonies; and such is now the necessity which constrains them to alter their former Systems of Government. The history of the present King of Great Britain is a history of repeated injuries and usurpations, all having in direct object the establishment of an absolute Tyranny over these States. To prove this, let Facts be submitted to a candid world.

He has refused his Assent to Laws, the most wholesome and necessary for the public good.

He has forbidden his Governors to pass Laws of immediate and pressing importance, unless suspended in their operation till his Assent should be obtained; and when so suspended, he has utterly neglected to attend to them.

He has refused to pass other Laws for the accommodation of large districts of people, unless those people would relinquish the right of Representation in the Legislature, a right inestimable to them and formidable to tyrants only.

He has called together legislative bodies at places unusual, uncomfortable, and distant from the depository of their public Records, for the sole purpose of fatiguing them into compliance with his measures.

He has dissolved Representative Houses repeatedly, for opposing with manly firmness his invasions on the rights of the people.

He has refused for a long time, after such dissolutions, to cause others to be elected; whereby the Legislative powers, incapable of Annihilation, have returned to the People at large for their exercise; the State remaining in the mean time exposed to all the dangers of invasion from without, and convulsions within.

He has endeavoured to prevent the population of these States; for that purpose obstructing the Laws for Naturalization of Foreigners; refusing to pass others to encourage their migrations hither, and raising the conditions of new Appropriations of Lands.

He has obstructed the Administration of Justice, by refusing his Assent to Laws for establishing Judiciary powers.

He has made Judges dependent on his Will alone, for the tenure of their offices, and the amount and payment of their salaries.

He has erected a multitude of New Offices, and sent hither swarms of Officers to harrass our people, and eat out their substance.

He has kept among us, in times of peace, Standing Armies without the Consent of our legislatures.

He has affected to render the Military independent of and superior to the Civil power.

He has combined with others to subject us to a jurisdiction foreign to our constitution, and unacknowledged by our laws; giving his Assent to their Acts of pretended Legislation:

For Quartering large bodies of armed troops among us:

For protecting them, by a mock Trial, from punishment for any Murders which they should commit on the Inhabitants of these States:

For cutting off our Trade with all parts of the world:

For imposing Taxes on us without our Consent:

For depriving us in many cases, of the benefits of Trial by Jury:

For transporting us beyond Seas to be tried for pretended offences:

For abolishing the free System of English Laws in a neighboring Province, establishing therein an Arbitrary government, and enlarging its Boundaries so as to render it at once an example and fit instrument for introducing the same absolute rule into these Colonies:

For taking away our Charters, abolishing our most valuable Laws, and altering fundamentally the Forms of our Governments:

For suspending our own Legislatures, and declaring themselves invested with power to legislate for us in all cases whatsoever.

He has abdicated Government here, by declaring us out of his Protection and waging War against us.

He has plundered our seas, ravaged our Coasts, burnt our towns, and destroyed the lives of our people.

He is at this time transporting large Armies of foreign Mercenaries to compleat the works of death, desolation and tyranny, already begun with circumstances of Cruelty & perfidy scarcely paralleled in the most barbarous ages, and totally unworthy the Head of a civilized nation.

He has constrained our fellow Citizens taken Captive on the high Seas to bear Arms against their Country, to become the executioners of their friends and Brethren, or to fall themselves by their Hands.

He has excited domestic insurrections amongst us, and has endeavoured to bring on the inhabitants of our frontiers, the merciless Indian Savages, whose known rule of warfare, is an undistinguished destruction of all ages, sexes and conditions.

In every stage of these Oppressions We have Petitioned for Redress in the most humble terms: Our repeated Petitions have been answered only by repeated injury. A Prince whose character is thus marked by every act which may define a Tyrant, is unfit to be the ruler of a free people.

Nor have We been wanting in attentions to our Brittish brethren. We have warned them from time to time of attempts by their legislature to extend an unwarrantable jurisdiction over us. We have reminded them of the circumstances of our emigration and settlement here. We have appealed to their native justice and magnanimity, and we have conjured them by the ties of our common kindred to disavow these usurpations, which, would inevitably interrupt our connections and correspondence. They too have been deaf to the voice of justice and of consanguinity. We must, therefore, acquiesce in the necessity, which denounces our Separation, and hold them, as we hold the rest of mankind, Enemies in War, in Peace Friends.

We, Therefore, the Representatives of the United States of America, in General Congress, Assembled, appealing to the Supreme Judge of the world for the rectitude of our intentions, do, in the Name, and by Authority of the good People of these Colonies, solemnly publish and declare, That these United Colonies are, and of Right ought to be Free and Independent States; that they are Absolved from all Allegiance to the British Crown, and that all political connection between them and the State of Great Britain, is and ought to be totally dissolved; and that as Free and Independent States, they have full Power to levy War, conclude Peace, contract Alliances, establish Commerce, and to do all other Acts and Things which Independent States may of right do. And for the support of this Declaration, with a firm reliance on the protection of divine Providence, we mutually pledge to each other our Lives, our Fortunes and our sacred Honor.

The foregoing Declaration was, by order of Congress, engrossed,
and signed by the following members:

John Hancock

NEW HAMPSHIRE
Josiah Bartlett
William Whipple
Matthew Thornton

MASSACHUSETTS BAY
Samuel Adams
John Adams
Robert Treat Paine
Elbridge Gerry

RHODE ISLAND
Stephen Hopkins
William Ellery

CONNECTICUT
Roger Sherman
Samuel Huntington
William Williams
Oliver Wolcott

NEW YORK
William Floyd
Philip Livingston
Francis Lewis
Lewis Morris

NEW JERSEY
Richard Stockton
John Witherspoon
Francis Hopkinson
John Hart
Abraham Clark

PENNSYLVANIA
Robert Morris
Benjamin Rush
Benjamin Franklin
John Morton
George Clymer
James Smith
George Taylor
James Wilson
George Ross

DELAWARE
Caesar Rodney
George Read
Thomas M'Kean

MARYLAND
Samuel Chase
William Paca
Thomas Stone
Charles Carroll, of Carrollton

VIRGINIA
George Wythe
Richard Henry Lee
Thomas Jefferson
Benjamin Harrison
Thomas Nelson, Jr.
Francis Lightfoot Lee
Carter Braxton

NORTH CAROLINA
William Hooper
Joseph Hewes
John Penn

SOUTH CAROLINA
Edward Rutledge
Thomas Heyward, Jr.
Thomas Lynch, Jr.
Arthur Middleton

GEORGIA
Button Gwinnett
Lyman Hall
George Walton

Resolved, That copies of the Declaration be sent to the several assemblies, conventions, and committees, or councils of safety, and to the several commanding officers of the continental troops; that it be proclaimed in each of the United States, at the head of the army.

The Articles of Confederation

Agreed to by Congress November 15, 1777; ratified and in force March 1, 1781

To all whom these Presents shall come, we the undersigned Delegates of the States affixed to our Names, send greeting. Whereas the Delegates of the United States of America, in Congress assembled, did, on the fifteenth day of November, in the Year of Our Lord One thousand Seven Hundred and Seventy seven, and in the Second Year of the Independence of America, agree to certain articles of Confederation and perpetual Union between the States of Newhampshire, Massachusetts-bay, Rhodeisland and Providence Plantations, Connecticut, New-York, New-Jersey, Pennsylvania, Delaware, Maryland, Virginia, North-Carolina, South-Carolina and Georgia in the words following, viz. "Articles of Confederation and perpetual Union between the states of Newhampshire, Massachusettsbay, Rhodeisland and Providence Plantations, Connecticut, New-York, New-Jersey, Pennsylvania, Delaware, Maryland, Virginia, North-Carolina, South-Carolina and Georgia.

Art. I. The Stile of this confederacy shall be "The United States of America."

Art. II. Each state retains its sovereignty, freedom and independence, and every Power, Jurisdiction and right, which is not by this confederation expressly delegated to the United States, in Congress assembled.

Art. III. The said states hereby severally enter into a firm league of friendship with each other, for their common defence, the security of their Liberties, and their mutual and general welfare, binding themselves to assist each other, against all force offered to, or attacks made upon them, or any of them, on account of religion, sovereignty, trade, or any other pretence whatever.

Art. IV. The better to secure and perpetuate mutual friendship and intercourse among the people of the different states in this union, the free inhabitants of each of these states, paupers, vagabonds and fugitives from Justice excepted, shall be entitled to all privileges and immunities of free citizens in the several states; and the people of each state shall have free ingress and regress to and from any other state, and shall enjoy therein all the privileges of trade and commerce, subject to the same duties, impositions and restrictions as the inhabitants thereof respectively, provided that such restriction shall not extend so far as to prevent the removal of property imported into any state, to any other state, of which the Owner is an inhabitant; provided also that no imposition, duties or restriction shall be laid by any state, on the property of the united states, or either of them.

If any Person guilty of, or charged with treason, felony, or other high misdemeanor in any state, shall flee from Justice, and be found in any of the united states, he shall, upon demand of the Governor or executive power, of the state from which he fled, be delivered up and removed to the state having jurisdiction of his offence.

Full faith and credit shall be given in each of these states to the records, acts and judicial proceedings of the courts and magistrates of every other state.

Art. V. For the more convenient management of the general interests of the united states, delegates shall be annually appointed in such manner as the legislature of each state shall direct, to meet in Congress on the first Monday in November, in every year, with a power reserved to each state, to recall its delegates, or any of them, at any time within the year, and to send others in their stead, for the remainder of the Year.

No state shall be represented in Congress by less than two, nor by more than seven Members; and no person shall be capable of being a delegate for more than three years in any term of six years; nor shall any person, being a delegate, be capable of holding any office under the united states, for which he, or another for his benefit receives any salary, fees or emolument of any kind.

Each state shall maintain its own delegates in a meeting of the states, and while they act as members of the committee of the states.

In determining questions in the united states, in Congress assembled, each state shall have one vote.

Freedom of speech and debate in Congress shall not be impeached or questioned in any Court, or place out of Congress, and the members of congress shall be protected in their persons from arrests and imprisonments, during the time of their going to and from, and attendance on congress, except for treason, felony, or breach of the peace.

Art. VI. No state without the Consent of the united states in congress assembled, shall send any embassy to, or receive any embassy from, or enter into any conference, agreement, or alliance or treaty with any King, prince or state; nor shall any person holding any office or profit or trust under the united states, or any of them, accept of any present, emolument, office or title of any kind whatever from any king, prince or foreign state; nor shall the united states in congress assembled, or any of them, grant any title of nobility.

No two or more states shall enter into any treaty, confederation or alliance whatever between them, without the consent of the united states in congress assembled, specifying accurately the purposes for which the same is to be entered into, and how long it shall continue.

No state shall lay any imposts or duties, which may interfere with any stipulations in treaties, entered into by the united states in congress assembled, with any king, prince or state, in pursuance of any treaties already proposed by congress, to the courts of France and Spain.

No vessels of war shall be kept up in time of peace by any state, except such number only, as shall be deemed necessary by the united states in congress assembled, for the defence of such state, or its trade; nor shall any body of forces be kept up by any state, in time of peace, except such number only, as in the judgment of the united states, in congress assembled, shall be deemed requisite to garrison the forts necessary for the defence of such state; but every state shall always keep up a well regulated and disciplined militia, sufficiently armed and accoutred, and shall provide and constantly have ready for use, in public stores, a due number of field pieces and tents, and a proper quantity of arms, ammunition and camp equipage.

No state shall engage in any war without the consent of the united states in congress assembled, unless such state be actually invaded by enemies, or shall have received certain advice of a resolution being formed by some nation of Indians to invade such state, and the danger is so imminent as not to admit of a delay, till the united states in congress asssembled can be consulted; nor shall any state grant commissions to any ships or vessels of war, nor letters of marque or reprisal, except it be after a declaration of war by the united states in congress assembled, and then only against the kingdom or state and the subjects thereof, against which war has been so declared, and under such regulations as shall be established by the united states in congress assembled, unless such state be infested by pirates; in which case vessels of war may be fitted out for that occasion, and kept so long as the danger shall continue, or until the united states in congress assembled shall determine otherwise.

Art. VII. When land-forces are raised by any state for the common defence, all officers of or under the rank of colonel, shall be appointed by the legislature of each state respectively, by whom such forces shall be raised, or in such manner as such state shall direct, and all vacancies shall be filled up by the state which first made the appointment.

Art. VIII. All charges of war, and all other expences that shall be incurred for the common defence or general welfare, and allowed by the united states in congress assembled, shall be defrayed out of a common treasury, which shall be supplied by the several states in proportion to the value of all land within each state, granted to or surveyed for any Person, as such land and the buildings and improvements thereon shall be estimated according to such mode as the united states in congress assembled, shall from time to time direct and appoint.

The taxes for paying that proportion shall be laid and levied by the authority and direction of the legislatures of the several states within the time agreed upon by the united states in congress assembled.

Art. IX. The united states in congress assembled, shall have the sole and exclusive right and power of determining on peace and war, except in the cases mentioned in the sixth article—of sending and receiving ambassadors—entering into treaties and alliances, provided that no treaty of commerce shall be made whereby the legislative power of the respective states shall be restrained from imposing such imposts and duties on foreigners, as their own people are subjected to, or from prohibiting the exportation of any species of goods or commodities whatsoever—of establishing rules for deciding in all cases, what captures on land or water shall be legal, and in what manner prizes taken by land or naval forces in the service of the united states shall be divided or appropriated—of granting letters of marque and reprisal in times of peace—appointing courts for the trial of piracies and felonies committed on the high seas and establishing courts for receiving and determining finally appeals in all cases of captures, provided that no member of congress shall be appointed a judge of any of the said courts.

The united states in congress assembled shall also be the last resort on appeal in all disputes and differences now subsisting or that hereafter may arise between two or more states concerning boundary, jurisdiction or any other cause whatever; which authority shall always be exercised in the manner following. Whenever the legislative or executive authority or lawful agent of any state in controversy with another shall present a petition to congress stating the matter in question and praying for a hearing, notice thereof shall be given by order of congress to the legislative or executive authority of the other state in controversy, and a day assigned for the appearance of the parties by their lawful agents, who shall then be directed to appoint by joint consent, commissioners or judges to constitute a court for hearing and determining the matter in question: but if they cannot agree, congress shall name three persons out of each of the united states, and from the list of such persons each party shall alternately strike out one, the petitioners beginning, until the number shall be reduced to thirteen; and from that number not less than seven, nor more than nine names as congress shall direct, shall in the presence of congress be drawn out by lot, and the persons whose names shall be so drawn or any five of them, shall be commissioners or judges, to hear and finally determine the controversy, so always as a major part of the judges who shall hear the cause shall agree in the determination: and if either party shall neglect to attend at the day appointed, without shewing reasons, which congress shall judge sufficient, or being present shall refuse to strike, the congress shall proceed to nominate three persons out of each state, and the secretary of congress shall strike in behalf of such party absent or refusing; and the judgment and sentence of the court to be appointed, in the manner before prescribed, shall be final and conclusive; and if any of the parties shall refuse to submit to the authority of such court, or to appear to defend their claim or cause, the court shall nevertheless proceed to pronounce sentence, or judgment, which shall in like manner be final and decisive, the judgment or sentence and other proceedings being in either case transmitted to congress, and lodged among the acts of congress for the security of the parties concerned: provided that every commissioner, before he sits in judgment, shall take an oath to be administered by one of the judges of the supreme or superior court of the state, where the cause shall be tried, "well and truly to hear and determine the matter in question, according to the best of his judgment, without favour, affection or hope of reward:" provided also, that no state shall be deprived of territory for the benefit of the united states.

All controversies concerning the private right of soil claimed under different grants of two or more states, whose jurisdictions as they may respect such lands, and the states which passed such grants are adjusted, the said grants or either of them being at the same time claimed to have originated antecedent to such settlement of jurisdiction, shall on the petition of either party to the congress of the united states, be finally determined as near as may be in the same manner as is before prescribed for deciding disputes respecting territorial jurisdiction between different states.

The united states in congress assembled shall also have the sole and exclusive right and power of regulating the alloy and value of coin struck by their own authority, or by that of the respective states—fixing the standard of weights and measures throughout the united states—regulating the trade and managing all affairs with the Indians, not members of any of the states, provided that the legislative right of any state within its own limits be not infringed or violated—establishing and regulating post-offices from one state to another, throughout all the united states, and exacting such postage on the papers passing thro' the same as may be requisite to defray the expences of the said office—appointing all officers of the land forces, in the service of the united states, excepting regimental officers—appointing all the officers of the naval forces, and commissioning all officers whatever in the service of the united states—making rules for the government and regulation of the said land and naval forces, and directing their operations.

The united states in congress assembled shall have authority to appoint a committee, to sit in the recess of congress, to be denominated "A Committee of the States," and to consist of one delegate from each state; and to appoint such other committees and civil officers as may be necessary for managing the general affairs of the united states under their direction—to appoint one of their number to preside, provided that no person be allowed to serve in the office of president more than one year in any term of three years; to ascertain the necessary sums of Money to be raised for the service of the united states, and to appropriate and apply the same for defraying the public expenses—to borrow money, or emit bills on the credit of the united states, transmitting every half year to the respective states an account of the sums of money so borrowed or emitted,—to build and equip a navy—to agree upon the number of land forces, and to make requisitions from each state for its quota, in proportion to the number of white inhabitants in such state; which requisition shall be binding, and thereupon the legislature of each state shall appoint the regimental officers, raise the men and cloath, arm and equip them in a soldier like manner, at the expense of the united states; and the officers and men so cloathed, armed and equipped shall march to the place appointed, and within the time agreed on by the united states in congress assembled: But if the united states in congress assembled shall, on consideration of circumstances judge proper that any state should not raise men, or should raise a smaller number than its quota, and that any other state should raise a greater number of men than the quota thereof, such extra number shall be raised, officered, cloathed, armed and equipped in the same manner as the quota of such state, unless the legislature of such state shall judge that such extra number cannot be safely spared out of the same, in which case they shall raise officer, cloath, arm and equip as many of such extra number as they judge can be safely spared. And the officers and men so cloathed, armed and equipped, shall march to the place appointed, and within the time agreed on by the united states in congress assembled.

The united states in congress assembled shall never engage in a war, nor grant letters of marque and reprisal in time of peace, nor enter into any treaties or alliances, nor coin money, nor regulate the value thereof, nor ascertain the sums and expenses necessary for the defence and welfare of the united states, or any of them, nor emit bills, nor borrow money on the credit of the united states, nor appropriate money, nor agree upon the number of vessels of war, to be built or purchased, or the number of land or sea forces to be raised, nor appoint a commander in chief of the army or navy, unless nine states assent to the same: nor shall a question on any other point, except for adjourning from day to day be determined, unless by the votes of a majority of the united states in congress assembled.

The congress of the united states shall have power to adjourn to any time within the year, and to any place within the united states, so that no period of adjournment be for a longer duration than the space of six Months, and shall publish the Journal of their proceedings monthly, except such parts thereof relating to treaties, alliances or military operations, as in their judgment require secrecy; and the yeas and nays of the delegates of each state on any question shall be entered on the Journal, when it is desired by any delegate; and the delegates of a state, or any of them, at his or their request shall be furnished with a transcript of the said Journal, except such parts as are above excepted, to lay before the legislatures of the several states.

Art. X. The committee of the states, or any nine of them, shall be authorised to execute, in the recess of congress, such of the powers of congress as the united states in congress assembled, by the consent of nine states, shall from time to time think expedient to vest them with; provided that no power be delegated to the said committee, for the exercise of which, by the articles of confederation, the voice of nine states in the congress of the united states assembled is requisite.

Art. XI. Canada acceding to this confederation, and joining in the measures of the united states, shall be admitted into, and entitled to all the advantages of this union: but no other colony shall be admitted into the same, unless such admission be agreed to by nine states.

Art. XII. All bills of credit emitted, monies borrowed and debts contracted by, or under the authority of congress, before the assembling of the united states, in pursuance of the present confederation, shall be deemed and considered as a charge against the united states, for payment and satisfaction whereof the said united states and the public faith are hereby solemnly pledged.

Art. XIII. Every state shall abide by the determinations of the united states in congress assembled, on all questions which by this confederation are submitted to them. And the Articles of this confederation shall be inviolably observed by every state, and the union shall be perpetual; nor shall any alteration at any time hereafter be made in any of them; unless such alteration be agreed to in a congress of the united states, and be afterwards confirmed by the legislatures of every state.

And Whereas it hath pleased the Great Governor of the World to incline the hearts of the legislatures we respectively represent in congress, to approve of, and to authorize us to ratify the said articles of confederation and perpetual union. Know Ye that we the undersigned delegates, by virtue of the power and authority to us given for that purpose, do by these presents, in the name and in behalf of our respective constituents, fully and entirely ratify and confirm each and every of the said articles of confederation and perpetual union, and all and singular the matters and things therein contained: And we do further solemnly plight and engage the faith of our respective constituents, that they shall abide by the determinations of the united states in congress assembled, on all questions, which by the said confederation are submitted to them. And that the articles thereof shall be inviolably observed by the states we respectively represent, and that the union shall be perpetual. In Witness whereof we have hereunto set our hands in Congress. Done at Philadelphia in the state of Pennsylvania the ninth day of July, in the Year of our Lord one Thousand seven Hundred and Seventy-eight, and in the third year of the independence of America.

The Constitution of the United States of America

[PREAMBLE]

We the People of the United States, in Order to form a more perfect Union, establish Justice, insure domestic Tranquility, provide for the common defence, promote the general Welfare, and secure the Blessings of Liberty to ourselves and our Posterity, do ordain and establish this Constitution for the United States of America.

ARTICLE I

Section 1

[LEGISLATIVE POWERS]

All legislative Powers herein granted shall be vested in a Congress of the United States, which shall consist of a Senate and House of Representatives.

Section 2

[HOUSE OF REPRESENTATIVES, HOW CONSTITUTED, POWER OF IMPEACHMENT]

The House of Representatives shall be composed of Members chosen every second Year by the People of the several States, and the Electors in each State shall have the Qualifications requisite for Electors of the most numerous Branch of the State Legislature.

No Person shall be a Representative who shall not have attained to the Age of twenty five Years, and been seven Years a Citizen of the United States, and who shall not, when elected, be an Inhabitant of that State in which he shall be chosen.

Representatives and *direct Taxes*[1] shall be apportioned among the several States which may be included within this Union, according to their respective Numbers, *which shall be determined by adding to the whole Number of free Persons, including those bound to Service for a Term of Years, and excluding Indians not taxed, three fifths of all other Persons.*[2] The actual Enumeration shall be made within three Years after the first Meeting of the Congress of the United States, and within every subsequent Term of ten Years, in such Manner as they shall by Law direct. The Number of Representatives shall not exceed one for every thirty Thousand, but each State shall have at Least one Representative; *and until such enumeration shall be made, the State of New Hampshire shall be entitled to chuse three, Massachusetts eight, Rhode-Island and Providence Plantations one, Connecticut five, New-York six, New Jersey four, Pennsylvania eight, Delaware one, Maryland six, Virginia ten, North Carolina five, South Carolina five, and Georgia three.*[3]

When vacancies happen in the Representation from any State, the Executive Authority thereof shall issue Writs of Election to fill such Vacancies.

---

1. Modified by Sixteenth Amendment.
2. Modified by Fourteenth Amendment.
3. Temporary provision.

House of Representatives shall chuse their Speaker and other Officers; and shall e sole Power of Impeachment.

ction 3

The Senate of the United States shall be composed of two Senators from each State, *chosen by the Legislature thereof*,[4] for six Years; and each Senator shall have one Vote.

Immediately after they shall be assembled in Consequence of the first Election, they shall be divided as equally as may be into three Classes. The Seats of the Senators of the first Class shall be vacated at the Expiration of the second Year, of the second Class at the Expiration of the fourth Year, and of the third Class at the Expiration of the sixth Year, so that one third may be chosen every second Year; *and if Vacancies happen by Resignation, or otherwise, during the Recess of the Legislature of any State, the Executive thereof may make temporary Appointments until the next Meeting of the Legislature, which shall then fill such Vacancies.*[5]

No Person shall be a Senator who shall not have attained to the Age of thirty Years, and been nine Years a Citizen of the United States, and who shall not, when elected, be an Inhabitant of that State for which he shall be chosen.

The Vice President of the United States shall be President of the Senate, but shall have no Vote, unless they be equally divided.

The Senate shall chuse their other Officers, and also a President pro tempore, in the Absence of the Vice President, or when he shall exercise the Office of President of the United States.

The Senate shall have the sole Power to try all Impeachments. When sitting for that Purpose, they shall be on Oath or Affirmation. When the President of the United States is tried, the Chief Justice shall preside: And no Person shall be convicted without the Concurrence of two thirds of the Members present.

Judgment in Cases of Impeachment shall not extend further than to removal from Office, and disqualification to hold and enjoy any Office of honor, Trust or Profit under the United States: but the Party convicted shall nevertheless be liable and subject to Indictment, Trial, Judgment and Punishment, according to Law.

Section 4

[ELECTION OF SENATORS AND REPRESENTATIVES]

The Times, Places and Manner of holding Elections for Senators and Representatives, shall be prescribed in each State by the Legislature thereof; but the Congress may at any time by Law make or alter such Regulations, except as to the Places of chusing Senators.

The Congress shall assemble at least once in every Year, and such Meeting shall be on the first Monday in December, unless they shall by Law appoint a different Day.[6]

Section 5

[QUORUM, JOURNALS, MEETINGS, ADJOURNMENTS]

Each House shall be the Judge of the Elections, Returns and Qualifications of its own Members, and a Majority of each shall constitute a Quorum to do Business; but a smaller Number may adjourn from day to day, and may be authorized to compel the Attendance of absent Members, in such Manner, and under such Penalties as each House may provide.

Each House may determine the Rules of its Proceedings, punish its Members for disorderly Behaviour, and, with the Concurrence of two thirds, expel a Member.

---

4. Modified by Seventeenth Amendment.

5. Modified by Seventeenth Amendment.

6. Modified by Twentieth Amendment.

Each House shall keep a Journal of its Proceedings, and from time to time publish the same, excepting such Parts as may in their Judgment require Secrecy; and the Yeas and Nays of the Members of either House on any questions shall, at the Desire of one fifth of those Present, be entered on the Journal.

Neither House, during the Session of Congress, shall, without the Consent of the other, adjourn for more than three days, nor to any other Place than that in which the two Houses shall be sitting.

Section 6

[COMPENSATION, PRIVILEGES, DISABILITIES]

The Senators and Representatives shall receive a Compensation for their Services, to be ascertained by Law, and paid out of the Treasury of the United States. They shall in all Cases, except Treason, Felony and Breach of the Peace, be privileged from Arrest during their Attendance at the Session of their respective Houses, and in going to and returning from the same; and for any Speech or Debate in either House, they shall not be questioned in any other Place.

No Senator or Representative shall, during the Time for which he was elected, be appointed to any civil Office under the Authority of the United States, which shall have been created, or the Emoluments whereof shall have been encreased during such time; and no Person holding any Office under the United States, shall be a Member of either House during his Continuance in Office.

Section 7

[PROCEDURE IN PASSING BILLS AND RESOLUTIONS]

All Bills for raising Revenue shall originate in the House of Representatives; but the Senate may propose or concur with Amendments as on other Bills.

Every Bill which shall have passed the House of Representatives and the Senate, shall, before it become a Law, be presented to the President of the United States: If he approve he shall sign it, but if not he shall return it, with his Objections to that House in which it shall have originated, who shall enter the Objections at large on their Journal, and proceed to reconsider it. If after such Reconsideration two thirds of that House shall agree to pass the Bill, it shall be sent, together with the Objections, to the other House, by which it shall likewise be reconsidered, and if approved by two thirds of that House, it shall become a Law. But in all such Cases the Votes of both Houses shall be determined by yeas and Nays, and the Names of the Persons voting for and against the Bill shall be entered on the Journal of each House respectively. If any Bill shall not be returned by the President within ten Days (Sundays excepted) after it shall have been presented to him, the Same shall be a Law, in like Manner as if he had signed it, unless the Congress by their Adjournment prevent its Return, in which Case it shall not be a Law.

Every Order, Resolution, or Vote to which the Concurrence of the Senate and House of Representatives may be necessary (except on a question of Adjournment) shall be presented to the President of the United States; and before the Same shall take Effect, shall be approved by him, or being disapproved by him, shall be repassed by two thirds of the Senate and House of Representatives, according to the Rules and Limitations prescribed in the Case of a Bill.

Section 8

[POWERS OF CONGRESS]

The Congress shall have Power

To lay and collect Taxes, Duties, Imposts and Excises, to pay the Debts and provide for the common Defence and general Welfare of the United States; but all Duties, Imposts and Excises shall be uniform throughout the United States;

To borrow Money on the credit of the United States;

To regulate Commerce with foreign Nations, and among the several States, and with the Indian Tribes;

To establish an uniform Rule of Naturalization, and uniform Laws on the subject of Bankruptcies throughout the United States;

To coin Money, regulate the Value thereof, and of foreign Coin, and fix the Standard of Weights and Measures;

To provide for the Punishment of counterfeiting the Securities and current Coin of the United States;

To establish Post Offices and post Roads;

To promote the Progress of Science and useful Arts, by securing for limited Times to Authors and Inventors the exclusive Right to their respective Writings and Discoveries;

To constitute Tribunals inferior to the supreme Court;

To define and punish Piracies and Felonies committed on the high Seas, and Offences against the Law of Nations;

To declare War, grant Letters of Marque and Reprisal, and make Rules concerning Captures on Land and Water;

To raise and support Armies, but no Appropriation of Money to that Use shall be for a longer Term than two Years;

To provide and maintain a Navy;

To make Rules for the Government and Regulation of the land and naval Forces;

To provide for calling forth the Militia to execute the Laws of the Union, suppress Insurrections and repel Invasions;

To provide for organizing, arming, and disciplining, the Militia, and for governing such Part of them as may be employed in the Service of the United States, reserving to the States respectively, the Appointment of the Officers, and the Authority of training the Militia according to the discipline prescribed by Congress;

To exercise exclusive Legislation in all Cases whatsoever, over such District (not exceeding ten Miles square) as may, by Cession of particular States, and the Acceptance of Congress, become the Seat of the Government of the United States, and to exercise like Authority over all Places purchased by the Consent of the Legislature of the State in which the Same shall be, for the Erection of Forts, Magazines, Arsenals, dock-Yards, and other needful Buildings;—And

To make all Laws which shall be necessary and proper for carrying into Execution the foregoing Powers, and all other Powers vested by this Constitution in the Government of the United States, or in any Department or Officer thereof.

Section 9

[SOME RESTRICTIONS ON FEDERAL POWER]

The Migration or Importation of such Persons as any of the States now existing shall think proper to admit, shall not be prohibited by the Congress prior to the Year one thousand eight hundred and eight, but a Tax or duty may be imposed on such Importation, not exceeding ten dollars for each Person.[7]

The Privilege of the Writ of Habeas Corpus shall not be suspended, unless when in Cases of Rebellion or Invasion the public Safety may require it.

No Bill of Attainder or ex post facto Law shall be passed.

No Capitation, or other direct, Tax shall be laid, unless in Proportion to the Census or Enumeration herein before directed to be taken.[8]

No Tax or Duty shall be laid on Articles exported from any State.

No Preference shall be given by any Regulation of Commerce or Revenue to the Ports of one State over those of another; nor shall Vessels bound to, or from, one State, be obliged to enter, clear, or pay Duties in another.

---

7. Temporary provision.

8. Modified by Sixteenth Amendment.

No Money shall be drawn from the Treasury, but in Consequence of Appropriations made by Law; and a regular Statement and Account of the Receipts and Expenditures of all public Money shall be published from time to time.

No Title of Nobility shall be granted by the United States: And no Person holding any Office of Profit or Trust under them, shall, without the Consent of the Congress, accept of any present, Emolument, Office, or Title, of any kind whatever, from any King, Prince, or foreign State.

Section 10

[RESTRICTIONS UPON POWERS OF STATES]

No State shall enter into any Treaty, Alliance, or Confederation; grant Letters of Marque and Reprisal; coin Money; emit Bills of Credit; make any Thing but gold and silver Coin a Tender in Payment of Debts; pass any Bill of Attainder, ex post facto Law, or Law impairing the Obligation of Contracts, or grant any Title of Nobility.

No State shall, without the Consent of the Congress, lay any Imposts or Duties on Imports or Exports, except what may be absolutely necessary for executing its inspection Laws: and the net Produce of all Duties and Imposts, laid by any State on Imports or Exports, shall be for the Use of the Treasury of the United States; and all such Laws shall be subject to the Revision and Control of the Congress.

No State shall, without the Consent of Congress, lay any Duty of Tonnage, keep Troops, or Ships of War in time of Peace, enter into any Agreement or Compact with another State, or with a foreign Power, or engage in War, unless actually invaded, or in such imminent Danger as will not admit of delay.

ARTICLE II

Section 1

[EXECUTIVE POWER, ELECTION, QUALIFICATIONS OF THE PRESIDENT]

The executive Power shall be vested in a President of the United States of America. *He shall hold his Office during the Term of four Years, and, together with the Vice President, chosen for the same Term, be elected, as follows*[9]

Each State shall appoint, in such Manner as the Legislature thereof may direct, a Number of Electors, equal to the whole Number of Senators and Representatives to which the State may be entitled in the Congress: but no Senator or Representative, or Person holding an Office of Trust or Profit under the United States, shall be appointed an Elector.

The electors shall meet in their respective States, and vote by ballot for two Persons, of whom one at least shall not be an Inhabitant of the same State with themselves. And they shall make a List of all the Persons voted for, and of the Number of Votes for each; which List they shall sign and certify, and transmit sealed to the Seat of the Government of the United States, directed to the President of the Senate. The President of the Senate shall, in the Presence of the Senate and House of Representatives, open all the Certificates, and the Votes shall then be counted. The Person having the greatest Number of Votes shall be the President, if such Number be a Majority of the whole Number of Electors appointed; and if there be more than one who have such Majority, and have an equal Number of Votes, then the House of Representatives shall immediately chuse by Ballot one of them for President; and if no Person have a Majority, then from the five highest on the List the said House shall in like Manner chuse the President. But in chusing the President, the Votes shall be taken by States, the Representation from each State having one Vote; A quorum for this Purpose shall consist of a Member or Members from two thirds of the States, and a Majority of all the States shall

---

9. Number of terms limited to two by Twenty-Second Amendment.

be necessary to a Choice. In every Case, after the Choice of the President, the person having the greatest Number of Votes of the Electors shall be the Vice President. But if there should remain two or more who have equal Votes, the Senate shall chuse from them by Ballot the Vice President.[10]

The Congress may determine the Time of chusing the Electors, and the Day on which they shall give their Votes; which Day shall be the same throughout the United States.

No Person except a natural born Citizen, or a Citizen of the United States, at the time of the Adoption of this Constitution, shall be eligible to the Office of President; neither shall any Person be eligible to that Office who shall not have attained to the Age of thirty five Years, and been fourteen Years a Resident within the United States.

In Case of the Removal of the President from Office, or his Death, Resignation, or Inability to discharge the Powers and Duties of the said Office, the Same shall devolve on the Vice President, and the Congress may by Law provide for the Case of Removal, Death, Resignation or Inability, both of the President and Vice President, declaring what Officer shall then act as President, and such Officer shall act accordingly, until the Disability be removed, or a President shall be elected.

The President shall, at stated Times, receive for his Services, a Compensation, which shall neither be increased nor diminished during the Period for which he shall have been elected, and he shall not receive within that Period any other Emolument from the United States, or any of them.

Before he enter on the Execution of his Office, he shall take the following Oath or Affirmation:—"I do solemnly swear (or affirm) that I will faithfully execute the Office of President of the United States, and will to the best of my Ability, preserve, protect and defend the Constitution of the United States."

Section 2

[POWERS OF THE PRESIDENT]

The President shall be Commander in Chief of the Army and Navy of the United States, and of the Militia of the several States, when called into the actual Service of the United States; he may require the Opinion, in writing, of the principal Officer in each of the executive Departments, upon any Subject relating to the Duties of their respective Offices, and he shall have Power to grant Reprieves and Pardons for Offences against the United States, except in Cases of Impeachment.

He shall have Power, by and with the Advice and Consent of the Senate, to make Treaties, provided two thirds of the Senators present concur; and he shall nominate, and by and with the Advice and Consent of the Senate, shall appoint Ambassadors, other public Ministers and Consuls, Judges of the supreme Court, and all other Officers of the United States, whose Appointments are not herein otherwise provided for, and which shall be established by Law: but the Congress may by Law vest the Appointment of such inferior Officers, as they think proper, in the President alone, in the Courts of Law, or in the Heads of Departments.

The President shall have Power to fill up all Vacancies that may happen during the Recess of the Senate, by granting Commissions which shall expire at the End of their next Session.

Section 3

[POWERS AND DUTIES OF THE PRESIDENT]

He shall from time to time give to the Congress Information of the State of the Union, and recommend to their Consideration such Measures as he shall judge necessary and expedient; he may, on extraordinary Occasions, convene both Houses, or either of them, and in Case

---

10. Modified by Twelfth and Twentieth Amendments.

of Disagreement between them, with Respect to the Time of Adjournment, he may adjourn them to such Time as he shall think proper; he shall receive Ambassadors and other public Ministers; he shall take Care that the Laws be faithfully executed, and shall Commission all the Officers of the United States.

Section 4

[IMPEACHMENT]

The President, Vice President and all civil Officers of the United States, shall be removed from Office on Impeachment for, and Conviction of, Treason, Bribery, or other high Crimes and Misdemeanors.

ARTICLE III

Section 1

[JUDICIAL POWER, TENURE OF OFFICE]

The judicial Power of the United States, shall be vested in one supreme Court, and in such inferior Courts as the Congress may from time to time ordain and establish. The Judges, both of the supreme and inferior Courts, shall hold their Offices during good Behaviour, and shall, at stated Times, receive for their Services, a Compensation, which shall not be diminished during their Continuance in Office.

Section 2

[JURISDICTION]

The judicial Power shall extend to all Cases, in Law and Equity, arising under this Constitution, the Laws of the United States, and Treaties made, or which shall be made, under their Authority;—to all Cases affecting Ambassadors, other public Ministers and Consuls;—to all Cases of admiralty and maritime Jurisdiction;—to Controversies to which the United States shall be a Party;—to Controversies between two or more States;—*between a State and Citizens of another State;*—between Citizens of different States,—between Citizens of the same State claiming Lands under Grants of different States, *and between a State,* or the Citizens thereof, *and foreign States, Citizens or Subjects.*[11]

In all Cases affecting Ambassadors, other public Ministers and Consuls, and those in which a State shall be Party, the supreme Court shall have original Jurisdiction. In all the other Cases before mentioned, the supreme Court shall have appellate Jurisdiction, both as to Law and Fact, with such Exceptions, and under such Regulations as the Congress shall make.

The Trial of all Crimes, except in Cases of Impeachment, shall be by Jury; and such Trial shall be held in the State where the said Crimes shall have been committed; but when not committed within any State, the Trial shall be at such Place or Places as the Congress may by Law have directed.

Section 3

[TREASON, PROOF, AND PUNISHMENT]

Treason against the United States, shall consist only in levying War against them, or in adhering to their Enemies, giving them Aid and Comfort. No Person shall be convicted of Treason unless on the Testimony of two Witnesses to the same overt Act, or on Confession in open Court.

The Congress shall have Power to declare the Punishment of Treason, but no Attainder of Treason shall work Corruption of Blood, or Forfeiture except during the Life of the Person attainted.

---

11. Modified by Eleventh Amendment.

ARTICLE IV

Section 1

[FAITH AND CREDIT AMONG STATES]

Full Faith and Credit shall be given in each State to the public Acts, Records, and judicial Proceedings of every other State. And the Congress may by general Laws prescribe the Manner in which such Acts, Records and Proceedings shall be proved, and the Effect thereof.

Section 2

[PRIVILEGES AND IMMUNITIES, FUGITIVES]

The Citizens of each State shall be entitled to all Privileges and Immunities of Citizens in the several States.

A Person charged in any State with Treason, Felony or other Crime, who shall flee from Justice, and be found in another State, shall on Demand of the executive Authority of the State from which he fled, be delivered up, to be removed to the State having Jurisdiction of the Crime.

No person held to Service or Labour in one State, under the Laws thereof, escaping into another, shall, in Consequence of any Law or Regulation therein, be discharged from such Service or Labour, but shall be delivered up on Claim of the Party to whom such Service or Labour may be due.[12]

Section 3

[ADMISSION OF NEW STATES]

New States may be admitted by the Congress into this Union; but no new State shall be formed or erected within the Jurisdiction of any other State; nor any State be formed by the Junction of two or more States, or Parts of States, without the Consent of the Legislatures of the States concerned as well as of the Congress.

The Congress shall have Power to dispose of and make all needful Rules and Regulations respecting the Territory or other Property belonging to the United States; and nothing in this Constitution shall be so construed as to Prejudice any Claims of the United States, or of any particular State.

Section 4

[GUARANTEE OF REPUBLICAN GOVERNMENT]

The United States shall guarantee to every State in this Union a Republican Form of Government, and shall protect each of them against Invasion; and on Application of the Legislature, or of the Executive (when the Legislature cannot be convened), against domestic Violence.

ARTICLE V

[AMENDMENT OF THE CONSTITUTION]

The Congress, whenever two thirds of both Houses shall deem it necessary, shall propose Amendments to this Constitution, or, on the Application of the Legislatures of two thirds of the several States, shall call a Convention for proposing Amendments, which, in either Case, shall be valid to all Intents and Purposes, as Part of this Constitution, when ratified by the Legislatures of three fourths of the several States, or by Conventions in three fourths thereof, as the one or the other Mode of Ratification may be proposed by the Congress; *Provided that no Amendment which may be made prior to the Year One thousand eight hundred and eight shall in any Manner affect the first and fourth Clauses in the Ninth Section of the first Article;*[13] and that no State, without its Consent, shall be deprived of its equal Suffrage in the Senate.

---

12. Repealed by the Thirteenth Amendment.

13. Temporary provision.

ARTICLE VI

[DEBTS, SUPREMACY, OATH]

All Debts contracted and Engagements entered into, before the Adoption of this Constitution, shall be as valid against the United States under this Constitution, as under the Confederation.

This Constitution, and the Laws of the United States which shall be made in Pursuance thereof; and all Treaties made, or which shall be made, under the Authority of the United States, shall be the supreme Law of the Land; and the Judges in every State shall be bound thereby, any Thing in the Constitution or Laws of any State to the Contrary notwithstanding.

The Senators and Representatives before mentioned, and the Members of the several State Legislatures, and all executive and judicial Officers, both of the United States and of the several States, shall be bound by Oath or Affirmation, to support this Constitution; but no religious Test shall be required as a Qualification to any Office or public Trust under the United States.

ARTICLE VII

[RATIFICATION AND ESTABLISHMENT]

The Ratification of the Conventions of nine States, shall be sufficient for the Establishment of this Constitution between the States so ratifying the Same.[14]

Done in Convention by the Unanimous Consent of the States present the Seventeenth Day of September in the Year of our Lord one thousand seven hundred and Eighty seven and of the Independence of the United States of America the Twelfth. *In Witness* whereof We have hereunto subscribed our Names,

---

14. The Constitution was submitted on September 17, 1787, by the Constitutional Convention, was ratified by the conventions of several states at various dates up to May 29, 1790, and became effective on March 4, 1789.

G:⁰ *WASHINGTON—*
Presidt. and deputy from Virginia

NEW HAMPSHIRE
John Langdon
Nicholas Gilman

MASSACHUSETTS
Nathaniel Gorham
Rufus King

CONNECTICUT
Wm. Saml. Johnson
Roger Sherman

NEW YORK
Alexander Hamilton

NEW JERSEY
Wil: Livingston
David Brearley
Wm. Paterson
Jona: Dayton

PENNSYLVANIA
B Franklin
Thomas Mifflin
Robt. Morris
Geo. Clymer
Thos. FitzSimons
Jared Ingersoll
James Wilson
Gouv Morris

DELAWARE
Geo: Read
Gunning Bedford jun
John Dickinson
Richard Bassett
Jaco: Broom

MARYLAND
James McHenry
Dan of St Thos. Jenifer
Danl. Carroll

VIRGINIA
John Blair—
James Madison Jr.

NORTH CAROLINA
Wm. Blount
Richd. Dobbs Spaight
Hu Williamson

SOUTH CAROLINA
J. Rutledge
Charles Cotesworth
Pinckney
Charles Pinckney
Pierce Butler

GEORGIA
William Few
Abr Baldwin

Amendments to the Constitution

Proposed by Congress and Ratified by the Legislatures of the Several States, Pursuant to Article V of the Original Constitution.

Amendments I–X, known as the Bill of Rights, were proposed by Congress on September 25, 1789, and ratified on December 15, 1791.

AMENDMENT I

[FREEDOM OF RELIGION, OF SPEECH, AND OF THE PRESS]

Congress shall make no law respecting an establishment of religion, or prohibiting the free exercise thereof; or abridging the freedom of speech, or of the press; or the right of the people peaceably to assemble, and to petition the Government for a redress of grievances.

AMENDMENT II

[RIGHT TO KEEP AND BEAR ARMS]

A well regulated Militia, being necessary to the security of a free State, the right of the people to keep and bear Arms, shall not be infringed.

AMENDMENT III

[QUARTERING OF SOLDIERS]

No Soldier shall, in time of peace be quartered in any house, without the consent of the Owner, nor in time of war, but in a manner to be prescribed by law.

AMENDMENT IV

[SECURITY FROM UNWARRANTABLE SEARCH AND SEIZURE]

The right of the people to be secure in their persons, houses, papers, and effects, against unreasonable searches and seizures, shall not be violated, and no Warrants shall issue, but upon probable cause, supported by Oath or affirmation, and particularly describing the place to be searched, and the persons or things to be seized.

AMENDMENT V

[RIGHTS OF ACCUSED PERSONS IN CRIMINAL PROCEEDINGS]

No person shall be held to answer for a capital, or otherwise infamous crime, unless on a presentment or indictment of a Grand Jury, except in cases arising in the land or naval forces, or in the Militia, when in actual service in time of War or in public danger; nor shall any person be subject for the same offence to be twice put in jeopardy of life or limb; nor shall be compelled in any criminal case to be a witness against himself, nor be deprived of life, liberty, or property, without due process of law; nor shall private property be taken for public use, without just compensation.

AMENDMENT VI

[RIGHT TO SPEEDY TRIAL, WITNESSES, ETC.]

In all criminal prosecutions, the accused shall enjoy the right to a speedy and public trial, by an impartial jury of the State and district wherein the crime shall have been committed, which district shall have been previously ascertained by law, and to be informed of the nature and cause of the accusation; to be confronted with the witnesses against him; to have compulsory process for obtaining witnesses in his favor, and to have the Assistance of Counsel for his defence.

AMENDMENT VII

[TRIAL BY JURY IN CIVIL CASES]

In suits at common law, where the value in controversy shall exceed twenty dollars, the right of trial by jury shall be preserved, and no fact tried by a jury, shall be otherwise reexamined in any Court of the United States, than according to the rules of the common law.

AMENDMENT VIII

[BAILS, FINES, PUNISHMENTS]

Excessive bail shall not be required, nor excessive fines imposed, nor cruel and unusual punishments inflicted.

AMENDMENT IX

[RESERVATION OF RIGHTS OF PEOPLE]

The enumeration in the Constitution, of certain rights, shall not be construed to deny or disparage others retained by the people.

AMENDMENT X

[POWERS RESERVED TO STATES OR PEOPLE]

The powers not delegated to the United States by the Constitution, nor prohibited by it to the States, are reserved to the States respectively, or to the people.

AMENDMENT XI

[PROPOSED BY CONGRESS ON MARCH 4, 1794; DECLARED RATIFIED ON JANUARY 8, 1798.]

[RESTRICTION OF JUDICIAL POWER]

The Judicial power of the United States shall not be construed to extend to any suit in law or equity, commenced or prosecuted against one of the United States by Citizens of another State, or by Citizens or Subjects of any Foreign State.

AMENDMENT XII

[PROPOSED BY CONGRESS ON DECEMBER 9, 1803; DECLARED RATIFIED ON SEPTEMBER 25, 1804.]

[ELECTION OF PRESIDENT AND VICE PRESIDENT]

The Electors shall meet in their respective states and vote by ballot for President and Vice-President, one of whom, at least, shall not be an inhabitant of the same state with themselves; they shall name in their ballots the person voted for as President, and in distinct ballots the person voted for as Vice-President, and they shall make distinct lists of all persons voted for as President, and of all persons voted for as Vice-President, and of the number of votes for each, which lists they shall sign and certify, and transmit sealed to the seat of the government of the United States, directed to the President of the

Senate;—the President of the Senate shall, in presence of the Senate and House of Representatives, open all the certificates and the votes shall then be counted;—The person having the greatest number of votes for President, shall be the President, if such number be a majority of the whole number of Electors appointed; and if no person have such majority, then from the persons having the highest numbers not exceeding three on the list of those voted for as President, the House of Representatives shall choose immediately, by ballot, the President. But in choosing the President, the votes shall be taken by states, the representation from each state having one vote; a quorum for this purpose shall consist of a member or members from two-thirds of the states, and a majority of all the states shall be necessary to a choice. And if the House of Representatives shall not choose a President whenever the right of choice shall devolve upon them, before the fourth day of March next following, then the Vice-President shall act as President, as in the case of the death or other constitutional disability of the President.—The person having the greatest number of votes as Vice-President, shall be the Vice-President, if such number be a majority of the whole number of Electors appointed, and if no person have a majority, then from the two highest numbers on the list, the Senate shall choose the Vice-President; a quorum for the purpose shall consist of two-thirds of the whole number of Senators, and a majority of the whole number shall be necessary to a choice. But no person constitutionally ineligible to the office of President shall be eligible to that of Vice-President of the United States.

AMENDMENT XIII

[PROPOSED BY CONGRESS ON JANUARY 31, 1865; DECLARED RATIFIED ON DECEMBER 18, 1865.]

Section 1

[ABOLITION OF SLAVERY]

Neither slavery nor involuntary servitude, except as a punishment for crime whereof the party shall have been duly convicted, shall exist within the United States, or any place subject to their jurisdiction.

Section 2

[POWER TO ENFORCE THIS ARTICLE]

Congress shall have power to enforce this article by appropriate legislation.

AMENDMENT XIV

[PROPOSED BY CONGRESS ON JUNE 13, 1866; DECLARED RATIFIED ON JULY 28, 1868.]

Section 1

[CITIZENSHIP RIGHTS NOT TO BE ABRIDGED BY STATES]

All persons born or naturalized in the United States, and subject to the jurisdiction thereof, are citizens of the United States and of the State wherein they reside. No State shall make or enforce any law which shall abridge the privileges or immunities of citizens of the United States; nor shall any State deprive any person of life, liberty, or property, without due process of law; nor deny to any person within its jurisdiction the equal protection of the laws.

Section 2

[APPORTIONMENT OF REPRESENTATIVES IN CONGRESS]

Representatives shall be apportioned among the several States according to their respective numbers, counting the whole number of persons in each State, excluding Indians not taxed. But when the right to vote at any election for the choice of electors for President and Vice-President of the United States, Representatives in Congress, the Executive and Judicial officers of a State, or the members of the Legislature thereof, is denied to any of the male inhabitants of such State, being twenty-one years of age, and citizens of the United States, or in any way abridged, except for participation in rebellion, or other crime, the basis of representation therein shall be reduced in the proportion which the number of such male citizens shall bear to the whole number of male citizens twenty-one years of age in such State.

Section 3
[PERSONS DISQUALIFIED FROM HOLDING OFFICE]

No person shall be a Senator or Representative in Congress, or elector of President and Vice-President, or hold any office, civil or military, under the United States, or under any State, who, having previously taken an oath, as a member of Congress, or as an officer of the United States, or as a member of any State legislature, or as an executive or judicial officer of any State, to support the Constitution of the United States, shall have engaged in insurrection or rebellion against the same, or given aid or comfort to the enemies thereof. But Congress may by a vote of two-thirds of each House, remove such disability.

Section 4
[WHAT PUBLIC DEBTS ARE VALID]

The validity of the public debt of the United States, authorized by law, including debts incurred for payment of pensions and bounties for services in suppressing insurrection or rebellion, shall not be questioned. But neither the United States nor any State shall assume or pay any debt or obligation incurred in aid of insurrection or rebellion against the United States, or any claim for the loss or emancipation of any slave; but all such debts, obligations and claims shall be held illegal and void.

Section 5
[POWER TO ENFORCE THIS ARTICLE]

The Congress shall have power to enforce, by appropriate legislation, the provisions of this article.

AMENDMENT XV
[PROPOSED BY CONGRESS ON FEBRUARY 26, 1869; DECLARED RATIFIED ON MARCH 30, 1870.]

Section 1
[NEGRO SUFFRAGE]

The right of citizens of the United States to vote shall not be denied or abridged by the United States or by any State on account of race, color, or previous condition of servitude.

Section 2
[POWER TO ENFORCE THIS ARTICLE]

The Congress shall have power to enforce this article by appropriate legislation.

AMENDMENT XVI
[PROPOSED BY CONGRESS ON JULY 2, 1909; DECLARED RATIFIED ON FEBRUARY 25, 1913.]

[AUTHORIZING INCOME TAXES]

The Congress shall have power to lay and collect taxes on incomes, from whatever source derived, without apportionment among the several States, and without regard to any census or enumeration.

AMENDMENT XVII

[PROPOSED BY CONGRESS ON MAY 13, 1912; DECLARED RATIFIED ON MAY 31, 1913.]

[POPULAR ELECTION OF SENATORS]

The Senate of the United States shall be composed of two Senators from each State, elected by the people thereof, for six years; and each Senator shall have one vote. The electors in each State shall have the qualifications requisite for electors of the most numerous branch of the State legislatures.

When vacancies happen in the representation of any State in the Senate, the executive authority of such State shall issue writs of election to fill such vacancies: *Provided,* That the legislature of any State may empower the executive thereof to make temporary appointments until the people fill the vacancies by election as the legislature may direct.

This amendment shall not be so construed as to affect the election or term of any Senator chosen before it becomes valid as part of the Constitution.

AMENDMENT XVIII

[PROPOSED BY CONGRESS DECEMBER 18, 1917; DECLARED RATIFIED ON JANUARY 29, 1919.]

Section 1

[NATIONAL LIQUOR PROHIBITION]

After one year from the ratification of this article the manufacture, sale, or transportation of intoxicating liquors within, the importation thereof into, or the exportation thereof from the United States and all territory subject to the jurisdiction thereof for beverage purposes is hereby prohibited.

Section 2

[POWER TO ENFORCE THIS ARTICLE]

The Congress and the several States shall have concurrent power to enforce this article by appropriate legislation.

Section 3

[RATIFICATION WITHIN SEVEN YEARS]

This article shall be inoperative unless it shall have been ratified as an amendment to the Constitution by the legislatures of the several States, as provided in the Constitution, within seven years from the date of the submission hereof to the States by the Congress.[1]

AMENDMENT XIX

[PROPOSED BY CONGRESS ON JUNE 4, 1919; DECLARED RATIFIED ON AUGUST 26, 1920.]

[WOMAN SUFFRAGE]

The right of citizens of the United States to vote shall not be denied or abridged by the United States or by any State on account of sex.

Congress shall have power to enforce this article by appropriate legislation.

AMENDMENT XX

[PROPOSED BY CONGRESS ON MARCH 2, 1932; DECLARED RATIFIED ON FEBRUARY 6, 1933.]

Section 1

[TERMS OF OFFICE]

The terms of the President and Vice President shall end at noon on the 20th day of January, and the terms of Senators and Representatives at noon on the 3rd day of

---

1. Repealed by the Twenty-First Amendment.

January, of the years in which such terms would have ended if this article had not been ratified; and the terms of their successors shall then begin.

Section 2

[TIME OF CONVENING CONGRESS]

The Congress shall assemble at least once in every year, and such meeting shall begin at noon on the 3rd day of January, unless they shall by law appoint a different day.

Section 3

[DEATH OF PRESIDENT-ELECT]

If, at the time fixed for the beginning of the term of the President, the President elect shall have died, the Vice President elect shall become President. If a President shall not have been chosen before the time fixed for the beginning of his term, or if the President elect shall have failed to qualify, then the Vice President elect shall act as President until a President shall have qualified; and the Congress may by law provide for the case wherein neither a President elect nor a Vice President elect shall have qualified, declaring who shall then act as President, or the manner in which one who is to act shall be selected, and such person shall act accordingly until a President or Vice President shall have qualified.

Section 4

[ELECTION OF THE PRESIDENT]

The Congress may by law provide for the case of the death of any of the persons from whom the House of Representatives may choose a President whenever the right of choice shall have devolved upon them, and for the case of the death of any of the persons from whom the Senate may choose a Vice President whenever the right of choice shall have devolved upon them.

Section 5

[AMENDMENT TAKES EFFECT]

Sections 1 and 2 shall take effect on the 15th day of October following the ratification of this article.

Section 6

[RATIFICATION WITHIN SEVEN YEARS]

This article shall be inoperative unless it shall have been ratified as an amendment to the Constitution by the legislatures of three-fourths of the several States within seven years from the date of its submission.

AMENDMENT XXI

[PROPOSED BY CONGRESS ON FEBRUARY 20, 1933; DECLARED RATIFIED ON DECEMBER 5, 1933.]

Section 1

[NATIONAL LIQUOR PROHIBITION REPEALED]

The eighteenth article of amendment to the Constitution of the United States is hereby repealed.

Section 2

[TRANSPORTATION OF LIQUOR INTO "DRY" STATES]

The transportation or importation into any State, Territory, or Possession of the United States for delivery or use therein of intoxicating liquors, in violation of the laws thereof, is hereby prohibited.

Section 3

This article shall be inoperative unless it shall have been ratified as an amendment to the Constitution by conventions in the several States, as provided in the Constitution, within seven years from the date of the submission hereof to the States by the Congress.

AMENDMENT XXII

[PROPOSED BY CONGRESS ON MARCH 21, 1947; DECLARED RATIFIED ON FEBRUARY 27, 1951.]

Section 1

[TENURE OF PRESIDENT LIMITED]

No person shall be elected to the office of President more than twice, and no person who has held the office of President or acted as President, for more than two years of a term to which some other person was elected President shall be elected to the office of the President more than once. But this Article shall not apply to any person holding the office of President when this Article was proposed by the Congress, and shall not prevent any person who may be holding the office of President, or acting as President, during the term within which this Article becomes operative from holding the office of President or acting as President during the remainder of such term.

Section 2

[RATIFICATION WITHIN SEVEN YEARS]

This article shall be inoperative unless it shall have been ratified as an amendment to the Constitution by the legislatures of three-fourths of the several States within seven years from the date of its submission to the States by the Congress.

AMENDMENT XXIII

[PROPOSED BY CONGRESS ON JUNE 16, 1960; DECLARED RATIFIED ON MARCH 29, 1961.]

Section 1

[ELECTORAL COLLEGE VOTES FOR THE DISTRICT OF COLUMBIA]

The District constituting the seat of Government of the United States shall appoint in such manner as the Congress may direct:

A number of electors of President and Vice President equal to the whole number of Senators and Representatives in Congress to which the District would be entitled if it were a State, but in no event more than the least populous State; they shall be in addition to those appointed by the States, but they shall be considered, for the purposes of the election of President and Vice President, to be electors appointed by a State; and they shall meet in the District and perform such duties as provided by the twelfth article of amendment.

Section 2

[POWER TO ENFORCE THIS ARTICLE]

The Congress shall have power to enforce this article by appropriate legislation.

AMENDMENT XXIV

[PROPOSED BY CONGRESS ON AUGUST 27, 1962; DECLARED RATIFIED ON JANUARY 23, 1964.]

Section 1

[ANTI-POLL TAX]

The right of citizens of the United States to vote in any primary or other election for President or Vice President, for electors for President or Vice President, or for Senator or

Representative of Congress, shall not be denied or abridged by the United States or any State by reason of failure to pay any poll tax or other tax.

Section 2
[POWER TO ENFORCE THIS ARTICLE]

The Congress shall have power to enforce this article by appropriate legislation.

AMENDMENT XXV
[PROPOSED BY CONGRESS ON JULY 6, 1965; DECLARED RATIFIED ON FEBRUARY 10, 1967.]

Section 1
[VICE PRESIDENT TO BECOME PRESIDENT]

In case of the removal of the President from office or his death or resignation, the Vice President shall become President.

Section 2
[CHOICE OF A NEW VICE PRESIDENT]

Whenever there is a vacancy in the office of the Vice President, the President shall nominate a Vice President who shall take the office upon confirmation by a majority vote of both houses of Congress.

Section 3
[PRESIDENT MAY DECLARE OWN DISABILITY]

Whenever the President transmits to the President pro tempore of the Senate and the Speaker of the House of Representatives his written declaration that he is unable to discharge the powers and duties of his office, and until he transmits to them a written declaration to the contrary, such powers and duties shall be discharged by the Vice President as Acting President.

Section 4
[ALTERNATE PROCEDURES TO DECLARE AND TO END PRESIDENTIAL DISABILITY]

Whenever the Vice President and a majority of either the principal officers of the executive departments, or of such other body as Congress may by law provide, transmit to the President pro tempore of the Senate and the Speaker of the House of Representatives their written declaration that the President is unable to discharge the powers and duties of his office, the Vice President shall immediately assume the powers and duties of the office as Acting President.

Thereafter, when the President transmits to the President pro tempore of the Senate and the Speaker of the House of Representatives his written declaration that no inability exists, he shall resume the powers and duties of his office unless the Vice President and a majority of either the principal officers of the executive department, or of such other body as Congress may by law provide, transmit within four days to the President pro tempore of the Senate and the Speaker of the House of Representatives their written declaration that the President is unable to discharge the powers and duties of his office. Thereupon Congress shall decide the issue, assembling within forty eight hours for that purpose if not in session. If the Congress, within twenty one days after receipt of the latter written declaration, or, if Congress is not in session, within twenty one days after Congress is required to assemble, determines by two-thirds vote of both Houses that the President is unable to discharge the powers and duties of his office, the Vice President shall continue to discharge the same as Acting President; otherwise, the President shall resume the powers and duties of his office.

AMENDMENT XXVI

[PROPOSED BY CONGRESS ON MARCH 23, 1971; DECLARED RATIFIED ON JULY 1, 1971.]

Section 1

[EIGHTEEN-YEAR-OLD VOTE]

The right of citizens of the United States, who are eighteen years of age or older, to vote shall not be denied or abridged by the United States or by any State on account of age.

Section 2

[POWER TO ENFORCE THIS ARTICLE]

The Congress shall have power to enforce this article by appropriate legislation.

AMENDMENT XXVII

[PROPOSED BY CONGRESS ON SEPTEMBER 25, 1789; DECLARED RATIFIED ON MAY 8, 1992.]

[CONGRESS CANNOT RAISE ITS OWN PAY]

No law varying the compensation for the services of the Senators and Representatives, shall take effect, until an election of representatives shall have intervened.

The Federalist Papers

NO. 10: MADISON

Among the numerous advantages promised by a well constructed Union, none deserves to be more accurately developed than its tendency to break and control the violence of faction. The friend of popular governments never finds himself so much alarmed for their character and fate, as when he contemplates their propensity to this dangerous vice. He will not fail therefore to set a due value on any plan which, without violating the principles to which he is attached, provides a proper cure for it. The instability, injustice, and confusion introduced into the public councils have, in truth, been the mortal diseases under which popular governments have everywhere perished, as they continue to be the favorite and fruitful topics from which the adversaries to liberty derive their most specious declamations. The valuable improvements made by the American constitutions on the popular models, both ancient and modern, cannot certainly be too much admired; but it would be an unwarrantable partiality to contend that they have as effectually obviated the danger on this side, as was wished and expected. Complaints are everywhere heard from our most considerate and virtuous citizens, equally the friends of public and private faith and of public and personal liberty, that our governments are too unstable, that the public good is disregarded in the conflicts of rival parties, and that measures are too often decided, not according to the rules of justice and the rights of the minor party, but by the superior force of an interested and overbearing majority. However anxiously we may wish that these complaints had no foundation, the evidence of known facts will not permit us to deny that they are in some degree true. It will be found, indeed, on a candid review of our situation, that some of the distresses under which we labor have been erroneously charged on the operation of our governments; but it will be found, at the same time, that other causes will not alone account for many of our heaviest misfortunes; and, particularly, for that prevailing and increasing distrust of public engagements and alarm for private rights which are echoed from one end of the continent to the other. These must be chiefly, if not wholly, effects of the unsteadiness and injustice with which a factious spirit has tainted our public administration.

By a faction I understand a number of citizens, whether amounting to a majority or minority of the whole, who are united and actuated by some common impulse of passion, or of interest, adverse to the rights of other citizens, or to the permanent and aggregate interests of the community.

There are two methods of curing the mischiefs of faction: the one, by removing its causes; the other, by controlling its effects.

There are again two methods of removing the causes of faction: the one, by destroying the liberty which is essential to its existence; the other, by giving to every citizen the same opinions, the same passions, and the same interests.

It could never be more truly said than of the first remedy, that it is worse than the disease. Liberty is to faction what air is to fire, an aliment without which it instantly expires. But it could not be a less folly to abolish liberty, which is essential to political life, because it nourishes faction, than it would be to wish the annihilation of air, which is essential to animal life, because it imparts to fire its destructive agency.

d expedient is as impracticable, as the first would be unwise. As long as the an continues fallible, and he is at liberty to exercise it, different opinions will be As long as the connection subsists between his reason and his self-love, his opinions s passions will have a reciprocal influence on each other; and the former will be objects which the latter will attach themselves. The diversity in the faculties of men, from which the rights of property originate, is not less an insuperable obstacle to a uniformity of interests. The protection of these faculties is the first object of Government. From the protection of different and unequal faculties of acquiring property, the possession of different degrees and kinds of property immediately results; and from the influence of these on the sentiments and views of the respective proprietors, ensues a division of the society into different interests and parties.

The latent causes of faction are thus sown in the nature of man; and we see them everywhere brought into different degrees of activity, according to the different circumstances of civil society. A zeal for different opinions concerning religion, concerning Government, and many other points, as well of speculation as of practice; an attachment to different leaders ambitiously contending for pre-eminence and power; or to persons of other descriptions whose fortunes have been interesting to the human passions, have in turn divided mankind into parties, inflamed them with mutual animosity, and rendered them much more disposed to vex and oppress each other, than to co-operate for their common good. So strong is this propensity of mankind to fall into mutual animosities, that where no substantial occasion presents itself, the most frivolous and fanciful distinctions have been sufficient to kindle their unfriendly passions, and excite their most violent conflicts. But the most common and durable source of factions has been the various and unequal distribution of property. Those who hold and those who are without property have ever formed distinct interests in society. Those who are creditors, and those who are debtors, fall under a like discrimination. A landed interest, a manufacturing interest, a mercantile interest, a moneyed interest, with many lesser interests, grow up of necessity in civilized nations, and divide them into different classes, actuated by different sentiments and views. The regulation of these various and interfering interests forms the principal task of modern Legislation, and involves the spirit of party and faction in the necessary and ordinary operations of Government.

No man is allowed to be judge in his own cause, because his interest would certainly bias his judgment and, not improbably, corrupt his integrity. With equal, nay with greater reason, a body of men are unfit to be both judges and parties at the same time; yet what are many of the most important acts of legislation but so many judicial determinations, not indeed concerning the rights of single persons, but concerning the rights of large bodies of citizens; and what are the different classes of legislators but advocates and parties to the causes which they determine? Is a law proposed concerning private debts? It is a question to which the creditors are parties on one side and the debtors on the other. Justice ought to hold the balance between them. Yet the parties are, and must be, themselves the judges; and the most numerous party, or in other words, the most powerful faction must be expected to prevail. Shall domestic manufacturers be encouraged, and in what degree, by restrictions on foreign manufacturers? are questions which would be differently decided by the landed and the manufacturing classes, and probably by neither with a sole regard to justice and the public good. The apportionment of taxes on the various descriptions of property is an act which seems to require the most exact impartiality; yet there is, perhaps, no legislative act in which greater opportunity and temptation are given to a predominant party to trample on the rules of justice. Every shilling with which they overburden the inferior number is a shilling saved to their own pockets.

It is in vain to say that enlightened statesmen will be able to adjust these clashing interests and render them all subservient to the public good. Enlightened statesmen will not always be at the helm. Nor, in many cases, can such an adjustment be made at all without taking into view indirect and remote considerations, which will rarely prevail over the immediate interest which one party may find in disregarding the rights of another or the good of the whole.

The inference to which we are brought is that the *causes* of faction cannot be removed and that relief is only to be sought in the means of controlling its *effects*.

If a faction consists of less than a majority, relief is supplied by the republican principle, which enables the majority to defeat its sinister views by regular vote. It may clog the administration, it may convulse the society; but it will be unable to execute and mask its violence under the forms of the Constitution. When a majority is included in a faction, the form of popular government, on the other hand, enables it to sacrifice to its ruling passion or interest both the public good and the rights of other citizens. To secure the public good and private rights against the danger of such a faction, and at the same time to preserve the spirit and the form of popular government, is then the great object to which our enquiries are directed. Let me add that it is the great desideratum by which alone this form of government can be rescued from the opprobrium under which it has so long labored and be recommended to the esteem and adoption of mankind.

By what means is this object attainable? Evidently by one of two only. Either the existence of the same passion or interest in a majority at the same time must be prevented, or the majority, having such co-existent passion or interest, must be rendered, by their number and local situation, unable to concert and carry into effect schemes of oppression. If the impulse and the opportunity be suffered to coincide, we well know that neither moral nor religious motives can be relied on as an adequate control. They are not found to be such on the injustice and violence of individuals, and lose their efficacy in proportion to the number combined together, that is, in proportion as their efficacy becomes needful.

From this view of the subject it may be concluded that a pure Democracy, by which I mean a Society consisting of a small number of citizens, who assemble and administer the Government in person, can admit of no cure for the mischiefs of faction. A common passion or interest will, in almost every case, be felt by a majority of the whole; a communication and concert results from the form of Government itself; and there is nothing to check the inducements to sacrifice the weaker party or an obnoxious individual. Hence it is that such Democracies have ever been spectacles of turbulence and contention; have ever been found incompatible with personal security or the rights of property; and have in general been as short in their lives as they have been violent in their deaths. Theoretic politicians, who have patronized this species of Government, have erroneously supposed that by reducing mankind to a perfect equality in their political rights, they would at the same time be perfectly equalized and assimilated in their possessions, their opinions, and their passions.

A Republic, by which I mean a Government in which the scheme of representation takes place, opens a different prospect and promises the cure for which we are seeking. Let us examine the points in which it varies from pure Democracy, and we shall comprehend both the nature of the cure and the efficacy which it must derive from the Union.

The two great points of difference between a Democracy and a Republic are: first, the delegation of the Government, in the latter, to a small number of citizens elected by the rest; secondly, the greater number of citizens and greater sphere of country over which the latter may be extended.

The effect of the first difference is, on the one hand, to refine and enlarge the public views by passing them through the medium of a chosen body of citizens, whose wisdom may best discern the true interest of their country and whose patriotism and love of justice will be least likely to sacrifice it to temporary or partial considerations. Under such a regulation it may well happen that the public voice, pronounced by the representatives of the people, will be more consonant to the public good than if pronounced by the people themselves, convened for the purpose. On the other hand, the effect may be inverted. Men of factious tempers, of local prejudices, or of sinister designs, may, by intrigue, by corruption, or by other means, first obtain the suffrages, and then betray the interests of the people. The question resulting is, whether small or extensive Republics are most favorable to the election of proper guardians of the public weal; and it is clearly decided in favor of the latter by two obvious considerations.

In the first place it is to be remarked that however small the Republic may be, the Representatives must be raised to a certain number in order to guard against the cabals of a few; and that however large it may be they must be limited to a certain number in order to guard against the confusion of a multitude. Hence, the number of Representatives in the two cases not being in proportion to that of the Constituents, and being proportionally greatest in the small Republic, it follows that if the proportion of fit characters be not less in the large than in the small Republic, the former will present a greater option, and consequently a greater probability of a fit choice.

In the next place, as each Representative will be chosen by a greater number of citizens in the large than in the small Republic, it will be more difficult for unworthy candidates to practise with success the vicious arts by which elections are too often carried; and the suffrages of the people being more free, will be more likely to centre on men who possess the most attractive merit and the most diffusive and established characters.

It must be confessed that in this, as in most other cases, there is a mean, on both sides of which inconveniencies will be found to lie. By enlarging too much the number of electors, you render the representative too little acquainted with all their local circumstances and lesser interests; as by reducing it too much, you render him unduly attached to these, and too little fit to comprehend and pursue great and national objects. The Federal Constitution forms a happy combination in this respect; the great and aggregate interests being referred to the national, the local and particular to the State legislatures.

The other point of difference is the greater number of citizens and extent of territory which may be brought within the compass of Republican than of Democratic Government; and it is this circumstance principally which renders factious combinations less to be dreaded in the former than in the latter. The smaller the society, the fewer probably will be the distinct parties and interests composing it; the fewer the distinct parties and interests, the more frequently will a majority be found of the same party; and the smaller the number of individuals composing a majority, and the smaller the compass within which they are placed, the more easily will they concert and execute their plans of oppression. Extend the sphere and you take in a greater variety of parties and interests; you make it less probable that a majority of the whole will have a common motive to invade the rights of other citizens; or if such a common motive exists, it will be more difficult for all who feel it to discover their own strength and to act in unison with each other. Besides other impediments, it may be remarked, that where there is a consciousness of unjust or dishonorable purposes, communication is always checked by distrust in proportion to the number whose concurrence is necessary.

Hence, it clearly appears that the same advantage which a Republic has over a Democracy in controlling the effects of faction is enjoyed by a large over a small republic—is enjoyed by the Union over the States composing it. Does this advantage consist in the substitution of representatives whose enlightened views and virtuous sentiments render them superior to local prejudices and to schemes of injustice? It will not be denied that the representation of the Union will be most likely to possess these requisite endowments. Does it consist in the greater security afforded by a greater variety of parties, against the event of any one party being able to outnumber and oppress the rest? In an equal degree does the increased variety of parties comprised within the Union increase this security? Does it, in fine, consist in the greater obstacles opposed to the concert and accomplishment of the secret wishes of an unjust and interested majority? Here again the extent of the Union gives it the most palpable advantage.

The influence of factious leaders may kindle a flame within their particular States but will be unable to spread a general conflagration through the other States: a religious sect may degenerate into a political faction in a part of the Confederacy; but the variety of sects dispersed over the entire face of it must secure the national Councils against any danger from that source: a rage for paper money, for an abolition of debts, for an equal division of property, or for any other improper or wicked project, will be less apt to pervade the whole body of the Union than a particular member of it; in the same proportion as such a malady is more likely to taint a particular county or district than an entire State.

In the extent and proper structure of the Union, therefore, we behold a republican remedy for the diseases most incident to Republican Government. And according to the degree of pleasure and pride we feel in being republicans ought to be our zeal in cherishing the spirit and supporting the character of federalist.

PUBLIUS
November 22, 1787

NO. 51: MADISON

To what expedient, then, shall we finally resort, for maintaining in practice the necessary partition of power among the several departments as laid down in the constitution? The only answer that can be given is that as all these exterior provisions are found to be inadequate the defect must be supplied, by so contriving the interior structure of the government as that its several constituent parts may, by their mutual relations, be the means of keeping each other in their proper places. Without presuming to undertake a full development of this important idea I will hazard a few general observations which may perhaps place it in a clearer light, and enable us to form a more correct judgment of the principles and structure of the government planned by the convention.

In order to lay a due foundation for that separate and distinct exercise of the different powers of government, which to a certain extent is admitted on all hands to be essential to the preservation of liberty, it is evident that each department should have a will of its own; and consequently should be so constituted that the members of each should have as little agency as possible in the appointment of the members of the others. Were this principle rigorously adhered to, it would require that all the appointments for the supreme executive, legislative, and judiciary magistracies should be drawn from the same fountain of authority, the people, through channels having no communication whatever with one another. Perhaps such a plan of constructing the several departments would be less difficult in practice than it may in contemplation appear. Some difficulties, however, and some additional expense would attend the execution of it. Some deviations, therefore, from the principle must be admitted. In the constitution of the judiciary department in particular, it might be inexpedient to insist rigorously on the principle: first, because peculiar qualifications being essential in the members, the primary consideration ought to be to select that mode of choice which best secures these qualifications; second, because the permanent tenure by which the appointments are held in that department must soon destroy all sense of dependence on the authority conferring them.

It is equally evident that the members of each department should be as little dependent as possible on those of the others for the emoluments annexed to their offices. Were the executive magistrate, or the judges, not independent of the legislature in this particular, their independence in every other would be merely nominal.

But the great security against a gradual concentration of the several powers in the same department consists in giving to those who administer each department the necessary constitutional means and personal motives to resist encroachments of the others. The provision for defence must in this, as in all other cases, be made commensurate to the danger of attack. Ambition must be made to counteract ambition. The interest of the man must be connected with the constitutional rights of the place. It may be a reflection on human nature that such devices should be necessary to control the abuses of government. But what is government itself but the greatest of all reflections on human nature? If men were angels, no government would be necessary. If angels were to govern men, neither external nor internal controls on government would be necessary. In framing a government which is to be administered by men over men, the great difficulty lies in this: You must first enable the government to control the governed; and in the next place oblige it to control itself. A dependence on the people is, no doubt, the primary control on the government; but experience has taught mankind the necessity of auxiliary precautions.

This policy of supplying, by opposite and rival interests, the defect of better motives, might be traced through the whole system of human affairs, private as well as public. We see it particularly displayed in all the subordinate distributions of power, where the constant aim is to divide and arrange the several offices in such a manner as that each may be a check on the other; that the private interest of every individual may be a sentinel over the public rights. These inventions of prudence cannot be less requisite in the distribution of the supreme powers of the State.

But it is not possible to give to each department an equal power of self-defense. In republican government, the legislative authority necessarily predominates. The remedy for this inconveniency is to divide the legislature into different branches; and to render them, by different modes of election and different principles of action, as little connected with each other as the nature of their common functions and their common dependence on the society will admit. It may even be necessary to guard against dangerous encroachments by still further precautions. As the weight of the legislative authority requires that it should be thus divided, the weakness of the executive may require, on the other hand, that it should be fortified. An absolute negative on the legislature appears, at first view, to be the natural defense with which the executive magistrate should be armed. But perhaps it would be neither altogether safe nor alone sufficient. On ordinary occasions it might not be exerted with the requisite firmness, and on extraordinary occasions it might be perfidiously abused. May not this defect of an absolute negative be supplied by some qualified connection between this weaker branch of the stronger department, by which the latter may be led to support the constitutional rights of the former, without being too much detached from the rights of its own department?

If the principles on which these observations are founded be just, as I persuade myself they are, and they be applied as a criterion to the several State constitutions, and to the federal Constitution, it will be found that if the latter does not perfectly correspond with them, the former are infinitely less able to bear such a test.

There are, moreover, two considerations particularly applicable to the federal system of America, which place that system in a very interesting point of view.

First. In a single republic, all the power surrendered by the people is submitted to the administration of a single government; and usurpations are guarded against by a division of the government into distinct and separate departments. In the compound republic of America, the power surrendered by the people is first divided between two distinct governments, and then the portion allotted to each subdivided among distinct and separate departments. Hence a double security arises to the rights of the people. The different governments will control each other, at the same time that each will be controlled by itself.

Second. It is of great importance in a republic not only to guard the society against the oppression of its rulers, but to guard one part of the society against the injustice of the other part. Different interests necessarily exist in different classes of citizens. If a majority be united by a common interest, the rights of the minority will be insecure. There are but two methods of providing against this evil: The one by creating a will in the community independent of the majority—that is, of the society itself; the other, by comprehending in the society so many separate descriptions of citizens as will render an unjust combination of a majority of the whole very improbable, if not impracticable. The first method prevails in all governments possessing an hereditary or self-appointed authority. This, at best, is but a precarious security;

because a power independent of the society may as well espouse the unjust views of the major as the rightful interests of the minor party, and may possibly be turned against both parties. The second method will be exemplified in the federal republic of the United States. Whilst all authority in it will be derived from and dependent on the society, the society itself will be broken into so many parts, interests and classes of citizens, that the rights of individuals, or of the minority, will be in little danger from interested combinations of the majority. In a free government the security for civil rights must be the same as that for religious rights. It consists in the one case in the multiplicity of interests, and in the other in the multiplicity of sects. The degree of security in both cases will depend on the number of interests and sects; and this may be presumed to depend on the extent of country and number of people comprehended under the same government. This view of the subject must particularly recommend a proper federal system to all the sincere and considerate friends of republican government: Since it shows that in exact proportion as the territory of the Union may be formed into more circumscribed Confederacies, or States, oppressive combinations of a majority will be facilitated; the best security, under the republican form, for the rights of every class of citizens, will be diminished; and consequently the stability and independence of some member of the government, the only other security, must be proportionally increased. Justice is the end of government. It is the end of civil society. It ever has been and ever will be pursued until it be obtained, or until liberty be lost in the pursuit. In a society under the forms of which the stronger faction can readily unite and oppress the weaker, anarchy may as truly be said to reign as in a state of nature, where the weaker individual is not secured against the violence of the stronger: And as, in the latter state, even the stronger individuals are prompted, by the uncertainty of their condition, to submit to a government which may protect the weak as well as themselves: So, in the former state, will the more powerful factions or parties be gradually induced, by a like motive, to wish for a government which will protect all parties, the weaker as well as the more powerful. It can be little doubted that if the State of Rhode Island was separated from the Confederacy and left to itself, the insecurity of rights under the popular form of government within such narrow limits would be displayed by such reiterated oppressions of factious majorities that some power altogether independent of the people would soon be called for by the voice of the very factions whose misrule had proved the necessity of it. In the extended republic of the United States, and among the great variety of interests, parties, and sects which it embraces, a coalition of a majority of the whole society could seldom take place on any other principles than those of justice and the general good; and there being thus less danger to a minor from the will of the major party, there must be less pretext, also, to provide for the security of the former, by introducing into the government a will not dependent on the latter, or, in other words, a will independent of the society itself. It is no less certain than it is important, notwithstanding the contrary opinions which have been entertained, that the larger the society, provided it lie within a practicable sphere, the more duly capable it will be of self-government. And happily for the *republican cause,* practicable sphere may be carried to a very great extent by a judicious modification and mixture of the *federal principle.*

PUBLIUS
February 6, 1788

The Anti-Federalist Papers

Essay by Brutus in the *New York Journal*

When the public is called to investigate and decide upon a question in which not only the present members of the community are deeply interested, but upon which the happiness and misery of generations yet unborn is in great measure suspended, the benevolent mind cannot help feeling itself peculiarly interested in the result.

In this situation, I trust the feeble efforts of an individual, to lead the minds of the people to a wise and prudent determination, cannot fail of being acceptable to the candid and dispassionate part of the community. Encouraged by this consideration, I have been induced to offer my thoughts upon the present important crisis of our public affairs.

Perhaps this country never saw so critical a period in their political concerns. We have felt the feebleness of the ties by which these United-States are held together, and the want of sufficient energy in our present confederation, to manage, in some instances, our general concerns. Various expedients have been proposed to remedy these evils, but none have succeeded. At length a Convention of the states has been assembled, they have formed a constitution which will now, probably, be submitted to the people to ratify or reject, who are the fountain of all power, to whom alone it of right belongs to make or unmake constitutions, or forms of government, at their pleasure. The most important question that was ever proposed to your decision, or to the decision of any people under heaven, is before you, and you are to decide upon it by men of your own election, chosen specially for this purpose. If the constitution, offered to your acceptance, be a wise one, calculated to preserve the invaluable blessings of liberty, to secure the inestimable rights of mankind, and promote human happiness, then, if you accept it, you will lay a lasting foundation of happiness for millions yet unborn; generations to come will rise up and call you blessed. You may rejoice in the prospects of this vast extended continent becoming filled with freemen, who will assert the dignity of human nature. You may solace yourselves with the idea, that society, in this favoured land, will fast advance to the highest point of perfection; the human mind will expand in knowledge and virtue, and the golden age be, in some measure, realised. But if, on the other hand, this form of government contains principles that will lead to the subversion of liberty—if it tends to establish a despotism, or, what is worse, a tyrannic aristocracy; then, if you adopt it, this only remaining assylum for liberty will be shut up, and posterity will execrate your memory.

Momentous then is the question you have to determine, and you are called upon by every motive which should influence a noble and virtuous mind, to examine it well, and to make up a wise judgment. It is insisted, indeed, that this constitution must be received, be it ever so imperfect. If it has its defects, it is said, they can be best amended when they are experienced. But remember, when the people once part with power, they can seldom or never resume it again but by force. Many instances can be produced in which the people have voluntarily increased the powers of their rulers; but few, if any, in which rulers have willingly abridged their authority. This is a sufficient reason to induce you to be careful, in the first instance, how you deposit the powers of government.

With these few introductory remarks, I shall proceed to a consideration of this constitution:

The first question that presents itself on the subject is, whether a confederated government be the best for the United States or not? Or in other words, whether the thirteen United States should be reduced to one great republic, governed by one legislature, and under the direction of one executive and judicial; or whether they should continue thirteen confederated republics, under the direction and controul of a supreme federal head for certain defined national purposes only?

This enquiry is important, because, although the government reported by the convention does not go to a perfect and entire consolidation, yet it approaches so near to it, that it must, if executed, certainly and infallibly terminate in it.

This government is to possess absolute and uncontroulable power, legislative, executive and judicial, with respect to every object to which it extends, for by the last clause of section 8th, article 1st, it is declared "that the Congress shall have power to make all laws which shall be necessary and proper for carrying into execution the foregoing powers, and all other powers vested by this constitution, in the government of the United States; or in any department or office thereof." And by the 6th article, it is declared "that this constitution, and the laws of the United States, which shall be made in pursuance thereof, and the treaties made, or which shall be made, under the authority of the United States, shall be the supreme law of the land; and the judges in every state shall be bound thereby, any thing in the constitution, or law of any state to the contrary notwithstanding." It appears from these articles that there is no need of any intervention of the state governments, between the Congress and the people, to execute any one power vested in the general government, and that the constitution and laws of every state are nullified and declared void, so far as they are or shall be inconsistent with this constitution, or the laws made in pursuance of it, or with treaties made under the authority of the United States.—The government then, so far as it extends, is a complete one, and not a confederation. It is as much one complete government as that of New-York or Massachusetts, has as absolute and perfect powers to make and execute all laws, to appoint officers, institute courts, declare offences, and annex penalties, with respect to every object to which it extends, as any other in the world. So far therefore as its powers reach, all ideas of confederation are given up and lost. It is true this government is limited to certain objects, or to speak more properly, some small degree of power is still left to the states, but a little attention to the powers vested in the general government, will convince every candid man, that if it is capable of being executed, all that is reserved for the individual states must very soon be annihilated, except so far as they are barely necessary to the organization of the general government. The powers of the general legislature extend to every case that is of the least importance—there is nothing valuable to human nature, nothing dear to freemen, but what is within its power. It has authority to make laws which will affect the lives, the liberty, and property of every man in the United States; nor can the constitution or laws of any state, in any way prevent or impede the full and complete execution of every power given. The legislative power is competent to lay taxes, duties, imposts, and excises;—there is no limitation to this power, unless it be said that the clause which directs the use to which those taxes, and duties shall be applied, may be said to be a limitation: but this is no restriction of the power at all, for by this clause they are to be applied to pay the debts and provide for the common defence and general welfare of the United States; but the legislature have authority to contract debts at their discretion; they are the sole judges of what is necessary to provide for the common defence, and they only are to determine what is for the general welfare; this power therefore is neither more nor less, than a power to lay and collect taxes, imposts, and excises, at their pleasure; not only [is] the power to lay taxes unlimited, as to the amount they may require, but it is perfect and absolute to raise them in any mode they please. No state legislature, or any power in the state governments, have any more to do in carrying this into effect, than the authority of one state has to do with that of another. In the business therefore of laying and collecting taxes, the idea of confederation is totally lost, and that of one entire republic is embraced. It is proper here to remark, that the authority to lay and collect taxes is the most important of any power that can be granted; it connects with it almost all other powers, or at least will in process of time draw all other after it; it is the great mean of protection, security, and defence, in a good government, and the great engine of oppression and tyranny in a bad one. This cannot fail of being the case, if we consider the contracted limits which are set by this constitution, to the late [state?] governments, on this article of raising money. No state can emit paper money—lay any duties, or imposts, on imports, or exports, but by consent of the Congress; and then the net produce shall be for the benefit of the United States: the only mean therefore left, for any state to support its government and discharge its debts, is by direct taxation; and the United States have also power to lay and collect taxes, in any way they please. Every one who has thought on the subject, must be convinced that but small sums of money can be collected in any country, by direct taxe[s], when the foederal government begins to exercise the right of taxation in all its parts, the legislatures of the several states will find it impossible to raise monies to support their governments. Without money they cannot be supported, and they must dwindle away, and, as before observed, their powers absorbed in that of the general government.

It might be here shewn, that the power in the federal legislative, to raise and support armies at pleasure, as well in peace as in war, and their controul over the militia, tend, not only to a consolidation of the government, but the destruction of liberty.—I shall not, however, dwell upon these, as a few observations upon the judicial power of this government, in addition to the preceding, will fully evince the truth of the position.

The judicial power of the United States is to be vested in a supreme court, and in such inferior courts as Congress may from time to time ordain and establish. The powers of these courts are very extensive; their jurisdiction comprehends all civil causes, except such as arise between citizens of the same state; and it extends to all cases in law and equity arising under the constitution. One inferior court must be established, I presume, in each state, at least, with the necessary executive officers appendant thereto. It is easy to see, that in the common course of things, these courts will eclipse the dignity, and take away from the respectability, of the state courts. These courts will be, in themselves, totally independent of the states, deriving their authority from the United States, and receiving from them fixed salaries; and in the course of human events it is to be expected, that they will swallow up all the powers of the courts in the respective states.

How far the clause in the 8th section of the 1st article may operate to do away all idea of confederated states, and to effect an entire consolidation of the whole into one general government, it is impossible to say. The powers given by this article are very general and comprehensive, and it may receive a construction to justify the passing almost any law. A power to make all laws, which shall be *necessary and proper*, for carrying into execution, all powers vested by the constitution in the government of the United States, or any department or officer thereof, is a power very comprehensive and definite [indefinite?], and may, for ought I know, be exercised in a such manner as entirely to abolish the state legislatures. Suppose the legislature of a state should pass a law to raise money to support their government and pay the state debt, may the Congress repeal this law, because it may prevent the collection of a tax which they may think proper and necessary to lay, to provide for the general welfare of the United States? For all laws made, in pursuance of this constitution, are the supreme lay of the land, and the judges in every state shall be bound thereby, any thing in the constitution or laws of the different states to the contrary notwithstanding.—By such a law, the government of a particular state might be overturned at one stroke, and thereby be deprived of every means of its support.

It is not meant, by stating this case, to insinuate that the constitution would warrant a law of this kind; or unnecessarily to alarm the fears of the people, by suggesting, that the federal legislature would be more likely to pass the limits assigned them by the constitution, than that of an individual state, further than they are less responsible to the people. But what is meant is, that the legislature of the United States are vested with the great and uncontroulable powers, of laying and collecting taxes, duties, imposts, and excises; of regulating trade, raising and supporting armies, organizing, arming, and disciplining the militia, instituting courts, and other general powers. And are by this clause invested with the power of making all laws, *proper and necessary*, for carrying all these into execution; and they may so exercise this power as entirely to annihilate all the state governments, and reduce this country to one single government. And if they may do it, it is pretty certain they will; for it will be found that the power retained by individual states, small as it is, will be a clog upon the wheels of the government of the United States; the latter therefore will be naturally inclined to remove it out of the way. Besides, it is a truth confirmed by the unerring experience of ages, that every man, and every body of men, invested with power, are ever disposed to increase it, and to acquire a superiority over every thing that stands in their way. This disposition, which is implanted in human nature, will operate in the federal legislature to lessen and ultimately to subvert the state authority, and having such advantages, will most certainly succeed, if the federal government succeeds at all. It must be very evident then, that what this constitution wants of being a complete consolidation of the several parts of the union into one complete government, possessed of perfect legislative, judicial, and executive powers, to all intents and purposes, it will necessarily acquire in its exercise and operation.

Let us now proceed to enquire, as I at first proposed, whether it be best the thirteen United States should be reduced to one great republic, or not? It is here taken for granted, that all agree in this, that whatever government we adopt, it ought to be a free one; that it should be so framed as to secure the liberty of the citizens of America, and such an one as to admit of a full, fair, and equal representation of the people. The question then will be, whether a government thus constituted, and founded on such principles, is practicable, and can be exercised over the whole United States, reduced into one state?

If respect is to be paid to the opinion of the greatest and wisest men who have ever thought or wrote on the science of government, we shall be constrained to conclude, that a free republic cannot succeed over a country of such immense extent, containing such a number of inhabitants, and these encreasing in such rapid progression as that of the whole United States. Among the many illustrious authorities which might be produced to this point, I shall content myself with quoting only two. The one is the baron de Montesquieu, spirit of laws, chap. xvi. vol. I [book VIII]. "It is natural to a republic to have only a small territory, otherwise it cannot long subsist. In a large republic there are men of large fortunes, and consequently of less moderation; there are trusts too great to be placed in any single subject; he has interest of his own; he soon begins to think that he may be happy, great and glorious, by oppressing his fellow citizens; and that he may raise himself to grandeur on the ruins of his country. In a large republic, the public good is sacrificed to a thousand views; it is subordinate to exceptions, and depends on accidents. In a small one, the interest of the public is easier perceived, better understood, and more within the reach of every citizen; abuses are of less extent, and of course are less protected." Of the same opinion is the marquis Beccarari.

History furnishes no example of a free republic, any thing like the extent of the United States. The Grecian republics were of small extent; so also was that of the Romans. Both of these, it is true, in process of time, extended their conquests over large territories of country; and the consequence was, that their governments were changed from that of free governments to those of the most tyrannical that ever existed in the world.

Not only the opinion of the greatest men, and the experience of mankind, are against the idea of an extensive republic, but a variety of reasons may be drawn from the reason and nature of things, against it. In every government, the will of the sovereign is the law. In despotic governments, the supreme authority being lodged in one, his will is law, and can be as easily expressed to a large extensive territory as to a small one. In a pure democracy the people are the sovereign, and their will is declared by themselves; for this purpose they must all come together to deliberate, and decide. This kind of government cannot be exercised, therefore, over a country of any considerable extent; it must be confined to a single city, or at least limited to such bounds as that the people can conveniently assemble, be able to debate, understand the subject submitted to them, and declare their opinion concerning it.

In a free republic, although all laws are derived from the consent of the people, yet the people do not declare their consent by themselves in person, but by representatives, chosen by them, who are supposed to know the minds of their constituents, and to be possessed of integrity to declare this mind.

In every free government, the people must give their assent to the laws by which they are governed. This is the true criterion between a free government and an arbitrary one. The former are ruled by the will of the whole, expressed in any manner they may agree upon; the latter by the will of one, or a few. If the people are to give their assent to the laws, by persons chosen and appointed by them, the manner of the choice and the number chosen, must be such, as to possess, be disposed, and consequently qualified to declare the sentiments of the people; for if they do not know, or are not disposed to speak the sentiments of the people, the people do not govern, but the sovereignty is in a few. Now, in a large extended country, it is impossible to have a representation, possessing the sentiments, and of integrity, to declare the minds of the people, without having it so numerous and unwieldly, as to be subject in great measure to the inconveniency of a democratic government.

The territory of the United States is of vast extent; it now contains near three millions of souls, and is capable of containing much more than ten times that number. Is it practicable for a country, so large and so numerous as they will soon become, to elect a representation, that will speak their sentiments, without their becoming so numerous as to be incapable of transacting public business? It certainly is not.

In a republic, the manners, sentiments, and interests of the people should be similar. If this be not the case, there will be a constant clashing of opinions; and the representatives of one part will be continually striving against those of the other. This will retard the operations of government, and prevent such conclusions as will promote the public good. If we apply this remark to the condition of the United States, we shall be convinced that it forbids that we should be one government. The United States includes a variety of climates. The productions of the different parts of the union are very variant, and their interests, of consequence, diverse. Their manners and habits differ as much as their climates and productions; and their sentiments are by no means coincident. The laws and customs of the several states are, in many respects, very diverse, and in some opposite; each would be in favor of its own interests and customs, and, of consequence, a legislature, formed of representatives from the respective parts, would not only be too numerous to act with any care or decision, but would be composed of such heterogenous and discordant principles, as would constantly be contending with each other.

The laws cannot be executed in a republic, of an extent equal to that of the United States, with promptitude.

The magistrates in every government must be supported in the execution of the laws, either by an armed force, maintained at the public expence for that purpose; or by the people turning out to aid the magistrate upon his command, in case of resistance.

In despotic governments, as well as in all the monarchies of Europe, standing armies are kept up to execute the commands of the prince or the magistrate, and are employed for this purpose when occasion requires: But they have always proved the destruction of liberty, and [are] abhorrent to the spirit of a free republic. In England, where they depend upon the parliament for their annual support, they have always been complained of as oppressive and unconstitutional, and are seldom employed in executing of the laws; never except on extraordinary occasions, and then under the direction of a civil magistrate.

A free republic will never keep a standing army to execute its laws. It must depend upon the support of its citizens. But when a government is to receive its support from the aid of the citizens, it must be so constructed as to have the confidence, respect, and affection of the people. Men who, upon the call of the magistrate, offer themselves to execute the laws, are influenced to do it either by affection to the government, or from fear; where a standing army is at hand to punish offenders, every man is actuated by the latter principle, and therefore, when the magistrate calls, will obey: but, where this is not the case, the government must rest for its support upon the confidence and respect which the people have for their government and laws. The body of the people being attached, the government will always be sufficient to support and execute its laws, and to operate upon the fears of any faction which may be opposed to it, not only to prevent an opposition to the execution of the laws themselves, but also to compel the most of them to aid the magistrate; but the people will not be likely to have such confidence in their rulers, in a republic so extensive as the United States, as necessary for these purposes. The confidence which the people have in their rulers, in a free republic, arises from their knowing them, from their being responsible to them for their conduct, and from the power they have of displacing them when they misbehave: but in a republic of the extent of this continent, the people in general would be acquainted with very few of their rulers: the people at large would know little of their proceedings, and it would be extremely difficult to change them. The people in Georgia and New-Hampshire would not know one another's mind, and therefore could not act in concert to enable them to effect a general change of representatives. The different parts of so extensive a country could not possibly be made acquainted with the conduct of their representatives, nor be informed of the reasons upon which measures were founded. The consequence will be, they will have no confidence in their legislature, suspect them of ambitious views, be jealous of every measure they adopt, and will not support the laws they pass. Hence the government will be nerveless and ineffi-cient, and no way will be left to render it otherwise, but by establishing an armed force to exe-cute the laws at the point of the bayonet—a government of all others the most to be dreaded.

In a republic of such vast extent as the United-States, the legislature cannot attend to the various concerns and wants of its different parts. It cannot be sufficiently numerous to be acquainted with the local condition and wants of the different districts, and if it could, it is impossible it should have sufficient time to attend to and provide for all the variety of cases of this nature, that would be continually arising.

In so extensive a republic, the great officers of government would soon become above the controul of the people, and abuse their power to the purpose of aggrandizing themselves, and oppressing them. The trust committed to the executive offices, in a country of the extent of the United-States, must be various and of magnitude. The command of all the troops and navy of the republic, the appointment of officers, the power of pardoning offences, the collecting of all the public revenues, and the power of expending them, with a number of other powers, must be lodged and exercised in every state, in the hands of a few. When these are attended with great honor and emolument, as they always will be in large states, so as greatly to interest men to pursue them, and to be proper objects for ambitious and designing men, such men will be ever restless in their pursuit after them. They will use the power, when they have acquired it, to the purposes of gratifying their own interest and ambition, and it is scarcely possible, in a very large republic, to call them to account for their misconduct, or to prevent their abuse of power.

These are some of the reasons by which it appears, that a free republic cannot long sub-sist over a country of the great extent of these states. If then this new constitution is calcu-lated to consolidate the thirteen states into one, as it evidently is, it ought not to be adopted.

Though I am of opinion, that it is a sufficient objection to this government, to reject it, that it creates the whole union into one government, under the form of a republic, yet if this objection was obviated, there are exceptions to it, which are so material and fundamen-tal, that they ought to determine every man, who is a friend to the liberty and happiness of mankind, not to adopt it. I beg the candid and dispassionate attention of my countrymen while I state these objections—they are such as have obtruded themselves upon my mind upon a careful attention to the matter, and such as I sincerely believe are well founded. There are many objections, of small moment, of which I shall take no notice—perfection is not to be expected in any thing that is the production of man—and if I did not in my conscience believe that this scheme was defective in the fundamental principles—in the foundation upon which a free and equal government must rest—I would hold my peace.

BRUTUS
October 18, 1787

Presidents and Vice Presidents

	PRESIDENT	VICE PRESIDENT
1	George Washington *(Federalist 1789)*	John Adams *(Federalist 1789)*
2	John Adams *(Federalist 1797)*	Thomas Jefferson *(Dem.-Rep. 1797)*
3	Thomas Jefferson *(Dem.-Rep. 1801)*	Aaron Burr *(Dem.-Rep. 1801)* George Clinton *(Dem.-Rep. 1805)*
4	James Madison *(Dem.-Rep. 1809)*	George Clinton *(Dem.-Rep. 1809)* Elbridge Gerry *(Dem.-Rep. 1813)*
5	James Monroe *(Dem.-Rep. 1817)*	Daniel D. Tompkins *(Dem.-Rep. 1817)*
6	John Quincy Adams *(Dem.-Rep. 1825)*	John C. Calhoun *(Dem.-Rep. 1825)*
7	Andrew Jackson *(Democratic 1829)*	John C. Calhoun *(Democratic 1829)* Martin Van Buren *(Democratic 1833)*
8	Martin Van Buren *(Democratic 1837)*	Richard M. Johnson *(Democratic 1837)*
9	William H. Harrison *(Whig 1841)*	John Tyler *(Whig 1841)*
10	John Tyler *(Whig and Democratic 1841)*	
11	James K. Polk *(Democratic 1845)*	George M. Dallas *(Democratic 1845)*
12	Zachary Taylor *(Whig 1849)*	Millard Fillmore *(Whig 1849)*
13	Millard Fillmore *(Whig 1850)*	
14	Franklin Pierce *(Democratic 1853)*	William R. D. King *(Democratic 1853)*

	PRESIDENT	VICE PRESIDENT
15	James Buchanan *(Democratic 1857)*	John C. Breckinridge *(Democratic 1857)*
16	Abraham Lincoln *(Republican 1861)*	Hannibal Hamlin *(Republican 1861)*
		Andrew Johnson *(Unionist 1865)*
17	Andrew Johnson (Unionist 1865)	
18	Ulysses S. Grant *(Republican 1869)*	Schuyler Colfax *(Republican 1869)*
		Henry Wilson *(Republican 1873)*
19	Rutherford B. Hayes *(Republican 1877)*	William A. Wheeler *(Republican 1877)*
20	James A. Garfield *(Republican 1881)*	Chester A. Arthur *(Republican 1881)*
21	Chester A. Arthur *(Republican 1881)*	
22	Grover Cleveland *(Democratic 1885)*	Thomas A. Hendricks *(Democratic 1885)*
23	Benjamin Harrison *(Republican 1889)*	Levi P. Morton *(Republican 1889)*
24	Grover Cleveland *(Democratic 1893)*	Adlai E. Stevenson *(Democratic 1893)*
25	William McKinley *(Republican 1897)*	Garret A. Hobart *(Republican 1897)*
		Theodore Roosevelt *(Republican 1901)*
26	Theodore Roosevelt *(Republican 1901)*	Charles W. Fairbanks *(Republican 1905)*
27	William H. Taft *(Republican 1909)*	James S. Sherman *(Republican 1909)*
28	Woodrow Wilson *(Democratic 1913)*	Thomas R. Marshall *(Democratic 1913)*
29	Warren G. Harding *(Republican 1921)*	Calvin Coolidge *(Republican 1921)*
30	Calvin Coolidge *(Republican 1923)*	Charles G. Dawes *(Republican 1925)*

	PRESIDENT	VICE PRESIDENT
31	Herbert Hoover *(Republican 1929)*	Charles Curtis *(Republican 1929)*
32	Franklin D. Roosevelt *(Democratic 1933)*	John Nance Garner *(Democratic 1933)*
		Henry A. Wallace *(Democratic 1941)*
		Harry S. Truman *(Democratic 1945)*
33	Harry S. Truman *(Democratic 1945)*	Alben W. Barkley *(Democratic 1949)*
34	Dwight D. Eisenhower *(Republican 1953)*	Richard M. Nixon *(Republican 1953)*
35	John F. Kennedy *(Democratic 1961)*	Lyndon B. Johnson *(Democratic 1961)*
36	Lyndon B. Johnson *(Democratic 1963)*	Hubert H. Humphrey *(Democratic 1965)*
37	Richard M. Nixon *(Republican 1969)*	Spiro T. Agnew *(Republican 1969)*
		Gerald R. Ford *(Republican 1973)*
38	Gerald R. Ford *(Republican 1974)*	Nelson Rockefeller *(Republican 1974)*
39	James E. Carter *(Democratic 1977)*	Walter Mondale *(Democratic 1977)*
40	Ronald Reagan *(Republican 1981)*	George H. W. Bush *(Republican 1981)*
41	George H. W. Bush *(Republican 1989)*	J. Danforth Quayle *(Republican 1989)*
42	William J. Clinton *(Democratic 1993)*	Albert Gore, Jr. *(Democratic 1993)*
43	George W. Bush *(Republican 2001)*	Richard Cheney *(Republican 2001)*
44	Barack H. Obama *(Democratic 2009)*	Joseph R. Biden, Jr. *(Democratic 2009)*
45	Donald J. Trump *(Republican 2017)*	Michael R. Pence *(Republican 2017)*
46	Joseph R. Biden, Jr. *(Democratic 2021)*	Kamala Harris *(Democratic 2021)*

Endnotes

CHAPTER 1

1. Erin Hinrichs, "Denied Unemployment Benefits, Minnesota High Schoolers Push for Reforms," *MinnPost,* October 1, 2020, www.minnpost.com/education /2020/10/denied-unemployment -benefits-minnesota-high-schoolers -push-for-reforms/; Zoe Jackson, "Minnesota Court Finds Jobless High School Students Can Access Pandemic Unemployment Benefits," *Star Tribune,* December 2, 2020, www.startribune .com/minn-court-jobless-high-school -students-can-access-pandemic -unemployment-aid/573267141/ (accessed 10/17/21).

2. V-Dem Institute, "Autocratization Turns Viral: Annual Democracy Report 2021," March 2021, www.v-dem.net/static /website/files/dr/dr_2021.pdf (accessed 1/26/22).

3. Steven Mintz, "Historical Context: The Constitution and Slavery," The Gilder Lehrman Institute of American History, www.gilderlehrman.org/history -resources/teaching-resource/historical -context-constitution-and-slavery (accessed 10/2/2021).

4. "2022 Ballot Measures," Ballotpedia, https://ballotpedia.org/2022_ballot _measures (accessed 8/23/22).

5. Harold Lasswell, *Politics: Who Gets What, When, How* (New York: Meridian Books, 1958).

6. Thomas H. Marshall, *Citizenship and Social Class,* vol. 11 (New York: Cambridge University Press, 1950).

7. U.S. Citizenship and Immigration Services, "Citizenship Rights and Responsibilities," https://my.uscis .gov/citizenship/information (accessed 4/10/22).

8. Kyle Dropp and Brendan Nyhan, "One-Third Don't Know Obamacare and Affordable Care Act Are the Same," *New York Times,* The Upshot, February 7, 2017, www.nytimes.com/2017/02/07 /upshot/one-third-dont-know-obamacare -and-affordable-care-act-are-the-same .html?_r=0 (accessed 12/28/17).

9. Annenberg Constitution Day Civics Survey, August 16–27, 2019, https://cdn .annenbergpublicpolicycenter.org/wp -content/uploads/2019/09/Annenberg _civics_2019_Appendix.pdf (accessed 1/19/20).

10. Joan Donovan, "Deconstructing Disinformation's Threat to Democracy," *The Fletcher Forum of World Affairs* 44, no. 1 (Winter 2020); Joe Heim, "'Disinformation Can Be a Very Lucrative Business, Especially if You're Good at It,' Media Scholar Says," *Washington Post,* January 19, 2021, www.washingtonpost .com/lifestyle/magazine/disinformation -can-be-a-very-lucrative-business -especially-if-youre-good-at-it-media -scholar-says/2021/01/19/4c842f06 -4a04-11eb-a9d9-1e3ec4a928b9_story .html (accessed 10/20/21); The Media Manipulation Casebook, https://media manipulation.org/ (accessed 10/20/21).

11. Pew Research Center, Global Attitudes & Trends, "Attitudes toward Elected Officials, Voting, and the State," February 26, 2020, pewresearch.org /global/2020/02/27/attitudes-toward -elected-officials-voting-and-the-state

/pg_2020-02-27_global-democracy
_02-1/ (accessed 3/21/20).

12. Pew Research Center, "Attitudes toward
Elected Officials, Voting, and the State."

13. Sidney Verba and Norman H. Nie,
Participation in America (New York:
Harper & Row, 1972).

14. U.S. Census Bureau, Population Clock,
www.census.gov/popclock/ (accessed
8/23/22).

15. Nicholas Jones et al., "2020 Census
Illuminates Racial and Ethnic
Composition of the Country," U.S.
Census Bureau, August 12, 2021, www
.census.gov/library/stories/2021/08
/improved-race-ethnicity-measures
-reveal-united-states-population
-much-more-multiracial.html (accessed
4/10/22).

16. Carter et al., *Historical Statistics of the
United States*, Table Aa145-184, Population, by Sex and Race: 1790–1990, 23.

17. Carter et al., *Historical Statistics of
the United States*, Table Aa145-184,
Population, by Sex and Race: 1790–1990,
23; Table Aa2189-2215, Hispanic
Population Estimates.

18. Campbell J. Gibson and Emily Lennon,
"Historical Census Statistics on the
Foreign-Born Population of the United
States: 1850–1990," February 1999,
www.census.gov/library/working
-papers/1999/demo/POP-twps0029
.html (accessed 4/10/22).

19. Carter et al., *Historical Statistics of the
United States*, Table Aa22-35, Selected
Population Characteristics.

20. Michael B. Katz and Mark J. Stern,
*One Nation Divisible: What America
Was and What It Is Becoming*
(New York: Russell Sage Foundation,
2006), 16.

21. Mae M. Ngai, *Impossible Subjects:
Illegal Aliens and the Making of Modern
America* (Princeton, NJ: Princeton
University Press, 2014).

22. Cristina Mora, *Making Hispanics:
How Activists, Bureaucrats, and
Media Constructed a New American*
(Chicago: University of Chicago
Press, 2014); Carter et al., *Historical
Statistics of the United States*, Table
Aa145-184, Population, by Sex and
Race: 1790–1990, 23.

23. Nicholas Jones et al., "2020 Census
Illuminates Racial and Ethnic
Composition of the Country: Asian
Population," U.S. Census Bureau,
August 12, 2021, www.census.gov
/library/stories/2021/08/improved
-race-ethnicity-measures-reveal-united
-states-population-much-more-multiracial
.html#:~:text=Asian%20Population,
people%20(4.8%25)%20in%202010
(accessed 3/18/22).

24. U.S. Census Bureau, "2020 American
Community Survey, 5-Year Estimates:
Selected Characteristics of the Native
and Foreign-Born Populations," https://
data.census.gov/cedsci/table?y=2020&d
=ACS%205-Year%20Estimates%20
Subject%20Tables&tid=ACSST5Y2020
.S0501 (accessed 3/18/22).

25. U.S. Census Bureau, "2020 American
Community Survey, 5-Year Estimates:
Selected Characteristics of the Foreign-
Born Population by Region of Birth:
Latin America," https://data.census.
gov/cedsci/table?y=2020&d=ACS%20
5-Year%20Estimates%20Subject%20
Tables&tid=ACSST5Y2020.S0506
(accessed 3/18/22).

26. U.S. Census Bureau, "2020 American
Community Survey, 5-Year Estimates:
Selected Characteristics of the Foreign-
Born Population by Region of Birth:
Asia," https://data.census.gov/cedsci
/table?y=2020&d=ACS%205-Year%20
Estimates%20Subject%20Tables
(accessed 3/18/22).

27. U.S. Census Bureau, "2020 American
Community Survey 5-Year Estimates:
Selected Characteristics of the Foreign-
Born Population by Region of Birth:
Europe," https://data.census.gov/cedsci
/table?y=2020&d=ACS%205-Year%20
Estimates%20Subject%20Tables&tid
=ACSST5Y2020.S0503 (accessed
4/10/22).

28. Bryan Baker, "Estimates of the Illegal
Alien Population Residing in the United
States: January 2015," Department of
Homeland Security, December 2018,
www.dhs.gov/sites/default/files
/publications/18_1214_PLCY_pops
-est-report.pdf (accessed 1/17/20).

29. *Plyler v. Doe*, 457 U.S. 202 (1982).

30. National Conference of State Legislatures, "Federal Benefit Eligibility for

Unauthorized Immigrants," February 24, 2014, www.ncsl.org/research /immigration/federal-benefits-to -unauthorized-immigrants.aspx (accessed 5/22/19); National Conference of State Legislatures, "Undocumented Student Tuition: Overview," March 14, 2019, www.ncsl.org/research/education /undocumented-student-tuition-overview .aspx (accessed 5/22/19).

31. Gallup, "Religion," https://news.gallup .com/poll/1690/religion.aspx (accessed 3/18/22).

32. Gallup, "Religion."

33. U.S. Census Bureau, "Demographic Trends in the 20th Century, Table 5: Population by Age and Sex for the United States: 1900 to 2000," www .academia.edu/1935231/Demographic _trends_in_the_20th_century (accessed 3/18/22); U.S. Census Bureau, "2020 American Community Survey, 5-Year Estimates: Age and Sex," https:// data.census.gov/cedsci/table?y=2020&d =ACS%205-Year%20Estimates%20 Subject%20Tables&tid=ACSST5Y2020 .S0101 (accessed 3/19/22).

34. World Bank, "Population Ages 65 and Above (% of Total)," http://data .worldbank.org/indicator/SP.POP .65UP.TO.ZS (accessed 3/19/22).

35. U.S. Census Bureau, "Urban and Rural," www.census.gov/programs-surveys /geography/guidance/geo-areas/urban -rural.html (accessed 1/25/22); Tim Henderson, "Shrinking Rural America Faces State Power Struggle," Pew Charitable Trusts, August 10, 2021, www.pewtrusts.org/en/research -and-analysis/blogs/stateline/2021/08 /10/shrinking-rural-america-faces-state -power-struggle (accessed 1/25/22).

36. See, for example, David B. Grusky and Tamar Kricheli-Katz, eds., *The New Gilded Age: The Critical Inequality Debates of Our Time* (Stanford, CA: Stanford University Press, 2012).

37. Edward N. Wolff, "Household Wealth Trends in the United States, 1962–2016: Has Middle Class Wealth Recovered?" NBER, November 2017, www.nber.org /papers/w24085 (accessed 10/1/21).

38. United States Federal Reserve, "Distri- bution of Household Wealth in the U.S. since 1989," www.federalreserve.gov /releases/z1/dataviz/dfa/distribute /table/ (accessed 3/19/22); Alexandre Tanzi and Mike Dorning, "Top 1% of U.S. Earners Now Hold More Wealth Than All of the Middle Class," Bloomberg Wealth, October 8, 2021, www.bloomberg .com/news/articles/2021-10-08/top-1 -earners-hold-more-wealth-than-the-u -s-middle-class (accessed 3/19/22).

39. U.S. Census Bureau, "Income and Poverty in the United States: 2020," September 14, 2021, www.census.gov /library/publications/2021/demo/p60 -273.html (accessed 3/19/22).

40. Neil Bhutta et al., "Disparities in Wealth by Race and Ethnicity in the 2019 Survey of Consumer Finances," September 20, 2020, Board of Governors of the Federal Reserve System, www.federalreserve .gov/econres/notes/feds-notes/disparities -in-wealth-by-race-and-ethnicity-in -the-2019-survey-of-consumer-finances -20200928.htm (accessed 10/1/21); Emily Moss et al., "Black-White Wealth Gap Left Black Households More Vulnerable," December 8, 2020, The Brookings Institution, www.brookings .edu/blog/up-front/2020/12/08/the -black-white-wealth-gap-left-black -households-more-vulnerable/ (accessed 10/1/21); Heather Long and Andrew Van Dam, "The Black-White Economic Divide Is as Wide as It Was in 1968," *Washington Post*, June 4, 2020, www .washingtonpost.com/business/2020/06 /04/economic-divide-black-households/ (accessed 10/1/21).

41. Jesse Sussell and James A. Thomson, "Are Changing Constituencies Driving Rising Polarization in the U.S. House of Representatives?" RAND Corporation Research Report RR-396-RC, 2015, www.rand.org/pubs/research_reports /RR896.html (accessed 1/15/18).

42. Herbert McClosky and John Zaller, *The American Ethos: Public Attitudes toward Capitalism and Democracy* (Cambridge, MA: Harvard University Press, 1984), 19.

43. J. R. Pole, *The Pursuit of Equality in American History* (Berkeley: University of California Press, 1978), 3.

44. Dan Murphy, "Economic Impact Payments," The Brookings Institution, February 2021, www.brookings.edu

/research/economic-impact-payments -uses-payment-methods-and-costs -to-recipients/ (accessed 10/5/21); Kevin Hassett and Matthew Jensen, "Here's How Much the COVID-19 Stimulus Will Cost You," *National Review*, March 18, 2021, www.nationalreview .com/2021/03/heres-how-much-covid-19 -stimulus-cost-you/ (accessed 10/5/21); Allison Prang and Veronica Dagher, "Debate Over Paid Family Leave Is Louder Than Ever," *Wall Street Journal*, October 30, 2021, www.wsj.com/articles /debate-over-paid-family-leave-is-louder -than-ever-11635564747 (accessed 10/5/21).

45. John Rawls, "Justice as Fairness: Political Not Metaphysical," *Equality and Liberty* (London: Palgrave Macmillan, 1991), 145–73; Rawls, *A Theory of Justice* (Cambridge, MA: Belknap Press of Harvard University Press, 1971).

46. *Obergefell v. Hodges*, 576 U.S. 644 (2015).

47. Martha Craven Nussbaum, *Frontiers of Justice: Disability, Nationality, Species Membership* (Cambridge, MA: Belknap Press, 2006).

48. L. Buchanan, Q. Bui, and J. K. Patel, "Black Lives Matter May Be the Largest Movement in U.S. History," *New York Times*, July 3, 2020, www.nytimes.com /interactive/2020/07/03/us/george -floyd-protests-crowd-size.html (accessed 10/7/21).

49. Barbara Ransby, *Making All Black Lives Matter: Reimagining Freedom in the Twenty-First Century* (Oakland: University of California Press, 2018); Deva Woodley, *Reckoning: Black Lives Matter and the Democratic Necessity of Social Movements* (Oxford, UK: Oxford University Press, 2021); Amna Akbar, "The Left Is Remaking the World," *New York Times*, July 11, 2020, www .nytimes.com/2020/07/11/opinion /sunday/defund-police-cancel-rent.html (accessed 10/5/21).

50. Harmeet Kaur, "Indigenous People across the US Want Their Land Back—and the Movement Is Gaining Momentum," CNN, November 26, 2020, www.cnn.com/2020/11/25/us/indigenous -people-reclaiming-their-lands-trnd /index.html (accessed 10/7/21); Claire

Elise Thompson, "Returning the Land," *Grist*, November 25, 2020, https://grist .org/fix/indigenous-landback-movement -can-it-help-climate/ (accessed 10/7/21).

51. Rawls, *A Theory of Justice*; Michael J. Sandel and T. Anne, *Liberalism and the Limits of Justice* (New York: Cambridge University Press, 1998); Iris Marion Young, *Justice and the Politics of Difference* (Princeton, NJ: Princeton University Press, 2011).

52. "Americans See Broad Responsibilities for Government; Little Change Since 2019," Pew Research Center, May 21, 2021, www.pewresearch.org/politics /2021/05/17/americans-see-broad -responsibilities-for-government-little -change-since-2019/ (accessed 3/19/22).

53. Pew Research Center, "Public Trust in Government: 1958–2021," May 17, 2021, www.pewresearch.org/politics/2021/05 /17/public-trust-in-government-1958-2021/ (accessed 10/12/21).

54. Pew Research Center, "Public Trust in Government, 1958–2021."

55. Joseph S. Nye, Jr., "Introduction: The Decline of Confidence in Government," in *Why People Don't Trust Government*, ed. Joseph S. Nye, Jr., Philip D. Zelikow, and David C. King (Cambridge, MA: Harvard University Press, 1997), 4.

CHAPTER 2

1. Jeffery C. Mays and Zachary Small, "Jefferson Statue Will Be Removed from N.Y.C. Council Chambers," *New York Times*, October 19, 2021, www.nytimes .com/2021/10/18/nyregion/thomas -jefferson-statue-ny-city-council.html (accessed 1/26/22).

2. Bill Chappell, "New York City Will Exile Thomas Jefferson's Statue from a Prominent Spot in City Hall," NPR, October 19, 2021, www .npr.org/2021/10/19/1047258467 /thomas-jefferson-statue-removal -new-york-city-council-chamber (accessed 10/20/21).

3. Joseph Guzman, "Thomas Jefferson Statue to Be Removed from New York City Council Chambers," *The Hill*, October 19, 2021, https://thehill.com /changing-america/respect/577446 -thomas-jefferson-statue-to-be

-removed-from-new-york-city-council (accessed 10/20/21).

4. Mays and Small, "Jefferson Statue Will Be Removed."

5. James Barron, "Removing a Statue of Thomas Jefferson from City Hall," *New York Times,* October 18, 2021, www .nytimes.com/2021/10/18/nyregion /removing-a-statue-of-thomas-jefferson -from-city-hall.html (accessed 10/21/21).

6. Edmund S. Morgan, *American Slavery, American Freedom* (New York: W. W. Norton, 2003); Robert G. Parkinson, *Thirteen Clocks: How Race United the Colonies and Made the Declaration of Independence* (Chapel Hill: University of North Carolina Press, 2021); Alan Taylor, *The Penguin History of the United States,* vol. 1, *American Colonies: The Settling of North America* (New York: Penguin, 2002); Sven Beckert, *Empire of Cotton: A Global History* (New York: Knopf, 2014); Walter Johnson, *River of Dark Dreams: Slavery and Empire in the Cotton Kingdom* (Cambridge, MA: The Belknap Press of Harvard University Press, 2013); Leslie M. Harris, *In the Shadow of Slavery: African Americans in New York City, 1626–1863* (Chicago: University of Chicago Press, 2004); Daina Ramey Berry, *The Price for Their Pound of Flesh: The Value of the Enslaved, from Womb to Grave, in the Building of a Nation* (Boston: Beacon Press, 2017).

7. Lisa Kahaleole Hall, "Strategies of Erasure: US Colonialism and Native Hawaiian Feminism," *American Quarterly* 60, no. 2 (2008): 273–80.

8. Gabrielle Tayac and Edwin Schupman, *We Have a Story to Tell: Native Peoples of the Chesapeake Region,* 2006, National Museum of the American Indian Education Office and the Smithsonian Institute, https://archive.org/details /chesapeakenativeamericans (accessed 1/24/22).

9. Robert N. Clinton, "The Proclamation of 1763: Colonial Prelude to Two Centuries of Federal-State Conflict over the Management of Indian Affairs," *Boston University Law Review* 69 (1989): 329.

10. Patrick Wolfe, *Settler Colonialism and the Transformation of Anthropology* (London: Continuum, 1999); Wolfe, "Settler Colonialism and the Elimina-

tion of the Native," *Journal of Genocide Research* 8, no. 4 (December 2006): 387–409.

11. The social makeup of colonial America and some of the social conflicts that divided colonial society are discussed in Jackson Turner Main, *The Social Structure of Revolutionary America* (Princeton, NJ: Princeton University Press, 1965).

12. Randall M. Miller and John David Smith, eds., *Dictionary of Afro-American Slavery* (Westport, CT: Greenwood Publishing Group, 1997).

13. John Hope Franklin and Evelyn Brooks Higginbotham, *From Slavery to Freedom* (New York: Knopf, 1956).

14. Harris, *In the Shadow of Slavery.*

15. Ira Berlin, *Many Thousands Gone: The First Two Centuries of Slavery in North America* (Cambridge, MA: Harvard University Press, 2009); Annette Gordon-Reed, *The Hemingses of Monticello: An American Family* (New York: W. W. Norton, 2009); Woody Holton, *Forced Founders: Indians, Debtors, Slaves, and the Making of the American Revolution in Virginia* (Chapel Hill: University of North Carolina Press, 2011); Parkinson, *Thirteen Clocks.*

16. See Carl Becker, *The Declaration of Independence* (New York: Knopf, 1942).

17. An excellent and readable account of the development from the Articles of Confederation to the Constitution will be found in Alfred H. Kelly, Winfred A. Harbison, and Herman Belz, *The American Constitution: Its Origins and Development,* 7th ed., vol. 1 (New York: W. W. Norton, 1991), chap. 5.

18. Quoted in Samuel Eliot Morrison, Henry Steele Commager, and William Edward Leuchtenburg, *The Growth of the American Republic,* 5th ed. (New York: Oxford University Press, 1962), 242.

19. Peter H. Wood, *Black Majority: Negroes in Colonial South Carolina from 1670 through the Stono Rebellion* (New York: W. W. Norton, 1996); Sylvia R. Frey, *Water from the Rock: Black Resistance in a Revolutionary Age* (Princeton, NJ: Princeton University Press, 2020).

20. Leslie Harris, "I Helped Fact-Check the 1619 Project. The Times Ignored Me," *Politico*, March 6, 2020, www.politico .com/news/magazine/2020/03/06/1619 -project-new-york-times-mistake -122248 (accessed 11/2/21).

21. Alfred F. Young, Ray Raphael, and Gary Nash, eds., *Revolutionary Founders: Rebels, Radicals, and Reformers in the Making of the Nation* (New York: Vintage, 2011).

22. Julie Zauzmer and Adrian Blanco, "More than 1,700 Congressmen Once Enslaved Black People. This Is Who They Were, and How They Shaped the Nation," *Washington Post*, January 10, 2022, www.washingtonpost.com/history /interactive/2022/congress-slaveowners -names-list/?itid=hp-top-table-main (accessed 1/11/22).

23. James Madison, Madison Debates, July 14, 1787, https://avalon.law.yale .edu/18th_century/debates_714.asp (accessed 11/2/21).

24. Alexander Hamilton, James Madison, and John Jay, *The Federalist Papers*, no. 71, ed. Clinton L. Rossiter (New York: New American Library, 1961).

25. *Federalist Papers*, no. 70.

26. Melancton Smith, quoted in Herbert J. Storing, *What the Anti-Federalists Were For* (Chicago: University of Chicago Press, 1981), 17.

27. *Federalist Papers*, no. 57.

28. *Federalist Papers*, no. 10.

29. "Essays of Brutus," no. 7, in Herbert J. Storing, *The Complete Anti-Federalist* (Chicago: University of Chicago Press, 1981).

30. "Essays of Brutus," no. 6, in Storing, *Complete Anti-Federalist*.

31. Storing, *What the Anti-Federalists Were For*, 28.

32. *Federalist Papers*, no. 51.

33. George Washington to Catharine Macaulay Graham, Letter, "A Great Experiment," January 9, 1790.

CHAPTER 3

1. Fabiola Cineas, "Here's How Hard It Is to Vote in Texas," Vox, July 22, 2021, www.vox.com/22585717/how-hard -to-vote-in-texas; Alexa Ura, "The Hard-Fought Texas Voting Bill Is Poised to Become Law. Here's What It Does," *Texas Tribune*, August 30, 2021, www .texastribune.org/2021/08/30/texas -voting-restrictions-bill/ (accessed 10/17/21).

2. Pietro S. Nivola, "Why Federalism Matters," Brookings Institution Policy Brief #146, October 2005, www .brookings.edu/wp-content/uploads /2016/06/pb146.pdf (accessed 7/15/19).

3. Lisa L. Miller, "The Representational Biases of Federalism: Scope and Bias in the Political Process, Revisited," *Perspectives on Politics* 50, no. 2 (June 2007): 305–21.

4. The public policy exception stems from developments in case law tracing back to the 1930s. In Section 283 of the Restatement (Second) of Conflict of Laws (1971) a group of judges and academics codified existing case law related to marriage: "A marriage which satisfies the requirements of the state where the marriage was contracted will everywhere be recognized as valid unless it violates the strong public policy of another state which had the most significant relationship to the spouses and the marriage at the time of the marriage." However, in *Baker v. General Motors Corp.*, 522 U.S. 222 (1998), the Supreme Court explicitly stated that its decision "creates no general exception to the full faith and credit command."

5. Adam Liptak, "Bans on Interracial Unions Offer Perspective on Gay Ones," *New York Times*, March 17, 2004, A22, www.nytimes.com /2004/03/17/us/bans-on-interracial -unions-offer-perspective-on-gay -ones.html.

6. *Loving v. Virginia*, 388 U.S. 1 (1967). The Lovings were charged with violating Virginia's miscegenation laws and were sentenced to one year in jail, which would be suspended if they left the state for 25 years. Five years later, with the assistance of the American Civil Liberties Union, the Lovings filed a motion to vacate their conviction. The Supreme Court heard the case and overturned the Lovings' conviction, finding Virginia's miscegenation law unconstitutional

under the due process clause and equal protection clause of the Fourteenth Amendment.

7. *Obergefell v. Hodges*, 576 U.S. ___ (2015).

8. *Hicklin v. Orbeck*, 437 U.S. 518 (1978).

9. A good discussion of the constitutional position of local governments is in Richard Briffault, "Our Localism: Part I, the Structure of Local Government Law," *Columbia Law Review* 90, no. 1 (January 1990): 1–115. For more on the structure and theory of federalism, see Larry N. Gerston, *American Federalism: A Concise Introduction* (Armonk, NY: M. E. Sharpe, 2007), and Martha Derthick, "Up-to-Date in Kansas City: Reflections on American Federalism" (1992 John Gaus Lecture), *PS: Political Science and Politics* 25 (December 1992): 671–75.

10. *McCulloch v. Maryland*, 17 U.S. 316 (1819).

11. *Gibbons v. Ogden*, 22 U.S. 1 (1824).

12. The Sherman Antitrust Act, adopted in 1890, for example, was enacted not to restrict commerce but rather to protect it from monopolies, or trusts, in order to prevent unfair trade practices and to enable the market again to become self-regulating. Moreover, the Supreme Court sought to uphold liberty of contract to protect businesses. For example, in *Lochner v. New York*, 198 U.S. 45 (1905), the Court invalidated a New York law regulating the sanitary conditions and hours of labor of bakers on the grounds that the law interfered with liberty of contract.

13. The key case in this process of expanding the power of the national government is generally considered to be *NLRB v. Jones & Laughlin Steel Corporation*, 301 U.S. 1 (1937), in which the Supreme Court approved federal regulation of the workplace and thereby virtually eliminated interstate commerce as a limit on the national government's power.

14. Morton Grodzins, *The American System*, ed. Daniel J. Elazar (Chicago: Rand McNally, 1966).

15. See Donald F. Kettl, *The Regulation of American Federalism* (Baton Rouge: Louisiana State University Press, 1983).

16. Brady Dennis and Juliet Eilperin, "California and Nearly Two Dozen Other States Sue Trump Administration for the Right to Set Fuel-Efficiency Standards," *Washington Post*, November 15, 2019, www.washingtonpost.com/climate-environment/2019/11/15/california-nearly-two-dozen-other-states-sue-trump-administration-right-require-more-fuel-efficient-cars/ (accessed 1/21/20).

17. The phrase "laboratories of democracy" was coined by Supreme Court Justice Louis Brandeis in his dissenting opinion in *New State Ice Co. v. Liebmann*, 285 U.S. 262 (1932).

18. W. John Moore, "Pleading the 10th," *National Journal*, July 29, 1996.

19. *United States v. Alfonso D. Lopez, Jr.*, 514 U.S. 549 (1995).

20. Timothy Conlan, *New Federalism: Intergovernmental Reform from Nixon to Reagan* (Washington, DC: Brookings Institution Press, 1988); U.S. Advisory Commission on Intergovernmental Relations, *Federal Regulation of State and Local Governments*.

21. Education Commission of the States, "50-State Comparison: Charter School Policies," January 2018, www.ecs.org/charter-school-policies/ (accessed 6/5/18).

22. Robert Jay Dilger and Richard S. Beth, "Unfunded Mandates Reform Act: History, Impact, and Issues," April 19, 2011 (Washington, DC: Congressional Research Service), 40, http://digital.library.unt.edu/ark:/67531/metadc40084/m1/1/high_res_d/R40957_2011Apr19.pdf (accessed 11/16/13).

23. Elissa Cohen et al., "Welfare Rules Databook: State TANF Policies as of July 2015," OPRE Report 2016-67 (Washington, DC: Office of Planning, Research and Evaluation, Administration for Children and Families, U.S. Department of Health and Human Services, 2016), www.acf.hhs.gov/sites/default/files/documents/opre/2015_welfare_rules_databook_final_09_26_16_b508.pdf (accessed 7/30/17); Mary Jo Pitzi, "Arizona Limits Poverty Aid to 1 Year; Strictest in U.S.," AZcentral.com, July 1, 2016, www.azcentral.com/story/news/politics

/arizona/2016/07/01/arizona-limits
-poverty-aid-1-year-strictest-us
/86499262/ (accessed 7/30/17).

24. Center for Budget and Policy Priorities, "States Must Continue Recent Momentum to Further Improve TANF Benefit Levels," www.cbpp.org/research/family -income-support/states-must-continue -recent-momentum-to-further-improve -tanf-benefit (accessed 1/21/22).

25. Kate Linthicum, "Obama Ends Secure Communities Program as Part of Immigration Action," *Los Angeles Times*, November 21, 2014, www .latimes.com/local/california/la-me -1121-immigration-justice-20141121 -story.html (accessed 8/16/15).

26. "Enhancing Public Safety in the Interior of the United States," Executive Order 13768, January 25, 2017, www.federal register.gov/documents/2017/01/30 /2017-02102/enhancing-public-safety -in-the-interior-of-the-united-states (accessed 7/27/17).

27. Camila Domonoske, "Judge Blocks Trump Administration from Punishing 'Sanctuary Cities,'" NPR, November 21, 2017, www.npr.org/sections/thetwo -way/2017/11/21/565678707/enter-title (accessed 2/18/18).

28. Tal Axelrod, "9th Circuit Rules in Favor of Trump Admin in 'Sanctuary City' Case," The Hill, July 12, 2019, https:// thehill.com/regulation/court-battles /452862-9th-circuit-rules-in-favor-of -trump-admin-in-sanctuary-city-case (accessed 7/15/19).

29. "DEA Raid of Southern California Illegal Marijuana Grow Operations Comes Following Obernolte, Garcia Letter to Attorney General Merrick Garland," June 8, 2021, https://obernolte .house.gov/media/press-releases/dea-raid -southern-california-illegal-marijuana -grow-operations-comes-following (accessed 4/19/22).

30. Local Solutions Support Center, "The Growing Shadow of State Interference: Preemption in the 2019 State Legislative Sessions," August 2019, https:// static1.squarespace.com/static/5ce4377 caeb1ce00013a02fd/t/5d66a3c36044f 700019a7efd/1567007722604/LSSC SiXReportAugust2019.pdf (accessed 3/21/20).

31. USAFacts, "Minimum Wage in America: How Many People Are Earning $7.25 an Hour?," September 18, 2019, https:// usafacts.org/articles/minimum-wage -america-how-many-people-are-earning -725-hour/?utm_source=bing&utm_ medium=cpc&utm_campaign=ND -Economy&msclkid=48726b90a0111afeef 7009cd3c75908e (accessed 4/19/22).

CHAPTER 4

1. *Tinker v. Des Moines Independent Community School District*, 393 U.S. 503 (1969).

2. *Morse v. Frederick*, 551 U.S. 393 (2007).

3. *Bethel School District No. 403 v. Fraser*, 478 U.S. 675 (1986).

4. David L. Hudson, Jr., "*Mahanoy Area School District v. B.L.* (2021)," *The First Amendment Encyclopedia*, https://mtsu .edu/first-amendment/article/1947 /mahanoy-area-school-district-v-b-l (accessed 11/13/21).

5. Alexander Hamilton, James Madison, and John Jay, *The Federalist Papers*, ed. Clinton Rossiter, no. 84 (New York: New American Library, 1961), 513.

6. *Federalist Papers*, no. 84, 513.

7. Clinton Rossiter, *1787: The Grand Convention* (New York: W. W. Norton, 1987), 302.

8. Rossiter, *1787*, 303. Rossiter also reports that "in 1941 the States of Connecticut, Massachusetts, and Georgia celebrated the sesquicentennial of the Bill of Rights by giving their hitherto withheld and unneeded assent."

9. *Barron v. Baltimore*, 32 U.S. 243 (1833).

10. The Fourteenth Amendment also seems designed to introduce civil rights. The final clause of the all-important Section 1 provides that no state can "deny to any person within its jurisdiction the equal protection of the laws." It is not unreasonable to conclude that the purpose of this provision was to obligate state governments as well as the national government to take positive actions to protect citizens from arbitrary and discriminatory actions, at least those based on race. Civil rights will be explored in Chapter 5.

11. For example, The Slaughterhouse Cases, 83 U.S. 36 (1873).

12. *Chicago, Burlington and Quincy Railroad Company v. Chicago*, 166 U.S. 226 (1897).

13. *Gitlow v. New York*, 268 U.S. 652 (1925).

14. *Near v. Minnesota*, 283 U.S. 697 (1931); *Hague v. C.I.O.*, 307 U.S. 496 (1939).

15. *Palko v. Connecticut*, 302 U.S. 319 (1937).

16. *Abington School District v. Schempp*, 374 U.S. 203 (1963).

17. *Engel v. Vitale*, 370 U.S. 421 (1962).

18. *Wallace v. Jaffree*, 472 U.S. 38 (1985).

19. *Kennedy v. Bremerton School District*, 597 U.S. __ (2022).

20. *West Virginia State Board of Education v. Barnette*, 319 U.S. 624 (1943). The case reversed an earlier decision, *Minersville School District v. Gobitis*, 310 U.S. 586 (1940), in which the Court upheld such a requirement and permitted schools to expel students for refusing to salute the flag. But the entry of the United States into a war to defend democracy in 1941, coupled with the ugly treatment to which the Jehovah's Witnesses children had been subjected, persuaded the Court to reverse itself and to endorse the free exercise of religion even when it may be offensive to the beliefs of the majority.

21. *Burwell v. Hobby Lobby Stores*, 573 U.S. 682 (2014).

22. *Roman Catholic Diocese of Brooklyn v. Cuomo*, 592 U.S. __ (2020).

23. *Abrams v. United States*, 250 U.S. 616 (1919).

24. *United States v. Carolene Products Company*, 304 U.S. 144 (1938), n4. This footnote is one of the Court's most important doctrines. See Alfred H. Kelly, Winfred A. Harbison, and Herman Belz, *The American Constitution: Its Origins and Development*, 7th ed. (New York: W. W. Norton, 1991), 2:519–23.

25. *Schenck v. United States*, 249 U.S. 47 (1919).

26. *Citizens United v. Federal Election Commission*, 558 U.S. 310 (2010).

27. *McCutcheon v. Federal Election Commission*, 572 U.S. 185 (2014).

28. *Chaplinsky v. State of New Hampshire*, 315 U.S. 568 (1942).

29. *Dennis v. United States*, 341 U.S. 494 (1951), upheld the infamous Smith Act of 1940 that provided criminal penalties for those who "willfully and knowingly conspire to teach and advocate the forceful and violent overthrow and destruction of the government."

30. *United States v. Schwimmer*, 279 U.S. 644 (1929).

31. *Tinker v. Des Moines Independent Community School District*.

32. *Bethel School District No. 403 v. Fraser*.

33. *Hazelwood School District v. Kuhlmeier*, 484 U.S. 260 (1988).

34. *Morse v. Frederick*.

35. *City Council v. Taxpayers for Vincent*, 466 U.S. 789 (1984).

36. *Bigelow v. Virginia*, 421 U.S. 809 (1975).

37. *Hague v. Committee for Industrial Organization*, 307 U.S. 496 (1939).

38. *NAACP v. Alabama*, 357 U.S. 449 (1958).

39. *Near v. Minnesota*, 283 U.S. 697 (1931).

40. *New York Times Co. v. United States*, 403 U.S. 713 (1971).

41. *Branzburg v. Hayes*, 408 U.S. 665 (1972).

42. *New York Times Co. v. Sullivan*, 376 U.S. 254 (1964).

43. See *Zeran v. America Online*, 129 F3d 327 (4th Cir. 1997).

44. *Roth v. United States*, 354 U.S. 476 (1957).

45. Concurring opinion in *Jacobellis v. Ohio*, 378 U.S. 184 (1964).

46. *Reno v. American Civil Liberties Union*, 521 U.S. 844 (1997).

47. *United States v. Williams*, 553 U.S. 285 (2008).

48. *United States v. Playboy Entertainment Group*, 529 U.S. 803 (2000).

49. *Brown v. Entertainment Merchants Association*, 564 U.S. 786 (2011).

50. *District of Columbia v. Heller*, 554 U.S. 570 (2008).

51. *McDonald v. Chicago*, 561 U.S. 742 (2010); *New York State Rifle and Pistol Association, Inc. v. Bruen*, 597 U.S. __ (2020).

52. *Horton v. California*, 496 U.S. 128 (1990).

53. *Mapp v. Ohio*, 367 U.S. 643 (1961). Although Mapp went free in this case, she was later convicted in New York on narcotics trafficking charges and served 9 years of a 20-year sentence.

54. For a good discussion of the issue, see Louis Fisher, *American Constitutional Law* (New York: McGraw-Hill, 1990), 884–89.

55. *United States v. Jones*, 565 U.S. 400 (2012).

56. *Maryland v. King*, 569 U.S. 435 (2013).

57. *Riley v. California*, 573 U.S. 373 (2014).

58. Edwin S. Corwin and J. W. Peltason, *Understanding the Constitution* (New York: Holt, 1967), 286.

59. *Benton v. Maryland*, 395 U.S. 784 (1969).

60. *Miranda v. Arizona*, 348 U.S. 436 (1966).

61. *Gideon v. Wainwright*, 372 U.S. 335 (1963).

62. *Furman v. Georgia*, 408 U.S. 238 (1972).

63. *Gregg v. Georgia*, 428 U.S. 153 (1976).

64. J. Baxter Oliphant, "Public Support for the Death Penalty Ticks Up," Pew Research Center, June 11, 2018, www .pewresearch.org/fact-tank/2018/06/11 /us-support-for-death-penalty-ticks -up-2018/ (accessed 2/3/20).

65. Death Penalty Information Center, "Facts about the Death Penalty," https:// deathpenaltyinfo.org/documents/ FactSheet.pdf (accessed 10/12/18).

66. *Kennedy v. Louisiana*, 554 U.S. 407 (2008).

67. *Snyder v. Louisiana*, 552 U.S. 472 (2008).

68. *Glossip v. Gross*, 576 U.S. ___ (2015).

69. *Timbs v. Indiana*, 586 U.S. ___ (2019).

70. *Olmstead v. United States*, 277 U.S. 438 (1928). See also David M. O'Brien, *Constitutional Law and Politics*, 6th ed. (New York: W. W. Norton, 2005), 1:76–84.

71. *Griswold v. Connecticut*, 381 U.S. 479 (1965).

72. *Roe v. Wade*, 410 U.S. 113 (1973).

73. *Dobbs v. Jackson Women's Health Organization*, 597 U.S. ___ (2022).

74. *Bowers v. Hardwick*, 478 U.S. 186 (1986).

75. *Lawrence v. Texas*, 539 U.S. 558 (2003).

76. *Lawrence v. Texas*. It is worth recalling here the provision of the Ninth Amendment: "The enumeration in the Constitution, of certain rights, shall not be construed to deny or disparage others retained by the people."

77. *Obergefell v. Hodges*, 576 U.S. ___ (2015).

78. *Bostock v. Clayton County*, 590 U.S. ___ (2020).

CHAPTER 5

1. Shannon Green, "Desmond Meade Helps Restore Voting Rights to Millions of Ex-Felons across Florida," *Orlando Sentinel*, February 5, 2019, www .orlandosentinel.com/opinion/os-ae -desmond-meade-ex-felon-voting-rights -20190130-story.html (accessed 7/27/19).

2. Stacey Abrams, "Desmond Meade," *Time*, April 17, 2019, https://time.com /collection/100-most-influential-people -2019/5567673/desmond-meade/ (accessed 7/27/19).

3. Green, "Desmond Meade Helps Restore Voting Rights."

4. Lawrence Mower, "Ron DeSantis Signs Amendment 4 Bill, Limiting Felon Voting," *Tampa Bay Times*, June 28, 2019, www.tampabay.com/florida -politics/buzz/2019/06/28/ron-desantis -signs-amendment-4-bill-limiting-felon -voting/ (accessed 7/27/19).

5. Lawrence Mower, "Florida Voting Rights Leader Desmond Meade Has Civil Rights Restored," *Tampa Bay Times*, October 9, 2021, www.tampabay.com /news/florida-politics/2021/10/09 /florida-voting-rights-leader-desmond -meade-has-civil-rights-restored/ (accessed 1/23/22).

6. Doug McAdam, Sidney Tarrow, and Charles Tilly, "Dynamics of Contention," *Social Movement Studies* 2, no. 1 (2003): 99–102; Sidney G. Tarrow, *Power in Movement: Social Movements and Contentious Politics*, 2nd ed. (Cambridge: Cambridge University Press, 1998); Doug McAdam, *Political Process and the Development of Black Insurgency, 1930–1970*, 2nd ed. (Chicago: University of Chicago Press, 1999).

7. Charles Tilly, *From Mobilization to Revolution* (New York: Random House, 1978).

8. Daniel Gillion, *The Loud Minority: Why Protests Matter in American Democracy* (Princeton, NJ: Princeton University Press, 2020).

9. Sidney Milkis and Daniel Tichenor, *Rivalry and Reform: Presidents, Social Movements, and the Transformation of American Politics* (Chicago: University of Chicago Press, 2019).

10. Alvin Tillery, *Between Motherland and Homeland* (Ithaca, NY: Cornell University Press, 2011); Michael Minta, *No Longer Outsiders: Black and Latino Interest Group Advocacy on Capitol Hill* (Chicago: University of Chicago Press, 2021).

11. David Garrow, "Hopelessly Hollow History: Revisionist Devaluing of *Brown v. Board of Education*," *Virginia Law Review* 80, no. 1 (February 1994): 151–60; Mark Tushnet, "The Significance of Brown v. Board of Education," *Virginia Law Review* 80, no. 1 (February 1994): 173–84; Tomiko Brown-Nagin, *Courage to Dissent: Atlanta and the Long History of the Civil Rights Movement* (New York: Oxford University Press, 2012).

12. Gerald Rosenberg, *The Hollow Hope: Can Courts Bring About Social Change?* (Chicago: University of Chicago Press, 1991); Michael J. Klarman, *From Jim Crow to Civil Rights: The Supreme Court and the Struggle for Racial Equality* (New York: Oxford University Press, 2004).

13. Jacquelyn Dowd Hall, "The Long Civil Rights Movement and the Political Uses of the Past," *Journal of American History* 91, no. 4 (2005): 1233–63.

14. *Dred Scott v. Sandford*, 60 U.S. 393 (1857).

15. Leon Litwack, *Been in the Storm So Long: The Aftermath of Slavery* (New York: Knopf, 1979); Eric Foner, *Reconstruction: America's Unfinished Revolution, 1863–1877* (New York: Harper & Row, 1988); Foner, *Give Me Liberty! An American History*, 6th ed. (New York: W. W. Norton, 2019).

16. Foner, *Give Me Liberty!*

17. August Meier and Elliott Rudwick, *From Plantation to Ghetto* (New York: Hill and Wang, 1976), 184–88; Nikole Hannah-Jones, "Our Founding Ideals of Liberty and Equality Were False," *New York Times Magazine*, August 18, 2019, 20–21.

18. *Plessy v. Ferguson*, 163 U.S. 537 (1896).

19. Equal Justice Initiative, *Lynching in America: Confronting the Legacy of Racial Terror*, 2017, https://eji.org/reports/lynching-in-america/ (accessed 2/22/22).

20. Robert Zangrando, *The NAACP Crusade against Lynching, 1909–1950* (Philadelphia: Temple University Press, 1980); Patricia Sullivan, *Lift Every Voice: The NAACP and the Making of the Civil Rights Movement* (New York: New Press, 2009); Megan Ming Francis, *Civil Rights and the Making of the Modern American State* (New York: Cambridge University Press, 2014).

21. *Brown v. Board of Education of Topeka, Kansas*, 347 U.S. 483 (1954).

22. The Supreme Court first declared that race was a suspect classification requiring strict scrutiny in the decision *Korematsu v. United States*, 323 U.S. 214 (1944). In this case, the Court upheld President Roosevelt's executive order of 1941 allowing the military to exclude persons of Japanese ancestry from the West Coast and to place them in internment camps. It is one of the few cases in which classification based on race survived strict scrutiny.

23. For good treatments of this long stretch of the struggle of the federal courts to integrate the schools, see Paul Brest and Sanford Levinson, *Processes of Constitutional Decision-Making: Cases and Materials*, 2nd ed. (Boston: Little, Brown, 1983), 471–80; and Alfred H. Kelly, Winfred A. Harbison, and Herman Belz, *The American Constitution: Its Origins and Development*, 6th ed. (New York: W. W. Norton, 1983), 610–16.

24. For a thorough analysis of the Office for Civil Rights, see Jeremy Rabkin, "Office for Civil Rights," in *The Politics of Regulation*, ed. James Q. Wilson (New York: Basic Books, 1980).

25. This was an accepted way of using quotas or ratios to determine statistically that Black people or other minorities were being excluded from schools or jobs and then, on the basis of that statistical

evidence, to authorize the Justice Department to bring suits in individual cases and class-action suits. In most segregated situations outside the South, it is virtually impossible to identify and document an intent to discriminate.

26. *Swann v. Charlotte-Mecklenberg Board of Education*, 402 U.S. 1 (1971).

27. *Milliken v. Bradley*, 418 U.S. 717 (1974).

28. Gary Orfield et al., *Harming Our Common Future: America's Segregated Schools 65 Years After Brown*, The Civil Rights Project at UCLA, 2019, www.civilrightsproject.ucla.edu /research/k-12-education/integration -and-diversity/harming-our-common -future-americas-segregated-schools -65-years-after-brown/Brown-65 -050919v4-final.pdf (accessed 8/9/22).

29. *Shelby County v. Holder*, 570 U.S. 529 (2013).

30. Brennan Center for Justice, "Voting Laws Roundup: February 2022," Report, www.brennancenter.org/our-work /research-reports/voting-laws-roundup -february-2022 (accessed 3/31/22).

31. Brennan Center for Justice, "The Impact of Voter Suppression on Communities of Color," Fact Sheet, January 10, 2022, www.brennancenter.org/our-work /research-reports/impact-voter -suppression-communities-color (accessed 3/31/22).

32. See Douglas S. Massey and Nancy A. Denton, *American Apartheid: Segregation and the Making of the Underclass* (Cambridge, MA: Harvard University Press, 1993), chap. 7.

33. *Loving v. Virginia*, 388 U.S. 1 (1967).

34. John David Skrentny, *The Minority Rights Revolution* (Cambridge, MA: Belknap Press of Harvard University Press, 2002).

35. See *Frontiero v. Richardson*, 411 U.S. 677 (1973).

36. See *Craig v. Boren*, 429 U.S. 190 (1976).

37. *Franklin v. Gwinnett County Public Schools*, 503 U.S. 60 (1992).

38. Jennifer Halperin, "Women Step Up to Bat," *Illinois Issues* 21 (September 1995): 11–14.

39. *Meritor Savings Bank v. Vinson*, 477 U.S. 57 (1986). See also Gwendolyn Mink, *Hostile Environment: The Political Betrayal of Sexually Harassed Women* (Ithaca, NY: Cornell University Press, 2000), 28–32.

40. *Burlington Industries v. Ellerth*, 524 U.S. 742 (1998); *Faragher v. City of Boca Raton*, 524 U.S. 775 (1998).

41. New Mexico had a different history because not many Anglos settled there initially. (*Anglo* is the term for a non-Hispanic White person, generally of European background.) Mexican Americans had considerable power in territorial legislatures between 1865 and 1912. See Lawrence H. Fuchs, *The American Kaleidoscope* (Hanover, NH: University Press of New England, 1990), 239–40.

42. *Hernandez v. Texas*, 347 U.S. 475 (1954).

43. Chris Zepeda-Millán, *Latino Mass Mobilization: Immigration, Racialization, and Activism* (New York: Cambridge University Press, 2017).

44. Gordon Chang, *Ghosts of Gold Mountain* (Boston: Houghton Mifflin Harcourt, 2019).

45. *Korematsu v. United States*, 323 U.S. 214 (1944).

46. Mitchell T. Maki, Harry H. L. Kitano, S. Megan Berthold, and Mazal Holocaust Collection, *Achieving the Impossible Dream: How Japanese Americans Obtained Redress* (Urbana: University of Illinois Press, 1999); Helen Yoshida, "Redress and Reparations for Japanese American Incarceration," National World War II Museum, August 13, 2021, www.nationalww2museum.org/war /articles/redress-and-reparations -japanese-american-incarceration (accessed 2/21/22).

47. *Ozawa v. United States*, 260 U.S. 178 (1922).

48. *United States v. Bhagat Singh Thind*, 261 U.S. 204 (1923).

49. Ian Haney-López, *White by Law: The Legal Construction of Race* (New York: New York University Press, 1996); Matthew Frye Jacobson, *Whiteness of a Different Color: European Immigrants and the Alchemy of Race* (Cambridge, MA: Harvard University Press, 1998); Mae M. Ngai, *Impossible Subjects: Illegal Aliens and the Making of Modern America* (Princeton, NJ: Princeton University Press, 2004).

50. *Johnson v. McIntosh*, 21 U.S. 543 (1823).

51. On the resurgence of Native American political activity, see Stephen Cornell, *The Return of the Native: American Indian Political Resurgence* (New York: Oxford University Press, 1990); and Dee Brown, *Bury My Heart at Wounded Knee* (New York: Holt, Rinehart, 1971).

52. See the discussion in Robert A. Katzmann, *Institutional Disability: The Saga of Transportation Policy for the Disabled* (Washington, DC: Brookings Institution Press, 1986).

53. Joseph Shapiro, *No Pity: People with Disabilities Forging a New Civil Rights Movement* (New York: Broadway Books, 1994); Skrentny, *The Minority Rights Revolution.*

54. For example, after pressure from the Justice Department, one of the nation's largest rental-car companies agreed to make special hand controls available to any customer requesting them. See "Avis Agrees to Equip Cars for Disabled," *Los Angeles Times*, September 2, 1994, D1.

55. For more, see Dale Carpenter, *Flagrant Conduct: The Story of* Lawrence v. Texas (New York: W. W. Norton, 2013).

56. *Romer v. Evans*, 517 U.S. 620 (1996).

57. *Obergefell v. Hodges*, 576 U.S. ___ (2015).

58. The Department of Health, Education, and Welfare (HEW) was the Cabinet department charged with administering most federal social programs. In 1980, when education programs were transferred to the newly created Department of Education, HEW was renamed the Department of Health and Human Services.

59. *Regents of the University of California v. Bakke*, 438 U.S. 265 (1978).

60. *Gratz v. Bollinger*, 539 U.S. 244 (2003).

61. *Grutter v. Bollinger*, 539 U.S. 306 (2003).

62. The Court reaffirmed the *Grutter* decision in 2013 in *Fisher v. University of Texas* when it rejected a white student's suit challenging the use of race as one factor among many in admissions decisions.

63. Adam Liptak and Anemona Hartocollis, "Supreme Court Will Hear Challenge to Affirmative Action at Harvard and U.N.C.," *New York Times*, January 24, 2022, www.nytimes.com/2022/01/24/us/politics/supreme-court-affirmative-action-harvard-unc.html (accessed 4/1/22).

64. *Plyer v. Doe*, 457 U.S. 202 (1982).

65. Sophia Jordán Wallace and Chris Zepeda-Millán, *Walls, Cages, and Family Separation: Race and Immigration Policy in the Trump Era* (New York: Cambridge University Press, 2020).

66. Amaney Jamal and Nadine Naber, *Race and Arab Americans Before and After 9/11: From Invisible Citizens to Visible Subjects* (Syracuse, NY: Syracuse University Press, 2008).

67. Katayoun Kishi, "Assaults against Muslims in U.S. Surpass 2001 Level," Pew Research Center, November 15, 2017, www.pewresearch.org/fact-tank/2017/11/15/assaults-against-muslims-in-u-s-surpass-2001-level/ (accessed 2/21/22).

68. Nazita Lajevardi, "The Media Matters: Muslim American Portrayals and the Effects on Mass Attitudes," *Journal of Politics* 83, no. 3 (2021): 1060–79.

69. Nazita Lajevardi, *Outsiders at Home: The Politics of American Islamophobia* (New York: Cambridge University Press, 2020).

70. Katherine Beckett and Megan Ming Francis, "The Origins of Mass Incarceration," *Annual Review of Law and Social Science* 16 (2020): 433–52.

71. A mandatory minimum is a sentence for a crime created by Congress in the 1980s, which courts must impose. At the federal level, most mandatory minimum sentences apply to drug offenses and depend on the type and weight of a drug, and judges cannot take into account mitigating circumstances.

72. Katherine Beckett and Bruce Western, "Governing Social Marginality: Welfare, Incarceration, and the Transformation of State Policy," *Punishment and Society* 3, no. 1 (2001): 43–59; Alexis Harris, *A Pound of Flesh: Monetary Sanctions as Punishment for the Poor* (New York: Russell Sage Press, 2016); Becky Pettit, *Invisible Men: Mass Incarceration and the Myth of Racial Progress* (New York: Russell Sage Press, 2012); Becky Pettit and Bruce Western, "Mass Imprisonment and the Life Course: Race and Class Inequality in U.S. Incarceration,"

American Sociology Review 69 (2004): 151–69; Bruce Western, "The Impact of Incarceration on Wage Mobility and Inequality," *American Sociology Review* 67 (2012): 526–46; Amy E. Lerman and Vesla M. Weaver, *Arresting Citizenship: The Democratic Consequences of American Crime Control* (Chicago: University of Chicago Press, 2014).

73. Federal Bureau of Prisons, "An Overview of the First Step Act," www.bop.gov /inmates/fsa/overview.jsp (accessed 4/1/22); White House, "President Donald J. Trump Is Committed to Building on the Successes of the First Step Act," Fact Sheet, April 1, 2019, https://trumpwhitehouse.archives.gov /briefings-statements/president-donald -j-trump-committed-building-successes -first-step-act/ (accessed 4/1/22).

74. Larry Buchanan, Quoctrung Bui, and Jugal Patel, "Black Lives Matter May Be the Largest Movement in U.S. History," *New York Times*, July 3, 2020, www .nytimes.com/interactive/2020/07/03 /us/george-floyd-protests-crowd-size .html (accessed 2/21/22).

75. "Amid Protests Majorities across Racial and Ethnic Groups Express Support for the Black Lives Matter Movement," Pew Research Center, June 12, 2020, https://pewresearch.org/social-trends /2020/06/12/amid-protests-majorities -across-racial-and-ethnic-groups -express-support-for-the-black-lives -matter-movement/ (accessed 5/12/22).

76. Keeanga-Yamahtta Taylor, *From #BlackLivesMatter to Black Liberation* (Chicago: Haymarket Books, 2016); Rogers M. Smith and Desmond King, "Racial Reparations against White Protectionism: America's New Racial Politics," *Journal of Race, Ethnicity, and Politics* 6, no. 1 (2021): 82–96; Alicia Garza, *The Purpose of Power* (New York: One World, 2020); Jamila Michener, "George Floyd's Killing Was Just the Spark. Here's What Really Made the Protests Explode," *Washington Post*, June 11, 2020, www.washingtonpost .com/politics/2020/06/11/george-floyds -killing-was-just-spark-heres-what -really-made-protests-explode/ (accessed 2/22/22).

CHAPTER 6

1. Suzanna Hupp, "In Their Own Words: The Gun Rights Advocate," *Texas Monthly*, March 23, 2016, www .texasmonthly.com/list/in-their-own -words/the-gun-rights-advocate/ (accessed 3/3/18).

2. Brianna Sacks, "After Florida School Shooting, Several Survivors and Victims' Parents Pan Trump's Idea to Arm Teachers," BuzzFeed News, February 24, 2018, www.buzzfeed .com/briannasacks/students-and -parents-react-to-armed-teacher -proposal?utm_term=.rtNPqM580# .xrVbnry1A (accessed 3/3/18).

3. Jeffrey M. Jones, "U.S. Preference for Stricter Gun Laws Highest since 1993," Gallup Social & Policy Issues, March 14, 2018, http://news.gallup.com/poll/229562 /preference-stricter-gun-laws-highest -1993.aspx (accessed 5/30/18).

4. Alvin Chang, "Gun Sales Usually Skyrocket after Mass Shootings. But Not This Time," Vox, March 7, 2018, www.vox.com/2018/3/7/17066352/gun -sales-mass-shooting-data (accessed 5/30/18).

5. Richard Wike and Katie Simmons, "Global Support for Principle of Free Expression, but Opposition to Some Forms of Speech: Americans Especially Likely to Embrace Individual Liberties," Pew Research Center, November 18, 2015, www.pewglobal .org/2015/11/18/global-support-for -principle-of-free-expression-but -opposition-to-some-forms-of-speech/ (accessed 11/18/15).

6. "In Views of U.S. Democracy, Widening Partisan Divides Over Freedom to Peacefully Protest," Pew Research Center, September 2, 2020, www.pewresearch .org/politics/2020/09/02/in-views-of -u-s-democracy-widening-partisan -divides-over-freedom-to-peacefully -protest/ (accessed 1/20/22).

7. Paul R. Abramson, "Political Attitudes in America: Formation and Change," *Political Science Quarterly* 98, no. 4 (April 1983): 694–96.

8. Lydia Saad, "U.S. Political Ideology Steady; Conservatives, Moderates Tie," Gallup, January 17, 2022, https://news .gallup.com/poll/388988/political

-ideology-steady-conservatives
-moderates-tie.aspx (accessed 1/20/22).

9. Hannah Gilberstadt and Andrew
Daniller, "Liberals Make Up the Largest
Share of Democratic Voters, but Their
Growth Has Slowed in Recent Years,"
Pew Research Center, January 17, 2020,
www.pewresearch.org/fact-tank
/2020/01/17/liberals-make-up-largest
-share-of-democratic-voters/ (accessed
1/20/22).

10. See Angus Campbell et al., *The American
Voter* (New York: Wiley, 1960), 147.

11. Anna Brown, "Most Democrats Who
Are Looking for a Relationship Would
Not Consider Dating a Trump Voter,"
Pew Research Center, April 24, 2020,
www.pewresearch.org/fact-tank/2020
/04/24/most-democrats-who-are
-looking-for-a-relationship-would
-not-consider-dating-a-trump-voter/
(accessed 5/17/22); Wendy Wang,
"The Partisan Marriage Gap Is Bigger
Than Ever," The Hill, October 27, 2020,
https://thehill.com/opinion/white
-house/522987-the-partisan-marriage
-gap-is-bigger-than-ever (accessed
5/17/22).

12. Eitan Hersh and Yair Ghitza, "Mixed
Partisan Households and Electoral
Participation in the United States,"
PLOS One, October 10, 2018, https://
doi.org/10.1371/journal.pone.0203997.

13. Betsy Sinclair, *The Social Citizen:
Peer Networks and Political Behavior*
(Chicago: University of Chicago
Press, 2012).

14. Raymond E. Wolfinger and Steven J.
Rosenstone, *Who Votes?* (New Haven,
CT: Yale University Press, 1980). See
also Steven J. Rosenstone and John
Mark Hansen, *Mobilization, Participa-
tion, and Democracy in America*
(New York: Macmillan, 1993).

15. Alan I. Abramowitz, *The Great
Alignment: Race, Party Transforma-
tion, and the Rise of Donald Trump*
(New Haven, CT: Yale University
Press, 2018).

16. Katherine Tate, *Black Faces in the
Mirror* (Princeton, NJ: Princeton
University Press, 1993).

17. Tate, *Black Faces in the Mirror*.

18. Juliana Menasce Horowitz, "Support
for Black Lives Matter Declined after
George Floyd Protests, but Has Remained
Unchanged Since," Pew Research Center,
September 27, 2021, www.pewresearch
.org/fact-tank/2021/09/27/support
-for-black-lives-matter-declined-after
-george-floyd-protests-but-has-remained
-unchanged-since/ (accessed 1/20/22).

19. "Hispanic or Latino Origin," U.S.
Census, www.census.gov/quickfacts
/fact/note/US/RHI725219#:~:text=for
%20racial%20categories.-,Definition,
%E2%80%A2Puerto%20Rican
(accessed 1/20/22).

20. Elizabeth Maltby et al., "Demographic
Context, Mass Deportation, and Latino
Linked Fate," *Journal of Race, Ethnicity
and Politics* 5, no. 3 (September 15,
2020): 509–36, www.cambridge.org
/core/journals/journal-of-race-ethnicity
-and-politics/article/abs/demographic
-context-mass-deportation-and-latino
-linked-fate/DCC6EB62D347D
1019929137B0F55E59A (accessed
3/8/22).

21. Abby Budiman, "Key Findings about
U.S. Immigrants," Pew Research Center,
August 20, 2020, www.pewresearch
.org/fact-tank/2020/08/20/key-findings
-about-u-s-immigrants/ (accessed
1/22/22).

22. Anna Brown and Renee Stepler,
"Statistical Portrait of the Foreign-Born
Population in the United States,
1960–2013," Pew Research Center,
September 28, 2015, www.pewhispanic.
org/2015/09/28/statistical-portrait-of
-the-foreign-born-population-in-the
-united-states-1960-2013-key-charts
/#2013-fb-origin (accessed 12/22/15).

23. Ana Gonzalez Barrera, Jens Manuel
Krogstad, and Luis Noe-Bustamante,
"Path to Legal Status for the Unauthorized Is Top Immigration Policy Goal
for Hispanics in U.S.," Pew Research
Center, February 11, 2020, www
.pewresearch.org/fact-tank/2020/02
/11/path-to-legal-status-for-the
-unauthorized-is-top-immigration
-policy-goal-for-hispanics-in-u-s/
(accessed 1/20/22).

24. "Shifting Public Views on Legal Immigration into the U.S.," Pew Research
Center, June 28, 2018, www.people

-press.org/2018/06/28/shifting
-public-views-on-legal-immigration
-into-the-u-s/ (accessed 1/15/20).

25. Amanda Barroso, "Key Takeaway on
Americans' Views on Gender Equality a
Century After U.S. Women Gained the
Right to Vote," Pew Research Center,
August 13, 2020, www.pewresearch
.org/fact-tank/2020/08/13/key-takeaways
-on-americans-views-on-gender-equality
-a-century-after-u-s-women-gained
-the-right-to-vote/ (accessed 10/20/20).

26. "Measuring Religion in Pew Research
Center's American Trends Panel," Pew
Research Center, January 14, 2021,
www.pewforum.org/2021/01/14
/measuring-religion-in-pew-research
-centers-american-trends-panel/
(accessed 1/20/22).

27. Michael Lipka, "Religious 'Nones' Are
Not Only Growing, They're Becoming
More Secular," Pew Research Center,
Fact Tank, November 11, 2015, www
.pewresearch.org/fact-tank/2015/11/11
/religious-nones-are-not-only-growing
-theyre-becoming-more-secular/
(accessed 11/11/15).

28. 2020 and 2022 Cooperative Comparative Election Studies, Harvard University,
https://cces.gov.harvard.edu (accessed
5/17/22).

29. See Richard Lau and David Redlawsk,
*How Voters Decide: Information Pro-
cessing during an Election Campaign*
(New York: Cambridge University Press,
2006).

30. Jacob R. Brown and Ryan D. Enos,
"The Measurement of Partisan Sorting
for 180 Million Voters," *Nature Human
Behaviour* 5, no. 8 (March 8, 2021):
998–1008, https://europepmc.org
/article/med/33686203 (accessed
1/22/22).

31. "Political Ideology by State," Pew
Research Center, 2014, www.pewforum
.org/religious-landscape-study/compare
/political-ideology/by/state/ (accessed
1/20/22).

32. John R. Zaller, *The Nature and Origins
of Mass Opinion* (New York: Cambridge
University Press, 1992).

33. Carroll Glynn et al., *Public Opinion*,
2nd ed. (Boulder, CO: Westview, 2004),
293. See also Michael X. Delli Carpini

and Scott Keeter, *What Americans
Know about Politics and Why It Matters*
(New Haven, CT: Yale University Press,
1996).

34. Delli Carpini and Keeter, *What
Americans Know.*

35. Adam J. Berinsky, "Assuming the Costs
of War: Events, Elites and American
Support for Military Conflict," *Journal
of Politics* 69, no. 4 (2007): 975–97;
Zaller, *Nature and Origins.*

36. James Druckman, Erik Petersen, and
Rune Slothuus, "How Elite Partisan
Polarization Affects Public Opinion
Formation," *American Political Science
Review* 107, no. 1 (February 2013): 57–79.

37. Nicholas Carr, *The Shallows: What
the Internet Is Doing to Our Brains*
(New York: W. W. Norton, 2011).

38. Benjamin I. Page and Robert Y. Shapiro,
*The Rational Public: Fifty Years of
Trends in Americans' Policy Preferences*
(Chicago: University of Chicago Press,
1992).

39. Christopher H. Achen and Larry M.
Bartels, *Democracy for Realists: Why
Elections Do Not Produce Responsive
Government* (Princeton, NJ: Princeton
University Press, 2016).

40. Christopher Wlezien, "The Public as
Thermostat: Dynamics of Preferences
for Spending," *American Journal
of Political Science* 39, no. 4 (1995):
981–1000.

41. Maltby et al., "Demographic Context,
Mass Deportation, and Latino Linked
Fate"; Rene R. Rocha, Benjamin R.
Knoll, and Robert D. Wrinkle, "Immi-
gration Enforcement and the Redis-
tribution of Political Trust," *Journal of
Politics* 77, no. 4 (October 2015).

42. See Julianna Pacheco, "Attitudinal
Policy Feedback and Public Opinion:
The Impact of Smoking Bans on
Attitudes toward Smokers, Secondhand
Smoke, and Anti-Smoking Policies,"
Political Research Quarterly 77, no. 3
(2013): 714–34; Barbara Norrander,
"The Multi-Layered Impact of Public
Opinion on Capital Punishment
Implementation in the American
States," *Political Research Quarterly* 53,
no. 4 (2000): 771–93; Suzanne Mettler
and Joe Soss, "The Consequences of

Public Policy for Democratic Citizenship: Bridging Policy Studies and Mass Politics," *Perspectives on Politics* 2, no. 1 (2004): 55–73; Andrea Hetling and Monika L. McDermott, "Judging a Book by Its Cover: Did Perceptions of the 1996 U.S. Welfare Reforms Affect Public Support for Spending on the Poor?" *Journal of Social Policy* 37, no. 3 (2008): 471–87; Joe Soss, "Lessons of Welfare: Policy Design, Political Learning, and Political Action," *American Political Science Review* 93, no. 2 (1999): 363–80; Joe Soss and Sanford F. Schram, "A Public Transformed? Welfare Reform as Policy Feedback," *American Political Science Review* 101, no. 1 (2007): 111.

43. Achen and Bartels, *Democracy for Realists.*

44. Malcolm E. Jewell, *Representation in State Legislatures* (Lexington: University Press of Kentucky, 1982).

45. Jacob S. Hacker and Paul Pierson, *Winner-Take-All Politics: How Washington Made the Rich Richer— and Turned Its Back on the Middle Class* (New York: Simon and Schuster, 2010).

46. Lawrence R. Jacobs and Robert Y. Shapiro, *Politicians Don't Pander: Political Manipulation and the Loss of Democratic Responsiveness* (Chicago: University of Chicago Press, 2000).

47. Larry M. Bartels, *Unequal Democracy: The Political Economy of the New Gilded Age* (Princeton, NJ: Princeton University Press, 2008).

48. Other authors have endorsed Bartels's view that government policy exacerbates income inequality. See, for example, Hacker and Pierson, *Winner-Take-All Politics.*

49. Herbert Asher, *Polling and the Public* (Washington, DC: CQ Press, 2001), 64.

50. Courtney Kennedy and Hannah Hartig, "Response Rates in Telephone Surveys Have Resumed Their Decline," Pew Research Center, February 27, 2019, www.pewresearch.org/fact-tank/2019/02/27/response-rates-in-telephone-surveys-have-resumed-their-decline/ (accessed 1/15/20).

51. Michael Kagay and Janet Elder, "Numbers Are No Problem for Pollsters, Words Are," *New York Times*, August 9, 1992, E6.

52. Ariel Edwards-Levy, "Here's What Pollsters Think Happened with 2020 Election Surveys," CNN, May 13, 2021, www.cnn.com/2021/05/13/politics/2020-polling-error-research/index.html (accessed 1/20/22).

53. Adam Berinsky, "The Two Faces of Public Opinion," *American Journal of Political Science* 43, no. 4 (1999): 1209–30; see also Adam Berinsky, "Political Context and the Survey Response: The Dynamics of Racial Policy Opinion," *Journal of Politics* 64, no. 2 (2002): 567–84.

54. Nate Silver, "Which Polls Fared Best (and Worst) in the 2012 Presidential Race," *FiveThirtyEight* (blog), November 10, 2012, http://fivethirtyeight.blogs.nytimes.com/2012/11/10/which-polls-fared-best-and-worst-in-the-2012-presidential-race/ (accessed 2/24/16).

55. David Redlawsk, Caroline J. Tolbert, and Todd Donovan, *Why Iowa? How Caucuses and Sequential Elections Improve the Presidential Nominating Process* (Chicago: University of Chicago Press, 2010).

CHAPTER 7

1. Alexis Wray, "Student Journalists at an HBCU Campus Newspaper Took on Racist Local Media—and Won," *Scalawag*, February 2, 2021, https://scalawagmagazine.org/2021/02/greensboro-hbcu-student-media-bias/ (accessed 11/3/21).

2. Poynter Institute, www.poynter.org/about/ (accessed 11/3/21).

3. Wray, "Student Journalists."

4. *New York Times v. United States*, 403 U.S. 713 (1971).

5. Kevin Loker, "Confusion about What's News and What's Opinion Is a Big Problem, but Journalists Can Help Solve It," American Press Institute, September 19, 2018, www.americanpressinstitute.org/publications/reports/survey-research/confusion-about-whats-news-and-whats-opinion-is-a-big-problem-but-journalists-can-help-solve-it/ (accessed 2/1/22).

6. Kirsten Worden and Michael Barthel, "Many Americans Are Unsure Whether Sources of News Do Their Own Reporting," Pew Research Center, December 8, 2020, www.pewresearch.org/fact-tank /2020/12/08/many-americans-are -unsure-whether-sources-of-news-do -their-own-reporting/ (accessed 2/1/22).

7. Bill Kovach and Tom Rosenstiel, *Blur: How to Know What's True in the Age of Information Overload* (New York: Bloomsbury, 2011).

8. Ashley Jardina and Michael Traugott, "The Genesis of the Birther Rumor: Partisanship, Racial Attitudes, and Political Knowledge," *Journal of Race, Ethnicity, and Politics* 4, no. 1 (November 20, 2018): 60–80.

9. Brian Rosenwald, *Talk Radio's America: How an Industry Took Over a Political Party That Took Over the United States* (Cambridge, MA: Harvard University Press, 2019).

10. Shanto Iyengar, *Media Politics* (New York: W. W. Norton, 2019).

11. Iyengar, *Media Politics.*

12. "Public Broadcasting Fact Sheet," Pew Research Center, June 29, 2021, www .journalism.org/fact-sheet/public -broadcasting/ (accessed 12/4/19); "Americans Who Mainly Get Their News on Social Media Are Less Engaged, Less Knowledgeable," Pew Research Center, July 30, 2020, www .pewresearch.org/journalism/2020 /07/30/americans-who-mainly-get -their-news-on-social-media-are-less -engaged-less-knowledgeable/ (accessed 2/1/22).

13. Iyengar, *Media Politics.*

14. Quoted in Rodney Tiffen, "Journalism in the Trump Era," *Inside Story*, February 24, 2017, http://insidestory .org.au/journalism-in-the-trump-era (accessed 4/4/18).

15. David Folkenflik, "AT&T Deal for Time Warner Casts Renewed Attention on CNN," NPR, October 25, 2016, www .npr.org/2016/10/25/499299869/at-t -deal-for-time-warner-casts-renewed -attention-on-cnn (accessed 5/21/18).

16. "Index of U.S. Mainstream Media Ownership," The Future of Media Project, Harvard University, https://

projects.iq.harvard.edu/futureofmedia /index-us-mainstream-media-ownership (accessed 2/1/22); "Pew's 2021 State of the News Media," Pew Research Center, August 3, 2021, www.press.org /newsroom/pews-2021-state-news -media (2/1/22).

17. For a criticism of the increasing consolidation of the media, see the essays in Patricia Aufderheide et al., *Conglomerates and the Media* (New York: New Press, 1997).

18. "The Role of Wire Services," Pew Research Center, December 3, 2015, www.pewresearch.org/journalism /2015/12/03/the-role-of-wire-services/ (accessed 2/1/22).

19. Neil Macker, "New Coverage of TV Station Owners: Sinclair and Nexstar Are the Two Biggest U.S. Operators," *Morning Star*, January 1, 2020, www .morningstar.com/articles/961093 /new-coverage-of-tv-station-owners (accessed 2/1/22).

20. David J. Garrow, *Protest at Selma: Martin Luther King, Jr., and the Voting Rights Act of 1965* (New Haven, CT: Yale University Press, 2001).

21. See Todd Gitlin, *The Whole World Is Watching* (Berkeley: University of California Press, 1980).

22. "How Black Lives Matter Reached Every Corner of America," *New York Times*, June 13, 2020, www.nytimes.com /interactive/2020/06/13/us/george -floyd-protests-cities-photos.html (accessed 2/1/22).

23. Doris Graber, ed., *Media Power in American Politics*, 5th ed. (Washington, DC: CQ Press, 2006).

24. Amber E. Boydstun, Stefaan Walgrave, and Anne Hardy, "Two Faces of Media Attention: Media Storms vs. General Coverage," *Political Communication* 31, no. 4 (2014): 509–31.

25. Larry M. Bartels, *Presidential Primaries and the Dynamics of Public Choice* (Princeton, NJ: Princeton University Press, 1988).

26. David P. Redlawsk, Caroline J. Tolbert, and Todd Donovan, *Why Iowa? How Caucuses and Sequential Elections Improve the Presidential Nominating*

Process (Chicago: University of Chicago Press, 2011).

27. Larry M. Bartels, *Unequal Democracy: The Political Economy of the New Gilded Age* (Princeton, NJ: Princeton University Press, 2008).

28. Robert Entman, "Framing: Toward Clarification of a Fractured Paradigm," *Journal of Communication* 43, no. 4 (1993): 51–58.

29. Shanto Iyengar and Donald R. Kinder, *News That Matters: Television and American Opinion* (Chicago: University of Chicago Press, 1987), 63; John Zaller, *The Nature and Origins of Mass Opinion* (New York: Cambridge University Press, 1992).

30. Elisa Shearer and Amy Mitchell, "Broad Agreement in U.S.—Even among Partisans—on Which News Outlets Are Part of the 'Mainstream Media,'" Pew Research Center, May 7, 2021, www .pewresearch.org/fact-tank/2021/05/07 /broad-agreement-in-u-s-even-among -partisans-on-which-news-outlets-are -part-of-the-mainstream-media/ (accessed 2/1/22).

31. Elisa Shearer, "More Than Eight in Ten Americans Get News from Digital Devices," Pew Research Center, July 12, 2021, www.pewresearch.org/fact-tank /2021/01/12/more-than-eight-in-ten -americans-get-news-from-digital -devices/ (accessed 2/1/22).

32. "The Washington Post Records 86.6 Million Unique Visitors in March 2019," *WashPost PR* (blog), April 17, 2019, www .washingtonpost.com/pr/2019/04/17 /washington-post-records-million-unique -visitors-march/ (accessed 12/4/19).

33. Aaron Smith and Monica Anderson, "Social Media Use in 2018," Pew Research Center, March 1, 2018, www .pewinternet.org/2018/03/01/social -media-use-in-2018/ (accessed 3/19/18).

34. "Digital and Nondigital Advertising Revenue," Pew Research Center, July 27, 2021, www.pewresearch.org/fact -tank/2021/07/27/6-key-takeaways -about-the-state-of-the-news-media -in-2020/ft_21-07-21_sotnmkeytake aways_5/ (accessed 2/1/22).

35. Laura Wamsley, "Big Newspapers Are Booming: 'Washington Post' to Add 60 Newsroom Jobs," NPR, December 27, 2016, www.npr.org/sections/thetwo -way/2016/12/27/507140760/big -newspapers-are-booming-washington -post-to-add-sixty-newsroom-jobs (accessed 1/22/18).

36. "Share of Newspaper Advertising Revenue Coming from Digital Adver- tising," Pew Research Center, July 29, 2021, www.pewresearch.org/journalism /chart/sotnm-newspapers-percentage -of-newspaper-advertising-revenue -coming-from-digital/ (accessed 2/1/22).

37. Wamsley, "Big Newspapers Are Booming."

38. Shearer, "More Than Eight in Ten Americans Get News from Digital Devices."

39. Shearer, "More Than Eight in Ten Americans Get News from Digital Devices."

40. Amy Mitchell, Elisa Shearer, and Galen Stocking, "News on Twitter: Consumed by Most Users and Trusted by Many," Pew Research Center, November 15, 2021, www.pewresearch.org/journalism /2021/11/15/news-on-twitter-consumed -by-most-users-and-trusted-by-many/ (accessed 2/1/22).

41. David B. Nieborg and Thomas Poell, "The Platformization of Cultural Production: Theorizing the Contingent Cultural Commodity," *New Media & Society* 20, no. 11 (April 2018): 4275–92.

42. Shearer, "More Than Eight in Ten Americans Get News from Digital Devices."

43. "Pew's 2021 State of the News Media."

44. "A Majority of Americans Say They Followed Election Results at Least Occasionally on Election Night," Pew Research Center, November 23, 2020, www.pewresearch.org/journalism /2020/11/23/a-majority-of-americans -say-they-followed-election-results-at -least-occasionally-on-election-night/ (accessed 2/1/22).

45. Michael Barthel, Elizabeth Grieco, and Elisa Shearer, "Older Americans, Black Adults, and Americans with Less Education More Interested in Local News," Pew Research Center,

August, 14, 2019, www.journalism .org/2019/08/14/older-americans-black -adults-and-americans-with-less -education-more-interested-in-local -news/ (accessed 12/4/19).

46. "Local TV News Fact Sheet," Pew Research Center, July 13, 2021, www .pewresearch.org/journalism/fact-sheet /local-tv-news/ (accessed 12/8/21).

47. Elisa Shearer, "Social Media Outpaces Print Newspapers in the U.S. as News Source," Pew Research Center, December 10, 2019, www.pewresearch.org/fact -tank/2018/12/10/social-media-outpaces -print-newspapers-in-the-u-s-as-a -news-source/ (accessed 12/4/19).

48. Shearer, "More Than Eight in Ten Americans Get News from Digital Devices."

49. Mason Walker, "Nearly a Quarter of Americans Get News from Podcasts," Pew Research Center, November 15, 2022, www.pewresearch.org/fact -tank/2022/02/15/nearly-a-quarter-of -americans-get-news-from-podcasts/ (accessed 2/1/22).

50. "Americans Who Mainly Get Their News on Social Media Are Less Engaged, Less Knowledgeable," Pew Research Center.

51. "Audio and Podcasting Fact Sheet," Pew Research Center, June 29, 2021, www.journalism.org/fact-sheet/audio -and-podcasting/ (accessed 2/1/22).

52. Shearer, "More Than Eight in Ten Americans Get News from Digital Devices."

53. Robert McChesney and John Nichols, *The Death and Life of American Journalism: The Media Revolution That Will Begin the World Again* (New York: Nation Books, 2010).

54. "Share of U.S. Ad Spend by Medium in 2009," Statista, www.statista.com /statistics/183704/us-advertising -spend-by-medium-in-2009/ (accessed 2/1/22).

55. Clay Shirky, *Here Comes Everybody: The Power of Organizing Without Organizations* (New York: Penguin Random House, 2009).

56. Shearer, "More Than Eight in Ten Americans Get News from Digital Devices."

57. Elizabeth Dwoskin and Craig Timberg, "Misinformation Dropped Dramatically the Week After Twitter Banned Trump and Some Allies," *Washington Post*, January 16, 2021, www.washingtonpost .com/technology/2021/01/16 /misinformation-trump-twitter/ (accessed 2/1/22).

58. Markus Prior, "News vs. Entertainment: How Increasing Media Choice Widens Gaps in Political Knowledge and Turnout," *American Journal of Political Science* 49, no. 3 (July 2005): 577–92.

59. "More Americans Now See the Media's Influence Growing Compared with a Year Ago," Pew Research Center, May 17, 2021, www.pewresearch.org/fact-tank /2021/05/17/more-americans-now-see -the-medias-influence-growing-compared -with-a-year-ago/ (accessed 2/1/22).

60. "More Americans Now See the Media's Influence Growing Compared with a Year Ago," Pew Research Center.

61. Jeffrey Gottfried, Galen Stocking, and Elizabeth Grieco, "Partisans Remain Sharply Divided in Their Attitudes about the News Media," Pew Research Center, September 25, 2018, www .journalism.org/2018/09/25/partisans -remain-sharply-divided-in-their -attitudes-about-the-news-media/ (accessed 12/4/19).

62. Jeffrey Gottfried, Mason Walker, and Amy Mitchell, "Americans' Views of the News Media During the COVID-19 Outbreak," Pew Research Center, May 8, 2020, www.journalism. org/2020/05/08/americans-views-of -the-news-media-during-the-covid-19 -outbreak/ (accessed 5/12/20).

63. Amy Wong, "'That's How Dictators Get Started': McCain Criticizes Trump for Calling Media 'the Enemy,'" *Washington Post*, February 8, 2017, www.washingtonpost.com/news/the -fix/wp/2017/02/18/thats-how-dictators -get-started-mccain-criticizes-trump -for-calling-media-the-enemy/?noredirect =on&utm_term=.90e929b9948d (accessed 5/21/18).

64. David Redlawsk, "Hot Cognition or Cool Consideration? Testing the Effects of Motivated Reasoning on Political Decision Making," *Journal of Politics* 6, no. 4 (2002).

65. Amy Mitchell, Mark Jurkowitz, J. Baxter Oliphant, and Elisa Shearer, "How Americans Navigated the News in 2020: A Tumultuous Year in Review," Pew Research Center, February 22, 2021, www.journalism.org/2021/02/22/how-americans-navigated-the-news-in-2020-a-tumultuous-year-in-review/ (accessed 2/1/22).

66. Andrew Guess, "(Almost) Everything in Moderation: New Evidence on Americans' Online Media Diets," *American Journal of Political Science* 65, no. 4 (2021): 1007–22.

67. "Media Bias Ratings," AllSides, www.allsides.com/media-bias/media-bias-ratings (accessed 3/25/20).

68. Omri Wallach, "How to Spot Fake News," Visual Capitalist, February 10, 2021, www.visualcapitalist.com/how-to-spot-fake-news/ (accessed 2/1/22).

69. Hannah Roberts, "This Is What Fake News Actually Looks Like—We Ranked 11 Election Stories That Went Viral on Facebook," Business Insider, November 17, 2016, www.businessinsider.com/fake-presidential-election-news-viral-facebook-trump-clinton-2016-11 (accessed 5/21/18).

70. Krysten Crawford, "Stanford Study Examines Fake News and the 2016 Presidential Election," *Stanford News*, January 18, 2017, http://news.stanford.edu/2017/01/18/stanford-study-examines-fake-news-2016-presidential-election/ (accessed 5/21/18).

71. Amy Mitchell et al., "Many Americans Say Made-Up News Is a Critical Problem That Needs to Be Fixed," Pew Research Center, June 5, 2019, www.journalism.org/2019/06/05/many-americans-say-made-up-news-is-a-critical-problem-that-needs-to-be-fixed/ (accessed 5/30/2020).

72. Cathy Cassata, "Doctors Debunk 9 Popular COVID-19 Vaccine Myths and Conspiracy Theories," Healthline, June 22, 2021, www.healthline.com/health-news/doctors-debunk-9-popular-covid-19-vaccine-myths-and-conspiracy-theories#Myth:-The-J&J-vaccine-was-created-from-fetal-tissue (accessed 2/1/22).

73. Shannon Bond, "Just 12 People Are behind Most Vaccine Hoaxes on Social Media, Research Shows," NPR, May 13, 2021, www.npr.org/2021/05/13/996570855/disinformation-dozen-test-facebooks-twitters-ability-to-curb-vaccine-hoaxes (accessed 2/1/22).

74. "Public Highly Critical of State of Political Discourse in the U.S.," Pew Research Center, June 19, 2019, www.people-press.org/2019/06/19/public-highly-critical-of-state-of-political-discourse-in-the-u-s/ (accessed 12/4/19).

75. Matthew A. Baum, "Preaching to the Choir or Converting the Flock: Presidential Communication Strategies in the Age of Three Medias," in *iPolitics: Citizens, Elections, and Governing in the New Media Era*, ed. Richard L. Fox and Jennifer M. Ramos (Cambridge: Cambridge University Press, 2012), 183–205.

76. Eli Pariser, *The Filter Bubble: What the Internet Is Hiding from You* (New York: Penguin Press, 2011).

77. Michael X. Delli Carpini and Scott Keeter, *What Americans Know about Politics* (New Haven, CT: Yale University Press, 1996); Cass Sunstein, *Republic.com* (Princeton, NJ: Princeton University Press, 2001).

78. Karen Mossberger, Caroline Tolbert, and Mary Stansbury, *Virtual Inequality: Beyond the Digital Divide* (Washington, DC: Georgetown University Press, 2003).

CHAPTER 8

1. Luke Broadwater, "With Biden's Agenda in the Balance, Lobbying Kicks into High Gear," *New York Times*, updated October 20, 2021, www.nytimes.com/2021/10/04/us/politics/biden-lobbying-congress.html (accessed 7/27/22).

2. Céilí Doyle, "How Will the Child Tax Credit Inside Biden's Stimulus Package Affect Rural Ohio?," *Columbus Dispatch*, March 19, 2021, www.dispatch.com/story/news/local/2021/03/19/how-child-tax-credit-affect-rural-ohio-american-rescue-plan-act/6941314002/ (accessed 12/10/21).

3. Seth Masket and Hans Noel, *Political Parties* (New York: W. W. Norton, 2021).

4. Masket and Noel, *Political Parties.*

5. John H. Aldrich, *Why Parties? A Second Look* (Chicago: University of Chicago Press, 2011).

6. James Madison, *The Federalist Papers*, ed. Clinton L. Rossiter (New York: New American Library, 1961), no. 10, https://guides.loc.gov/federalist-papers/text-1-10 (accessed 2/1/22).

7. Lilliana Mason, *Uncivil Agreement: How Politics Became Our Identity* (Chicago: University of Chicago Press, 2018).

8. Todd Donovan and Shaun Bowler, *Reforming the Republic: Democratic Institutions for the New America* (Upper Saddle River, NJ: Prentice Hall, 2003).

9. E. E. Schattschneider, *The Semisovereign People: A Realist's View of Democracy in America* (Boston: Cengage, 1975).

10. Anthony Downs, *An Economic Theory of Democracy* (New York: Harper, 1957).

11. Stephen Gruber-Miller, "Chuck Grassley Says He Tried to Remind President That Tariffs 'Brought About Adolf Hitler,'" *Des Moines Register*, May 15, 2019, www.desmoinesregister.com/story/news/politics/2019/05/15/chuck-grassley-tariffs-donald-trump-brought-great-depression-hitler-world-war-2-smoot-hawley-trade/3683407002/ (accessed 3/1/22).

12. Thomas Mann and Norman J. Ornstein, *It's Even Worse Than It Looks: How the American Constitutional System Collided with the New Politics of Extremism* (New York: Basic Books, 2016).

13. Rachel M. Blum, *How the Tea Party Captured the GOP: Insurgent Factions in American Politics* (Chicago: University of Chicago Press, 2020).

14. Sean M. Theriault, *Party Polarization in Congress* (New York: Cambridge University Press, 2008).

15. David Hawkings, "Ahead, the First Pure Party-Line Modern Tax Cut?," *Roll Call*, October 31, 2017, www.rollcall.com/news/hawkings/party-line-tax-cut (accessed 8/15/18).

16. Donovan and Bowler, *Reforming the Republic*. See also Marty Gilens, *Affluence and Influence: Economic Inequality and Political Power in America* (Princeton, NJ: Princeton University Press, 2014).

17. Jacob R. Brown and Ryan D. Enos, "The Measurement of Partisan Sorting for 180 Million Voters," *PubMed*, 2021.

18. Adrian Blanco, Kevin Schaul, and Ashlyn Still, "How Redistricting Is Shaping the 2022 U.S. House Map," *Washington Post*, December 16, 2021, www.washingtonpost.com/politics/interactive/redistricting-tracker-map/?itid=mr_politics_4 (accessed 4/27/22).

19. For an excellent analysis of the parties' role in recruitment, see Paul Herrnson, *Congressional Elections: Campaigning at Home and in Washington* (Washington, DC: CQ Press, 1995).

20. Katherine Schaeffer, "Far More Americans See 'Very Strong' Partisan Conflicts Now Than in the Last Two Presidential Election Years," Pew Research Center, March 4, 2020, www.pewresearch.org/fact-tank/2020/03/04/far-more-americans-see-very-strong-partisan-conflicts-now-than-in-the-last-two-presidential-election-years/ (accessed 4/30/20).

21. Donald Green, Bradley Palmquist, and Eric Schickler, *Partisan Hearts and Minds* (New Haven, CT: Yale University Press, 2004).

22. Anthony Downs, *Economic Theory of Democracy* (New York: Harper & Row, 1957).

23. Green, Palmquist, and Schickler, *Partisan Hearts and Minds.*

24. Mason, *Uncivil Agreement.*

25. "Party Affiliation," Gallup, https://news.gallup.com/poll/15370/party-affiliation.aspx?msclkid=8c3beb2bc63611ecb493a29563ce3f6b (accessed 4/27/22).

26. Donovan and Bowler, *Reforming the Republic.*

27. Bruce E. Keith et al., *The Myth of the Independent Voter* (Berkeley: University of California Press, 1992).

28. Samara Klar and Yanna Krupnikov, *Independent Politics: How American Disdain for Parties Leads to Political Inaction* (Cambridge: Cambridge University Press, 2016).

29. "Beyond Red vs. Blue: The Political Typology," Pew Research Center, November 9, 2021, www.pewresearch.org/politics/2021/11/09/beyond-red-vs-blue-the-political-typology-2/; 2020

Cooperative Election Study, Harvard University, https://cces.gov.harvard.edu/ (accessed 4/27/22).

30. "Political Independents: Who They Are, What They Think," Pew Research Center, March 14, 2019, www.people -press.org/2019/03/14/political -independents-who-they-are-what -they-think/ (accessed 1/16/20); Lilliana Mason, "A Cross-Cutting Calm: How Social Sorting Drives Affective Polarization," *Public Opinion Quarterly* 80, no. S1 (2016): 351–77.

31. "Beyond Red vs. Blue: The Political Typology"; 2020 Cooperative Election Study.

32. "Behind Biden's 2020 Victory," Pew Research Center, June 30, 2021, www .pewresearch.org/politics/2021/06/30 /behind-bidens-2020-victory/ (accessed 4/27/22).

33. "Behind Biden's 2020 Victory."

34. Shaun Bowler, Gary Segura, and Stephen Nicholson, "Earthquakes and Aftershocks: Race, Direct Democracy, and Partisan Change," *American Journal of Political Science* 50 (January 2006): 146–59.

35. "Amid Campaign Turmoil, Biden Holds Wide Leads on Coronavirus, Unifying the Country," Pew Research Center, October 9, 2020, www.pewresearch.org /politics/2020/10/09/amid-campaign -turmoil-biden-holds-wide-leads-on -coronavirus-unifying-the-country/ (accessed 6/18/22); "National Exit Polls: How Different Groups Voted," *New York Times*, www.nytimes.com /interactive/2020/11/03/us/elections /exit-polls-president.html?msclkid =67f03730c63911ecb21803c037d3b27b (accessed 4/27/22); "Behind Biden's 2020 Victory."

36. Shanto Iyengar, Gaurav Sood, and Yphtach Lelkes, "Affect, Not Ideology: A Social Identity Perspective on Polarization," *Public Opinion Quarterly* 76, no. 3 (2012): 405–31; Shanto Iyengar and Sean J. Westwood, "Fear and Loathing across Party Lines: New Evidence on Group Polarization," *American Journal of Political Science* 59, no. 3 (2015): 690–707.

37. Alan Abramowitz, *The Great Realignment: Race, Party Transformation, and the Rise of Donald Trump* (New Haven, CT: Yale University Press, 2018).

38. "Partisan Antipathy: More Intense, More Personal," Pew Research Center, October 10, 2019, www.pewresearch .org/politics/2019/10/10/how-partisans -view-each-other/ (accessed 4/27/22).

39. Gregory A. Huber and Neil Malhotra, "Political Homophily in Social Relationships: Evidence from Online Dating Behavior," *Journal of Politics* 79, no. 1 (2017): 269–83.

40. Karen Gift and Thomas Gift, "Does Politics Influence Hiring? Evidence from a Randomized Experiment," *Political Behavior* 37 (2015): 653–75.

41. John G. Bullock et al., "Partisan Bias in Factual Beliefs about Politics," *Quarterly Journal of Political Science* 10 (2015): 519–78.

42. Ryan E. Carlin and Gregory J. Love, "The Politics of Interpersonal Trust and Reciprocity: An Experimental Approach," *Political Behavior* 35 (2013): 43–63.

43. Jacob R. Brown and Ryan D. Enos, "The Measurement of Partisan Sorting for 180 Million Voters," *Nature Human Behaviour* 5 (2021), doi.org/10.1038 /s41562-021-01066-z.

44. For a discussion of third parties in the United States, see Daniel Mazmanian, *Third Parties in Presidential Elections* (Washington, DC: Brookings Institution Press, 1974).

45. Lee Drutman, *The Business of America Is Lobbying: How Corporations Became Politicized and Politics Became More Corporate* (New York: Oxford University Press, 2015).

46. Kay Lehman Schlozman, Henry E. Brady, and Sidney Verba, *Unequal and Unrepresented: Political Inequality and the People's Voice in the New Gilded Age* (Princeton, NJ: Princeton University Press, 2018), Table 8.3.

47. Center for Responsive Politics, "Lobbying Database: Ranked Sectors," www .opensecrets.org/federal-lobbying/ranked -sectors?cycle=2021 (accessed 6/16/22).

48. Drutman, *The Business of America Is Lobbying*, 13.

49. Schlozman, Brady, and Verba, *Unequal and Unrepresented*, Table 8.3.

50. G. William Domhoff, "The Rise and Fall of Labor Unions in the U.S.," Who Rules America?, February 2013, https://whorulesamerica.ucsc.edu/power/history_of_labor_unions.html (accessed 9/10/19); Bureau of Labor Statistics, "Union Members – 2021," January 20, 2022, www.bls.gov/news.release/pdf/union2.pdf (accessed 9/24/22).

51. Sean McElwee, "How Unions Boost Democratic Participation," *American Prospect*, September 16, 2015, https://prospect.org/article/how-unions-boost-democratic-participation (accessed 9/10/19).

52. Schlozman, Brady, and Verba, *Unequal and Unrepresented*, Table 8.3.

53. Anthony J. Nownes, *Interest Groups in American Politics*, 2nd ed. (New York: Routledge, 2013).

54. Schlozman, Brady, and Verba, *Unequal and Unrepresented*, Table 8.3.

55. David B. Truman, *The Governmental Process* (New York: Knopf, 1951).

56. Mancur Olson, Jr., *The Logic of Collective Action* (Cambridge, MA: Harvard University Press, 1965).

57. See, for example, the Singles Section of the New Jersey Sierra Club: www.sierraclub.org/new-jersey/sierra-singles (accessed 9/4/19).

58. E. E. Schattschneider, *The Semisovereign People: A Realist's View of Democracy in America* (New York: Holt, Rinehart and Winston, 1960).

59. Kay Lehman Schlozman and John T. Tierney, *Organized Interests and American Democracy* (New York: Harper and Row, 1986), 60.

60. Jesse M. Crosson, Alexander C. Furnas, and Geoffrey M. Lorenz, "Polarized Pluralism: Organizational Preferences and Biases in the American Pressure System," *American Political Science Review* 114, no. 4 (2020): 1117–37.

61. Dara Z. Strolovitch, *Affirmative Advocacy: Race, Class, and Gender in Interest Group Politics* (Chicago: University of Chicago Press, 2007); Cathy J. Cohen, *The Boundaries of Blackness: AIDS and the Breakdown of Black Politics* (Chicago: University of Chicago Press, 1999).

62. Richard L. Hall and Alan V. Deardorff, "Lobbying as Legislative Subsidy," *American Political Science Review* 100, no. 1 (February 2006): 69–84.

63. Center for Responsive Politics, "Lobbying Database," www.opensecrets.org/Lobby/ (accessed 12/10/21).

64. See Sean McMinn and Kate Ackley, "Lobbying Hits $3.9 Billion in Trump's First Year," Roll Call, January 23, 2018, www.rollcall.com/news/politics/lobbying-trump-first-year; Derek Kravitz and Alex Mierjeski, "Trump's Appointees Pledged Not to Lobby After They Leave. Now They're Lobbying," ProPublica, May 3, 2018, www.propublica.org/article/trump-appointees-pledged-not-to-lobby-after-they-leave-now-lobbying (accessed 9/5/19).

65. U.S. PIRG, "Lobbyist Registrations Hit 18-Year Low," January 30, 2017, https://uspirg.org/news/usp/lobbyist-registrations-hit-18-year-low (accessed 9/5/19).

66. For discussions of lobbying, see Allan J. Cigler and Burdett A. Loomis, eds., *Interest Group Politics* (Washington, DC: CQ Press, 1983). See also Jeffrey M. Berry, *Lobbying for the People* (Princeton, NJ: Princeton University Press, 1977).

67. Brookings Institution, *Vital Statistics on Congress*, Table 5.1, February 8, 2021, www.brookings.edu/multi-chapter-report/vital-statistics-on-congress/ (accessed 9/5/21).

68. Drutman, *The Business of America Is Lobbying*, 33–34.

69. *Brown v. Board of Education of Topeka, Kansas*, 347 U.S. 483 (1954).

70. *Obergefell v. Hodges*, 576 U.S. 644 (2015).

71. *Dobbs v. Jackson Women's Health Organization* 597 U.S. ___ (2022).

72. Christine Day, *AARP: America's Largest Interest Group and Its Impact* (Westport, CT: Praeger, 2017).

73. Jacob S. Hacker and Paul Pierson, *Winner-Take-All Politics: How Washington Made the Rich Richer, and Turned Its Back on the Middle Class* (New York: Simon and Schuster, 2010).

74. Frank R. Baumgartner et al., *Lobbying and Policy Change: Who Wins, Who Loses, and Why* (Chicago: University of Chicago Press, 2009).

75. Hall and Deardorff, "Lobbying as Legislative Subsidy."

76. Kevin M. Esterling, *The Political Economy of Expertise: Information and Efficiency in American National Politics* (Ann Arbor: University of Michigan Press, 2004).

77. Amy McKay and Susan Webb Yackee, "Interest Group Competition on Federal Agency Rules," *American Politics Research* 35, no. 3 (May 2007): 336–57.

78. Ida A. Brudnick, "Congressional Salaries and Allowances: In Brief," Congressional Research Service, April 11, 2018, https://crsreports .congress.gov/ (accessed 9/24/19).

79. James Madison, *The Federalist Papers*, no. 10.

CHAPTER 9

1. Edward Fitzpatrick, "Rhode Island's Youngest State Legislator: An Advocate for the Working Class," *Boston Globe*, April 14, 2021, www.bostonglobe.com /2021/04/14/metro/rhode-islands -youngest-state-legislator-an-advocate -working-class/?event=event12 (accessed 12/11/21).

2. Susan Matthis Johnson, "Youngest Black Legislator in America Ready to Get to Work for WV," *Charleston Gazette-Mail*, January 6, 2019, www.wvgazettemail .com/life/youngest-black-legislator -in-america-ready-to-get-to-work /article_9f22e066-ab68-5f18-90be -a79fe0868dfc.html; Adeel Hassan, "Freshman in College, Freshman in the Capitol: West Virginia's 19-Year-Old Lawmaker," *New York Times*, January 27, 2019, www.nytimes.com/2019/01/27 /us/caleb-hanna-bio-facts-republican -gop.html (accessed 12/11/21).

3. Aaron C. Davis, "The Attack: The Jan. 6 Siege of the U.S. Capitol Was Neither a Spontaneous Act nor an Isolated Event," *Washington Post*, October 31, 2021, www.washingtonpost.com/politics /interactive/2021/jan-6-insurrection -capitol/?itid=lk_interstitial_manual _5&itid=lk_interstitial_manual_6 (accessed 1/15/22).

4. John Gramlich, "What Makes a Good Citizen? Voting, Paying Taxes, Following the Law Top List," Pew Research Center, July 2, 2019, www.pewresearch.org /fact-tank/2019/07/02/what-makes -a-good-citizen-voting-paying-taxes -following-the-law-top-list/ (accessed 12/6/19).

5. Sidney Verba, Kay Lehman Schlozman, and Henry E. Brady, *Voice and Equality: Civic Voluntarism in American Politics* (Cambridge, MA: Harvard University Press, 2005), chap. 3, for kinds of participation; 66–67 for prevalence of local activity.

6. Michael P. McDonald, "American Voter Turnout in Historical Perspective," in *The Oxford Handbook of American Elections and Political Behavior*, ed. Jan Leighley (New York: Oxford University Press, 2010), 125–43.

7. Todd Donovan and Shaun Bowler, *Reforming the Republic: Democratic Institutions for the New America* (Upper Saddle River, NJ: Pearson Education, 2004).

8. Meredith Rolfe, *Voter Turnout: A Social Theory of Political Participation* (New York: Cambridge University Press, 2012).

9. Lee Rainie et al., "Social Media and Political Engagement," Pew Research Center, October 19, 2012, www .pewinternet.org/2012/10/19/social -media-and-political-engagement/ (accessed 6/24/14).

10. Helen Margetts et al., *Political Turbulence: How Social Media Shape Collective Action* (New York: Oxford University Press, 2017).

11. Angus Campbell et al., *The American Voter* (New York: Wiley, 1960); Steven Rosenstone and John Mark Hansen, *Mobilization, Participation, and Democracy in America* (New York: Macmillan, 1993); Kay Lehman Scholzman, Sidney Verba, and Henry E. Brady, *The Unheavenly Chorus: Unequal Political Voice and the Broken Promise of American Democracy* (Princeton, NJ: Princeton University Press, 2012).

12. "Voting and Registration in the Election of November 2020," U.S. Census Bureau, April 2021, www.census.gov/data/tables /time-series/demo/voting-and-registration /p20-585.html (accessed 1/15/22).

13. "Voting and Registration in the Election of November 2020."

14. Sidney Verba and Norman H. Nie, *Participation in America: Political Democracy and Social Equality* (New York: Harper and Row, 1972).

15. "Voting and Registration in the Election of November 2020."

16. Jessica Trounstine, *Segregation by Design: Local Politics and Inequality in American Cities* (New York: Cambridge University Press, 2018).

17. Jan E. Leighley and Jonathan Nagler, "Individual and Systemic Influences on Turnout: Who Votes? 1984," *Journal of Politics* 54, no. 3 (1992): 718–40.

18. "2016 Election Exit Polls," *Washington Post*, November 29, 2019, www .washingtonpost.com/graphics/politics /2016-election/exit-polls/ (accessed 12/6/19); Ruth Igielnik, Scott Keeter, and Hannah Hartig, "Behind Biden's 2020 Victory," Pew Research Center, June 30, 2021, www.pewresearch.org /politics/2021/06/30/behind-bidens -2020-victory/ (accessed 1/15/22).

19. Kevin Morris and Coryn Grange, "Large Racial Turnout Gap Persisted in 2020 Election," Brennan Center for Justice, August 6, 2021, www.brennancenter .org/our-work/analysis-opinion/large -racial-turnout-gap-persisted-2020 -election (accessed 1/15/22).

20. Matt Barreto and Gary Segura, *Latino America: How America's Most Dynamic Population Is Poised to Transform the Politics of the Nation* (New York: Public Affairs, 2014).

21. "The Gender Gap Fact Sheet," Center for the American Woman and Politics, January 2017, https://cawp.rutgers.edu /sites/default/files/resources/ggpresvote .pdf (accessed 3/16/2020).

22. Bruce E. Cain, Todd Donovan, and Caroline J. Tolbert, *Democracy in the States: Experiments in Election Reform* (Washington, DC: Brookings Institution Press, 2008).

23. "Automatic Voter Registration," National Conference of State Legislatures, January 12, 2022, www.ncsl.org/research /elections-and-campaigns/automatic -voter-registration.aspx (accessed 5/26/22).

24. "Same Day Voter Registration," National Conference of State Legislatures, September 20, 2021, www.ncsl.org /research/elections-and-campaigns /same-day-registration.aspx (accessed 1/15/22).

25. Michael Hanmer, *Discount Voting: Voting Registration Reforms and Their Effects* (New York: Cambridge University Press, 2009); Melanie Springer, *How the States Shaped the Nation: American Electoral Institutions and Voter Turnout, 1920–2000* (Chicago: University of Chicago Press, 2014); Mary Fitzgerald, "Greater Convenience but Not Greater Turnout: The Impact of Alternative Voting Methods on Electoral Participation in the United States," *American Politics Research* 33, no. 6 (2005): 842–67; Craig Leonard Brians and Bernard Grofman, "When Registration Barriers Fall, Who Votes? An Empirical Test of a Rational Choice Model," *Public Choice* 99 (1999): 161–76; Michael Ritter and Caroline J. Tolbert, *Accessible Elections: How the States Can Help Americans Vote* (New York: Oxford University Press, 2020).

26. "Early In-Person Voting," National Conference of State Legislatures, January 17, 2022, www.ncsl.org/research/elections -and-campaigns/early-voting-in-state -elections.aspx (accessed 3/17/22).

27. "Voting Laws Roundup: December 2021," Brennan Center for Justice, December 21, 2021, www.brennancenter .org/our-work/research-reports/voting -laws-roundup-december-2021 (accessed 1/15/22).

28. "Voter ID Laws," National Conference of State Legislatures, www.ncsl.org/research /elections-and-campaigns/voter-id.aspx (accessed 1/15/22).

29. "Republicans and Democrats Move Further Apart in Views of Voting Access," Pew Research Center, April 22, 2021, www.pewresearch.org/politics /2021/04/22/republicans-and-democrats -move-further-apart-in-views-of-voting -access/ (accessed 1/15/22).

30. Zoltan Hajnal, Nazita Lajevardi, and Lindsey Nielson, "Voter Identification Laws and the Suppression of Minority Votes," *Journal of Politics* 79, no. 2 (2017): 363–79; but see Justin Grimmer et al., "Obstacles to Estimating Voter ID Laws' Effect on Turnout," *Journal of*

Politics 80, no. 3 (2018): 1045–51; Zoltan Hajnal, John Kuk, and Nazita Lajevardi, "We All Agree: Strict Voter ID Laws Disproportionately Burden Minorities," *Journal of Politics* 80, no. 3 (2018): 1052–59; see also Justin Grimmer and Jesse Yoder, "The Durable Differential Deterrent Effects of Strict Photo Identification Laws," *Political Science Research and Methods* (2021): 1–17.

31. Rene R. Rocha and Tetsuya Matsubayashi, "The Politics of Race and Voter ID Laws in the States: The Return of Jim Crow?" *Political Research Quarterly* 67, no. 3 (2014): 666–79.

32. Enrico Cantoni and Vincent Pons, "Strict ID Laws Don't Stop Voters: Evidence from a U.S. Nationwide Panel, 2008–2018," *Quarterly Journal of Economics* 136, no. 4 (2021): 2615–60.

33. Lonna Rae Atkeson et al., "A New Barrier to Participation: Heterogeneous Application of Voter Identification Policies," *Electoral Studies* 29, no. 1 (2010): 66–73; Lonna Rae Atkeson et al., "Who Asks for Voter Identification? Explaining Poll-Worker Discretion," *Journal of Politics* 76, no. 4 (2014): 944–57; Bernard L. Fraga and Michael G. Miller, "Who Do Voter ID Laws Keep from Voting?," *Journal of Politics* 84, no. 2 (2022), www.journals.uchicago.edu /doi/abs/10.1086/716282.

34. Sarah Zimmerman, "Illinois Protecting against Russian Election Tampering," *U.S. News and World Report*, February 28, 2018, www.usnews.com/news/best -states/illinois/articles/2018-02-28 /illinois-protecting-against-russian -election-tampering (accessed 5/14/18).

35. David P. Redlawsk, Caroline J. Tolbert, and Todd Donovan, *Why Iowa? How Caucuses and Sequential Elections Improve the Presidential Nominating Process* (Chicago: University of Chicago Press, 2010).

36. State legislatures determine the system by which electors are selected. Almost all states use this "winner-take-all" system. Maine and Nebraska, however, provide that one electoral vote goes to the winner in each congressional district and two electoral votes go to the winner statewide.

37. Jeffrey Karp and Caroline J. Tolbert, "Polls and Elections: Support for Nationalizing Presidential Elections," *Presidential Studies Quarterly* 40, no. 4 (2010): 771–93.

38. Stephen Ansolabehere and James Snyder, "Campaign War Chests and Congressional Elections," *Business and Politics* 2 (2000): 9–34.

39. Gary W. Cox and Eric Magar, "How Much Is Majority Status in the U.S. Congress Worth?," *American Political Science Review* 93 (1999): 299–309.

40. "Two-Thirds of Presidential Campaign Is in Just 6 States," Nationalpopularvote .com, www.nationalpopularvote.com /campaign-events-2016 (accessed 5/14/18); Daron Shaw, *The Race to 270: The Electoral College and the Campaign Strategies of 2000 and 2004* (Chicago: University of Chicago Press, 2006).

41. John Geer, *In Defense of Negativity: Attack Ads in Presidential Campaigns* (Chicago: University of Chicago Press, 2006).

42. Nicholas Confessore and Karen Yourish, "$2 Billion of Free Media for Donald Trump," *New York Times*, March 16, 2016, www.nytimes.com/2016/03/16 /upshot/measuring-donald-trumps -mammoth-advantage-in-free-media .html (accessed 7/25/18).

43. D. Sunshine Hillygus and Todd G. Shields, *The Persuadable Voter: Wedge Issues in Political Campaigns* (Princeton, NJ: Princeton University Press, 2009). Bush's campaign focused on wedge issues—issues where voters' preferences diverge from those of their political party. By targeting Democratic voters with messages focusing on Bush's opposition to same-sex marriage, the campaign hoped to convince socially conservative Democrats to cast a ballot for Bush rather than for his opponent.

44. Sasha Issenberg, *The Victory Lab: The Secret Science of Winning Campaigns* (New York: Crown, 2012).

45. Alan S. Gerber and Donald P. Green, "The Effects of Canvassing, Telephone Calls, and Direct Mail on Voter Turnout: A Field Experiment," *American Political Science Review* 94, no. 3 (2000): 660.

46. Gerber and Green, "The Effects of Canvassing."

47. Robert M. Bond et al., "A 61-Million-Person Experiment in Social Influence and Political Mobilization," *Nature* 489 (2012): 295–98.

48. Katerina Eva Matsa and Kristine Lu, "10 Facts about the Changing Digital News Landscape," Pew Research Center, September 14, 2016, www.pewresearch .org/fact-tank/2016/09/14/facts-about -the-changing-digital-news-landscape/ (accessed 10/16/16).

49. Morris P. Fiorina, "The (Re)Nationaliza-tion of Congressional Elections," *Hoover Institution Essay, No. 7*, October 19, 2016, www.hoover.org/research /renationalization-congressional -elections (accessed 11/7/22).

50. "Trump, the 2018 Election and Beyond," Pew Research Center, November 15, 2018, www.people-press.org/2018/11/15 /4-trump-the-2018-election-and-beyond (accessed 11/7/22).

51. Morris P. Fiorina, *Unstable Majorities* (Stanford, CA: Hoover Institution Press, 2017).

52. Josh Pacewicz, *Partisans and Partners* (Chicago: University of Chicago Press, 2016).

53. Kim Hart, "Most Democrats See Republicans as Racist, Sexist," Axios, November 12, 2018, www.axios.com /poll-democrats-and-republicans -hate-each-other-racist-ignorant-evil -99ae7afc-5a51-42be-8ee2-3959e43ce320 .html (accessed 11/7/22).

54. Elaine Kamarck and Norman Eisen, "Democracy on the Ballot—How Many Election Deniers Are on the Ballot in November and What Is Their Likelihood of Success?" Brookings Institution, October 7, 2022, www.brookings.edu /blog/fixgov/2022/10/07/democracy -on-the-ballot-how-many-election -deniers-are-on-the-ballot-in-november -and-what-is-their-likelihood-of-success/ (accessed 11/7/22).

55. Henry Olsen, "My Predictions for the 2022 Midterm Elections," *Washington Post*, November 7, 2022, www.washingtonpost .com/opinions/2022/11/07/midterm -elections-2022-prediction-house-senate -forecast/ (accessed 11/7/22).

56. "Midterm Voting Intentions Are Divided, Economic Gloom Persists: Inflation Continues to Dominate Americans' Economic Concerns," Pew Research Center, October 20, 2022, www.pewresearch.org/politics /2022/10/20/the-midterm-elections -and-views-of-biden/ (accessed 11/7/22).

57. "Midterm Voting Intentions Are Divided, Economic Gloom Persists."

58. Janice Kai Chen, Chris Alcantara, and Emily Guskin, "How Different Groups Voted According to Exit Polls and AP VoteCast," *Washington Post*, November 10, 2022, www.washingtonpost.com /politics/2022/11/08/exit-polls-2022 -elections/ (accessed 11/13/22).

59. "Midterm Voting Intentions Are Divided, Economic Gloom Persists."

60. "Midterm Voting Intentions Are Divided, Economic Gloom Persists."

61. Katherine Schaeffer and Ted Van Green, "Key Facts about U.S. Voter Priorities Ahead of the 2022 Midterm Elections," Pew Research Center, November 3, 2022, www.pewresearch.org/fact-tank /2022/11/03/key-facts-about-u-s-voter -priorities-ahead-of-the-2022-midterm -elections/ (accessed 11/7/22).

62. Chen, Alcantara, and Guskin, "How Different Groups Voted."

63. "Midterm Voting Intentions Are Divided, Economic Gloom Persists."

64. U.S. Election Project, "2022 General Election," www.electproject.org/2022g (accessed 11/13/22).

65. Kati Perry, Luis Melgar, Kate Rabinow-itz, and Dan Keating, "Where Voter Turnout Exceeded 2018 Highs," *Washington Post*, November 9, 2022, www.washingtonpost.com/politics /interactive/2022/voter-turnout-2022 -by-state/ (accessed 11/9/22).

66. "2022 Election: Young Voters Have High Midterm Turnout, Influence Critical Races," Circle, Tufts University, https:// circle.tufts.edu/2022-election-center (accessed 11/7/22).

67. Chen, Alcantara, and Guskin, "How Different Groups Voted"; Perry, Melgar, Rabinowitz, and Keating, "Where Voter Turnout Exceeded 2018 Highs."

68. "2022 Election: Young Voters Have High Midterm Turnout."

CHAPTER 10

1. Marguerite Reardon, "Section 230: How It Shields Facebook and Why Congress Wants Changes," CNET, October 6, 2021, www.cnet.com/news/section-230-how -it-shields-facebook-and-why-congress -wants-changes/ (accessed 11/15/21).

2. Marcy Gordon, "Senator Asks Facebook CEO to Testify on Instagram and Kids," Associated Press, October 20, 2021, https://apnews.com/article/technology-business-data-privacy-mark-zuckerberg-richard-blumenthal-28b2d3f962cc85afe9ca1fba2d30437b (accessed 11/15/21).

3. Cecilia Kang, "Facebook Whistle-Blower Urges Lawmakers to Regulate the Company," *New York Times*, October 5, 2021, www.nytimes.com/2021/10/05/technology/facebook-whistle-blower-hearing.html (accessed 11/15/21).

4. Barbara Ortutay and David Klepper, "Facebook Whistleblower Testifies: Five Highlights," Associated Press, October 5, 2021, https://apnews.com/article/facebook-frances-haugen-congress-testimony-af86188337d25b179153b973754b71a4 (accessed 11/15/21).

5. David Mayhew, *Congress: The Electoral Connection* (New Haven, CT: Yale University Press, 1974).

6. Jennifer E. Manning, *Membership of the 116th Congress: A Profile* (Washington, DC: Congressional Research Service, March 31, 2020), https://fas.org/sgp/crs/misc/R45583.pdf (accessed 4/8/20).

7. Manning, *Membership of the 116th Congress.*

8. For a discussion, see Benjamin Ginsberg, *The Consequences of Consent* (New York: Random House, 1982), chap. 1.

9. Norman J. Ornstein et al., *Vital Statistics on Congress* (Washington, DC: Brookings Institution Press, 2017), Tables 5–3 and 5–4, www.brookings.edu (accessed 3/22/18); Norman J. Ornstein, Thomas E. Mann, and Michael J. Malbin, *Vital Statistics on Congress 2008* (Washington, DC: Brookings Institution Press, 2009), 111–12.

10. Linda Fowler and Robert McClure, *Political Ambition: Who Decides to Run for Congress* (New Haven, CT: Yale University Press, 1989); Alan Ehrenhalt, *The United States of Ambition: Politicians, Power, and the Pursuit of Office* (New York: Three Rivers Press, 1992).

11. OpenSecrets, "Reelection Rates over the Years," www.opensecrets.org/elections-overview/reelection-rates (accessed 11/15/20).

12. OpenSecrets, "Reelection Rates over the Years."

13. Autumn Johnson, "Union Sanitary District Dedicates New Green Energy Facility," Patch, April 6, 2015, https://patch.com/california/unioncity/union-sanitary-district-dedicates-new-green-energy-facility (accessed 2/18/20).

14. Diana Evans, *Greasing the Wheels: Using Pork Barrel Projects to Build Majority Coalitions in Congress* (New York: Cambridge University Press, 2004).

15. Mayhew, *Congress: The Electoral Connection.*

16. Mark Hugo Lopez and Paul Taylor, "The 2010 Congressional Reapportionment and Latinos," Pew Research Center, January 5, 2011, www.pewhispanic.org/2011/01/05/the-2010-congressional-reapportionment-and-latinos/ (accessed 2/24/14).

17. Adam Liptak, "Supreme Court Rebuffs Lawmakers over Independent Redistricting Plan," *New York Times*, June 29, 2015, www.nytimes.com/2015/06/30/us/supreme-court-upholds-creation-of-arizona-redistricting-commission.html (accessed 9/14/15).

18. *Rucho v. Common Cause*, 588 U.S. __ (2019).

19. *Shelby County v. Holder*, 570 U.S. 529 (2013).

20. Richard Fenno, Jr., *Home Style: House Members in Their Districts* (Boston: Little, Brown, 1978).

21. Richard E. Cohen, "Crackup of the Committees," *National Journal*, July 31, 1999, 2210–16.

22. See, for example, the announcement of an agreement on the Agricultural Act of 2014, House Committee on Agriculture, "House–Senate Negotiators Announce Bipartisan Agreement on Final Farm Bill," press release, http://agriculture.house.gov/news/documentsingle.aspx?DocumentID51220 (accessed 9/21/15).

23. Norman J. Ornstein et al., *Vital Statistics on Congress* (Washington, DC: Brookings Institution and American Enterprise Institute, July 2013), chap. 5, www.brookings.edu/research/reports/2013/07/vital-statistics-congress-mann-ornstein (accessed 6/13/16).

24. Barbara Sinclair, *Unorthodox Lawmaking: New Legislative Processes in the U.S. Congress,* 5th ed. (Washington, DC: CQ Press, 2016).

25. Walter Oleszek, *Congressional Procedures and the Policy Process* (Washington, DC: CQ Press, 2019), 170.

26. Oleszek, *Congressional Procedures*, 182.

27. Congressional Research Service, https://crsreports.congress.gov/ (accessed 10/9/21); see also Doug Andres, "Congress and Why Process Matters" (master's thesis, Johns Hopkins University, 2015).

28. David M. Herszenhorn, "Failed Spending Bills Pile Up in Senate as Budget Agreement Breaks Down," *New York Times*, July 12, 2016, A11, www.nytimes.com /2016/07/12/us/politics/failed-spending -bills-pile-up-in-senate-amid-dispute -over-budget-deal.html (accessed 9/17/16).

29. John W. Kingdon, *Congressmen's Voting Decisions* (New York: Harper and Row, 1973), chap. 3; R. Douglas Arnold, *The Logic of Congressional Action* (New Haven, CT: Yale University Press, 1990).

30. Eric Lipton and Ben Protess, "Banks' Lobbyists Help in Drafting Financial Bills," *New York Times*, May 23, 2013, https://dealbook.nytimes.com/2013/05 /23/banks-lobbyists-help-in-drafting -financial-bills/ (accessed 9/21/15); Michael Corkery, "Citigroup Becomes the Fall Guy in the Spending Bill Battle," *New York Times*, December 12, 2014, https://dealbook.nytimes.com/2014/12/12 /citigroup-becomes-the-fall-guy-in-the -spending-bill-battle/ (accessed 9/21/15).

31. Norman J. Ornstein and Thomas E. Mann, *Vital Statistics on Congress* (Washington, DC: Brookings Institution, 2018), Table 6-4.

32. Geoffrey C. Layman, Thomas M. Carsey, and Juliana Menasce Horowitz, "Party Polarization in American Politics: Characteristics, Causes, and Consequences," *Annual Review of Political Science* 9 (2006): 83–110.

33. For example, Fredreka Schouten, "Club for Growth Plans New Push in House Races," *USA Today*, August 17, 2015, www.usatoday.com/story/news /politics/onpolitics/2015/08/17/club-for -growth-plans-new-push-in-house -races/81220646/ (accessed 9/21/15).

34. *United States v. Pink*, 315 U.S. 203 (1942). For a good discussion of the problem, see James W. Davis, *The American Presidency* (New York: Harper and Row, 1987), chap. 8.

35. U.S. House, "Impeachment," http://history .house.gov/Institution/Origins-Development /Impeachment/ (accessed 4/18/14).

CHAPTER 11

1. Julie Turkewitz, "Trump Slashes Size of Bears Ears and Grand Staircase Monuments," *New York Times*, December 4, 2017, www.nytimes.com /2017/12/04/us/trump-bears-ears .html. This account also draws on Krystal D'Costa, "On Indigenous People's Day, the Fight for Bears Ears Remains Unresolved," *Anthropology in Practice* (blog), *Scientific American*, blog, October 8, 2018, https://blogs .scientificamerican.com/anthropology -in-practice/on-indigenous-peoples -day-the-fight-for-bears-ears-remained -unresolved/; Bears Ears Country, "An Interview with Charles Wilkinson," June 18, 2019, www.bearsearscountry .com/blog/2019/6/18/an-interview -with-charles-wilkinson; "A Proclamation on Bear Ears National Monument," The White House, October 8, 2021, www.whitehouse.gov/briefing-room /presidential-actions/2021/10/08/a -proclamation-on-bears-ears-national -monument/; Deepa Shivaram, "Biden Restores Protections for Bears Ears Monument, 4 Years After Trump Downsized It," NPR, October 8, 2021, www.npr.org/2021/10/07/1044039889 /bears-ears-monument-protection -restored-biden (accessed 11/21/21).

2. Shivaram, "Biden Restores Protections."

3. These statutes are contained mainly in Title 10 of the U.S. Code, Sections 331, 332, and 333.

4. The best study covering all aspects of the domestic use of the military is that of Adam Yarmolinsky, *The Military Establishment* (New York: Harper and Row, 1971). Probably the most famous instance of a president's unilateral use of the power to protect a state "against domestic violence" was President Grover Cleveland's dealing with the Pullman strike of 1894. The famous Supreme Court case that ensued was *In re Debs*, 158 U.S. 564 (1895).

5. In *United States v. Pink*, 315 U.S. 203 (1942), the Supreme Court confirmed that an executive agreement is the

legal equivalent of a treaty, despite the absence of Senate approval. This case approved the executive agreement that was used to establish diplomatic relations with the Soviet Union in 1933. An executive agreement, not a treaty, was used in 1940 to exchange "fifty over-age destroyers" for 99-year leases on some important military bases.

6. *United States v. Nixon*, 418 U.S. 683 (1974); Mark J. Rozell, *Executive Privilege*, 3rd ed. (Lawrence: University Press of Kansas, 2010).

7. For a different perspective, see William F. Grover, *The President as Prisoner: A Structural Critique of the Carter and Reagan Years* (Albany: State University of New York Press, 1988).

8. A third source of presidential power is implied from the provision for "faithful execution of the laws." This is the president's power to impound funds—that is, to refuse to spend money Congress has appropriated for certain purposes. One author referred to this as a "retroactive veto power" (Robert E. Goostree, "The Power of the President to Impound Appropriated Funds," *American University Law Review* 11 [January 1962]: 32–47). This impoundment power has been used freely and to considerable effect by many modern presidents, and Congress has occasionally delegated such power to the president by statute. But in reaction to the Watergate scandal, Congress adopted the Congressional Budget and Impoundment Control Act of 1974, which was designed to circumscribe the president's ability to impound funds by requiring that the president spend all appropriated funds unless both houses of Congress consented to an impoundment within 45 days of a presidential request. Therefore, since 1974, the use of impoundment has declined significantly. Presidents have had either to bite their tongues and accept unwanted appropriations or to revert to the older and more dependable but politically limited method of vetoing the entire bill.

9. For more on the veto, see Robert J. Spitzer, *The Presidential Veto: Touchstone of the American Presidency* (Albany: State University of New York Press, 1989).

10. "Bush to Veto Congress Waterboarding Ban," National Public Radio, February 19, 2008, www.npr.org/2008/02/19/19168008/bush-to-veto-congress-waterboarding-ban (accessed 8/9/22).

11. John Yoo, *The Powers of War and Peace* (Chicago: University of Chicago Press, 2003). See also Dana D. Nelson, "The 'Unitary Executive' Question," *Los Angeles Times*, October 11, 2008, www.latimes.com/opinion/la-oe-nelson11-2008oct11-story.html (accessed 4/20/18).

12. See Eric Posner and Adrian Vermeule, *The Executive Unbound: After the Madisonian Republic* (Chicago: University of Chicago Press, 2011).

13. "Unchecked Abuse," *Washington Post*, January 11, 2006, www.washingtonpost.com/wp-dyn/content/article/2006/01/10/AR2006011001536.html (accessed 3/25/18).

14. Theodore J. Lowi, *The End of Liberalism*, 2nd ed. (New York: W. W. Norton, 1979), 117.

15. Louis Fisher, "The Unitary Executive and Inherent Executive Power," *Journal of Constitutional Law* 12, no. 1 (February 2010): 586.

16. Louis Fisher, "Invoking Inherent Powers: A Primer," *Presidential Studies Quarterly* 37, no. 1 (March 2007): 1–22.

17. John Gramlich, "Holder Sees Constitutional Basis for Obama's Executive Actions," Roll Call, January 29, 2014, www.rollcall.com/news/holder_sees_constitutional_basis_for_obamas_executive_actions-230528-1.html?pg=1 (accessed 4/20/18).

18. *Trump v. Hawaii*, 585 U.S. ___ (2018).

19. Harold C. Relyea, "National Emergency Powers," Congressional Research Service, 2007, http://fas.org/sgp/crs/natsec/98-505.pdf (accessed 3/27/18).

20. Matthew Crenson and Benjamin Ginsberg, *Presidential Power: Unchecked and Unbalanced* (New York: W. W. Norton, 2007), 341–42.

21. A substantial portion of this section is taken from Theodore J. Lowi, *The Personal President* (Ithaca, NY: Cornell University Press, 1985), 141–50.

22. The actual number is difficult to estimate because, as with White House staff, some EOP personnel, especially in

national security work, are detailed to the EOP from outside agencies.

23. Article I, Section 3, provides that "the Vice-President . . . shall be President of the Senate, but shall have no Vote, unless they be equally divided." This is the only vote the vice president is allowed.

24. Samuel Kernell, *Going Public: New Strategies of Presidential Leadership*, 3rd ed. (Washington, DC: CQ Press, 1997); also Jeffrey K. Tulis, *The Rhetorical Presidency* (Princeton, NJ: Princeton University Press, 1987).

25. James MacGregor Burns, *Roosevelt: The Lion and the Fox* (New York: Harcourt, Brace, 1956), 317.

26. Kernell, *Going Public*, 79.

27. Claire Cain Miller, "How Obama's Internet Campaign Changed Politics," *New York Times*, November 7, 2008, https://bits.blogs.nytimes.com/2008 /11/07/how-obamas-internet-campaign -changed-politics/ (accessed 4/7/14); David Plouffe, *The Audacity to Win: The Inside Story and Lessons of Barack Obama's Historic Victory* (New York: Viking, 2009).

28. "Presidential Job Approval Center," Gallup, https://news.gallup.com /interactives/185273/presidential -job-approval-center.aspx (accessed 3/14/14).

29. Lowi, *Personal President*.

30. Lowi, *Personal President*, 11.

31. "Presidential Job Approval Center."

32. Sidney M. Milkis, *The President and the Parties* (New York: Oxford University Press, 1993), 128.

33. Milkis, *President and the Parties*, 160.

34. Nadja Popovich, Livia Albeck-Ripka, and Kendra Pierre-Louis, "The Trump Administration Is Reversing Nearly 100 Environmental Rules. Here's the Full List," *New York Times*, October 15, 2020, www.nytimes.com/interactive /2019/climate/trump-environment -rollbacks.html (accessed 10/4/19).

35. Terry M. Moe and William G. Howell, "The Presidential Power of Unilateral Action," *Journal of Law, Economics, and Organization* 15, no. 1 (January 1999): 133–34.

36. Harold C. Relyea, "Presidential Directives: Background and Overview," Congressional Research Service, November 26, 2008, http://fas.org/sgp /crs/misc/98-611.pdf (accessed 3/25/18).

37. Adam L. Warber, *Executive Orders and the Modern Presidency* (Boulder, CO: Lynne Rienner Publishers, 2006), 118–20.

38. *Dames & Moore v. Regan*, 453 U.S. 654 (1981).

39. Philip Cooper, *By Order of the President* (Lawrence: University Press of Kansas, 2002), 201.

40. Edward S. Corwin, *The President: Office and Powers*, 5th ed. (New York: NYU Press, 1984), 283.

41. *National Labor Relations Board v. Noel Canning*, 573 U.S. 513 (2014).

CHAPTER 12

1. Annie Sneed, "Forever Chemicals Are Widespread in U.S. Drinking Water," *Scientific American*, January 22, 2021, www.scientificamerican.com/article /forever-chemicals-are-widespread-in -u-s-drinking-water/ (accessed 10/24/21).

2. Hannah Rappleye, David Douglas, and Anne Thompson, "A 'Forever Chemical' Contaminates Drinking Water near Military Bases," NBC News, December 16, 2019, www.nbcnews.com/health /cancer/forever-chemical-poisons -drinking-water-near-military-bases -n1101736 (accessed 10/24/21).

3. Sneed, "Forever Chemicals Are Widespread."

4. Justine McDaniel and Laura McCrystal, "Biden's EPA Plans to Tackle the 'Forever Chemicals' That Contaminated Drinking Water in Philly Region and U.S.," *Philadelphia Inquirer*, October 18, 2021, www.inquirer.com/news/pfas-epa -biden-chemicals-water-contamination -20211018.html (accessed 10/24/21).

5. Government Accountability Office, "Operation Warp Speed," GAO-21-319, February 11, 2021, www.gao.gov/products /gao-21-319 (accessed 10/27/21).

6. Amy B. Zegart, *Spying Blind: The CIA, the FBI, and the Origins of 9/11* (Princeton, NJ: Princeton University Press, 2009).

7. Paul C. Light, "A Cascade of Failures: Why Government Fails, and How to Stop It," Brookings Institution, July 14,

2014, www.brookings.edu/research
/a-cascade-of-failures-why-government
-fails-and-how-to-stop-it/ (accessed
8/5/17).

8. Thanks to Andy Rudalevige for this
   formulation.

9. Environmental Protection Agency,
   "Regulations for Emissions from
   Vehicles and Engines: Light-Duty
   Vehicle Greenhouse Gas Regulations
   and Standards," www.epa.gov
   /greenvehicles/light-duty-vehicle
   -greenhouse-gas-regulations-and
   -standards (accessed 7/9/16).

10. Anna M. Phillips, "Biden, Reversing
    Trump Order, Announces Tougher
    Car Pollution Standards," *Los Angeles
    Times*, August 5, 2021, www.latimes
    .com/politics/story/2021-08-05/biden
    -expected-to-reverse-trump-and
    -announce-tougher-car-pollution
    -standards (accessed 10/21/21).

11. Margaret Cronin Fisk et al., "Volkswagen
    Agrees to $15 Billion Diesel-Cheating
    Settlement," Bloomberg News, June 28,
    2016, www.bloomberg.com/news
    /articles/2016-06-28/volkswagen-to
    -pay-14-7-billion-to-settle-u-s-emissions
    -claims (accessed 7/8/16).

12. Gary Bryner, *Bureaucratic Discretion*
    (New York: Pergamon Press, 1987).

13. Nicholas Bagley, "Legal Limits and the
    Implementation of the Affordable Care
    Act," *University of Pennsylvania Law
    Review* 164, no. 7 (2016): 1715–52.

14. Li Zhou, "Many Small Businesses Are
    Being Shut Out of a New Loan Program
    by Major Banks," Vox, April 7, 2020,
    www.vox.com/2020/4/7/21209584
    /paycheck-protection-program-banks
    -access (accessed 5/4/20).

15. Alex Guillén, "Impact of Supreme
    Court's Climate Ruling Spreads," *Politico*,
    July 20, 2022, www.politico.com/news
    /2022/07/20/chill-from-scotus-climate
    -ruling-hits-wide-range-of-biden-actions
    -00045920 (accessed 8/17/22).

16. Office of Management and Budget,
    Historical Tables, "Table 16.2, Total
    Executive Branch Civilian Full-Time
    Equivalent (FTE) Employees, 1981–
    2020," www.whitehouse.gov/omb
    /historical-tables/ (accessed 12/12/19).

17. Congressional Research Service,
    "Selected Homeland Security Issues
    in the 116th Congress," November 26,
    2019, https://fas.org/sgp/crs/homesec
    /R45701.pdf (accessed 12/10/19).

18. For example, see Government Accountabil-
    ity Office, *High-Risk Series: Substantial
    Efforts Needed to Achieve Greater Prog-
    ress on High-Risk Areas*, March 2019,
    www.gao.gov/assets/700/697245.pdf
    (accessed 12/10/19).

19. In 2019, the Trump administration
    announced plans to dismantle the
    OPM. For more history, see David
    Rosenbloom, *Public Administration*
    (New York: Random House, 1986),
    186–221; Charles H. Levine and Rosslyn
    S. Kleeman, *The Quiet Crisis of the Civil
    Service: The Federal Personnel System
    at the Crossroads* (Washington, DC:
    National Academy of Public Adminis-
    tration, 1986).

20. David E. Lewis, "Patronage Appoint-
    ments in the Modern Presidency:
    Evidence from a Survey of Federal
    Executives," Vanderbilt University Center
    for the Study of Democratic Institutions,
    Working Paper 01-2009, www.vanderbilt
    .edu/csdi/research/files/CSDI-WP-01
    -2009.pdf (accessed 10/21/21).

21. Vice President Gore's National Partnership
    for Reinventing Government, "Appendix F,
    History of the National Partnership for
    Reinventing Government: Accomplish-
    ments, 1993–2000, A Summary," http://
    govinfo.library.unt.edu/npr/whoweare
    /appendixf.html (accessed 3/28/08).

22. President Barack Obama, First Inaugural
    Address, January 21, 2009, https://
    obamawhitehouse.archives.gov/blog
    /2009/01/21/president-barack-obamas
    -inaugural-address (accessed 8/5/17).

23. Kate Rogers, "USDA's Plan to Relocate
    Research Agencies to the Midwest
    Unleashes a Brain Drain," CNBC, July
    22, 2019, www.cnbc.com/2019/07/22
    /usdas-plan-to-move-research-agencies
    -to-midwest-starts-a-brain-drain.html
    (accessed 11/14/19).

24. Office of Personnel Management,
    "Executive Branch Civilian Employment
    Since 1940," www.opm.gov/policy-data
    -oversight/data-analysis-documentation
    /federal-employment-reports/historical
    -tables/executive-branch-civilian

-employment-since-1940/ (accessed 4/24/20); United States Postal Service, "Number of Postal Employees Since 1926," https://about.usps.com/who -we-are/postal-history/employees -since-1926.pdf (accessed 4/24/20); George M. Reynolds and Amanda Shendruk, "Demographics of the U.S. Military," Council on Foreign Relations, April 24, 2018, www.cfr.org/article /demographics-us-military (accessed 10/13/18).

25. Bureau of Labor Statistics, Current Employment Statistics, "Table B-1a, Employees on Nonfarm Payrolls by Industry Sector and Selected Industry Detail, Seasonally Adjusted," www.bls .gov/web/empsit/ceseeb1a.htm (accessed 4/21/20).

26. John J. Dilulio, Jr., *Bring Back the Bureaucrats: Why More Federal Work- ers Will Lead to Better (and Smaller!) Government* (West Conshohocken, PA: Templeton Press, 2014); Kimberly J. Morgan and Andrea Louise Campbell, *The Delegated Welfare State* (New York: Oxford University Press, 2011).

27. Jennifer L. Selin and David E. Lewis, *Sourcebook of United States Executive Agencies*, 2nd ed. (Washington, DC: Administrative Conference of the United States, 2018).

28. Richard E. Neustadt, *Presidential Power and the Modern Presidents: The Politics of Leadership from Roosevelt to Reagan* (New York: Free Press, 1990), 29.

29. Daniel P. Gitterman, *Calling the Shots: The President, Executive Orders, and Public Policy* (Washington, DC: Brookings Institution Press, 2017).

30. Brian Naylor, "Neera Tanden Withdraws as Nominee for Office of Management and Budget," NPR, March 2, 2021, www .npr.org/2021/03/02/970543130/tanden -withdraws-as-omb-nominee (accessed 10/21/21).

31. Selin and Lewis, *Sourcebook of United States Executive Agencies*, 21.

32. White House, "Statement from the Press Secretary Regarding the President's Coronavirus Task Force," January 29, 2020, https://trumpwhitehouse.archives .gov/briefings-statements/statement -press-secretary-regarding-presidents -coronavirus-task-force/ (accessed 5/4/20); Tarini Parti and Chad Day, "Biden's Task Forces Take on Covid-19, Climate Change," *Wall Street Journal*, February 13, 2021, www.wsj.com/articles /bidens-task-forces-take-on-covid-19 -climate-change-11613228400 (accessed 10/21/21).

33. Selin and Lewis, *Sourcebook of United States Executive Agencies*, 27.

34. David M. Cohen, "Amateur Government: When Political Appointees Manage the Federal Bureaucracy," CPM Working Paper 96-1, Brookings Institution, 1996, www.brookings.edu/wp-content/uploads /2016/06/amateur.pdf (accessed 12/12/19).

35. William G. Howell, *An American Presidency: Institutional Foundations of Executive Politics* (Boston: Pearson, 2015).

36. Selin and Lewis, *Sourcebook of United States Executive Agencies*, 34.

37. Food and Drug Administration, "Learn about FDA Advisory Committees," June 21, 2018, www.fda.gov/patients/learn-about -patient-affairs-staff/learn-about-fda -advisory-committees (accessed 12/12/19).

38. Will Feuer, "Nursing Homes with More Minority Residents Had 3 Times as Many Covid Deaths as Those with More Whites, Study Finds," CNBC, February 10, 2021, www.cnbc.com/2021/02/10 /nursing-homes-with-more-minority -residents-had-more-covid-deaths -study.html (accessed 10/21/21); Blaire Bryant and Sarah Gimont, "Senate Finance Committee Holds Hearings on COVID-19 in Nursing Homes as CMS Eases Visitation Guidelines," National Association of Counties blog, March 23, 2021, www.naco.org/blog/senate -finance-committee-holds-hearing -covid-19-nursing-homes-cms-eases -visitation-guidance (accessed 10/21/21); see Mathew D. McCubbins and Thomas Schwartz, "Congressional Oversight Overlooked: Police Patrols versus Fire Alarms," *American Journal of Political Science* 28, no. 1 (1984): 165–79.

39. Charlie Savage and Peter Baker, "Trump Ousts Pandemic Spending Watchdog Known for Independence," *New York Times*, April 7, 2020, www.nytimes .com/2020/04/07/us/politics/trump -coronavirus-watchdog-glenn-fine.html

(accessed 3/16/22); Peter Baker, "Trump Moves to Replace Watchdog Who Identified Critical Medical Shortages," *New York Times*, May 4, 2020, www .nytimes.com/2020/05/01/us/politics /trump-health-department-watchdog .html (accessed 8/11/22).

40. Government Accountability Office, "About GAO," www.gao.gov/about/ (accessed 12/8/19).

41. Congressional Research Service, "About CRS," www.loc.gov/crsinfo /about/ (accessed 12/8/19).

42. Congressional Budget Office, "Introduction to CBO," www.cbo.gov/about /overview (accessed 12/8/19).

43. Consumer Financial Protection Bureau, "Creating the Consumer Bureau," www.consumerfinance.gov/about-us /the-bureau/creatingthebureau/ (accessed 12/7/19); "How the Consumer Financial Protection Bureau Came into Creation," NPR, November 28, 2017, www.npr.org/2017/11/28/567057893 /how-the-consumer-financial-protection -bureau-came-into-creation (accessed 12/7/19).

44. Andrew Prokop, "Read: The Whistleblower Complaint about Trump and Ukraine," Vox, September 26, 2019, www.vox.com/2019/9/26/20884022 /whistleblower-complaint-trump -ukraine-read (accessed 11/14/19).

45. See Aram A. Gavoor and Daniel Miktus, "Oversight of Oversight: A Proposal for More Effective FOIA Reform," *Catholic University Law Review* 66, no. 3 (Spring 2017): 528.

46. Alison Young, "Congress Demands Details of Secret CDC Lab Incidents Revealed by *USA Today*," *USA Today*, January 17, 2017, www.usatoday.com /story/news/2017/01/17/congress-wants -details-of-cdc-lab-accidents/96551636/ (accessed 11/14/19).

47. U.S. Department of Veterans Affairs, "Veterans Access, Choice, and Accountability Act of 2014 Fact Sheet," www.va .gov/opa/choiceact/documents/choice -act-summary.pdf (accessed 8/6/17).

48. Dominic Gates, "Flawed Analysis, Failed Oversight: How Boeing, FAA Certified the Suspect 737 MAX Flight Control System," *Seattle Times*, March 17, 2019, www.seattletimes.com /business/boeing-aerospace/failed -certification-faa-missed-safety-issues -in-the-737-max-system-implicated-in -the-lion-air-crash/ (accessed 11/4/19).

49. Selin and Lewis, *Sourcebook of United States Executive Agencies*, 85–87.

CHAPTER 13

1. This account based on Executive Order No. GA-38 Relating to the Continued Response to the Covid-19 Disaster, July 29, 2021, https://gov.texas.gov /uploads/files/press/EO-GA-38_continued _response_to_the_COVID-19_disaster _IMAGE_07-29-2021.pdf; Disability Rights Texas, "Mask Mandate Ban Violates Federal Law," press release, November 10, 2021, www.disabilityrightstx .org/en/press_release/federal-lawsuit -texas-mask-mandate-ban; Reis Thebault and Timothy Bella, "Texas Schools Can Require Masks after Federal Judge Overturns Abbott's Ban," *Washington Post*, November 11, 2021; Daniel Marin, "Resolution to Texas School Mask Battle 'Could Take Months' Despite Ruling," KXAN, November 11, 2021, www.kxan .com/news/texas/resolution-to-texas -school-mask-battle-could-take-months -despite-ruling/ (accessed 11/13/21).

2. U.S. Courts Statistical Tables, www .uscourts.gov/statistics-reports/analysis -reports/statistical-tables-federal -judiciary (accessed 5/27/22).

3. For limits on judicial power, see Alexander Bickel, *The Least Dangerous Branch* (Indianapolis, IN: Bobbs-Merrill, 1962).

4. *Worcester v. Georgia*, 31 U.S. 515 (1832).

5. Martin Shapiro, "The Supreme Court: From Warren to Burger," in *The New American Political System*, ed. Anthony King (Washington, DC: American Enterprise Institute, 1978).

6. See "Developments in the Law—Class Actions," *Harvard Law Review* 89 (1976): 1318.

7. Donald Horowitz, *The Courts and Social Policy* (Washington, DC: Brookings Institution Press, 1977).

8. Michael A. Fletcher, "Obama Criticized as Too Cautious, Slow on Judicial Posts," *Washington Post*, October 16, 2009, www.washingtonpost.com/wp-dyn

/content/article/2009/10/15/AR200910 1504083.html (accessed 3/1/10).

9. Brandon Bartels, "It Took Conservatives 50 Years to Get a Reliable Majority on the Supreme Court. Here Are Three Reasons Why," *Washington Post*, June 29, 2018, www.washingtonpost.com/news /monkey-cage/wp/2018/06/29/it-took -conservatives-50-years-to-get-a-reliable -majority-on-the-supreme-court-here -are-3-reasons-why/ (accessed 12/3/21).

10. John Bowden, "Timeline: Brett Kavanaugh's Nomination to the Supreme Court," The Hill, October 6, 2018, https://thehill .com/homenews/senate/410217-timeline -brett-kavanaughs-nomination-to -the-supreme-court (accessed 10/16/18).

11. *Marbury v. Madison*, 5 U.S. 137 (1803).

12. *National Federation of Independent Business v. Sebelius*, 567 U.S. 519 (2012).

13. "Acts of Congress Held Unconstitutional in Whole or in Part by the Supreme Court of the United States," General Printing Office, www.gpo.gov/fdsys /pkg/GPO-CONAN-2013/pdf/GPO -CONAN-2013-11.pdf (accessed 4/20/14).

14. This review power was affirmed by the Supreme Court in *Martin v. Hunter's Lessee*, 14 U.S. 304 (1816).

15. *United States v. Jones*, 565 U.S. 400 (2012).

16. *Riley v. California*, 573 U.S. 373 (2014).

17. Michael A. Genovese and Robert J. Spitzer, *The Presidency and the Constitution* (New York: Palgrave Macmillan, 2005).

18. *Hamdi v. Rumsfeld*, 542 U.S. 507 (2004).

19. *National Labor Relations Board v. Noel Canning*, 573 U.S. 513 (2014).

20. *Trump v. Hawaii*, 585 U.S. ___ (2018).

21. *Roe v. Wade*, 410 U.S. 113 (1973).

22. Robert Scigliano, *The Supreme Court and the Presidency* (New York: Free Press, 1971), 162. For an interesting critique of the solicitor general's role during the Reagan administration, see Lincoln Caplan, "Annals of the Law," *New Yorker*, August 17, 1987, 30–62.

23. Edward Lazarus, *Closed Chambers* (New York: Times Books, 1998), 6.

24. Sarah Isgur, "The New Trend Keeping Women Out of the Country's Top Legal Ranks," Politico, May 5, 2021, www .politico.com/news/magazine/2021 /05/04/women-supreme-court-clerkships -485249 (accessed 12/3/21).

25. *Smith v. Allwright*, 321 U.S. 649 (1944).

26. Jeffrey A. Segal and Harold J. Spaeth, *The Supreme Court and the Attitudinal Model Revisited* (New York: Cambridge University Press, 2002).

27. *McCutcheon v. Federal Election Commission*, 572 U.S. 185 (2014).

28. Charles Krauthammer, "Why Roberts Did It," *Washington Post*, June 29, 2012, www.washingtonpost.com/opinions /charles-krauthammer-why-roberts -did-it/2012/06/28/gJQA4X0g9V _story.html (accessed 4/22/14).

29. *Dobbs v. Jackson Women's Health Organization*, 597 U.S. ___ (2022).

30. Alexander Hamilton, James Madison, and John Jay, *The Federalist Papers*, no. 10, 78, ed. Clinton Rossiter (New York: New American Library, 1961).

CHAPTER 14

1. Ben Casselman, "Child Tax Credit's Extra Help Ends, Just as Covid Surges Anew," *New York Times*, January 2, 2022, www.nytimes.com/2022/01/02 /business/economy/child-tax-credit .html (accessed 1/28/22).

2. Casselman, "Child Tax Credit's Extra Help Ends."

3. Half of the year-long tax credit was distributed monthly over the last six months of 2021, and the other half was distributed to eligible households in a lump sum after they filed their 2021 taxes in early 2022.

4. Casselman, "Child Tax Credit's Extra Help Ends."

5. Alfred Lubrano, "What Happened to Those in Poverty with the Child Tax Credit Expansion Ended?," *Philadelphia Inquirer*, January 9, 2022, www.inquirer .com/news/philadelphia/child-tax-credit -expansion-biden-administration-poverty -20220109.html (accessed 1/28/22).

6. Tax Foundation, "2022 Tax Brackets," November 10, 2021, https://taxfoundation .org/2022-tax-brackets/ (accessed 5/30/22).

7. There is an additional 1.45 percent tax on all income without limit that funds Medicare benefits, and an additional 0.9 percent Medicare tax for high earners (individuals earning over $200,000 and

couples earning over $250,000) that was introduced by the Affordable Care Act.

8. The *Federal Register* is the daily publication of all official acts of Congress, the president, and the administrative agencies. A law or executive order is not legally binding until it is published in the *Federal Register*.

9. Ronald Reagan, Inaugural Address, January 20, 1981, www.presidency.ucsb .edu/documents/inaugural-address-11 (accessed 4/27/14).

10. Pew Research Center, July 8–18, 2021 poll, https://ropercenter.cornell.edu /ipoll/study/31118536/questions#2a97 d8a9-aa81-4d18-83cf-3d8e954c8876 (accessed 1/8/22).

11. Pew Research Center, "As Sequester Deadline Looms, Little Support for Cutting Most Programs," U.S. Politics & Policy, February 22, 2013, www.people -press.org/2013/02/22/as-sequester -deadline-looms-little-support-for -cutting-most-programs/ (accessed 4/27/14).

12. See, for example, Paul Krugman, "The Bankruptcy Boys," *New York Times*, February 21, 2010, www.nytimes.com /2010/02/22/opinion/22krugman .html?_r50 (accessed 4/27/14).

13. Office of Management and Budget, Historical Table 8.3, "Percentage Distribution of Outlays by Budget Enforcement Act Category: 1962–2026," www.whitehouse.gov/omb/historical -tables/ (accessed 3/11/22).

14. Pew Research Center, "Section 2: Government, Regulation, and the Social Safety Net," U.S. Politics & Policy, October 5, 2017, www.people-press.org /2017/10/05/2-government-regulation -and-the-social-safety-net/ (accessed 10/6/17).

15. "Executive Order on Increasing the Minimum Wage for Federal Contractors," April 27, 2021, www.whitehouse.gov /briefing-room/presidential-actions /2021/04/27/executive-order-on-increasing -the-minimum-wage-for-federal -contractors/ (accessed 1/7/22).

16. Amina Dunn, "Most Americans Support a $15 Federal Minimum Wage," Pew Research Center, April 22, 2021, www .pewresearch.org/fact-tank/2021/04/22 /most-americans-support-a-15-federal -minimum-wage/ (accessed 1/8/22).

17. Economic Policy Institute, "Minimum Wage Tracker," January 1, 2022, www .epi.org/minimum-wage-tracker/ (accessed 1/7/22).

18. Social Security Administration, "Contribution and Benefit Base," www.ssa.gov /oact/cola/cbb.html (accessed 1/23/22).

19. Social Security Administration, "Social Security Fact Sheet: 2022 Social Security Changes," www.ssa.gov/news /press/factsheets/colafacts2022.pdf (accessed 1/23/22).

20. John R. Kearney, "Social Security and the 'D' in OASDI: The History of a Federal Program Insuring Earners against Disability," *Social Security Bulletin* 66, no. 3 (2006), www.ssa.gov /policy/docs/ssb/v66n3/v66n3p1.html (accessed 6/7/17).

21. Workers must have lost their job through no fault of their own. For a full description of the program, see Chad Stone and William Chen, "Introduction to Unemployment Insurance," Center on Budget and Policy Priorities, July 30, 2014, www.cbpp.org/research /introduction-to-unemployment -insurance (accessed 11/18/15).

22. Ali Safawi and Cindy Reyes, "States Must Continue Recent Momentum to Further Improve TANF Benefit Levels," Center on Budget and Policy Priorities, December 2, 2021, www.cbpp.org /research/family-income-support /states-must-continue-recent-momentum -to-further-improve-tanf-benefit (accessed 1/27/22).

23. Department of Health and Human Services, Office of the Assistant Secretary for Planning and Evaluation, "HHS Poverty Guidelines for 2022," https:// aspe.hhs.gov/topics/poverty-economic -mobility/poverty-guidelines (accessed 1/27/22).

24. Center on Budget and Policy Priorities, "State Fact Sheets: Trends in State TANF-to-Poverty Ratios," November 30, 2020, www.cbpp.org/research /family-income-support/state-fact -sheets-trends-in-state-tanf-to-poverty -ratios (accessed 3/6/22).

25. Suzanne Mettler, *The Submerged Welfare State* (Chicago: University of Chicago Press, 2011); Christopher

Faricy, *Welfare for the Wealthy* (New York: Cambridge University Press, 2015).

26. U.S. Congress, Joint Committee on Taxation, "Estimates of Federal Tax Expenditures for Fiscal Years 2016–2020," January 30, 2017, www.jct.gov/publications .html?func=startdown&id=4971 (accessed 5/29/17). Note that there are tax breaks in the corporate tax code as well, but the tax breaks for individuals and households account for about 80 percent of the total.

27. New America Foundation, "Federal, State and Local K–12 School Finance Overview," June 29, 2015, http://atlas .newamerica.org/school-finance (accessed 7/10/16).

28. David K. Cohen and Susan L. Moffitt, *The Ordeal of Equality: Did Federal Regulation Fix the Schools?* (Cambridge, MA: Harvard University Press, 2009).

29. For a positive view of the standards, see Sonja Brookins Santelises, "Abandoning the Common Core Is Taking the Easy Way Out," *Equity Line* (blog), March 31, 2014, https://edtrust.org/the-equity -line/abandoning-the-common-core -is-taking-the-easy-way-out/ (accessed 4/3/18); for a critique see Valerie Strauss, "The Coming Common Core Meltdown," *Washington Post*, January 23, 2014, www.washingtonpost.com /blogs/answer-sheet/wp/2014/01/23 /the-coming-common-core-meltdown (accessed 5/11/14).

30. Valerie Strauss, "The Successor to No Child Left Behind Has, It Turns Out, Big Problems of Its Own," *Washington Post*, December 7, 2015, www .washingtonpost.com/news/answer-sheet /wp/2015/12/07/the-successor-to-no -child-left-behind-has-it-turns-out-big -problems-of-its-own/ (accessed 7/11/16).

31. Erica L. Green, "Private and Religious School Backers See Broad Victory in Supreme Court Decision," *New York Times*, July 1, 2020, www.nytimes .com/2020/07/01/us/politics/private -religious-schools-supreme-court.html (accessed 7/14/20).

32. Jaison R. Abel and Richard Deitz, "Despite Rising Costs, College Is Still a Good Investment," Federal Reserve Bank of New York, June 5, 2019, https:// libertystreeteconomics.newyorkfed .org/2019/06/despite-rising-costs -college-is-still-a-good-investment.html (accessed 5/12/20).

33. College Board, *Trends in Student Aid 2019*, November 2019, 28, https:// research.collegeboard.org/pdf/trends -student-aid-2019-full-report.pdf (accessed 12/15/19).

34. The Institute for College Access and Success, *Student Debt and the Class of 2018*, September 2019, https://ticas .org/wp-content/uploads/2019/09 /classof2018.pdf (accessed 12/16/19).

35. Henry J. Kaiser Family Foundation, "Total Monthly Medicaid and CHIP Enrollment," www.kff.org/health -reform/state-indicator/total-monthly -medicaid-and-chip-enrollment (accessed 1/30/22).

36. Henry J. Kaiser Family Foundation, *Medicaid: A Primer—Key Information on the Nation's Health Coverage Program for Low-Income People*, March 1, 2013, 26, www.kff.org/medicaid/issue -brief/medicaid-a-primer/ (accessed 6/2/16).

37. U.S. Department of Health and Human Services, "HHS Poverty Guidelines for 2022," https://aspe.hhs.gov/topics /poverty-economic-mobility/poverty -guidelines (accessed 5/30/22).

38. *National Federation of Independent Businesses v. Sebelius*, 567 U.S. 519 (2012).

39. Kaiser Family Foundation, "Status of State Action on the Medicaid Expansion Decision," October 1, 2020, www.kff .org/health-reform/state-indicator /state-activity-around-expanding -medicaid-under-the-affordable -care-act (accessed 10/12/20).

40. Jennifer Steinhauer, "House Votes to Send Bill to Repeal Health Law to Obama's Desk," *New York Times*, January 6, 2016, www.nytimes.com /2016/01/07/us/politics/house-votes-to -send-bill-to-repeal-health-law-to -obamas-desk.html (accessed 7/11/16).

41. Maureen Groppe, "Record 14.5 Million Americans Sign Up for Obamacare During Open Enrollment for 2022 Plans," *USA Today*, January 27, 2022, www.usatoday.com/story/news/politics /2022/01/27/biden-touts-record

-obamacare-enrollment-14-5-million/9234349002/ (accessed 1/27/22).

42. James Krieger and Donna L. Higgins, "Housing and Health: Time Again for Public Health Action," *American Journal of Public Health* 92, no. 5 (May 2002): 758–68.

43. John E. Schwarz, *America's Hidden Success*, 2nd ed. (New York: W. W. Norton, 1988), 41–42.

44. Congressional Budget Office, *Federal Housing Assistance for Low-Income Households*, September 2015, www.cbo.gov/sites/default/files/114th-congress-2015-2016/reports/50782-lowincomehousing-onecolumn.pdf (accessed 5/29/17).

45. National Low Income Housing Coalition, *FY22 Budget Chart for Selected HUD and USDA Programs*, October 18, 2021, https://nlihc.org/sites/default/files/NLIHC_HUD-USDA_Budget-Chart_FY22.pdf (accessed 1/27/22); Joint Committee on Taxation, "Estimates of Federal Tax Expenditures, for Fiscal Years 2020–2024," www.jct.gov/publications/2020/jcx-23-20/ (accessed 1/27/22).

46. Chloe N. Thurston, *At the Boundaries of Homeownership: Credit, Discrimination, and the American State* (New York: Cambridge University Press, 2018).

47. Trymaine Lee, "A Vast Wealth Gap, Driven by Segregation, Redlining, Evictions and Exclusion, Separates Black and White America," *New York Times Magazine*, August 14, 2019, www.nytimes.com/interactive/2019/08/14/magazine/racial-wealth-gap.html (accessed 12/16/19).

48. U.S. Census Bureau, "Income and Poverty in the United States: 2020," September 2021, Figure 8, www.census.gov/library/publications/2021/demo/p60-273.html (accessed 1/27/22).

49. U.S. Census Bureau, "Income and Poverty in the United States," Figure 1.

50. U.S. Census Bureau, "Income and Poverty in the United States," Table B-5.

51. U.S. Census Bureau, "Quick Facts: United States 2021," www.census.gov/quickfacts/fact/table/US/PST045221 (accessed 1/27/22).

52. AARP, *Annual Report 2020*, www.aarp.org/content/dam/aarp/about_aarp/annual_reports/2021/2020-aarp-annual-report.pdf (accessed 1/27/22); Center for Responsive Politics, "AARP Profile: Summary," www.opensecrets.org/orgs/aarp/summary?id=D000023726 (accessed 1/27/22); AARP, "Public Policy Institute Experts," www.aarp.org/ppi/experts/ (accessed 1/27/22).

53. Christopher Howard, *The Hidden Welfare State: Tax Expenditures and Social Policy in the United States* (Princeton, NJ: Princeton University Press, 1999).

54. U.S. Congress Joint Committee on Taxation, "Estimates of Federal Tax Expenditures for Fiscal Years 2020–2024," www.jct.gov/publications/2020/jcx-23-20/ (accessed 1/24/22).

55. Center on Budget and Policy Priorities, "A Quick Guide to SNAP Eligibility and Benefits," January 6, 2022, www.cbpp.org/research/food-assistance/a-quick-guide-to-snap-eligibility-and-benefits (accessed 1/24/22).

56. Rachel Garfield, Kendal Orgera, and Anthony Damico, "The Coverage Gap: Uninsured Poor Adults in States That Do Not Expand Medicaid," Kaiser Family Foundation, March 21, 2019, www.kff.org/medicaid/issue-brief/the-coverage-gap-uninsured-poor-adults-in-states-that-do-not-expand-medicaid/ (accessed 12/15/19).

57. U.S. Census Bureau, "Income and Poverty in the United States: 2020," Figure 9, Figure 1, and Table B-9.

58. Thurston, *At the Boundaries of Homeownership;* Jamila Michener, *Fragmented Democracy: Medicaid, Federalism, and Unequal Politics* (New York: Cambridge University Press, 2018); Matthew Desmond, *Evicted: Poverty and Profit in the American City* (New York: Crown, 2016); Monique W. Morris, *Black Stats: African Americans by the Numbers in the Twenty-First Century* (New York: New Press, 2014).

59. U.S. Census Bureau, "Income and Poverty in the United States: 2020," Table B-5.

60. For an argument that children should be given the vote, see Paul E. Peterson, "An Immodest Proposal," *Daedalus* 121, no. 4 (Fall 1992): 151–74.

CHAPTER 15

1. This account is based on Deborah Lockridge, "Intermodal Chassis Tariffs: 'Timing Couldn't Be Worse,'" HDT Trucking Info, May 7, 2021, www.truckinginfo.com/10142921/intermodal-chassis-tariffs-timing-couldnt-be-worse (accessed 12/10/21); Juliana Tornabene, "Stoughton Manufacturer Cites Labor Shortage for Wage Increase Decision," WMTV NBC15.com, September 21, 2021, www.nbc15.com/2021/09/21/stoughton-manufacturer-cites-labor-shortage-wage-increase-decision/ (accessed 12/10/21); and Binyamin Appelbaum, "Trump Wanted to Punish China. We're Still Paying for It," *New York Times*, November 24, 2021, www.nytimes.com/2021/11/24/opinion/trucking-trump-biden-tariffs.html (accessed 11/26/21).

2. Lockridge, "Intermodal Chassis Tariffs."

3. Rupert Smith, *The Utility of Force: The Art of War in the Modern World* (New York: Vintage, 2008).

4. D. Robert Worley, *Shaping U.S. Military Forces: Revolution or Relevance in a Post–Cold War World* (Westport, CT: Praeger Security International, 2006).

5. Colin S. Gray, "The Implications of Pre-emptive and Preventive War Doctrines," Strategic Studies Institute, July 2007, www.jstor.org/stable/resrep11587#metadata_info_tab_contents (accessed 8/1/14).

6. Kelebogile Zvobgo and Meredith Loken, "Why Race Matters in International Relations," *Foreign Policy*, June 19, 2020, https://foreignpolicy.com/2020/06/19/why-race-matters-international-relations-ir/ (accessed 11/26/21).

7. Kurt M. Campbell and James B. Steinberg, *Difficult Transitions: Foreign Policy Troubles at the Outset of Presidential Power* (Washington, DC: Brookings Institution Press, 2008).

8. U.S. Senate, "Treaties," www.senate.gov/artandhistory/history/common/briefing/Treaties.htm (accessed 4/15/18).

9. P. D. Miller, "Organizing the National Security Council: I Like Ike's," *Presidential Studies Quarterly* 43, no. 3 (2013): 592–606.

10. Ivo H. Daalder and I. M. Destler, *In the Shadow of the Oval Office: Profiles of the National Security Advisers and the Presidents They Served* (New York: Simon and Schuster, 2009).

11. Department of Defense, "About," January 27, 2017, www.defense.gov/About/ (accessed 7/23/18).

12. Mark Riebling, *Wedge: From Pearl Harbor to 9/11* (New York: Touchstone, 2002).

13. Benjamin Ginsberg, *The Worth of War* (New York: Prometheus Books, 2014), chap. 5.

14. Alexander Hamilton, James Madison, and John Jay, *The Federalist Papers*, ed. Clinton L. Rossiter (New York: New American Library, 1961; repr., New York: Signet Classics, 2003), no. 418 (Signet edition).

15. For information on current U.S. sanctions programs, visit U.S. Department of the Treasury, "Sanctions Programs and Country Information," www.treasury.gov/resource-center/sanctions/Programs/Pages/Programs.aspx (accessed 6/1/14).

16. Loveday Morris, "Yazidis Who Suffered Genocide Are Fleeing Again," *Washington Post*, March 21, 2017, www.washingtonpost.com/world/middle_east/yazidis-who-suffered-genocide-are-fleeing-again-but-this-time-not-from-the-islamic-state/2017/03/21/6392fe26-0353-11e7-9d14-9724d48f5666_story.html?noredirect=on&utm_term=.c2dbf2c8c6a1 (accessed 4/15/18).

17. Scott Shane and Mark Mazzetti, "Inside a Three-Year Russian Campaign to Influence U.S. Voters," *New York Times*, February 16, 2018, www.nytimes.com/2018/02/16/us/politics/russia-mueller-election.html (accessed 4/15/18).

18. Shane and Mazzetti, "Inside a Three-Year Russian Campaign to Influence U.S. Voters."

19. Elias Groll, "Feds Quietly Reveal Chinese State-Backed Hacking Operation," *Foreign Policy*, November 30, 2017, www.foreignpolicy.com/2017/11/30/feds-quietly-reveal-chinese-state-backed-hacking-operation/ (accessed 4/15/18).

20. Jonathan Watts and Kate Connolly, "World Leaders React after Trump Rejects Paris Climate Deal," *The Guardian*, June 1, 2017, www.theguardian.com/environment/2017/jun/01/trump-withdraw-paris-climate-deal-world-leaders-react (accessed 4/15/18).

Credits

PHOTOGRAPHS

Chapter 1: Page 2: Erin Scott/Bloomberg via Getty Images; p. 4: Scott Takushi/MediaNews Group/St. Paul Pioneer Press via Getty Images; p. 8: Bettmann/Corbis via Getty Images; p. 9: Reproduced by permission of The Economist Intelligence Unit; p. 11: REUTERS/Evelyn Hockstein/Alamy Stock Photo; p. 22: FREDERIC J. BROWN/AFP via Getty Images; p. 23: B Christopher/Alamy Stock Photo; p. 24: Courtesy of April Lawson; p. 29: Scott Takushi/Media News Group/St. Paul Pioneer Press via Getty.

Chapter 2: Page 30: Chip Somodevilla/Getty Images; p. 32: Nancy Siesel/ZUMA Press/Newscom; p. 35: IanDagnall Computing/Alamy Stock Photo; p. 40: Sarin Images/Granger, NYC — All rights reserved.; p. 42: The History Collection/Alamy Stock Photo; p. 45: Samuel Jennings (active 1789-1834). Liberty Displaying the Arts and Sciences or The Genius of America Encouraging the Emancipation of the Blacks, 1792. Oil on canvas. 60 1/4" x 74". Library Company of Philadelphia. Gift of the artist, 1792.; p. 61: Bryan Olin Dozier/NurPhoto/Shutterstock; p. 62: Nancy Siesel/ZUMA Press/Newscom.

Chapter 3: Page 64: Sergio Flores/Bloomberg via Getty Images; p. 66: Courtesy of Britney Hyman; p. 71: Christian Petersen/Getty Images; p. 74: Courtesy of Domingo Morel; p. 75: Derek Davis/Portland Portland Press Herald via Getty Images; p. 85: Ilene MacDonald/Alamy Stock Photo; p. 89: AP Photo/Skip Foreman; p. 91: Courtesy of Britney Hyman.

Chapter 4: Page 92: Maren Hennemuth/picture alliance via Getty Images; p. 94: Danna Singer; p. 101: Meegan M. Reid/Kitsap Sun via AP; p. 106: Clay Good/ZUMA Press; p. 111: Brandon Bell/Getty Images; p. 116: Bettmann/Getty Images; p. 123: Danna Singer.

Chapter 5: Page 124: GHI Vintage/Universal History Archive/Universal Images Group via Getty Images; p. 126: SCOTT MCINTYRE/The New York Times/Redux; p. 128 (left): REUTERS/Alamy Stock Photo; p. 128 (right): Okamoto/Interim Archives/Getty Images; p. 129 (left): Bettmann Archive/Getty Images; p. 129 (right): Paul Morigi/Getty Images for HRC; p. 132 (left): Lanmas/Alamy Stock Photo; p. 132 (right): Historic Collection/Alamy Stock Photo; p. 137: Bettmann/Getty Images; p. 146: Eliot Elisofon/The LIFE Picture Collection/Shutterstock; p. 150: Alex Wong/Getty Images; p. 154: Kent Sievers/The World-Herald via AP; p. 155: Stephanie Keith/Getty Images; p. 157 (left): Nicolaus Czarnecki/METRO US/ZUMAPRESS.com/Alamy Live News; p. 157 (right): Joe Raedle/Getty Images; p. 159: SCOTT MCINTYRE/The New York Times/Redux.

Chapter 6: Page 160: GEORGE FREY/AFP via Getty Images; p. 162 (left): Jay Mallin/ZUMAPRESS.com/Alamy live news; p. 162 (right): Tom Brenner/The New York Times/Redux; p. 171: REUTERS/Alamy Stock Photo; p. 176 (left): Everett Collection Historical/Alamy Stock Photo; p. 176 (right): Twitter/@realDonaldTrump; p. 180: CALVIN AND HOBBES © 1994 Watterson. Reprinted with permission of Andrews McMeel Syndication. All rights reserved.; p. 186: Courtesy of Neil Newhouse/Public Opinions Strategies; p. 187: Courtesy of American Broadcasting Company, Inc.; p. 188 (left): Bettmann/Getty Images; p. 188 (right): Lionel Hahn/ABACAPRESS.com/Sipa via AP Images; p. 189 (left): Jay Mallin/ZUMAPRESS.com/Alamy live news; p. 189 (right): Tom Brenner/The New York Times/Redux.

Chapter 7, America Side by Side (p. 199): Adapted from Global Press Freedom in Peril from Freedom and the Media 2019, Media Freedom: A Downward Spiral, by Sarah Repucci. © 2019 Freedom House. Reprinted by permission of Freedom House.

Chapter 7, Who Are Americans (p. 211): Charts adapted from "More than eight-in-ten Americans get news from digital devices," Pew Research Center, Washington, DC (January 2021) https://www.pewresearch.org/fact-tank/2021/01/12/more-than-eight-in-ten-americans-get-news-from-digital-devices/.

Figure 7.2 (p. 215): Chart adapted from "Broad agreement in U.S. – even among partisans – on which news outlets are part of the 'mainstream media,'" Pew Research Center, Washington, DC (May 2021) https://www.pewresearch.org/fact-tank/2021/05/07/broad-agreement-in-u-s-even-among-partisans-on-which-news-outlets-are-part-of-the-mainstream-media/.

Figure 8.3 (p. 243): Graph reprinted by permission of Catalist from "What Happened in 2020." By Yair Ghitza and Jonathan Robinson. Interactive Data Visualizations by Chase Stolworthy, Edited by Aaron Huertas, Site design by Melissa Amarawardana. https://catalist.us/wh-national/.

Glossary / Index

1954 Supreme Court decision that struck down the "separate but equal" doctrine as fundamentally unequal; this case eliminated state power to use race as a criterion of discrimination in law and provided the national government with the power to intervene by exercising strict regulatory policies against discriminatory actions

Buckley v. Valeo, 285, 286

Budget and Accounting Act (1921), 350

budget deficit, 443, 452 the amount by which government spending exceeds government revenue in a fiscal year

budget process, 331–32
See also government spending
congressional oversight and, 338
congressional "power of the purse" and, 331, 488
foreign policy and, 488, 489
presidency and, 350, 359, 365, 445

"Build Back Better (BBB)" Plan, 360

burden of proof, 130, 143, 152 the responsibility of an individual, organization, or government to provide sufficient evidence in support of a claim in court

bureaucracy the complex structure of offices, tasks, rules, and principles of organization that is employed by all large-scale institutions to coordinate the work of their personnel
See also Executive Office of the President;

government regulation; *specific agencies, e.g. Food and Drug Administration*
administrative law and, 406
agency creation, 366
civil rights and, 136, 139
Congress and, 365, 422
congressional staff agencies, 256, 322
delegated powers of, 354, 422
Department of Defense and, 487
employment in, 140, 152, 445
foreign policy and, 488
independent agencies, 358, 446
intelligence agencies and, 489–90
judicial review and, 422
privatization and, 445
rule-making, 256, 259, 354, 365–66, 406
size of, 358, 365
Supreme Court and, 414, 422, 427

Burke, Tarana, 144

Burwell v. Hobby Lobby Stores, 101–2

Bush, George H. W., 355, 433, 488

Bush, George W., and administration
ballots and, 277, 280
education policy and, 68, 459
election of 2000 and, 244, 277, 280, 288
foreign policy and, 478
inherent powers and, 355
Iraq War and, 364
judicial review and, 422
micro-targeting and, 288
Muslim Americans and, 155
September 11, 2001, terrorist attacks and, 68, 350, 364, 488

Supreme Court appointments and, 433
tax policy and, 443
unitary executive theory and, 352
veto and, 350–51
voter mobilization, 290

Bush, Maggie, 278

Bush Doctrine, 478, **483** foreign policy based on the idea that the United States should take preemptive action against threats to its national security

business interests
See also employment; financial industry; wealthy Americans, influence of
American Revolution and, 34
Articles of Confederation and, 40
congressional decision-making and, 435
corporate taxes, 181, 232, 441, 443
corruption and, 194
federalism and, 78
foreign policy and, 490
government regulation and, 78, 447, 452–53
influence of, 259
interest groups for, 247, 252, 253, 259
lobbying by, 222, 223, 247, 435
media ownership, 198, 200, 207, 210, 219
media profit motives, 197–98, 200, 210, 212
national monuments and, 343
political ideologies and, 168
political parties and, 226, 228, 230, 240, 294

political polarization and, 175

religion and, 174

Republican Party and, 235, 240

Supreme Court and, 294, 415, 417, 433, 434, 435–36

Tea Party movement, 232

conservatives, 166 today this term refers to those who generally support the social and economic status quo and are suspicious of efforts to introduce new political formulas and economic arrangements; conservatives believe that a large and powerful government poses a threat to citizens' freedom

See also conservatism

constituencies, 57, 305, 334, *334* the residents in the areas from which officials are elected

See also constituency service

constituency service (casework), 311, 312, 314

Constitution, U.S., 41–62

See also Bill of Rights; civil rights; expressed powers; federalism; Founding; political culture; *specific amendments, e.g. Fourteenth Amendment*

amendment process, 53, *54*

amendments to, *54–55*

on appropriations, 57

vs. Articles of Confederation, *47–48*

civil liberties in original, 95

comity clause, 53, 72–73

commerce clause, 77–79, 86

content of, 31–32

court system and, 406, 410, 412

economic policy and, 441

elastic clause, 50, 61, 69

federal government power in, 50

federalism in, 56, 57, 67–69, 71–73

framers of, 43, *43*, 95

full faith and credit clause, 72

Great Compromise, 41–42, 47

implied powers in, 78, 352, 354, 355

judicial review and, 420–21

on justice, 23

on liberty, 20

limits on federal government in, 56–58, *56, 57,* 61

local governments and, 73

necessary and proper clause, 50, 69, 78

originalism and, 433–34

on presidency, 50, 52, 345–46, 369–70

provisions of, 47–50, 52–58

ratification of, 48, 53, 56, 59–61, 95

on recess appointments, 370

slavery and, 44–46, *45,* 77

supremacy clause, 53, 61, 69, 420–21

on Supreme Court, 52, 412, 432

on Supreme Court jurisdiction, 408, 424

on vice presidency, 359

Constitutional Convention (1787), 41–46, 95, 420

constitutional government, 7 a system of rule in which formal and effective limits are placed on the powers of the government

Consumer Product Safety Act (1972), 352

Consumer Product Safety Commission (CPSC), 352, 448, 461

consumer protection, 352, 447, 461

See also Food and Drug Administration; government regulation

containment, 477 a policy designed to curtail the political and military expansion of a hostile power

contraceptive care. *See* birth control

contract cases, 405–6

contracting, 445, 489, 490 the power of government to set conditions on companies seeking to sell goods or services to government agencies

See also privatization

contributory programs, 17, 452, 454–56, **455,** 465–66 social programs financed in whole or in part by taxation or other mandatory contributions by their present or future recipients

See also Social Security

cooperative federalism, *81,* **81** a type of federalism existing since the New Deal era in which grants-in-aid have been used strategically to encourage states and localities (without commanding them) to pursue nationally defined goals; also known as *intergovernmental cooperation*

Coronavirus Aid, Relief, and Economic Security Act (CARES Act), 450

See also Covid-19 stimulus legislation

death penalty, 117
debates, political, 288
Declaration of
    Independence, 20, 21,
    31, 36–37, 42, 127
Declaration of Sentiments
    and Resolutions, 142
de facto, 136 literally,
    "by fact"; refers to
    practices that occur
    even when there is no
    legal enforcement, such
    as school segregation
    in much of the United
    States today
de facto segregation, 136
defendant, 405 the
    one against whom a
    complaint is brought in a
    criminal or civil case
Defense, Department of
    (DoD), 108, 358, 487,
    488, 489
defense industry, *257*, 295,
    475, 490
    See also military
Defense of Marriage Act
    (DOMA) (1996), 72
**Deferred Action for
    Childhood Arrivals
    (DACA), 154**, 435,
    435 a government
    program intended to
    allow undocumented
    immigrants who were
    brought to the United
    States as minors to
    legally remain in the
    country to study or work
DeJonge v. Oregon, 98
de jure, 135, 139 literally,
    "by law"; refers to legally
    enforced practices, such
    as school segregation
    in the South before the
    1960s
de jure segregation, 135, 139
DeLay, Tom, 259
delegated powers, 354, 365
    constitutional powers
    that are assigned to one
    governmental agency but
    are exercised by another
    agency with the express
    permission of the first

**delegates (in political parties),
    280** representatives to
    national party conventions
    who vote according to
    the preferences of voters
    in caucus and primary
    elections
    See also national
        conventions
**delegates (member of
    Congress role), 306**
    representatives who
    vote according to the
    preferences of their
    constituencies
democracy, 5, **7** a system of
    rule that permits citizens
    to play a significant part
    in the governmental
    process, usually through
    the election of key public
    officials
    civil liberties and, 103
    direct, 8
    federalism and, 83
    flawed, 9
    foreign policy and, 482
    Founders' distrust of, 8,
        47–48, 49, 52, 60
    importance of media to,
        192, 193
    interest groups and, 246
    international comparisons,
        51, *51*
    military force and, 495
    political knowledge and,
        178–79
    political parties' role in,
        226–27
    as political value, 164
    racial justice movement
        and, 157–58
    Supreme Court and, 417
Democratic National
    Committee (DNC), 234
    Watergate scandal and,
        195, 349, 359
Democratic Party
    See also political ideology;
        political parties;
        *specific presidents,
        e.g. Obama,
        Barack, and
        administration*

Affordable Care Act and,
    360, 461
budget process and,
    332
civil rights movement
    and, 230
congressional committee
    system and, 321
democratic socialism
    and, 168
divisions within, 225,
    293–94, 439
economic policy and,
    450
election of 2018 and,
    360
election of 2020 results
    and, 296, 297
evolution of, 228, 230,
    231–32
federal government
    power and, 27
filibuster and, 328, 332
gender and, 272
government regulation,
    452–53
government role in
    economy and, 450
House caucus, 319
liberalism and, 175
national conventions,
    281
New Deal and, 230, 291
party identification, *239*
policy issues and, 237,
    293–94
primary elections and
    caucuses and, 202,
    294–95
progressive caucus, 293,
    294, 296
Russian election
    interference
    investigations and,
    338
social media and, 364
superdelegates, 281
Supreme Court
    appointments and,
    416, 417, 433
voter demographics
    and, 240, 242,
    270, 272
voting by mail and, 296
voting rights and, 71

democratic socialism, 168
demographics, 13–14, *15*,
 16–18, *19*
 See also voter
  demographics;
  specific categories,
  e.g. age
 candidate characteristics
  and, 292
 Congress and, 307–8,
  307, *309*, *310*, *313*
 federalism and, 67
 federal judges and, *419*
 Founding and, 43, *43*
 history of, 13–14, *15*
 immigration and, 13–14,
  16–17, *16*, *147*
 linked fate and, 172, 174
 news sources and, *211*
 political ideologies and,
  167, 168–69, *169*
 presidency and, *361*
 ratification debates and,
  60
 Supreme Court justices,
  417
 Supreme Court law
  clerks, 427
 vice presidency and, *360*
demonstrations. *See* protest
Dennis v. United States, 104
Department of Homeland
 Security (DHS), 68, 86,
 352
deregulation, 231, 295, **448**
 a policy of reducing or
 eliminating regulatory
 restraints on the conduct
 of individuals or private
 institutions
descriptive representation
 (Congress), 307–8, *307*,
 307, *309*, *310*, *313* a
 type of representation
 in which representatives
 have the same racial,
 gender, ethnic,
 religious, or educational
 backgrounds as their
 constituents; it is based
 on the principle that
 if two individuals are
 similar in background,
 character, interests, and
 perspectives, then one

can correctly represent
 the other's views
African Americans, 263,
 271, *310*
 Latino/a/x Americans,
  310
 political participation
  and, 271
 ratification debates
  and, 59
 voter decisions and, 292
 women, *310*
desegregation. *See*
 segregation/
 desegregation
deserving/undeserving
 concept of social policy,
 468
détente, 477
deterrence, 477–78, **477**,
 478 an effort to prevent
 hostile action by
 promising to retaliate
 forcefully against an
 attacker
Development, Relief, and
 Education Act for Alien
 Minors (DREAM Act),
 154, *154*, 435
devolution, 84–86, **84**
 policy to remove a
 program from one
 level of government by
 delegating it or passing
 it down to a lower level
 of government, such
 as from the national
 government to the state
 and local governments
DeVos, Betsy, 143, 460
Dewey, Thomas, *188*
diffusion, 85
digital news
 See also news websites
 advertising and, 212
 citizen journalism and,
  196, 212
 civility/incivility and,
  220
 consumers of, *211*
 evaluating, 218
 media ownership and,
  207, 210, 212

media technology
  companies and,
  210, 212
 misinformation and,
  192, 197, 212–13
 news aggregators and, 208
 newspapers and, 207,
  208, 210
 political knowledge and,
  11, 178, 220
 on social media, 208–9,
  212–13
digital political
 participation, **268**, 287,
 364 activities designed
 to influence politics
 using the internet,
 including visiting a
 candidate's website,
 organizing events online,
 and signing an online
 petition
diplomacy, 484, *486*,
 487, 491–92, **491** the
 representation of a
 government to other
 governments
direct-action politics, 10, *11*
 See also protest
direct democracy, **8** a
 system of rule that
 permits citizens to vote
 directly on laws and
 policies
directives, presidential, 368
Director of National
 Intelligence (DNI), 488
Disability Rights Education
 and Defense Fund, 149
disabled Americans
 civil rights, 85, *85*, 149
 health care and, 461
 political participation,
  277
 welfare programs and,
  455, 461
discretionary spending, 452
discrimination, **131** the use
 of any unreasonable
 and unjust criterion of
 exclusion, 0
 See also gender
  discrimination;
  racial discrimination

unitary executive theory and, 352, 354

Executive Office of the President (EOP), 358–59, *358*, 363–64, 365, 484 the permanent agencies that perform defined management tasks for the president; created in 1939, the EOP includes the OMB, the Council of Economic Advisers (CEA), the NSC, and other agencies
See also executive branch

executive orders, 343, **366**, *367*, 368 rules or regulations issued by the president that have the effect and formal status of legislation
See also specific policy issues, e.g. immigration policy

executive power expansion, 363–69
administrative strategy, 352, 365–66, *367*, 368–69
checks and balances and, 369–70
civil rights and, 139
Congress and, 346
executive agreements and, 484, 489
judicial review and, 422
national security policy and, 483, 484
public appeals and, 363–64
unitary executive theory and, 352, 354

executive privilege, 349–50, **349** the claim that confidential communications between a president and close advisers should not be revealed without the consent of the president

expressed powers, 49–50, **50**, **69**, **346** specific powers granted by the Constitution to Congress

(Article I, Section 8) and to the president (Article II)
Bill of Rights and, 57
of federal government, 50, 57, 67, 69, 78
of presidency, 346–52, 355
extraordinary renditions, 355

F

Facebook
See also social media
algorithms and, 212, 217, 302, 303
congressional oversight and, 302–4, 338
elections and, 212–13
hate speech and, 106
January 6 U.S. Capitol insurrection and, 213
lobbying by, 303–4
misinformation on, 212, 213, 217, 302–4
news on, 208, 212, 213
Russian election interference and, 217
voter mobilization and, 288, 290
fact-checking, 193, 194, 212, 217, 218
FactCheck.org, 217
Fair Housing Act (1968), 140
Fair Housing Amendments Act (1988), 140–41
fairness, 23 impartial decision making; the quality of treating people equally, free from discrimination
fake news. *See* misinformation
Families First Coronavirus Response Act, 450, *452*
family, political socialization by, 171, *171*
Farmer, James, *128*
Faubus, Orval, 347
FCC (Federal Communications Commission), 219

FDR. *See* Roosevelt, Franklin Delano, and administration
Federal Bureau of Investigation (FBI), 213, 346, 349
Federal Communications Commission (FCC), 219
Federal Election Campaign Act (1971), *285*
federal government
See also federal government power; federalism; public policy
in Articles of Confederation, 38, 57
benefits from, *87*
Bill of Rights and, 96–97, 99
civil rights movement and, 136, *138*, 139, 347, *347*
Constitutional limits on, 56–58, *56*, *57*, 61
grants-in-aid, 79–81, *80*, *81*, 84–85, 86, *87*, 139, 152
federal government power
See also federalism; Federalists; limited government
civil liberties and, 95
civil rights and, 84, 127, 139
economic policy and, 27, 76, 79
expressed powers, 49, 57, 67, 69, 78
growth in, 76, 77–79, 230
national security policy and, 68
New Deal and, 27, 76, 79, 230, 352
political ideologies and, 165, 166, 168
political parties and, 230, 232
Progressive movement and, 165
supremacy clause and, 53, 61, 69, 420–21

Fourth Amendment, 114, 119, 421
See also due process of law
Fox Corporation, 200
Fox News, 203, 209, 216
framers of the Constitution, 43, *43*, 95
See also Founding
framing, 203, 205, 208 the process of presenting information from a certain perspective in order to shape the audience's understanding of that information
France, 476, 492
franchise. See voting rights
Frankfurter, Felix, 430, 433
Frazier, Darnella, 196
freedom. See liberty
freedom of assembly, 97, *98*
freedom of association, 108
freedom of religion, *98*, 100–102, *101*
freedom of speech, 103–4, 106–8
   campaign finance and, 104, 434
   commercial speech, 107
   fighting words, 104
   hate speech, 104, 106
   political speech, 103–4, 193
   as political value, 164
   protest and, 106, 107–8, 265
   selective incorporation and, 97, *98*
   speech-plus, 107
   strict scrutiny and, 103
   student speech, 92–94, *94*, 106–7, *106*
   symbolic speech, 107–8
   violence and, 109
freedom of the press, 108–9
   international comparisons, 193, *199*
   libel and slander and, 108–9

media and, 192, 193, 195–96
   as political value, 164
   pornography and obscenity and, 109
   prior restraint and, 108
   selective incorporation and, 97, *98*
Freedom Rides, *138*
free exercise clause, 101–2, **101** the First Amendment clause that protects a citizen's right to believe and practice whatever religion they choose
See also freedom of religion
free media, 287
free riders, 249 those who enjoy the benefits of collective goods but did not participate in acquiring or providing them
free trade, 480
frontloading, 280 the moving up of presidential primaries by states to provide those states greater influence on the selection of candidates
fugitive slave clause, 77
full faith and credit clause, 72 provision from Article IV, Section 1, of the Constitution requiring that the states normally honor the public acts and judicial decisions that take place in another state
Fulton, Robert, 78
fundraising. See campaign finance

G
gag rules. See closed rules
gambling, 149
Gannett corporation, 200
Gardner, Cory, 297
Garland, Merrick, 416
Garrity, W. Arthur, Jr., 414

gatekeeping, 201, 203
gay rights movement, 150, 258
See also LGBTQ civil rights
gender
See also demographics; gender discrimination; transgender Americans
   cruel and unusual punishment and, 117
   federal judges and, *419*
   political parties and, 240, *241*, 272
   presidency and, *361*
   public opinion and, 174
   social composition of Congress and, *309, 310*
   vice presidency and, *360*
   voter demographics and, 174, 272
gender discrimination
   in education, 143
   in employment, 143
   international comparisons, *145*
   Supreme Court on, 142–43
gender gap, 174, 272 a distinctive pattern of voting behavior reflecting the differences in views between women and men
general elections, 274–75, **275** regularly scheduled elections involving most districts in the nation or state, in which voters select officeholders; in the United States, general elections for national office and most state and local offices are held on the first Tuesday after the first Monday in November in even-numbered years (every four years for presidential elections)

investment, 447, 448

Iowa, 280

Iran, 475, 478, 484, 486, 487, 499

Iraq, 495

Iraq War, 155, 355, 364, 494

iron triangles, 256–57, **256,** *257* stable, cooperative relationships that often develop among a congressional committee, an administrative agency, and one or more supportive interest groups; not all of these relationships are triangular, but iron triangles are the most typical

IRS (Internal Revenue Service), 369

Islamophobia, 155–56, **155** the fear of and discrimination against Islam or people who practice Islam

isolationism, 168, 295, **476,** 477, 478–79, 480 avoidance of involvement in the affairs of other nations

Israel, 490, 493, 499

issue networks, 256–57, **256** loose networks of elected leaders, public officials, activists, and interest groups drawn together by specific policy issues

Italy, 496

J

Jackson, Andrew, 228, 413

Jackson, Henry M., 312

Jackson, Ketanji Brown, *416,* 417

Jackson, Robert H., 430

January 6 U.S. Capitol insurrection (2021) House select committee on, 321, 338–39, 349 as insurrection, 265

political polarization and, 336

social media and, 212–13

trust/distrust in media and, 214

Japanese American internment, 14, *146,* 148

Jay, John, 59

Jefferson, Thomas Declaration of Independence and, 37 as enslaver, 30–31, 37 on freedom of religion, 100 judicial review and, 420 political parties and, 228 statue removal, 30–31, *32*

Jeffersonian Republicans (Antifederalists), 59, 95, 228

Jewish Americans, 17, 272, 490 *See also* religion

Jim Crow era *See also* civil rights movement Compromise of 1877 and, 133 federalism and, 83–84 *Plessy v. Ferguson* and, 134–35 racial violence, 134 school segregation/ desegregation and, 134–36 voting restrictions, 266, 271, 430

Jim Crow laws, 134–35, **134** laws enacted by southern states following Reconstruction that discriminated against African Americans *See also* Jim Crow era; segregation/ desegregation

job discrimination. *See* employment

John Lewis Voting Rights Advancement Act, 65, 334

Johnson, Andrew, 348

Johnson, Lyndon B., and administration, *138* affirmative action and, 152, 368 civil rights movement and, *128,* 129, 230 War on Poverty, 81

Joint Chiefs of Staff, 487

joint committees, 321 legislative committees formed of members of both the House and Senate

joint resolutions, 323

Jones, Doug, 297

journalism of affirmation, 197 the putting forth of opinion and information that is consistent with the consumer's preexisting beliefs

journalism of assertion, 197 the publishing or broadcasting of information or opinion as quickly as possible, with minimal fact-checking

journalism/journalists, 194–97 *See also* digital news; media adversarial, 195–96 citizen journalism, 196–97, 212 mainstream news organizations and, 194–95, 205 media ownership and, 210 opinion-driven, 197 principled, 194–95, 205, 210 tolerance and, 220

judicial activism, 434 judicial philosophy that posits that the Court should go beyond the words of the Constitution or a statute to consider the broader societal implications of its decisions

judicial branch, 23, 52, 57, 368, 413–14 *See also* court system; Supreme Court

civility/incivility and,
219–20
civil rights movement
and, 136, 201, *202*
congressional elections
and, 312
evaluating, 218
framing by, 203, 205,
208
freedom of the press
and, 192, 193
government regulation
of, 109, 219
importance to
democracy, 192,
193
influence of, 201–4, *202*,
214
leaks, 195–96
media technology
companies, 210,
212
national conventions
and, 281
newspapers, 207, 210,
248
news sources, 204–5,
206, *211*
ownership of, 198, 200,
207, 210, 212, 219
political knowledge and,
193, 194, 198, 203,
210, 220
political participation
and, 193, 194
political polarization
and, 214–16, *216*,
243
politicians' use of, 176,
176, 178, 195, 201,
202, 209, 268
presidential power and,
363–64
primary elections and
caucuses and, 280
priming by, 203
profit motives in,
197–98, 200, 210,
212
public broadcasting, 198,
210
public opinion and, 163
public policy and, 201
radio, 176, *176*, 209–10,
363

roles of, 193–94, *194*
sensationalism in, 200
television, 109, 200, 201,
202, 209, 287, *363*
trust/distrust in, 213–14,
215
media echo chambers,
215–16, **215** closed
communication systems
in which individual
beliefs are amplified or
reinforced by repetition;
they may increase social
and political polarization
because users do not
encounter opposing
views
media monopolies, 200
giant, often global,
corporations that control
a wide array of media,
including television
networks, movie studios,
record companies, cable
channels, book and
newspaper publishers,
and digital media outlets
Medicaid, 456, 461 a
federally and state-
financed, state-operated
program providing
medical services to low-
income people
ACA expansion of, 461,
462–63, 467
federalism and, 79–80
welfare reform and, 456
medical care. *See* health
care
medical marijuana, 86, 88,
88
Medicare, 452, **455,** 461,
465 a form of national
health insurance for
elderly people and
disabled people
memoranda, presidential,
368
men
See also gender
death penalty and, 117
economic inequality and,
465
law clerk demographics
and, 427

mass incarceration and,
156
Supreme Court
demographics
and, 417
voting rights, 133, 265,
266
Meta/Facebook, 210
See also Facebook
#MeToo movement, 144
Mexican American
Legal Defense and
Educational Fund
(MALDEF), 144
Mexican Americans, 144,
174, 242
See also Latino/a/x
Americans
Mexico, 144, 154, 168, 174,
476, *486*
See also immigration
policy
Michigan, 89, 296
Microsoft, 210
micro-targeting, 288 a
campaign strategy
that uses data and
demographics to identify
the interests of small
groups of like-minded
individuals and deliver
tailored ads or messages
designed to influence
their voting behavior
middle/upper classes, 18,
466
See also socioeconomic
status; wealthy
Americans,
influence of
midterm elections, 273
congressional elections
that do not coincide with
a presidential election;
also called off-year
elections
See also congressional
elections
Mijente, 154
military
civil rights and, *138*,
347, *347*
Congress and, 489
defense industry, *257*,
475, 489

multiple referral, 330–31, **330** the practice of referring a bill to more than one committee for consideration

multiracial Americans, 14, 16

Muse, Hayat, 2–4, *4*

Muslim Americans, 17, 155–56, *156*
See also religion

Muslim ban, 154, *155*, 156, 355, 368, *421*, 422, 472

mutually assured destruction (MAD), 477

Myanmar, 482

N

NAACP (National Association for the Advancement of Colored People), 134–35, 136, *138*, 149, 258, 271, 428

NAACP v. Alabama, 108

Nader, Ralph, 244

NAFTA (North American Free Trade Agreement), 480–81

NARAL Pro-Choice America, 248

National American Woman Suffrage Association (NAWSA), 142

national conventions, 280–81

national debt, 443 the total amount of money the government has borrowed

National Defense Authorization Act (2019), 369

National Defense Education Act (1958), 459, 460

National Emergencies Act (1976), 356

National Federation of Independent Business, 247

national government. *See* federal government; federalism

National Governors Association, 459

National Indian Youth Council, 149

National Institutes of Health (NIH), 461

national monuments, 342–43, *344*

National Origins quota system, 13–14

National Public Radio (NPR), 198, 210

National Rifle Association (NRA), 246, 248, 337

national security adviser, 359, 484, 486

National Security Agency (NSA), 346, 355, 488

National Security Council (NSC), 346, **359**, 484, 486 a presidential foreign policy advisory council composed of the president, the vice president, the secretary of state, the secretary of defense, and other officials invited by the president

national security policy, 475–80
See also foreign policy; military

Department of Defense and, 487

energy policy and, 476, 480

federal government power and, 68

foreign military assistance, 196, 294, 493

freedom of speech and, 103–4

institutional presidency and, 359

intelligence agencies and, 346, 355, 475, 487–88, 489–90

military spending and, 295, 332, 475, 478, *479*, 489

National Taxpayers Union, 248

national unity, 47, 52–53, 67, 72, 300

National Welfare Rights Organization, 659

nation-states, 478 political entities consisting of a people with some common cultural experience (nation) who also share a common political authority (state), recognized by other sovereignties (nation-states)

Native Americans
See also demographics; voter demographics

citizenship, 13, 14, 149

court system and, 413

Founding and, 23, 30

landback movement, 26

land removal, 23, 30, 33–34, 37, 148–49, 228, 476

national monuments and, 342–43, *344*

precontact populations, 33

in U.S. population, 13

natural disasters, 71, 347, 364, 481

Naturalization Act (1790), 14

NBC, 209

Near v. Minnesota, 98, 108

Nebraska, 235

necessary and proper clause, 50, **69**, 78 Article I, Section 8, of the Constitution, which provides Congress with the authority to make all laws "necessary and proper" to carry out its expressed powers

negative ads, 234, 287

negative partisanship, 243–44, **243** a phenomenon in which people form strong opinions against a political party rather than in support of one

Nevada, 280, 296

Never Again MSD, 161

New Deal
   federal government
       power and, 27, 76,
       79, 230, 352
   government role in
       economy and, 449
   grants-in-aid, 79
   health care and, 461
   housing policy and, 464
   political parties and,
       230, 291, 293
   socioeconomic status
       and, 18
   Supreme Court and,
       434–35
New Federalism, 84
   attempts by Presidents
   Nixon and Reagan to
   return power to the
   states through block
   grants
New Hampshire, 280
Newhouse, Neil, 186–87,
   186
New Jersey Plan, 41 a
   framework for the
   Constitution that
   called for equal state
   representation in the
   national legislature
   regardless of population
news aggregators, 208
   websites that pull
   together news from a
   wide range of online
   sources and make
   them available on one
   platform or page; news
   aggregators can be a
   way to avoid partisan or
   filtered news, providing
   a broad overview of the
   news of the day from
   many sources
Newsmax, 205
news media. *See* digital
   news; media
Newsom, Gavin, 8
newspapers, 195, 200, 207,
   210
news websites, 207, 208,
   210 digital sites that are
   owned and managed by
   newspapers, follow the
   principles of journalism,

and deliver content like
   that of print newspapers,
   with similar story layout
   for all users regardless of
   location, demographic
   characteristics,
   partisanship, or friend
   networks
   See also digital news
New York State, 102, 112
New York Times, 194, 196,
   207
*New York Times Co. v.
   Sullivan,* 109
*New York Times Co. v.
   United States* (Pentagon
   Papers case), 108, 196
Nexstar Media Group, 200
9/11. *See* September 11,
   2001, terrorist attacks
Nineteenth Amendment,
   142, 267 amendment
   that guaranteed the right
   to vote to women
Nixon, Richard, and
   administration
   devolution and, 84
   foreign policy and, 483
   pardon, 347
   regulatory review and,
       365
   resignation, 349, 359
   southern strategy, 230,
       231
   Vietnam War and, 201
   Watergate scandal, 195,
       349, 359
No Child Left Behind Act
   (NCLB) (2001), 68, 459
nomination, 281
   See also primary
       elections and
       caucuses
noncontributory programs,
   456–57, **456,** *457*
   social programs that
   provide assistance to
   people on the basis
   of demonstrated
   need rather than any
   contribution they have
   made
non-state actors, 475
   groups other than
   nation-states that

attempt to play a role in
   the international system;
   terrorist groups are one
   type of non-state actor
nonworking poor, 468
North American Free Trade
   Agreement (NAFTA),
   480–81
North Atlantic Treaty
   Organization (NATO),
   479–80, 494, 498
North Carolina, 89, *89,* 136
North Dakota, 276
North Korea, 7, 478, 484,
   487, 499
NSC (National Security
   Council), 346, 359 a
   presidential foreign
   policy advisory council
   composed of the
   president, the vice
   president, the secretary
   of state, the secretary
   of defense, and other
   officials invited by the
   president
nuclear weapons, 477, 478,
   478, 486, 489, 490,
   498–99
nullification, 83

O

Obama, Barack, and
   administration
   anti-terrorism and, 355,
       484
   approval ratings, 364
   big data and, 288
   birther conspiracy and,
       197, *198*
   Democratic Party and,
       360
   descriptive
       representation
       and, 263
   economic conditions
       and, 231
   education policy and, 68,
       459
   environmental policy
       and, 351
   executive orders and,
       366
   federalism and, 68

the final 10 days of a legislative session

podcasts, 209, 210

polarization, 337 the deep ideological distance between the two parties
See also political polarization

police power, 71, 99 power reserved to the state government to regulate the health, safety, and morals of its citizens

policing. *See* criminal justice system; law enforcement

policy feedback, 180

policy issues. *See* public policy

political action committees (PACs), 234–35, **234**, 246, 283, **284**, *285*, 287 private groups that raise and distribute funds for use in election campaigns

political appointees, 487

political culture, 20–23, 20, 26 broadly shared values, beliefs, and attitudes about how the government should function; American political culture emphasizes the values of liberty, equality, and justice
See also equality of opportunity
Americans' views of government, 27–28
civil rights and, 127
equality, 5, 21–22
Founding and, 20, 21, 23, 32, 33
justice, 23, 26, 163
liberty, 5, 10, 20–21, 26, 84, 131, 163, 164, 192
slavery and, 44, *45*
unfinished nature of, 23, 26, 32

political efficacy, 12 the belief that one can influence government and politics

political equality, 22 the right to participate in politics equally, based on the principle of "one person, one vote"
See also civil rights; voting rights

political ideology, 163 a cohesive set of beliefs that forms a general philosophy about the role of government
See also conservatism; liberalism; political polarization
demographics and, *167*
interest groups and, 248, 252
media and, 203, 205
party activists and, 239
political knowledge and, 178
political parties and, 169, 235, 237, 240, 293, 336
public opinion and, 164–66, *167*, 168–69
regional differences and, 175
social groups and, 174–75
Supreme Court and, 433, 434

political knowledge, 11 information about the formal institutions of government, political actors, and political issues
digital news and, 11, 178, 220
elites and, 178, 194
informational shortcuts and, 178
limits of, 11–12, 178
media and, 193, 194, 198, 203, 210, 220
media profit motive and, 198
political ideology and, 178
political polarization and, 178
public opinion and, 176, 178–79, 193
social media and, 178

political participation, 265–72
See also protest; voter turnout; voting rights
African Americans, 133, 139
collective action and, 128
contacting your member of Congress, 316–17
digital, 268, 364
equality and, 22
federalism and, 68
local governments and, 74–75
media and, 193, 194, 201
organized labor and, 247
political efficacy and, 12
political parties and, 225
political power and, 8, 10
political socialization and, 172
as political value, 164
racial injustice protests (2020) and, 265–66
voting rights and, 266–68

political parties, 225 coalitions of people who form a united front to win control of government and implement policy
See also political polarization; primary elections and caucuses
campaign finance and, 226, 234–35
caucuses and, 280, 319
congressional campaign committees and, 235
congressional decision-making and, 335, 337
congressional elections and, 311
congressional leadership, 235, 318–19, 325–26, 330, 331, 336
criticisms of, 226–27

poverty

> See also economic inequality; socioeconomic status

children and, 438, 469

cruel and unusual punishment and, 117

housing policy and, 464

nonworking poor, 468

race and, 271, 468, 469

social policy and, 439, 453, 454, 455, 456, 461, 469

welfare programs and, 465–66

women and, 468–69, *469*

working poor, 466–68

Powell, Jerome, *446*, 447

precedents, 306, 430, 432, 436 prior cases whose principles are used by judges as the basis for their decision in a present case

preclearance, 139, 140, 315, 334

preemption, 82, 89, *89* the principle that allows the national government to override state or local actions in certain policy areas; in foreign policy, the willingness to strike first in order to prevent an enemy attack

presidency, 342–70

> See also executive branch; executive power expansion; presidential elections; *specific presidents and administrations, e.g. Obama, Barack, and administration*

approval ratings, 364

broadcast media and, 176, *176*, 195, 363

budget process and, 350, 359, 365, 445

civil rights movement and, *128*, 129, 137, *138*

Constitution on, 50, 52, 345–46, 369–70

death in office, 359–60

demographics of, *361*

executive agreements, 484, 489

executive orders, 343, 366, *367*, 368

expressed powers of, 346–52, 355

foreign policy and, 50, 339, 348, *348*, 355, 483–84, 486, 488

head of state role, *348*, 360, 362, *486*

implied powers, 55, 352, 354, 355

inherent powers, 355–56

institutional structure, 357–60, *358*, 362

international comparisons, *353*, 358

judicial power of, 347–48

lawmaking and, 329–30, 350, 365–66

legislative initiative, 350, 365

media agenda setting and, 201

oath of office, *345*

political parties and, 360

powers of, 50

proclamations, 343, 368

social media and, 176, *176*, 364

social movement strategy and, *128*, 129

take care clause and, 345, 352

term limits, 369

trust/distrust in government and, 27

unitary executive theory, 352, 354

vesting clause, 345, 352

veto power, 50, 56, 329–30, 350–51, *351*

presidential appointments

Cabinet, 358

checks and balances and, 56, 370

congressional advice and consent powers and, 339

expressed powers and, 348–49

federal judges, 414–15

Federal Reserve Board, 446

recess, 370, 422

Supreme Court, 415–17, *416*

presidential elections, 380–82

> See also elections; electoral college; *specific elections, e.g.* election of 2016

debates, 288

international comparisons, 281

media agenda setting and, 202

national party conventions, 280–81

primary elections and caucuses, 280

social media and, 212

vice presidency and, 359

voter mobilization, 364

Presidential Succession Act (1947), 359–60

press, freedom of the, 97, *98*, 108–9, 164, 192, 193, 196

preventive war, 477, 478, 483 a policy of striking first when a nation fears that a foreign foe is contemplating hostile action

primary elections, 274–75, 274 elections held to select a party's candidate for the general election

> See also primary elections and caucuses

equality of opportunity
and, 439, 455,
458–59
grants-in-aid and,
79–80, 86, 153
Great Depression and,
453–54, *454*
health care and, 460–64,
463
history of, 453–54, *454*
housing and, 464
lobbying and, 222–23,
224
noncontributory
programs, 456–57,
457
political ideologies and,
166, 168
public health and,
460–61
state variations in,
456–57, *457*
tax expenditures
(shadow welfare
state), 457–58,
464, 466
welfare reform, 85–86,
456, 469
social regulation, 447
See also government
regulation
Social Security, 455 a
contributory welfare
program into which
working Americans
contribute a percentage
of their wages and from
which they receive cash
benefits after retirement
or if they become
disabled
aging population and, 17
constituencies for, 465,
466
Earned Income Tax
Credit and, 467
spending on, 452
tax policy and, 442, 443
Social Security Act (1935),
456, 468–69
Social Security Disability
Insurance (SSDI), 455
socioeconomic status,
270 status in society
based on level of

education, income, and
occupational prestige
See also demographics;
economic
inequality;
poverty; voter
demographics;
wealthy
Americans,
influence of
campaign finance and,
270
colonial America, 34
death penalty and, 117
education policy and,
459, 460
Medicare and, 455
political knowledge and,
178
political participation
and, 277
political parties and,
226, 240, *241*
public opinion and, 175
public-opinion polls and,
185
public policy influence
and, 181
social composition of
Congress and, 308
Social Security and, 455
tax expenditures and,
458, 464, 466
tax policy and, 443, *451*
unrepresented interests
and, 252, 253
in U.S. population, 18
voter registration and,
276
voter turnout and, 270,
271
voting rights based on, 7,
22, 265, 266
sociological representation.
See descriptive
representation
sodomy laws, 150
soft news, 198
soft power, 481, 495–96
solicitor general, 427 the
top government lawyer
in all cases before the
Supreme Court where
the government is a
party

solidary benefits, 252
selective benefits of
group membership that
emphasize friendship,
networking, and
consciousness-raising
Sotomayor, Sonia, *416*, 417
South
See also civil rights
movement;
Jim Crow era;
Reconstruction;
regional
differences
African Americans in
public office, 139
apportionment and, 314
political parties and,
230, *231*
school desegregation
resistance, 135–36,
137
states' rights and, 81,
83–84
Three-Fifths Compromise
and, 44
South Carolina, 202, 280,
295
Southeast Asia Treaty
Organization (SEATO),
494
Southern Christian
Leadership Conference
(SCLC), 136
Southern Manifesto, 83–84
southern strategy, 230, *231*
Soviet Union, collapse of,
477, 494
Speaker of the House,
235, **319**, 325, 330,
360 the chief presiding
officer of the House
of Representatives;
the Speaker is the
most important party
and House leader
and can influence the
legislative agenda,
the fate of individual
pieces of legislation,
and members' positions
within the House
special concurrences, 430
SpeechNow.org v. FEC, 284,
285

activities desired by the government, reward political support, or buy off political opposition

substantive representation, 59–60, **308** a type of representation in which a representative is held accountable to a constituency if they fail to represent that constituency properly; this is incentive for the representative to provide good representation when their personal background, views, and interests differ from those of their constituency

suburban areas, 140, 240

suffrage, 266 the right to vote; also called *franchise*
See also African American voting rights; voting rights; women's suffrage

Sugar Act (1764), 34

superdelegates, 281 (in the Democratic Party) an unelected party member/leader who is free to support any candidate for the presidential nomination at the party's national convention. They are only allowed to vote if no candidate has a majority after the first round of voting

Super PACs, 234–35, **284,** 285, 287 nonprofit independent political action committees that may raise unlimited sums of money from corporations, unions, and individuals but are not permitted to contribute to or coordinate directly with parties or candidates

Supplemental Nutrition Assistance Program (SNAP), 456, 461, 467, 467, 468 the largest antipoverty program, which provides recipients with a debit card for food at most grocery stores; formerly known as food stamps

Supplemental Security Income (SSI), 456

supply-side economics, 450, 452 an economic theory that posits that reducing the marginal rate of taxation will create a productive economy by promoting levels of work and investment that would otherwise be discouraged by higher taxes

supremacy clause, 53, 61, 69, 420–21, **420** Article VI of the Constitution, which states that laws passed by the national government and all treaties are the supreme law of the land and superior to all laws adopted by any state or any subdivision

Supreme Court, 412–13
See also specific cases, e.g. Dred Scott v. Sanford
on abortion, 107, 119–20, 258, 425, 436
access to, 424–26
on affirmative action, 153, 432
on Affordable Care Act, 102, 420, 462
anti-terrorism and, 422
appointments to, 232, 294, 415–17, 416, 435–36
on Bill of Rights, 96
on birth control, 119
bureaucracy and, 414, 422, 427
on campaign finance, 104, 287, 434

caseload, 411, 426
chief justice, 413
circuit courts and, 412
on citizenship, 148
class-action suits and, 414
on commerce clause, 77–79, 86
on commercial speech, 107
conference, 430
Constitution on, 52, 412, 432
on Covid-19 public health measures, 102
on cruel and unusual punishment, 117
current justices, 416
democracy and, 417
demographics, 417
on double jeopardy, 97, 115
on education policy, 460
on eminent domain, 97
on exclusionary rule, 114
on executive privilege, 349
federal government power and, 77–79, 83
on freedom of religion, 100–102, 101
on freedom of speech, 92–94, 97, 103–4, 106–7, 108, 109
on freedom of the press, 97, 108, 109, 196
on gender discrimination, 142–43
on gun rights/gun control, 84, 111–12
on immigration policy, 17, 153
influences on, 432–36
on inherent powers, 355
interest groups and, 427–28
on interracial marriage, 72, 141, 152
on Japanese American internment, 148
judicial restraint/ activism, 433–34

unfunded mandates, 85, 459 laws or regulations requiring a state or local government to perform certain actions without providing funding for fulfilling the requirement

unicameral legislature, 41 a legislative assembly having only one chamber or house

unions. *See* organized labor

unitary executive theory, 352, 354

unitary systems, 67, *70* centralized government systems in which lower levels of government have little power independent of the national government

United Auto Workers, 247

United Kingdom, 492

United Mine Workers, 247

United Nations (UN), 492 an organization of nations founded in 1945 to be a channel for negotiation and a means of settling international disputes peaceably

United States–Mexico–Canada Agreement (USMCA), 480–81, 480 a trade treaty between the United States, Canada, and Mexico to lower and eliminate tariffs among the three countries

United States v. Bhagat Singh Thind, 148

United States v. Grubbs, 114

United States v. Jones, 114

United States v. Lopez, 84

United States v. Nixon, 349

United States v. Playboy Entertainment Group, 109

United We Dream, 154

universities. *See* higher education

unorthodox lawmaking, 325, 330–32, **330** a set of legislative procedures that deviates from regular order; reflects a greater level of control from party leaders and less deliberation from members

upper classes. *See* middle/upper classes; wealthy Americans, influence of

urbanization, 17 *See also* urban/rural divisions

urban/rural divisions, 17–18, 240, 336

USA PATRIOT Act (2001), 68

U.S. Chamber of Commerce, 247

U.S. Court of Appeals for the Federal Circuit, 409, 412

U.S. Court of Federal Claims, 409

U.S. Court of International Trade, 409

U.S. Foreign Service, 486–87

U.S. International Trade Commission (ITC), 473

U.S. Public Health Service, 461

Uvalde school shooting (2022), *111*, 112

V

values (beliefs), 5, 163, 164, *165* basic principles that shape a person's opinions about political issues and events *See also* political culture

venue shopping, 68

vesting clause, 345, 352

veto, 50, 56, 329–30, 329, 350–51, *350, 351*, 368 the president's constitutional power to turn down acts of Congress; a presidential veto may be overridden by a two-thirds vote of each house of Congress

vice presidency, 359–60, *360*

Vietnam War
  adversarial journalism and, 195–96
  deterrence and, 477–78
  freedom of the press and, 108, 195–96
  media and, 201
  political repercussions of, 495
  protest and, 92, 106, 268
  voting rights and, 267–68

Virginia Plan, 41 a framework for the Constitution that called for representation in the national legislature based on the population of each state

voter demographics
  election of 2016, 232, 270, 271, 272
  election of 2018, 272
  election of 2020, *243*, 270, 271, 272, 295, 342, 343
  political parties and, 133, 226, 231, *241*, 242–43, *242, 243,* 272
  turnout and, 270–72, 466

voter fraud concerns, 140, 276

voter ID laws, 140, 277

voter mobilization
  digital political participation and, 268
  election of 2020, 226, 299–300
  personal contact and, 288, *290*
  political parties and, 225, 226
  presidential elections and, 364
  social media and, 268, 288, 290

voter registration, *275*, 276–77, 278–79